A
LITERARY
HISTORY
OF
FRANCE

A LITERARY HISTORY OF FRANCE

General Editor: P. E. CHARVET
Fellow of Corpus Christi College, Cambridge

THE MIDDLE AGES
by JOHN FOX
Professor of French at the University of Exeter

RENAISSANCE FRANCE 1470–1589
by I. D. McFARLANE
Professor of French Literature, University of Oxford

THE SEVENTEENTH CENTURY 1600–1715
by P. J. YARROW
Professor of French at the University of Newcastle upon Tyne

THE EIGHTEENTH CENTURY 1715–1789
by ROBERT NIKLAUS
Professor of French at the University of Exeter

THE NINETEENTH CENTURY 1789–1870
by P. E. CHARVET

THE NINETEENTH AND TWENTIETH CENTURIES 1870–1940
by P. E. CHARVET

A LITERARY HISTORY OF FRANCE

RENAISSANCE FRANCE

1470-1589

A LITERARY
HISTORY OF FRANCE

Renaissance France
1470-1589

I. D. McFARLANE

Professor of French Literature, University of Oxford

LONDON & TONBRIDGE
ERNEST BENN LIMITED

BARNES & NOBLE BOOKS
NEW YORK

First published 1974 by Ernest Benn Limited
Sovereign Way, Tonbridge, Kent and
25 New Street Square, Fleet Street, London, EC4A 3JA
and Harper & Row Publishers Inc.
Barnes & Noble Import Division
10 East 53rd Street, New York 10022

Distributed in Canada by
The General Publishing Company Limited, Toronto

© I. D. McFarlane 1974

Printed in Great Britain

ISBN 0 510–32205–0

ISBN 06–494700–9 (U.S.A.)

FOREWORD BY THE GENERAL EDITOR

IN HIS QUEST for the past, the historian proper deals with a variety of evidence, documentary and other, which is of value to him only for the light it sheds on events and on the men who played a part in them. The historian of literature has before him documents in manuscript or print that exist in their own right, books and ever more books, as the centuries unfold. Within the space allotted to him, his first task must be to give the maximum amount of relevant information about them, but if he is to avoid producing a mere compilation of unrelated and therefore meaningless facts, he is bound to organise his matter into some sort of pattern.

Time itself does this for him to some extent by keeping alive the memory of those writers and books that retain their relevance, and, often enough, setting one school of writers against another, as successive generations seek to establish their own originality by revolt against their immediate predecessors.

At whatever point in time the historian of literature may stand, he is bound to adopt as a basis of his work the patterns time gives him, although he knows well enough that, just as the tide and the waves may alter the patterns they themselves are for ever imprinting on the sands of the sea shore, time, bringing with it changing tastes and values, will alter these patterns, at least in detail or emphasis.

Within these broad natural patterns come problems of arrangement. Here inevitably a degree of arbitrariness creeps in. Some writers are dubbed precursors, as though they themselves had consciously played the role of prophet in a wilderness, others are marked down as 'epigoni' – poor fellows! Had they but known! – others again are lumped together because they are seen to have in common the characteristics of an age, though they may have had no relations with each other; chronology must often be sacrificed to the need of tidiness. Thus does the historian of literature try to create from the vigorous and confused growth he is faced with, at least on the surface, an ordered garden, where the reader may wander and get an impression to store away in his memory, of neatness and controlled change, an impression helpful, indeed indispensable, as a preliminary to the study of the subject, but not to be confused with the reality.

Nor is this all. Should the historian of literature, need he, smother his personal responses? And if he should (which we doubt and indeed have not tried to do), is this really possible? Within the kindly Doctor Jekyll, recording in detached tones his literary history, seeking to give an objective picture of an age, explaining, elucidating, lurks Mr Hyde, the critic, ready to leap out at the reader on the slightest provocation and wreak his mischief. As in all of us, the levels of his personality that may respond to stimuli are numerous: intellectual, emotional, moral, spiritual; more numerous still the sources of interest whence the stimuli may come: historical and social psychological, linguistic and stylistic, aesthetic. Literature is a vast catchment area all these streams flow into; a book, a great book is like a burning glass that concentrates the rays of human experience into one bright point; it burns itself into our memories and may even sear the soul.

If he be wise, Mr Hyde the critic will use as his criterium of judgement only the degree to which he feels his own experience has been enriched, his own perceptiveness extended. Thus will he avoid being too rigid or narrow in his attitudes and avoid the temptation of for ever seeking some underlying principle that controls the whole mechanism. Since the corpus of a writer's work is the expression of his experience, since the writer belongs to a given age, a given people, the works may easily become the pretext for an exercise in individual or national psychology. Conversely, the idea of race, the age, the accumulated legacy of history – its momentum, in a word – may be invoked as cause and explanation of the works. Or again, since the works have their place in one or more given art-forms, they may be seen as no more than moments in the evolution of these.

Such ideas and unifying theories have their value no doubt; the people, the society, the age, the art-forms all bear on the question, but who is to assess their impact? They leave the mystery of individual genius and of artistic creation intact; to emphasise them at the expense of the latter is really using the history of literature for other ends. Admittedly books do not spring from nothing, but whether we consider them historically or critically, in the last resort they stand, as we observed at the outset of this foreword, in their own right, and their value depends upon their impact on the individual; every book has three aspects: what the author meant to express, what the book contains, and the image the reader carries away with him; this latter changes with every reader of the book and depends as much upon himself as upon the book and the author.

From its early beginnings in the ninth century down to the present day, French literature can claim a continued existence of 1100 years. What country, besides our own, can boast such literary wealth, such resource, such powers of renewal? The authors of this history, the first of its kind in English, have been only too well aware of the difficulties attendant upon so vast an enterprise. Their hope is that it may give to all readers of French literature a coherent background against which parti-cular periods or writers may be studied and enjoyed in greater depth.

P. E. C.

PREFACE

THE chronological limits of this volume are indicated by the beginnings of printing in France (*c.* 1470) and the sunset of the Valois (1589); so far as the end of our period is concerned, the choice of authors who spill over into the seventeenth century has been determined in some measure by the terms of reference conferred by Professor P. J. Yarrow on his volume. Three main principles underlie my approach to the sixteenth century: in the first place, we are dealing with a period which is unlikely to be familiar to the reader in the way that the volumes already published in this series may legitimately assume is the case for the authors they consider. At the same time, a student who goes on to the Renaissance period may well be eager to make rapid progress, since his motivation has been enriched by his previous knowledge of the seventeenth century and literature since 1800. I have therefore deemed it right to offer some sections that deal with basic aspects of the Renaissance world-picture; but I have also given a certain amount of more advanced bibliographical information which I hope will help the reader to get to grips quickly with primary sources. In the second place, I have tried to make the reader aware of the present state of Renaissance studies in the field of French literature; there will inevitably be an interval between the composition of my text and the moment of publication, so I should make it clear that I have not been able to take full account of research published since autumn 1971, though here and there I have made some exceptions. And thirdly, I have tried to provide the reader with a personal interpretation of the sixteenth century. Clearly, these three principles may not always make ideal bedfellows; but I am convinced that, even though a fairly objective survey of a period of literature is far from useless, it is more important that the reader should feel that what I have to say is not just potted information, but the result of experience and genuine response. Charles du Bos once wrote:

Je n'attache vraiment de prix qu'à ce qui, dans la vie intellectuelle, peut devenir consubstantiel à la conscience . . . Consubstantiel, tout est là. Ou la littérature nous est, nous devient, nous deviendra consubstantielle, ou, pour lui appliquer le mot de Pascal sur la philosophie, elle 'ne vaut pas une heure de peine'. (*Approximations*, VII, 325)

In his own register, he was no doubt echoing something of Rabelais's recognition that 'Science sans conscience n'est que ruyne de l'âme'. Stress will therefore be on the texts and on the cultural matrix out of which they grew; biographical material will be reduced to a minimum, though something must be said on the groups and circles in which ideas and sensibility take shape.

A number of early difficulties face any reader approaching French Renaissance literature: spelling, for instance. Though I have tried as far as possible to respect the spelling(s) of the times, I have on occasion made some concessions. A glossary is also supplied to help with terms that must occur in the text, especially in the fields of literary genre, rhetoric, and theology. The Bibliography is divided into footnotes dealing with specific authors, texts and points as they crop up, and the General section. These bibliographies make no claim to completeness, but they will help in the first steps of further reading and they will also express on my part a sense of gratitude to books and colleagues from whom I have profited. Certain valuable monographs, published too late for me to make proper use of their findings, are noted by means of an asterisk. (Except where stated otherwise, English titles are published in London and French ones in Paris.)

Where possible, 'modern' editions are indicated, as the originals may be difficult of access; but it must be admitted that some of these 'modern' editions are stopgaps, and in any case the reader will wish to consult as soon as possible original editions; to this end, I have given locations of the works under scrutiny. These locations are naturally incomplete, but I have made a point of noting the existence of books in the United Kingdom; British libraries are very much better endowed in Renaissance French books than is commonly supposed.

The reader will therefore soon find himself on the way to the bibliographical world: in every *seiziémiste* there lurks a bibliophile. But he ought to equip himself in other ways too: one cannot embark seriously on a study of Renaissance France without a competent knowledge of Latin, and to that should be added Italian; nor would some acquaintance with Greek, German, and Dutch come amiss. In an age where men of culture discussed religion as we discuss politics, a familiarity with the Bible is essential; the more I read in sixteenth-century literature, the more I regret not having had some theological training.

I have tried, so far as I can, to avoid using emotionally charged terms such as 'Baroque' or 'Mannerism'. I would not wish to diminish the worth of Baroque criteria for a re-evaluation of much fine poetry written towards the end of the century, but I suspect that such terms are more useful after one has established first-hand acquaintance with the literature in question, and should not be bandied about prematurely. Had it been possible, I should have avoided the terms 'humanism', 'Renaissance', 'classicism', but this has not always been practicable.

Finally, I believe that the reader will find much in the sixteenth century that is, as the phrase goes, 'relevant to our own age'. The Renaissance is essentially a time of crisis, of transition from certain structures and sets of values to new ones; and in consequence, it is a period in which men are forced to ask themselves fundamental questions, but (or should one say and?) also a period of immense vitality, in which all possible responses to the human condition are represented and sometimes apprehended in the web of literary genius. Tower of Babel or think-tank, the Renaissance raises in acute form all sorts of vital questions, not least the two cardinal ones of the relations between authority (tradition) and self-realisation, and of those between commitment and detachment, on which, of course, Montaigne provides such illuminating reflections towards the end of the century. Nor is it a coincidence that the poetic criteria formulated since the days of Mallarmé and Valéry have enabled us to savour the splendid poetry written from Scève onwards with greater understanding and approval. To come to grips with the Renaissance is one way of grasping issues ever-present to us today; this of course does not imply that there are easy short-cuts to understanding the mental structures and categories within which the

Renaissance mind tackled those problems. And it will be necessary to encounter humanists such as Pierre de La Ramée (Ramus), Guillaume Postel, or Jean Bodin, whose work is essential to the understanding of the French Renaissance, but who fall in great measure outside the scope of a book concerned primarily with its literary manifestations.

It remains for me to acknowledge many debts to colleagues, friends, and predecessors; without them it would have been impossible to write this book and, though space may prevent explicit recognition of debts in the text from time to time, I have tried to bring the fruits of their research and judgement to a wider public.[1] More substantial obligations must gladly be expressed: in the first place, I owe a particular debt to my friends Richard Sayce and Terence Cave who read the typescript in its entirety and offered many helpful and wise suggestions to its great profit; a more distant debt in time, but equally important, I acknowledge to Gladys Dickinson who first opened my eyes to the Renaissance. And I also wish to thank my wife, not only for encouragement and patience over many years, but for her critical perusal of the text from which she removed many stylistic warts and excrescences.

I. D. MCF.

Oxford
March 1973

NOTE

1. This includes unpublished dissertations, whose authors, now colleagues, have kindly allowed me to consult them. I have, however, mentioned two theses (by Dr Hindley and Dr Gouna), of whose existence I became aware too late to profit by their conclusions.

CONTENTS

FOREWORD BY THE GENERAL EDITOR   ix

PREFACE   xiii

LIST OF ABBREVIATIONS   xxiii

INTRODUCTION   1
I. Geography and Political Structures, 1. II. Language, 5. III. The Renaissance World-Picture, 7. IV. Conception of Poetry, 10

PART I

1 EARLY HUMANISM AND THE
   RHÉTORIQUEURS   21
I. Historical Outlines until 1529, 21. II. Early Humanism, 25. III. Early Printing, 28. IV. Neo-latin Poetry, 29 V. The *rhétoriqueurs*, 31. VI. *Rhétoriqueur* Poetry, 31. VII. Jean Lemaire de Belges (1473–?1524), 40. VIII. Early Historiography, 45: Jean d'Auton (1467–1528), 47; Jean Lemaire de Belges, 49; Philippe de Commynes (1445–1509), 50; *Rhétoriqueur* Prose Style, 51; *Histoire de Bayart* (1527), 53. IX. Claude de Seyssel (1450–?1520), 53. X. Early Drama, 55; The *mystères*, 55; The *moralité*, 56; The *sottie*, 58; The *farce*, 59; Other Genres, 60; Marguerite de Navarre (1492–1549), 61. Conclusion to Part I, 63. Appendix to Part I, 64

PART II

2 FRANCIS I AND THE DEVELOPMENT
   OF FRENCH CULTURE   71
I. Historical Outlines, 71. II. Emergence of a New Cultural Climate, 73. III. Renaissance Themes, 75. IV. The Study of Greek, 78. V. Printing, 79. VI. Educational Reform, 80. VII. Guillaume Budé (1467–1540), 82.

xvii

VIII. Religious Developments, 83. IX. Lefèvre d'Etaples (*c.* 1450–1536), 84. X. Erasmus (?1469–1536), 86

3 POETRY DURING THE REIGN OF FRANCIS I 90
I. General Survey, 90. II. Latter-day *Rhétoriqueurs*, 93: Jean Marot (?—?1526), 94; Jean Parmentier (1494–1529), 96; Eustorg de Beaulieu (?1495–1552), 97; Roger de Collerye (?1470–1537), 97; Minor Figures, 98; Jean Bouchet, 99; François Habert, 100; Bonaventure des Périers, 102. III. Neo-latin Poetry, 103. IV. Clément Marot (*c.* 1496–1544), 104. V. The *querelle des amyes* – Neoplatonism – Aulic and anti-Aulic Themes, 115: Neoplatonism, 117; Antoine Héroët (?1492–1568), 118; Further Developments, 120; Philibert de Vienne, 123. VI. Marguerite de Navarre, 125. VII. Transitional Figures, 129: Charles Fontaine (1514–?), 129; Charles de Sainte-Marthe and Mellin de Saint-Gellais, 130; Hugues Salel (1504–53), 131; Peletier du Mans (1517–1582), 132. VIII. Towards a more Conscious Promotion of the Vernacular as a Means of Literary Expression, 135: Translations, 136; French Poetic Theory, 138; The *Deffense et illustration* (1549), 140

4 HUMANISM AND LITERATURE IN LYONS DURING THE FIRST HALF OF THE SIXTEENTH CENTURY 147
I. General Survey, 147: Symphorien Champier (1471–?1539), 148; *Collège de la Trinité*, 150; Neo-latin Activity, 151; Printing, 152. II. Maurice Scève (*c.* 1500–60), 153. III. Pernette du Guillet, 161. IV. Louise Labé (?1520–1565), 162

5 PROSE FICTION UNDER FRANCIS I 167
I. The Novel, 167: *Jehan de Paris* (1533), 167; Foreign Novels, 168; Helisenne de Crenne, 169; Theodose Valentinian, 170. II. François Rabelais (?1494–?1553), 171: *Pantagruel*, 172; *Gargantua*, 174; *Tiers Livre*, 178; *Quart Livre*, 185; The Fifth Book, 187. Appendix: The Emergence of the Epistolary Genre, 190

PART III

6 THE REIGN OF HENRY II – POLITICAL AND CULTURAL BACKGROUND 195
I. Political Outlines, 195. II. Social and Intellectual

Background, 198. III. The Court, 198. IV. Humanism,
199. V. Neoplatonism, 202. VI. Neo-stoicism, 205. VII.
Scepticism and Rationalism, 205. VIII. Occultism, 206

7 THE DEVELOPMENT OF PROSE AND THE
WIDENING OF MAN'S HORIZONS 211
I. The Dialogue, 211: *Cymbalum Mundi* (1537), 213;
Pontus de Tyard, 215; Etienne Pasquier – *Le Monophile*
(1554), 216; Louis Le Caron (?1534–1613), 217; Guy de
Bruès, 220; Jacques Tahureau (1565), 221. II. Emergence
of New Attitudes to Scientific Study, 224: André Thevet
(?1504–92), 225; N. de Nicolay, 227; Pierre Belon (1517–
1564), 228; Ambroise Paré (?1509–90), 229; Bernard
Palissy (*c.* 1510–90), 231

8 DEVELOPMENTS IN NARRATIVE FICTION
AFTER 1550 234
I. General Survey (including Earlier Activity), 234:
Jeanne Flore, 238; La Motte Roullant, 239; Noël du
Fail (?1521–91), 240; Claude de Taillemont (?1504–
?1558), 241; *Comptes du monde aventureux* (1555), 242:
Marguerite de Navarre and her *Heptaméron*, 243; Bona-
venture des Périers (1510–44), 249; Henri Estienne (1531–
1598), 251; P. Boaistuau and F. de Belleforest, 252;
Jacques Yver's *Printemps*, 253; Bénigne Poissenot –
L'Esté (1583), 254; Developments at End of Period:
E. Tabourot, Gabriel Chappuys, Guillaume Bouchet,
N. de Cholières, 255

9 THE PLÉIADE 260
I. Introduction, 260. II. Neo-latin Poetry, 262. III.
Pontus de Tyard (1521–1605), 264. IV. Joachim du
Bellay (1523–60), 266. V. Rémy Belleau (1528–77), 276.
VI. Jean-Antoine de Baïf (1532–89), 281. VII. Etienne
Jodelle (1532–73), 284. VIII. The Pléiade and the Pro-
vinces, 287: Etienne Forcadel (*c.* 1518–73), 287; Marc-
Claude Buttet (1530–86), 288. IX. Poets Associated with
Poitiers, 289; Vauquelin de la Fresnaye (*c.* 1535–1606),
289; Jacques Tahureau (1527–55), 290; Charles Toutain,
291; Scévole de Sainte-Marthe (1533–1623), 291. Appen-
dix, 293

10 PIERRE DE RONSARD (1524–85) 297
I. The *Odes*, 298. II. The *Amours*, 300. III. The Philo-
sophical Poet, 305. IV. The Court Poet, 309. V. The
Committed Poet, 313. VI. The Later Poetry, 316. VII.
Ronsard's Poetic World, 319

PART IV

11 THE WARS OF RELIGION   331
    I. Historical Outlines from 1559, 331. II. Calvinism and
    its Relevance to Literary Developments, 336. III. Jean
    Calvin (1509–64), 337. IV. The Calvinist Conception of
    Literature, 343. V. Fields of Calvinist Literary Activity,
    345: The Theatre, 345; Théodore de Bèze – *Abraham
    sacrifiant* (1550), 345; Louis des Masures – *Tragédies
    saintes* (1566), 346; Non-dramatic poetry. Meditations,
    347; Political Theory, 350. VI. Agrippa d'Aubigné – *Les
    Tragiques*, 352

12 POETRY UNDER CHARLES IX AND HENRY III 364
    I. General Survey, 364: The Court, 364; Literary *Salons*
    and Groups. Types of Poetry Composed, 368; Neo-latin
    Poetry, 370. II. Love-Poetry, 373: Amadis Jamyn
    (?1540–93), 373; Philippe Desportes (1546–1606), 374;
    D'Aubigné – *Le Printemps*, 376. III. 'Scientific' Poetry,
    379: Peletier du Mans – *Amour des Amours* (1554), 379;
    Maurice Scève – *Microcosme*, 382; Guy Lefèvre de la
    Boderie (1541–98), 384; Saluste du Bartas (1544–90), 387;
    Beroalde de Verville (1556–?1629), 390; Isaac Habert
    (?1560–?), 392. IV. Religious Poetry, 394: Anne des
    Marquets (?–1588), 397; Georgette de Montenay
    (1540–?), 398; Jacques de Billy (1535–81), 399; Jean de
    Sponde (1557–94), 403; Jean-Baptiste Chassignet (?1578–
    ?1635), 406. V. Committed, Satirical, and *Moraliste*
    Poetry, 409. VI. Conclusion, 418

13 THE THEATRE AFTER THE ADVENT
    OF THE PLÉIADE   424
    I. Tragedy, 424: Tragedy-Theory, 425; Jodelle, 427;
    Jacques Grévin – *Jules César* (1561), 430; Gabriel
    Bounyn – *La Soltane* (1561), 431; A. de Rivaudeau –
    Aman (1566), 432; Jean de la Taille (?1533–?1617), 435;
    Robert Garnier (c. 1545–90), 437. II. Comedy, 442:
    Survey and Theory, 442; Etienne Jodelle – *L'Eugène*,
    444; Jacques Grévin, 445; Rémy Belleau – *La Reconnue*,
    446; Jean de la Taille – *Les Corrivaus* (1573), 447; Pierre
    de Larivey (?1540–1619), 448; François d'Amboise, 450;
    Odet de Turnèbe – *Les Contens*, 450; Pierre Le Loyer –
    Nephelococugie, 451. III. Tragicomedy, 452; R. Garnier
    – *Bradamante* (1582), 452. IV. Conclusion, 453. Chrono-
    logical Table of Plays, 454

14 PROSE WRITERS AND THE STUDY OF MAN
    IN HIS HISTORICAL AND POLITICAL
    CONTEXTS   458
    I. The Study of History, 458: Etienne Pasquier, 461.
    II. Writers of Memoirs, 462: Blaise de Montluc (1502–
    1577), 462; Pierre de Bourdeille (Brantôme) (c. 1534–
    1614), 464; Marguerite de Valois (1553–1615), 465. III.
    Mid-century Political Thought, 467: Jean Bodin – *De la
    Republique* (1580), 468; Etienne de la Boétie (1530–63),
    470. IV. *La Satyre Menippée*, 472. V. Conclusion, 474

15 MICHEL DE MONTAIGNE (1533–92)   477
    Appendix: *Le Journal du Voyage*, 499

    RETROSPECT AND PROSPECT   501

    FURTHER READING AND STUDY   511

    GENERAL BIBLIOGRAPHY   516

    GLOSSARY   528

    A NOTE ON DATING   533

    INDEX   535

Abbreviations

AGB	Association Guillaume Budé (has its own *Bulletin*)
Ars	Bibliothèque de l'Arsenal, Paris
ASNS	*Archive für das Studium der neueren Sprachen*
BHR	*Bibliothèque d'Humanisme et Renaissance*
BM	British Museum
BN	Bibliothèque Nationale, Paris
BSHP	*Bulletin de la Société de l'Histoire du Protestantisme Français* (the Society's library is in Paris)
CAIEF	*Cahiers de l'Association Internationale des Etudes Françaises*
CDU	Centre de Documentation Universitaire, Paris
CL	*Comparative Literature*
ECr	*L'Esprit Créateur*
EUL	Edinburgh University Library
FMLS	*Forum for Modern Language Studies*
FRC	*French Renaissance Classics*
FS	*French Studies*
HR	*Humanisme et Renaissance* (subsequently became *BHR*)
MC	Manchester University, Christie Collection
MLN	*Modern Language Notes*
MLQ	*Modern Language Quarterly*
MLR	*Modern Language Review*
MPh	*Modern Philology*
MRy	Manchester, Rylands Library
NLS	National Library of Scotland, Edinburgh
O	Oxford, Bodleian Library
PMLA	*Publications of the Modern Language Association of America*
PSG	Paris, Bibliothèque Sainte-Geneviève
RF	*Romanische Forschungen*
RHLF	*Revue d'Histoire Littéraire de la France*

RR	*Romanic Review*
RRen	*Revue de la Renaissance*
RSH	*Revue des Sciences Humaines*
RSS	*Revue du Seizième Siècle*
SATF	Société des Anciens Textes Français
SF	*Studi Francesi*
SHF	Société de l'Histoire de France
SPh	*Studies in Philology*
StA	Library, University of St Andrews
STFM	Société des Textes Français Modernes (published by Didier)
THR	*Travaux d'Humanisme et Renaissance* (Droz, Geneva)
TLF	*Textes Littéraires Français* (published by Droz, Geneva)
ZFSL	*Zeitschrift für französische Sprache und Literatur*
ZRP	*Zeitschrift für Romanische Philologie*

Dates of the relevant Kings of France

1483–98	Charles VIII
1498–1515	Louis XII
1515–47	Francis I
1547–59	Henry II
1559–60	Francis II
1560–74	Charles IX
1574–89	Henry III
1589–1610	Henry IV

INTRODUCTION

BEFORE we come to grips with the literary developments of the period, we ought to cast an eye over one or two aspects of what one might call the cultural infrastructure. The Renaissance Frenchman lives in a land that is geographically different from the France of today; he employs a language, or languages, that will be affected by the geography and the political structures of his country; and he will have a conception of the world that is basically pre-Copernican.

I. GEOGRAPHY AND POLITICAL STRUCTURES[1]

At the beginning of our period, that is during the reign of Louis XI, the frontiers of France were more confined than today; the north-east was particularly fluid and remained so for most of the sixteenth century and even later, but to the south Savoy was outside the territory. The face of the country will be affected by two factors: the foreign policy of a succession of kings, involved in conflict with England, or Italian states, or the Holy Roman Emperor, leads to alternate expansion and contraction of the frontiers; and within the country there were still areas that asserted a certain independence of the Crown. Dauphiné (1349) and Provence (1463) were already linked to the kingdom, but were not considered fully part and parcel, since the monarch was obeyed there by virtue of his being dauphin of Dauphiné and count of Provence. Only after the death of Charles the Bold did Burgundy become assimilated (1478), but in several cases the official recognition of a change in status was not necessarily matched by popular, local assent. Brittany was related to France under Charles VIII and Louis XII because these kings both married Anne of Brittany, but it was not until 1532 that full union was sought and reached. In the south-west, the lands of the kings of Navarre enjoyed autonomous status, and even in the seventeenth century the kings of France maintain the style ' . . . et de Navarre'. Calais remained in English hands until 1558 and the north-eastern frontier was to remain unstable for a long time to come; moreover, Alsace-Lorraine was not yet part of the realm. The lands of the Bourbon family were absorbed during the first half of Francis I's reign; but the Nivernais enjoyed a privileged and indeed curious position. The Pope's jurisdiction extended over Avignon and the Venaissin. Throughout our period, therefore, there is, apart from one or two pockets of resistance, a gradual spread of royal power, and though the wars of religion will seriously threaten central authority, the advance towards a firmer conception of monarchy is a steady one.

This patchwork pattern of authority was also reflected at commercial level: communications were poor and dangerous, the roads usually deplorable,[2] the rivers often encumbered by stationary boats and mills (as for instance the Rhône at Lyons). Trade was further hampered by local tolls and taxes, and there was no standardised currency in the land. Couriers were still sporadic, except at royal and university level. Paris, though the centre of France, was not unambiguously so over the whole period, either politically or culturally. Demographic statistics are difficult to come by, but the capital was probably not much larger than sixteenth-century Venice, and under Henry II it has been suggested that it contained some 210,000 inhabitants; but it was regularly afflicted by plagues. Geographically it was well placed, acting as a thoroughfare between north and south, with a further main road to Orléans. Two arteries crossed the city, corresponding roughly to the rue Saint-Denis and the rue Saint-Martin, and in early times the Ile de la Cité had provided a useful refuge. In the Middle Ages, development occurred to the north, and on the South Bank colleges and religious settlements took root. At the beginning of our period, the city was fairly static; between Charles VII and Louis XII, almost nothing had been constructed, the city being surrounded with walls consolidated during the later Middle Ages. Bridges across the Seine linked the three parts, but often collapsed under the numerous houses they carried; towers anchored the chains that were slung across the river in time of flood or other emergency. During the sixteenth century the face of the city changes more rapidly: in spite of pestilence, the population appears to have increased at some rate; the royal family, disliking the old tower of the Louvre, plans the reconstruction of the area and incorporates it within the fortifications of the city; and some effort is made to improve and build roads. A number of churches are built, completed, or modified (Saint-Gervais, Saint-Etienne du Mont, Saint-Eustache).[3]

Outside Paris, the main towns were those which had a university, a *parlement*, or both: the outstanding exception was Lyons which had neither, but enjoyed special privileges and stood at the crossroads between Italy and the north, and Spain and Germany (see below, pp. 147–8). The second town of the realm was held to be Rouen, but foreigners often spoke highly of Orléans, whose university was celebrated for civil law, not taught in Paris. Among the universities, Poitiers remained an important cultural centre: its links with poets influenced by the Pléiade are well known, and later its law faculty became closely associated with an absolutist view of the monarchy. Bourges had its moment of glory when Alciat taught there and Marguerite de Navarre gave it her support and with Orléans played some part in the diffusion of Lutheran ideas. Toulouse, on the other hand, founded to resist heresy, was a distinguished centre of law, but the town with its religious fanaticism and intellectual conservatism became the target for humanist abuse and scorn (*Tolosa barbara*). The other important university was Montpellier, celebrated throughout the centuries for its medical studies. The main harbour towns were Marseilles, trading with Morocco and the Levant, and especially when the New World opens up, La Rochelle, Bordeaux, Nantes; the northern ports also had military value – Dieppe, Saint-Malo, and Le Havre which was completed in 1547.

During the sixteenth century the structure of government becomes increasingly complex: this is due in part to the development of a more systematic legal organisation, to a growing presence of what nowadays one would call civil servants, and also to the need of a better financial network brought about by expensive foreign policies, the development of court life, and later by the ravages of civil war. Major innovations were introduced under Francis I, but later kings also played their part in building the system. Government was assured through high officials, many of whom formed part of the *Maison du Roi*, and by a hierarchy of councils and committees. Certain posts were of exceptional importance, though the duties and competence are not always easy to determine with precision. Of the state officials, the *Connétable* and the *Chancelier* were the most influential. The *Connétable*, with a smaller staff at his disposal than the *Chancelier*, was the king's lieutenant in all things military, and his authority was all the greater at a time when the need for a permanent army became obvious. He was in charge of military discipline and had certain representational functions, but because his post was potentially a very powerful one, it was not always filled. The *Chancelier*, with his large administrative staff, was the Viceroy in the field of justice and head of the magistrature; he presided over the Council in the king's absence and was Keeper of the Royal Seal. We shall find the names of various *Chanceliers* appearing frequently in ceremonial and encomiastic verse, such as Antoine du Prat, François Olivier, and Michel de l'Hôpital, who were enlightened, if not always disinterested, humanists. The *Grand Aumônier*, concerned with matters religious and charitable, also had a say in the appointment of the Royal Readers, see below, p. 81) and, it seems, in ecclesiastical preferment.

The post of *Grand Maître* was influential but that of the *Grand Chambrier* was only filled sporadically.

The administration of justice was a complex affair: to begin with the church still had its own courts for certain offences, and royal justice did not always prevail in the *justices seigneuriales* or *municipales*, though these rights were gradually eroded with the extension of royal authority through the land. Where the king's power prevailed, there were special courts or authorities with their own field of competence (*Table de Marbre, Connétablie, Prévosts des Maréchaux*), and exceptional means of dispensing justice were available through the *Grand Conseil*, the *juridictions extraordinaires*, the *Requêtes du Palais*, and the *Requêtes de l'Hôtel*; but the normal course of justice ran through the *bailliages*, the *sénéchaussées*, later the *présidiaux*, but especially the eight *parlements* of which the *Parlement de Paris* came to be the most powerful: it claimed to be the supreme court of appeal, it registered the royal decrees, it enjoyed, off and on, powers of censorship, much resented by the Sorbonne, it considered itself to have the 'manutention et tuition de la chose publique', in other words it saw itself as the spokesman of the national conscience, and it exercised ambulant justice by means of the *Grands Jours*. It thus came to wield considerable political authority and distinguished itself often by a strongly gallican attitude in religious matters. Its relations with the provincial *parlements*, which tended to voice local interests and also saw themselves as representatives of the governed, were not always harmonious; but during the sixteenth century, there is an evolution, checkered and hesitant at times, towards the increased authority of central institutions and justice. In the second half of the century, we shall notice, from the literary point of view, an ever closer association between letters and the legal world. This is also a period in which the study of law, not only common law, but Roman law, assumes substantial proportions, and these studies, scholarly in their own right, also serve to give theoretical support to the growing prestige of central authority and more especially of monarchy by divine right. With the political solution found by Henry IV, absolutist theory will be furthered by the desire for order, unity, and identity that characterises the final years of the century, at a time when the claims of the Huguenots have been, to say the least, circumscribed. In this context, the members of the legal profession acquire yet more standing in the social and political structure, partly because of their increased role, but also because of their growing numbers and the marked tendency for legal posts to be confined to a limited family network; a survey of the various repertories of the *parlements* reveals a recurrence of the same family names, and a pattern of resignations in favour of some relative.

Finally, what of the structure of church authority? At the beginning of our period, France was divided into fourteen ecclesiastical provinces, with well over a hundred dioceses, though figures fluctuate inevitably with the variations in national frontiers, and the bishops in the Comtat Venaissin constituted an atypical case. Though the bishop had full powers of jurisdiction in his diocese, his position was always weakened by the unresolved problems of the relation between the bishops, the monastic orders, and the Pope: this question impinged, for instance, on nomination to benefices, but also on matters of justice, where the bishop might be caught between the claims of royal justice and those of the Pope. This last problem was one of many that finally led to the Concordat between Francis I and the Pope (see below, p. 23); but gallicanism is not the only factor that will raise difficulties, for we are entering the period when questions of doctrinal and moral reform become burning issues.

II. LANGUAGE[4]

During the Renaissance, the French language develops with a rapidity that disconcerts many contemporaries: Tory in his *Champfleury* (1529), wrote: 'aujourdhuy est changé en mille façons du language qui estoit il y a cinquante ans', and at the end of the century Montaigne observed that

Selon la variation continuelle qui a suivy le nostre [langage] jusques à cette heure, qui peult esperer que sa forme presente soit en usage, d'icy à cinquante ans? . . . et depuis que je vis, s'est altéré de moitié. (Essais, III, ix)

This fluidity was indeed one of the arguments invoked for maintaining the cultural supremacy of Latin; and even by the middle of the century – firm statistics are hard to come by – it seems that half of the books printed were still in Latin. The case for Latin rested in part on the vested interests of the Church, universities, and schools, and in a more limited measure, science; but those who wished to make their mark by the printed word valued a tongue that transcended national frontiers and the ravages of time. Many French poets tried to vie with Italy by composing Neo-latin verse; and of the Pléiade only Ronsard remained faithful to the vernacular, all his friends taking out insurance policies with posterity in Latin verse. Ronsard and Marot are translated into Latin until the end of the century; and Pasquier, who had an interesting exchange with Turnèbe on the respective merits of the two languages, later published a considerable amount of Latin poetry. Moreover, many contemporaries thought that French was not yet a suitable vehicle for graver themes, and this suspicion colours Du Bellay's *Deffense*. Nevertheless, the counter-arguments gathered momentum: national-

ism, increasing throughout the Renaissance, must work in favour of
the vernacular. Some wondered whether Latin, for all its powers of
endurance, could really keep pace with developments in science and
culture – and in this context medicine and biology are important.
The influence of the Reformers, who sought to reach the Christian
without intermediary and to let him read the Scriptures in his own
tongue, cannot be ignored; and, even more significant is the gradual
spread of royal authority through the *parlements* and the legal
system: the edict of Villers-Cotterets (1539) upheld the claims of
French over Latin and marks the culmination of a series of efforts
by central authority in this direction. And in the long run, the growing prestige of the Court, no longer peripatetic, and indeed of Paris
as the capital, will count for much. At all events, the sixteenth
century sees the appearance of hosts of grammarians preoccupied
with describing the language, establishing rules for grammar, pronunciation and spelling reforms (Tory, Palsgrave, Meigret, La
Ramée, Estienne, etc.); and all this must be seen against a background of increasing cultural nationalism, but also in the context of
the development of printing, for the printers will gradually promote
the standardisation of print and therefore of spelling. Many linguistic reformers were printers, though it must also be said that
humanist learning often introduced aberrations in the field of spelling on so-called etymological grounds.

The French language at this time, and especially in its printed and
literary aspects, is a genuine entity; the dialectical elements have
probably been overestimated, though Paris did not exert yet as great
an influence as in the seventeenth century. In pronunciation, apart
from the incursus of unwonted elements from humanist or popular
sources (e.g., the hesitation over intervocalic–r–/–z–), one notices a
gradual levelling-out of sounds (*au* = *o*, and sounds may conflate,
ain/*ein*/*in*); and some consonants will fade in specific positions,
though humanism will on occasion try to check this evolution.[5] A
modern reader will notice certain phonetic differences by a careful
look at the rhymes of sixteenth-century poets. Generally speaking,
two tendencies may be observed in the written tongue: on the one
hand, there is a marked increase in vocabulary, brought about partly
by the acquisition of new knowledge, the influence of classical vocabulary on form and meaning, the needs of the translators, a broadening of intellectual discussion in the vernacular, the recommendations
of the Pléiade on dialectalisms, neologisms, and archaisms. And on
the other hand, perhaps as an unconscious counterweight, attempts
are made to ensure greater clarity. The sixteenth-century prose sentence is often a rather loose baggy thing, and though syntactical
structures often remain quite complicated, clarifications are introduced little by little: the need for the article before the noun and the

pronoun before the verb; efforts to formulate rules for the agreement of the past participle; gradual standardisation of the conjugations; the emergence of a more sophisticated system of articles (especially the indefinite and the partitive); the fading of the passe-partout *que* in favour of clearer subordination (the forms *lequel*, etc., owe something to humanist influence); all these features make for greater control and ease of communication, though word order, in spite of some development between Rabelais and Montaigne, is still much more flexible than it will be in the following century. There are of course different levels of literary utterance at which the authors of the sixteenth century write: in poetry, the classical and medieval theory of the three styles is still very vigorous, and, as we shall see, the role of rhetoric is extremely important; but in the field of prose, we shall find a different approach among the humanists, who are affected by classical models and sometimes by the fashionable Ciceronianism, and among the authors of scientific treatises and of memoirs who stress their non-humanist formation (e.g., Ambroise Paré or Montluc) and who in spite of some concessions to a more self-conscious style pride themselves on a natural utterance. Even so, with the advent of printing and the widening of educational activity, the demands of the public will apply certain pressures to authors, whatever their origin; and if it may be sometimes difficult to define the public or publics for whom books are published, their role is an ever increasing one.

III. THE RENAISSANCE WORLD-PICTURE[6]

Renaissance man saw the world in a very different perspective from people today. No doubt for the average man, the assumptions on which he based his picture remained medieval, but during our period various influences, classical, Italian, scientific, will introduce shifts of attitude, and theological discussion will often centre on such key problems as man's psychology in the context of free-will, the relations between the different domains of the mind, and so forth. The discussions of such problems are not always easy to follow, partly because linguistic difficulties may arise, partly because the thinking can be muddled, especially in a period when syncretist tendencies are very much in evidence. Nevertheless, some 'working model', even if it glosses over vital areas of debate, is useful as an initial framework of reference. A student of literature may not wish to explore the more technical treatises in which these matters are considered; but he will not understand many references and assumptions in prose and poetry if he makes no attempt to understand the Renaissance world-picture.

Though the words *achriste* and *athée* are frequently bandied about in acrimonious argument, there seem to be few atheists on the ground; most people would accept the view that there was a unity in the Universe and that man's destiny was to be interpreted in Christian fashion. The Universe, created *ex nihilo* (though there was also the aristotelian view), was geocentric. Round the earth there circled the spheres (usually nine or ten), and their music was inaudible to fallen man. Beyond the spheres the *habitaculum Dei*, and in between these the *primum mobile*. An important distinction in the structure of the Universe was marked by the moon: what lay beyond it was created in a perfect blend of the four elements, was therefore immortal and situated where the air was pure. In the *sublunar* world, the elements blended imperfectly and the air was foul and infested. The moon and stars were believed to exert a considerable influence upon man's destiny (within theologically acceptable limits) – hence the overlap between astronomy and astrology. For most people God and Nature were identical, but with classical influences, the distinction was visible, and with it the difference between *fatum, fortuna*, and providence. If Nature was differentiated, she was hastily subjected to the divine will. In the Universe, and acting as links between God and man, were the angels who, though they enjoyed free-will, never acted against God's wishes. They were divided into various orders, though experts often differed in their classifications, and the Neoplatonic currents brought their own variations upon these themes.

Man's place in this system was viewed in the light of the Fall. He was, however, the highest form of being in this world, since he partook of both divine and terrestrial being; and in consequence he acted as a link between the phenomena in the world. Physically, he was an imperfect compound of four elements, seen in the body as four humours (but here too there was a division of opinion between Galen and Hippocrates). These elements have nothing to do with modern elements, but are connected with certain prime characteristics of matter. They had a series of cognate manifestations: *fire*, choler, hot and dry, bitter, gall, summer; *air*, blood, hot, moist, sweet, spring; *water*, phlegm, cold, moist, tasteless, rain, winter; *earth*, melancholy, cold and dry, *aigre*, spleen, autumn. These parallels, within the context of the body, affected matters of balance: for instance, if the humours went beyond their part of the body, they gave rise to illnesses, so that phlegm mounting to the brain induced diseases such as apoplexy or 'catarrh'. Humans could be classified according to various temperaments, depending on whether they were divided according to humours or to the qualities inherent in the elements. The links between the elements and the humours manifesting themselves in the body were called spirits. Natural spirits rose from the liver and penetrated the body through the veins; vital spirits, created in the heart (with the help of air from the lungs), entered the body through the arteries; and the animal spirits appear to be some refinement of the vital spirits, but functioning in the brain, so that they became the link between the body and the soul.

On the question of psychosomatic relations, opinions were divided, and these differences were to have important consequences. There was (i) the vegetative soul, which linked man with the animal kingdom and was concerned with procreation, growth, and nutrition. Then came (ii) the sensible soul, subdivided in divers fashions. The exterior part concerned the five senses and the communication of sense data to the brain, whereas the interior had special functions or faculties: commonsense, imagination, memory, spatially associated with the front, middle, and rear of the brain. The sensible soul was, for some, divisible into the concupiscible and the irascible. It contained the faculties of knowing and desiring. Then (iii) the rational soul, which distinguished man from the rest of the world, was what was left in him of the divine and angelic after the Fall. It possessed two chief characteristics: understanding with judgement and the will. Life was therefore seen as a struggle in part between passions and reason, and ethics aimed at restoring the proper equilibrium of forces; passion might blind the will and the understanding as well as contribute something positive. Nevertheless, there were shades of opinion on the relations and differences between reason, will, and passion.[7] The position of the imagination, usually thought of as irresponsible and linked with the passions, was also slightly ambiguous. Finally, there persisted the medieval attitude to woman's 'inferiority', an attitude determined in part by her role in *Genesis*, but also by physiological structure.

With the emergence of neo-stoicism, the stress becomes greater on the value of self-knowledge as a step towards moral progress; but the concept of virtue remains very complex. Theologically it constitutes the opposite of sin, but it can also be the control of the passions by the reason, the preservation of order in the human economy. It also becomes associated with the golden mean, and for some too, with certain social connotations, so that it impinges on what was later to become *honnêteté*. On the other hand, with the reappraisal of theological positions, discussion brought in the problem of free-will and determinism, and the role and measure of grace. It will take more than the century of the Renaissance to reach, in a modern context, a satisfying and acceptable solution to the nexus of problems relating to synergism. These problems enter the literary domain, as even a superficial perusal of Rabelais will show; and though certain distinctions may be blurred in poetic contexts, this is by no means always the case and one must try to grasp the different resonance of words such as *sors, providence, destin, fortune.*

IV. CONCEPTION OF POETRY[8]

Though the problem of poetry is more circumscribed than matters just considered, it is one that should form part of the prolegomena to Renaissance literature. For readers coming after the Romantic movement, Renaissance poetry requires some mental readjustment and an awareness that different principles underlie its composition. The humanist poet did not claim originality by the assertion of his personality, he was suspicious of the workings of the imagination, he did not set so high a premium on sincerity as the Romantic writer, and he normally regarded himself as being under certain obligations towards the public for whom he was writing. As in the case of the Renaissance world-picture, I shall offer a working model of Renaissance poetic theory, on the understanding that I am simplifying the position and not taking into account the variations that any given poet may develop on certain points.

The poet considers himself the guardian of traditional values and one able to communicate truths to a public which enjoys a lesser measure of sophistication. At all times, poets have been concerned to offer a serious, worthwhile justification of their practice; and in the Renaissance this wish must be seen against the background of a theocentric view of the Universe and of a society in which the poet can play a meaningful role. An 'aesthetic' definition is suspect to many, because the imagination is not accorded any standing in traditional psychology, and is seen to introduce 'aberrations' into the proper representation of truth. The poet is not trying, therefore, to invent a world of his own: he represents what is already there, but by virtue of his privileged position, he is better placed to do so. Throughout the sixteenth century, there runs the theme of the *vates*, the inspired seer whose main function is to communicate what he sees. This conception is associated in particular with the Pléiade and the Neoplatonic tradition so flourishing in the middle third of the century, but we find traces of it in the *rhétoriqueurs* and earlier. For many this initiate status of the poet sets him apart; but the public for whom he writes is also privileged in that it forms an élite and is far removed 'du sot Peuple au vil gain intentif' (Scève). This view of the public stems partly from social causes (the poet's links with the Court), partly from literary tradition (Petrarchism), partly too from the close links between poetry, scholarship, and humanism: one of the battle-cries of the Neo-latins and the Pléiade is directed against *le monstre Ignorance*. There is room for other ideas: the Calvinists were bound to take a different view of the literary public, poets were quite aware that much of their activity did not fit into such exalted categories; and it comes as no surprise that Du Bellay, in his *Deffense*, should have seen fit to touch upon topics such as the

place of learning, the usefulness of poetry as entertainment, and
upon its accessibility or otherwise to a wider public.

At the same time, poets are very anxious to justify their place in
the order of society, and this status determines a sizeable portion of
their activity. The poet is not merely a versifier, he may be a chronicler and enjoy some position at Court; he will participate in court
ceremonial; he may act as a mouthpiece for political attitudes and
actions; he may well be involved in the religious debates of the civil
wars; he is, broadly speaking, an articulate patriot. All these commitments will condition in high degree the genres in which he works;
many will be of serious purpose, but others will have entertainment
as their end, and in some cases the poet will compose verse for the
benefit of some royal personage – it is not certain, for instance,
whether Francis I's poems are always by his hand or by, say, Mellin
de Saint-Gellais; and there will be a current of encomiastic poems
engendered by the need for protection in high quarters. In the later
part of the sixteenth century, patronage will undoubtedly continue,
but many poets, often members of the judiciary (like Pasquier or
Scévole de Sainte-Marthe), will write poetry for *délassement* without
financial motive.

Poetry may often be the expression of a group. The whole output
of the *rhétoriqueurs* is closely bound up with a certain social structure. There are also the numerous competitions: some are annual,
such as the activities of the *puys* (Rouen, Toulouse), others are occasional, for instance as the *blason* competition seemingly organised by
Marot, or the variations on the flea found on the bosom of Mme
des Roches during the *Grands Jours* at Poitiers. *Salons* are only
coming into existence in the last third of the century, but they become
centres for forms of precious poetry.[9] A particular genre that develops after 1550 is the collective *tombeau*. This may be a tribute by
friends and colleagues to some respected personage, but it may go
further. When Dolet organised the *tombeau* of the dauphin in 1536,
he took advantage of the occasion to break a lance in favour of Neo-
latin poetry; and later in the century, *tombeaux*, usually in Latin
and French (and sometimes other languages were added), will be
used at the same time for political and religious ends. Groups may
also reveal themselves in the abundant *vers liminaires* that introduce volumes of poetry or scholarship: these poems are rarely of
great literary interest, but they often shed light on the groups in
which the author moved. The conditions in which such poetry is
born encourage virtuosity and preciosity, so that the habits of the
rhétoriqueurs, so often derided by later critics, tend to recur in
certain social conditions, though classical sources such as the *Greek
Anthology* may restore some respectability to these devices. It is significant that a society poet like Etienne Pasquier should devote some

enthusiastic pages to the *rhétoriqueurs* in his *Recherches de la France.*

The poet's rejection of 'originality' is well reflected in his attitude to authority and tradition. When Du Bellay attacked the French heritage, far from him the thought that the poet should burn his boats and strike out on his own: on the contrary he recommended the close imitation of foreign models, exercises in imitation, and a fruitful study of the classics. Time and again we find poets indulging in extended translation, or introducing echoes more or less prolonged of earlier authors. Moreover, the poet sets to work by using common-place themes (*topoi*) whose history can often be traced back through medieval times to classical antiquity. Many of these themes are edifying, and the gnomic element is an important one in Renaissance poetry: we find it in the emblem, the *icon*, it may form the *pointe* of a sonnet or *dizain*, it may appear as a string of *sententiæ* in drama. And less moral themes will be justified on the Martialian ground: *lasciua est nobis pagina, uita proba* (Epig. 1. 4). There are various grounds for this acceptance of a respectable authority: it links the poet with a well-established tradition, which may facilitate a sympathetic hearing and confers value on the imitator; it can also enrich the harmonics of a poem by the use of echoes, or tags, or even overt reference. And when Ronsard experiments in the *style bas* of the Marie cycle, his claims to be 'naïf' merely show him to be following a tradition different from the Petrarchan tone of the earlier *Amours.*

The poet must not only be inspired and defer to respected traditions, he must be an excellent craftsman; throughout the century the *arts poétiques* devote much space to problems of form, versification, and style; their impact is reinforced by dictionaries of rhyme, or of epithets, and by manuals of rhetoric which play a very important role. For the poet of the fifteenth century, poetry is the *art de seconde rhétorique*, and the links between poetry and rhetoric are indissoluble throughout the period. The manuals, concerned more normally with technique than with matters of general principle, tend to have something to say in four domains.

(i) Genre

Here as elsewhere, authority is very important, and as the century progresses, more effort is made to define the nature, content, and form of each genre. Though Du Bellay and others tried to oust the older genres, these did in fact have tough powers of resistance – even Lefèvre de la Boderie will work in the *chant royal* and several, banned in the *Deffense*, tend to return by the back door with slightly different names. In any case there was often an evident overlap between the genres: once the metrical distinction observed in Latin between the elegy and the epistle vanished in French, we find a considerable identity between the two; and the eclogue may extend from the full court, allegorical poem to something that is not far from a meditation with a bare minimum of pastoral frills. On one occasion, Ronsard observed that the elegy had acquired very wide range of reference, and certain poems are defined by a different genre in later editions of his works.

(ii) Versification

In a period when 'new' genres are being acclimatised and the language is evolving fairly rapidly – so much so that it has been suggested that syntactical developments have helped the move from the decasyllable to the alexandrine in the more exalted style[10] – theorists and practitioners have much to say. The principle of *alternance*, already affirmed by more than one *rhétoriqueur*, will acquire *droit de cité* with the Pléiade, and more especially after the second edition of the *Amours*, though of course the process is not finished overnight. On the other hand, the rule about the rhyming of simple and compound words of similar root is still embryonic. The caesura has almost entered its 'modern' phase, and the older epic and lyric caesuræ are therefore on their way out by the middle of the century. Hiatus, which does not offend the Renaissance ear as much as the classical, is frequently practised; but more attention is paid to problems of *enjambement*. There are still a number of grammatical licences allowed in the interest of rhyme and scansion, and Malherbe will feel it his duty to attack some of them.

(iii) Vocabulary

We are in an era of rapid enrichment of the language, and the aristocratic view of poetry will encourage a certain *recherche* in the use of words: the role of the classical renaissance here need hardly be stressed. At the same time, there is a search for the more concrete term, and political and religious involvement will play some part in the development of satirical style. Du Bellay advocated the use of neologisms, archaisms, dialectalisms, and technical words; and the second half of the century sees a marked development of the 'scientific' poem which by definition requires technical vocabulary: this may stretch from astronomy to hunting and geographical description.

(iv) Rhetoric

We have seen that the tradition of rhetoric is well established in poetry; but the humanist poet, brought up in colleges where classical rhetoric is an important element of the curriculum, will also study classical writers such as Cicero and Quintilian; he will have composed Latin verse according to rhetorical rules, and he will have studied figures and tropes and the whole business of the *disposition des matières*. When Barthélemy Aneau, in the *Quintil Horatien*, criticised some of Du Bellay's early poems, he was adopting the standpoint of the traditional rhetorician who feels that rules are being unnecessarily violated. The choice of vocabulary will be determined, in great measure, by the style (and therefore tone) in which one is writing; and certain figures will be more suitable in this or that context. The use of *sententiæ* is often stressed in dramas (and elsewhere) by the use of inverted commas; zeugma and chiasmus are considered to have valuable emotive functions; periphrasis or *antonomasia* plays an important part; and theorists devote much space to 'comparisons' by which are also meant images and metaphors. *Prosopopoeia* is a frequent device (especially in poems composed about the sufferings of France in the civil wars), but there are many others, with which one soon becomes familiar (*anadiplosis, adunaton, repetitio, correctio, compar* or *isocolon*, etc.).[11] Rhetoric also stressed the logical structure of poetry, and one will find that some of the finest poems of, say, Scève or Ronsard, including *Mignon, allon voir*, are built on a tight dialectical foundation. Rhetoric, of course, had played an immense role in the Renaissance humanists' scale of values. Its role in relation to philosophy had been discussed by the Italians, by Erasmus and Budé, nor must one forget La Ramée's attitude in *La Dialectique*, in which he assigns priority to rhetoric as a means of exploring reality.

The connection between poetry and music is far from negligible, though it is a fluctuating one. The *rhétoriqueurs*, in their beginnings, were poets *and* musicians; some of their poetic genres have a structure that can only be understood in terms of music; and Eustache Deschamps lamented the growing gap between the two arts (*musique naturelle* and *musique artificielle*). In the sixteenth century the number of poets who were sufficiently competent to set their poems to music was probably small (including Eustorg de Beaulieu, Mellin de Saint-Gellais, and probably Scève), but many poems are soon set to music, as can be seen from the magnificent volumes published by Attaingnant after 1528. Many humanists did feel that there were strong links between music and poetry, and more than one poet could perform on some instrument; the song seems to predominate over other forms of music in our period.[12] A strong tradition of court music persists from the fifteenth century, through the *rhétoriqueurs* at the Court of Burgundy and in the Netherlands, and reinforced by links with Italy: Okeghem, Obrecht, Josquin des Prés, *maître de chapelle* to Louis XII, who often works in the *ballade* form, but is not insensitive to humanist texts. Francis I's Court encouraged musicians, many of whom came from Italy; the popularity of the *chanson* and the need for ceremonial music ensured employment. One notices a general tendency towards secularisation, a fondness for programme music, as well as a transcending of polyphonic structures, which may explain Josquin's eclipse for some decades after his death. The emergence of Calvinism makes its own contribution to musical developments, and several distinguished composers (Certon, Goudimel, Bourgeois) had Huguenot sympathies. Certain printers make a name for themselves by publishing music (Attaingnant, J. Moderne, the Beringen brothers), and the main centres are Paris and Lyons.

Music was of course studied as part of the normal college curriculum; but in the second half of the century it received a boost through the interest taken in Neoplatonism. Music is seen as fitting into an ethical conception of the Universe: it is capable, in certain modes, of calming the passions and preparing man for the next step in his spiritual reascent. Music's pacificatory and purifying powers apply not only to the individual, but to the group: hence the views expressed by Le Jeune and other members of Baïf's Academy on music's power to moderate feelings in the religious wars. Since music, poetry, and religion are linked, certain genres will be preferred in this climate: the love-song, both sacred and profane, the Psalms, the *ballet de cour*, in which both Baïf and Thibault took a leading part. The *ballet de cour* was an allegorical presentation of the contemporary situation, created in the hope that it might lead to an easing of tensions.[13] With dancing, acting, elaborate scenery and machinery, an early form of synaesthetic art was enacted in which members of the royal family took part. Certain modes were preferred, such as the Dorian, considered conducive to peaceful sentiment; but since words were as important as the music, polyphony gives way to part-singing performed rhythmically in unison.

The Pléiade had, however, taken an interest in music from its beginnings, as can be seen in the 1552 edition of Ronsard's *Amours*, which contains a number of settings by contemporary musicians to which the sonnets may be sung. Ronsard affirmed a clear connection between a capacity to understand music and a properly developed moral nature; Binet tells us that for him 'sans la musique la poésie était presque sans grâce, comme la musique sans la mélodie des vers inanimés est sans vie'. So Ronsard composed 'vers mesurés à la lyre' (to be distinguished from Baïf's 'vers mesurés à l'antique', on which see below, p. 283); this meant that, given the settings by Goudimel, Certon, Jannequin, and Muret to serve for various sonnet structures, the basic form must be rigidly maintained and the *alternance des rimes* observed. Of course, the fusion between poetry and music is only partial: one tune is used for sonnets similar in structure, but very different in content, and we are equally far away from the early *rhétoriqueurs* and the world of Duparc and Fauré. The importance of music is a theme that recurs frequently in Ronsard; it is also true that many of his poems were set to music by composers in the last third of the century. Yet one must ask whether his affirmations of theory really contribute much to the proper union of the two arts in practice; he did not compose the settings himself, he was not so well equipped musically as some of his poetic predecessors, and very often for him music becomes a source of imagic evocation of poetry (*La Lyre*). I doubt if Ronsard really did anything to stem the growing separation between music and poetry; his finest poems stand on their own. Nevertheless, the end of the century is notable for the attempts made by members of the Pléiade and others to bring the two arts into some sort of symbiosis; and even rather dry texts like Pibrac's quatrains will find a composer to provide settings.

To sum up: in approaching sixteenth-century poetry, one must set aside the critical commonplaces of later times, though certain recent shifts in sensibility have helped us to rediscover the poets of the Counter-reformation. We must not be put off by frequent recurrence of *topos* and theme, not be oversuspicious of rhetoric. Originality will be revealed in the ways a poet varies his use of a theme, by what he leaves aside, by his choice of devices from the traditional armoury, by his feeling for poetic patterns and his sense of language. So many of the better poets are experimenting with the French tongue; we also need to acquire familiarity with the poetic traditions whose echoes are often exploited; and above all, this is poetry that should be read aloud, so that we may seize the delicate rhythmic experiments which even the minor poets are able to indulge in with some success.

NOTES

1. L. Mirot, *Manuel de Géographie historique de la France*, 1948 (Part I); R. Doucet, *Les Institutions de la France au XVIᵉ siècle*, 2 vols., 1948; G. Zeller, *Les Institutions de la France au XVIᵉ siècle*, 1948.

2. Charles Estienne, *La guide des chemins pour aller et venir par tous les pays de France*, 1552 (also 1553; Lyons, 1566 and 1580) (BM). Modern ed. J. Bonnerot, 2 vols., 1936.

3. On the history of Paris, see General Bibliography.

4. N. S. Bement, *French Modal Syntax in the Sixteenth Century*, Ann Arbor, 1934; F. Brunot, *Histoire de la langue française des origines à 1900*, t. II, *Le Seizième Siècle*, 1906; G. Gougenheim, *Grammaire de la langue française du seizième siècle*, Lyons, 1951; E. Huguet, *Dictionnaire de la langue française au seizième siècle*, 1925– ; P. Rickard, *La Langue française au seizième siècle*, 1968*.

5. C. Thurot, *De la Prononciation française depuis le commencement du XVIᵉ siècle*, 2 vols., 1881–83.

6. A. O. Lovejoy, *The Great Chain of Being*, Cambridge, Mass., 1936; Herschel Baker, *The Dignity of Man*, 1947; E. M. W. Tillyard, *The Elizabethan World Picture*, 1943; A. K. Varga, 'Poésie et cosmologie au XVIᵉ siècle', *Lumières de la Pléiade*, 1966, pp. 135–55.

7. Anthony Levi, *French Moralists. The Theory of the Passions 1585 to 1649*, Oxford, 1964; G. S. Brett, *A History of Psychology*, 3 vols., 1912.

8. R. J. Clements, *Critical Theory and Practice of the Pléiade*, Cambridge, Mass., 1942; H. Franchet, *Le Poète et son œuvre d'après Ronsard*, 1923; W. F. Patterson, *Three Centuries of French Poetic Theory*, 2 vols., Ann Arbor, 1935; and the most recent survey Grahame Castor, *Pléiade Poetics*, 1964. Various sixteenth-century theoreticians will be mentioned later. The approach to poetry is of course in many important respects a special case of the more general problem of the approach to literature; but major issues are debated with reference to poetry in the first place by many theoreticians.

9. L. Clark Keating, *Studies on the Literary Salon in France 1550–1615*, Cambridge, Mass., 1941.

10. C. Camproux, 'Langue et métrique. A propos du décasyllabe des Epîtres de Marot', *Le Français Moderne*, 1964.

11. Common terms are explained in the Glossary; more extended treatment in L. A. Sonnino, *A Handbook to Sixteenth-century Rhetoric*, 1968.

12. D. P. Walker, 'Musical Humanism in the 16th and early 17th Centuries', *Music Review*, II (1941) and III (1943); G. Reese, *Music in the Renaissance*, 1954; and vols. II and III of the *New Oxford History of Music*.

13. Margaret McGowan, *L'Art du ballet de cour en France 1581–1643*, 1963.

PART I

Chapter 1

EARLY HUMANISM AND
THE RHÉTORIQUEURS

THE first phase of our period stretches roughly from the beginnings of printing until the middle 1520s: the brilliant period of Francis I's reign, in which so much of the intellectual ferment of the French Renaissance finds its way into literature, starts after the king's return from captivity and the homecoming of the royal children; and though the *rhétoriqueur* tradition does not die out overnight, one can note something of a break about 1525, with the death of Crétin and the imminent appearance of Clément Marot; a similar break is also observable in Neo-latin poetry with the publication of Salmon Macrin's *Carminum libellus* in 1528.

I. HISTORICAL OUTLINES UNTIL 1529

The second half of Louis XI's reign may be seen as an attempt to bring about the centralisation of government under the king. There was plenty to be done after the Hundred Years' War. The king had to take ruthless measures against certain families that stood in his path, such as Armagnac, Saint-Pol, Nemours; in other cases, a subtle arrangement of marriages served to bring regions into the royal domain. In particular, Louis XI sought to counter the ambitions of the Orléans family, and Louis d'Orléans, subsequently Louis XII, was married to the king's deformed and sterile daughter Jeanne. The toughest opponent, however, remained Burgundy: Charles the Bold tried, by force, guile, or treachery, to consolidate possessions which hardly formed a unity, geographical, political, or otherwise, but his stubborn efforts were halted only by his death at the battle of Nancy (1477). Nevertheless, the problem still remained, and Louis was not the only person to grasp the importance of whom Charles's daughter Mary would marry. In the diplomatic activity that ensued, Mary never forgave Louis XI for his behaviour, and she married Maximilian of Austria (1477), with immeasurable consequences for France in the sixteenth century. Nevertheless, after

Mary's death from a fall (1482), the Flemings preferred to entrust her daughter Margaret to France's dauphin, and by the treaty of Arras in the same year, Louis obtained a sizeable portion of Burgundian territory – though Brittany lay outside his power – and the sixteenth century will see a consolidation of his work. The king also did much to improve communications and institutions: certain *parlements* were created, fairs were encouraged, roads were developed, the royal *poste* established, attempts made to standardise weights and measures; and it was during his reign that printing became a reality in Paris. In literature, his reign was that of Villon and Commynes, though the latter's Memoirs were published only in Francis I's reign.

The early years of the young Charles VIII (1483–98) show little change of pattern: his sister Anne de Beaujeu, acting as regent, succeeds in checking the centrifugal tactics of various noble families. A fairly peaceful foreign policy results in internal prosperity, and it is during these years that much is done to rewrite common law. From 1491 things change: Charles, nurtured on chivalric ideals, soon falls a prey to the Italian mirage. In Italy the claims to the kingdom of Naples lay open and for a short while the complex situation of peninsular politics was favourable to French intervention. After a period of diplomatic preparation to immobilise potential dangers (Henry VII and Ferdinand of Aragon), Charles VIII took the opportunity of the death of Fernando of Naples (1494) to invade the peninsula. Militarily, the French quickly made gains, but the inevitable diplomatic backlash, led by Venice, began to work against them: in the long run, the invasion was militarily indefensible come what might, but Charles's action not only succeeded in altering the kaleidoscope of Italian intrigue to his own detriment, but provoked the active interest of the Emperor Maximilian and also of Spain. Charles VIII died (1498) before the full implications of his policy became clear, and his successor Louis XII in fact did not question his wisdom; indeed the Neapolitan claims were reinforced by Louis's pretensions to Milan. His reign is marked by a great deal of military and diplomatic activity that yields very poor results. The Italian wars are concentrated into two main periods: first, up till 1504, when Louis has to retreat after initial successes, and 1509–13, when Italy, under the vigorous leadership of a new Pope, Julius II, markedly xenophobic, succeeds in pushing the French king back; towards the end of the campaign France is invaded and is in conflict not only with Italy, but with Spain and England. The impact of the Italian wars on the emerging Renaissance of France has been frequently described, and perhaps in exaggerated terms; it is, however, true that the French were struck by many aspects of Italian culture and also by courtly life, which

French monarchs will try to emulate. Moreover, the kings use their courtier-poets in the service of propaganda, and the ephemeral victories against Italians and English are sung in Latin and French verse, while the anti-papal sentiments of the people often find expression in the theatre. In military terms, Louis's ambitions in Italy, encouraged by his vanity and lack of judgement, were a continuing drain on the country's resources, but he was not the only French monarch to be blind to Claude de Seyssel's view:

Et en tel cas, s'il n'y avoit point de remède de s'assurer du pays sans continuer celle garnison (qui fût pour forcer les paysans), ne seroit bien conseillé un Prince d'en entreprendre la conquête pour le garder. . . . Car toutes nations et gens raisonnables aiment mieux être gouvernés par ceux de leur pays et de la nation mêmes (qui connoissent leurs mœurs, lois et coutumes et ont le même langage et manière de vivre comme eux) que par estrangers. (*La Grant Monarchie de France*, V, chapters vi and ix)

At home, in spite of protests against the level of taxation caused by the Italian wars, Louis's government was considered fairly enlightened; and the king and his adviser, the cardinal d'Amboise, showed some interest in cultural developments, even if this interest was not always altruistic.

In 1515 Francis I succeeds to the throne, and the Italian pattern repeats itself once again. Francis, maintaining the claims of his predecessors, opens his reign with a brilliant campaign, which ended in a peace very favourable to France. Moreover, the opportunity was taken to conclude the Concordat with Pope Leo X (1516): this was not registered by the *Parlement* for another two years, for though it did in fact satisfy many gallican demands, including the nomination of bishops, it was widely thought that too great concessions had been made by the government. For some years, peace is maintained: the death of Julius II and also of Ferdinand of Aragon simplify matters and diplomacy reduces the tension between France and the Habsburgs. However, the lull was only a temporary one, for the confrontation between France and Germany could not be long delayed. After Maximilian's death (1519), great activity surrounded the election of his successor; in spite of Francis's efforts, Charles V received the votes, and his elevation presented an inevitable threat to France, through his authority both in Germany and Spain and his claims in Italy and Burgundy. Within a year, hostilities broke out in sporadic form; the kingdom of Navarre was also in difficulties. Francis soon invaded Italy, and over several years the situation was fairly fluid. However, the disaster of Pavia (1525), in which Francis I was taken prisoner, altered the picture. After his release, the French king had no scruples in breaking his undertakings and formed the League of Cognac; in the following year he invaded Italy once again. In this situation Francis benefited from the fear of other European countries that Charles V was growing too powerful. Moreover, things took a turn for the better with the Peace of Cambrai (1529), for Charles, with worries abroad (Turkey) and also at home (the Lutheran question), was anxious for an easing of pressures. As a result of this treaty, Francis lost ground in Italy, but his claims to Burgundy were recognised.

The religious question was not confined to Germany; in France eyes were steadily fixed on developments across the Rhine. Already the Reuchlin affair, centred on the study of Hebrew, had compelled the attention of the Sorbonne; then the events that led to the ex-communication of Luther (1520) caused anxiety in France lest similar problems arose there too. Lutheran tracts had been circulating with increasing frequency and the new doctrines were attracting people in high places. Moreover, there had been reforming, evangelical stirrings in France itself: on the one hand, there was a widespread conviction that the Church needed to put its house in order, and on the other hand, humanists like Lefèvre d'Etaples and his disciple Guillaume Briçonnet were exerting considerable influence, Lefèvre by his editions of biblical texts, Briçonnet by his attempts to reform his diocese of Meaux and by his spiritual authority over Marguerite de Navarre and members of her circle. No doubt the moderate reformist tendencies of such humanists were unfortunate in coinciding with happenings in Germany, for the Sorbonne, quickly identified with intellectual obscurantism, saw in any such tendency the presence of Lutheranism – and the term 'Lutheran' is used in a very broad sense indeed, to include the 'evangelicals' as well as the stricter followers of the German leader. In 1521 the *Parlement* condemned Lutheran doctrines; but the king, at this stage, was more open-minded than Sorbonne or *Parlement*. When he was in captivity, his mother Louise, acting as regent, was far more inclined to listen to the Pope and the Sorbonne and encouraged repression. Things improved for the holders of new ideas on the king's return, but after an outrage committed against the image of the Virgin Mary, he took a sterner line, and Berquin, who had benefited earlier from his leniency, was condemned to the stake in 1529. Francis's attitude to the new currents will remain equivocal, partly for political reasons, but partly also because of the influence of his sister Marguerite de Navarre and, as has been suggested, his own ambiguous religious attitude.

1529 is a convenient date at which to interrupt the historical narrative. It corresponds to a shift of emphasis in the conflict between the French king and the Habsburg monarchy; and at home, on the cultural plane, we have already noted that a change of climate is under way. Moreover, Francis I's support of cultural developments, however fulsomely he is praised by contemporaries and later generations of humanists, is distinctly modest before 1530. Finally, the economic state of the country was far from brilliant: the Italian wars were a persistent sore, and France suffered more than her share of plague and social unrest (e.g., the Lyons *Rebeyne* in 1529).

II. EARLY HUMANISM

At the beginning of our period, humanists were very much aware of the need for reform. The thesis that there is a complete break between the generation of Robert Gaguin and the humanism of the Cols and Nicolas de Clamanges has probably been exaggerated,[1] but many suspected that Paris had ceased to be the Athens of the North. At philosophical level, the century-old struggle between realists and nominalists had resulted in a victory for the latter and the followers of William of Ockham. Realism never died out completely, but the predominance of Ockhamism in the fifteenth-century Sorbonne, whatever impetus it may have given to fideism, was bound to paralyse philosophical discussion and to create a gap between programme and values for living. One cannot therefore be surprised at the growing distaste for scholasticism, Ockhamist or Scotist, and indeed against the traditional view of Aristotle. If the rut into which theology, the goal of education, had sunk raised protest, it was understandable that the pedagogic structures of the university should also come under fire. In 1452 Cardinal d'Estouteville had drawn up new statutes, but later attempts to enforce them met with only partial success. There were precise points on which forward-looking humanists were critical: the low ebb to which Latinity had sunk; the medieval form of exegesis with its quadruple system (historical, allegorical, anagogical, and tropological); the sluggish reliance on antiquated manuals; the financial position of most colleges (except the Sorbonne and the Collège de Navarre); and the living conditions in Paris. More broadly, the state of the university was symptomatic of the state of the Church; many orders had fallen into disrepute and had ceased to follow their rule, voices were raised against pluralism and its corollary absenteeism, gallican sentiment criticised various practices that benefited the Popes (*annates*, etc.). Nevertheless, in the last thirty years or so of the fifteenth century, a serious attempt is made by humanists to restore some order; all these humanists were brought up in the ecclesiastical tradition and fully recognised the close connection between education and the state of the Church.

First, many orders did attempt to reform themselves, though opposition was encountered. In some cases, the impetus came from outside France – there is a close connection between the Collège de

Montaigu, reformed by Jean Standonck, and the Brothers of the Common Life at Windesheim, who stressed the return to an inner religion and the study of sources rather than of medieval commentary; but the Mathurins were reformed by Robert Gaguin (1497). The process took over a century to complete (for instance, the Trappists were very late in the field), and the monks remained a target for censure, fun, and abuse, partly because of their failure to harmonise rule and behaviour, partly because of their ecclesiastical privileges (especially in the matter of justice). And the higher clergy was often worldly in outlook and concerned with the financial benefits of preferment. Second, genuine efforts were made to halt decay in the university, at both administrative and pedagogic levels. College libraries were enriched: Rabelais's pouring of scorn on Saint-Victor masks the fact that it was a remarkable storehouse of learning with an impressive collection of Neoplatonic works. Leading humanists also try to interest king and nobles; extensive patronage perhaps does not exist in this field for the time being, but there are notable *Mécènes*: the two Rochechouarts and Etienne Poncher, not to mention members of the wealthy Briçonnet and Ruzé families. Encouragement is given to foreign scholars to visit Paris. Some, like Beroaldo the Elder, came for a spell; others, and especially teachers from the Low Countries, with which Gaguin had close contacts, came to stay (Gilles de Delft, Petrus de Ponte). Finally, attempts are made to improve the Latinity of the university, and here the circle of Robert Gaguin is all-important. Latinity was not just a matter of cultural pride, humanists thought that the man who really knew Latin held the key to all knowledge, and that education based on proper Latin instruction was in the moral interest of the student. Classical learning is not of course a substitute for Christianity, but as some Church Fathers suggested, something that harmonises with it and can prepare men for the Christian life. This aim was implemented in divers ways: efforts were made to supplement, if not to oust, medieval manuals, by making available welltried manuals of Italian origin, or by the preparation of new textbooks. Suitable texts were also printed, though the full force of Italian scholarship was not to hit France awhile (the Aldine press is set up in 1494); stress is laid on edifying works: the Latin moralists are popular, Ovid and Vergil continue to enjoy their medieval celebrity, and contemporary Latin writers are pressed into service, for as yet there is little distinction made between Vergil and the modern Swan of Mantua, Baptista Spagnuoli. Public lectures on literature begin to be held towards the end of the century; and much is done to raise the standard of Latin verse composition on which great stress is laid. This interest is not confined to Paris: Caen stands out as an attractive centre of pioneering humanism, with its distinguished rector Guillaume de la Mare, and Poitiers and Orléans will also become prominent.

In this context, Robert Gaguin's achievement is a remarkable one.[2] In many ways he remains medieval in outlook; for him the main task was to bring religion and education back to their pristine excellence, and the Latin world was a training ground for the Christian mind. He was no great scholar in his own right – his numerous administrative and ambassadorial duties kept him too busy – but he and his circle did much to promote the flow of Renaissance currents. He encouraged the return to classical texts, shorn of foggy commentators, and placed more value on the apparatus of contemporary scholarship; he quickly grasped the long-term benefits of printing; he seems to have quickened cultural communications with other countries, as a perusal of his letters will show; he brought foreign scholars to Paris, he himself travelled widely in Italy and the Low Countries, and helped to create a climate of receptivity in France. And though his outlook is ecclesiastical and late-medieval, his stress on the value of rhetoric as part of the educational process is significant. Behind his lifework there lies a staunch patriotism, which is reflected especially in his historical writings; and he imparts vigorous momentum to the study of Latin verse and to Neo-latin composition. Nevertheless, his humanist generation marks the point of departure, the fruits of his labours will appear on the trees of the next generation.

After his death, Robert Gaguin appears to be fairly quickly forgotten, except in the field of historiography; and this is probably true of some of his literary friends and admirers such as Pierre de Bur or Nicolas Horry. Nevertheless, the first fifteen years of the sixteenth century, in spite of a certain literary aridity, are decisive for intellectual developments. The colleges and universities are entering a healthier phase, new *instruments de travail* are being fashioned, and scholars of note are nearing their maturity, Charles de Bouelles, Lefèvre d'Etaples, and Guillaume Budé, though their impact on the literary world will come somewhat later. Contacts with Italy are increasing, both through book publication and personal contacts: French humanists will soon consider the *voyage d'Italie* as an essential part of their formation; scholars like Lascaris and Jérome Aléandre help to stimulate Greek studies. Though the example of Italian humanism is becoming increasingly important, one must recognise that French reactions are still selective, and that humanists are far more interested, for instance, in the writings of the Carmelite Baptista Spagnuoli than in the poems of Marullus, so much read a decade or more later. Moreover, relations with the Low Countries remain very close, and a number of pedagogues teaching in Paris colleges are of Flemish origin. Having made these reservations, it is right to say that French humanism is already aware that something new is in the air, that medieval ideas are making way for others. It is also a time when new religious currents are making themselves felt: Lefèvre d'Etaples had shown interest in Raymon Lull and Bouelles was a disciple of Nicolas of Cusa. Nor is the moment far off when the theological implications of philological research will become very clear. Though still strongly based on the universities, humanism is already spreading further; we shall find evidence of its presence in courtly circles and among enlightened ecclesiastics such as Bishop Jean des Pins.

III. EARLY PRINTING[3]

Before the appearance of printing, scholars had been well aware of the importance of the written word; when the printed book, thanks mainly to Gutenberg, came into being by the conjunction of various factors – movable types, metal founts, paper, suitable ink, and so forth – many humanists were quick to understand its significance. In France, Paris led the field; this was due in part to royal encouragement, but chiefly to the initiative of Gaguin, Fichet, and Heynlin. In 1470 the first book was printed, Gasparino da Barzizzi's *Epistolarum libri*, from a press in the vicinity of the Sorbonne. Significantly it was a book by an Italian humanist of Ciceronian persuasion and printed in roman type; the books that followed were Guillaume Fichet's *Rhetorica* and a work by Valla. Nevertheless, in spite of the humanists' percipience, and though Paris soon attracted a number of other publishers, often of German origin, development along the early lines after the first two years, in which twenty titles were brought out, slackened compared with progress in northern Italy and in some measure Lyons, where many pseudo-Aldines were to be printed and which was the only other printing-centre capable of holding a candle to Paris. In the capital, financial and university influences determined the type of book published, so that the main production consisted of Church Fathers, mystics, scholastics, devotional works; but romances and popular literature also had a ready market. Renouard calculated that, up to 1515, less than 30 per cent of the annual output was devoted to humanist works, over 50 per cent being of a religious character. At this stage, little is done for vernacular literature; even in 1528, less than a sixth of the books printed in Paris are in the French language.

Nevertheless, though Lyons for various reasons attracted printers throughout the century, it rarely initiated new techniques, and Paris remained the magnet. It is significant that Josse Bade (yet another scholar from Flanders) should have a spell in Lyons training under Trechsel whose daughter he married, and then move to Paris, where he published for over thirty years. Bade's career is an epitome of humanist publishing: he was first and foremost a scholar and a teacher; he set about editing texts, doing what he could to incorporate the latest scholarship by means of a grammatical and a thematic commentary; he also brought earlier manuals up to date. His editions included modern Latin writers, a certain range of classical authors (excluding for instance the elegists), Erasmus, theological works; and his taste shows him to be intellectually a kinsman of Gaguin, for there is still something medieval about his outlook. Nevertheless, he does not close his door to currents from abroad, and his *officina* becomes a centre for the leading humanists of his time: Lefèvre d'Etaples, Jacques Toussaint, Danès, and Vatable, and more modest pedagogues such as Nicole Dupuys. Bade, moreover, came to be linked with the Estienne family, through the marriage of his daughter Pernelle to Robert I; the other daughters married Jean de Roigny, Michel Vascosan, and Jacques Dupuis I. This suggests, from the outset, the extraordinary interrelationships between the various printing-houses. Of all these, the most remarkable are the Estiennes who remain in business for a century and a half. Henri I published some 121 volumes and was a close friend of Lefèvre, Budé, and the Du Bellays;[4] his son Robert I, also very impressive, will symbolise, in Francis I's reign, the transition from Renaissance to Reformation in the printing world, for the book trade does much not only to spread humanism, but to promote the interests of Protestantism. Robert's son, Henri II, is perhaps the most distinguished member of the dynasty: a very great scholar, he is also a most active printer (often doing much to further Greek studies), a writer passionately interested in the welfare of the French tongue, and a convinced Calvinist. Other printers will become important, such as Simon de Colines and Michel Vascosan, but in the first stage of French humanism it is Josse Bade and Robert Estienne who do most to spread the results of scholarship and pedagogy abroad.

IV. NEO-LATIN POETRY[5]

Though Neo-latin poetry does not reach very great heights in the early decades of our period, it is still an interesting aspect of cultural activity, and all the more so as we shall see that the claims of the vernacular as a serious vehicle for poetic sensibility have still to be debated publicly. For Gaguin and his circle, a good Latinity was the indispensable requisite of a Christian mind, and poetry had as its main mission the praise of God's glory. Though Gaguin himself indulged in a certain amount of light verse, the main output of himself and his friends was religious in character; but strenuous efforts were made to improve stylistic and metrical competence. The verse produced by Gaguin's circle is copious, but it is forgotten fairly soon in the sixteenth century, partly because the standard of Latinity, though a great improvement on what had gone before, left much to be desired in the eyes of the next, more scholarly generation. And in any case, the range of thematic taste among Gaguin's followers was soon to prove too narrow. In the first fifteen years of the sixteenth century, colleges do much to introduce higher standards: not only is more attention paid to the language, but various manuals on prosody are printed. Works of reference like Ravisius Textor's *Specimen epithetorum* (1518) will go through numerous, augmented editions, and gradually humanists become more aware of what Italy has to offer in the way of Latin verse. Even so, Mantuan still enjoys a privileged position and he will have a distinguished disciple in the French writer Pierre Rosset. During Louis XII's reign, two main features appear so far as literary output is concerned: on the one hand, humanists will publish a lot of occasional verse laced with religious compositions, not only in Paris, but also in the provinces: Poitiers and its neighbourhood seem to produce a few poets, and Guillaume de la Mare of Caen is fairly prolific: his work poses one curious problem, in that he appears to be influenced by the *Greek Anthology* at a time when it must have been very difficult indeed for him to lay his hands on that collection. Under the influence of Mantuan a number of eclogues are written, often with a pedagogic end in view. And on the other hand, the Neo-latin poet gains a footing at Court, where he often sings the victories of France against Italy and England (Forestier, Valeran de Varanne, Humbert de Montmoret, Germain de Brie); throughout the century, the French kings will have Latin poets as well as French ones to compose poems on court matters and events of greater national significance. Faustus Andrelinus, who emigrated from Italy before the beginning of the century, is awarded the title of *poeta regius* and no doubt sets a pattern in encomiastic verse.

At court level, and also at the *puys*, a relationship develops between the emerging Neo-latin writers and the *rhétoriqueurs*. Anne of Brittany had Jean Lemaire, Jean Marot, and Germain de Brie in her entourage; and we shall see some overlap of theme between the two literary currents, and also some interchange of techniques: for instance, when Guillaume du Bellay as a young man composes a versified abbreviation of Deguileville's *Pèlerinage de l'homme*, he will add some Latin poems of an anagrammatic nature. Some poetic texts will be rendered into the other tongue. And one must presume that these contacts helped to introduce humanist currents into *rhétoriqueur* writing; but the *rhétoriqueurs* belonged to a tradition of poetry that went further back than the neo-classical exercises of Gaguin and his friends.

V. THE RHÉTORIQUEURS[6]

At the outset it should be stressed that the term *rhétoriqueurs*, used to describe the currents of poetry forming the subject of the present chapter, comes very late into critical vocabulary; the poets themselves were not called by this name in their own times. On the other hand, they do have an unmistakable family air, and if the present term did not exist, another would certainly have to be found.

In the reigns of Charles VIII and Louis XII, literature flourishes under the aegis of the Church, the Court, and, discreetly, a nascent humanism. Somewhat spurned and derided by modern critics, it is strongly conditioned by the social pressures of the times, and in several ways it forms a springboard for later developments. The origins of this literature go back some way and are associated with the Court of Burgundy, but a number of poets transfer their allegiance to the French Court and patronage. They resemble each other by their professional status, ecclesiastic, their duties at Court, their close personal links and sense of discipleship, and their conception of poetry. Indeed their resemblances are so great that their identities are not always very easy to distinguish, and even some poets who were less connected with the Court followed the tone and style of the established *poncif*. These writers tend to work in certain fields: the theatre, historiography, and religious and court poetry.

VI. RHÉTORIQUEUR POETRY[7]

Their conception of poetry was a noble one, more noble indeed than much of their practice would suggest. They believed in the gift of inspiration – Deschamps had said that this natural faculty could not be 'aprise a nul, se son propre couraige naturalement ne s'i applique' – but equally insisted on a high technique patiently acquired. Indeed, what posterity reproaches them with chiefly is their sacrifice of *fond* to *forme*, but like La Bruyère they doubtless thought that 'tout est dit' and that their business was to develop variations on themes accepted and valued. They also held that poetry was an art for the élite: hence their stress on erudition, complex technique, but also their use of a style sharply distinct from everyday parlance, both in verse and in an elevated prose known as *poetrie*. Furthermore, they stressed the need to harmonise the disciplines of music and poetry, which Deschamps felt had become estranged in his day. Originally their links with music were strong: Machaut was a musician of genius as well as a poet, and certain poetic forms are best understood in a musical context; but, though the *rhétoriqueurs* continued to interest themselves in music – both Crétin and Lemaire wrote *déplorations* on celebrated composers – the poetic forms do acquire gradually an independent existence. Nonetheless, the view of poetry remained an exalted one.

Much of their output was religious in inspiration, and it was often associated with the activities of the *puys*, yearly festivals at which prizes were awarded for the best compositions on the theme of the Immaculate Conception.[8] There were strict rules for these exercises, and each *puys* tended to specialise in certain forms: thus at Lille the *amoureuse* and the *serventois* prevailed, whereas at Dieppe it was the *chant royal* and at Béthune the *pastourelle*. At Rouen, where things appear to have got under way from 1486, *palinods*, *chants royaux*, *ballades*, and *rondeaux* were acceptable. The term *Epigramme* is sometimes used to cover the poems, which were normally written in French, but could also be composed in Latin, though at Toulouse prizes for the latter were awarded at a later date. The *puys* flourished more or less throughout the sixteenth century, but by their rigid adherence to formal convention and the nature of their theme, they remain marginal to poetic development; at the same time they keep alive certain poetic structures which reappear in serious authors at the end of the century, such as Lefèvre de la Boderie. In their other religious poems, the *rhétoriqueurs* show little feeling; considerations of rhyme and metrical dexterity, a fondness for acrostic and pattern verses transform the poem all too often into gymnastic, but here and there a certain unaffected simplicity may be found:

> De tout mon cueur humblement te salue,
> Pour la grandeur de ta haulte value,
> Royne du Ciel, de la terre et la mer,
> Pardonne moy se j'oze au reclamer
> Ton sainct nom mettre en ma bouche polue.
> Delaissant voe [*voix*] estrange et dissolue,
> Vueil par pensée honneste et resolue
> Te bien servir, et loyaument aymer
> De tout mon cueur.
> Tu fuz comme es de Dieu si bien voulue,
> Que pour sa mere et fille preesleue
> Dame te feit des vertus renommer;
> Telle te doy en la terre nommer,
> Et telle aussi seras escripte et leue,
> De tout mon cueur. (G. Crétin, K. Chesney ed., 48)

The alembicated idiom is also reduced in the versified lives of the saints which become very popular towards the end of the fifteenth century, no doubt because of the wider audience for which such texts were destined.

It is, however, in their court activity that these poets were most prolific. Here their position was not always very enviable: they were rarely paid for their poetic services but rather for other functions; some might be secretaries or librarians, and as they were normally in holy orders, might hold some benefice. Yet there were advantages: they found themselves in a society of relative refinement and, through their commitments, might travel and come into contact with residents of other countries: this is certainly true of Lemaire, and indeed of Gaguin who wrote occasionally in the vernacular. These circumstances explain in some measure the nature of their writing, and also perhaps the presence of elements that announce later Renaissance writers. Their love verse and pastime compositions were much appreciated, as is shown by both the proliferation of the *rondeau* as a suitable medium and by the courtly manuscript anthologies that have come down to us.[9] But there were more formal occasions for which the poets would be expected to write and indeed plan – *entrées* and other royal ceremonies. More important, they served as a means of propaganda for central policies, celebrating military expeditions and famous victories. During the Italian wars, many poems of an epic or near-epic character are written in both French and Latin, combining a measure of realism with the apparatus of Vergilian tradition. Jean Marot's *Voyage de Gênes* is an example of this formula, though it contains other elements as well, for the *rhétoriqueurs*, like so many French poets, are rarely successful in organising large-scale poetic structures; and Lemaire de Belges writes in celebration of political and military matters in which Margaret of Austria or her lieutenants were involved. Closely allied in practice was the exploiting of the *déploration* which celebrated the death of some illustrious person. Obituary verse could also take the form of the *complainte* (a variation on the *lai*), but the *déploration* was the genre of high ritual. Crétin composed a *Déploration ... sur le trespas de feu Okergan* (sc. Okeghem) and a *Plainte* on Guillaume de Bissipat.[10] These compositions are often very elaborate: thematically they not only honour the dead, but set him or her up as an example to be followed: the way of facing death is often stressed, and the text abounds in *sententiæ*. The metre and stanzaic form are varied, and prose may be interleaved with the verse (a practice not confined to this genre). Medieval devices, such as the dream, the garden, allegory, are pressed into service; Christian figures of allegory and classical goddesses appear together, and an almost pastoral atmosphere is sometimes achieved. The language, as would be expected, is highflown and heavily latinised, but two features tend to clog the mechanism: the stress laid on rhyme and the excessive taste for enumeration. The final impression is thus one of ornate alembication lacking in vitality. Rhyming indulgence can lead to unintelligibility as in Crétin's *Apparition du Mareschal sans reproche, feu Messire Jacques de Chabannes,* a poem which on the other hand has an interesting section on the difficulties facing eyewitnesses when they try to recapture events in which they were involved. The pastoral idiom reappears in a kind of *Genethliacon* for the dauphin born in 1517 (Crétin, no. xli); here the bucolic allegory is explained towards the end, with Galatée standing for 'la chose publique'.

In poetry of this nature the moralising element looms large. It may occur in a *déploration* of a royal personage, in which case the themes resemble those of the *Lunettes des Princes,* a genre that is very popular and paints a picture of the ideal king: as Seneca had said, one of the duties of poets was to give advice to monarchs. It will also appear in the *chant royal* and *ballade,* but especially in the *débat,* in which two contraries are presented: among the more popular categories are the straight discussion of moral issues, comparisons of persons of differing social standing, debates on love, contrasts of animals trying to prove their superiority over one another. In many such poems *blason* techniques inevitably come to the fore. The moralising may spill over into satire, and occurs frequently within the field of drama. There are the traditional attacks on the failings of the Church and its representatives; and if poets tend to support royal policies, they also attack war, taxation, false counsellors. This political moralising is to be found in poems like *Le gouvernement des trois estatz* and in edifying texts bearing titles that begin with *Doctrinal, Miroir, Lunettes.* The *doctrinals* can, however, cover a very wide thematic range.

The satire of this period, whether on traditional or political topics, is substantial in quantity, and can sometimes be very lively and closer to popular style than in some of the poems we have been considering. The spirit of Villon and the *fabliau* lives on, and even writers like Molinet[11] can turn out extremely free verse. The satirical tradition may be reinforced by imports from Germany (e.g., Bade's edition of Sebastian Brant's *Narrenschiff*), and it is no coincidence that at the turn of the century the classical moralists (Juvenal, Martial, Persius) are popular and often edited; but the refinements of Erasmian and Lucianic satire have yet to come.

Satire is often directed into anti-feminine channels, with special insistence on the theme of marriage. Here the prose *Quinze Joyes de mariage,*[12] but also the *Matheolus,* are regular sources of inspiration, and it is characteristic that these topics should be dealt with in an apparently dignified genre (e.g., *Complainte du nouveau marié*) or based on a parodic treatment of sacred texts (*Les tenebres du mariage, De profundis des Amoureux*); this parodic principle can be developed in other paths, as in *La lethanie des bons compagnons*, and the interplay of sacred and profane levels is a marked feature at this time. The 'religious' vehicle can be treated humorously in the sermon, which is often in verse and which, as a monologue, comes very close to dramatic form: indeed, the dramatic monologue enjoys a prolonged success (see below, p. 60). More generally, dignified genres are sometimes adapted to ends other than was originally intended: as examples one may mention a *Testament de Martin Luther*, where the villonesque structure is pressed into the service of religious propaganda, and in a different vein, the notorious *Triomphe de treshaulte et puissante Dame Verolle royne du puys d'Amour*; the *verollez* often figure as part of an anti-erotic attitude (*Le patrenostre des verollez*, etc.).

The range of genre exploited by these poets is very wide indeed. Among the popular ones are comparisons between women from different parts of the country (e.g., Jean Marot's poem contrasting women from Paris and Lyons, spiced with some flattery of the king); prognostications in verse, which by their loose structure and sometimes ridiculous statements make one think of an embryonic *coq-à-l'âne*; curious, extended compositions, in which technical matters, allegory, and courtly flattery blend more or less happily: such is the well-known *Livre du faulcon*,[13] which against all expectation contains a substantial amatory element. However, the *rhétoriqueurs* tend to be associated with a number of other genres whose possibilities they explored thoroughly.

One of these is the *epistle*, whose literary origin was Ovid rather than Horace, and which appears under three chief forms: the straightforward letter expressing the poet's sentiments or those of some living person on whose behalf he is acting; the love-epistle clearly derived from the *Heroides*; and what some critics have termed the *artificial* epistle. This refers to the composition of a letter sent by one person to someone he or she could never possibly have met (a technique also developed in Fontenelle's *Dialogue des Morts* or Landor's *Imaginary Conversations*). The situation allows for the discussion of some moral theme, often from two points of view, so that the epistle can verge on the *débat*. These epistles, which in the amatory mode are close to the elegy, usually remain stereotyped, and only occasionally can a poet like Lemaire make something of them; they tend to be impersonal and bear little resemblance to Marot's incursions into the field. Other genres which attract the *rhétoriqueurs* are the *temples* – more extended and giving scope for elaborate allegorical structures, sometimes with a *débat* scheme introduced – and the *testament*, stemming in great measure from Villon and allowing a rather wider range of feeling, sometimes of a playful or satiric character.

Very often, however, the theme is slight, and the genre is thought of more by its form than by its content. For instance, it is not uncommon for the *blason* to be considered a light, sometimes loose poem – one thinks of the *blason* competition in the mid-thirties – but Molinet's *Blason des armes de nostre Redempteur* is obviously very serious in its matter. In the *fatras*, the thematic point of departure is minimal, and originally seems to have been a basis for improvisation – a fair amount of poetry in this period and indeed in the whole century originates in extempore form, whether Latin or French be the language employed. A couplet might be given, and a member of the circle would be invited to produce a poem in strict form, in which the rhymes would be determined by the given couplet, whose first line would form the first line of the improvisation; its last line would also close the invention. The form had to be respected without argument: eleven lines with the rhyme-scheme Aabaabbabaʙ; the *fatras* could be *simple* or *double*, and it could be further subdivided into *possible* (with recognisable and serious content) or *impossible* (where comprehensibility counted for little). For the most part we are dealing with an *amusette*, but the use of the ambiguous or incomprehensible in verse could make it a precursor of the *énigme* or the *coq-à-l'âne* used under Francis I for satirical and possibly religious purpose.

The *rhétoriqueurs* put much effort into the small genres, *chant royal*, *ballade*, *rondeau*, which were governed by complex rules affecting metrical pattern, rhymes, and sounds of words. The *rondeau* often treats of love, though there is room for other themes and word-play is extensive: the love *rondeau* may range from sophisticated idealism to something much more earthy, and correspondingly the tone may be highly self-conscious or come close to the spoken word. Originally, an eight-line structure seems to have been the basis: after a period of elaboration, poets reverted to a simpler treatment, but in our period, greater variations became the order of the day, with the following schemes occurring frequently: abaʌabAʙ and aaʙʙaaaʙ. Great attention was paid to rhyme which not only was *riche*, but could be *équivoquée* (an example from Molinet illustrates the principle: *Sansonnet, sans son net, sans sonnet, sans son est*); other types of rhyme employed were *couronnée*, *batelée annexée*, *emperière*, or *fratrisée*. An example of complex rhyming is described by its author: 'On peult faïre aussi autre maniere d'equivoques masles par ryme double couronnée à double unisonance':

Par discors cors   ja pris en recordz corps
Creux garniz nidz   ou as mes amys mys,
En consortz sortz   tant que en ressortz sors
Hors joliz lictz   non sentantz delictz lis . . .

The exercise may be further complicated by acrostic, word-play with numerals (XI doit montrer XII et gent . . .), texts that 'make sense' also if read backwards. There are Latin poems that have a second meaning if read as if they were French, *rondeaux* capable of being read in twelve fashions, as one author, Nicole du Puys, explained in a prefatory poem:

> Ce rondeau a double couronne
> Est fait à trois coups planieres
> Et si est la sentence bonne
> En le lisant en six manieres
> Ainsi sont qui gardent leur rang
> Six rondeaulx contenus en ung
> Et qui les sçait mettre a l'enuers
> Peult voir douze rondeaulx divers.[14]

All this, of course, in honour of the Virgin Mary. The systematic repetition of sounds, either by alliteration or by the multiplied use of some root, was strongly advocated. In *poetrie*, refinement could be hardly sought in similar fashion, but authors were encouraged in the arts of rhetoric to use words of Latin colour, and sometimes lists were provided. In consequence, we find texts such as the opening of André de la Vigne's *Ressource de la Chrestienté*:

Accumulé de liqueur vaporeuse, perplexe de vigilante vacacion, perturbé de sens, desnué d'avoir et de voir, offusqué par le dormitoire qui lors coaguloit le sens naturel de ma personne avec boursoufleuse oysiveté: qui permettoit à mon organe taisibilité, à mon serveau ruralité, à mon ame bestialité, à mes membres labilité, à mon engin débilité, repous à sensualité et au corps seul felicité et utilité naturelle. . . .[15]

The learned word replaces the 'vocable de commun entendement', enumeration with repeated balance and order is employed mercilessly, the pair of words is preferred to the single. In all this content is sicklied over by a paste of meaningless jargon, and the modern reader echoes Jules Lemaître's comment after reading a symbolist text: 'Vous comprenez? Moi non plus'. One can only be dismayed by the immense gap between serious purpose and futile practice.

It is, however, essential not to lose sight of this serious purpose and not to contrast too favourably the later sixteenth century with the literature of Louis XII's reign, as if such alembication faded after Marot. The *rhétoriqueurs* maintained their position and prestige for a long while yet; their works were regularly reprinted during the first half of the sixteenth century, and indeed beyond, and Du Bellay's attack on the old French school hardly implies a defunct tradition. Moreover, certain of these precious habits persisted, but under new labels (Book XVI of the *Greek Anthology* is a useful source) and the poetic prose we find in the pastoral during the

1570s bears an uncanny resemblance to what we have been examining. Literature of this sort flourishes within a closed society or group.

At a higher level, nevertheless, the *rhétoriqueurs* set a respectable example. Their concept of poetry, as we have seen, was a dignified, indeed an aristocratic, one, very similar to the Pléiade's in certain respects. They laid vigorous stress on the acquisition of technique – in fact, they made some contribution to poetic development by their interest in *alternance*, in the alexandrine, and in *terza rima*; and they were aware of the need to enrich poetic language. Some of the genres in which they worked were continued by their successors: the epistle, the embryonic eclogue, the dream, and genres associated with the more formal poetry of court ceremonial. A perusal of an anthology such as the *Jardin de Plaisance* will reveal the considerable thematic range of these poets. Some of their poetic habits last longer than is often realised: the presence of allegory, rhetorical practices such as the ternary phrase, stress on epithets, enumeration, negative presentation of theme, *sententiæ*, the *topos* of poetic humility (Crétin speaks of 'mon escript rural et mecanique'); the exploitation of themes such as Envy, Fortune's wheel, enemies at Court, the five manifestations of love, life as a preparation for death, and many others. The fact that the Pléiade could innovate so much depends in part on the continuum already provided by the national tradition, which the *rhétoriqueurs* helped to transmit. In another respect one may wonder whether the *rhétoriqueurs* do not anticipate later taste; Valéry once wrote that Latin verse had reached a stage where 'il devient si conscient de ses moyens que la tentation de les employer pour le plaisir de s'en servir et de les développer à l'extrême, passe le besoin vrai, primitif et naïf de s'exprimer'. This comment might be taken as a stick with which to beat the *rhétoriqueurs*, and yet are there not times when this enjoyment of language in itself generates an unsuspected vitality of its own?

> . . . Et vont disant que par tous les bons dieux
> Le serviront de cueur, de corps et de yeulx.
> L'une paistrit, l'aultre chauffe le four,
> L'autre s'en va en ung grant carrefour,
> Et faict dresser, qui qu'en groumelle ou gronde,
> A tous venans la belle table ronde:
> Tartres, flannetz, talemouzes, pastez
> De gros canars, et gras pigeons pattez
> Mectent sur table; ung haulte compte et songe esse
> De oyr cryer a puissance largesse.
> Tout va dehait: pastoureaulx, pastourelles,
> Grans et petits, sauttereaulx, sautterelles,
> Ont du plaisir et lyesse habondance.
> On chante, on rit, qui le corps a bon, dance. . . .
> (G. Crétin, Poem lxiv, lines 159 ff., K. Chesney ed., 287)

The context no doubt encourages linguistic exuberance, but from time to time one feels that the words take over and we are moving into a sort of Surrealist world. And indeed how far away are we here with gastronomic cheer and verbal fireworks, from Rabelais who himself, when in a mood to compose verse, reverts to *rhétoriqueur* traditions? Crétin and Molinet, in particular, seem able on occasion to take verbal wing and go beyond the *poncif* of their art; and this is an aspect of their activity that is likely to appeal to a generation accustomed to the explorations of Surrealism.

Furthermore, it is sometimes overlooked that the *rhétoriqueurs*, by their fairly extensive translation activity, introduce new material into the literature of their time. Octovien de Saint-Gellais's rendering of the *Metamorphoses* is well enough known, but he also translated Aeneas Sylvius's *Ystoire de Eurialus et de Lucrece*,[16] thus filling a gap indigenous authors had neglected and satisfying a need of contemporary sensibility. The value of his version is suggested by its lasting success – it was reprinted just over a century after its first appearance (1493/1599). The *rhétoriqueurs*, though encased in their rigid set of conventions, were not blind to what was going on beyond the frontiers of France.

From time to time one comes across references to Italian writers who were to affect the French Renaissance, or mention of some theme or concern that indicates new trends. Petrarch is mentioned; some of his work had been known for a long time, and French printings of some texts come out during Louis XII's reign; but sometimes the *rhétoriqueurs* show knowledge of him (Robertet, Crétin, Marot). Moreover, a few of them were in touch with Parisian humanist circles, and aspects of Italian culture were known to them; nevertheless, the awareness of new horizons is still more noticeable in the Latin writings of the period, and the *rhétoriqueurs'* attitude is in great measure late medieval; their view of Petrarch is circumscribed, and they refer much more frequently to their poetic predecessors, like Chastellain and Deschamps: professional solidarity probably encourages the closed outlook. Nevertheless, it would be wrong to discount signs of change: the *rhétoriqueurs'* understanding of the classical tradition seems rather richer and more open-minded than in the past, and they have a more alert awareness of their role in the active, contemporary world. And there is at least one poet whose *vision du monde* and literary ability mark him off from the others – Jean Lemaire de Belges.

VII. JEAN LEMAIRE DE BELGES[17] (1473–?1524)

Lemaire's distinction was evident to sixteenth-century readers: Marot, Ronsard, Rabelais, and Du Bellay all rated him highly and set him apart from the rank and file. Though his training under Molinet and his conception of poetry show up his poetic affiliation, Lemaire does seem in various ways to be ahead of his times. He had connections with the humanist world (Gaguin), and later, after he had transferred his allegiance from Margaret of Austria to Anne of Brittany, he was able to meet younger scholars like Germain de Brie, even if his classical culture for all its breadth did not extend to a knowledge of Greek. His acquaintance with things Italian is wide-ranging and fruitful: he had occasion to travel in the peninsula, and as he spent some time in Lyons, he could not fail to meet persons, like Symphorien Champier, familiar with Italian culture. He had some knowledge of Dante and refers to later poets like Serafino d'Aquila; nor could the *Concorde des deux langages* have been composed without a keen appreciation of what Italy had to offer. But Lemaire marks an advance not merely by keener insight into new trends, but by a greater poetic originality: he developed sufficient taste and aesthetic sense to avoid the worst *rhétoriqueur* pitfalls, he succeeded in making poetry a more personal affair, and he was able to inject into it the vitality which convention and technical excess had stifled in his colleagues. The most convenient way to approach his poetry is to take three texts available in modern editions, the *Plainte du Désiré*, the *Epistres de l'Amant vert*, and the *Concorde*.

The *Plainte* appeared in 1509 from the press of Jean de Vingle, together with the *Légende des Venitiens* and the *Regretz de la Dame infortunée*, written in honour of Margaret of Austria's brother recently deceased. The *Plainte* was probably composed earlier, to celebrate the death of the comte de Ligny (December 1503), who took a prominent part in certain Italian expeditions, but appears to have fallen from favour after 1500; Lemaire assumes that this turn of fortune hastened his death, and he accordingly makes Envy play a role in the poem. The plan is simple: two speeches by *Painture* and *Rhetorique* respectively, flanked by three short prose passages – a prologue giving the setting, an *entr'acte* between the speeches, and an epilogue explaining the origin of the work. The *Plainte* is strongly coloured by the *rhétoriqueur* tradition: the mixture of prose and verse, two allegorical figures involved in what verges on a *débat*, the presence of several *topoi*, and numerous stylistic devices (doublets, epithets, enumeration, word-play). Nevertheless, Lemaire is able to curb linguistic exuberance: one has only to compare his restraint with Molinet's athleticism in the *Epitaphe de Simon Marmion, Painctre (Faictz et Ditz,* II, 824). He does not go to inordinate lengths in his search for unusual vocabulary, jingles, or erudition; and by introducing two speeches, he not only helps to dramatise his material, but adds themes and feelings that go beyond the nominal subject. The qualities of painting and poetry are discussed, a dialogue which allows the poet to refer copiously to the state of literature in his own time, and *en passant* to musicians, who are invited to sing the praise of the Count, a generous patron of the arts:

> Ung grave accent, musicque larmoiable
> Est bien seant à ce dueil piteable,
> Pour parfournir noz lamentacions.
> A toy, Josquin, en priere amiable
> Le deffunct mande estre tant serviable
> Qu'on puist chanter sa complainte louable
> Sur tes motetz et compositions.
> Fais doncq ung chant ainsi que de tenebres,
> Sans mignotise et sans point d'illecebres
> Remply de dueil en ses proportions:
> Comme on faisoit es granz pompes funebres
> Jadis à Romme, ou aux festes celebres
> D'Isis, querant par troux et par latebres
> Son mary mort, aumoins par fictions.
> (Yabsley ed., p. 81)

Lemaire is surely following a tradition in developing the theme of the efficacy of an art, but what is worth noting here is the way in which he has shifted the focus from the theme of death to the praise of art and life. The poem is by no means free from stilted and stylised elements, but we can already see Lemaire making a more supple use of his idiom.

This gradual emancipation is more evident in the *Epistres de l'Amant vert*; the first epistle (1505) celebrated the death of a parrot killed by a dog in Margaret's absence. At this time, Lemaire had been engaged on the *Palais d'honneur femenin* and the rather tedious *Couronne Margaritique,* written to console the queen on the death of her third husband; the *Epistre* therefore came in the nature of a diversion. It found its way around various Courts in manuscript, and its success no doubt prompted the sequel, composed towards the end of 1505, and considerably revised before publication, partly because Lemaire had by then moved to Anne of Brittany's Court and was impelled to change the proportions of homage paid to the two queens, partly because the text was too long. The epistle, in decasyllables and *rimes plates,* was, as we have seen, an established *rhétoriqueur* genre and the celebration of a pet animal has a long pedigree back to classical times; indeed Lemaire may have been influenced by a poem of Statius. The link between the parrot and love is not new, since in the medieval scheme of symbolism, green is the sign of passion. But when all is said and done, Lemaire has renewed the genre: he introduces a considerable range of mood, and if there is perhaps some satiric handling of traditional themes applied to a parrot, the bird nevertheless serves as a mask for the expression of delicate feeling. If we take a verse letter by Molinet, say the one to Florimond Robertet:

> Chef d'œuvre exquis, sintilant Florymond,
> Soleil luysant au franc assuré throsne,
> Les grandz vertuz de ton champ flory m'ont
> Bouté en train, si qu'à ton flory mont
> Mon epistolle indigne se patrone;
> Ton pere estoit filz de nostre matronne,
> La réthorique, et je crois que tel es:
> Nam sequitur patrem sua proles. . . .
>
> (Dupire ed., II, p. 842)

we can see how the sustained preciosity simply does not come to life. Turn then to the lines uttered by the Amant vert:

> Ainsi dira la bergiere au corps gent
> Aux pelerins et à mainte autre gent,
> Que voulentiers la mienne histoire orront
> Et de pitié, peut-être ploureront,
> Et semeront des branches verdelettes,
> Sur mon tumbel, et fleurs et violettes,
> Puis s'en iront comptant par mainte terre
> Comment Amours m'ont fait cruelle guerre,
> Par quoy sera mon bruit trop plus ouvert
> Que du Vert Conte ou du Chevalier Vert;
> Et sera dit l'Amant vert noble et preux,
> Quand il morut vray martyr amoureux.
> Et oultreplus, à ma tumbe, de nuyt,
> Quand tout repose et que la lune luyt,
> Viendront Silvan, Pan, et les demydieux
> Des bois prouchains et circonvoisins lieux,
> Et avec eux les fees et nymphettes,
> Tout alentour faisans joyeux festes,
> Menans deduit en danses et caroles
> Et en chansons d'amoureuses parolles . . .
>
> (Frappier ed., pp. 13–14, lines 257–76)

Here we are in a different world: Lemaire has managed to remove solemnity and stiffness from the genre, without overstepping into buffoonery, and to achieve a good deal more besides. He has introduced a note of wistful and therefore personal *badinage*, such as will be developed soon by Marot, quite different from the faceless and ineffectual efficiency of technique displayed by his masters. He has created atmosphere by the treatment of the setting, which is not just a catalogue of conventional details: there is harmony between the bird's mood and the countryside where his tomb will be set up;

allegorical figures are avoided, and Lemaire is content to rely on a discreet evocation of the classical mythological fauna (whom we shall find again in Ronsard). A contrast is established between the quiet of the tomb and the graceful movements of the dancers, and the intimacy of the scene is enhanced by the use of diminutives (*verdelettes, oiselets*). We are presented with a passage of clear, classical delicacy, which also derives from the poet's handling of language. He maintains the doublets and the *coupe ternaire* of his colleagues, but he avoids the heavier artillery of tradition: rhymes and word-play are reduced to a minimum, enumeration is less obvious than even in the *Plainte du Désiré*, cumbersome latinisms are eschewed. Over and above this, note the care with which Lemaire controls the phrase and restores line and flow to the verse. There has been attention paid to the selection of verbs of motion, to word-balance (especially in the placing of adjectives), to varying the pauses within the line, and to the judicious use of *enjambement*. The final unity of tone is ensured by a blend of delicate emotion and a certain detachment which allows the poet complete control of his material.

The second epistle, like other second helpings, is less attractive. Here the dead bird finds its way down to the Underworld and we are given a rapid sketch of the place through its eyes; but something has happened to the parrot since we last met it. It has been reading a lot of Vergil and may even have turned over the leaves of the *Divine Comedy*, so that true to its nature it begins to recite uncritically what it has learned. Poetically, this means an unfortunate return to *rhétoriqueur* enumeration (the catalogue of animals), a failure to capture atmosphere. In the list of animals we become aware of a feeling of admiration for the poet's cleverness, and this shift of focus harms the general effect. Finally, the element of homage seems more laboured than in the first epistle, especially as the parrot is not only speaking to its mistress.

The *Concorde* is a much more substantial work: not only has Lemaire evolved artistically, but the poem is strengthened by a firm intellectual framework. Its shape is reminiscent of the *Plainte*'s: two blocks of poetry surrounded by prose prologue, *entr'acte*, and epilogue. After an introduction in which Lemaire suggests that the Italian and French tongues should work in harmony and not in opposition, he goes on to describe the Temple of Venus and that of Minerva. In order to develop this cultural symbiosis, we must seek to live under the sign of Wisdom rather than of Love. Apart from the theme of cultural collaboration, which strikes an unmistakably new note, the artificial framework is very much in the *rhétoriqueur* tradition: symmetrical pattern of prose and verse, temples, allegorical figures, edifying tone, and a fair sprinkling of linguistic devices (alliterations, refined latinisms). In a sense, this language seems to mark a regression from that of the *Amant vert*; but Lemaire, singing some graver theme, is bound by the tradition of sustained rhetoric; even so, the abuses are infrequent and masked by some startling novelties.

The first is precisely the theme of cultural harmony between Italy and France. Lemaire has not gone so far as to tackle the problem of Latin and the vernacular (though Crétin encouraged him to write in French), but he gives unstinted welcome to Italian culture without any hint of that anti-Italianism which is so often a feature of French humanist writing. He gives practical expression to his hopes in that the description of the Temple of Venus is in *terza rima* (though his treatment departs from the Italian); the Temple of Minerva is presented in alexandrines. One must, however, not take logic too far, for Lemaire condemns the Temple of Venus as unsuitable for cultural progress.

The next surprise is to be found in that same description of the Temple of Venus. In the prose, Lemaire makes it abundantly clear that it is Minerva and not Venus who is to be followed; but in the poetry, Venus enjoys a much finer innings than Minerva who is given 108 lines to her rival's 616, and Lemaire seems more at ease in *terza rima* than in the alexandrine. Beneath the moralising, ecclesiastical, and *rhétoriqueur* surface of the poet's personality, there is a full-blooded hedonist ready to break through. One will notice, *inter alia*, the warm, lavish picture of the temple itself, which incorporates Christian and pagan elements and is situated in Lyons, perhaps because Lyons was the meeting-point of the two cultures, but also certainly because of the myth that linked Fourvières with a *forum Veneris*. Once again, Lemaire gives a handsome role to music: this is in the tradition, but his treatment goes further in its auditive exuberance. More important is the remarkable tribute to Nature, and with the density of suggestion he carries, Lemaire can truly be said to herald Ronsard. There is on the one hand a powerful portrayal of aspects of Nature and on the other he apostrophises Old Age and advises us to gather the rosebuds while we may. Here he shows a gift for the memorable line, something not shared by many *rhétoriqueurs*:

> Trop est grief fais que de vieulx devenir,
> D'avoir passé le joly temps d'esté
> Le riche automne où n'a nul revenir.
> (lines 475–7)

Such is the vitality of the text that even the allegorical figure Genius, the archpriest of Venus, ceases to be rigid and hollow and seems to take on flesh and blood. Obviously Lemaire has expressed something very deep-seated here, and these few hundred lines break new ground. The rest of the poem no doubt becomes something of an anti-climax: Minerva gets rather short shrift and we may feel callously that wisdom, like virtue, is its own reward; Lemaire does his best to convince us that the rarified heights on which stands her temple constitute our Ultima Thule; but when the satyr sings the glories of the spirit, we wonder whether he is not tired or mendacious. In short, the impact of this remarkable poem hardly corresponds to the author's stated intentions; and if it had, we should have been the poorer.

Some discussion has arisen as to whether Lemaire's insights were conscious or not; on balance I am inclined to think that his achievement was greater and perhaps other than he realised. As a poet he restored vitality to his writing and infused values into technique; whereas the *rhétoriqueurs* had what one might call an atomic view of poetry, Lemaire, shifting the relations between syntax, sound, and meaning, conferred a more organic character on poetic language. Through his work shines a poetic personality, and in his best compositions there is an awareness of the world in which he is taking part. The substance of poetry is not taken for granted and experience informs his more articulate utterance.

VIII. EARLY HISTORIOGRAPHY

The *rhétoriqueurs* were not only poets, they were chroniclers. In Italy and France, a close connection was understood between poetry and history, which, in the eyes of some, were taken to be different methods of describing truth, though both used eloquence as the medium of expression. The discussion goes on right through the Renaissance: we find traces of it in Ronsard's preface to his *Franciade*, but the relationships between the two activities are accepted a long time earlier. In his *Bref sommaire* of 1531, Télin, whose attitude is very similar to that of the *rhétoriqueurs*, includes a definition of history: it is

le tesmoignage des temps, lumiere de verité, nourrice & vie de la memoire, enseigneresse et maistresse d'escolle a nostre vie et mesnagiere d'ancienneté.

All the major *rhétoriqueurs* took some interest in the events of their times and left accounts for posterity; some were more ambitious and composed histories of France (Lemaire de Belges and Robert Gaguin, whose work was translated into French). They followed a series of well-known annalists, Blondel, Chastellain, Olivier de la Marche; one will find scattered references in their verse to their views on history and they were of the opinion that the historian conferred immortality by his art. In most cases, historiography

remained within the confines of the chronicle or annals – a chronological account of events, or nearly so, was considered right. Very
few of these authors can be said to have evolved a clear concept of
history, beyond what was implicit in their activity. Indeed, so long
as Christian medieval attitudes persisted, little progress was likely
to be made: these writers no doubt assumed that events were in
accordance with some divinely preordained pattern, and the
Augustinian conception of history as a struggle between good and
evil was accepted by many. Within the circumscribed framework of
national history the concept of the rise, apogee, and decline of kings
or periods could find a place (the theme of Fortune's wheel is a
constant one), but the classical conception of a cyclical development
of history, such as was entertained by a number of later Renaissance
humanists, has no place here; nor can one claim that these
chroniclers had yet acquired clear ideas on the periodicisation of
history, though this feature, characteristic of emergent Renaissance
attitudes, is round the corner. The run-of-the-mill chronicler did
not set his sights high enough to formulate a personal view of history; his activity was determined in great measure by more mundane
considerations.

The chronicler was the servant of the Court and expressed the
interests of the king and entourage in his annals. He therefore tends
to narrate the glories of some princely house or to justify policies
undertaken, and these aims may be achieved in both the chronicle
and the epic or para-epic poem, a number of which are written in
Latin (e.g., Blarrorivus's *Nanceis*, printed in 1518, but written
earlier, and the poems inspired by the wars with England and
Italy). Many of the *rhétoriqueurs* had a tincture of classical reading
and had more than a nodding acquaintance with the Roman
historians; there is also evidence that Livy was not unknown to
some kings. The influence of Roman historiography is no doubt
rather diffuse at this time, but it seems to express itself in three
main ways: in the search for accuracy (though this urge is often
obscured by other factors); in the tendency to see the record of
history as an example for rulers – and we have noted the current
fashion for *Miroirs des Princes*; and finally in a concern for style,
showing itself in a *style soutenu*, the composition of speeches
(usually imaginary),[18] portraits, *débats*, and *sententiæ*. The further
implications of Roman historiography were probably hidden from
the majority, though the patriotic, committed character of Livy and
others must have been evident, especially in an age where culture is
developing strong nationalist traits. The exemplary element is very
pronounced: princes are praised for their military prowess, but also
for the way in which they may live up to the ideal of royal behaviour, which includes a due encouragement of the arts. The *topos*

warning kings against courtiers and false flatterers is current and sometimes introduced as a measuring staff. (It recurs frequently much later, too, in a work like George Buchanan's *History of Scotland*, 1579.)

The claims to a measure of accuracy are genuine enough, but in practice many factors of a national or local nature can warp the picture. An obvious example is the manner in which the number of persons slain in some battle is handled. Moreover, royal involvement and the persistence of the chivalric ideal determine the type of events selected for treatment; military events play a preponderant part, but occasionally there enters attention to the motives underlying such happenings. For similar reasons, well-worn legends preserve the appearance of historical fact: the prime example is that of the Trojan origin of the French kings, which Lemaire, for instance, is very keen to exploit at the expense of the Venetians. Narrative may also be distorted by allegorical preoccupations. All in all, we have a deeply ingrained conservatism that will hamper innovation: it will be a long time before historians take the discovery of America seriously. In any case, the chroniclers are still heavily dependent on medieval sources for their material, a debt which they variously recognise. Moralising and stylistic considerations also reduce the historical relevance of much of what they have to say. On the other hand, their staunch patriotism will have the effect of reducing among French humanists the contempt for the 'Dark Ages': the standing of Charlemagne, for instance, is never questioned, and the ideal of chivalry is bolstered by these chroniclers, who moreover, by their uncritical praise of kings, make some contribution to the growing support for an absolutist conception of kingship, so popular in humanist circles in the near future.

Such a panorama of generalities may give the impression that all these chroniclers were cast in the same mould; but though they do have a family air, there is considerable variety from one author to another: the standard of accuracy, the particular weight given to public events or private insights, to patriotic or psychological interest, and of course the literary qualities, for some excel in the portrait, others in a *style soutenu* seeking to bring out the splendour of events, yet others in a lively realism. I shall therefore concentrate on a few figures, who have estimable qualities and who represent different facets of the historiographical activity under Charles VIII, Louis XII, and the young Francis I.

Jean d'Auton (1467–1528)[19]

A Benedictine monk, Jean d'Auton, figures among the *rhétoriqueurs* by his occasional poetry, but his chronicles, published first in the eighteenth century, are much more substantial, though they cover a short period, the middle years of Louis XII's reign (1499–1507). He starts his career as an unofficial historian, 'non presumant sur ceulx a quy par raison l'office en appartient', but enjoys apparently the patronage of Anne of Brittany before coming under Louis XII's wing. His period of favour is short-lived and after the accession of Francis I, we rather lose sight of him. Jean d'Auton went to considerable trouble to obtain material, both at first hand and from reliable witnesses, though he emerges as a collector of public events rather than as an analyst of political motive, and indeed he does not give the impression of being 'on the inside': at one stage he mentions his inability to gain access to significant documents. His mind is more ocular than intellectual and we are given a rather flat account of events as they occur. There is an occasional relief from this objective attitude, especially when he is conscious of his official function; and though he does not reach the extremes of alembication we find in so much *rhétoriqueur* prose, he may latinise his style, in spite of little tendency to classical colouring: learned adjectives (*voragineux, turbineux*) and the involved sentence that proceeds through chains of consecutive, causal, and relative links:

> Celuy qui portoit l'enseigne aprocha de tant que, joignant du boulevart, se mist a pied ferme et, nonobstant coups d'artillerie et de pierres dont il estoit batu de toutes parts, ne voulut desmarcher ne reculer ung seul pas par craincte de mort, dont a la fin ne fut exempt, car il mourut sur le champ, avec d'autres assez. (I, 127)

This lack of control is a feature of his writing; on occasions of moment, superlatives and hyperbolic comparisons may be used, but his tone remains generally sober, though classical allusions and speeches make their expected appearance. Relief also comes from the rather timid peeping-through of his kindly, humane personality. His purpose in writing is to praise famous men and immortalise them by the pen:

> Or, a la fin que partye ou relicque
> Des faictz louables de nos Françoys modernes
> Puissent durer immortels et eternes,
> Par vrays escriptz, en convient mencion
> Faire aux futurs et clere ostencion,
> Et tant a plein leurs biensfaictz publier
> Que on ne puisse jamais les oublyer,
> Comme jadis ont esté plus d'ung cent
> D'hommes dignes de regnom florissant,
> Voyre de telz qui, de fresche memoire,
> Ont a la mort perdu louange et gloire,
> Pour n'a avoir mys pour eulx main a la plume.
>
> (I, 116–17)

This theme is closely linked with the glory of France and French-men who he declares are the direct heirs of Rome in fame 'Ainsi que Dieu l'a permys et voulu'; and it is this pride in national tradition that recurs time and again in the chronicles of the period. Jean d'Auton can interest the historian by his relative objectivity; for the historian of literature his claims are modest enough, but he does seek to introduce a measure of sobriety into his style.

Jean Lemaire de Belges

Of all the historical writings of the time, the *Illustrations de Gaule* were the most immediately popular, and though they strike a modern reader as fiction rather than fact, they were widely read until the middle of the century and beyond: both Ronsard and Etienne Pasquier had some regard for the work. It purports to trace the early history of France from the days of Troy – Lemaire, less critical than Gaguin, does much to popularise the Trojan legend that reappears in the *Franciade* – and by his adoption of John of Viterbo's theory that there was an *Hercule gaulois*, he gives wide-spread currency to a legend that will find favour far into the century.[20] There are many fruitful strands in the *Illustrations*: for a start, the moral considerations that lie behind Paris's attitude to his two successive wives are very much in keeping with contemporary climate of opinion. More important, though, is the manner in which Lemaire gives expression to certain national sentiments connected with the emergence of the French Renaissance. By the themes of the Trojan origins and the *Hercule gaulois*, Lemaire promotes the theory of Gaul's cultural primacy: his confused scheme of history, which brings in biblical history, classical mythology, and Gaulish kings, with the help of an elaborate genealogical tree, links Gaul with Greece, so that Roman culture is seen to be a product rather than a source of Western culture. Early on we thus see a certain reaction to Italy's claims to supremacy in the field of letters. Lemaire's patriotism is also revealed by his use of the vernacular, 'ce langage François, que les Italiens par leur mesprisance acoustumée appellent barbare (mais non est)'. He takes the opportunity to praise Paris as the 'mere et maistresse souveraine des estudes de tout le monde, plus que jadis nulles Athenes, ne nulles Rommes'. We have seen elsewhere Lemaire's conviction that French culture had as much to offer as the Italian, and here he is also concerned to show the qualities of the French language as a cultural medium. Admittedly his style is that of a *rhétoriqueur* enjoying a splendid Indian summer: his description of love as 'grand calefaction d'amoureuse concupiscence' is not very happy, and one can detect the unfortunate effects of his writing on so sensitive a mind as Helisenne de Crenne; despite all this, the *Illustrations* are a gesture

in favour of the vernacular. Finally, the work, with its patriotic
inspiration, is the expression of a certain ideal of behaviour, and it
shows at the same time how the domains of the chronicle, the novel,
and the romance may overlap. A number of 'classical' scenes are
presented through the lens of medieval behaviour (jousting, to give
one example); and Lemaire has offered the reader a stylised view of
Nature (not all that remote from Ronsard) and of gracious living
that is renewed rather than displaced by the *poncif* of the *Amadis*
or the Pléiade. Lemaire is continually surprising us by transcending
the categories in which we try to enclose him, and the *Illustrations'*
success is to be explained by its ability to play on so many strings of
contemporary sensibility: it stands at the crossroads between the
late medieval era and the Renaissance. Somewhere he points to the
need to get behind 'l'escorce des fables artificielles'; if we apply
this method to his own fiction, we shall realise the wide-ranging
interest of his excursion into national history, which will also play
its part in muting the average humanists' contempt for the Middle
Ages.

Philippe de Commynes[21] (*1445–1509*)

With Commynes we enter yet another world of historiography.
Not of course that his chronicles fail to share characteristics we have
noticed in other writers: the noting of events *sub specie Dei*, the role
of fortune, the *exemplary* character of his writing. On the other
hand, he has often first-hand experience of the events he is narrating
and when he cannot be present, he fills in the gaps 'par communications de leurs ambassades, par lettres, et par leurs instructions'. Even so, his claims are excessive on occasion: he is inaccurate
about the events he may have witnessed, his chronology can be
ragged – though he is endowed with an interesting topographical
memory – and recent scholars have seen in his work the effect of a
bad conscience brought about by his switch of allegiance – he moved
from Charles the Bold to Louis XI. Yet, when all is said and done,
there remains a remarkable achievement. Commynes's own rather
disillusioned view of life prevents him from believing in the chivalric
outlook: he notes his first experience of the buffets of fortune: 'C'est
la premiere fois que j'euz jamais congnoissance que les choses de ce
monde sont peu estables'. He does not indulge in fanciful descriptions of battles, he always refers slightingly to the way in which
figures are exaggerated. He entertains a less rosy opinion of
monarchs, their motives, and their behaviour. Somewhere he draws
a contrast between two types of prince, but to the profit of neither;
and he injects a sober, incisive realism into the memorable portraits
he offers of kings. In his eyes all men are imperfection – only God is
perfect, and His representatives on earth are not automatically

infected by the workings of divine right. In these circumstances, the patriotic urge plays little role; what interests Commynes are the conclusions to be drawn from political behaviour – indeed politics appeal to him far more than warfare or court life; and his steady popularity in the sixteenth century – shown by various editions, a serious commentary from the pen of Denys Sauvage in 1549, a translation into Latin – is due in part at least to comments on statesmanship and government. Commynes is not averse from comparing the behaviour of different nations: thus the English are contrasted with the French in their habits of fighting, but also in their manner of conducting public affairs. In life he sees a mixed bag – 'partout il y a du bien et du mal' – and he hopes that his analyses will help readers to profit from the past; the moralist is deeply present, but not to the damage of his insight:

Ainsi, en tous estatz, y a bien affaire à vivre en ce monde et faict Dieu une grande grace à ceulx à qui il donne bon sens naturel. (I, 253)

These virtues are mirrored in his style; Commynes maintains, as one might expect, various elements of the tradition – the themes of fortune and ingratitude, speeches, *sententiæ, exempla*; but there is less search for superlative and hyperbole or other means to inflate the event. There is also less humanist colouring in his vocabulary, and he is not afraid of inserting popular idiom. He is precise and does not allow the structure of his sentence to be affected by rhetorical ideals, though it must not be assumed that the complex structure eludes him. He seeks clarity (note, for instance, his use of the definite article and the personal pronoun); he has a welcome command of the nuance – the portrait of Louis XII springs to mind; and he captures the movement of a scene. There is little variation in emotion, and this imparts a monochrome effect to much of his writing; but perhaps already we have the glimmerings of a classical clarity, and one can understand why Pasquier enjoyed reading Commynes. Unlike so many of his contemporaries writing with their rose-tinted spectacles on, he tends to observe the seamy side of existence, and his terser, more abrasive passages come as a pleasant change from inflated rhetoric.

Rhétoriqueur prose style[22]

It may be convenient to mention here some characteristics of prose style at this time, though there are authors like Commynes who fight shy of the *rhétoriqueur* idiom. Prose is used for chronicles (though verse is also employed), the adaptation of prose romances, and the novel, such as it is then. We have pointed to an overlap of these genres, and this is reflected in the style. There will be individual variations, of course, and the novel and *conte* will not aim quite so high; but the authors with whom we are concerned have a certain family air, determined in part by their professional formation and the public for whom they write. Let us take a short passage from Lemaire's *Illustrations*:

Adoncq Paris tout esmerveillé et transmué d'une vision si nouvelle se dressa sur pieds en sursault, et d'un grand zele ardant se print à courir après elles et treslegierement qu'il ne sembloit point fouler l'herbe de ses plantes. Et tant fit, qu'il en rataignit une legierement fuyant, de laquelle les cheveux aureins voletoient en l'air par dessus ses espaules. Si la retint doulcement par les plys undoyans de sa robe gentille et lui dist humblement en ceste maniere: 'O deesse specieuse, quelle que tu soyes, ou nom de la clere Diane, plaise à ta grace et courtoisie demourer un petit (saulve ta bonne paix) et me vouloir dire quelle est l'assemblée de ces nobles nymphes, que j'ay presentement veues. Car oncques nulle chose ne desiray tant sçavoir que ceste cy'. Lors la gracieuse nymphe qui se sentit arrestée, se retourna promptement et d'une chere semblable à coursée, luy dist ainsi: 'Quelle hardiesse te meut, o jeune adolescent Royal? ne de quelle fiance presumes tu de mettre la main aux nymphes (qui sont demydeesses) en leur faisant violence' . . . Le noble enfant Paris Alexandre, quand il ouyt la nymphe ainsi parler imperieusement et hautainement, tout craintif et plain de tremeur, s'enclina en terre, comme estonné et moitié ravy tant de sa merveilleuse eloquence comme de sa souveraine beauté et la voulut adorer comme une deesse celeste. . . (I, xxiv)

The first thing to strike one is the artificiality of this style, so self-conscious as to verge on the stilted. There is an obviously classical colour – even the presentation of the speakers is slightly reminiscent of Vergil; Lemaire borrows words from Latin (*aureins, specieuse*) or developed from a classical root, he exploits the *incise*, the relative clause opening with *lequel*, though the frequent liking for absolute participial phrases is not shown up here. He searches carefully for the epithet, and often presents it in binary form – a feature that reappears right down to Montaigne – or reinforces it by a straight superlative, a consecutive construction, or a comparison. These are all devices intended to strengthen the affective quality of the passage, but at the expense of forward movement. The static impression of much of this prose is also given by the fondness for speeches, which have their own *style soutenu*. The adverb in *-ment* is often present (Scève may have learned from Lemaire in this respect), and too great a break between sentences is avoided, by the use of adverbs and conjunctions (*car, et*). The final sentence of the passage is constructed with particular care, with its first main verb situated in the centre of an ample epithetic development, and terminated by a much shorter clause in which, however, the force is achieved by the comparison on which the passage ends. We gain an impression of sustained rhetoric, slow-moving and heavily charged with emotion; but when we read on for a further half-dozen pages, the impact is gradually reduced, because once we have familiarised ourselves with the armoury of rhetorical device, we are rarely surprised or shaken from the lulling effect of similar rhythms and tones. Yet this style will not die out entirely with the passing of the *rhétoriqueurs*.

Histoire de Bayart (*1527*)[23]

The *Très joyeuse, plaisante et recréative histoire du gentil-Seigneur de Bayart* is a commemorative biography of a valiant knight. The author, whose identity is still in doubt, assures us that his aim is not to write for some patron but to honour the perfect knight 'sans peur et sans reproche'. Some of the techniques we have noticed elsewhere recur in this work – the speeches, care with little details, dramatisation, hyperbole, and there is a patriotic, italophobe attitude on the part of the author when he is referring to contemporary events, on which he sometimes airs his views: thus he wonders whether Louis XII's marriage to Anne of Brittany was wise. But he also shows humanity, as when he protests against unnecessary severity towards the vanquished. Nevertheless, the life strikes one less as a realistic biography than as a development of a chivalric romance, for the work, an *exemplum* of extended scale, is essentially an extolling of knightly virtues. This type of existence is described in loving detail, with tourneys and splendid encounters; the enemy always loses thousands whereas the French suffer minimal loss. We have also a glimpse of courtly love, when Bayart is loved platonically by a married lady; he is defined as the 'filz adoptif de Dame Courtoisie'. The events are recounted with a great battery of superlatives ('tant honorablement que impossible seroit de plus', etc.); the hero is perfection incarnate, and we seem to have slipped from the world of reality into some fairy-tale; it comes as no surprise that Tristan and Gawain are mentioned and that reference is made to the *Roman de la Rose*: in fact, reality and dream blend easily in this narrative which, in addition, has a thoroughly Christian tone. The language, though perhaps not as rich as that of Lemaire and other chroniclers of high standing, is quite sophisticated. A work such as this, still extremely readable today, shows how narrow was the gap between the chronicle and the romance: we know how Charles VIII's outlook was influenced by his reading of romances, and under Henry II we shall find that the novel tends to embody once again the chivalric ideal.

IX. CLAUDE DE SEYSSEL[24] (1450–?1520)

Seyssel composed the *Louenges du Roy Louis XII* (1508); and perhaps his 'translations' of various classical historians (Appian, Thucydides, Xenophon), published posthumously in 1527, may have made a modest contribution to historiography, but his fame rests on

La Grant Monarchie de France (1518); written for the benefit of Francis I, it is in various ways a remarkable work. Seyssel was an old man when he composed the treatise, and it reflects his own experience in the world of politics. Throughout the sixteenth century, the political thinking of most humanists will work in support of an absolute monarchy in France, though the medieval 'democratic' attitudes are current in the 1520s with the works of Almain and John Major and will re-emerge in the second half of the century when Huguenots turn their attention to political theory. Yet, as early as Francis I's reign, there are numerous signs of a less critical conception of monarchy by divine right: the theme is sounded in Ferrault's work, and Budé will also support it. In this context, Seyssel's little volume presents some originality. In the first place, the author adopts a pragmatic approach: he accepts the idea of the Christian monarch, but he is not concerned to offer us a theory born in the abstract. In his view, monarchy appears to work better than aristocracy or democracy and its chances of survival are greatest. It is certainly the best form of government for France, and his purpose is to outline the conditions in which it may continue to survive. These conditions he sets down in the light of experience. The work is divided into five parts, and there are a number of themes we shall encounter elsewhere: criticism of the present state of the Church, the dangers involved in aggressive wars and occupation of a foreign country (Seyssel is obviously thinking of the Italian wars), the level at which taxation can be maintained, that is a level which is seen to be tolerable to those taxed. Seyssel appeals to political sense and the experience of history:

Et davantage je n'ai écrit chose en particulier que ne puisse prouver par raison politique, par autorité approuvée et par exemple d'histoire authentique, ainsi qu'ont fait ceux qui ont composé les traités des polices et choses publiques tant en grec qu'en latin, qui presque tous ont été gens clercs et non ayants experience de la plus grande partie de ce qu'ils écrivaient, lesquels toutefois je n'ai pu voir fraîchement en composant cette mienne fantaisie pour la brieveté du temps que j'ai eu à le faire . . . (*Prohème*)

He then lists the constraints that can be placed on a monarchy whose power in theory is absolute. The king is limited by the Christian religion: if he behaves in a manner contrary to Christianity, he is betraying his mission. He is bound by a series of laws and customs, and by those whose duty is to enforce them: Seyssel places these under the titles of *Justice* and *Police*, and sees in their continuing efficacy the persistence of tradition. Yet, in principle, he is not prepared to accept what we would now call a constitutional monarchy, but his arguments may have had some appeal to a later generation of humanists, especially those of Huguenot inclination.

Seyssel's treatise is also valuable in that, apart from the conventional series of *Miroirs des princes*, it is an attempt to discuss political theory in the vernacular, and at an early date. The author, like others who appeal to experience rather than to learning, stresses the relative simplicity and familiarity of his language:

... et si n'ai voulu suivre le style ni user de termes d'aucun qui en ait écrit, ains en style bas et familier, par termes communs et usités, et sans alléguer grands raisons, ni autorités. ... (ibid.)

And like such authors, his rejection of the erudite and alembicated is mingled with an occasional attraction for a style for which he was not professionally trained. The work shows signs of the rush with which it was set down, and there is some loss of sentence control. On the other hand, Seyssel does maintain a straightforward and down-to-earth attitude, and his text can be read with enjoyment; and in other ways he is close to the humanists, by his concern with the contemporary world and by an evident national pride.

X. EARLY DRAMA

Throughout this phase, drama forms an important part of the literary spectrum, but the sociological conditions of its existence explain its very pronounced conservatism. The more ambitious spectacles, which sometimes lasted for days, were closely related to the life of the town in which they were performed, and they were intimately built into the religious tradition. They were in consequence characterised by an element of repeated ritual, dramatic as well as religious, and often performed by and for a specific audience with its own traditions and stock responses. In these circumstances, such plays are less sensitive to the new currents of the Renaissance – except perhaps about the Court or, to a limited extent, in religious propaganda – but they allow the author, often a *rhétoriqueur*, to indulge his fancy rather more than in the genres with which we have so far been concerned. At the same time, the thematic material of the plays was often traditional: successful plays of an earlier time are revamped or plundered by authors who are often anonymous or dubiously identified. This is one of the reasons why it is so difficult to date farces, where contemporary allusion is rare and satire is of a general character. For clarity of exposition, we shall break the material down into genres, but it must be recognised that genres are not absolutely rigid, though persistent traits may be identified within a specific genre.

The mystères[25]

The most ambitious plays were the *mystères*, whose links with the liturgical drama are easily seen. They embraced plays based on the

Old Testament, passion plays, and others concerned the Virgin Mary or saints or miracles. In the course of time, the term *mystère* seems to have become rather elastic, since towards the middle of the sixteenth century a distinction was made between sacred and profane mysteries. Plays on saints would be performed on the appropriate day and would be conditioned to a large extent by local pressures. They were often written for specific guilds, which had their patron saints, and they were, as often as not, performed indoors. Some plays could be of very great length: the *Mystère des Apôtres*, performed in 1536 at Bourges, lasted some forty days. They were highlights of the year in the towns where they were acted: put on with great splendour and complexity, they involved many of the inhabitants as well as providing commercial incentives by attracting custom from outside the walls.[26] The financing of such enterprises was a matter of public concern and the staging seems to have been put in the hands of a *facteur* or *conducteur de secrets* who was a man of considerable ability and drive and who, if successful, might well be sought after all over the country (Jean Bouchet for instance). The plays, very varied in their structure, called for highly developed stagecraft and the *feintes* appear to have been remarkable for their power of illusion. In many towns, the *Confrérie de la Passion* had a great say – in Paris a virtual monopoly of sacred plays – but this is not a time in which regular, professional troupes exist; some professional actors may be around, but in these large-scale compositions, local amateur talent was called upon, with female parts acted by youths, while in long parts doubling was frequent. Music played an important part, but seemingly as a source of effect rather than closely integrated to the text; choirs were recruited from local churches and the instrumentalists sat in the 'heaven'. Instrumental music was suitable in the scenes concerning heaven or pastoral, and it might also serve to indicate pauses or support mime, though not much appears to be known about the nature of the music.[27] The stage itself could be very elaborate, especially outdoors: it was made up of a series of 'mansions' (*décor simultané*) and indications could be given either by *écriteaux* or through the prologue. Heaven was traditionally represented to the left of the spectators and hell to the right. Outdoors the 'wheeled' stage was also used and there is some evidence to suggest that the stage could be constructed in the form of a semi-circle, surrounded by the spectators; but the search for perspective that characterises the Italian Renaissance stage does not make its appearance yet awhile.[28]

The *mystères*, usually of great length, were as broad as life in the matters they represented; sometimes they were so vast that parts only might be performed separately. These plays were a curious compound of allegory and grim realism, which was alleviated by a multiplicity of characters and scenes of farcical comedy. Though the professed aim was edifying, the authors also pandered to public taste, and a general lowering of tone is implied by the decree of 1548 banning *mystères* in Paris. A certain number of *mystères* were composed during the first half of the century, and, since the authors were *rhétoriqueurs*, one may find in the plays performed during the emergence of humanism elements of classical colour and a certain widening of thematic material.

Various factors lead to the decline of the genre: the ban in Paris, the disruption of the religious wars which would affect any full-scale attempts to launch a performance, the fading of the *rhétoriqueurs*, the development of new trends in the theatre; nevertheless, the tradition died hard: not only do we find some latter-day writers like Duval (1545)[29] and Lecoq still active, but performances do take place in the provinces well on in the second half of the century.

The moralité[30]

In the sixteenth century the miracle play is on the wane; a few texts that belong to our period are extant, but humanist and Huguenot pressures seem to have contributed to its decline and it hardly forms part of the literary scene. On the other hand, the *moralité* has a much greater vitality and attracts at least one writer of distinction, Marguerite de Navarre. It was still very much alive when Sebillet (1512–89) wrote his *Art poëtique françoys* in 1548. It could be serious or 'pleasant', and its two main traits were 'le Decore des personnes observées à l'ongle, et la convenance et apte reddition du Moral et allegorie'; it was this edifying factor that distinguished it from the *sottie* or *farce*, at least in theory, for the line is not always easy to draw between these genres. Some critics credit the *moralité* with greater technical sophistication than the other two genres possess, but this is an unreliable yardstick, though on occasion singing and dancing appear to have been an additional feature. Up to a point, length is a determining characteristic: in about 1535, the *moralité* was said to run to 1,000–1,200 lines, but the remarkable *Condamnacion de Bancquet* is much longer, whereas others can often be slim affairs. Though some historical *moralités* exist, contemporary reference is very marked. Many of these plays are anonymous, but the majority are connected with the *Basoche*, since the authors were usually *clercs*. It is assumed that in a performance a series of plays were put on: *cry, sottie, moralité, farce*. The satirical element in the *moralité* is usually extensive, but in the sixteenth century it can spill over into the political arena and be involved in religious controversy, as in *Science et Asnerye* (*c.*1530) which though orthodox in outlook is extremely harsh in its criticism of the Church. The characters vary greatly in number but, except in the historical plays, tend to be allegorical figures representing attitudes, vices or virtues, or, if the play approaches farce, types. In the more extended plays there was a considerable variety and indeed complexity of metre and the 'artificial' forms such as the *rondeau* fitted in easily. The most sophisticated and interesting is perhaps the *Condamnation de Bancquet*, printed in 1507, not only because of its technical brilliance, but also because it is unusual in its dramatisation of a trial, knowledgeably presented by its author Nicolas de la Chesnaye, who was a doctor of canon and civil law.[31]

The sottie[32]

The *sottie*, usually performed in Paris by the *Enfants sans souci*, closely associated with the *Basoche*, was so called because of the regular presence of the fool or *sot*. Thought to have been originally a curtain-raiser, it becomes a genre in its own right; it tends to be much shorter than the *moralité* and for that reason would have fewer characters. By the time Sebillet was writing, the *sottie* was more or less fused with the farce:

Car le vray suget de la Farce ou Sottie Françoise, sont badinages, nigauderies, et toutes sotties esmouvantes à ris et plaisir.

but this is not true of the earlier period, when the *sottie*, which usually had a basic allegorical element, was more serious in intention. The *sottie* is usually in octosyllables, whereas the farce shows more metrical variety, but even here a dogmatic distinction cannot be drawn. The *sot* and *sotte* are characterised in their speech by a rapid flow of words that may verge on the unintelligible, a formula that allows for daring allusion. The thematic range is wide: sometimes the author confines himself to broad, traditional targets: André de la Vigne's *Sotise à huit personages* (*c.*1507, Toulouse), which is markedly longer than the norm, stages the *Monde* surrounded by various *sots*, representing different pillars of society (e.g., *sot dissolu* = the Church; *sot trompeur* = tradesmen; and *Sot ignorant* and *Sotte folle* who stand for the people). The 'plot' is of the thinnest and imagines *Monde* overrun by the *sots* who find it impossible to live in the chaotic world they have tried to substitute for the real one. Here we have the traditional complaints about the manner in which the Church, the nobility, and the law have failed in their duty towards the people; but in Pierre Gringore's *Sottie contre le Pape Jules II* (Paris, 1512),[33] the customary attack on the Church is sharpened for political reasons, but is also presented in ambiguous fashion to safeguard the author. *Mère Sotte* appears in a series of garbs: first she is seen as the Church ('le temporel vueil acquerir') deserted by *Bonne Foy*, then when she tries to make the nobles follow her policy, she discloses her military dress; once her identity is revealed, reference is made to the genuine Church and the *Mère sotte*, as a scapegoat, is placed on the shelf. The text is liberally spiced with flattery of Louis XII, and one sees how the theatre, no less than the other work of the *rhétoriqueurs*, is pressed into political service. Brantôme, speaking of the *clercs de la Basoche*, tells us that Louis XII

... leur permettoit qu'ils parlassent de luy et de sa cour, mais non pourtant desreglement, mais sur-tout qu'ils ne parlassent de la reyne sa femme en façon quelconque; autrement qu'ils les feroit tous pendre.

Generally speaking, the authorities were very sensitive to the impact made by the theatre and the edicts frequently show the degree of censorship that could be imposed. Gringore's *Sotye nouvelle des Croniqueurs* (Paris, 1515), which is lacking in plot and characterisation, includes traditional criticism of the Estates, sketches a portrait of the good Prince, and ends with support for the military expedition setting off for Italy. The speech, everyday in vocabulary, though not devoid of rhetorical rhythms, is vigorous, but also peppered with *sententiæ*; it appears to contain a number of veiled, yet pointed, allusions to contemporaries. Later *sotties* will tend to support the Establishment at religious level, though criticism of behaviour will continue. Rather akin to the *sottie* is the *satire* (Latin *satura*), as for instance Roger de Collerye's *Satire pour les habitants d'Auxerre* (1530) which combines in rather chaotic form bits of social criticism with comments on the return of peace and discreet flattery intended for high quarters.

The farce[34]

The *farce*, whose source-material goes back to the *fabliau* and the *nouvelle*, and sometimes the *causes grasses* of the *Basoche*, tends to be shorter than the *sottie*, to have a greater metrical variety, to rely on social types, and to approach good-natured caricature rather than acrimonious satire; it may possess a more satisfactory dramatic structure with fewer characters, who for their part are more 'real' than allegorical. Nevertheless, it is not always easy to fit these plays into tidy categories: for instance, there was performed *c.* 1523 in Rouen a *Farce morale de troys Pelerins et Malice*, which in addition to traditional criticism attacks the Lutherans and, more pointedly, disapproves the involvement of women in government; the *Farce de Maistre Jehan Jenin, vray Prophete à deux personnages* (*Recueil Trepperel* 32), some 350 lines long, makes fun of medieval methods of teaching and in tone reminds one slightly of Rabelais's first book. The uncommitted farce, with its limited cast, often has a symmetrical plot (a – b – a), is usually in octosyllabic verse, sprinkled sometimes with *rondeau* and *ballade* forms; domestic problems are exploited and the formula tricker-tricked is common. Slapstick and unconcern for niceties abound and the level of some farce is low, but there is a racy vitality of language that can still be appreciated.

Other genres

Though the genres just mentioned cover most of the dramatic material still extant, there are two other forms worth noting. The first is the *sermon joyeux* which can be seen as an intermediate form between drama and the sermon – and Franciscan sermons were often very pithy, as one discovers in reading Menot and Maillard; the parodic sermon seems to have been performed before the *mystère*, but was also found in other contexts; a text like the *Sermon de l'Endouille* shows how risqué the parodic sermon could be. The *monologue*,[35] in octosyllables and *rimes plates* and, according to the contemporary theoretician Drusac, about 200 lines long (though many overrun this norm), could be so composed as to give the impression that several characters were involved. It could have satirical elements, but more often than not, came close to being a *conte dramatisé*. Themes such as love, drink could serve as a basis, but the monologue was often delivered by what one might loosely call a professional person, though the intention was essentially comic, either directly or at the expense, in part, of the *persona*. Some popular varieties concerned the *valet* or the *chambrière à louer*. The tone of self-publicity was much in evidence and could be linked with salacious allusions, as in the *Ramoneur* where the sexual theme is thinly disguised. One character that was popular was the soldier; so popular indeed that this type of monologue may go back to the fifteenth century, but throve throughout the Renaissance and might well be reprinted more than once. Such is the *Franc-Archier de Bagnolet*, reprinted in 1532.[36] The *franc-archier*, who had reappeared in the military set-up, was disliked for his conduct and cowardice, and so made a splendid target. The matamoresque trait, with comic mock-epic developments on occasion, formed the core, but play can be made of the shift of level from unawareness to insight. The charlatan feature, suitably deflated after the build-up, was a source of comedy, but the *franc-archier*'s sexual prowess is another mainspring of humour. A distant imitation of this monologue occurs in the *Franc-Archier de Cherré* (1544 and 1580). The genre appealed by a combination of features: comic narrative (where the tale might be more important than the character), character-study, social reference, and linguistic vitality, and one can see in it a source for Marot's epistles. Theatrically, it usually served as a curtain-raiser, and it seems that sometimes the monologue was helped by a secondary character who, by brief intervention, acted as a foil for the soliloquist.[37] Some of the techniques have no doubt found their way also into Rabelais.

These, then, are the genres that flourish in the theatre of the time. The college theatre, more sophisticated in form and speech, exists too, but it does not yet rise to any significant literary level. What strikes one about all this dramatic material is its great acceptability throughout the period and, as corollary, its pronounced conservatism. The public does not appear to have sought much in the way of innovation and prefers variations on well-tried themes; in any case, many texts seem to go back quite a long way in their essentials. The literary value of these plays is often modest; and, though one may detect here and there traces of the nascent humanism, the religious and social premises on which the plays were built tended to keep them remote from both literary distinction and from the new currents of the Renaissance. Drama is the area of literary activity which takes longest to enter a new phase of development. It does more than just linger on in the provinces, and some genres may retain their usefulness in the new climate: one Joachim de Coignac publishes *La desconfiture de Goliath* at Geneva in 1551, and ten years later Conrad Badius prints his *Comédie du Pape malade*,[38] which draws on traditional forms of comedy for its effects. The Calvinists, with their desire to keep literature in touch with the wider public, maintain for a time dramatic forms that originally commanded a wide audience in France.

Marguerite de Navarre[39] *(1492–1549)*

One author who exploits traditional structures, and relatively late in our period, is Marguerite de Navarre. Her plays, published only in part during her lifetime, are usually divided into sacred (essentially the tetralogy, including the *Comedie de la Nativité de Jésus-Christ*) and profane, but whatever the genres and categories we use, all her drama is bound up with her evangelical faith, bordering upon the mystical. The titles (*Comedies, Eclogue, Farce*) serve imperfectly to indicate some structural differences: the 'biblical' comedies are closely linked with the *mystère*, though they are much shorter, whereas the profane plays, akin to the *moralité*, differ essentially in the type of character taking part. In the *Comedie du Trespas du Roy* the shepherds are allegorical figures with a thin veneer of Renaissance pastoral; thematically the *leitmotiv* is divine love. In the Eclogue on the death of Francis I, there is no real dramatic progression, but rather a lyrical effusion expressing the belief that the king, now dead on earth, lives on in eternity. Some of the other plays are constructed on a system of progressive 'initiation': for instance, the farce *Le Mallade* contains four characters; the sick man is looking for a cure, his wife suggests recourse to popular medicines and old wives' remedies, but is sent to fetch the doctor. In the meanwhile, the *Chambriere* advises faith rather than professional prescription, so that the doctor is somewhat sceptical when he arrives to find the patient cured. The symbolism of the character is clear in religious terms: the sick man is average humanity in need of succour; his wife represents a somewhat limited, worldly cure; the doctor stands for the professional; and the *Chambriere* (note her humble estate) provides the real spiritual cure, which is Faith. A similar structure supports the *Comedie de Mont de Marsan*, though a substantial role is given to the *chanson*, whose religious text is accompanied, according to custom, by profane tunes. Here four different attitudes are expressed, but with less dramatic characterisation than in the farce: the *Mondaine* symbolises the worldly and the sensual, the *Superstitieuse* stands for the *bien-pensant*, the pharisaic practitioner of religion whose attitude to the world is, contrariwise, too puritan. Then comes *La Sage* who stresses the role of man on earth, endowed with reason; she also expresses various evangelical ideas, but does not represent the last stage of man's evolution, partly perhaps because she stresses 'science', which so often in Marguerite's writings is viewed with suspicion. The final state of mind is embodied by the *Bergère* (Ravie) who, like a sort of *anima*, sings with perfect trust and love and in great *simplesse*. These allegorical figures inevitably invite discussion about their exact meaning – this is particularly true of the puzzling *Trop prou peu moins* – but their religious character is not in doubt. Sometimes Marguerite is thinking in more general terms, at others she writes a play with obvious contemporary reference, so that a satiric note may be introduced, as in *L'Inquisiteur*, where the persecutor of the faithful is himself converted by the children. For some critics, the 'earlier' plays are connected with the political attempts to ensure religious unity during the 1530s, but dating difficulties and the lack of obvious internal reference militate against such an interpretation. The tone of the plays may vary widely from the lighter *bluette* to something very intense. Rarely, however, does the situation become really dramatic; we often have the equivalent of a *débat*, but the dialogue, a statement of attitude, is static, though in *Le Mallade*, *L'Inquisiteur*, and the *Comedie à dix personnages* some interaction of character does occur. In all probability the profane plays were composed after the biblical, and they were usually intended for performance at her Court. There is little search for literary or humanist decoration; given Marguerite's distrust of 'science' and of literary embellishment, one can understand that she found the medieval idiom to her taste; and if we do hear echoes, they are likely to come from the Bible, sometimes from songs or psalm paraphrases by Marot. She varies her metre frequently (though the norm remains the octosyllable) and she does not go beyond *rhétoriqueur* conventions. Structurally, there is no evident development, but perhaps the plays become more lyrical in their expression of her mysticism.

CONCLUSION TO PART I

The period we have surveyed is a curious one. It is undoubtedly characterised by the early workings of intellectual ferment – a rethinking of philosophical principles, a reappraisal of the traditional hierarchy of intellectual activity (e.g., the relations between philosophy and 'eloquence'), a serious concern with religious reform, both inward and institutional, a similar concern with pedagogic betterment, the awareness of a new dimension introduced by the printed book and of philological method – all this is present and reinforced by sensitivity to what is happening beyond the frontiers of France. Nevertheless, this new *conscience* takes time to invade existing structures. The full impact of Guillaume Budé and Lefèvre d'Etaples has yet to come, though Budé has already completed his major works, and one might well ask what was the immediate effect of that impressive and yet solitary figure Charles de Bouelles (*Bovillus*). The full consequences of philological research are not yet evident, though a close interest was taken in the Reuchlin affair which involved the study of Hebrew. Moreover, certain aspects of the Italian Renaissance were making little headway as yet; French humanists, at this time, often have close links with the Low Countries and their sympathies and attitudes are compatible with the Northern Renaissance, from which Erasmus had still to sever certain bonds. Gaguin and his friends seem to be the sorcerer's apprentices of a later generation.

A further feature of the period is the moderate extent to which this early humanism seeps into vernacular literature, where the structures are still late-medieval and not likely to renew themselves except in detail. Where national interest is involved, there is some parallelism between Neo-latin and vernacular writing (epic, narrative chronicle, military encomium); but the religious, dramatic, and non-lyrical qualities of poetry are very tenacious. We do find, especially in Jean Lemaire and Robert Gaguin, an awareness of things stirring, but they rarely assimilate from Italy anything that does not fit into the late-medieval framework of their minds. As an example, Gaguin knows of Ficino, but to what extent does that knowledge become consubstantial with his inner life, if at all? Of course, various elements we have mentioned will come into critical focus shortly, under the stimulus of a rapidly developing situation in the political and religious fields. In this context, Erasmus will have a cardinal role to play; but so far, little of this filters into the vernacular literature, and it is indeed surprising that the old-time structures should have remained so long impervious to these new pressures. The conditions in which literature maintains its activity are somewhat conservative: the influence of the Court, where Burgundian structures have been taken over in part, does little to change the face of the chronicle or of the minor *rhétoriqueur* genres. In the field of drama, the audiences, for which production so often means revamping of earlier models, are hardly likely to accept fundamental changes, even if the *sottie* can on occasion be used in the interest of political or religious propaganda. In consequence much of the literature produced at this time has an anonymous character; anyone trained along certain lines and active in a certain social and political context could serve up something more or less adequate. Only two authors seem to stand out with sufficient originality to transcend the conventions of their times, and for rather different reasons: Jean Lemaire undoubtedly has imaginative urges that raise him from the rank and file of the *rhétoriqueurs* and Commynes's more personal standpoint allows him to breathe a certain life into the jejune form of the chronicle. And both had achieved a mastery of language that showed them to be ahead of their times.

APPENDIX TO PART I

The lack of distinctive personality we have detected in so many *rhétoriqueurs* allowed us to treat them in a more general survey, with the signal exception of Jean Lemaire. Undoubtedly, these *rhétoriqueurs* have their own traits – a greater or lesser moral preoccupation, a more developed religious concern, special interest in formal or metrical matters, and so forth: it is therefore proper to include a list of the more prominent poets, with mention of some of their writings. There are also various manuscript sources which coincide only in part with published work: e.g., BN ms. fçs 2205–6, 2228, 2266, 14982 or nouv. acq. fçse 1158 (which contains compositions by Octovien de Saint-Gellais). Below we give some contemporary editions and also, where they exist, modern critical editions. In a number of cases, the dating of early editions is a tricky affair and problems of attribution may also arise.

Anthologies: *La Chasse et le départ d'amours*, A. Vérard, 1509 (BM); another ed. undated (BN). *Le Jardin de plaisance et fleur de rhétorique*, A. Vérard, ?1503. (The BM has this and three other printings, the dates of which are approximate.) Modern edition by A. Piaget and E. Droz, SATF, 2 vols., 1910, 1925.

Alexis, Guillaume: *Le Blason des faulses Amours*, 1486 (BN, which has two other undated editions). The BM has the 1493 and 1497 editions. *Œuvres poétiques*, ed. A. Piaget and E. Picot, SATF, 3 vols., 1896–1908.

Auton, Jean d': *Les epistres envoyées au roy treschrestien*, Lyons, 1509 (BM, BN). *Chroniques*, ed. R. de Maulde La Clavière, 4 vols., 1889–95.

Bourgouync, Simon: *Lespinette du jeune prince conquerant le royaulme de bonne renommée*, A. Vérard, 1508 (BM, BN).

Chastellain, G.: *Le Temple [de] Jehan Boccace . . .*, G. Du Pré, 1517 (BM, BN). *Œuvres . . .* ed. Kervyn de Lettenhove, Brussels, 8 vols., 1863–66.

Coquillart, Guillaume: *Les œuvres*, G. Du Pré, 1532 (BM). Mod. ed. C. d'Héricault, 1857.

Crétin, Guillaume: *Chantz royaulx, oraisons et aultres petitz traictez*, Paris, 1527; n.d.; n.d. (all BN). *Œuvres poétiques*, ed. Kathleen Chesney, SATF, 1932.

Gringore, Pierre: *Le C[h]asteau dAmours*, 1500 (BM, BN). *Le Chasteau de labour*, 1500 (BM). *Sensuyvent les fantasies de Mere Sotte*, ?1520 (BM). *Les folles entreprises*, 1507 (BM). *Les menus propos*, 1521 (BM). *Rondeaux en nombre trois cens cinquante*, 1527 (BM). *Œuvres complètes*, ed. C. d'Héricault and A. de Montaiglon, 2 vols., 1858–77.

Ivry, Jean d': *Les Triumphes de France . . . Epistre aux Romains . . . L'Origine de Francoys*, 1508 (BN). *Scrinium medicine*, ?1519 (BM).

La Marche, Olivier de: *Le Chevalier deliberé*, 1500 (BN); 1493 (BM). *Mémoires*, ed. H. Beaune and J. d'Arbaumont, 4 vols., 1883–88. These were edited also by Denys Sauvage (1561 and 1562, BM).

La Vigne, André de: *La Louenge des roys de France*, 1507 (BM, BN). *Le Vergier d'honneur. . . . De l'entreprise et voyage de Naples*, n.p., n.d. (BN), ?1520 (BM).

Le Franc, Martin: *Le champion des dames*, ?Lyons, 1490 (BM); 1530 (BM, BN). *L'estrif de fortune et de vertu*, 1519 (BM, BN). Modern ed. of *Le Champion des Dames*, ed. A. Piaget, Vol. I, Lausanne, 1968. See O. Roth, *Estrif de Fortune et Vertu von Martin Le Franc*, Berne, 1970.

Meschinot, Jean: *Les lunettes des princes auec aulcunes balades et additions*, Paris, 1505, 1522; Rouen, 1530; Lyons ?1530 (all BM).

Molinet, Jean: *Les faictz et dicts*, Paris, 1531, 1537, 1540 (all BM). Modern ed. Noël Dupire, SATF, 3 vols., 1936–39.

Robertet, Jean: In MS. until recently published *Œuvres*, ed. Margaret Zsuppàn, *TLF*, 1970.

Saint-Gellais, Octovien: *Le sejour d'honneur*, Paris, 1519 (BM, BN); ?1520 (BM). An ed. in progress for Oxford B. Litt. *Le Vergier d'honneur*, Paris, ?1520 and ?1525 (BM) (with Blaise d'Auriol, *La chasse et depart damours*).

NOTES

1. General surveys include: Franco Simone, *Il Rinascimento francese*, Turin, 1961, reprinted 1965 (abbreviated translation Gaston Hall, London, 1969); A. Renaudet, *Préréforme et humanisme à Paris pendant les premières guerres d'Italie*, 1916, 2nd revised ed. 1953; A. A. Tilley, *The Dawn of the French Renaissance*, Cambridge, 1918. On medieval philosophy, see E. Gilson, *History of Christian Philosophy in the Middle Ages*, 1955.

2. *Epistolæ et orationes*, ed. L. Thuasne, 1903, 2 vols.; F. Simone, 'Robert Gaguin ed il suo cenacolo umanistico, I', *Aevum*, XIII (1939).

3. L. Febvre and H.-J. Martin, *L'Apparition du livre*, 1958; P. Renouard, *Bibliographie des impressions et des œuvres de Josse Bade Ascensius, imprimeur et humaniste, 1462–1535*, 3 vols., 1909.

4. Elizabeth Armstrong, *Robert Estienne, Royal Printer*, Cambridge, 1954.

5. D. Murarasu, *La poésie néo-latine et la Renaissance des lettres antiques en France (1500–1549)*, 1928; A. Hulubei, *L'Eglogue en France au XVIᵉ siècle*, 1938.

6. H. Guy, *Histoire de la poésie française au XVIᵉ siècle*, vol. I, *L'Ecole des Rhétoriqueurs*, 1910.

7. For the predecessors of the generation with which we are concerned, see Nigel Wilkins, *One Hundred Ballades, Rondeaux and Virelais from the late Middle Ages*, 1969, which provides musical settings of the period, analyses the structures, and gives a good indication of the quality that could be achieved in this type of poetry.

8. The rules for the *puys* at Rouen are preserved in Oxford (Bodleian, Ms Douce 379), and are reproduced in *Fleurs de rhétorique*. ed. Kathleen Chesney, Oxford, 1950, p. 37. The contemporary anthology *Le Jardin de Plaisance et Fleur de Rhétorique*, Paris, 1501 (BM) is available in facsimile in two vols., SATF, 1910, 1925. G. Leba *Les Palinods et les poètes dieppois*, Dieppe, 1904; J.-A. Guiot, *Les Trois Siècles palinodiques*, 2 vols., Dieppe-Paris, 1898; J. C. Dawson, *Toulouse in the Renaissance*, New York, 1912.

9. e.g., BN ms. fçs 19182, BN nouv. acq. 477, and Lille 402, reproduced in *Poèmes de transition (XV–XVIᵉ siècle)* . . . ed. Marcel Françon, Cambridge, Mass., and Paris, 1939.

10. Crétin's *Œuvres poétiques* have been edited by Kathleen Chesney, SATF, 1932.

11. J. Molinet, *Les Faictz et Dictz*, ed. N. Dupire, 3 vols., SATF, 1936–39. Molinet, who lived from 1435 to 1507, was associated with the Burgundian Court; he may have composed music on occasion. His works are still very popular in the 1530s.

12. Modern ed. J. Rychner, *TLF*, 1963.

13. The BM has two early eds., ?1490 and ?1520.

14. *Palinods, Chants royaux, Ballades, Rondeaulx, et Epigrammes à l'honneur de l'immaculée Conception de la toute belle mère de dieu Marie (Patrone des Normans)* . . . , Paris, n.d. (BN). These poems were composed for the *puys* at Rouen.

15. Quoted K. Chesney, *Fleurs de rhétorique*, p. 40, from a ms. source; the printed versions (in the *Vergier d'honneur*, BN, O) vary considerably, and show the earnest attention paid by the *rhétoriqueur* to this style of writing.

16. Published in 1493. The Latin original was also popular in France: the

BM has five editions up till *c.* 1500 of this work whose author became Pope Pius II.

17. Works: *Le Temple d'honneur et de vertus*, 1504 (BN), ed. H. Hornik, *TLF*, 1957; *La Plainte du Désiré* and other works, Lyons, 1509 (BM), ed. of *Plainte* by D. Yabsley, 1932; *Illustrations de Gaule*, ?1510–13 (BM, BN); *La Concorde des deux langages*, 1513 (BN), ed. J. Frappier, *TLF*, 1947; *Epistres de l'Amant vert*, Lyons, 1510, in vol. I of *Illustrations*, ed. J. Frappier, *TLF*, 1948; *La difference des scismes* ..., Lyons, 1514 (BM, BN); J. Stecher edited the *Œuvres complètes*, Louvain, 4 vols., 1882–91, but a new ed. is required. On Lemaire see Ph.-A. Becker, *Jean Lemaire, der erste humanistische Dichter Frankreichs*, Strasbourg, 1893; P. Spaak, *Jean Lemaire de Belges, sa vie, son œuvre et ses meilleures pages*, 1927; P. Jodogne, 'L'orientation culturelle de Jean Lemaire de Belges', *CAIEF*, May 1971; and the same author's exhaustive study **Jean Lemaire de Belges, écrivain franco-bourguignon*, Brussels, 1972.

18. The taste persists; see, for instance, F. de Belleforest, *Harangues militaires*, 1573(O).

19. *Chroniques*, ed. R. de Maulde La Clavière, 4 vols., 1889–95.

20. F. Simone, 'Une entreprise oubliée des humanistes français', *Humanism in France*, ed. A. H. T. Levi, Manchester, 1970, pp. 106–31; R. E. Asher, 'Myth, legend and history in Renaissance France', *SF*, 39 (1969), 409–19; M. R. Jung, *Hercule dans la littérature française du XVI*ᵉ *siècle*, *THR*, 1966.

21. The first part of the *Mémoires* (originally called *Chroniques*) came out in 1524 (BM), the second in 1528/29 (BM). Modern ed. J. Calmette and G. Durville, 3 vols., 1924–25. See G. Charlier, *Philippe de Commynes*, Brussels, 1945, and J. Dufournet, *La Destruction des mythes dans les Mémoires de Philippe de Commynes*, Geneva, 1966. See also *Historiens et Chroniqueurs du Moyen Age*, ed. A. Pauphilet (Pléiade).

22. J. Rasmussen, *La Prose narrative française du XV*ᵉ *siècle*, Copenhagen, 1958.

23. Copies of the original edition in BM and BN; edition in *SHF*, no. 180, 1878. A strong case has been made out for attributing authorship to Jaques de Maille.

24. Three editions appear in the sixteenth century: 1518, 1541, and 1557 (all three in the BN; the BM holds the first two). See the recent ed. by Jacques Poujol, 1961.

25. R. Lebègue, *La Tragédie religieuse en France. Les Débuts (1514–1573)*, 1929.

26. Cf. the testimony of Jean Bouchet, *Les Annales d'Acquitaine*, Poitiers, 1545, fol. MM v, under year 1533: 'On joua aussi la passion & resurrection, troys sepmaines après ou environ, en la ville de Saulmeur, où je vis d'excellentes fainctes'. At Poitiers, a passion play 'en ung theatre faict en rond' lasted eleven days.

27. H. M. Brown, *Music in the French Secular Theatre 1400–1550*, Cambridge, Mass., 1963.

28. The *Confrérie* in Paris did sometimes engage the *Enfants sans souci* to undertake the comic interludes in the *mystères*. The *Confrérie* was the first troupe to stage plays indoors regularly, initially at the Hôtel de la Trinité, later at the Hôtel de Bourgogne.

29. *Théâtre mystique de Pierre Du Val* ..., ed. E. Picot, 1882.

30. Apart from information in R. Lebègue, op. cit., and Grace Frank, *The Medieval French Drama*, Oxford, 1954; see also H. G. Harvey, *The Theatre of the Basoche*, Cambridge, Mass., 1941; Emile Picot, 'Les moralités polémiques ou la controverse religieuse dans l'ancien théâtre français', *BSHP*, 1887, 1892, 1906.

31. The text is available in E. Fournier, *Le Théâtre français avant la Renaissance (1430–1550)*, 1872; this anthology with E.-L.-N. Viollet-le-Duc, *Ancien théâtre françois*, 10 vols., 1854–57, though outdated in scholarly respects, remains useful.

32. E. Picot, *Recueil général des sotties*, 3 vols., SATF, 1902–12.

33. C. Oulmont, *Pierre Gringore*, 1907.

34. Three important collections of farces exist: one in the BM; the second

in the Royal Library, Copenhagen (printed in *Nouveau recueil de farces françaises des XV⁰ et XVI⁰ siècles*, ed. E. Picot and C. Nyrop, 1880); and the *Recueil Trepperel*, ed. E. Droz, vol. I, 1933, and with the help of H. Lewicka, vol. II, Geneva, 1964. On the distinction between *sottie* and farce, see L. C. Porter, 'La farce et la sotie', *ZRP*, 1959, and Barbara C. Bowen, *Les Caractéristiques essentielles de la farce française et leur survivance dans les années 1550–1620*, Urbana, 1964. The same author has edited *Four French Farces* for the Blackwell series.

35. E. Picot, 'Le Monologue dramatique dans l'ancien théâtre français', *Romania*, 1886–88.

36. *Le Franc-Archier de Bagnolet suivi de deux autres monologues dramatiques*, ed. I. Polak, Geneva, *TLF*, 1966.

37. See also *Le Pionnier de Seurdre*. Monologue dramatique récité à Angers, ed. E. Picot, 1896.

38. Modern ed. by Helen A. Shaw, Philadelphia, 1934. On the comic language of the plays see H. Lewicka, *La Langue et le style du théâtre comique* . . . , Warsaw, 1960.

39. *Théâtre profane*, ed. V.-L. Saulnier, Geneva, *TLF*, 1947, 1963; see also V.-L. Saulnier, 'Etudes critiques sur les comédies profanes de Marguerite de Navarre', *BHR*, 1947. Brantôme informs us that 'Elle composoit souvent des comédies et des moralités qu'on appeloit en ce temps là des pastorales, qu'elle faisoit jouer et représenter par les filles de sa cour'. Some of her plays were published in the *Marguerites de la Marguerite des Princesses*, 1547.

PART II

Chapter 2

FRANCIS I AND THE DEVELOPMENT OF FRENCH CULTURE

I. HISTORICAL OUTLINES

FRANCIS I's reign has been variously assessed, but whatever its deficiencies, to his contemporaries it appeared a period of brilliant cultural enlightenment and progress. It is also a period in which the monarchy accelerates its evolution from its medieval status to something that foreshadows seventeenth-century absolutism; this is a process that goes hand-in-hand with the emergence of a more aggressive nationalism, resentful culturally of Italy and politically opposed to Germany. This trend is reflected in various ways. In the first place, the administrative arms of the monarchy are gradually strengthened: the king does not interest himself in the States General and the *Parlement* of Paris is brought to heel; the regional *parlements* become more and more instruments of central policy, and during the reigns of Francis I and Henry II the structures of the law are reinforced. Second, the theoreticians of monarchy move away gradually from the concept of a ruler limited by the control of law and certain traditional brakes, as had for instance been suggested by Claude de Seyssel in his *Grant Monarchie* (see above, pp. 53–4); and the humanists themselves (Erasmus, Budé, and others) do much to further the concept of the benevolent despot. Professional *jurisperiti* like Antoine du Moulin, as early as the 1530s, advance absolutist ideas, and the vigorous study of Roman law, developed at first especially in Toulouse, tends to work also in this direction. Towards the end of the century, absolutist views will be strongly represented by professors of law at Poitiers. One way and another, there will emerge strong theoretical support for the political ascendancy of the king. Finally, Francis I, like his immediate predecessors, is fully aware of the influence that can be exerted by the Court. On the one hand, the Court becomes a means of display and, with its cultural trappings, is developed partly in imitation of Italian manners. It is during Francis I's reign that Fontainebleau is created,[1] and to that end a host of Italian artists and craftsmen are imported; Italian men of letters are also in

71

evidence at Court, and one of the tutors to the royal children is
Tagliacarne (Theocreno), a minor Neo-latin poet. Castiglione's
Courtier, published in 1528 and translated twice into French ten
years later,[2] had expressed the hope that Francis would become the
ideal monarch:

But if kind fate will have it that Monseigneur d'Angoulême succeed to the
crown, as is hoped, then I think that just as the glory of arms flourishes and
shines in France, so must that of letters flourish there also with the greatest
splendour. (trs. Charles Singleton)

Much will be done, not only to encourage architecture and the
visual arts, but also letters, and we shall note an upsurge in the
patronage offered to writers and scholars; it is in 1530 that the
Royal Readerships are somewhat belatedly founded (on patronage,
see below, p. 74). And on the other hand, the Court will become
more and more a centre for the nobility, which is brought gradually
into the king's orbit. The tensions between king and noblemen,
revealed partly in the increased granting of titles, but also in the
political allegiances of the civil wars, will not be resolved in the
immediate future, but the beginnings of the process are already
visible. Francis I also accelerates the rise of the *noblesse de robe*,
with the creation of offices sold for economic profit. The magistracy,
partly on this account, will tend to become more inbred and group-
conscious in a period of rapid expansion, but this will also work to
the advantage of central authority.

At the same time, Francis has to contend with the continuing
problem of Charles V. For various reasons, the conflict is marked
by fewer overt military confrontations. Charles's own situation was
not reassuring: he had clashes with the Protestants at home, and by
virtue of his political claims in Italy, he also came into strife with
the Pope. There was trouble with the Moors and their attacks on
Spain, and, a cardinal factor, he was gravely disturbed by the
growing Turkish threat. He was powerful, but his lines were widespread and the channels of communication very long. It was therefore not too difficult for Francis to play upon these problems. This
explains why he found it expedient to conclude pacts with the
Turks; and though the religious problem at home had been
exacerbated by Cop's rectorial address (1533), the *Affaire des
Placards* in the following year, and the appearance of Calvin in
Geneva not so long after, where he was to set up a centre of propaganda and effective strategic planning, Francis was nevertheless
motivated by political considerations to negotiate with various
German princes whose sympathies were clearly Lutheran. Finally,
his Italian dream had not completely evaporated: he did much to
reorganise the army – descents into Italy were no longer the initially

easy forays Charles VIII had known – but his outlook, doubtless influenced by the *Connétable* Anne de Montmorency, appears to have been more prudent than in his earlier days. Whatever the truth of the matter, only minor wars break out between Charles V and France. In 1535, the death of Francesco Sforza prompted Francis I to claim Milan for a nephew, and in the spring of the following year, he invaded Italy through Savoy which had refused him passage. There followed various sorties by Charles, one into Provence, another into Picardy; but peace was patched up with the Truce of Nice (1538), which left Francis with gains in Piedmont and Savoy, but no guarantee of lasting peace. Hostilities broke out again in 1542, when Francis attacked on various fronts; but in the course of the next two years, Charles V and Henry VIII league together against France, and Francis agrees to the Peace of Crépy (September 1544). This resulted in France breaking with Turkey, but certain provisions of the treaty were null and void by the death of the duc d'Orléans before he could marry either Charles's daughter or his niece. In practice, things returned more or less to their state at the time of the treaty of Nice. A state of war persisted with England until 1550. The last years of Francis I's reign, therefore, go out with a whimper: the economic condition of the country was still unsatisfactory, and the various attempts at financial reform still fell short of the ideal; matters on the religious front were a cause of anxiety, with persecution achieving no clear results. Francis himself was in poor health, and cultural activities appear to be somewhat reduced, at a time when the new generation had not yet shown itself, though premonitory signs are visible especially in the provinces. Francis I died in 1547 within a short time of Henry VIII of England; and his sister Marguerite de Navarre was to disappear in 1549. Politically and culturally, a new era was at hand. We must now return to the earlier years of Francis's reign and have a closer look at its intellectual ferment.

II. EMERGENCE OF A NEW CULTURAL CLIMATE

The middle 1520s, for various reasons, mark a turning-point in the cultural development of France. We already noted that the heyday of the *rhétoriqueurs* was past; though their traditions will by no means die out overnight, Guillaume Crétin and Lemaire de Belges are dead by 1525, and a year or so later Jean Marot will follow them into the grave, so that the very strong group-consciousness of those poets tends to break up. In any case, humanist pressures and a new style at Court will find the rising Clément Marot more to its taste. Court life will pick up again after the return of Francis I from captivity and that of his children held in Spain as hostages for his good behaviour. Though his patronage of the arts may have been exaggerated, it was nonetheless very considerable; he was very aware of the prestige that could be enjoyed by a prominent Court, he understood the national importance of cultural development, and if his own tastes were superficial, he was not without artistic accomplishments himself. We have seen how he attracted Italian artists to help in the building of Fontainebleau; he patronised many humanists, played an important part in the creation of the Royal Readerships, took an interest in the collection of manuscripts for the Royal Library (with the advice and enterprise of Jan Lascaris), appointed the first royal printer (Robert Estienne I), and had a number of humanists around him in court posts, such as Salmon Macrin, Theocreno, Du Chastel, and others. Nor was he the only patron in high places; his sister, Marguerite de Navarre, extended a helping hand to many men of letters and also protected those whose evangelical leanings had brought them into conflict with the Sorbonne. And among the *grands seigneurs* are several patrons of liberal and generous outlook: particularly notable are the members of the Du Bellay family, Jean bishop of Paris and Guillaume de Langey who befriended Rabelais among others, the cardinal de Lorraine, Bishop Philippe de Cossé, the Bohiers, and the less sympathetic Antoine du Prat – their names recur frequently in the writings of scholars and writers who had good cause to sing their praises. In the provinces, too, patronage was fairly extensive; Jean des Pins had been an early supporter of new humanist currents; Sadoleto had formed an interesting group around him in Carpentras, the cardinal de Tournon, though strictly orthodox, exercised patronage on a useful scale, and there were several rich families in Lyons (the Scèves, the Vauzelles, etc.)who played a prominent role in the cultural life of the town.

However, in the mid-1520s, the main Renaissance impetus is to be found in the colleges of Paris and the centres closely linked with university life. The scholars forming the generation of humanists who grew up in the heyday of Guillaume Budé and Lefèvre d'Etaples, both still active, are forming their own pupils and shaping the character of French humanism for the next few decades: men like Vatable, Danès, Oronce Finé, and Jacques Toussaint are well established, and there seem to be an unusually high number of interesting scholars from abroad studying in Paris at that time; it must indeed have been a most exciting moment to be a student then. To begin with, a wider range of classical culture is becoming accessible to the younger generation: first, Latin poets whom Gaguin's contemporaries shunned, become widely read: Tibullus, Catullus, Propertius, and the lyrical odes of Horace; second, a corresponding widening of the spectrum is to be found in the knowledge of Italian humanists – Marullus, Pontanus, the Strozzi, Angeriano, and others; third, the study of Greek is taking serious root, and this will have serious consequences, for philological studies, for the penetration of various streams of Greek thought, and for religious debate. At the same time, a new wave of printers has entered the scene; though Josse Bade is still alive, humanists are turning to Robert Estienne and Simon de Colines in Paris and to Gryphius in Lyons. Two other features deserve mention: on the one hand, Neo-latin poetry, with its serious pretensions to deflate Italy's cultural supremacy, has entered a stimulating phase quite different from what we saw during the reign of Louis XII and strongly promoted by the poems of Salmon Macrin, who becomes the leader of a vigorous current of poetic activity when the vernacular is still groping towards new poetic forms and inspiration. And on the other, we are in a period of intense pedagogic reappraisal and expansion. It comes as no surprise, of course, that many of the pioneers in educational reform are scholars interested in Greek as well as in Latin and men strongly affected by the new religious ideas; for here too, with the advent of Luther, and also the mature impact of Erasmus and Lefèvre d'Etaples, the religious problem is reaching a climax. Nor is it a coincidence that, in this period of intellectual and spiritual ferment, Ignatius Loyola and Jean Calvin should be studying at the same time in the Collège de Montaigu, though Loyola soon moved to Sainte-Barbe, whose intellectual climate was rather more open-minded. We must examine various facets of this vital activity and also the work of one or two men whose role is crucial; but before-hand, a word might be opportune here on the penetration of various ideas and themes that are traditionally associated with the French Renaissance.

III. RENAISSANCE THEMES[3]

The Renaissance is often described in terms of certain key themes – the dignity of man, the *vita activa*, and so forth, but a few pre-liminary words of caution should be sounded. It is true that a great number of important concerns were voiced early in Italy; but one must not consider the French Renaissance as being the product of various humanist imports from Italy, however impressive the Italian presence may be. Moreover, many themes that do have Italian ancestry do not come into France, as it were, overnight and *en bloc*. France's move into the Renaissance complex is not to be dissociated from the simultaneous religious ferment that is a main preoccupation for most of the century.[4] Certain themes acquire a particular relevance as circumstances permit, authors too develop importance that may vary from decade to decade, so that their impact occurs in successive stages; nor should the appearance of some 'theme' be separated from the intellectual atmosphere in which it is found. Examples of these points come easily to mind: a text by Philip Beroaldo, first printed in Paris in 1493, turns up in translation some fifty years later; Plutarch is by no means unknown in the early part of the sixteenth century, but he only acquires a significant popularity after Amyot has completed his translation towards the time of the civil wars; can one say that the theme of *dignitas hominis*, present in the curious *Exhortation* of Jean Parmentier (1531), has the same resonance as it has in the writings of Charles de Bouelles, active twenty years before and in many ways more 'modern' than Parmentier? It is also right to say that, very often in France, as indeed elsewhere, various Renaissance themes are discussed in a context of polarisation: so that, if we find a treatment of the dignity of man in one author, we may well find its counterpart, the *miseria hominis*, elsewhere, or in another text of the same author. The evolution of a more 'modern' conception of man is a slow affair, with hesitations and reticences, and such is the mental structure of man that he may well appear 'advanced' in one field and highly reactionary in another. On almost every topic of contemporary interest, we find the presence of an anguished discussion of the *pro* and *con*, a discussion which may be exacerbated, indeed envenomed, by the religious situation. It is therefore not surprising to find literary forms of discussion and ambivalency common in the sixteenth century: the medieval *débat* may live on or be replaced by the *dialogue*, and especially after 1550, the drama, in which the *personæ* present different aspects of a matter of principle; the mania for encyclopædias of knowledge, heavily dosed with varying interpretations of phenomena, the search for syncretism in religious matters, the predilection for anthologies and *compendia*, all this points to an intense awareness of the need to inquire into fundamentals, but not always an ability to take a decision, let alone a series of decisions in a clear direction, though certain issues will be clarified by the religious question. On the other hand, it is possible to identify a number of areas in which discussion shows that new attitudes are in the process of being formed.

Like Romanticism, the Renaissance marks a stage in the development of Western civilisation when man feels compelled to search for new values and to find new structures, intellectual, political, social, and religious, to replace those which, consciously or not, he feels are ceasing to be meaningful. He may consider them outworn or in need of basic revision, but as they stand they resemble bark rather than sap. When political and economic structures are undergoing change, man finds himself asking questions about his identity, his role in the world, and his relationships with others. He will be stimulated in this by new political alignments, fresh religious yearning, and in the Renaissance context, the classical world will play an essential role; but coming to terms with a situation that is so rapidly evolving will take time. Various pressures may be particularly significant: the role of Neoplatonism, the rediscovery of the Church Fathers, the emergence of a more empiric attitude to science, all these are important; and yet others, such as the discovery of the New World or the publication of Copernican theory, will simply not impinge on many humanist minds.

What the Renaissance is working towards is a total reassessment of the human condition, of man's place in the scheme of things; and it is round certain key themes that discussion will take place. First, man as the microcosm, who stands between God and the subhuman part of the Universe: the concept is well established, but it is given a new scrutiny, perhaps along the axis dignity/misery of man; and at one end of the spectrum stands Jean Calvin, with Pico della Mirandola and probably Charles de Bouelles at the other. A more middle-of-the-road attitude will be taken, for instance, by the Jesuits or those who believe in some form of synergism between God and Man. But this fundamental problem is closely linked to others: first, the problem of free-will, which forms part of the Rabelaisian fabric. Second, does man, whose nature partakes of the human and the divine, direct his life with a view on the afterlife or on existence *hic et nunc*: *vita activa* or *vita contemplativa*? To identify the Renaissance way of life with the former and the medieval outlook with the latter is surely too simplified, especially when many monastic orders are successfully reforming their rule and new ones will be founded under the stimulus of the Counter-reformation. Nevertheless, a more favourable view seems to emerge of man as a social animal with a duty towards his neighbour and his country. Life is not merely the preparation for death – though the theme persists from medieval texts down to Montaigne. Celibacy is no longer praised to the exclusion of marriage; and the Calvinists, for all their fundamental attitude towards man's state of disgrace, advocate economic virtues, banking, family life. The ambivalent attitude of humanists to the Court (parade or merely *paraître*) is significant in this context. And since behaviour becomes a matter of rethinking, we shall come across numerous revaluations of the ethical consequences of man's psychology: the relations between the will, the reason, and the passions are tirelessly debated, as are the dangers but also the merits of the passions in the economy of human existence; are we to dominate our passions or 'jouyr loiallement de nostre estre', and does Ronsard's poetry not express sometimes a

tension between the suffering caused by passions and the knowledge
that without feeling we simply do not exist?

Whatever the variety of different attitudes expressed, there is an
undoubted drift in the direction of laicisation, of a greater concern
with what man should do with his life on this earth; and it is no
accident that much humanist thinking is devoted to the problem of
education. This involves a rethinking of the traditional hierarchy of
disciplines and arts – the relations between philosophy and language,
the role of eloquence, the nature of language. In the Renaissance
theology probably loses some of her status as the queen of disciplines, and what we broadly call social sciences begin to loom larger
in the humanist mind: political theory, legal studies, historiography,
and the study of natural sciences and mathematics undergo a process
of rejuvenation. All these are disciplines which can help man to
further his destiny upon earth; and of course, the Renaissance
humanist will spend a lot of time also on the ways and means by
which knowledge can be imparted under new conditions. Once
again, Paris will give an impressive lead to the Western world by its
originality in pedagogic experiment and reform.

These new and many pressures encourage men to review their
conception of wisdom: discussions may centre round the contrast
between divine and human wisdom, between knowledge and ignorance, between the wisdom of the solitary and that of the socially
committed, and it is interesting to note the appearance of books that
deal with these problems: in France, we find Bouelles's *De Sapientia*
at the beginning of the century and Charron's *De la Sagesse* at the
end; but the themes of judgement and experience, so fruitfully
matured in Montaigne's essays, are also prominent. Most of the texts
with which we are concerned reveal this gradual shift towards a
concept of wisdom that develops through contact with everyday
experience; nevertheless, the Renaissance world is not totally devoid
of solitaries; on the other hand, many contemporaries for whom the
vita activa was a valid way of life would probably agree that real
wisdom could only be found within God. In France, the humanist
debate is conducted in the context of the equally important religious
conflict, and in a way that did not affect the evolution of Italian
humanism; to distinguish the French Renaissance from the Reformation (and the Counter-reformation) is to ignore certain aspects
of the polarisation of Renaissance thinking on matters of vital
concern.

IV. THE STUDY OF GREEK[5]

The study of Greek goes back some way. In the second half of the
fifteenth century, we have records of itinerant teachers active in

Paris, and one or two *rhétoriqueurs* may have had a smattering of Greek, as for instance Guillaume de Bissipat. Lefèvre d'Etaples learned some rudiments from Georgius Hieronymus, and Jan Lascaris, who later acquired numerous manuscripts for the Royal Library, also did some teaching. Stimulus for Greek studies came understandably from Italy and more especially from the circle of Aldus Manutius, the famous Venetian printer. Further encouragement was given by Jérome Aléandre: he taught for two spells in Paris and for a time at Orléans, which during the early decades of the sixteenth century is an important humanist centre (1508–12). It is, however, in the Paris of the 1510s that the first great French scholars, after Lefèvre, acquire their command of Greek, in circumstances that are not as clear as we would wish: Guillaume Budé; Jacques Toussaint (*Tusanus*), who trained Nicolas Bourbon to translate from the *Greek Anthology* into Latin verse and also taught Jean Dorat; Vatable who, as a scholar of Hebrew, is referred to as the French Reuchlin; Pierre Danès. From 1528 on, thanks to the initiative of Simon de Colines, the printing of Greek texts will be facilitated, and Robert Estienne will later publish the first pocket edition of the New Testament. Though certain aspects of Greek culture will be vitally important for the development of French humanism and letters, it must be remembered that knowledge of the Greek world was hampered in part by the resistance of the Sorbonne, in whose eyes Greek and Hebrew were suspect because of the threat posed by philological research to the theological tradition and which therefore delayed the foundation of the royal readerships. One should also be careful not to overestimate the number of French humanists throughout the century who were really at home in the Greek language: it is noteworthy how many Greek texts are translated, not only into French, but also into Latin, so that a firsthand knowledge of Greek texts may have been less extensive than one might assume. Nevertheless, this does not imply that Greek studies fail to play an essential part in literary developments and of course in religious matters, where linguistic skills and patristic knowledge become very important.

V. PRINTING[6]

It is during the reign of Francis I that French printing comes into its own. The various scholar-printers connected with the Estienne family (including Simon de Colines and Michel Vascosan) help to determine the character of the book trade. There is, first of all, a growing desire to improve the book as such: black-letter tends to regress, and is replaced by roman and italic which, developed by the

Aldine press, is imported by Simon de Colines. Further interest in
type is shown by Geoffroy Tory (*Champfleury*, 1529).[7] The attempt,
rather later, to introduce *lettres de civilité*, was confined to Lyons
and does not seem to have progressed very far. With the desire to
spread culture more rapidly comes the attempt to reduce the size
of the book, and Robert Estienne in particular plays a leading part
in developing the pocket-sized volume. During Francis I's reign we
note a very marked increase in output and the settling in France of
distinguished printers such as Wechel and Gryphius who set up
business in Paris and Lyons respectively. Robert Estienne offers an
excellent example of printing activity: in his work we see the
transition from the early Renaissance to the Reformation. He continues in Josse Bade's footsteps by providing manuals and textbooks
– his own *Thesaurus* will, for instance, supersede the original
Calepinus; he will publish a wider range of classical texts, develop
the printing of Greek (note his Eusebius of 1544–46), and break
some ground in Hebrew, though his son Henri II will go much
further in these directions. He will also make his mark by rendering
sacred texts available to as wide a public as possible: in 1523 he
brings out his New Testament; in 1534 he publishes a pocket
edition; and in 1540 he prints a new edition of the Bible, so that it
is hardly surprising he falls foul of the Sorbonne. His relative Simon
de Colines[8] follows similar technical paths, abandoning Gothic,
developing italic, and producing pocket editions; more than Robert
Estienne, he helped to bring down the price of books and also concerned himself with problems of illustration. He was sympathetic to
the new religious ideas, as was Michel Vascosan, whose full development, however, comes later. Of the other printers, perhaps Dolet is
the most interesting, setting up in Lyons and producing some fine
work before his untimely death in 1546; but there were many men
of distinction engaged in the printing trade who contributed towards
the rapid development of the book. These men play an important
part in the diffusion of humanist culture, pedagogic reform, and
new religious currents, but by pressures of an economic order they
introduce technical advances and, in the fullness of time, contribute
to the standardisation of spelling. Some of them were scholars of
high calibre, such as Dolet, Turnèbe, and certain members of the
Estienne family.

VI. EDUCATIONAL REFORM[9]

The current of reform that was already strong under Charles VIII
and Louis XII continues to swell, and the 1520s, in particular, show
a remarkable concern with educational method. This is brought

about, not only by the recognised need to improve techniques, but by the conviction that the aims of education were shifting in a world that was itself changing rapidly. Whereas, in earlier times, the arts course would be seen essentially as a preparation for those going on to theological study, this is no longer the case. The altered relationships between philosophy, philology, and eloquence were bound to be reflected in pedagogic attitudes, and the enlarged awareness of the classical world must also have repercussions in the classroom. Moreover, the emerging religious attitudes will play their part, and there is no need to stress the importance which the Calvinists and the Jesuits were soon to attach to education. In Paris, certain colleges appear to have been more active in educational reform than others – the outstanding example is probably Sainte-Barbe – but the ferment was widespread. The concern with improved methods for teaching Latin is prominent, much care is taken with Latin verse composition, for many the place of Greek studies is a matter for serious discussion; and there is naturally a reflection of these preoccupations in the printing of new manuals, the importing of successful ones from abroad, the attempts to modernise older textbooks. The excitement spreads soon to the provinces, where towns are anxious to have their educational structures reformed, but troubles will arise, of a religious nature, in certain areas, since so often educational reform and religious renewal are closely linked. Calvinist education owes much to men who had studied or taught in Paris – Calvin, Sturm of Strasbourg, Mathurin Cordier, whose book on spoken Latin became a classic; the group associated with Sainte-Barbe and which included men such as the Gouveas, Nicolas de Grouchy, Visagier, Guérente, George Buchanan, is involved in the reform of the Collège de Guyenne at Bordeaux; and some of the *Barbistes* go on later to implement changes at Coimbra.[10] When Buchanan, returned home, is asked for his opinion on certain educational reforms, he expresses views that bear a close kinship with the ideas he acquired in Paris in the 1520s. Lyons and Nîmes also seek to improve the quality of their teaching. In short, the ramification of these ideas is very impressive. At the highest level the establishment of the Royal Readerships (1530) will allow scholarship in certain fields to develop without the surveillance of the Sorbonne; and it is in these years that are laid the foundations of French scholarship that will reach such remarkable heights in the middle of the century, scholarship on which the members of the Pléiade will be nourished. Outside Paris, Orléans continues to enjoy prestige, though it will soon enter a decline; Bourges, ephemerally in the limelight, partly through Marguerite de Navarre's interest, partly too through the presence for a while of the legist Alciat, will make its mark. Both these towns attract men who will be much affected by the new religious currents – it was at Bourges that Théodore de Bèze came under the influence of Melchior Wolmar. Toulouse will remain the butt of humanist invective for its orthodox conservatism; but it plays some part in the development of law studies.

VII. GUILLAUME BUDÉ[11] (1467–1540)

Of the French scholars active in the first quarter of the sixteenth century, Guillaume Budé is surely the most eminent. He is remembered for two massive works, the *Annotationes in quattuor et viginti Pandectarum libros* (1508) and the *De Asse* (1515), of which, on the king's command, an *Epitome* was printed in 1522; but he continued to publish right into the 1530s: his *De studio literarum* (1532) is still worth reading, and the *Commentarii linguæ græcæ* (1529) constitute an important milestone in Greek studies. Though his two main works survey numerous aspects of Roman civilisation, they are also, as it were, a sort of pantechnicon for the storing of Budé's vast scholarship and his views on many topics. To begin with, they reveal the new humanist attitudes towards classical studies, shunning earlier commentaries and interpretations in favour of a deeper understanding of the Latin language; and Budé, who shares the patriotic zeal of other French humanists, is not slow to refer to the way in which the torch of learning has passed from Italy to French territory. Budé's scholarship is impressive by any standard, but it is significant too for the outlook that underlies it: his sense of contemporary involvement appears everywhere and is symptomatic of the links discerned by humanists between learning and the *vita activa*. The comparative method often allows him to illuminate some point in Roman history by reference to the Greek world, but also to contemporary times. He may mention areas where improvements could be made, as in the field of taxation or warfare; he praises the benefits of printing; he has much to say on the training of the ruler; and stresses connections between political and cultural development – in the *Epitome*, in particular, space is devoted to emperors who interested themselves in culture and gave suitable patronage. On the other hand, Budé does not attempt to harmonise the classical and modern worlds nor to indulge in any religious syncretism: in the *De transitu Hellenismi ad Christianismum* (1535), published a year after the *Affaire des placards* and therefore in a more vigilant climate, he maintains a clear distinction between classical philosophy and Christianity. In any case, his concern is less theological than moral: he thinks that the Church has fallen into disrepute for its loss of moral fibre, and he has some trenchant things to say about Julius II, indulgences, and pluralism; but his views are also coloured by gallican tendencies. In some ways, Budé remains late-medieval in his outlook, but he mirrors ideas that were in the air, emphasising the importance of moral regeneration, the primacy of moral attitude over rites and gestures, the significance of Christ in the elevation of man's being. On the other hand, he was strongly opposed to anything that might lead to schism, but he was not the only humanist of his generation whose son or children went over to Calvinism (Salmon Macrin, Nicole Bérault). However, both by his attitude on matters of religion and by his emphasis on philological training, he furthers trends that are about to get under way, and his impact is brought about, not only by his published works, but also by his personal contacts and his very considerable correspondence.

VIII. RELIGIOUS DEVELOPMENTS

We have noted the stirrings of religious reform before the beginning of the century. The critics of abuse were numerous and vocal, not only among enlightened humanists, but also among the preachers, such as Menot, Maillard, and Raulin.[12] The Church itself was endeavouring to put its house in order, though often against much opposition, as Jean de Bourbon found in the course of his activity at Cluny; reforming zeal led in some cases to division within the order (as happened with the Franciscans). However, before 1480 sizeable efforts had been made to reform the Benedictine order; various assemblies, notably that of Tours in 1493, had also furthered the cause of improvement. But such progress as was made was patchy, discontinuous, and certainly nothing like fast enough to contain the criticisms of the more advanced partisans. In addition to internal momentum, various currents flow in from outside, of which three can be briefly mentioned. The first is the impact of the Brothers of the Common Life of Windesheim, whose stress on inner reform (devotio moderna) underlies their activities; they were associated in some measure with reforming attempts in Paris, and Jean Standonck, the severe Principal of Montaigu, was inspired by their ideals. Second, the growing impact of the classical world, by textual contact, by connections with Italian humanism already imbued with ideals from ancient writers, remains an important factor. The impact is various and may be characterised by doubts as well as by enthusiasm, but in a period of critical reassessment, classical texts often offer useful formulations, a sharpening of focus on certain problems, a support for tendencies already present within France. Among the authors who command a great deal of interest in the coming decades will be Cicero (often acting as a filter); Plato, with his commentator Ficino; Seneca; Lucian; and of course the Church Fathers, who benefit from the new philological approach to texts. And thirdly, no humanist could be insensible to what was happening in Germany. Interest had already been aroused by the Reuchlin affair, for Reuchlin, known to Lefèvre d'Etaples among others, was carrying on the same struggle in the Hebrew field as was the Frenchman on behalf of Greek studies. Then came the more important issue of Lutheranism, and by 1521 the Sorbonne has condemned Luther on certain points of doctrine. The term 'Lutheran' will come to be used indiscriminately by contemporaries to denote any reformist tendency, so that the evangelicals, inspired by Erasmus who had taken issue with Luther on the matter of free-will, are lumped together with others whose orthodoxy is suspect. The impact of Lutheran ideas during the 1520s was very considerable: we know that many texts found their way through the book trade, and that Marguerite de Navarre took an interest in them.[13] In a general way, it would seem that Luther's writings affected French readers at three different levels: there is the critical aspect, and criticisms of the Pope and various abuses would be welcome to gallican ears anyhow; there is, rather later, the Luther who commands attention by his rejection of points of doctrine; and there is also the man who wrote texts of a more devotional nature, in harmony with a mystical tradition well established on the other side of the Rhine. In more extreme form, Luther was formulating attitudes which were already far from embryonic in France. And in this internal development, a major role is played by Lefèvre d'Etaples.

IX. LEFÈVRE D'ÉTAPLES[14] (c. 1450–1536)

Though Budé's work obviously had implications for the development of religious attitudes, it was Lefèvre who made the greatest mark among Frenchmen of his generation. He would no doubt have considered himself a defender of late medieval piety, and certainly no iconoclast; but he ended by incurring the displeasure of the Sorbonne and seeking refuge with Marguerite de Navarre. By temperament he reveals some affinities with Robert Gaguin: he saw in education through the classics a step towards moral development; he shared the contemporary desire to clear religious tradition of the useless commentaries that blurred the truth of the texts. He understood the potential offered by printing for the world of education and for the religious man. We tend to forget that he tried to improve traditional pedagogy by writing treatises on mathematics and astronomy for the *quadrivium;* he also sought to refurbish aristotelian studies by editing or having edited newer commentaries on the main

texts, and to make accessible to French scholars Latin translations
of the philosopher's work undertaken in Italy. His strictly theological interests, therefore, take time to emerge. He went on to
organise new editions of the Church Fathers: Basil, 1505, 1508;
Cyril of Alexandria, 1508; Origen, 1512; and Origen will, on
account of his unorthodox views, play a special part in the religious
reappraisals to come. There were two other fields in which Lefèvre
himself showed himself to be a pioneer. On the one hand, he took
an intense interest in the writings of mystics and Neoplatonists, an
interest that was furthered by journeys to Italy and Germany, one
of which allowed him to discover some unknown manuscripts of
Nicolas of Cusa. He was also well connected with the Brothers of
the Common Life and almost certainly came under the influence of
John of Mauburn, one of the Brothers sent to reform various houses
in Paris in 1490. His zeal in publishing mystical texts is astonishing:
he did much to spread knowledge of Raymon Lull, Nicolas of Cusa,
Denys the Areopagite and also turned his attention to Marsilio
Ficino. And on the other hand, he set himself to edit various biblical
texts, among which the most important were a revised Latin version
of St Paul, with commentary (1512), and his edition of the New
Testament; the *Psalterium quincuplex* (1509), usually attributed to
him, may be the work of someone else, but his translation of the
Bible, including some 'corrections' from the Greek texts (1523), is a
milestone, given the spirit of the times. By his concern for the inner
life, the stress on St Paul and also on certain mystical writers,
Lefèvre anticipates the Reformation, though on doctrinal points he
remains conservative. His importance reveals itself, not only through
his editorial activities, but through personal contacts; and here,
Guillaume Briçonnet assumes significance as his eminent disciple,
for he was at the centre of the Groupe de Meaux and, at one time,
confessor to Marguerite de Navarre. Lefèvre placed scholarship at
the service of religion, nor indeed did he make excessive claims for
his own erudition; he was much more concerned with religious
improvement, through the removal of moral blemish and intellectual
accretion, and his mystical leanings impart a strong emotive character to his religion. He stands as a sort of halfway house between the
earlier humanists and the generation of 1520 in his religious attitude,
but the impact of his work coincides with the Lutheran crisis, so
that his conflict with the redoubtable Noel Beda is quite understandable once the Sorbonne saw in any move towards reform the
suspicion of heresy.

X. ERASMUS (? 1469–1536)[15]

Erasmus had studied in Paris before the end of the fifteenth century; and in some ways he resembles the humanists of the age of Gaguin and Lefèvre: he saw education as a means towards greater moral improvement, and stressed the role that the classics could play in that context. He edited a number of ancient authors, including Cicero, Seneca, and among the Greeks Aristotle and Demosthenes; but he was no Ciceronian nor did his tastes extend to the Roman elegists; his moral outlook inclined him to prefer Prudentius to Catullus, and several modern Latin writers to ancient authors. This outlook is also reflected in his own Latin poetry which is distinctly late-medieval in flavour. He felt it was part of his mission to make more texts available to students, but, very conscious of the links that should exist between the classical world and the modern, he began to comment in a contemporary spirit. His *Adagia* (1500) began, he tells us, from the chance requests of some friends and were intended to be little more than an annotated anthology of ancient wisdom, but the second edition (1508) and the greatly augmented one of 1515 convert them into dynamic vehicles of religious and social criticism, in which the commentary verges on something very like the essay. This is also true of the *Colloquia*, which expand the school dialogue into an expression of an attitude towards contemporary issues. The *Encomium moriæ* (1511) moves beyond the pedagogic field and is a Lucianic satire of obscurantism and old-world theological attitudes, but also turns a critical eye on other aspects of the modern scene and, by its ambivalent techniques of satire, opens up a much wider debate on the issue of wisdom and ignorance; such is its range that it can find a public today through popular editions. In this work, Erasmus offered humanists a mode of expression, which both implied an awareness of the polyvalency of important current themes and offered literary techniques whose ambiguity was not without use in an age of religious polarisation: irony, paradox, pseudo-encomium, all this and more will make its way in the literary idiom of the coming decades. Erasmus put forward a coherent and highly articulate criticism of church abuses, he attacked religion that did not go beyond outward gesture, he had much to say on contemporary issues such as taxation, warfare, unsatisfactory rulers, and so forth. He also expressed himself in renovated genres and in a Latin which was accessible to a wider public; one has only to compare his lucid, sensitive, and fast-moving style with the turgid gibberish that passes for Latin in some of Josse Bade's prefaces. And in this context, it is not only the *Adagia*, *Colloquia*, and *Encomium moriæ* that are relevant; no student of the Renaissance, however tyronic, can afford to ignore the fascinating Correspondence of Erasmus, which forms an intellectual microcosm of the period.[16]

Important though Erasmus is as a critic of his times, it would be quite wrong to present him solely as a negative writer. The texts just mentioned have enjoyed the greatest literary circulation, but Erasmus had much more of a positive nature to offer his contemporaries who like him were concerned in promoting a more genuine Christian way of life. Erasmus is the author of the *Enchiridion militis christiani* (1508), and if this is not vintage writing, its immense impact cannot be gainsaid. More important, Erasmus plays a leading role in the edition of the Church Fathers, Cyprian, Hilary, and his beloved Jerome; he discovered Lorenzo Valla's *Adnotationes* on the New Testament and published them in 1505; in 1516 he brought out the first edition of the New Testament in Greek. And in due course he was drawn into religious controversy with Luther, whose attitude to free-will he felt obliged to reject. In short, he was in the forefront of religious controversy.

Erasmus's religious attitude has been subjected to a great variety of conflicting interpretations. In his own time, he found himself between two fires, denounced by Luther on the one hand, and attacked by the orthodox on the other for his semi-Pelagian views. He himself considered that he remained within the pale of orthodoxy, but that did not prevent his works being put on the Index. He has also attracted criticism for an over-rational approach to the Scriptures, and his oblique, sometimes sibylline form of expression has inclined readers to see in him a man who was not fully committed in his religious outlook, to think of him perhaps as a kind of Renaissance Renan. Recent research has tended to move in the opposite direction, and it is clear that his impact, at religious level, on his younger contemporaries was immense. He was less of a scholar than Budé or probably Lefèvre, but he achieved a great deal in developing the humanist, philological approach to texts; he was prominent in making the Church Fathers an essential part of the spiritual landscape – his own debt to Augustine, as well as to Jerome, has been emphasised recently; and he diffused a complex of Christian attitudes that spread far and wide.[17] Nor can his role in educational advances be ignored, and at literary level he evolves techniques of *vulgarisation* that will find a ready audience. It is true of course that Erasmianism may not find an immediately fruitful expression in French vernacular texts, if one excludes Rabelais and in some measure Marot; but, on the other hand, some writers may simply not have thought it prudent to publish their works – a good example is found in the early poems of Charles Fontaine; and one must not forget that Erasmian attitudes find their way quickly into Neo-latin poetry during the 1530s. Equally important, Erasmus has given a certain colour and character to the humanist climate of these years, and his influence will persist in differing forms for a very long time.

All in all, this is an immensely exciting period; it not only helps to crystallise religious attitudes, it also lays the foundations of the French humanism that will nourish French writers, in Latin and in the vernacular, until the Pléiade and beyond. The general tone of these years is markedly Christian, and as we have seen evangelical; the work of, say, Charles de Bouelles, whose *De Sapientia* develops ideas we associate with Pico della Mirandola and, with the expected references to humility and Godfearing, stresses man's role in acquiring knowledge and the exercise of his will, has perhaps a muted impact at this time, though we shall find his name mentioned by Etienne Dolet and themes reminiscent of his works in Scève's *Microcosme*.[18] Even so, there is a clear impression abroad among humanists that they are living in a new epoch, different from that of an older generation, and that it is one in which France will culturally come into her own.

NOTES

1. J.-J. Champollion-Figeac, *Le Palais de Fontainebleau*, 1866; L. Dimier, *Fontainebleau*, 1911; F. Gébelin, *Les Châteaux de la Renaissance*, 1927; T. G. Jackson, *The Renaissance of Roman Architecture*, III, *France*, Cambridge, 1923; A. Blunt, *Art and Architecture in France 1500–1700*, 1953.

2. Jacques Colin's version appeared in 1537 (BN); revised by Mellin de Saint-Gellais and Etienne Dolet in the following year (BM, BN). Another version was provided by Gabriel Chappuys (BM has copy of Lyons, 1580).

3. E. Garin, *Italian Humanism*, Oxford, 1965; Eugene Rice, *The Renaissance Idea of Wisdom*, Cambridge, Mass., 1958; L. Sozzi, 'La *dignitas hominis* dans la littérature française de la Renaissance', *Humanism in France*, ed. A. H. T. Levi.

4. Nor from the pressures that well up from a national *prise de conscience*.

5. E. Egger, *L'Hellénisme en France*, 2 vols., 1869; J. E. Sandys, *A History of Classical Scholarship*, 3 vols., Cambridge, 1921; J. Paquier, *Jérôme Aléandre de sa naissance à la fin de son séjour à Brindes (1480–1529)*, 1900; A. Lefranc, *Histoire du Collège de France depuis ses origines jusqu'à la fin du Premier Empire*, 1893; L. Delaruelle, 'L'Etude du grec à Paris de 1514 à 1530', *RSS*, 1922.

6. See General Bibliography.

7. Available in BM and MRy, and in reprint (FRC): see A.-J. Bernard, *Geoffroy Tory, peintre et graveur . . .*, 1865.

8. See General Bibliography. Bio-bibliography of Vascosan, by C. Du Bus, in BN, Réserve.

9. W. H. Woodward, *Studies in Education during the Age of the Renaissance 1400–1600*, 1906; S. D'Irsay, *Histoire des universités françaises et étrangères*, 2 vols., 1933–35.

10. J. Quicherat, *Histoire de Sainte-Barbe, collège, communauté, institution*, 3 vols., 1860; E. Gaullieur, *Histoire du Collège de Guyenne*, 1874; T. Braga, *Historia da Universidade de Coimbra*, t. I (1289–1555), Lisbon, 1892; M. Brandão, *A Inquisicão e os professores do Colégio das Artes*, I, Coimbra, 1948; C.-G.-A. Schmidt, *La Vie et les travaux de Jean Sturm*, Strasbourg, 1855; E. Puech, *Un Professeur au XVIe siècle, Mathurin Cordier*

..., Montauban, 1896; M.-J. Gaufrès, *Claude Baduel et la Réforme des études au XVIe siècle*, 1880.

11. The BN and BM have first editions of the works mentioned and also of the *Epistolae* (1520) and the *Opera omnia*, Basel, 1557; EUL has the 1524 ed. of the *Annotationes*, St A the *De studio litterarum* (1532). See L. Delaruelle, *Guillaume Budé, les origines, les débuts, les idées maîtresses* and *Répertoire analytique et chronologique de la correspondance de Guillaume Budé, 1907*; J. Bohatec, *Budé und Calvin*, Graz, 1950.

12. O. Maillard, *Œuvres françaises*, ed. A. de la Borderie, Nantes, 1877; Michel Menut, *Sermons choisis*, ed. J. Nève, 1924; A. J. Krailsheimer, *Rabelais and the Franciscans*, Oxford, 1963.

13. W. G. Moore, *La Réforme allemande et la littérature française* ..., Strasbourg, 1930.

14. C. H. Graf, *Essai sur la vie et les écrits de Jacques Lefèvre d'Etaples*, Strasbourg, 1842. The major texts will be found in BM and BN; M. A. Screech has reproduced the first ed. of *Epistres et Evangiles pour les cinquante & deux sepmaines de l'An*, Geneva, 1964.

15. There is a vast bibliography, swollen if not always enriched by recent centenary junketings; I confine myself to general works that give advice for further reading: R. H. Bainton, *Erasmus of Christendom*, New York, 1969; J. Huizinga, *Erasmus of Rotterdam*, New York, 1923; W. Kaiser, *Praisers of Folly*, 1964; M. M. Phillips, *Erasmus and the Northern Renaissance*, 1949; J.-C. Margolin, *Erasme par lui-même*, 1965; Preserved Smith, *Erasmus*, New York, 1923. Various key texts are available in translation: Craig R. Thompson, *The Colloquies of Erasmus*, Chicago, 1963; M. M. Phillips, *The Adages of Erasmus*, Cambridge, 1964 (shortened version, *Erasmus on his Times*, Cambridge, 1967); *Praise of Folly*, translation by Betty Radice, introduction by Anthony Levi, Harmondsworth, 1971; R. Himelick, *The Enchiridion of Erasmus*, Bloomington, 1963.

16. *Opus Epistolarum Desiderii Erasmi Roterodami*, ed. P. S. Allen and H. M. Allen, Oxford, 1906–41; impeccably edited with polymathic notes.

17. J.-B. Pineau, *Erasme, sa pensée religieuse*, 1924; C. Béné, *Erasme et Saint Augustin, THR*, 1969.

18. The *Liber de Sapientia* will be found in the volume containing the *Liber de Intellectu*, ?1510 (BM, BN, O, EUL); see J. Dippel, *Versuch einer systematischen Darstellung der Philosophie des Carolus Bovillus*, Würzburg, 1865, and Eugene Rice, op. cit.

Chapter 3

POETRY DURING THE REIGN OF FRANCIS I

I. GENERAL SURVEY[1]

THIS period is extremely rich in poetic activity, but it is also a very varied one, in which a number of currents may be discerned. In the first place, the *rhétoriqueur*, less well established and threatened by new pressures, is far from moribund; not only do we find a steady number of poets working in the old idiom, but the writings of the *rhétoriqueurs* are still sufficiently acceptable to justify reprints until the time of the Pléiade, and manuscript sources suggest considerable popularity as well. Evangelically inspired poetry will not, for obvious reasons, always find its way into print; but it is curious to observe Charles Fontaine and Marguerite de Navarre often using *rhétoriqueur* forms as a vehicle for their Christian sentiments. Among the forces that help to modify the poetic climate one may mention a growing awareness of the classical world, the development of court life, and pedagogic factors.

We have seen that classical writers are being subjected to fresh humanist scrutiny and that authors, hitherto neglected, are coming into their own. Vergil and Ovid still hold pride of place, but Horace the lyric poet and the elegists, as well as the *Greek Anthology*, are finding a public, though the odes of Horace command greater attention at first among the Neo-latin poets. The epigrammatists, such as Martial and Ausonius, also become popular; but no doubt the example of the classics is reinforced by their utilisation in the texts of Italian humanist poets who are now widely read. A latinisation of the genres is under way: the elegy, under Marot's encouragement, comes to stay;[2] the epistle, already well installed in the *rhétoriqueur* world, undergoes renovation; and the eclogue, partly under court influence, enjoys some success. The epigram and the epitaph take over from older genres, the *chanson* and the *complainte*; but too rigid distinctions should not be drawn. The *chanson*, with its popular origins, no doubt introduced more flexible and lively tones into poetry, and it was very popular in the musical settings published by Attaingnant from 1528 onwards; but it was felt by some poets to be vulgar, and the epigram with its classical harmonics would be more acceptable. However, if we turn to Sebillet's *Art poétique françoys* (1548), it is quite clear that the frontiers between *chanson* and *épigramme* are extremely tenuous; and, from another angle, we have seen that, in spite of theoretical definitions, genres can be very flexible: the eclogue in particular can range from full-scale stylised courtly form to something approaching a meditation. Yet, it is true that there is a shift from old forms to new, a shift that will be consecrated by the poets of the Pléiade. Contact with classical sources will also favour a new look at rhetorical techniques: here school and college syllabus plays a part, but the stylistic features of Vergil, Claudian, Cicero, as well as the perusal of classical treatises on rhetoric, will widen the gap between new poets and the *rhétoriqueurs*. Classical sources do something to reinforce the aristocratic view of poetry which will also be fed by Petrarchan currents, and this will affect attitudes towards poetic language.

The influence of the Court, as earlier, remains decisive, but the atmosphere under Francis I is rather different from what we associate with Louis XII and Anne of Brittany. Throughout the century, the presence of women at Court increases, a process which, as Brantôme reiterates, began with Anne of Brittany:

Ce fut la premiere qui commença la grande cour des dames que nous avons veue depuis elle jusqu'a ceste heure.

The role of the Court as part of the state apparatus assumes growing proportions; the example of Italian Courts was not lost upon French kings, and the success of the contemporary *Courtier*, by Castiglione (1528, translated into French 1537) is no coincidence.[3] Literature will take its share of a court life that manifests itself also in the building of Renaissance *châteaux*, the encouragement of the visual arts, and the development of musical taste: *chansons* are popular at Court and there is evidence that Francis I liked psalm paraphrases set to music.[4] Poetry contributes to the propaganda system of the monarchy, celebrating the prowesses of French king and military leaders and also reviling France's enemies; and the events of the Court – births, marriages, deaths – will promote a considerable output of encomiastic verse. The needs of entertainment are also numerous, and the Court will have its accredited poets, Marot and Saint-Gellais for the vernacular, Salmon Macrin for Latin poetry. The Court is peopled or frequented by humanists, sometimes of foreign origin, who also make their presence felt. All this means that writers are expected to provide compositions that are wider in thematic range and in tone than what we have seen among the late *rhétoriqueurs*; and higher standards of elegance and urbanity seem to be the order of the day. There are, of course, other centres of

cultural activity than Francis's Court and entourage; Marguerite de
Navarre will have her own Court and more precisely defined
interests, and Lyons will for a time become the pacemaker in certain
poetic developments.

In a period where humanism is so closely connected with pedagogic reform, one would hardly expect edifying and didactic poetry
to suffer any decline. Moreover, it is now that printers, especially in
Lyons, are very aware of the valuable symbiosis to be created
between word and picture, a connection encouraged in any case by
Horatian literary doctrine. The clearest example at the strictly
pedagogic level is the *icon*, in which potted wisdom of the ancients
is presented by means of an *exemplum*. In Neo-latin poetry, the
distich or tetrastich is the usual formal medium for this type of
poetry: at first, it may serve historical ends, and because of its
pedagogic links, tends to be a predominantly Latin genre, but later
in the century it acquires further value, especially in Protestant
circles, as a means of religious propaganda. Nevertheless, a moralising form, with illustrations, can be found in the vernacular, the
blason or *devise*. Certain authors have a particular liking for this
formula, Gilles Corrozet with his *Hecatomgraphie* (1540, with three
further editions in the next eight years),[5] or Guillaume de la Perrière
with his *Morosophie* (1553);[6] this latter work also had its Latin
counterpart, nor is this case isolated, for Pierre Coustau produced
his *Pegma* in the same year in Latin, followed very rapidly by a
French version.[7] These works are, however, already determined in
some of their characteristics by the massive success of Alciat's
Emblems,[8] which literally enjoyed hundreds of editions in Europe,
both in Latin and in vernacular renderings. The date, perhaps
indeed the existence, of the presumed first edition, is still a matter of
debate, but from the 1531 edition onwards, the popularity of the
work was never in doubt. The formula – a picture, motto, followed
by a short poem, and possibly an exegesis – did not necessarily make
for good poetry, but it helped to popularise a wide range of themes,
some of which were already to be found in Erasmus's *Adagia*, it
fostered the taste for *sententiæ* and gnomic poetry (sometimes, I
suspect, without accompanying illustration), and it served as a
stimulus to more serious poetry, not only in France, but in England:
the names of Scève and of Daniel spring readily to mind – and the
genre had some vogue also in the Low Countries. The emblem
technique is also used for religious ends, as in the case of Georgette
de Montenay, whose book will also be published in Lyons. Other
cognate developments include the *Picta poesis* by Barthélemy
Aneau (Lyons, 1552), the fashion for quatrains based on biblical
texts and illustrated by suitable pictures (e.g., Claude Paradin,
Quadrins historiques de la Bible). These latter were extremely

successful: first published in 1555 at Lyons, they were frequently reprinted throughout the century, and they were also used for dinner services made at Limoges – examples of these may be seen in the Victoria and Albert Museum. All this didactic poetry, which often has mnemonic value, may only be marginal to literature proper, but it is a feature of Renaissance writing that must not be ignored.

One or two further points about poetic composition may be briefly mentioned. As in previous decades, the enjoyment of extempore verse is widespread; besides, it seems that more than a few poets liked working in two languages. We have seen that, for pedagogic reasons, some humanists translated Greek models into Latin verse, but we have also just noted the appearance of parallel texts in Latin and French, often by the same author. Rabelais has an interesting remark in this connection:

. . . descripvoient quelques plaisans epigrammes en latin, puis les mettoient par rondeaux et ballades en langue françoyse. (I, xxiv.)

This quotation also hints at a further feature, the social or communal nature of much writing. This is a period in which some interesting poetry emerges from group activity: in the Latin sector, one can point to the various poets of the Lyons *sodalitium* whose epigrams often answer one another, or the attempt by Dolet to organise the *Tombeau du Dauphin* in 1536. Towards the same time, there is the famous *blason* competition in which Clément Marot took the leading part; and there are good grounds for believing that the *querelle des amyes* (see below, pp. 115–23) started as a *divertissement* between authors who were on excellent terms with each other.

The period is dominated, of course, by Clément Marot, but it would be too facile to see it other than as very varied and, above all, transitional in character.

II. LATTER-DAY RHÉTORIQUEURS

We have mentioned the continuing success of the *Rhétoriqueurs*; they gradually lose their foothold at Court – Jean Marot is perhaps the last court *rhétoriqueur*[9] – and are more active in the provinces. In any case, the organisation of the *puys* or *palinods* helps to preserve older poetic traditions, and it is curious how many budding poets will continue to compete for the annual prizes. That there was a market for older-style verse is indicated, not only by numerous reprints of Molinet, Crétin, and others, but by the frequently published anthologies whose themes, idiom, and forms belong to an earlier tradition: here are some examples:

1535   *Petit traicté contenant en soy la fleur de toutes joyeusetez* (also reprinted).
1538   *S'ensuyvent les trois cents cinquante Rondeaulx,*
1540(?) *La Fleur de vraye poesie francoyse* (also 1541, 1543, 1548).
1552   *Recueil de tout soulas et plaisir ...*
1557   *Histoire ioyeuse contenant les passions et angoisses d'un martyr amoureux d'une dame.*
1570   *L'amoureux passe-temps.*

The love-poetry of the *banny de lyesse* and the *esclave de fortune* will continue to be marketable for a while, though no doubt these anthologies are more dilute, less alembicated than the major *rhétoriqueurs* and show the absorption of neo-petrarchan elements. A sophisticated expression of love requires a high degree of stylisation, and it is not surprising that Scève owes something to the *rhétoriqueurs* or that Helisenne de Crenne's prose reminds us of Lemaire de Belges. The tradition survives, partly because it takes time for the Marotic idiom to establish itself, partly because in the 1530s some interesting poetic developments are occurring more especially in the Neo-latin domain, partly because the later disciples are not completely impervious to new fashions; but also because *rhétoriqueur* and Petrarchan or humanist poets are not totally opposed on all points of principle; on the contrary they have a certain amount in common, and it will often happen that in the more recent poetry old wine is being offered under new labels. Allegory, word-play, formal alembication do not die with the *rhétoriqueurs*; but they need to be revitalised in a new climate of existential and literary opinion. One final point: where the highest degree of elaboration and sophistication is required in, say, formal court poetry, the stylistic differences can be narrowed to a remarkable degree.

Jean Marot (?–?1526).

We shall now review a few poets whose roots are in the *rhétoriqueur* tradition, but space will not allow a close survey of their work. Jean Marot was at the Court of Anne of Brittany and of Francis I, but his works were not published until after his death.[10] He left the impression of an amiable man who relied on his wits to make up for his lack of formal education, and the preface to his *Recueil* says that we should admire him for having 'tant bien escript sans scauoir aulcunes lettres ne Grecques ne Latines'; so that the classical veneer his writing appears to have on occasion derives either from his *rhétoriqueur* predecessors or from manuals of second-hand information. His career allows him to work in the usual genres: *doctrinal, epistle, rondeau,* and *chant royal,* and he was present at the military events he describes in his *Voyage de Gênes* and *Voyage de Venise,* in which poetry and prose rub shoulders. He took part in the Rouen *puy* of 1520, and it is very likely that some of his work is not extant. He impresses most when he is at his simplest and most natural:

> Vous avez tort de luy estre contraire
> Au pauvre cueur qui s'est voulu fortraire
> De liberté en gettant en vos lacz
> Pour estre serf, & jamais ne fust las
> De bien servir pour vostre grace attraire.
>
> Et neantmoins que peine veult sallaire
> Si n'ha il eu de vous pour son bien faire
> Fors que rigueur, dont souvent dit helas
>   Vous aves tort.
>
> Parquoy me plains de vous, & vostre affaire
> Deuant amour quant pour le satisfaire.
> L'auez plongé au(x) grandz fleuues & lacz,
> De desespoir, ou il est sans soulas,
> Pardonnes moy si ie ne m'en puys taire,
>   Vous aves tort. (*Rondeau* vii)

What, however, is more interesting is that Jean Marot is aware of Italian poetry and has translated or adapted texts of Serafino dell'Aquila:

> S'il est ainsi que ce corps t'abandonne,
> Amour commandes & la raison ordonne
> Que je te laisse en gaige de ma foy
> Le cueur ja tien, car par honneste loy
> Aulcun ne doibt reprendre ce qu'il donne.
>
> Ne croy plus jamais qu'aillieurs il s'abandonne!
> Plus tost la mort (sans que Dieu luy pardonne)
> Le puisse prendre & meurtrir devant toy
>   S'il est ainsi.
>
> Si Faulx Rapport qui les amantz blasonne
> Te vient disant que j'ayme autre personne,
> Tu respondras: Meschant, point ne le croy,
> Car j'ay son cueur; & corps sans cueur, de foy
> Ne peult aymer; la raison y est bonne
>   S'il est ainsi. (*Rondeau* xxx)

Since it is possible that Marot wrote this poem in the early years of Francis's reign, it shows an early penetration of the Italian writer into France. However, Marot's most substantial works are his accounts of the Genoa campaign (1507) and the second campaign against Venice. Here, of course, the genre will often require the use of rhetorical devices consonant with the writing of history, and Marot remains a docile follower of the tradition; when he prefers to use his eyes – and his accounts appear to be generally reliable – he is more straightforward, but he can be desperately prosaic:

Lan Mil Cinq Cens & Neuf du moys de May,
Le premier iour a Millan arriua.
Nobles manans en triumphant arroy
Vont au deuant long temps a que le Roy,
Si grant Noblesse ensemble ne trouua,
Chascun adonc son cheual esprouua
Deuant le Roy Millanoys sont pennades
Faisans en laer mille saulx & ruades.

Lors quau Chasteau le Roy fist son entree,
France on cria de cueur & de couraige,
Lartillerie adonques cest monstree,
Mais une piece est rompue & oultrée,
Dont il advint trop merueilleux dommaige
Car elle occist ung gentil homme & paige
Par les esclatz dont furent assignez,
Pour celon dit en ung commun langaige
En toute feste en a de mal disnez.

(BM copy, 1537, fol. 63 v)

Marot probably remained in print in great measure because of his
son's presence; but the other *rhétoriqueurs* whose works are published in the 1530s are not markedly superior. On the other hand,
they are not linked with the Court, and their individual destinies
introduce, from time to time, new features into their writing.

Jean Parmentier (1494–1529)

Parmentier, a native of Dieppe, tried his hand at genres that are
characteristic of the *rhétoriqueur*: he left a translation of Sallust,
wrote a morality play that was performed at Dieppe in 1527, and
composed a number of poems in strict form. His works were published posthumously in 1531[11] and were not reprinted in the sixteenth
century. Poetically his writings are not very inspiring, but they
present a few points of interest. Parmentier was a seafarer who met
his death in the East Indies, and his poems make use of technical
vocabulary (naval and cosmographic) to elaborate the conventional
themes concerning the Virgin Mary. Moreover, though he is
strongly anti-Lutheran and asserts his orthodoxy more vigorously
than some *rhétoriqueurs*, he has composed a surprising *Exhortation
contenant les merveilles de Dieu et de la dignité de l'homme*; this
work, his most substantial poem apart from the morality, sings the
wonders of God's creation in tones which take us beyond the
expected world of the *rhétoriqueurs* by its combination of greater
cosmic awareness and a delicate use of the Psalms; but it is also
original, given its date of publication, for the way in which themes
associated with Pico della Mirandola on the dignity of man find
their way into this Dieppe poet. Nevertheless, though man's privileged position is emphasised, he is firmly situated under God's
authority. The poem is also impressive for passages of sustained

tone, but it does suffer linguistically from a lack of stamina and resonance. Parmentier's relatively few poems – others said to have been composed have not survived – show a man trying to go beyond the framework of *rhétoriqueur* tradition in a number of ways, but his restricted imagination means that intention is more praiseworthy than realisation.

Eustorg de Beaulieu (?*1495–1552*)

Two other poets whose work appeared in the 1530s resemble each other in that they led nomadic lives, so that their work shows no trace of court influence, but appears at its best in the satiric vein. Eustorg de Beaulieu published his *Divers Rapportz* in 1537, though his rather tedious *Gestes des solliciteurs* had come out in 1529.[12] Much of his writing is in the fixed forms (*rondeaux* and *ballades*) and he cultivates the epistle in conventional fashion. There may be some discreet innovation in his *blasons*, *chansons*, and *coq-à-l'âne*, but whatever humanist colouring he may have acquired, it does not come through in his verse. He is perhaps rather unusual at this time in that he was a fully trained musician, was organist of a cathedral, and left three settings to *chansons* of his own composition. The vein in which he is most successful, however, is the satiric; here he succeeds in maintaining momentum and can make fair use of a more popular idiom on occasion:

> La Court courut, court & courra,
> Mais tel apres elle a couru
> Qu'en lieu d'estre secouru
> En couchant meschef encourra
> Toutesfois, quand il recourra
> Devers Madame Flatterie,
> (Pourveu qu'en sçachant Flater rye)
> Je croy qu'elle le secourra.
> (Pegg ed., p. 195)

but even here, the liking for word-play tends to take precedence. Of Beaulieu's life little is known, and even less has left traces in his poetry. We would hardly have suspected that he had Calvinist leanings,[13] though later in his career he turns up in Switzerland.

Roger de Collerye (?*1470–1537*)

Roger de Collerye resembles Beaulieu by his fidelity to older forms, the avoidance of the grand style, a preference for the satiric mode, and little interest in love-poetry.[14] Like Beaulieu too he is only marginally affected by the example of Marot – though the former may have imitated the poet of Cahors in one or two respects. Roger's poems have a greater raciness, often prefer the particular to the general, and reveal a more marked verbal sprightliness:

Voyant les barbes non rasées,
Dont plusieurs font leurs risées,
Bigarreures non abolyes,
Nous engendrent melencolyes,
Car ce sont choses mal prisées.

Les dames se sont advisées
D'estre en leurs habitz desguisées,
Cointes, bragardes, et jolyes,
    Voyant les barbes.

Or, les nations divisées
Gectent dessus eulx leurs visées
De voir régner tant de folyes
Qui ne sont pas aux omelyes
Que Bede a jadis devisées
    Voyant les barbes. (Lachèvre ed., p. 55)

Though in Holy Orders, Collerye appears to have had a poverty-stricken life, and his poetry assumes a much more personal character than does Beaulieu's. Religious inspiration is exceptional in his verse, and he is at his best when he writes in the tradition of the *Basoche*.

Minor figures

The allegorical love tradition, influenced by Ovid, persists in authors such as Michel d'Amboise (*fl.* 1540),[15] who published in 1536 his *Epistres veneriennes*, though they had been written earlier, and also his *Penthaire de l'esclave fortuné*. He tells us that he studied 'es Cretiennes, Marotiennes & Bouchetiques' to improve his verse, that he suffered from *inscience*, but also owed something to his friendship with Gilles Corrozet. His verse combines *rhétoriqueur* sophistication with occasionally very frank statement, but he appears aware of the Roman elegists and Angeriano. Love themes also may be found in the *Tuteur d'Amour* of Gilles d'Aurigny,[16] who gives proof of attractive qualities in minor, inconsequential poetic trifles, but whose main contribution probably lies in the field of translation. The older frameworks still seem capable of coping, up to a point, with more contemporary preoccupations: a useful example is Claude Colet, who published in 1544 his *L'Oraison de mars aux dames de la Court ... plus l'Epistre de l'amoureux de vertu* (2nd edition, 1548).[17] Colet makes use of the traditional *débat*, allegorical elements, a fairly strong structure of argument and rhetoric; but his *fond* is up to date, with some interesting comments on war, its effects upon the common soldier, its evil economic consequences (influence of Erasmus?). Also Colet introduces a number of religious considerations in a tone that is strongly evangelical; attention is drawn to Christ's sacrifice, and he refers to Him as 'Nostre Saulveur, nostre

Espoux, nostre Frere'. Colet was a friend of Gilles d'Aurigny, and like him was active as editor and translator; he edited the letters of Helisenne de Crenne and translated the ninth book of the *Amadis de Gaulle*. The large amount of satire he is alleged to have composed has not survived.

Jean Bouchet (1476–?1557)

Of all these writers who remain faithful to the older forms only one attains some literary stature: Jean Bouchet.[18] He makes his mark as poet, impresario of *mystères*, and annalist; and among his friends numbers Ardillon, Claude Cottereau, and François Rabelais, which suggests rightly that this late-medieval figure was not insensitive to new trends. His output was impressive, and a number of his works were reprinted up till his death in 1555. Some writings go back as far as the reign of Louis XII, and throughout the presence of allegory and satire is widespread. His *Labyrinth de fortune*, published in 1521, but composed earlier, is a poetic treatment of the *ars vivendi*, for which he consulted many theologians and which is presented with plentiful use of allegorical techniques. *Veritable doctrine* conquers *humaine discipline*, and space is devoted to describing the evils of this world, hypocrisy, *gloria*, blasphemy, and so forth. The narrative is set in the symbolic topography of the *rhétoriqueur* tradition; Bouchet refers to Jean d'Auton in gratitude for the interest he took in the preparation of this work. He also gives us his view of poetry: 'En poesie il ny a que mensonge/Poetes sont communement menteurs', and they can only remain on the right road if they have 'la science, lart, le sçauoir, lesprit, lexperience' to prevent them falling by the wayside:

> Je nescriptz rien qui ne soit approuvé
> Et par histoire ou bon acteur prouvé
> Et si je nay doulx et fluant langaige
> Je nay pas eu de nature ce gaige
> Plus advenant est un don naturel
> Que le sçauoir dhomme artificiel.
> (fol. GG ii r, in 1532 ed.)

His view of Nature and his treatment of love themes remain stilted and old-fashioned, and a didactic spirit is normally at work. Yet a wider range of interests, with some awareness of contemporary issues, is revealed by his *Epistres*. A letter to an *escolier* outlines a programme of study; faith in God, wide reading accompanied by specialisation in some subject, practice in *bien escrire*, avoidance of too much rest, indulgence in sport and play, a proper attitude to teachers; elsewhere Bouchet interests himself in the problem of free-will; and in his ideas, biblically inspired, on kingship, he comes near to Rabelais:

Et parce appert si tout bien on rumine
Que la guerre est permise aux chrestiens
Si faicte elle est par princes terriens
Pour bien de paix, & publicque concorde
Pour des foulez avoir misericorde,
Et subvenir aux pouvres opprimez,
Pour relever ceulx qui sont supprimez,
Pour deprimer forces et tyrannies,
Et pour punir crimes & villanies,
Quand on ne peult aultrement corriger
Les delinquans, ne leurs vices purger.
Semblablement pour ses terres defendre
Aussi sa vie, en ce on ne peult mesprendre,
Ne pour son bien avoir et retirer.
Pourveu qu'a Dieu on se vueille tirer
Pour obtenir secours & adiutoire,
Et que le tout en redoute a sa gloire . . .
                              (Ep. xxxvi)

Perhaps these edifying urges reduce in part the tendency to word-play, erudite vocabulary, abuse of epithet, and over-rich rhyme that we have come to associate with many *rhétoriqueurs*, though Bouchet's criticism of a friend's style suggests a more florid conception of writing than the quotation we have just given would imply. Yet his verse remains flat and imprisoned in the couplet without any search for varied rhythms. Bouchet was for all that interested in formal matters; some ideas are found as early as the foreword to his *Angoysses & remedes d'amours du traverseur en son adolescence*, where he acknowledges his debt to writers such as Clopinel, Castel, Lemaire, Meschinot. He followed Lemaire in trying his hand at *terza rima*; and a later statement is worth recalling:

Et neantmoins de maistre Ian le Mare
Georges aussi, la reigle non vulgaire
Ie t'ay rescript quant a synalumpher
La quadrature, & le metre lympher,
Et amolir par rime femenine
Incontinent apres la masculine
I'entends es vers qu'on nomme leonins
Comme ceux cy, car les vers masculins
Et femenins faictz de deux a deux metres
Ont la doulceur des carmes penthametres. . . .

but his advocacy of *alternance* in *rimes croisées* was not immediately heeded; and his reputation was no doubt eclipsed by the arrival of the Pléiade. Though he was not insensitive to the winds of change, I doubt if he was adaptable as his almost exact contemporary Salmon Macrin was in the domain of Latin poetry.

François Habert

François Habert is a very minor talent, but he affords a striking example of the persistence of *rhétoriqueur* idiom into the 1560s,[19] with only a slight concession to the metrical practices of the younger generation (e.g., regular *alternance* and exploiting of the alexandrine). He brought out nearly fifty different volumes, some of which were reprinted late in the century; his work lies in the field of translation (Horace, Ovid, *Quatrains de Caton*), a large amount of encomiastic verse produced when he was court poet to Henry II, and finally a number of edifying poems in old-style presentation. His *Jeunesse du Banny de Lyesse* (1541) shows him to be influenced also by Marot, though a strong didactic and religious vein is present:

> Semblablement couché par ton escript
> Quelle a son cœur tout mis en Jesus Christ
> Aimant sa loy, qui tousjours se descœuvre
> Ferme en la foy qui est morte sans l'œuvre. . . .
> (fol. 45 v–46 r)

an orthodox view confirmed by the Latin tag *Fides sine operibus mortua est*. Habert likes the epistle, the *rondeau*, the *ballade*, the *dizain*, the *déploration*, and of course *rhétoriqueur* word-play. In his *Philosophe parfaict* and the following *Temple de Vertu*, he develops a strongly Christian view of the sage, whose wisdom is linked with prudence, the rejection of *avarice*, and timidity, but who above all must follow Christian doctrine ('sans foy chrestienne, ne peult estre parfaict Philosophe'), mortifying the flesh, conquering 'le monde', and overcoming 'les malings espritz'. The sage, in order to enter the temple of Virtue, must follow the books of Christian tradition and not classical authors (many of whom Habert had in fact translated):

> Non poinct Virgile aux fables de Priam,
> Non point Ovide aux amours impudicques,
> Non poinct Homere aux guerres heroicques,
> Non d'Alexandre ou Daire Roy de Perse,
> Faicts vertueux, non Catule ou Properse,
> Encores moins le Romant de la Rose
> Où il n'y a que vanité enclose,
> Car en ce lieu ces livres ne sont point,
> C'est pour ceulx là que lubrique amour poingt.
> (lines 238 ff.)

But Cicero and Aristotle are admitted as servers in the cult. This moral preoccupation comes to the surface in many other volumes, notably in the *Temple de Chasteté*, in which Habert adds his own footnote to the *querelle des amyes* (on which see below, pp. 122–3). Though he is in so many ways a backwoodsman, Habert stays fairly close to circles where new ideas are developing, witness his connections with the Jean de Brinon poets and also the Court, but his poetic forms remain resolutely in an older tradition.

Bonaventure des Périers

In considering these authors at some length, I have no intention of rescuing them from a deserved poetic oblivion; but they must be mentioned as a persistent element of the literary landscape, and their quantitative presence is abundant proof. On the other hand, they are not totally impervious to new trends, though this statement refers more to the thematic content. The fact that they no longer belonged to the centres of dynamic development – humanist circles and Court – except marginally or sporadically, may explain certain features in a Parmentier or a Roger de Collerye. Yet the obvious success of Jean Bouchet and François Habert shows that taste, beyond vanguard circles, was evolving, as one would expect, much more slowly. The influence of Marot impinges on some later poets of a conservative nature, but their capacity for self-renewal is limited. One curious feature is that several prose-writers, who belong in many respects to the vanguard of literary achievement, revert to *rhétoriqueur* idiom when they write poetry; two examples spring to mind. One is Rabelais who occasionally introduces a poem into his text, the other is Bonaventure des Périers, whose poetic output is quite substantial.[20] When he writes *Des roses*, developing the theme of 'Gather ye rosebuds while ye may', he becomes lost in word-play on *roses* and *rosée*:

> . . . Las! a peine sont nées
> Ces belles fleurs qu'elles sont ja fanées.
> . . . Vous donc, jeunes fillettes,
> Cueillez, bientost les roses vermeillettes
> A la rosée, ains que le temps lors vienne
> A desseicher; et tandis, vous souvienne
> Que ceste vie, à la mort exposée,
> Se passe ainsi que roses ou rosée. (Lacour ed., I, pp. 70–2)

He will describe Nature as if it were a *locus amœnus* of medieval inspiration, and he refers approvingly to 'le rosier de maistre Jean de Meung'. Word-play also occurs in a religious poem to Marguerite de Navarre, and even where evangelical inspiration is present, the verse remains flat and pedestrian:

> Quand premier ma rustique Muse
> Pleine de grand' legereté,
> Qui de nature ne s'amuse
> Volontiers qu'a joyeuseté . . .
> Mais c'estoit son intention
> De parler de la loy du Christ. (I, 156)

Simplicity may be required by the dictates of evangelical direction, and it is true that in his occasional satirical poems, some humanist elegance, movement, and incisiveness are evident, but his poetic key remains generally low.

III. NEO-LATIN POETRY[21]

Between the heyday of the *rhétoriqueurs* and the emergence of the Pléiade, Neo-latin poetry plays a substantial role on the literary scene. With the advent of a new wave of humanism, we find a number of poets who wish to break fresh ground in Latin composition. There are two features that deserve mention: on the one hand, the *renouveau poétique* of Salmon Macrin who in his *Carminum libellus* (1528) has abandoned the idiom he had adopted towards the end of the reign of Louis XII, in favour of lyric poetry, influenced by Horace, the Roman elegists, and the Italian humanist poets. During the 1530s, he publishes a large number of substantial volumes of verse, from the two books of *Lyrica* in 1530 down to the three books of Odes in 1540. His stock at this time is extremely high; he is appointed *cubicularius regius c.* 1533 and becomes the undisputed leader of French humanist poets. And on the other hand, a number of interesting humanists, slightly younger and trained in Paris during the 1520s, move out into the provinces, partly to carry out pedagogic reforms in various towns, partly because their religious outlook induced caution; many of them coalesce in Lyons during the years 1536–38, where Dolet for a brief spell succeeds in giving them a certain collective sense of unity, and they publish an impressive amount of poetry while they are connected with the town. These poets, including Macrin, are important on a number of counts. In the first place, they believe that French cultural supremacy over the Italians is to be achieved by means of Neo-latin poetry, and many of their epigrams reflect this concern (Macrin, Bourbon, Visagier, Sussannée, etc.). In the second place, they introduce a number of themes and thematic areas which will help to renew poetic inspiration; obviously, there are supporting influences, direct acquaintance with primary classical sources and derivative Italian works, but the Latin poetry produced in France enjoys a certain prestige. Macrin, in particular, develops Horatian themes that will catch on slightly later in the vernacular as the Pléiade moves into view: exploitation of Nature, local patriotism, the passage of time, but also themes associated with court activities. Macrin and several members of the Lyons *sodalitium* will provide embryonic love cycles, in which Petrarchan and Neo-catullan themes are developed; they also stress an aristocratic view of poetry and their strongly nationalist sentiments are similar to those we associate with the Pléiade. Third, these poets work in genres that will shortly be exploited in the vernacular; we have mentioned the love cycle, but there is also the ode, the epigram, the epitaph, the eclogue, the *xenium*, the elegy, the *basium*, the *votum*. And neo-classical drama is appearing in colleges, notably at the Collège de Guyenne, where Buchanan wrote his *Jephthes* and *Baptistes*, and where, it seems, Gentien Hervet translated his *Antigone*, published in 1541. Finally, one must point to the close relations that existed between these Neo-latins and vernacular writers whose contribution to French poetry is marked by humanist influence. Before Scève began to work on his *Délie* he was closely linked with members of the Lyons *sodalitium*, was admired by them as a Latin poet, and was later to use Neo-latin sources for his sequence. Marot was friendly with Macrin, he also was warmly defended by Jean Visagier, whose interest in the Martialian epigram (1536–38) corresponds with Marot's. Macrin was known to Ronsard, who began in Latin verse and must have known of the Neo-latin's contribution to the Latin ode, and also to Joachim du Bellay, who writes an ode to him; moreover, we can find echoes of Macrin's writings in the work of both these poets. And when the Pléiade is turning its attention to neo-classical drama, Buchanan will be teaching in Paris; some of his audience will work in the genre, and his *Jephthes*, published in 1554, will be reprinted three years later. These various points lend substance to the view that Neo-latin poetry acts as a sort of John the Baptist to the Pléiade and that the aspirations of the 1550 generation derive from the same humanist matrix as do those of the Neo-latins in the 1530s. Humanist poetry flourishes for a time in the middle of Francis I's reign, partly because humanist energy is directed into those channels and assumes a certain poetic coherence, but also because there is a generation gap in the vernacular between the major *rhétoriqueurs* and the Pléiade which even the dominating presence of Clément Marot does not fill completely; and in any case some of his achievement will be to prepare the ground for the Pléiade through his contacts with the humanist world.

IV. CLÉMENT MAROT (*c.* 1496–1544)[22]

Until fairly recently, Marot's standing in the eyes of posterity has been high, but the criteria that are now fashionable for poetic appraisal have worked against him, even if one makes allowance for the fact that the traditionally favourable assessment was itself onesided, in that it introduced an unnecessary Marot-Ronsard antithesis. In particular, the ascendancy of late sixteenth-century poetry has damaged Marot's reputation. Nevertheless, his place in the development of French poetry is unassailable, and his importance throughout the French Renaissance can hardly be overestimated. It is in great measure through him that the transition from the *rhétoriqueurs* to the Pléiade took place, but polemic and later achievements have

probably masked this. The approach to his poetry is hardly facilitated by the very complicated problems arising in connection with
various manuscript sources, editions, and attributions; and dates of
composition can often be exasperatingly vague.[23]

At the outset of his career, Marot stands firmly in the *rhétoriqueur*
tradition, partly because, like those writers, he is a court poet working in similar social conditions, partly because, through his father
and his admiration more especially for Jean Lemaire de Belges, he
continues in their path; it is also believed generally that he 'edited'
the *Roman de la Rose* in 1526. At all events, nearly all his compositions up to about 1526 belong to the tradition; and his translation
work (Vergil and Lucian) echoes an activity of the *rhétoriqueurs*. His
first substantial poem, the *Temple de Cupido*, written in 1515, when
he was page to Nicolas de Neufville, reveals him to be a fairly docile
disciple. Originally called the *Queste de ferme Amour*, it brings on
parade a series of allegorical figures to celebrate the marriage of
Francis, still duc d'Angoulême, and Claude de France; the use of
the *locus amœnus*, the catalogues of natural phenomena, and naturally the temple itself (with which is associated the vocabulary of the
Christian Church):

> De Requiem les messes sont aubades,
> Sierges, Rameaulx, & Sieges la verdure,
> Où les Amans font rondeaulx & ballades . . .
> (lines 383–5, *Œuvres lyriques*, C. A. Mayer, ed., p. 106)

all this, as well as the characteristic rhetoric of the tradition, even in
diluted form, light up its kinship. Written in stanzas of alternating
metre, the *Temple* is rather ill-constructed, with curious variations
in tone, ranging from high-flown passages to breezy reference; but
the text is more spacious than one might expect, one notes an interesting allusion to Petrarch and the theme of Cupid's two arrows, and
there is some rhythmic vitality here and there. Many of the early
poems reveal little originality, whether they be *complaintes, rondeaux,* or *chansons* or the *Epistre de Maguelonne*, based on a medieval romance and incomprehensible without previous knowledge of
the source. Marot also competes at the Rouen *puy* in 1521 with an
absurd *Chant Royal de la Conception;* he indulges in *rébus* and
riddle; and a *ballade De la naissance de feu Monsieur le daulphin
Françoys* (1517) gives us an idea of the progress Marot will make a
few years later:

> Quand Neptunus, puissant Dieu de la Mer,
> Cessa d'armer Carraques & gallées,
> Les Gallicans bien le deurent aymer
> Et reclamer ses grands undes sallées,
> Car il voulut en ces basses vallées
> Rendre la Mer de la Gaule haultaine

Calme & paisible ainsi qu'une fontaine;
Et, pour oster Mathelotz de souffrance,
Faire nager en ceste eau claire & saine. . . .
(lines 1–7, *Œuvres diverses*, C. A. Mayer ed., p. 149)

Here we have the triumph of hollow rhetoric, the studied production of meaninglessness, a pattern of ornate irrelevance, in which the nymphs, in spite of their legendary tendency to sea-sickness, take to the waves in the dauphin's (dolphin's) honour and quieten the storm. The early *epistres*, such as the *Petite Epistre au Roy* or the *Epistre du despourveu à ma Dame la Duchesse d'Alençon & de Berry, sœur unique du Roy* (*c.* 1519), betray the same dependence on tradition; so far, the circumstances of the Court, to which Marot had been appointed, only serve to maintain him in the *poncif*. In the early *ballades*, he appears more at ease, livelier when he is handling subjects linking him with the *Basoche*, such as the *Cry du Jeu de l'Empire d'Orléans*:

Laissez à part voz vineuses Tavernes,
Museaulx ardans, de rouge enluminez;
Renjeunissez, saillez de vos Cavernes,
Vieulx accropiz, par aage examinez. . . .
(lines 1–4, ibid., p. 140)

And perhaps in the *Epistre du camp d'Atigny* (*c.* July 1521), which is also a *rhétoriqueur* reportage of historical events, we can notice some rudiments of a poetic personality.

It is after 1526, to give an approximate date, that a change in Marot's writing becomes discernible. In the first place, the literary climate is altering, and the sharpening of religious issues has some impact on his development. In 1526 Marot was thrown into prison; the circumstances of his detention are still obscure, but from this time on, he was a marked man in the eyes of the Sorbonne. From the literary point of view, both personal destiny and humanist currents help to bring out his individuality, and the more or less rapid rejection of *rhétoriqueur* genres is matched by a new sensitivity to classical sources of inspiration. It is now that his gifts for satire come to the fore: *L'Enfer* is a powerful work, one of the most sustained from his pen, though it is somewhat disorganised and only in part satirical. Marot still continues old habits by his use of a classical framework with allegorical elements: instead of giving us portraits of the judges with whom he was involved, he evokes Rhadamanthus and Minos, throwing in an unsuccessful sketch of Cerberus for measure. The rejection of this source of realism may have reduced the efficacy of the satire, which comes off in the detail rather than in the overall structure. However, Marot soon shifts attention to himself, and his self-portrait is marked by a pleasing freshness of tone in the recall of youth; he also shows his ability to vary tones and insert some

dramatic movement. His remarks on religion are intentionally ambiguous and he disclaims any connection with Lutheranism, but he
also reproaches the Church for not preaching the Gospel with sufficient fervour, emphasises the fundamental wickedness of man, and
complains how little is done to counteract it.

Once satire enters his work, it stays.[24] It recurs in the epigrams,
which become frequent from precisely this period onwards, and
the early one on Semblançay's death is rightly famous.[25] During the
1530s, as we have seen, the epigram becomes a regular form of expression for the Neo-latin poets (who were sometimes writing them
earlier in their Paris colleges), and towards 1537, the Lyons *sodalitium* shows a liking for the Martialian formula. In more ways than
one Marot helps to introduce into the vernacular trends that were
already apparent in the Neo-latin domain. Boyssonné's charge that
'Marotus latine nescivit' may be well-founded, so far as the heights
of scholarship are concerned, but Marot, more than any other poet
of his generation, widens the spectrum of classical influence in
French poetry, by the range of genres he exploited as well as by the
themes he handled. Some of his earliest work involved translation
from Vergil; later he turned his mind to Ovid, and most important,
to the Psalms; he also rendered some epigrams from Martial and the
Histoire de Leander et Hero. Moreover, he was fully aware of the
benefits that might accrue from the Renaissance, and he associated
them closely with the elimination of ignorance and the enrichment
of learning:

> Et d'aultre part (dont nos jours sont heureux)
> Le beau verger des lettres plantureux
> Nous reproduict ses fleurs à grands jonchées
> Par cy devant flaistries & seichées
> Par le froid vent d'ignorance & de sa tourbe
> Qui hault sçavoir persecute & destourbe,
> Et qui de cueur est si dure ou si tendre
> Que verité ne veult ou peult entendre.
> O Roy heureux, soubs lequel sont entrés
> (Presque periz) les lettres & Lettrés.
>> (*L'Enfer* lines 367–76, *Œuvres satiriques,*
>> C. A. Mayer ed., p. 69)

In his epigrams, Marot explores a fairly wide range of themes;
as in the Neo-latins, we have anecdotic poems, satirical cameos, also
lighthearted love-poems in which Petrarchan elements are visible:

> *D'Anne qui luy jecta de la neige*
> Anne (par jeu) me jecta de la Neige,
> Que je cuidoys froide, certainement:
> Mais c'estoit feu, l'experience en ay je,
> Car embrasé je fuz soubdainement.
> Puis que le feu loge secretement
> Dedans la Neige, où trouveray je place

Pour n'ardre point? Anne, ta seule grace
Estaindre peult le feu que je sens bien,
Non poinct par Eau, par Neige ne par Glace,
Mais par sentir ung feu pareil au mien.
(Ep. xxiv, *Les Epigrammes*, C. A. Mayer ed., p. 115)

Here we have a Petrarchan conceit, with its antithesis and demonstrative colour, a good example of a genre that will run riot in volumes of minor verse before the Pléiade.[26] Sometimes Marot sketches out a *grivois* anecdote, common indeed in contemporary Neo-latin collections:

D'un Advocat jouant contre sa femme & de son clerc
Un advocat jouoit contre sa femme
Pour un baiser que nommer n'oserois.
Le jeu dit tant & si bien à la Dame
Que dessus luy gaigna des baisers troys.
'Or, ça, dit elle (amy); à ceste foys,
Jouons le tout pendant qu'estes assis.
– Quoy, respond il, le tout, ce seroient six?
Qui fourniroit à un si gros payement?
Alors son clerc de bon entendement
Luy dist, ayant de sa perte pitié;
'Ayez bon cueur, Monsieur, certainement
Je suys content d'en estre de moytié!
(Ep. ccli, ibid., pp. 301–2)

Here we have no doubt, a fusion of classical sources (Ausonius, Martial) with vestiges of the *conte* in this type of epigram, which can also be directed against *cordeliers* in their relations with women, lawyers, doctors; the satire may be slight, giving a touch of colour to the outline of a tale. Marot prefers the *huitain* and *dizain*, and once he finds his feet in the genre, the shorter *rhétoriqueur* forms tend to vanish; but tone and themes also show how far Marot and his contemporaries are moving from the older school. In the more satirical epigrams of his maturity, he is indebted not so much to Horace or Juvenal as to Martial, who helps to bring out a talent already well fledged some ten years earlier. Two subdivisions of the epigram may be mentioned here: the *étrennes*, which belong in the main to 1538 – though some appear to go back to 1531 – and therefore at a time when Marot was translating Martial and was on friendly relations with Jean Visagier, whose *Xenia* appears towards the same time. These are trifles, sometimes with a sting in the tail:

A Bye
Voz graces en faict & dict
Ont credit
De plaire, Dieu sçait combien:
Ceulx qui s'y congnoissent bien
Le m'ont dit.
(Etr. xxxiii, *Œuvres diverses*, p. 258)

And there is the epitaph; as a genre it is already common currency
with the *rhétoriqueurs*, but is richly exploited by the contemporary
Neo-latins, not only at the more exalted level of court ceremonial
(though here the *déploration* or eclogue may be the most appropriate form), but as a peg on which the author may hang his virtuosity and wit. There are variations in the form of address, the author
speaking in his own voice, or using the *débat* form, or the *prosopopœia* in which the deceased may deliver a posthumous speech either
to the traveller passing by or to a beloved relative still on earth, a
mode which allows for the development of some edifying *topos*. The
epitaph may concern imaginary characters, usually of comic quality,
it may be the occasion for word-play – and here the influence of
Ausonius, Martial, and the *Greek Anthology* is evident. In the hands
of some authors, the genre can virtually merge with the emblem or
the *icon* (by way of the *exemplum*). Marot himself ranges widely in
tone and theme; he may toss off an imaginary obituary at the expense of a monk:

> Cy gist Cordellier Semydieux,
> Dont ces vieilles fondent en larmes
> Pource qu'il les confessoyt mieulx
> Qu'Augustins, Jacobins ne Carmes.
> (Epitaphe xii, ibid., p. 200)

but he may also adopt the elevated style not normally associated
with him, as in the epitaph of Christophe de Longueil, a distinguished humanist who died young:

> O Viateur, cy dessoubz gist Longueil!
> A quoy tient il que ne meines long dueil
> Quand tu entends sa vie consommée?
> N'as tu encore entendu Renommée,
> Par les Climatz, qui son renom insigne
> Va publiant à voix, trompe & buccine?
> Si as pour vray: mais si grande est la gloire
> Qu'en as ouy, que tu ne le peulx croire.
> Va donc lire (pour en estre asseuré)
> Ses beaulx escriptz de stille mesuré:
> Lors seulement ne croiras son hault prix,
> Mais aprendras, tant sois tu bien appris.
> Si te sera son bruit tout veritable,
> Et la grandeur de ses faictz profitable.
> (Epitaphe ii, ibid., pp. 191–2)

Not vintage Marot, but interesting in that it shows how, when he
sings of a vanguard humanist in solemn tones, he reverts to *rhétoriqueur*, depersonalised idiom.

The epigram, then, reveals Marot's ability to vary key and also
his gifts for satire on a small scale. These talents appear in another
satirical genre, the *coq-à-l'âne*, of which Marot wrote four between

1530 and 1536. The origins of the genre are complex,[27] but Marot
seems to have been the chief force in establishing it in its own right,
though Eustorg de Beaulieu gives the appearance of having composed one slightly earlier. Sebillet defines the poem thus:

> ...et tu peus voir encor en ce Poëme, que nous avons descouvert puisnagueres:
> et l'ont ses premiers autheurs nommé, Coq à l'asne, pour la variété incon-
> stante des non coherens propos, que les François expriment par le proverbe
> du saut du Coq à l'asne. Sa matiere sont les vices de chacun, qui y sont
> repris librement par la suppression du nom de l'autheur (*sc.* des vices). Sa plus
> grande elegance est sa plus grande absurdité de suite de propos qui est
> augmentée par la ryme platte et les vers de huit syllabes. L'exemplaire en est
> chez Marot, premier inventeur des Coqs à l'asne, et premier en toutes sortes
> autheur d'iceus, si tu ne les veus recercher de plus loin. (F. Gaiffe ed.,
> pp. 167–8)

The *coq-à-l'âne* is recognisable by satirical intent and a wilful
disorder; we are presented with a kaleidoscope of words whose underlying pattern is not always too obvious; word-play, amusing associations, and serious purpose are all intertwined. The genre has been
traced, in some measure, to the *sottie* tradition and the *fatrasie*;
whatever the precise links, the genre corresponds in high degree to
the needs filled by these other genres in earlier times, and this type
of enigma-satire is all the more welcome in a period when ambiguity
of utterance has many advantages, and allows a writer sniping at
dangerous things to duck behind a parapet of apparent nonsense;
all this of course apart from the almost surrealist pleasure in seeing
what words will do, such as is often to the fore in Rabelais. Marot
renews tradition by presenting his *coq-à-l'âne* in epistolary form and
by injecting, it seems, something of the Lucianic spirit. At all events,
the edge of the satire is now sharper, with Marot violently attacking
persons unnamed, or commenting acidly on war *à propos* of the
invasion of Provence. The poems, with the exception of the third
(Venice, 1536), are marked by a verve and a quick-wittedness that
hold the reader's attention to the very end.

Marot's concern with the classics, so evident in the genres discussed
earlier, is patent in the elegies; the great majority are published in
1533 and naturally owe something to Ovid for the amatory inspiration, but in addition to classical sources, at a time when the Roman
elegists are making headway in France, Marot draws on *rhétoriqueur*
practice. Though on three occasions he tries to take the genre beyond
the confines of what Sebillet called the 'epistre amoureuse', these
elegies do not possess great literary interest:[28] the *topoi* are developed
without overmuch zest, the poet affirms the constancy of his love,
regrets that reality has not given substance to his dream; his mistress's radiance would save him the trouble of lighting his candle at
night, she and the month of May are one and the same, the lover is
disturbed by false rumours and by that perennial stage-property the

Envieux. All this is very conventional, nor does it make amends by any originality in the handling of language; moreover, Marot seems rather ill at ease in a genre whose tone demands tempos that are less than congenial. Historically speaking, the elegies help to establish the genre in French literature, and several of Marot's followers will try their hand at this type of composition which ceases to be a mere love elegy to become a medium for some range of personal expression.[29] Perhaps Marot handles amatory themes more successfully in the *chansons* of which the bulk were composed in the first years of his career; not because they are more 'sincere' or 'felt', but because they show up his qualities in a genre that does not require development or depth, but fancy, elegance, a sense of form, metrical agility, and liveliness, not to say naughtiness:

> Pourtant, si je suis Brunette,
> Amy, n'en prenez esmoy,
> Aultant suis ferme & jeunette
> Qu'une plus blanche que moy;
> Le Blanc effacer je voy.
>
> Couleur Noire est tousjours une;
> J'ayme mieulx donc estre Brune
> Avecques ma fermeté,
> Que Blanche comme la Lune
> Tenant de legiereté.
>
> (*Œuvres lyriques*,
> Mayer ed., pp. 202–3)

It is in the *epître* that Marot really finds his form.[30] This genre was practised by the *rhétoriqueurs*, who identified it with two features: love as its matter, decasyllables in *rimes plates* as its metrical structure; but Sebillet's definition, coming after Marot, shows in some degree what the latter had made of it:

L'epistre Françoise faite en vers, ha forme de missive envoyée à la personne absente, pour l'acertener ou autrement avertyr de ce tu veus qu'il sache, ou il desire entendre de toy, soit bien, soit mal: soit plaisir, soit desplaisir: soit amour, soit haine. Par ce moien tu discours en l'Epistre beaucoup de menues choses et de differentes sortes sans autre certitude de suget propre à l'Epistre. Et en un mot, l'Epistre Françoise n'est autre chose qu'une lettre missive mise en vers: comme tu peus voir aus Epistres d'Ovide tant Latines que Françoises: et aus Epistres de Marot, et autres telz famés Poëtes. (Gaiffe ed., pp. 153–4)

Sebillet in fact attempts to make the elegy a subdivision of the epistle, in that it is more restricted in subject, less concerned with trivia than with love, 'triste et flebile' in tone. Du Bellay, for his part, tended to see the *epistre* as familiar and therefore incapable of elevated development. Both genres, however, are said by Sebillet to be written normally in decasyllables with *rimes plates*, but some latitude is allowed for the metre of the epistle; Marot uses as well the trisyllable, the quadrisyllable, and the octosyllable.

Obviously the epistle is a genre in which the poet can do much as he pleases; he can be familiar or sustained, vary length, tone, and mood to his liking and according to the context. Marot may start by adopting some *rhétoriqueur* conventions, but he ends up by making it a vehicle of personal expression. This means a real reduction in metrical fireworks (though Marot will never be blind to possibilities in that direction), the elimination of allegorical elements, a closing of the gap between poetry and everyday life. Since most of the epistles concern the poet's personal circumstances and needs, the old routine devices are no longer valid and the poet must maintain the reader's interest in his affairs. The *Epistre à son Lyon Jamet*, the first in whch his real voice can be heard, still shows a Marot dependent to some extent on tradition. The start, for instance,

> Je ne t'escry de l'amour vaine & folle,
> Tu voys assez s'elle sert ou affolle;
> Je ne t'escry ne d'Armes ne de Guerre,
> Tu voys qui peult bien ou mal y acquerre ...
> (Epît. x, *Les Epîtres*, C. A. Mayer ed., p. 127)

and so on for twelve lines, opens on the *topos* of negative intention, used later by Du Bellay in his *Regretz*, and therefore of enumeration. Marot also has recourse to allegory in the form of the fable; but he soon gets into his stride, revealing a gift for story-telling, an eye for the characteristic gesture, and a smart sense of rhythm. There is an engaging use of familiar language and effective passing reference of satiric intent; and the poem as a whole is given a satisfying balance of proportions. In the *Epistre au Roy* (xi), seeking release from prison, Marot shows full mastery of his idiom; narrative and tempo are governed with a sure hand, and he displays a telling wit. He is able to see a situation from all angles, so that the narrative, in addition to its sequence of events, acquires a further dimension of movement. Marot has mastered the art of seeing himself, as it were, from outside; he is both actor and spectator. In this we may detect elements of the traditional dramatic monologue finding their way into the epistle, but Marot has developed the role of the fool or clown, which allows for entertainment, but also for ambiguity, for a successful blend of involvement and detachment, though deep emotional commitment is rare before the period of exile and a closer acquaintance with Ovid's Euxine poems induce a broader maturation of his art – even so, certain passages in the *Epistre au Roy pour avoir esté desrobé* (xxv) seem to go deeper than usual. In this framework, Marot brings to the surface a feeling for the revelatory trait, sometimes a nice sense of caricature, an ability to develop irony through verbal gymnastics. In all this he creates a judicious blend of the ridiculous and the fanciful, but also of parody and caricature. Above all, he is sharply sensitive to the reactions of the addressee, hence the impression he sometimes gives of the barrister-at-play or indeed of the journalist. Where he has a cause to defend, he works not so much through the inner coherence of his argument as upon the feelings of his listener or reader.

Marot's success depends, in the last analysis, greatly on his handling of language; and here he had to divest himself of the monotony of tone and the too-static rhythms that characterise certain forms of the *rhétoriqueur* tradition. He turns in part to a more popular current – the pupil of Villon has not forgotten the master's lessons – and he seeks to narrow the interval between life and letters. He often gives the feeling that you are being spoken to, that you are in the presence of a cheerful Ancient Mariner. He also possesses a love of words for their own sake, and this quality makes one think of Rabelais on occasion:

> J'avois ung jour Valet de Gascogne,
> Gourmand, Yvroigne, & asseuré Menteur,
> Pipeur, Larron, Jureur, Blasphemateur,
> Sentant la Hart de cent pas à la ronde,
> Au demeurant le meilleur fils du monde,
> Prisé, loué, fort estimé des Filles
> Par les Bordeaulx, & beau joueur de Quilles . . .
> (Epît. xxv, ibid., pp. 171–2)

where enumeration, mixture of levels, and ambiguities play their part. The Pléiade were to reproach Marot for the nature of his success which they saw as a failure to construct a genuinely poetic language different from everyday speech. It is also true that his poetry has fewer images of high quality than any other poet of standing in the century. He writes with his eye on his audience, he is more concerned with what its members think than his own inmost feelings; he often depends on the outside world for stimulus, and this world is essentially human, for though he occasionally manifests a sense of Nature (especially when youthful memories are involved),[31] his muse is essentially urban. His poetry therefore gives an impression of intelligence and alertness, but rarely of depth.

It would nevertheless be unfair to picture Clément Marot as nothing more than a buffoon, a Till Eulenspiegel; there are poems where strong feelings come to the surface, particularly on religious matters. We may take a very long time to discern the outline of his religious evolution – we are ill informed about the crucial years 1528–33, and in addition, though there are naturally constants in Marot's world-picture, it must also be recognised that, chameleon-like, he is very sensitive to the colour of the milieu in which he happens to be. At all events, he was certainly thought to harbour heretical views by contemporaries of various religious beliefs. He is harsh in his criticism of the Church, he has provocative things to say on the subject of monasticism, he certainly had evangelical leanings at different periods of his life. The *Deploration de Florimond Robertet,* in its original text of 1527, was strongly evangelical in its attitude to justification by faith and to the questions of purgatory and predestination. Twenty-five years or so in the neighbourhood of Marguerite de Navarre's entourage must have left some mark upon him. His attacks on the Pope may go beyond the limits of orthodox outcry, and his observations on the Mass and justification by works may have raised eyebrows, perhaps too his silences might connect him with evangelicals in the eyes of some. He certainly hoped for a more inward religion; he also spoke up for freedom of speech and of reading, he advocated greater toleration, and he was a lone opponent of judicial torture. And if his views coincided with neither Lutheranism nor Calvinism, he had to leave his country twice because of ecclesiastical opposition.[32] Nevertheless, whatever the final word may be on his religious convictions, one must admit that when he turns to serious thoughts in his poetry, Marot loses some of his characteristic qualities. He seems at his best in certain forms of the epigram or in those epistles where he interposes a *persona* between himself and his audience. When he speaks in his own right, tempo, language, and tones may be sacrificed. At deeper levels, the inner life, as it manifests itself in his poetry, seems to lack the required vitality; Marguerite de Navarre, by contrast, even though she does not re-create poetic form, manages to overcome certain limitations by the sheer sustained force of her feeling. In Marot this rarely occurs; he is at his best, more often than not, when stimulus comes from without. This may be one reason why he achieves comparative success with his psalm paraphrases, composed between 1533 and 1543 but never completed.[33] In this activity, he was probably encouraged by his links with Marguerite's circle and of course he had, as a given starting-point, the sacred text. Recent research has detected a considerable fidelity to the original text (chiefly through the intermediary of Olivetan), with its strongly set articulations. The relative simplicity of his rhetoric bridges the religious desiderata of evangelical paraphrase and the more vital aspects of his own poetic imagination – here, as in the *chansons*, some formal characteristics may be determined in part by the needs of musical accompaniment. Marot's mastery of language is confined to certain bands of experience and is as it were rectilinear rather than complex and imagic. He often comes into his own when a certain self-consciousness, that can be dramatised, coloured by irony and switch of standpoint, asserts its presence.

Nevertheless, Marot's historical importance as a transitional figure, particularly in the matter of form, is incontrovertible. It is he who takes poetry beyond the limits in which the *rhétoriqueurs* worked, by exploring new genres whose origins go back to the classi-

cal world, by experimenting in new metrical patterns, by a widening
of thematic range, and finally by injecting life and movement into
the poetic line. Before the Pléiade he sensed the need for renewal
through fresh contacts with classical authors, he also contributed in
modest fashion to the acclimatisation of Petrarchan conventions. He
worked in *terza rima*, developed the resources of the decasyllable,
and by his search for metrical variety in the Psalms he can be said to
anticipate the Pléiade's use of the ode. He was one of the first
Frenchmen to write a sonnet, though claims have been advanced for
the priority of Mellin de Saint-Gellais and also Jean Bouchet.
Poetic language in his hands becomes more supple, more responsive,
more dynamic, even though it lacks resonance and complexity. The
extraordinary success of the *Adolescence Clementine* reflects contemporary urges towards a new type of poetry,[34] and this success persists throughout the century, in spite of Pléiade opposition; significantly Marot and Ronsard are the two poets who are most frequently
set to music and translated into Latin verse. There are, of course,
limitations of sensibility, and Marot, coming earlier, will not achieve
the linguistic mastery of a Ronsard; but his poetic qualities were
such that they often allowed later generations to rank him above
Ronsard and as one representative of the Gallic muse. The formula
devised by Boileau ('élégant badinage') may do Marot less than
justice; ironically, it helped to keep his reputation afloat, whereas
poets such as Scève, D'Aubigné, Sponde had to wait for the aftermath of Symbolism before their true stature was understood.

V. THE QUERELLE DES AMYES — NEOPLATONISM — AULIC AND ANTI-AULIC THEMES

In the early 1540s a number of poems were composed around the
theme of the *Amye de court*. The success of this *querelle* may be
judged, not only from several editions of Antoine Héroët's works –
six editions within two years – but also by the appearance of editions
that included the main compositions in question: most of them
followed the translation of Guevara's *Mespris de la court* (1544,
1545, 1546), but this work is not contained in the 1547 edition of
the *Opuscules d'amour*; on the other hand, the original compilation
went through another five editions before 1568. All this makes it an
outstanding best-seller, and the reasons for this merit some attention.
Several strands are involved: in the first place, it is necessary to distinguish the *querelle des femmes* from the *querelle des amyes*.[35] The
former is, of course, nothing new, having roots well developed in the
Middle Ages, and the pros and cons of woman's estate are discussed
frequently by the *rhétoriqueurs*: woman is seen as inferior to man

both on physiological and on theological grounds, but defenders also come to her rescue. In the 1530s, the *querelle* comes to the surface again: no doubt, the increasing presence of women at Court has something to do with it; we are also in a period when Petrarchism is making headway. The anti-feminist position may be associated with anti-humanist obscurantism; it did not escape the notice of contemporaries that the ardent anti-feminist Gratien du Pont was also a cultural backwoodsman.[36] As early as 1537 Almanque Papillon had published his *Victoire et triumphe d'Argent contre Cupido*,[37] and Charles Fontaine had replied in the form of a *débat* concluded by a judicial decision. Then in 1537 and 1538, there appeared two translations of Castiglione's *Courtier*, which had been printed in Italian in 1528. It aroused a great deal of interest in France, not only for the topics it raised, but also because the work's origins were associated in some measure with Francis I when he was still duc d'Angoulême. Moreover, it provided a theoretical correlative of the Court as it was developing in France at that time. It offered a portrait of the ideal courtier: it had much to say on his training, developed important ideas on the relations between Courtier and Prince, and also devoted a lot of space to the presence of ladies at Court. It introduced much else *chemin faisant*: it offered a code of behaviour based on the relations between reason and the passions, it emphasised the value of letters and of music, it supported the criterion of *usage* in behaviour and in language – and discussions of these points allow observations on the advantages of the vernacular and on the nature of the comic seen as an awareness of incongruity. The active and the contemplative lives are also subjected to scrutiny; but above all it gave the reader a very convenient formulation of Platonic love: it provided a psychological infrastructure, and stressed the connection between love and beauty as well as goodness. Other Platonic themes – man as the microcosm, the theory of the two loves, the body as an earthly prison – these and more were introduced into a text whose form of presentation was an urbane dialogue. In other words, this accessible text plays a by no means negligible part in the diffusion of Platonic ideas; this aspect and the praise of the courtly life become substantial themes of the *querelle des amyes*. Not so very long after, the counter-theme finds a defender in Antonio de Guevara's *El menosprecio de corte*, a work that enjoys an immense vogue in France, exercises considerable influence upon La Taille and Montaigne, and brings grist to the mill of the enemies of the *amye*.

The *querelle*[38] is opened by La Borderie in 1542, when he publishes his notorious *Amye de court*, which not only tilted at the placing of woman upon a pedestal – cleverly argued with a woman as mouthpiece – but also drew upon the pro-aulic tradition:

J'estime là mon trophée & ma gloire,
De pouvoir vaincre estant femme mortelle,
Par artifice une deité telle . . .
(1547 ed. of *Opuscules*, p. 112)

The lady finds safety in numbers and, without sacrificing her virtue, is happy to use her charms to increase her worldly possessions at the expense of wealthy persons and others at Court. Love in fact should and can be resisted by *Honneur, Dissimulation*, and so forth. The poem is not simply anti-petrarchan, it is the assertion of security values: beauty lasts but a short while and honour, once lost, cannot be regained. Therefore love should be subordinated to marriage, though the lady naturally hopes to have the best of both worlds, by marrying the ideal husband as well as making the safe marriage: The *amye* takes delight in dominating men, but there is also a curious theological side to her arguments: though the body is corrupt, the spirit, nearer to God, can inhibit the prompting of the flesh. The poem ends on an invocation to 'O bienheureuse, — vraye Amour future'.

La Borderie's poem naturally drew fire, with two writers providing rejoinders – Antoine Héroët and Charles Fontaine. Héroët's composition *La Parfaicte Amye* is the most impressive poem thrown up by the *querelle*; it also raises the issue of Neoplatonic penetration into France at this time.

Neoplatonism[39]

Neoplatonism can be detected here and there throughout the century, but it comes to the surface at literary level in two main waves, first in the entourage of Marguerite de Navarre, and second in the works of certain members of the Pléiade; both these 'moments' are in some measure linked together. Broadly speaking, Neoplatonism is associated with the work of Marsilio Ficino, the Florentine humanist who tried to harmonise Platonism and Christianity and whose commentaries no doubt had more direct and indirect influence than the writings of Plato himself. Ficino, as we have seen, had had contacts with French humanists of an earlier generation; some of his works were translated before 1500, his *De religione christiana* was printed in Paris and possibly Lyons in 1510, and he may have been studied in some Paris colleges. A step forward was taken by Lefèvre d'Etaples who had some role in introducing Ficino's works to Marguerite de Navarre and the Groupe de Meaux. Translations of Plato's dialogues take time to appear in print, but they are often inspired by Marguerite; texts begin to come out from 1533 on: *Charmides* (1533), *Phaedo* (1536), *Io* 1546), *Crito* (1547). Individual texts had appeared in Greek in Paris from 1529 onwards, and one must not forget that ancient Neoplatonists were also attracting interest. In

addition to serious works of scholarship, there were the various
Italian treatises on Platonic love, which were becoming widely read
in France, sometimes in the original, more often in translation:
Castiglione's *Courtier*, Leone Ebreo's *Dialoghi d'Amore* (translated
1551), Bembo's *Asolani* (translated 1545 by Jean Martin and reprinted 1553, 1576). Ficino's writings appear in French print during
the 1540s and 1550s more especially. Finally, some Platonic strands
become wound up with Petrarchan themes, though the two currents,
carried to their logical conclusion, must diverge; indeed some writers,
like Héroët, whose verse *Androgyne* is based on the *Symposium*,
were careful to distinguish the two.

The immense success of Neoplatonism, however loose its definition, is very understandable. At philosophical and religious level, it
offered something that many found lacking in the aristotelian tradition: it accorded proper importance to feeling, it harmonised with
a number of evangelical concerns and in some cases with mystical
leanings, and it may have been understood by some as granting a
larger role to free-will in man, who could thereby contribute effectively to his own salvation. In other words, it appealed strongly to the
spirituality of the period. It may also have added a few elements to
the cosmology of the century (e.g., the Great Chain of Being); but
there were inevitably points on which the Christian and the Platonic
outlooks could not be reconciled (e.g., metempsychosis, pre-existent
memory). In the first period under review, it also colours philosophical or religious poetry.

At the same time, Neoplatonism, by its special doctrine of love,
enriches the themes of poetry that develop after, say, 1540 and
often in the entourage of Marguerite de Navarre. To some extent
it blends with Petrarchism,[40] and Neoplatonic themes will persist
in love-poetry throughout the period. And finally, by the special
place it allows to poetry in the structure of things, it appeals to
writers anxious to improve the status of poetry in the eyes of the
public. Nevertheless, these ideas, promoted by the translation of
the *Io* in 1546 do not acquire full momentum until the appearance
of the Pléiade, though the theory of poetic fury is by no means a
newcomer to the scene.

Antoine Héroët (?1492-1568)[41]

A number of essential Platonic themes are stated in Héroët's *La
Parfaicte Amye* (1542). Very little is known of his early life, but a
distich from his pen is printed *c.* 1514, and he may well have been
associated then in Paris with scholars who had some knowledge of
Greek. Héroët, later to become bishop of Digne, had already adapted
Platonic texts on the *Androgyne*; he was familiar with certain
Ficinian writings, and in his chief composition his Neoplatonic out-

look leads him to take issue with La Borderie's *Amye de court*. He himself eschews literary embellishment:

> PARFECTION d'amour sera mon livre
> Intitulé: pour lequel accomplir
> Il n'est besoing de fables le remplir;
> D'inventions poëtiques je n'use,
> En invocquant ou Erato la Muse
> Ou Apollo. . . .
>
> (I, 22–7)

He claims no interest in mythological origins, but is concerned with single love, which is perfect and lasting, unaffected by time or old age, existing for itself and not for ulterior motive. This love, coming from heaven, is mutual between two partners and helps them to find themselves in each other; perfect love also casts out fear. It does not seek to bruit itself abroad (Héroët, like the Petrarchans, shuns 'la vulgaire et sotte multitude'); and space is given over to the woman who platonically loves outside marriage:

> Puis que l'amy, qui l'esperit possede,
> Corps et beaulté de moy s'amye cede
> A qui n'en chault, à qui mal s'en acquicte
> (I, 357–9)

a theme which recurs in the *Délie*. The lover will find 'tout ce qu'il veult' through her, whose perfection comes from him:

> Sans vraye amour, sans foy, et sans sçavoir,
> Rien ne se peult attaindre n'y avoir.
> (I, 493–4)

When two souls, which knew each other previously in heaven, meet again in 'corps propices', they experience perfect love. Héroët here touches upon the subject of the androgyne, due to recur later. The first book of the poem is somewhat disjointed: this derives in part from the fact that he wishes to refute certain points raised in the *Amye de court*, but this is also the book in which he relies most heavily upon the *Courtier*. In the remaining two books, the poet concerns himself much more closely with various Platonic doctrines; he traces in greater detail the theme of the immortality of the soul and also the manner in which love creates beauty in woman and leads us to a perfect knowledge of God. The beauty of the body anticipates the 'bonté' of the soul; our earthly life is a 'prison mondaine', but love gives us the 'souvenance' of the original spirit. In this second book, Héroët allows himself some excursions in which, among other things, he asserts his distance from classical wisdom and perhaps stresses his orthodoxy. He attacks the Stoics for their wrong attitude to life and death, he criticises the Epicureans for their deistic interpretation of the Universe, and finally he treats himself to a dig at the Calvinists for their views of the soul in its passage between life and resurrection. He includes an interesting passage on the Blessed Isles, which could have well have been read by Ronsard, a warm admirer of Héroët. Book III which, of the three, is perhaps closest to the original Platonic text (*Symposium*), justifies the existence of love upon earth; it ensures the continuity of the human species, it gives a relative happiness here below (Héroët is careful to affirm that life is essentially ugly, a pale shadow of the real thing), it reduces the forces of ignorance – though here again, real knowledge is beyond the world, and all we can aspire to is awareness of our ignorance. Héroët also discusses the relations between spiritual beauty and health, even if he gets tied up in discussing the possible illness of the loved one for reasons that are far from clear or at least creditable.

However, Héroët recognises that he is painting an ideal: only a few can know this love upon earth. His poem is a fairly comprehensive treatise on love, written in a spare style that makes few concessions to literary ornament — a rare image, some ternary movement, and exclamations — but he remains nearer to Marguerite de Navarre than to what we shall find a bit later in Pléiade times. Just occasionally, some colour filters into his verse, usually when he turns his gaze outwards and has some dry comments to make on attitudes foreign to that of the *parfaicte amye*, as for instance when he attacks Petrarchism, but this does not add up, aesthetically, to very much. What impresses is the dignity and sincerity of the line. However, it must not be forgotten that Héroët is not simply writing a didactic poem, for the subject-matter is presented through the mind of a woman who loves, beyond marriage, a man who is dead. She is trying to find the correlation of her emotions with the Platonic ideas her lover had taught her; but she confesses to some misunderstandings, and there is some interval between what one may call the 'doctrine' and her love which is centred on the man who is therefore not just a gateway to higher spirituality, though such themes are undoubtedly 'stated' in the text; and one wonders to what extent this counterpoint was grasped by contemporaries.

Further developments

The other rejoinder to La Borderie was Charles Fontaine's *Contr'amye de court* (1543). This poet, as we have seen, had already entered the lists against Almanque Papillon; he was connected with the Lyons *sodalitium*, had undertaken the *voyage d'Italie*, and had become increasingly attracted to Platonism. His *contr'amye* in fact draws extensively on the *Symposium* and the *Phaedrus* as well as on Ficinian sources, in order to refute La Borderie. She, the daughter of a merchant – an anti-aulic touch – has made love, so intensely praised by her father, the centre of her life. It is love that makes the Universe go round, it harmonises the elements in man, it has strong ties with virtue; it is disinterested, but plays a great part in creating arts and sciences; it rejects dissimulation; and finally, it is, not the consequence of gold, but 'la fruition de la beauté'. This last point allows Fontaine to introduce the *topos* of poverty and happiness, to which must be added the important association of love with marriage – rare in poetry at the time, except in Salmon Macrin. This summary shows that the poem is markedly didactic in flavour, and indeed many of the compositions associated with the *querelle* barely stretch beyond versified prose, with little concern for poetic quality. Nevertheless, these poems commanded some attention: thus Paul Angier in his *L'experience* (1544) came to the defence of the *Amye de court*, suggesting that Fontaine had misunderstood the lady whose life is governed surely by godliness and not cupidity; moreover, *folle amour* is something that goes against reason and orderly living. For all that, his refined *Honneste amant* is hardly the answer to the *amye*'s prayer for a rich fool of a husband, and Angier has to distort Fontaine's conception of love to advance his own defence of love in marriage which has religious overtones. Additional material was included in subsequent editions: the *Accroissement d'Amour* is printed in 1545, and in the following year Almanque Papillon's *Le nouvel amour* – a story about Jupiter ordering the disputing Venus and Cupid to join forces again in the interests of humanity. Venus represents more passionate love, Cupid a less sensual feeling that should be confined to one woman. Papillon's solution is therefore one of refined realism from which emotion is not excluded; his poem is furthermore a vehicle for courtly flattery of Francis I. In 1547, the *Opuscules* contained another poem, La Borderie's *Discours du voyage de Constantinople*, allegedly sent by the author to his *amyes* left in France; the travel sections and the love themes do not mingle very happily, and there is a further inflation of patriotic fervour. The text does contain some passages of interest as reportage, but the work has only a tenuous link with the other *opuscules*.

The *querelle* encouraged other authors to contribute. In 1545 Antoine du Moulin published a volume which, in addition to developing the *rhétoriqueur* theme of the 'Dames de Paris', offered a pleasant satire of Héroët (*L'Amante loyalle qui depuis a esté variable*): the lady has striven to put the theories of the *parfaicte amye* into practice, but after a period of frustration, discovers that the *Amye de court* takes a more realistic view of things – a playful *bluette* by the man who in the same year was writing the preface to Pernette du Guillet's poems.

A year later, Gilles d'Aurigny published his *Tuteur d'Amour* (BM, BN). A minor figure who tends to work like a parasite on others – he contributes to the edition of Martial d'Auvergne's *Arrests d'Amours*, adapts Erasmus to monarchist ends in his edition of the *Institution du Prince*, dabbles in religious verse, if we accept the rumour that he composed thirty psalm paraphrases – D'Aurigny is, as we have suggested, a late *rhétoriqueur*. His 1546 volume works chiefly in traditional forms, but he wished to play some part in the *querelle*, as Claude Colet's liminary *dizain* tells us:

> Tous ceulx qui ont veu la parfaicte amye,
> Peuvent iuger estre un œuvre parfaict,
> L'amye aussi de cour non endormye,
> Merite un bien grand louenge en effect:
> La contr'amye est un œuvre bien faict,
> Et le nouvel amour semblablement.
> Brief tous ceulx la ont escript haultement:
> De Cupido & de Venus aussi,
> Mais si d'iceulx as tu contentement,
> Moins n'en auras en lisant cestuy cy.

So many had talked of the miseries of love that Gilles felt it necessary to take measures:

> Et pensoy lors combien grande seroit
> L'utilité qui l'amour dompteroit.

There follows a lengthy poem, compounded of mythological figures from pagan antiquity, late-medieval romance castles, and at the end Petrarchan themes, to describe how the poet tries to capture Cupid who takes his revenge by making him lovesick. The mythological court *débat* of the *Nouvel Amour* may have suggested the framework of Gilles's composition. He apologises for not having dealt with Cupid's revenge on the gods who had been accomplices in his temporary captivity. The poem, inevitably, adds up to very little in the context of the *querelle*, but in the following poems, Gilles defines his view of love:

> I'ay arresté que ce n'est autre chose
> Qu'une vertu, qui se tient ferme & close
> Entre deux cœurs, d'une façon si haulte,
> Qu'on n'y peult veoir seulement une faute.

and he links love with marriage in a poem about a nobleman's grief for his dead wife who was

> . . . . l'estincelle
> De vray amour & d'honneste courage,
> Tout procedant de noble mariage.

This theme is to be found also in François Habert's *Nouvelle Venus* (1547); we have seen some of his other work in which he attacks *folle amour* and warns against the promptings of the flesh (see above, p. 101). In 1547 his stance has not altered, except that he stresses the need for love to be closely connected with marriage and to be understood in a biblical context. This is of course a theme that is acquiring relevance in the developing religious atmosphere.

In the same year there appeared the charming *Compte du Rossignol*,[42] usually attributed to Gilles Corrozet, whose *Blasons Domestiques* have their niche in the history of descriptive poetry. Here the tale owes something to Caviceo's *Peregrino*: the lover seeks satisfaction of his mistress, but she tells him first to study and adds that she will gratify his wish when he has solved the riddle of the mating lark. When, with the help of an old woman, he does so, the lady points the moral of the lark, namely that satisfied love loses its savour and price:

> Puis, tout ainsi qu'un homme qui travaille
> Par un vain songe et du dormir s'esveille,
> Il commença premier à se mouvoir
> Et l'amour fol, lequel souloit avoir,
> S'esvanouit comme un songe menteur;
> Puis, l'amour saint, de tant de biens autheur,
> Entra chez luy, avecques fermeté
> De non tenter jamais la chasteté
> De telle dame, à laquelle il voua
> Le chaste amour, et elle l'avoua . . .
> (Montaiglon, VIII, 73)

Yolande, who wishes to 'changer l'amour en amytié honneste', affirms the power of reason and will over the passions, and points to the links between learning and love. Some Neoplatonism may have brushed off on to her, but much of the tale, with its *rhétoriqueur* allegories, belongs still to a medieval world. What raises the poem above the average is a gift for lively narrative within the older mode.

The *querelle* is interesting, first because of its ability to induce authors of various temperament and attitude to contribute, second because it brings to articulate discussion, not only problems concerning the nature of love, but also Neoplatonic and religious themes as well as topics that centre on the Court. From a strictly literary point of view, these poets are conservative and draw extensively on the *art de seconde rhétorique*; thematically they attract attention for nearly ten years. It may be that the *querelle* began as a theme with variations among friends or colleagues; nevertheless, it succeeds in touching on a number of topics that shed much light on the sensibility of these years preceding the Pléiade.

Philibert de Vienne

To conclude this section, a word would be appropriate on a prose text which nevertheless belongs to the same period and climate of thought. *The Philosophe de Court*, written by Philibert de Vienne, came out in 1543.[43] It owes something to Castiglione, though no direct reference is made to the *Courtier*, and is also inspired by Cicero, whose *decorum naturale* is advanced as one standard of behaviour. The prologue is addressed to the *Amye de Vertu* (another sign of affiliation), and the case for the courtly way of life is set out in a fairly systematic manner as a result of discussions held in the previous year. It is, however, this reasonableness of presentation which heightens the fundamentally satiric intent of the book. We are told that man must not live in an ivory tower, that he must make himself useful to others, that we must distinguish between primitive nature, basically good, and our secondary nature, debased and likely to warp our judgement. We are also informed, with quotations from the classical world, that virtue must be valued for itself. Then the devil shows his hoof: the only way to correct our secondary nature is to follow 'la mode de court'. Honour is our reward and glory; 'L'honneur & la reputation sont la fin de nostre vertu, sans lesquelz nostre vertu ne seroit rien'. We must dissemble, if this will help us to please others better, and we shall follow the style of each Court, since each milieu develops its own *mores*. Four virtues will propel us towards this end: prudence, justice, magnanimity, temperance, which last prevents us from lapsing into excess or vice, for virtue is, in the last analysis, the *via media* between two vices. On the road, the author pokes much fun at the scholar and pedant, and his satirical outlook comes through his academic presentation of the argument. To this may be added digs at astrologers and Christian fundamentalists, and some clever satiric portraits are etched. Tongue in cheek, the author touches on many topics that will acquire currency: glory, know thyself, appearance and reality, nature. What is original is the technique; it is of course our old friend the paradox – a technique that is well developed in Erasmus and in Rabelais, but will also acquire momentum from Italy. Philibert does not adopt a rumbustious tone – though he refers to Jean des Sentonneures (*sic*); he exploits dead-pan presentation, and very effective it is too, and the book ends on the observation that 'La vraye Philosophie est le mespris et contemnement de Philosophie'. He shows a neat ironic sense in the way he presses four genuine virtues into dubious service; in spite of the scholastic division into subsections and of the academic paraphernalia, they become somewhat warped. The book is a satire on the scholar as well as on the courtier; it is also an excellent illustration of the way in which the French Renaissance adopts a complex attitude to values and themes which form part and parcel of that Renaissance.

VI. MARGUERITE DE NAVARRE[44]

At first blush, Marguerite's poetry might seem to have little to catch the eye of the modern reader; its thematic range is relatively narrow, and apart from a few 'profane' poems like *La Coche*, which offers a fascinating blend of courtly and Neoplatonic love themes in a medieval *débat*, she tends to confine herself to religious poetry, and within that framework to a restricted number of topics. In her choice of genres and her use of allegory she looks back to the Middle Ages, though she may allow herself some technical experiments (as, for instance, in the *terza rima* and the alexandrine); and her poetic language is often characterised by a flat fluidity, uninterrupted by linguistic initiative, rhetorical virtuosity, or rhythmic flair. Yet to leave it at that would be extremely unfair; it is true that she shows little search for literary effect, any more than does Héroët, but we shall find more variety than might appear immediately, there is some range in metrical practice, and above all, when religious inspiration is upon her, her verse acquires an incandescent quality that is rarely matched elsewhere in French Renaissance poetry. Undoubtedly her poetic activity has been underestimated; and of course, if we except the vestigial composition of the *puys* and *palinods* and on the other hand the efforts of the Neo-latin poets to write religious verse, there is really rather little work being done in this field under Francis I. This is partly to be explained by the fact that religious poetry might well be inspired by the new evangelical currents, and if so, two alternative consequences would result: either the poets might restrict themselves to the Neo-latin medium (Salmon Macrin, Nicolas Bourbon, Jean Visagier in more modest measure), or poets writing in the vernacular might be reluctant to publish. This is certainly the case with Charles Fontaine; and it is equally true that Marguerite's poems were only printed in part during her lifetime. She seems to have written poetry throughout the greater part of her maturity: her *Miroir de l'âme pecheresse*, printed in 1531, condemned by the Sorbonne in 1533, also translated by young Elizabeth of England, was her first publication; then, after some sporadic printing of poems, a more substantial collection appeared in the *Marguerites de la Marguerite* (1547), followed by the *Suyte*. But the *Prisons* and the *Navire*, among others, were to lie in manuscript until Abel Lefranc turned his attention to them; and in the last few years scholars have been providing a welcome number of critical editions.

Marguerite is in fact one of the few poets of that period able to sustain her theme in extended fashion, and the qualities that pierce through in the *Heptaméron* – descriptive power, narrative momentum, lightness of touch – come to her help in the writing of verse too.

The essential theme, as in the *Heptaméron*, is love, but the accent here is on the religious. The comparison between sacred and profane love recurs in her writings: in *La Mort et resurrection d'Amour*, in *La Coche* (where the different attitudes are reflected in metrical variety), and also in the *Distinction du vray Amour*, a series of *dizains* where one sees the Petrarchan idiom, admittedly very dilute, recruited in a higher service:

> Amour, remply de pitié et de zelle,
> D'amour mourant toucha la legiere aille,
> Et l'arracha du corps trop tendre et beau:
> La trousse print, et ses trectz avec elle,
> L'arc impiteux et la corde cruelle,
> Aussi l'espais et ignorant bandeau;
> Le tout il mit en ung feu si nouveau
> Que leur chaleur [il] convertit en glace;
> Sans oublier de Venus le flambeau,
> Dont ce sainct feu toute navrure efface.
>
> (Lefranc ed., 301–2)

But Marguerite also writes *chansons spirituelles* and poems which are essentially devotional – various *oraisons* in which a well-known genre is directed towards evangelical meditation. In these poems, one can detect the disciple of Lefèvre d'Etaples and Guillaume Briçonnet, who was her confessor for a time in the 1520s, and stressed the striving of the soul towards spiritual fulfilment. If one or two early compositions indicate Lutheran influence, the later ones show a wider spectrum of inspiration enriched by her evangelical contacts, her interest in Neoplatonism, and her reading of mystical writers; themes such as the following come to the surface: man's miserable state in the world, Christ's redeeming role, man's reunion with spiritual perfection through certain mystical processes. Marguerite lays more emphasis on the good and the beautiful; the themes of hell and punishment hold little appeal for her.

The *summa* of her poetic activity is undoubtedly the *Prisons*, which develop majestically like some river from a modest source. The poem is divided into three books, each one considerably longer than its predecessor. The overall structure is comparatively simple, for we are shown the stages in its pilgrimage of the human soul through its prisons, three in number: earthly love, ambition, and learning. This quasi-epic structure is not new in her poetry: the manuscript *Petit œuvre devot et contemplatif* belongs to a similar type. On to this trellis Marguerite weaves an ever increasingly complex foliage of themes, and in this poem one senses that here is the testament of her life; almost all the themes that inform her other compositions are gathered together here, and threaded into an ascent to spiritual truth and life. And though the final stage is the absorption of the soul in its spiritual home, and therefore a renunciation of the earthly life, presented as temptation and *paraître*, the subject is abundantly enriched by the expression given to experiences which, once undergone, must be discarded. Marguerite seems, in her mystical ecstasy, to have turned her back on so much of what the Renaissance claims to stand for: human love, wide-ranging experience throughout the world, the inexhaustible wealth of learning, symbolised by architectural features that crumble to dust. The poem is presented therefore as a pilgrim's progress (compare Guillaume de Deguileville's *peregrinatio*, so popular in medieval and early Renaissance times); but Marguerite has embellished its structure by constant reference to Dante's *Divine Comedy* which she knew perhaps better than any of her French contemporaries. Less ambitious in scope than the *Comedy*, it is nonetheless a most impressive piece of sustained composition. It is presented in the form of a *prosopopœia*: just as Héroët spoke through the mouth of an *amye*, so does Marguerite offer her song through that of an *amy*. The first canto, which deals with earthly love, is remarkably detailed in its analysis of feeling in a lover who persists in his prison until infidelity releases him from his infatuation. Some have seen in this episode a poetic refraction of Marguerite's feeling for her first husband, but such associations are hardly essential to an understanding of the poem's general import. Prison is preferred to liberty, and that is a measure of human failing:

> O belle tour, ô paradis plaisant,
> O clair paradis du soleil reluysant,
> Où tout plaisir se voit en ung regard!
> Las! qu'il me plaist d'estre icy seulle à part
> Pour contempler vostre perfection,
> Vostre beauté, vostre condition;
> Par quel amour ne par quel artifice
> Peut estre faict si parfaict edifice?
> Fi des chasteaux, des villes, des palais!
> Au pris de vous ilz me semblent tous laidz.
> Boys et jardins, blez, vignes et prairies
> Dignes n'estoyent sinon de moqueries,
> Ayant esgard au plaisir de ce lieu
> Qui passe tout fors celluy de veoir Dieu . . .
>   (ibid., 125–6)

It is as if the medieval *locus amœnus* had been distorted to these special ends, and undoubtedly the poem owes much to earlier tradition. The canto ends with the prison in ruins, and the lover, now free, is on the threshold of wider horizons. The second canto describes him roaming the world, interested in the Church, concerned to become a perfect Courtier. This book gives an imposing sense of space and wide-ranging vision, a vision which conveys both excitement in earthly experience and at the same time awareness of its deficiencies. This feeling is reinforced by the meeting with the old man who carries the analysis further and tells the author that his progress is hampered by three vices, love, ambition, and avarice, and that he must take the path of learning if he is to advance further. This leads on to the third book, the longest by far, and of intricate richness. It opens with the exploration of all branches of learning; here Marguerite captures the Renaissance's thirst after polymathy and also, I think, its desire to reconcile classical learning with Christian teaching. The *amy* does in fact turn his attention then to the study of religion and the Scriptures; but soon he comes to realise his nothingness. The rest of the book introduces a series of themes and episodes which prepare him and the reader for the final apotheosis of the soul: a contrast is established between *Tout* (God) and *Rien* (the human being), a contrast which was already developed in another poem (*Chansons spirituelles*, viii). This is followed up by an attack on *cuyder* (pride), the affirmation of *Celluy qui est*, reference to the more merciful law of Christ that comes to replace the harsh edicts of the Old Testament, four exemplary deaths (of persons closely associated with Marguerite, including Francis I, whose death forms the subject of another fine poem, *La Navire*), the episode of the mystical vision. Central to the climax of the poem is the figure of Christ the Redeemer; here theology gives way to adoration, and we see the confluence of the mystical current and the inner yearning to be found in the evangelicals of her generation. It is difficult to convey the impressive harmony of tone and sustained experience that gives this poem its peculiar quality. Certain topics have received separate expression in other poems – one thinks of the *Triomphe de l'Agneau*, itself a further illustration of her gift for elevated writing, in spite of some padding; but in this pilgrimage are garnered the fruits of a lifetime. I can think of no other poem of such prolonged inspiration in the religious domain before D'Aubigné's *Tragiques*; and indeed here and there one may come upon themes to be developed in greater detail some fifty years hence, for Marguerite's work, after all, forms an essential link in the chain of Christian spirituality running from the age of Lefèvre down to the Counter-reformation. D'Aubigné's poem is of course, in some ways, not comparable, with its epic description of humanity through the arches of the centuries, its caustic satire, its immense linguistic energy; but in their rejection, not without a full awareness, of certain Renaissance values – earthly love, the Court, learning, worldly success – the *Prisons* are in some measure a harbinger of D'Aubigné's great poem.

VII. TRANSITIONAL FIGURES

We must now turn our attention to several poets who occupy a respectable position in the literary landscape of Francis I, who are by no means insensitive to new stirrings and who, in their writings, provide links between an earlier conception of poetry and that of the Pléiade. In any case, their own output spans the years before and after the publication of the *Deffense et Illustration* in 1549, and though only one of them, Jacques Peletier du Mans, seems to twentieth-century eyes to stand out, they reflect developing attitudes and practice in poetry.

Charles Fontaine (1514-?)[45]

We have already met Fontaine as a participant in the *querelle des amyes*; recently, however, his portrait has been broadened by the discovery of manuscript poems that belong to his youth, and reveal the impact made on him by evangelical currents in the 1530s. These sentiments are expressed in a large number of poems that are couched in traditional forms (*chant royal, rondeau*, etc.), which shows that these were not incapable of adapting themselves to new currents of inspiration; but one can understand why they remained unpublished at the time. I give one example of Fontaine's writing in this vein:

> Le cueur à Dieu, l'affection au monde
> Ne peult avoir celluy qui se dit munde.
> Vous ne povez à deux maistres servir,
> Dit Jesus Christ. Te veulx tu asservir
> A Dieu? Fuys donc le monde comme immunde.
>
> Fuys l'ennemy de cent pas à la ronde.
> Aussi ta chair qu'elle ne te surunde.
> Lors tu pourras entierement ravyr
>   Le cueur à Dieu.
>
> Ta chair fuyras par traveil qui confonde
> Ton ennemy, par œuvre en qui se fonde
> Amour de Dieu que tu doibs poursuyvir;
> Le monde aussi, par desir pour suyvir
> Tous gens de bien purs et nectz comme l'onde,
>   Le cueur à Dieu.
>   (Scalamandré ed., p. 224)

On the other hand, we do not find very many traces of these preoccupations in his later published verse. He has a chameleonic response to the *milieux* in which he moves; his beginnings are, poetically, also linked with Marot, on whose behalf he speaks up, with Bonaventure des Périers and Jean Visagier, when the poet is in exile. We find him moving in the literary circles of Lyons: and in these

years, he is near Héroët and Marguerite de Navarre, he is known to
members of the Neo-latin *sodalitium*, and he has some relations with
the Collège de la Trinité. His *Fontaine d'Amours* (1545)[46] reflects up
to a point some of the Neo-latin formulae then popular, but the
Marot example is also present. In his epigrams he betrays some
influence of Martial, whose maxim he repeats on the distinction
between art and morals in private life. For him, poetry is now 'ces
petites choses joyeuses', and the poet must have 'ie ne sçay quoy de
gayeté naturelle, sans laquelle (i'ose dire) ne se peut appeler Poëte'.
A substantial portion of the volume is devoted to elegies and epistles,
though in the domain of love the distinction between the two is not
very marked, except perhaps in so far as the epistles deal with one
rather drawn-out affair. The pace of development is leisurely, and
though a mild Petrarchism may be detected, the discursive element is
very much to the fore. Fontaine makes little attempt to enrich his
verse with imagery, and when he does, the effect can be odd:

> Car ma doulceur n'est sucre de Madaire,
> Mon cœur ne va ainsi qu'un dromadaire . . .
> (p. 83)

Clearly we have some Ovidian and Marotic influence here, but
Fontaine's conception of woman is hardly as exalted as in the
Contr'amye. We find little to announce a new phase in French
poetic evolution; but when the Pléiade does appear, Fontaine shows
considerable sympathy for its aims. His view of the poet is decidedly
more dignified, and he tries his hand at newer genres such as the
ode (*Ruisseaux*, 1555).[47] What stays in the memory of the reader is
an amiable personality who makes some contribution to the Platonic
debate and also to the development of translation, but whose poems
lack character for all their gentle charm and relaxed tone and remain
essentially a discreet *écho sonore* of the literary world.

Charles de Sainte-Marthe and Mellin de Saint-Gellais

Among the other *poetæ minores*, brief mention may be made of
Charles de Sainte-Marthe and Mellin de Saint-Gellais. The former,
whose *Poésie françoise* appeared in 1540, shows similar transitional
features;[48] he remains faithful to Marot, he supports the claims
of the vernacular, and he has made some use of the Petrarchan
tradition. One may detect a strong influence of Marguerite de
Navarre – in whose memory he wrote an impressive funereal *Oratio*
– on his conception of Platonic spiritual love, but I must confess that
I find his verse bald and barren. Mellin de Saint-Gellais[49] (1491–
1558) presents something of a puzzle: in his lifetime, he enjoyed
very great prestige as a court poet, perhaps in part because he took
great care to commit little of his writing to print. What we have –
and there are also problems of attribution – is very slight, and one is

tempted to think that today he would be lucky to obtain employment as a writer of mottoes for Christmas crackers. Nevertheless, he has some interest as a cog in the machinery of literary history, and his very success is an indication of taste at Court. His evolution follows that of his times: in his youthful days, he exploited a certain range of *rhétoriqueur* forms, but he soon turned to the epigram. His poems are usually slight in length and substance – and many of them were probably written for accompaniment by the lute, of which he was an accomplished player. In spite, or perhaps because, of his weakness and facility, he is something of a crossroads. He has close connections with the Neo-latins – a certain number of Latin poems by him are extant – and he helped no doubt to acclimatise themes already present in their collections of verse. He translates a few Latin epigrams (e.g., Martial) and he contributes to the diffusion of Horace. In his youth he spent some years in Italy, and especially at Bologna, and well versed in Italian literary developments, he translates and adapts texts from Ariosto, Aretino, Petrarch; his rendering of the *Sophonisbe*, performed posthumously in 1559, is a minor landmark in the development of tragedy. He takes his part in fashioning court entertainment (*mascarades* and *cartels*), and he experiments in new metrical forms, the *terza rima*, the sonnet, nor should one refuse him an undeniable technical competence. Had he lived a century later, this abbé would have frolicked gracefully from *salon* to *salon*, composing ephemera and playing a delicate role in the creation of an urbane society, where refinement and trifling mingled happily.

Hugues Salel (1504–53)[50]

Salel's activity spans the vital years 1534–53; he is a real mirror of poetic fashion, which he also anticipates occasionally, and though rarely capable of imaginative flights, he turns out polished compositions that reveal an awareness of linguistic possibilities. His first work, the *Dialogue non moins utile que delectable* (1534), takes place between Jupiter and Cupid on themes that some critics have thought to be congenial to Marguerite de Navarre – and Salel is in great measure a court poet. This extended poem shows his dependence on the *rhétoriqueur* tradition: the dream, the *sylva* with its conventional features, the *débat*, the overt emphasis on rhetoric – triads, epithets, high proportion of latinisms, diminutives, adverbs in *–ment*, present-participial phrases, occasional archaisms; and the metrical elements and rhymes form part of the same pattern. However, Salel is very much in the swim, through his presence at Court, his contacts with Marot and Lyons, his humanist friends; and he has some scholarship, as is shown in his translation of Homer for whom he had an unbounded admiration. His later ceremonial poems are sensitive to evolving fashion: he contributes an *eglogue marine* to the *Tombeau*

of the dauphin in 1536, and this composition, influenced naturally by
Sannazaro but also Marot, is the first of its kind in France. The
Chasse royale, though heavily dependent on allegory, has interesting
passages on the art of hunting, thus anticipating the cynegetic poems
of later decades. The *Chant poétique* for Henry II, in which the
theme of Pan and Syrinx (present in the 1534 poem) recurs, shows
how Salel has adapted *rhétoriqueur* ingredients to a new style of
court poetry, to create a work in which allegory and mythology are
more closely associated with royal personages.

Salel's writing is often indebted to Marot, but like Marot he owes
something to the climate in which humanists were penning Neo-latin
verse in the 1530s; he translates Petrarch, also Pontano, he moves
from *rhétoriqueur* forms to the epigram, he turns out amusing satiric
dizains, he composes some epitaphs, he adapts Ausonius. He is not
averse from experimenting in new poetic structures, *terza rima*, the
sonnet, the ode. He works in the field of love-poetry, using Petrarchan themes in the *Chapitres* (i.e., *capitoli*), but the effect tends to
be wooden and academic. Religious poetry as such does not figure;
but he takes a serious, indeed aristocratic, view of his art. In poem
61, the writer is termed a 'scavant', and *bon sçavoir* is identified
with *vertu* in the *Epistre de Dame poesie*. Just occasionally one
notices the hint of a Platonic theme (poem 68). We can see Salel
moving with the times, but in his themes he never sunders with the
past: the Petrarchan poems are peopled with various allegorical
figures from the *Roman de la Rose*, and his conception of love often
has a courtly ring about it; his treatment of Nature, basically old-
style, acquires a superficially classical veneer late in his life, though
of course the more formal genres maintain *rhétoriqueur* elements
with some ease. A serious artist, he is esteemed by a number of
poets active in the middle of the century.

Peletier du Mans (1517-82)[51]

Peletier has not received the acclaim he deserves; he is of course
overshadowed by the poets he encouraged, but he was also their precursor in many respects. In his polymathy he united the arts and
sciences, he offered insights into poetic theory which anticipate the
future, and was something of a pioneer in scientific poetry. His view
of poetry, first outlined in his translation of Horace's *Ars poetica*
(1541), is an exalted one and harnessed to *sapientia*, and expects
from the poet an almost Promethean attitude:

N'estime son esprit incapable de perfection: embrasse par cogitation
l'universe structure des choses, respire un vouloir invincible et un desir
insatiable.

His own *Œuvres poétiques* came out in 1547, from the press of
Michel Vascosan who publishes the works of many of his friends and

colleagues (Elie Vinet, Pierre de Montdoré, Nicolas de Grouchy, Buchanan). The volume contained the first fruits of Ronsard and a prefatory text addressed to Francis I, in which Peletier referred to his translation of Homer, also included: he attached some value to translation as a means of improving the literary language, without of course sacrificing fidelity to the original:

> Mais il convenient garder la maiesté
> Et le naïf de l'ancienneté.

In the preamble to his rendering of twelve Petrarch sonnets (the rhyme-scheme of which differs slightly from the original), he points to the need for combining fidelity and sensitivity to 'la diction'. He also includes three renderings of Horace, and may be one of the sources for the interest taken by the Pléiade in this poet. These versions are followed by the *vers lyriques de l'invention de l'auteur*, in which his support for the vernacular is evident:

> J'escri en langue maternelle,
> Et tasche à la mettre en valeur:
> Affin de la rendre eternelle,
> Comme les vieux ont fait la leur:
> Et soutien que c'est grand malheur
> Que son propre bien mespriser
> Pour l'autruy [i.e., Latin] tant favoriser
> (fol. 82 v)

We should be able to achieve as much as the ancients did in their mother tongue; moreover, we cannot hope to rival Vergil by composing in Latin. One must think of the French who will understand poetry in their own tongue, which is not by any means as 'lourde' as some will have. In any case, the classics are there to enrich, not to supplant, national resources:

> S'il y a de la pauvreté
> Qui garde que tu ne composes
> Nouveaux motz aux nouvelles choses?
> Si mesme à l'exemple te mires
> De ceulx là que tant tu admires.
> (*A un poète qui n'escrivoit qu'en latin*, fol. 83)

The inspiration of this volume is mixed indeed, but certain features predominate. There are a few love-poems, rarely rising above precious flirtation or memories of Martial; more substantial are the pieces devoted to persons in high places. Peletier, like Salmon Macrin, is very aware of the change of climate at Court since the death of Francis I, and he hopes for the return of better times, not only politically but culturally. Marguerite de Navarre is often sung, and a poem to Henry II develops the *topos* of the ideal monarch. Particularly interesting are the poems on Nature. Peletier treats the commonplace of *rus* against *urbs* in a poem inviting Ronsard to the countryside, and in a more formal, extended *débat* entitled *Les louanges de la Court*, which weaves various aulic themes and links the courtier with the soldier.

It is, however, the seasonal poems that catch our attention. The structure of the individual poems in the cycle is sometimes wayward, but they have an unmistakable identity of their own. Peletier often interposes a counter-theme, which may give the text a slightly bitter-sweet tone. Though care is taken with the rhetorical devices (epithets, enumeration, binary and ternary patterns), the poems are not elaborately learned, imagery and comparisons are discreetly employed, and here and there a more personal note creeps in, with a relative 'realism' of description. The *blason* technique, present elsewhere in the volume too, is used on a more ambitious scale, with the result that Peletier imparts to his text an almost medieval flavour. In *L'hyver*, he achieves effect by unadorned description but ends in the major key with thoughts of hunting, the warm log-fire, the coming spring, and the pleasures of living on one's capital. At the same time, the poet's scientific interest in Nature peeps through; the Zodiac is brought in more than once and we are made aware of the wider world about us. In *A ceulx qui blament les mathematiques*, Peletier praises the discipline, especially for its application to astronomy, and he talks of

> La facture & grande merveille
> De la ronde machine.
> (fol. 77 v)

He expresses his admiration of the divine pattern and dwells on the passing of time; these are thoughts that will assume greater significance later on.

Peletier did not set too high a price on his poetic ability:

> Car Poesie en moy, n'est, Dieu mercy,
> Le meilleur don, & n'est le pire aussi
> Que par faveur m'aient departi les Cieux.
> (*A M. de St Gellais*, fol. 101)

and to this view he was to adhere. To be sure, he maintains a certain dryness of line that is apparent in other transitional figures (Salel and Denisot), nor is there much attempt to renovate poetic language, though Peletier insists on a decent rhetorical standard. Yet there is much of positive value in this admirer of Marot: poetic criteria that foreshadow the Pléiade, a determined effort to experiment in divers metrical structures, a new sensitivity to Horace, a personal reaction to Nature. Intellectual content is far from negligible in his poetry, but there is a firmness of language and a delicate sense of detail that give flavour to his verse. He has some control of line, if not always of the larger poetic scheme; with its relative lack of warmth and colour, his poetry makes one think of an etching. Later he was to display a greater depth of poetic sensitivity (see below, pp. 379–81).

VIII. TOWARDS A MORE CONSCIOUS PROMOTION OF THE VERNACULAR AS A MEANS OF LITERARY EXPRESSION

We have remarked that the struggle between French and Latin was not to be settled overnight: there was something to be said for Latin if it could prove France's cultural supremacy, and the aristocratic view of literature (and this means in great measure poetry in this context), so prevalent in humanist circles, lends some support to Latin, especially when many accept that the French language is underdeveloped. The fact that rhetoric plays so important a part in poetry may help to blur the linguistic issue, at any rate for a while. Nevertheless, momentum is gathering in favour of the vernacular. Some time back, Jean Lemaire had broken a lance in favour of French, and Claude de Seyssel had noted that there were important connections between political and linguistic *rayonnement*:

Car premierement par le moyen des grandes et glorieuses conquêtes qu'avez faites en Italie, n'y a quartier maintenant en icelle où le langage français ne soit entendu par la plupart des gens: tellement que, là où les Italiens réputoient jadis les Français barbares tant en mœurs qu'en langage, à présent s'entrentendent sans truchement les uns les autres et si s'adeptent les Italiens . . . aux habillements et manière de vivre de France . . . Aussi est la langue françoise moult publiée en plusieurs autres provinces et nations d'Europe, pour la continuelle communication que les Princes et Peuples d'icelle ont avec eux et vos sujets, plus grande beaucoup qu'ils n'ont eu, bien longtemps a.
    (*Exorde de Justin*, in J. Poujol's ed. of *La Grant Monarchie*, pp. 66–7)

Geoffroy Tory, in his *Champfleury* (1529), had also championed its cause vigorously. It is in the 1540s that things move rather quickly, and indeed to such a tune that many have felt Du Bellay was doing little more than pushing an open door in 1549. One notices some hesitation among humanists that ends in favour of the vernacular: this is the case with Maurice Scève; and Dolet, so long a staunch advocate of Latin, crosses over in his *Maniere de bien traduire d'une langue en autre* (1540), in which he uses an argument that will enjoy some currency in favour of the vernacular, namely that the Romans, for all they owed to Greek civilisation, had developed the potential of the Latin language, and that other countries coming later should follow the same principle. Thomas Sebillet in his *Art poetique françoys* (1548), sensing like others a close connection between poetic and linguistic progress, saw in Henry II's reign sure signs of excellent things to come:

Maintenant [la poésie] rencontre soubz la prudence et divin esprit de Henri Roy second de ce nom, et premier de vertu, téle veneration de sa divinité, que l'esperance est grande de la voir dedans peu d'ans autant sainte et autant auguste que elle fut soubz le Cesar Auguste.

(F. Gaiffe ed., 1932, pp. 14-15)

His general standpoint was a well-balanced one, for though he recognised the need for fertilisation from outside, he refused to discard what the national heritage had to offer.

Translations

The shift of emphasis is reflected also in the rapidly increasing publication of works concerned with the improvement of spelling, pronunciation, punctuation, and grammar. Matters of spelling are discussed not only by grammarians, for instance the original Louis Meigret, but by poets such as Peletier du Mans, Guillaume des Autelz, Barthélemy Aneau, Jean-Antoine de Baïf; many humanists close to the Pléiade concern themselves with grammatical questions; and the problems often filter into theories of poetry. It is also in the middle third of the century that the art of translation assumes massive proportions. The *rhétoriqueurs* had already made translation a characteristic feature of their activity; and Seyssel, himself a translator of classical historians, had had interesting things to say about the benefits of this exercise, which were not only intellectual and scientific, but a means of enriching the language. It is clear too that humanists were often encouraged to translate by patrons in high quarters. When the problem of the vernacular becomes more prominent in the 1540s we find that it also involves discussion of methods and principles of translation. Among the works Dolet planned to 'illustrer' his mother tongue, he included *La maniere de bien traduire d'une langue en une aultre*, a short treatise in which he laid down five principles, of which the third runs:

. . . en traduisant il ne se fault pas asseruir jusques à là, que l'on rende mot pour mot. (1545 ed., fol. G r)

and, though he will respect the intentions of the original, he recognises 'la propriété de l'une & l'autre langue' and is therefore opposed to an approach that prefers the letter to the spirit of the text. This view is in fact widespread, though certain translators will make it the excuse for an unwarranted freedom of action. Peletier du Mans devotes a whole chapter of his *Art poétique* to translation, and his views are no doubt fairly representative, in spite of the Pléiade's strictures at one time:

Somme, un traducteur n'a jamais le nom d'Auteur. Mais, pour cela, veux-je decourager les Traducteurs? nanni, et moins encore les frustrer de leur louange deue; pour estre, en partie, cause que la France a commencé à gouster les bonnes choses. Et mesmes il leur demeure un auantage, que s'ils traduisent bien et choses bonnes: le nom de leur Auteur fera vivre le leur: et certes ce n'est pas peu de chose que d'avoir son nom escrit en bon lieu. Et bien souvent ceux qui sont inventeurs, se mettent au hasard de vivre moins que les Traducteurs d'autant qu'une bonne Traduction vaut trop mieux qu'une mauvaise invention. Davantage, les Traductions, quand elles sont bien faites, peuvent beaucoup enrichir une Langue. (Boulanger ed., p. 106)

It is therefore not surprising that many authors indulge in some exercise of translation; and in the middle third of the century, we see the emergence of the professional translator. A good example is Jean Martin who is responsible for the French versions of Caviceo's *Il Peregrino* (1528), Horus Apollo (1543), Sannazaro's *Arcadia* (1544), Serlio's treatise on architecture and Bembo's *Asolani* (both 1545), *Le Songe de Poliphile* (1546), Vitruvius (1547), L. B. Alberti (1553) and finally Raimond Sebond (1557), all key texts or authors in the development of the French Renaissance.[52] And there are others such as Herberay des Essarts, who opened the series of translations of the *Amadis*, and Boaistuau, François de Belleforest, and his friend François d'Amboise, whose activities are remarkable in range and quantity. These figures, though their own literary claims may be modest, are very important as cultural intermediaries: Belleforest for instance makes a significant contribution to the diffusion of the *novella* by his rendering of Bandello, but also to Counter-reformation *spiritualité* with his translation of Granada.

The fields of translation are, obviously, very broad indeed. Though Latin is still the *lingua franca* of humanists, texts of classical Rome are translated, notably Vergil, Ovid, and the historians; but Greek, less widely mastered, makes a greater impact through French translations. Italian texts are frequently rendered into French, and to a lesser degree Spanish, but English authors are in the background. Translation undoubtedly helps to fill literary or cultural gaps and encourages French authors to venture into new genres: classical tragedy (cf. Lazare de Baïf's version of a Greek play), the pastoral (Sannazaro), the novel and short story which is still below par in reputation, dialogue literature – and here one thinks not only of Lucian and of Plato, but also of the numerous Italian treatises couched in dialogue form – and finally comedy. Translation is not confined to prose: Amadis Jamyn completes Salel's verse translation of the *Iliad* and a minor author like Guillaume Belliard will publish in 1578 his *Premier Livre de Poemes* which consists mostly of versions of Ovid, Petrarch, and Ariosto.[53] In the last third of the century more especially we shall also note the popularity of translations or paraphrases of sacred texts: the practice has special virtue in the eyes of the

Calvinists, but will gradually spread in Catholic circles as well – a useful example is Desportes's psalm paraphrases.

In addition to lending impetus to genres hitherto neglected or in need of renovation, translation communicates ideas; a great deal of the wisdom of the classical world enters France this way as well as by Latin channels. And one notices more than a trickle of translations of works recounting journeys to hitherto unknown parts of the globe (e.g., N. de Grouchy's 1553 version of a Portuguese work). Finally, as Peletier du Mans saw, this activity must have contributed something to the development of the language. The extent of this influence has been variously estimated, but it seems that contemporaries, who were aware of French vernacular's claims as a rival to Latin, stressed the virtues of translation to this end. There is evidence that Amyot, the translator of Plutarch and other authors, was held, in his times as well as later, to be an early master of French prose style; and we also have knowledge of the precepts he himself wished to put into practice.[54] Amyot possesses an acute sense of choice in vocabulary, but he is also particularly concerned about the structure of his sentences, not only in the matter of balance, but also as regards length and sound. For him, the language is to be heard and not merely read; and one may detect in his prose the lineaments of the classical period and its chief characteristic, *nombre*. Generally speaking, the main contribution of translation here was in the field of vocabulary, often in matters of intellectual, abstract discourse; but translators of worth would feel compelled to exercise the muscles of the vernacular in finding adequate syntactical equivalents of the foreign phrase and also in adapting the vocabulary of other tongues beyond mere *calque*.

French Poetic Theory[55]

During the 1540s, one of the signs of things to come is the appearance of a considerable number of critical writings on poetry. Of course, the *rhétoriqueur* tradition had not died out entirely: *c.* 1525 an anonymous compiler had brought out an augmented version of Molinet's treatise, which was reprinted in Poitiers *c.* 1550. In 1521 Pierre Fabri had published his *Grant art de pleine rhétorique*; and in the 1530s the tradition is still alive. Jean Bouchet is, as usual, in full spate; and in 1531 Guillaume Télin publishes his *Bref sommaire*.[56] This curious work, which owes much to St Augustine, introduces some new notes by its stress on divine inspiration ('diuine maniere d'infusion de grace') and on the vatic quality of the poet:

Il est assauoir que l'office des poetes est de bailler les choses convertement et faindre soubz autre semblance et figure.

Télin also seeks to define the genres according to classical criteria and he claims some knowledge of Valla, like whom he stresses the privileged position of eloquence. Nevertheless, his own poetry links him up with tradition, and there is no evidence that his work had much of an audience. Gratien du Pont's treatise dates from 1539,[57] and as one would expect from this backwoodsman, makes no concessions to modernity. In the 1540s, however, the climate begins to change, and the claims of the vernacular and a plea for the renewal of French poetry go hand in hand. One of the earliest texts is Peletier du Mans's preface to his translation of Horace's *Ars poetica* (1541): he emphasised the need for bettering national literature and suggested the sources that might be useful, classical and Italian. At the same time he introduced Horace into the debate, and the Latin poet's ideas will come to play a vigorous part in the forthcoming revival. Peletier is an undoubted harbinger of the Pléiade by his accent on classical culture, his interest in technical and linguistic matters, but he will not reject the national heritage. His contribution to poetic theory becomes more apparent in the *Art poétique* he published in the mid-fifties (see below, p. 142).

The next important tract was Thomas Sebillet's *Art poétique françoys* (1548).[58] It rather took the wind out of Du Bellay's sails, as he made very similar points: in the very first chapter he gives a Platonic *raison d'être* for poetry, he sees it as the product of divine 'fury', natural talent, and also art or technique. Like Peletier he preaches assimilation of what Italy and classical antiquity have to offer, he sees the benefits of good translations for the language; but he is no extremist. On the one hand, he refuses to turn his back on the national tradition, which he sees descending in direct line from the classical era; and when he considers specific genres, there are earlier French poets, notably Marot, whom he warmly recommends as models. And on the other hand, he sees that a wholesale imitation of the classics would be harmful, if not useless. There is virtue in the introduction of new genres – he is the first to pay serious attention to the sonnet, and in the field of the ode he recommends Pindar and Horace, but he is fully aware of the basic differences between Latin and French versification, so that he has nothing favourable to say about *vers mesurés à l'antique*, which are beginning to appear on the market. On the contrary, he proposes the exploitation of the alexandrine whch not so long before theorists were deprecating for its archaic character. He makes a conscientious attempt to define seriously the genres he studies, nor does he try to fit them into traditional categories, though he is far from rejecting forms such as the *rondeau*. He emerges as an admirer more especially of Marot and Saint-Gellais, and this was what the Pléiade resented. He also mentions approvingly transitional figures who will be well thought of by the Pléiade: Salel and Scève, and others whom he calls 'savants'. Finally, he expresses misgivings about the present state of the French theatre. The success of Sebillet's treatise is apparent from the fact that it was reprinted six times over the next thirty years.

The Deffense et illustration (1549)

Du Bellay's *Deffense* is important, not so much perhaps for its ideas, most of which were already 'in the air', as for providing a springboard for a reasonably coherent group of poets endowed with much talent. The pamphlet, which owes much to Speroni, is an unequal affair in which Du Bellay tries to ride with different saddles on Pegasus. After all, his hand had been forced by Sebillet, and the work shows signs of hasty composition. The main points can be reviewed fairly concisely. First, the renewal of the language: French is potentially rich as a vehicle of poetic and scientific communication, but it is underdeveloped compared with other cultures that also go back to a common origin. Polemics compel Du Bellay to develop the theory of imitation and translation with some contortions, to avoid approval of predecessors; hence the working-out of the rather nebulous principle of *innutrition*. In any case, borrowing from other cultures is fertile only if it can be grafted on to something already present and vital in the host. Du Bellay's specific recommendations include adaptation of classical words, use of neologisms, technical words, archaisms, *provignement*, and some syntactical points such as the use of the article before an adjective or infinitive to substantival ends, the wider use of the article and the personal pronouns. Here we have in Du Bellay the urge to enrich the language balanced by the sense that basic principles of clarity be respected.

In the field of literature, Du Bellay's poet should make use of erudition – the principle of aristocratic poetry is accepted, as well as that of the divine source of inspiration coupled with the destruction of Ignorance. The poet should develop genres that have proved their worth in classical and Italian literature, at the expense of 'obsolete' forms practised by earlier French writers, cultivate a more critical use of rhetoric – judicious choice of epithet, search for tonally proper vocabulary, periphrasis or *antonomasia*, technical improvements concerning rhyme, hiatus, and the *coupe*. Much of this is rather patchwork, and some points are not developed as they deserve, but one can see what Du Bellay is aiming at behind the smokescreen of polemic. He is not only defending the potential of the vernacular as a poetic medium, he is making out a case for poetry as a serious activity with valid functions. He himself has a delicate sense of what the French language can stand in the way of innovation and borrowing, and no more than Ronsard will he go the lengths of later followers. Both poets stress the need for relying on one's ear and innate taste; they also emphasise the importance of craftsmanship, without which inspiration will pass through the poet's mind like a sieve.

The standpoint adopted by Du Bellay was hardly likely to go unchallenged, and one may mention three areas of resistance. First, the claims of Latin will still be asserted, even by humanists very close to the Pléiade such as Adrien Turnèbe and Marc-Antoine Muret, though the debate does not take an acrimonious turn. Second, the pagan and 'aesthetic' implications of Pléiade doctrine will be attacked by Bèze and other representatives of a Calvinist attitude to art. And third, Du Bellay will be answered by writers who may often be sympathetic to innovation, but not at the expense of the previous French poets. Sebillet, understandably, offered a reply in the preface to his translation of the *Iphigénie* (1549, 1550), though his later relations with the Pléiade were very harmonious; Guillaume des Autelz, not yet part of the Pléiade fraternity, also provides a rejoinder,[59] but the most pungent answer was the *Quintil Horatien*, generally assumed to be from the pen of Barthélemy Aneau, whose own creative writings, as we shall see, belong to an older tradition.[60] The counter-arguments to the *Deffense* ran along broadly similar lines: above all, there was the refusal to throw the national tradition overboard, and therefore the use of consecrated poetic genres is upheld. Reservations are made about the uncritical or impossible imitation of foreign models; in addition, excessive stress on learning is condemned, and here no doubt the practice of the Marotic poets is tacitly supported, though in the case of Bèze a more 'democratic' conception of art is involved on religious grounds. In all this, both sides undoubtedly had valid points to make: and whereas the traditionalists seem to have been worried about poetry mirroring too limited, albeit serious, bands of experience, the Pléiade wished to elevate the status of poetry and free it from a too static conception of rhetoric.

The rejoinders to the *Deffense* did not themselves go unanswered, and this debate encourages the appearance of a number of *arts poétiques* in the next few years: Claude de Boissières, 1554; Peletier du Mans, 1555, Antoine Foclin (or Fouquelin), 1555; P. de Courcelles, 1557; and Ronsard, 1565. In this ferment, the role of La Ramée, concerned with the status of rhetoric, is important and is reflected in his *Dialectique* published in 1555. The same year sees the appearance of Adrien Turnèbe's edition of Aristotle's *Ars poetica*, important in its own critical right, but also because of the reappraisal of Aristotle that is going on in Paris towards this time. To these may be added various prefaces to creative writings and philosophical dialogues in which the nature of poetry is discussed *passim* (e.g., Pontus de Tyard or Louis le Caron); and most important, both by its ambitious scope

and by the influence it was to exercise, is J. C. Scaliger's posthumous
Poetice, printed in 1561 and strongly coloured by aristotelian
ideas.[61] Some of his ideas may well have been circulating in humanist
circles some ten years earlier, since Scaliger's prestige and connections were impressive, but understandably it was the printed statement that made the most impact. Fouquelin's treatise reflects his
discipleship of *La Ramée*, but Ramist ideas appear to have had more
influence in Protestant countries and especially England; in any case,
Ramus's own central concerns were not literary, though he naturally
sought to fit literary phenomena into his scheme of things. Peletier,
whom we have seen as a middle-of-the-road precursor, amplifies his
previous statements in the *Art poétique* of 1555, organises the positive
content of Pléiade poetics in more systematic fashion, but also pays
tribute to earlier poets, including Héroët, who seems to enjoy high
standing during the reigns of Henry II and Charles IX. On the
status of poetry, on the need for enrichment from abroad, on the
value of classical genres and the sonnet to be exploited, Peletier
echoes what had by then been recognised in French literature; like
the Pléiade he urges the composition of an epic. However, his conception of poetry is more 'popular' than that of the Pléiade; this
implies, if not xenophobia, at least a guarded acceptance of foreign
models, suspicion of excessive erudition, obscurity, overmuch *style
soutenu*, a preference for poetry that is direct rather than oblique in
its utterance and places clear statement before periphrasis.

Yet, throughout the debate, we discern an unmistakable patriotism
on all sides, a recognition that renewal is inevitable, a clear support
for the claims of French over Latin, but also a suspicion of the hermetic and obscure – after all, the Pléiade themselves moderate the
excessive claims they enthusiastically made for an erudite and aristocratic poetry. With the exception of Barthélemy Aneau, and for a
time Guillaume des Autelz, all these theorists have more or less close
connections with the dynamic Parisian centres of humanism and
literature; and this cohesion, going well beyond theories, helps to
give impetus to the development of poetry during the coming
decades.

However, before we scrutinise the work of the Pléiade, we must
take a look at what was going on in and about Lyons; for the various
poets associated with the city, and especially Scève, seem to anticipate in their practice many of the ideas that will be taken up by the
Pléiade. Moreover, the Lyons poets are producing poetry of a high
order at a time when elsewhere in France achievement remains
modest.

NOTES

1. Some aspects of this period are considered by H. Guy, *Histoire de la poésie française au XVI° siècle*, vol. II, *Clément Marot et son école*, 1926. The Lyons poets are examined below, pp. 153–65.

2. See General Bibliography for monographs on the several genres.

3. The *Courtier* is available in an English version by Charles S. Singleton in the Anchor Book series, New York, 1959.

4. *Chanson and Madrigal 1480–1530*, ed. J. Haar, Cambridge, Mass., 1964; G. Dottin, 'Aspects littéraires de la chanson musicale à l'époque de Marot', *RSH*, 1964.

5. Copies in BM and BN; his *Blasons domestiques* (BN) came out in 1539.

6. La Perrière's works are published at Lyons; in addition to the *Morosophie* (BM, BN), there are *Le Théâtre des bons engins*, 1536 (BM), 1539 (BM, BN) but published at Paris, and 1545 (BN); and *Le Miroir politique*, 1555 (BM, BN). On this author see article by G. Dexter, *BHR*, 1954.

7. The translation was by Lanteaume de Rieu. Both versions in BM, BN.

8. H. Green, *Andrea Alciati and his Book of Emblems*, 1872.

9. Unless we count François Habert, still active under Henry II.

10. A. Ehrlich, *Jean Marots Leben und Werke*, 1902; E. M. Rutson, *The Life and Works of Jean Marot*, Oxford B.Litt. thesis; C. A. Mayer and D. Bentley-Cranch, 'Le premier Pétrarquiste Français, Jean Marot', *BHR*, 1965. *Les deux heureux voyages de Genes & Venise*, 1532 (BM, BN); *Le Recueil*, ?1533 (Ars), often reprinted in editions of Clément Marot's *Adolescence Clémentine*.

11. Jean Parmentier, *Œuvres poétiques*, éd. crit. Françoise Ferrand, *TLF*, 1971. The BN holds the one copy known to have survived in a public library. See also K. von Pasadovsky-Wehner, *Jean Parmentier (1494–1529), Leben und Werk*, Munich, 1937; and J. C. Lapp, 'An explorer poet: Jean Parmentier', *MLQ*, 1945.

12. *Les Divers Rapportz*, éd. crit. M. A. Pegg, *TLF* 107, 1964; see also Nanie Bridgman, 'Eustorg de Beaulieu Musician', *Musical Quarterly*, 1951. The BM holds the first ed. of the *Gestes* and the 1537 ed. of the *Divers Rapportz*.

13. That is, not in the *Rapportz*, though discreet hints of evangelism are detectable. In later works, published in Switzerland, even the titles betray the zeal of the neophyte.

14. *Œuvres*, ed. Charles d'Héricault, 1855; *Roger de Collerye et ses Poésies dolentes, grivoises et satiriques*, ed. F. Lachèvre, 1942. The *Œuvres* were published in 1536 (BN).

15. *L'Esclave fortuné*, Lyons, 1535 (BN); *Cent Epigrammes*, s.d. (BN); *Epistres Veneriennes*, 1536 (BM), n.d. (BN); *Le Secret d'amours*, 1542 (BN).

16. Held by BM and BN (1546 ed.).

17. Both eds. held by BM, the 1544 by BM.

18. A. Hamon, *Un Grand Rhétoriqueur poitevin, Jean Bouchet (1476–1557?)*, 1901. On Bouchet historian see below, p. 459. Considerable holdings of this voluminous author in BM, BN, and O; NLS holds four titles. Reprint of *Epistres morales et familieres du traverseur*, *FRC*, 1969, introduction by J. J. Beard.

19. Very prolific (Cioranescu has 49 entries), he published his first work, *Le passetemps et songe du Triste*, in 1529; he translated Cato, Horace, Ovid, and Nicolas Brizard. Among his writings may be mentioned: *La Jeunesse du Banny de Lyesse*, 1541 (BM, BN, O); *Le Philosophe Parfaict*, 1542 (BN, modern ed. H. Franchet, 1923); *Le songe de Pantagruel*, 1542 (BN); *Le temple de Chasteté*, 1547, also 1549 (BM, BN). See J.-C. Margolin, 'Erasme, prince des Bergers', *BHR*, 1967.

20. *Recueil des œuvres*, Lyons, 1544 (BM, BN). *Œuvres françaises*, ed. L. Lacour, 2 vols., 1856; A. Chenevière, *Bonaventure des Périers, sa vie, ses poésies*, 1886; Ph.-A. Becker, *Bonaventure des Périers als Dichter und Erzähler*, Vienna, 1924. See below for his *contes* and the *Cymbalum Mundi*.

21. D. Murarasu, op. cit., P. van Tieghem, 'La littérature latine de la Renaissance', *BHR*, 1944; I. D. McFarlane, 'Jean Salmon Macrin (1490–1557)', *BHR*, 1959–60.

22. *L'Adolescence clementine*, 1532 (BM, BN); *La Suite de l'Adolescence clementine*, 1533 (BN); *Les Œuvres*, 1538 (BN); *Les Psaumes*, 1542. Modern ed. by C. A. Mayer, London: *Les Epîtres*, 1958; *Œuvres satiriques*, 1961; *Œuvres lyriques*, 1964; *Œuvres diverses*, 1966; *Les Epigrammes*, 1970. Critical studies: P. Villey, *Marot et Rabelais*, 1923; Ph.-A. Becker, *Clément Marot, sein Leben und seine Dichtung*, Munich, 1926; J. Plattard, *Marot, sa carrière poétique et son œuvre*, 1938; P. Jourda, *Marot, l'homme et l'œuvre*, 1950, revised ed. 1967; P. M. Smith, *Clément Marot, Poet of the Renaissance*, 1970. C. A. Mayer, **Clément Marot*, 1972.

23. C. A. Mayer, *Bibliographie des Œuvres de Clément Marot*, 2 vols., *THR*, 1954.

24. C. E. Kinch, *La Poésie satirique de Clément Marot*, 1940.

25. *Epigrammes*, ed. C. A. Mayer, p. 129 (xliii).

26. The source of the poem will be found in the *Latin Anthology*, which also inspires a sonnet on the same theme by Pierre de Brach; but the antithetical elements are easily assimilated to the Petrarchan style.

27. C. A. Mayer, 'Coq-à-l'âne; Définition, invention, attributions', *FS*, 1962; H. Meylan, *Epîtres du Coq à l'âne*, *THR*, 1956.

28. V.-L. Saulnier, *Les Elégies de Clément Marot*, 1952, new ed. 1968.

29. C. M. Scollen, *The Birth of the Elegy in France, 1500–1550*, *THR*, 1967.

30. J. Vianey, *Les Epîtres de Clément Marot*, 1962.

31. See Liverpool doctorate by A. James.

32. P. Le Blanc, *La Poésie religieuse de Clément Marot*, 1955; C. A. Mayer, *La Religion de Marot*, *THR*, 1960; M. A. Screech, *Marot évangélique*, Geneva, 1967.

33. *Les Psaumes de Clément Marot*, ed. S. J. Lenselinck, Assen, 1969; M. Jeanneret, *Poésie et tradition biblique au XVIᵉ siècle*, 1969.

34. See C. A. Mayer, *Bibliographie de Marot* for details and locations.

35. E.-V. Telle, *L'Œuvre de Marguerite d'Angoulême, reine de Navarre et la querelle des femmes*, Toulouse, 1937; L. L. Richardson, *The Forerunners of Feminism in French Literature of the Renaissance*, I, Baltimore, 1929; K. König, *Die literarische Ehrenrettung der Frau in Frankreich während der ersten Hälfe des 16ten Jahrhunderts*, Dresden, 1909; R. Kelso, *Doctrine for the Lady of the Renaissance*, Urbana, 1956.

36. See his *Controverses des sexes masculin et feminin*, Toulouse, 1534 (BM, BN).

37. Copy in BN.

38. M. A. Screech, 'An interpretation of the *Querelle des Amyes*', *BHR*, 1959.

39. Abel Lefranc, *Grands Ecrivains français de la Renaissance*, 1914; J. Festugière, *La Philosophie de l'amour de Marsile Ficin et son influence sur la littérature française au XVIᵉ siècle*, 1941; N. Robb, *Neoplatonism of the Italian Renaissance*, 1935; R. Lebègue, 'Le Platonisme en France au XVIᵉ siècle', AGB, Congrès de Tours-Poitiers, 1954; W. Mönch, *Die italienische Platonrenaissance und ihre Bedeutung für Frankreichs Literatur- und Geistesgeschichte (1450–1550)*, Berlin, 1936; R. V. Merrill and R. J. Clements, *Platonism in French Renaissance Poetry*, New York, 1957; E. F. Meylan, 'L'évolution de la notion d'amour platonique', *BHR*, 1938; A. H. T. Levi, 'The Neoplatonist Calculus', *Humanism in France*. The terms Platonism and Neoplatonism are sometimes bandied about as if they were interchangeable, which may lead to serious confusion.

40. On Petrarchism see also below, pp. 154–5, 261. Poets may combine Petrarchan and Platonic motifs, but Petrarchism remains more courtly and Platonism more spiritual in essential principle.

41. The first ed. is rare (Manchester, Stuttgart), but another ed. of the same year is in BM. I have used the 1547 ed. of the *Opuscules d'amour* (BM) and the *Œuvres poétiques*, ed. F. Gohin, *STFM*, 1909.

42. Original ed. in BN; reprinted in the Montaiglon-Rothschild anthology.

43. C. A. Mayer, '*L'honnête homme*, Molière and Philibert de Vienne's

Philosophe de Court', *MLR*, 1951; Annette Porter, 'Philibert de Vienne', *BHR*, 1965; D. Javitch, 'The Philosopher of the Court: a French satire misunderstood', *CL*, 1971; P. M. Smith, *The Anti-courtier Trend in Sixteenth-century French Literature*, *THR*, 1966.

44. *Marguerites de la Marguerite des Princesses*, 1547 (BM, BN, MRy, O), 2nd ed. 1554 (BM). Modern ed. F. Frank, 4 vols., 1873; reprint *FRC*; *Les Dernières Poésies*, ed. Abel Lefranc, 1896; *La Navire*, ed. R. Marichal, *TLF*, 1956; *Petit œuvre devot et contemplatif*, ed. H. Sckommodau, Frankfurt, 1960; *La Coche*, ed. R. Marichal, *TLF*, 1971; *Chansons spirituelles*, ed. G. Dottin, *TLF*, 1971. See H. Sckommodau, *Die religiösen Dichtungen Margaretes von Navarre*, Cologne, 1955.

45. R. L. Hawkins, *Maistre Charles Fontaine, Parisien*, Cambridge, Mass., 1916; this must be supplemented by Grace Frank, 'The early work of Charles Fontaine', *MPh*, 1925, and R. Scalamandré, *Un poeta della Preriforma: Charles Fontaine*, Rome, 1970, who publishes the poems of the ms. Vat. Reg. lat. 1630 without the Pauline epistles.

46. The BM has the 1545 Lyons ed., the BN the 1546. The BM holds a number of Fontaine's works, and EUL the translation of Artemidorus on dreams.

47. Copy in BN; the work was originally published in Lyons.

48. C. Ruutz-Rees, *Charles de Sainte-Marthe (1512–1555)*, New York, 1910; Ph.-A. Becker, *Aus Frankreichs Frührenaissance*, Munich, 1927. Copy of the *Poésie françoise* in BN.

49. *Œuvres*, Lyons, 1547 (BN); *Œuvres poétiques*, Lyons, 1574 (BM, BN) and 1582 (BM). *Œuvres complètes*, ed. P. Blanchemain, 3 vols., 1873. See M.-J. Molinier, *Mellin de Saint-Gellais*, 1910.

50. *Dialogue* in work by J. Dupré, ?1534 (BM); *Eglogue marine*, 1536 (BN); *Les œuvres* (1539) (BM, BN). Modern ed. in L.-A. Bergougnioux, *Un Précurseur de la Pléiade: Hugues Salel de Cazals-en-Quercy*, 1929; A. Hulubei, 'Etude sur quelques œuvres poétiques d'Hugues Salel (1504–1553)', *HR*, 1935.

51. Translation of Horace, *Art poétique*, 1545 (BM, BN); his own *Art poétique*, Lyons, 1555 (BM, BN); *Les œuvres poétiques*, 1547 (BM, BN, NLS, EUL), modern ed. M. Françon, Rochecorbon, 1958; *L'Amour des amours*, Lyons, 1555 (BN); *La Savoye*, Annecy, 1572 (BM, BN), modern ed. C. Pagès, Moutiers, 1897; *Louanges*, 1581 (BN). Modern ed. of *L'Art poétique*, A. Boulanger, Strasbourg, 1930. See C. Jugé, *Jacques Peletier du Mans*, Le Mans, 1907; Becker, *Aus Frankreichs Frührenaissance*.

52. P. Marcel, *Jean Martin*, 1927.

53. Copy in BM.

54. Amyot translated Heliodorus, *L'histoire ethiopique*, 1547 (BM, BN, frequently reprinted); Longus, *Les amours, pastorale de Daphnis et Chloe*, 1559 (BN); Plutarch's *Lives*, 1559 (BM, BN, NLS), 1565 (BM, BN), 1567 (BM, BN, Kilkenny); and *Œuvres morales et meslees*, 1572 (BN, often reprinted). See A. Cioranescu, *Vie de Jacques Amyot*, 1941; R. Sturel, *Amyot traducteur des Vies parallèles de Plutarque*, 1909; R. Aulotte, *Amyot et Plutarque*, *THR*, 1966.

55. W. F. Patterson, *Three Centuries of French Poetic Theory*, 2 vols., Ann Arbor, 1935.

56. Copy in BM; see J. E. Clark, 'An early XVIth-century art *poétique* by Guillaume Télin', *BHR*, 1969.

57. *Art et science de rhétorique metrifiée*, Toulouse, 1539 (BN).

58. Frequently reprinted: first ed. 1548 (BN); Lyons, 1551 (Troyes, NLS), 1555 (BM, BN), Lyons, 1556 (BN), 1564 (Ars), 1573 (BN), Lyons, 1576 (Ars). This suggests the work was more popular than the *Deffense et illustration*. Modern ed. F. Gaiffe, *STFM*, 1930.

59. *Replique aux furieuses defenses de Louis Meigret*, 1551 (BM, BN); see M. L. M. Young, *Guillaume des Autelz, a Study of his Life and Works*, *THR*, 1961.

60. H. Chamard, 'La date et l'auteur du Quintil Horatien', *RHLF*, 1898, thinks it appeared *c.* beginning March 1550. The text can be read in the Lyons 1551 ed. of Sebillet's *Art poétique*.

61. *Poetices libri septem,* Lyons (printed in Geneva), 1561 (BM, BN, NLS). See V. Hall jnr, *Life of Julius Caesar Scaliger (1484–1558), Trans. Amer. Philosoph. Society,* n.s. vol. 40, pt. 2, 1950; G. Saintsbury, *A History of Criticism and Literary Taste in Europe,* Edinburgh–London, 1900–04; J. E. Spingarn, *A History of Literary Criticism in the Renaissance,* New York, 1899; B. Weinberg, 'Scaliger versus Aristotle', *MPh,* 1942; V. Hall jnr, 'Scaliger's defense of poetry', *PMLA,* 1948.

Chapter 4

HUMANISM AND LITERATURE IN LYONS DURING THE FIRST HALF OF THE SIXTEENTH CENTURY[1]

I. GENERAL SURVEY

LYONS'S prosperity goes back to the fifteenth century; it had, of course, excellent geographical advantages, standing at the crossroads between Paris and Italy, and Germany and Spain. In the fifteenth century, its fairs began to flourish, thanks to benevolent patronage by the kings who accorded them various privileges; and during the Italian wars, the town often served as a military headquarters. In general, it had no doubt benefited from the opening-up of Mediterranean trade, and in the Renaissance it became a far from negligible centre of banking. It had early taken advantage of the developments in printing, though in the first decades its outlook had been determined less by humanist considerations than by economic factors; and, though Lyons will be the major provincial printing centre in the sixteenth century, it remains fairly conservative in the types of books it publishes until the 1530s, if we except the trade it conducted in pseudo-aldines; nor does it appear to have made substantial contributions to technical advances in book production, though later it distinguished itself in typography, ornament, and illustration.

A very high percentage of the population was Italianate; this factor no doubt helped the spread of Italian humanism and literature when French minds were becoming increasingly aware of what the peninsula had to offer, and the Lyons printers will do much to increase the circulation of texts from Italy. Petrarch and Boccaccio are frequently printed in the town, both in the original and in French translation, and certain Spanish authors too come to be known through the activities of Lyons editors. Alberti, Ariosto, Castiglione, Dante are also represented; it seems that the vogue for the tale, both Italian and French, is linked in some measure with Lyons, since so many of the texts are published there; and the fortunes of Petrarch will be furthered, not only by editions of his work, but by the alleged discovery of Laura's tomb at Avignon, made by Maurice Scève, in 1533 and by the latter's own contribution to Petrarchism a decade later. Other fields in which Lyons printers distinguished themselves were emblem books and works of an aphoristic nature (Alciat, Girard), which included illustrated books of biblical quatrains; and also music – here the brothers Beringen and Jacques Moderne were figures to be reckoned with.[2] It is notoriously difficult to assess just how many books were printed in any given town during the sixteenth century, but one estimate suggests 25,000 for Paris and 13,000 for Lyons; and the years 1530–50 are particularly rich for Lyons from our point of view.

At this time, Lyons had other advantages: Calvin was organising his Church at Geneva, and Lyons, so close to the frontier, was exposed to the new winds of religion. In this context, the fact that the town had neither *parlement* nor university may have made it more attractive to humanists for whom Paris after the *Affaire des Placards*, and indeed earlier, was not very congenial. One must not assume that heresy-hunting was unknown in the city, far from it; and there were also economic troubles (e.g., the Rebeyne, 1529), with a tiresome mendicant problem into the bargain. Those placed by the king in authority were not always liberal in their thought, though many of them seem to have encouraged men of learning and letters. On balance, however, the 1530s were lively and stimulating years for the town: economic impulses, persecution in other countries, Francis I's initiative in attracting artists and men of culture from Italy, all these factors introduce further elements into the population; the drift of humanists from Paris and elsewhere is also significant; the presence of the Court in 1536 adds impetus. And to the encouragement given by Vice-roys, Court, and higher clergy, should be added the patronage of the local rich families (Trivulce, Vauzelles, Scève, etc.). Finally, links between cultivated Lyons circles and groups in neighbouring towns are close: Sadoleto is bishop of Carpentras, and Tarascon also has some interesting humanists, including the learned nun Claude de Bectoz. We shall now look briefly at various figures, in chronological order, who made an important contribution to the cultural life of Lyons in the first half of the century; we shall also mention the Collège de la Trinité and special features relevant to literary developments.

Symphorien Champier (1471-?1539)[3]

In the early days, the cultural scene of Lyons, which was frequented at one time by Jean Lemaire and Jean Perréal, is dominated by Symphorien Champier. A voluminous writer, who did not always make concessions to his readers – and much of his work is in Latin – he manifests attitudes that bear some kinship with those of Gaguin and his circle; and for him life and learning are devoted to the improvement of man's moral nature and to the greater glory of God. Champier was something of a polymath and a staunch patriot: he praises Paris as the Athens of the North:

> . . . ainsi Paris en nostre temps est aorné de toutes sciences & illumine & nourrist de sapience tout le residu des chrestiens. (*Le nef des Princes*, 1527, fol. m ii)

and he also has kind things to say of Rouen, Orléans, Toulouse, and Lyons, though the unfortunate town of Narbonne is dismissed as 'la latrine du monde et la plus basse cité que on sache des autres pays de France'. Lyons, however, claims his local patriotism. He made a very considerable reputation as a doctor, and his views on the training of the medical profession, the problem of classical authority in medicine, and the place of the practitioner in the social framework show him to be an alert and shrewd thinker. His excursions into poetry anchor him firmly in the *rhétoriqueur* tradition, and one has to admit that his writing is often turgid and stodgy. Nevertheless, he deserves our attention in a number of ways. In the first place, there is his attitude towards Italian culture. He is thoroughly awake to the rich developments in the peninsula, but at the same time he is very sensitive to criticisms that may be made of the culture of his own country; he shares that cultural patriotism that is so marked a feature of French humanism. In his *Duellum epistolare Galliae et Italiae summatim complectens*, he recognises the distinction of certain Italian writers, but speaks up stoutly for Frenchmen such as Froissart, Molinet, Chastellain, and Saint-Gellais. And a similar pride informs his historiographical writings, however much they give him the appearance of an uncritical compiler: there is a trickle of new wine in these rather old-fashioned vessels. And this is true of another very important aspect of his work: he may write *Le nef des princes* or *Le nef des dames vertueuses*, like any rank-and-file *rhétoriqueur*, but we cannot fail to be astonished when the first of these works is found to contain quotations from the *Timaeus* and an extract 'Ex argumento Marcilii ficini in apologiam Socratis', and the second offers us the *Livre de vraye amour*, containing important statements based on a Ficinian Platonism.[4] It is not absolutely clear how Champier became acquainted with Ficino: was it through Italian contacts, or through his friends in Paris? for we know that Ficino was being read in the French capital before the end of the fifteenth century. No doubt Champier tailors Ficino's outlook to fit in with his own view of life; nonetheless this is an important and early penetration of Neoplatonism into French literature ('amour n'est autre chose que de chose belle et honneste'); and the stories contained in this third book of the *Nef* illustrate certain Platonic relationships:

L'homme qui aime meurt: et en amour est une mort et deux resurrection.

This work must clearly have found a receptive audience: published originally in 1503, it is reprinted in 1515 and 1531. Even so, when he is at his most active, Champier is not quite in the mainstream: perhaps ahead of his time in Lyons he does not maintain very close contacts with the capital. On the other hand, his works are still very current in the 1530s; and if his literary talent is inferior to his learning, he plays a useful part in the diffusion of Neoplatonism, he chooses on occasion to use the vernacular to discuss philosophical ideas, he has an up-to-date attitude to the relations between erudition, moral formation, and experience, and he develops attitudes to French culture that will soon be widely accepted.

Collège de la Trinité

We mentioned that Lyons had no university; but like other towns affected by humanist currents it was very keen to keep abreast of pedagogic developments. In 1527 the Collège de la Trinité was founded: its career was somewhat checkered, but it claims our attention on two counts. In the first place, it was one of the *foci* in Lyons likely to attract humanists of some distinction, and among the men who taught there were Jean Raynier, Gilbert Ducher, Charles de Sainte-Marthe, and possibly Claude Bigothier. If one looks at the texts edited by, say, Jean Raynier, for use in the college, one gains the impression that the establishment was perhaps not as advanced as all that, but it does play some positive role during the 1530s. Secondly, its principal was Barthélemy Aneau;[6] he is a rather curious figure who combines a certain traditionalism with new ideas. He translated More's *Utopia*, and works by Erasmus and Cicero; and like Bèze, he was a pupil of Melchior Wolmar at Bourges, which doubtless explains the Calvinist sympathies that were partly the cause of his death in an affray in 1561. He prepared an edition of Alciat's *Emblems* in 1549, the success of which prompted him to compose some of his own, an undertaking that was also inspired by the availability of suitable woodcuts in a printer's workshop; and the *Picta poesis* came out in separate Latin and French editions in 1550. All this suggests a somewhat advanced outlook on his part; on the other hand, his ventures into French literature reveal a more conservative outlook. It is almost certain that he was the author of the *Quintil Horatien*, the anonymous rejoinder to the *Deffense* of Joachim du Bellay; in this work, he emerges as the representative of a more traditional view of rhetoric and poetry, but also shows himself capable of satiric writing. In 1539, he published a *Nativeté* which is essentially a collection of Christmas carols strung together; and in 1542 his *Lyon marchant* was performed by the pupils of the college.[7] This eccentric – some have said absurd – composition is hardly theatrical and owes a good deal to tradition. It is really a

Satyre françoyse which partly develops the old *rhétoriqueur* game of comparing towns, in this case Paris, Rouen, Lyons, and Orléans, and partly gives a thinly disguised allegory of foreign affairs since 1524, with special reference to Francis I's dealings with England and Charles V. There is also a section on the death of the dauphin (1536) and fulsome praise of the monarch. Aneau treats himself to some puns:

> Non droict levé d'ond la mer sera trouble
> En un bout, laine est tondue, et descouble
> Le rochier fort auec ses unanimes . . .
> [c. *Anne Boulaine* in margin of text]

The characters form a mixture of classical figures, town representatives, and allegories such as *Verité*, who at one stage is found in a cave, and also quotes Psalm 85 in Latin. Aneau uses the decasyllable as the dominant metre, but he also introduces *rondeaux*; he belongs to a moralising tradition that is strong in Lyons and emerges especially in the emblem and quatrain books. In all this it is difficult to see much sensitivity to new currents of inspiration. His later work includes an *Alector, histoire fabuleuse* and the *Premier livre de la nature des animaux.*

In the 1530s stimulus is provided by various factors. In the first place, the royal Court arrived in Lyons in February 1536; and though Francis I was not permanently in residence – the military situation hardly allowed it – the presence of the Court itself affects the world of letters; and the death of the dauphin in that year gave impetus to encomiastic poetry. Associated with the Court are various statesmen well known for their interest in letters and humanism; these include Cardinals Jean de Lorraine and Guillaume du Bellay. Nor should one forget the close connections between Marguerite de Navarre and Lyons: she stayed on more than one occasion in the city, and it is hardly necessary to stress the favour she showed to poets and men with evangelical leanings; among those who benefited from her patronage were Bonaventure des Périers and Dolet.

Neo-latin activity

Coinciding with this presence of the Court is the flow of humanists and Neo-latin poets to Lyons in the middle of the decade. This is an important phenomenon: the issue between Latin and the vernacular is far from decided, indeed many poets believe that they can prove their superiority over the Italians by writing in Latin. Moreover, a great number of themes, rhetorical techniques, and humanist attitudes will be found in these poets which anticipate the Pléiade: (see above, p. 103) and to these one should add the appearance of a worthwhile current of religious inspiration. The congregation of many of these poets in Lyons – Dolet, Bourbon, Visagier, Sussannée (briefly), Ducher – is expressed in two chief ways. On the one hand, Dolet organises the *Tombeau du Dauphin* (1536): the collective volume is in French and Latin, but the Latin element is very considerable, and the volume can be seen not only as a suitable piece of humanist court poetry, but as an attempt to establish the claims of Latin poetry in Renaissance France. And on the other hand, Lyons sees the publication of a number of important collections of verse by these humanists, between 1536 and 1538 in particular, though the first editions of volumes by Bourbon and Dolet had appeared earlier. These poets have a family air, with the exception of the one-time *meneur du jeu* Etienne Dolet, who for all his humanist dedication, does not write religious poetry, compose love cycles, or depart from a Ciceronian view of Latinity. In addition to the exploring of areas just mentioned, these men derive from the intellectual (and religious) climate of Paris in the late 1520s; they all owe something to the example of Salmon Macrin, who, rather older, is now *cubicularius regius* and follows the Court in its peregrinations, and they mark a break with the conception of poetry favoured by an earlier generation of humanists. Moreover, they have fairly close contacts with poets who have chosen to write in the vernacular: Marot is on friendly terms not only with Macrin but with Jean Visagier. Equally interesting is that Scève is closely connected with this group and is admired by its members for his promise in the field of Latin poetry.

Printing

It is towards this time that Sebastien Gryphe (Gryphius) is at the height of his printing activity. Of German origin, he had settled in Lyons and rapidly became the outstanding printer of his generation there. He published editions of the classics, Latin and Greek, modern school manuals, works by leading humanists such as Erasmus, Budé, and, locally, Sadoleto, the volumes of Latin poetry that are becoming an important feature of humanism; but, as is so often the case in the Renaissance, the *officina* is not only a centre of publication, it is a meeting-place for humanists, and in addition to scholars writing in Latin we find Rabelais, Marot, and Scève in close touch with him. His efforts will be reinforced by those of Dolet who publishes an impressive number of volumes during his comparatively short career, including works of scholarship, classical editions, a few books in French, and a number of works whose religious orthodoxy was suspect. Later printers of repute include the de Tournes and Guillaume Roville (or Rouillé). In short, a conjuncture of events conspired to make Lyons for a while the undoubted centre of humanist and literary activity in France. Moreover, a number of important poets belong to Lyons, and to these we must now turn.

II. MAURICE SCÈVE (c. 1500–1560)[8]

With the appearance of the *Délie* in 1544, French poetry enters upon a new, decisive phase, even if the merits of this Petrarchan sequence were evident at the time to only a handful of the Happy Few. One naturally compares Scève with Marot, the contemporary master: Scève writes for himself, careless of reputation and audience, whereas one can hardly imagine Marot without his public. Scève has tried his hand in a number of minor genres, though ranging less widely than Marot; but his main effort goes into two works that ripened over the years and which still occupy a unique position in the development of French Renaissance poetry – the *Délie* and the *Microcosme*. And though it would be unfair to deny Marot's claims to write serious poetry when the mood took him, I doubt if one can grant him the richness of inner experience that is so distinctive in Scève's poetry.

Scève was closely connected with cultured society in Lyons and particularly with the humanist circles we have just mentioned. Traces of the connections appear in the *Délie*, and more especially in a translation of a poem by Jean Visagier (Diz. 89). Moreover, Scève does not break firmly with the national past, for we come upon tricks of style, textual echoes, and even occasional themes that take us back to the *rhétoriqueurs* and Jean Lemaire de Belges in particular. And one could also point to lines where some kinship with Marot was recognisable. Nevertheless, more than any poet of his generation, Scève looks to the future, not only in the way in which he is able to graft Italian models on to the French tradition, but also in the creation, quite simply, of a new poetic language in his fashioning of a masterpiece of Renaissance poetry. And to anyone approaching the sixteenth century for the first time, Scève gives a masterclass in the way the stock conventions and commonplaces can be transmuted into patterns of exceptional beauty.

Much speculation has arisen about the origins of the sequence; whatever the truth of the matter, the poet underwent some sentimental crisis in the middle 1530s, reopening perhaps the wounds of an earlier experience that occurred, according to one *dizain*, some fifteen years before. The *Délie* is thematically, therefore, the record of the rise, zenith, and final assimilation of an experience lasting over a number of years. One must, however, not expect all the poems to be fully integrated to the main themes at a high level of intensity: on the one hand, a fair number of trifling *dizains* (e.g., anecdotes about Venus and Cupid) pepper the text, and on the other, there are poems containing political or contemporary reference (such as those concerning the Connétable de Bourbon, whose death occurred in 1527), some of which were in all probability written independently, but have a greater or lesser thematic relevance. The sequence has an un-mistakable unity, but we should perhaps not demand too rigid a cohesion of this kind in a Renaissance cycle.

The expression of the poet's experience is coloured by the poetic and philosophic currents spreading into France at the time. The 'psychology' that underlies the poet's description of his varying moods is conventional enough, but its presentation may be sharp-ened to some extent by the contemporary fashion for analysis; and it is well known that most of the final *dizains* are adaptations, some-times near translations, of Sperone Speroni, an Italian writer of Neo-platonic persuasion. Undoubtedly, Scève is well aware of Platonic currents: they manifest themselves in certain themes (the *innamorata* as the incarnation of divine perfection), various images, and also phrases or terms. Due attention must be paid to the presence of key terms of this nature which had a clear, identifying resonance for contemporaries, both in the poetic field and in the world of theo-logical discussion. Nevertheless, I am not convinced that the *Délie* should be taken as a fundamentally Platonic sequence; in spite of several 'spiritualising' motifs and of *dizains* where religious experi-ence is present, the poet's journey, for all its enrichment of inner life and for all the benefit Délie's influence has upon him, hardly amounts to a Platonic ascent towards spiritual purification; in some ways, the metaphysical dimension is conspicuous by its absence.

The more compelling presence, in the literary and conceptual tradition, is surely Petrarch;[9] and in the development of French poetry this is vital. Before Scève, we find little sustained love-poetry in Renaissance France: the *rhétoriqueurs* did not ignore erotic themes and indeed they sometimes put woman on a pedestal, but their poetic achievement in this domain is negligible. Marot's excur-sions into love-poetry are somewhat disappointing, tending either to flatness or to triviality; and though we find a certain diffusion of Petrarchan themes in the poetry of the 1530s and early 1540s, clear patterns have hardly been established. Scève, with his *Délie*, puts his stamp on the evolution of love-poetry for the rest of the century, and his dependence on Petrarch, far from indicating a poverty of imagin-ative substance, is immensely fruitful, and it must not be forgotten that Scève organises his Petrarchan material to fit the pattern of his own experience. Petrarchism, at a time when France is still finding her way poetically, provides a ready-made store of themes, struc-tures, and terminology on which to build; admittedly the term Petrarchism is unsatisfactory, for it means both more and less than what we associate with Petrarch himself, and it attracts to itself elements that often occur in very different contexts. The motifs we call Petrarchan recur throughout our period: the first moment of love, either through Cupid's arrow or the *innamorata*'s gaze, the spiritual nature of her presence, the description of her beauty (often with the aid of jewel imagery), the agency of fear as a destroyer of love, despondency in solitude among natural surroundings, divers possessions of the beloved (glove, mirror, ring, etc.), the dream, the 'moment privilégié', the haughtiness and coldness of the lady, the jealousy episode, the several events that lead to the ending of the relationship, also some anecdotal situations in which the beloved is compared with Venus or is involved with other mythological figures – these motifs and others form the common currency of the tradition. They are often expressed by means of a series of rhetorical devices: antithesis, the *pointe* in the final line, *anaphora, adunaton*, stock imagery, binary and ternary sentence structures, *sententia, exclamatio, gradatio*; features of local geography may be introduced, and the poet may draw on mythological legend or even biblical allusion to develop his theme. The structural elements are equally important: first, a short poem of complex fabric, second the sequence (though Petrarch and some of his followers may not confine themselves to one poetic form such as the sonnet). The originality of a writer sometimes seems elusive to a modern reader, but it may be determined by the choice he makes from this rich arsenal, so that his own group of themes and stylistic devices will mark him off from the rest of his contemporaries. It is not sufficient to track down 'sources' and leave it at that; such displays of erudition, as John Press once said:

exhibit that remarkable combination of intellectual acuteness and imaginative blindness which is so depressing to contemplate. All that they say is logically impeccable and totally irrelevant.

A closer scrutiny reveals that the poet, if he has any imaginative force, will be assimilating these elements in such a way that they form an essential part of his poetic world. Scève in fact is very discriminating in his borrowing, his literal appropriation is infrequent and occurs for specific purposes. More than many neo-petrarchans, he prefers the master to his followers: not that he ignores the Tebaldeos and the Chariteos of this world, but he learns more from Petrarch himself. And when he borrows from Petrarch, he takes only what illuminates and enriches his own experience. Moreover, he maintains his independence in two other cardinal ways. On the one hand, he has not taken imitation so far as to replace the *dizain* by the sonnet, as the members of the Pléiade were to do. Scève has given no explanation for this decision: timidity or fidelity to a national form? In view of his experiments elsewhere, timidity can hardly be the reason, and it may well be that Scève wished to work in a form that was not only part of the poetic heritage of France, but also allowed him a greater density of structure. And on the other hand, he has done something rather unusual in marrying the sequence to the emblem tradition.[10] He has set out the 449 *dizains* in groups of nine, each group prefaced by an emblem which illustrates an episode, an object, or a person by a picture, surrounded by a motto that usually finds its way into the last line of the following *dizain*; it may have to be altered slightly for metrical reasons, but it serves as a sort of conceit, as is consistent with the Petrarchan tradition. A number of problems arise in connection with these emblems: their origin, the relation of emblem and motto, Scève's possible contribution to the series; and satisfactory explanations have yet to be found. However that may be, Scève was making use of a genre which had become exceedingly popular through the publication of Alciat's *Emblemata*, a work that runs through many editions and is frequently printed in Lyons. The pedagogic element of the genre is not taken by Scève further than the *pointe*, but it may harmonise with the dialectical structure he often gives to his *dizain*; and the visual presentation is meant to reinforce the effect produced by the word (*Ut picta poesis*). Attempts to see in the mathematical symmetries of the lay-out some link with the hermetic tradition have not proved very convincing: any significance that may lie in that direction is not likely to enhance the poetic worth of the sequence, nor can one confidently point to a normal unity of inspiration in the nine poems that follow any particular emblem.

However, Scève reveals his originality particularly in his pioneer efforts to renew French poetic utterance. The fact that he moves towards this time from Neo-latin to the vernacular is significant: we saw that he was closely associated with the humanists who hoped to assert French cultural supremacy over the Italians by success in the Neo-latin field, but he, like Etienne Dolet, undergoes a change of heart, and of course other humanists are working in the same direction. He will maintain an aristocratic conception of poetry, such as we find in the Petrarchan tradition and soon in the Pléiade, and he will therefore not follow in the path of, say, Marot, but rather try to shape a language that is distant from everyday reality and composed of highly stylised elements. On the other hand, he will not aim to impress by the display of erudition; though he is a highly trained humanist, it is curious how rarely Scève draws overtly on classical authors to enrich the harmonics of his verse. Some of his 'scientific' imagery may seem a trifle alembicated, but we are still a long way from Ronsard's Pindaric indulgence. At the same time, working in the *dizain* requires considerable economy of means, and his language will distinguish itself by its density and concentration.

So far as vocabulary is concerned, Scève naturally accepts the terminology of the Petrarchan idiom in which he is working, but he adapts it to French needs. Like the humanist he is, he allows himself a fair number of latinisms – and in any case, this was a characteristic of much *rhétoriqueur* writing; but what is interesting is the habit he has of enriching words of Latin origin by restoring to them certain nuances they had lost with the passage of time. He may also indulge, though rarely, in a Latin construction; on the other hand, Italianisms are surprisingly rare for an inhabitant of Lyons working in the Petrarchan style, but this is perhaps precisely a sign of his desire to 'illustrer la langue française'. He appears to invent only a handful of words – something like twenty – and they rarely stand out like a sore thumb, as did Ronsard's *contumax* in an early edition of the *Amours*. His marked predilection for adverbs in *-ment* may owe something to Petrarchan style, but the *rhétoriqueurs* also saw poetic merits in their use, and for Scève they often function like a *point d'orgue*. On two points of syntax, he anticipates the Pléiade programme: he makes judicious use of the article before the infinitive and also before the adjective which are thereby substantivised.

Though Scève's vocabulary is for the most part elevated, we must look elsewhere for the means that allow the *dizains* to combine density, stress, movement, and poetic resonance. In the syntax, Scève obtains remarkable effects of concision by his use of apposition, participial phrases (which are not only short but permit of an openness of relation with other parts of the sentence), repetition, suppression of the verb. Nevertheless, there needs to be some counterbalancing search for movement, if the *dizain* is not to become clogged; and Scève betrays a fine awareness of sentence-pattern in relation to *dizain* structure. Here, sequences, *incises, enjambement* are among the devices introduced with a sure hand in the construction of *dizains* whose dominant pattern is 4 + 4 + 2, but can be varied with startling results.

All these instruments are valuable, indeed indispensable; but Scève goes further in the extent to which he exploits the harmonics of imagery, a field in which his immediate predecessors are often weak. It is not that his images are especially original in their reference, apart perhaps from some scientific images which tend to be too sophisticated, verging on the precious; but they contribute immensely to the resonance of the poems. Even Délie's name has imagic connotation; to see in it an anagram of *l'idée*, as some have done, is quite in keeping with sixteenth-century habits, but such an interpretation would limit the lady's role to the Platonic field, and this would not really square with the impression given by the sequence as a whole. In Diz. 22 the author has himself pointed to Délie's links with Diana in her manifestation as the moon and as Hecate (which suggests suffering after death). Elsewhere she is identified with Libytina, the Roman goddess of corpses who represented another aspect of Diana. The conventional association of Diana the huntress with chastity is not prominent; on the other hand, Diana inevitably conjures up the idea of Apollo, so that the themes of sun and moon recur regularly; indeed, one of the main contrasts in the work is that of light and dark, which is closely related to that of absence and presence. There are further possible associations with Apollo, the god of health, medicine, knowledge, and poetry, but these features are not exploited in any systematic fashion. Nevertheless, the range of reference evoked by Délie's name is considerable and mirrors the pattern of the whole sequence.

Scève draws for his imagery on classical mythology, though without undue self-consciousness, geography (links with local features and rivers, and standard imagery of the type 'from Tagus to Ganges'), contemporary political events, science and technology; some of these sources of poetic reference will be found in the Petrarchan idiom, *mutatis mutandis*, but Scève also exploits biblical imagery, in particular from the Old Testament (Exodus), so that his absence from Délie is on occasion tinged by the introduction of the themes of guilt and exile.

Two *dizains* may serve here, however inadequately, to give a glimpse of Scève's achievement. Dizain 1 runs thus:

> L'Œil trop ardent en mes jeunes erreurs
> Girouettoit mal caut à l'impourveue :
> Voicy (ô paour d'agreables terreurs)
> Mon Basilisque avec sa poingnant' veue
> Perçant Corps, Cœur, & Raison despourveue,
> Vint penetrer en l'Ame de mon Ame.
>   Grand fut le coup, qui sans tranchante lame
> Fit que vivant le Corps, l'Esprit desvie,
> Piteuse hostie au conspect de toy, Dame,
> Constituée Idole de ma vie.

This is a most impressive opening: for Scève, more than for, say, Ronsard in the *Amours* or even Du Bellay, the *coup de foudre* is an event to which he will return time and again. And the importance of this experience is revealed not merely by the place it occupies at the very outset, but by the way in which the poet handles it. There is a discreet echo of Petrarch in the first line (*jeunes erreurs*, the noun incidentally having an amorous connotation in Petrarch, in Latin verse, and in poets such as Pontus de Tyard). Further Petrarchan motifs develop the main theme: the eye, compared to a basilisk, pierces the lover's heart, without bloodshed, and Scève introduces two antitheses in lines 3 and 8; otherwise, the poem carries an unmistakable resonance of its own. The workings of vocabulary, sentence-control, syntax, imagery, to which I alluded earlier, are all very much in evidence here. *Girouettoit* is in all probability a neologism, and both *conspect* and *Constituée* have had some of their Latin harmonics restored to them. As for word order, note the placing of *Girouettoit* and *Grand* (inverted), that is words denoting motion and feeling, at the beginning of the line. Syntactically, there is nothing of great note, but sentence-control is very skilful, with *incises*, ternary movement, *enjambement*, chiasmus, invocation, and the carrying of the final sentence through four lines before it reaches its climax. The tone of the poem is heightened by the scattering of religious terms, so that our entry to the sequence occurs with an impressive degree of *elevation*. Thematically, the *dizain* marks the shift from idle play to fixation of the poet's feelings; and the first *dizain* is not simply a fitting prelude to the sequence, but a challenge of high linguistic order.

The second *dizain* selected (Diz. 58) is perhaps less remarkable in some ways, but it displays Scève's mastery in building up his poem to a triumphant climax:

> Quand j'apperceus au serain de ses yeux
> L'air esclarcy de si longue tempeste,
> Jà toute empeinct au prouffit de mon mieulx,
> Comme un vainqueur d'honnorable conqueste,
> Je commençay à eslever la teste:
> Et lors le Lac de mes nouvelles joyes
> Restangna tout, voire dehors ses voyes
> Assez plus loing, qu'oncques ne fit jadis.
> Dont mes pensers guidez par leurs Montjoyes
> Se paonnoient tous en leur hault Paradis.

Now there are, to be sure, elements less forceful than in the first *dizain*. The first five lines – and this is something that occurs in other *dizains* from time to time – do not seem to promise anything out of the ordinary; they have no particular colour, the comparison employed is modest in its effect, and the image of the tempest in line 1 might seem trite obedience to the Petrarchan tradition. One might also feel that the second half of line 8 was conventionally hyperbolic as in any old-world novel. Nevertheless, the poem has considerable power. To begin with, it is robustly articulated: unusual by its division into two sentences (in line 9 *Dont* runs on with little break from the previous line and the full stop has less than its full value), it is carefully balanced; the subordinate clause of four lines leans on the main clause of line 5 which acts as the release-mechanism for the second half of the poem. Here we not only have the movement maintained and indeed quickened, but this half is richly studded with imagery. First the lake of his *joyes* (not an entirely new image, since water is often a symbol of love) is developed into an image of progress and successful journey: if we take *empeinct* in the sense of 'pushed, moving towards', then we have a slight hint given of this movement in the first half. *Montjoyes* has the meaning of 'milestones' or 'commemorative barrows', and in this context marks the poet's amorous advance, with the help of a play on words that is perfectly acceptable. Particularly interesting is the word *Restangna*, which like *Constituée* in Diz. 1 has been reinvigorated by its original meaning in

Latin ('overflow'), and which also stands out by virtue of its place in the line. The final line fittingly crowns the whole poem with its upward sweep, its triumphant close (with the inverted adjective allowing *Paradis* to reverberate), and the use of what appears to be a most successful imagic neologism – *Se paonnoient*. Here as elsewhere, the movement is from darkness to light, but the presence of the beloved is almost eclipsed in the overwhelming delight of the poet. In Scève, however pedantic the process may appear at first blush, the careful noting of linguistic originality enhances immeasurably the value we may set upon his poetry.

Scève's high quality emerges, I hope, from these analyses. He possesses mastery of imagery in an unusual degree, and that at a time when French poetry lacked enterprise in this field. It is this quality that, above all, gives his writing its density and its luminosity; Scève is a pioneer in his ability to exploit to the full the potential of an image, by combining it with other poetic effects, by careful preparation of its entry, by the way too in which he can confer on a final image the power to light up, as it were retrospectively, the whole fabric of a *dizain*. For he is also a master of structure: his liking for imagery from the fields of science and architecture suggests a precise mind concerned with formal matters and aware of the problems of stress and balance. His finest *dizains* owe their success to this quality, flanked by a sure linguistic sense and a sensibility that is characterised by a high intellectual awareness. Behind the poems lie not only emotions, but mind; and sometimes his writing reminds us of Mallarmé and Valéry. These are all poets whose verse gives the impression of powerful emotional forces held in balance by equally powerful aesthetic and intellectual controls. In Scève the impression of cohesion is prominent: no loose strands, no *chevilles*, no marking time. And this closeness of texture is accompanied by a very delicate sense of tempo. His best work gives an impression of finely chiselled delicacy and strength, compelling the attention of the reader, whose imagination is fully engaged. Scève's eclipse for so many centuries is a measure of the inadequacy of those classical criteria of literary excellence that have dominated the French scene all too long.

Historically, Scève's impact may in consequence appear rather slight, for even his contemporaries were put off by his 'mots nouveaux' (Sebillet) and his hermetic appearance. Nevertheless, he did exercise a seminal influence upon some poets of the Pléiade generation, notably Du Bellay and Pontus de Tyard – nor was his example ignored by Ronsard. In fact, he was very much a precursor: his claims for a more aristocratic view of poetry, the need for renewal of the poetic language, the exploration of foreign models, all these points will be found in the *Deffense* of 1549. Scève also produced the first *canzoniere* in France[11] and gave stature and status to love-poetry; he may have helped to tip the balance in favour of French; he foresaw in his practice the urgency of various syntactical innovations; he showed the part that could be played by imagery in poetic structure. We tend to judge him on the merits of the *Délie*, and this is no doubt justifiable; but he was also a poet of some range. He produced a little court verse – the *Arion* is a homage to the dauphin – and contributed to the Lyons *entrée* of 1549; nor should we forget his enchanting *Saulsaye* which in its way marks a turning-point in pastoral;[12] and later in life, like Ronsard, he turned to scientific poetry (see below, pp. 382–4). Eclipsed in his time by the *prince des poètes* he stands as a sort of poetic John the Baptist, whose full genius has come to be recognised only in our time.

III. PERNETTE DU GUILLET[13]

The total absence of contemporary reference to this poetess, beyond the preface to her *Rimes* published in 1545, is curious and has led to some speculation on her identity, and even on her reality. Whatever the truth of the matter, the *Rimes* present her in relationship with Maurice Scève, for some of the poems and the *Délie* answer one another; Scève is praised for his virtue, his eloquence, and his *hault sçavoir*. Pernette has written several compositions in Italian and her general debt to Italian sources needs no stressing: the third *Elegie* is in *terza rima* and the *Desespoir* poem in particular is influenced by the Italian version of the genre. She does not for all that break with French tradition, and several features link her with the Marotic school; in an epistle she proclaims her admiration of both Petrarch and Jean de Meung, and she makes use of allegorical figures to express various attitudes of mind.

The *Rimes* treat of Pernette's unfulfilled love for the poet, a love that comes to be more and more sublimated in Neoplatonic terms; indeed the Platonic element is, proportionately and qualitatively, more to the fore than in the *Délie*. Though Pernette responds thematically in a number of poems to Scève's sequence and resembles him sometimes in her psychological analyses and even the dialectical idiom, her poetry rarely emits a Scevian resonance. There is virtually no obscure or dense writing, the role of learning is reduced, though evidence is there that it exists, and above all, she fails to exploit imagery in a comparable degree. Where she achieves a striking measure of expression is in the uncomplicated description of her passion, a straightforward utterance where alembication and intricate imagery are absent. To be sure, a few poems come close to preciosity, but they are not among the best. Pernette works in a variety of structures, and even her shortest epigrams can reveal an impressive blend of control and simplicity.

Je suis tant bien que je ne le puis dire,
Ayant sondé son amytié profonde
Par sa vertu, qui à l'aymer m'attire
Plus que beaulté: car sa grace, et faconde
Me font cuyder la premiere du monde.

(Epigramme xvii)

More frequently, these themes are in the minor mode, for she subordinates herself to her lover in her sense of inadequacy; ecstasy is
reserved for those poems where spiritual elevation is the central
concern. Her works, which fill only a small volume, found a ready
public as no less than four editions came out between 1545 and 1552,
a success greater than that of the *Délie* to which nowadays they
form a modest pendant.

IV. LOUISE LABÉ (?1520–65)[14]

Louise Labé is remembered by a handful of writings, which a
fanciful view of her biography has not helped to elucidate. Her work
consists of a *Débat de la folie et de l'amour* (c. 1555), three elegies,
and some two dozen sonnets. The *Débat*, which seems to have enjoyed some success in the sixteenth century, treats of a quarrel
between Love and Folly who had scratched out his eyes and then
blindfolded him; though the substance of the text consists of speeches
by Apollo and Mercury defending Love and Folly respectively, these
are preceded by several scenes (called *discours*) in which the events
leading up to the debate are presented to the reader; and there is a
short coda in which Jupiter defers judgement for many centuries,
realising that the two characters can get along very well together.
The general structure is thus medieval, with its debate and allegorical
forms, though some dramatic touches are introduced. On the other
hand, the material of the debate reflects two different aspects of the
Renaissance mind. There is first the defence of love, in which a series
of *topoi*, partly of Neoplatonic colour, are developed: love as the
force which makes the world go round, the principle of harmony
that unites men so different in outward character, love rather than
glory as the motivation towards a better life, love as the inventor of
music; and in this apology, critics have rightly discerned the influence
of Italian models, Bembo, Castiglione, and perhaps others. Then, the
praise of Folly, which immediately conjures up the name of Erasmus,
and with good cause, adopts a different tone – indeed, one of the
features of the work is the range of tones introduced. Here we have
something reminiscent of the pseudo-encomium, such as is found in
Lucian, in Buchanan's *Pro Læna* (c. 1540), or Rabelais's praise of
debts. Folly is presented as the salt of life, the principle of activity,
without whom existence would be a sorry affair. Folly is then closely

associated with Love, and some pleasant asides are made at the expense of the Stoics and their shunning of passion. Towards the end, the tones of the two apologies begin to converge: 'Car si c'est vray amour, il est grand et vehement, et plus forte que toute raison'. However, the finale verges on the Rabelaisian and there may in fact be some echoes of the Pantagruel epic:

Ne laissez perdre cette belle Dame, qui vous ha donné tant de contentement avec Genie, Jeunesse, Bacchus, Silene, et ce gentil Gardien des Jardins [i.e., Priapus.]

Louise Labé shows a confident, happy command of French prose, where both rhetorical period and a tripping, jolly phrase can coexist successfully. And though, according to tradition, the apologies are supported by the evidence of time-honoured authority, the style does not become laboured as a result, and the author carries her learning lightly.[15]

For posterity, however, it is the sonnets rather than the *Débat* or the elegies, valuable for some biographical details, that have stolen the limelight. Discussion of these texts has been obscured by the scandal-loving or knightly approach adopted in speculations about her life; and the lack of obvious erudition – compared with the Pléiade's early Petrarchan displays – has led critics to interpret the set of sonnets through Romantic spectacles: Magny, who was in Lyons in 1552, has been mentioned, and more recently suggestions have been made about the poetess's connection with Marot and the Dauphin Henry. According to her own statements, she fell in love at the age of sixteen with someone who did not respond, and some thirteen years later, her memories were still sufficiently raw for her to compose these poems. The generally Petrarchan nature of the series will be obvious, though only Sonnet iii has been identified as an undoubted imitation, and certain themes tend to recur: the distance between lover and loved, the contrast between the harmony of the gods and the lovers' discords, the lute, the solar *topos*, themes of night, solitude, the discreet use of mythology to imagic ends, and of course the very use of the sonnet form. There is also a *basium*; on the other hand, there is no clear progression in the order of the sonnets, but rather different facets of an englobing experience. What strikes one immediately is the intensity of the passion, and its unambiguous expression; yet it would be rash to think that this is poetry without artifice:

> Oh si j'estois en ce beau sein ravie
>   De celui là pour lequel vois mourant:
>   Si avec luy vive le demeurant
>   De mes courts jours ne m'empeschoit envie:
> Si m'acollant me disoit: chere Amie,
>   Contentons nous l'un l'autre, s'asseurant

> Que jà tempeste, Euripe, ne Courant
> Ne nous pourra desjoindre en nostre vie:
> Si de mes bras le tenant acollé,
> Comme du Lierre est l'arbre encercelé,
> La mort venoit, de mon aise envieuse:
> Lors que souef plus il me baiseroit,
> Et mon esprit sur mes levres fuiroit,
> Bien je mourrois, plus que vivante, heureuse.
>
> (Sonnet xiii)

The working of love through the theme of death is carried with skilled control to a triumphant affirmation; and the sentence structure is specially notable, with its repetition of conditional clauses so organised that the main clause is confined to the final line where an *incise* including a conceit brings the sonnet to a radiant close. Louise Labé has a delicate sense of the placing of her stress words, both at the caesura and at the end of the line, and she makes striking use of repetition (root *mour-* and *acollé*). She is perhaps less sure in her handling of imagery: line 7, with its ternary movement, works with decreasing effect, and *Euripe* does not bear out its imagic promise; then in line 10 the comparison of the lover with ivy, even though he is welcomed as a messenger of death, may disconcert. As a general rule, she does not rely on imagery to the same extent as Scève, and it is indeed unlikely that she owes very much to him; her language is less *recherché*, and she rarely attains his density; on the other hand, she can create the *point d'orgue* capable of reverberating in the reader's mind:

> Tant que mes yeulx pourront larmes espandre
> A l'heur passé avec toy regretter:
> Et qu'aux sanglots et souspirs resister
> Pourra ma voix, et un peu faire entendre:
> Tant que ma main pourra les cordes tendre
> Du mignard lut, pour tes graces chanter:
> Tant que l'esprit se voudra contenter
> De ne vouloir rien fors que toy comprendre:
> Je ne souhaitte encore point mourir.
> Mais quand mes yeus je sentiray tarir,
> Ma voix cassée, et ma main impuissante,
> Et mon esprit en ce mortel sejour
> Ne pouvant plus montrer signe d'amante:
> Priray la Mort noircir mon plus cler jour.
>
> (Sonnet xiv)

Here again we have the theme of death, but expressed in very different fashion: the sense of time, but also timelessness, suggested by the very desire that death shall blot out everything when the poetess ceases to have strength to sing her love. The structure of the sonnet differs from the previous one discussed in that, instead of thirteen lines of subordinate clauses pressing towards the single main-clause line, we have a scheme in which two important lines are isolated: $4/4+1, 2/2+1$. There is a very clear pattern of symmetries and balances, in which the elements are linked by temporal conjunctions (*tant que . . . quand*); notice also the skilful use of modals (*pourra* in varying positions, *vouloir*) and the way in which the movement goes against the conventional expectation of the sonnet. The tone of the poem is further determined by the choice of adjectives, the stress on sound (*sanglots, voix, entendre, lut, chanter, voix cassée*) and on the eyes, and the final antithesis of day and death. In all this, there is an avoidance of erudite allusion, of significant reliance on imagery, but an experienced handling of rhetorical instruments – including enumeration and invocation of which she makes a very personal use – and an exceptional feeling for sonnet structure, in which the last line, Petrarchan in its essential device, goes far beyond any commonplace trickery and illuminates the whole poem, as it were, retrospectively. It is the peculiar blend of passion and rhetoric that gives Louise Labé's sonnets their character, linked with a choice of vocabulary that seeks no obvious literary effect in its own right. Intensity and supplication, but also a modification of the Petrarchan idiom, in that the lover, though absent and probably aloof, is not placed on a pedestal, but enwrapped in the incandescence of her feeling. In consequence, Louise Labé has carved for herself a niche in the Petrarchan gallery which sets her apart from so many of the master's French neophytes.

After Louise Labé, Lyons has less to contribute to the development of French poetry, though it still remains a very important printing centre, and a point of entry for further Italian and Spanish influence. Economic troubles beset the town in later decades, but Lyons's prestige was bound to wane, once cultural life had been restored to its brilliance and vigour in the capital. Lyons gave asylum and the possibility of organized expression in the 1530s to Neo-latin currents, whose presence helps to acclimatise themes, attitudes, and genres that will become successful in the vernacular a little while later; it makes an equally important contribution by its development of a new style of poetry, Petrarchan in inspiration very often, but carrying the seeds of further development in French terms. It is no doubt possible to exaggerate the links between the Lyons circles and the budding Pléiade; nevertheless, these links are real, both at personal and at literary level. The Lyons poets fill the gap between the death of Marot and the advent of the Pléiade; and by their choice of style and idiom they accelerate a process that had been only timidly foreseen by the later representatives of the so-called Marotic school. The Lyons poets raise French love-poetry to heights it had not known for a very long time, and they also make an important contribution to the development of new poetic structures and of a new poetic language.

NOTES

1. A. Kleinclausz, *Histoire de Lyon*, vol. I., *Des Origines à 1595*, Lyons, 1939; F. Buisson, *Sébastien Castellion*, vol. I 1892, ch. ii; R. C. Christie, *Etienne Dolet*, 1899, ch. iv; V.-L. Saulnier, *Maurice Scève*, 1948, vol. I. ch. v–vi; J. B. Wadsworth, *Lyon 1473–1503: the Beginning of Cosmopolitanism*, Cambridge, Mass., 1962; H.-J. Martin (ed.), *Cinq Études lyonnaises*, Geneva–Paris, 1966.

2. S. F. Pogue, *Jacques Moderne, Lyons Music Printer of the XVIth century*, *THR*, 1969; also Oxford D.Phil. thesis by N. Dobbins (1972).

3. P. Allut, *Etude biographique et bibliographique sur Symphorien Champier*, Lyons, 1859; *Cinq Études lyonnaises*, ed. H.-J. Martin. Several unpublished dissertations have recently been completed on Champier, but an up-to-date general survey is badly needed. Though much of his writing belongs to earlier decades, he is still prominent in the 1530s.

4. *Le livre de vraye amour*, ed. James B. Wadsworth, 'S Gravenhage, 1962; W. Mönch, op. cit.

5. J. L. Gerig, 'Le Collège de la Trinité à Lyon avant 1540', *RRen*, 1908.

6. J. L. Gerig, 'Barthélemy Aneau, a study in humanism', *RR*, 1911 and 1913.

7. Published in 1541 (BM). See V.-L. Saulnier, 'Le théâtre de Barthélemy Aneau', *Mélanges Gustave Cohen*, 1950.

8. V.-L. Saulnier, *Maurice Scève*, 2 vols., 1948–49, and the series of volumes in course of publication by Enzo Giudici on *Maurice Scève poeta della Délie*, 1966– ; D. Coleman, 'Les Emblesmes dans la *Délie* de Maurice Scève', *SF*, 1964. Editions of the *Délie* by E. Parturier, *STFM*, 1916, 1931, 1966; and by I. D. McFarlane, Cambridge, 1966; Scolar reprint of first edition by D. B. Wilson, 1972. See also A. Falbe, *Die Dichtung Maurice Scèves: Komposition, Struktur, Bilder*, Berlin, 1964.

9. J. Vianey, *Le Pétrarquisme en France au XVIᵉ siècle*, Montpellier, 1909; Leonard Forster, *The Icy Fire*, Cambridge, 1969; J. U. Fechner, *Der Antipetrarkismus*, Heidelberg, 1966.

10. M. Praz, *Studies in Seventeenth-Century Imagery*, 2nd ed., Rome, 1964; A. Henkel and A. Schöne, *Emblemata, Handbuch zur Sinnbildkunst des XVI. und XVII. Jahrhunderts*, Stuttgart, 1967; G. de Tervarent, *Attributs et symboles dans l'art profane, 1450–1600. Dictionnaire d'un langage perdu*, *THR*, 1958.

11. The *Centuries* of the lawyer Jean de Boyssonné, who also left interesting Latin poetry, may have some claims to priority in this respect; but the exact date of their composition is still in doubt, and they remained in manuscript until fairly recently.

12. Texts available in B. Guégan's ed. of *Œuvres poétiques complètes*, 1927, and E. Giudici, *Maurice Scève Bucolico e Blasonneur*, Naples, 1965, and *Le Opere Minori di Maurice Scève*, Naples, 1959. *Saulsaye* ed. M. Françon, Cambridge, Mass., 1959.

13. *Rymes*, Lyons, 1545,1546 (BN); modern ed. by V. E. Graham, *TLF*, 1968. See also V.-L. Saulnier, 'Etude sur Pernette du Guillet et ses Rymes', *BHR*, 1944, and E. Giudici's monographs on Scève's *Délie*.

14. *Euures*, Lyons, 1555 (BM, BN) and 1556 (BM, BN). Modern eds. by B. Jourdan, 1953, E. Giudici, 1960, K. Varty (announced). See also D. O'Connor, *Louise Labé, sa vie et son œuvre*, 1926; F. Zamaron, *Louise Labé dame de franchise: sa vie, son œuvre, le texte des élégies, et sonnets, son entourage littéraire*, 1968; L. E. Harvey, *The Aesthetics of the Renaissance Love Sonnet*, Geneva, 1962; E. Giudici, *Louise Labé e l'Ecole lyonnaise*, Naples, 1964.

15. E. Giudici, *Il Canzoniere. La Disputa di Follia e di Amore*, Parma, 1955.

Chapter 5

PROSE FICTION UNDER FRANCIS I

I t is during the reign of Francis I that prose fiction gets properly under way. There is evidence that this form of literature was rather despised by writers; on the other hand, there is consider-able demand, especially it seems among women readers. At all events, until the 1530s little creative work is produced at home, and demand is satisfied partly by the printing of medieval romances, which often go through more than one edition, partly by the translation of Italian and Spanish works. Over fifty medieval romances were pub-lished during the century; Arthurian legends were to become very popular at Court, where the chivalric tradition still has its sup-porters. To simplify the presentation of material that rapidly assumes ample proportions, I shall deal in this chapter with the more ex-tended form of fiction; I shall reserve for later the discussion of the *conte* and *nouvelle*: in any case, this division also reflects *grosso modo* the fact that, though a number of authors, connected in some degree with Marguerite de Navarre, interest themselves in the shorter forms during the 1540s, it is during the following decade that this writing comes into print and finds a steady flow of imitators.

In the extended structure there are two main currents: the romance or 'sentimental' novel and Rabelais with his imitators. The first, though still a rather modest trickle, attracts writers of talent.

I. THE NOVEL[1]

Jehan de Paris[2] (*1533*)

One of the first novels to appear in the 1530s, *Jehan de Paris* was reprinted several times, but it dates from the last decade of the fifteenth century, and the identity of its author is still in doubt. The narrative centres on the young King of France, whose father had, after ensuring the authority of the King and Queen of Spain, accepted their promise that their child would marry whomsoever he wished. With the passing of the years, the Spanish couple forgot their pledge and were on the point of marrying their daughter to the elderly King of England, when the news reached France. The young King, disguising himself as the bourgeois Jehan de Paris, undertakes the journey to Spain at the same time as the English King; after a fairy-tale display of splendour and strength, he wins the Spanish princess to the discomfiture of the King of England who makes his way home with despatch and his tail between his legs. The story, which claims to be no more than an 'histoire joyeuse', a 'passe-temps', draws in fact on the tradition of the romance and fairy-tale, with the impeccable hero to whom nothing is denied. The disguised Frenchman, after speaking in riddles to the King of England, also belongs thereby to a tradition. At the same time, one can read the work as a eulogy of France and her king; all the Spanish kings bow before him, and at a moment when his identity has yet to be revealed. His standards – the dispensing of justice and the fear of God – are emphasised; and above all, a hyperbolic contrast is established between him and the English King, who is presented as the elderly lover of a farce, whose soldiers are drowned in the river when all Frenchmen cross safely, and have no idea how to protect themselves from the rain. There are a few remarks against the feudal barons, keen to make war as they have been subjected to peace for an un-conscionable time. All this gives the work a mixture of lively satirical comment and fairy-tale atmosphere. Internal evidence has suggested that the author may well have been acquainted with the Court of Anne of Brittany and Charles VIII. The style, though still of the fifteenth century, is uncluttered and made brisk by the skilful use of dialogue and a sense of the dramatic tableau. In places, there are hints of a sense of psychological detail, and the author always gives the impression of being in control of his material. He tends to give all he describes a larger-than-life quality and we are introduced to a world of incredible sumptuousness and integrity; the villains, if there are any, remain in the background and any failure to keep one's word is readily made good.

Foreign novels

During this decade, reliance is still placed on foreign sources for the reading public. Octovien de Saint-Gellais had before 1500 trans-lated Aeneas Sylvius's *Histoire d'Euryale et Lucrece*, and the French versions of Ovid may have appealed in this context to contem-porary sensibility; but it is above all the appearance of the Spanish novel, usually in the minor key, that sets the tone. Maurice Scève's translation of *Flamete* by Juan de Flores, published in 1535 and 1536, is fairly well known; but Diego de San Pedro commands a larger public: his *Carcel de Amor*, translated as the *Prison d'Amors*, was first published in Paris in 1526, but it went through several reprints, including the bilingual edition of 1552 and 1567. Herberay des Essarts, whose role as a translator of romances is substantial, rendered the same writer's *Petit traité de Arnalte et Lucenda* in

1539: such was the success of this work that it enjoyed nearly twenty editions before the end of the century. A further text of his, *Le debat des deux gentilzhommes espanolz sur le fait d'amour*, was printed in 1541. And Herberay goes on to translate, in part to embroider on, the famous *Amadis de Gaule* (see below, pp. 236–7). To these Spanish works must be added the Italian contribution: though one associates the Italian authors with the *nouvelle*, and often the lighthearted sort, more sombre tones also make themselves heard in their work. In the 1530s, Boccaccio's reputation is well established, but Caviceo's *Peregrino* commands an extraordinary success (translated in 1527, it is reprinted in 1528, 1531, 1535, 1540). In contemporary poetry, Petrarchism is beginning to assert itself on a broad front, but little of this seems to filter into the novel, though one wonders whether in the fairly near future some Neoplatonic harmonics may not be added to a conception of love in these novels which is often tragic or unfulfilled: it is not a coincidence that the tale of the *Châtelaine de Vergi* should find its way into the *Heptaméron*. And in the novel, rather than in the *nouvelle*, we may find a significant edifying tendency.

Helisenne de Crenne[3]

In this context, Helisenne de Crenne's *Angoysses douloureuses qui procedent d'amours* (1538) is a milestone, and a successful one, for it went through seven, perhaps more, editions. The authoress's real name was Marguerite de Briet, and she divides her work into three parts; these appear slightly heterogeneous in that the first section, which recounts Helisenne's infatuation for a young man of lower rank than herself, ends in her incarceration by her husband, whereas the two other sections belong much more closely to the *roman d'aventures*: they describe the endless experiences of the young man and his friend in their search for the heroine and remind us of Arthurian romance, with the male lover spiritualising his emotions by a series of travels and lengthy frustrations. The first section, apparently based on Marguerite de Briet's own life, has interested critics to the exclusion of the rest, partly because it is more realistic and psychologically profound, partly because the style of the later sections becomes even more alembicated and latinised than ever. The opening lines of the *amy*'s letter give us some idea of this style:

Ma dame, puisque la libere faculté de parler à vous pour vous enucleer mon amoureuse conception ne m'est permise, j'ay esté contrainct par la persuasion du filz Venus vous escripre la presente. Et pour vous certiorer de l'extremité où l'amour excessif m'a conduict, debvez sçavoir que lors que premierement dressay ma veue sur vos yeulx verds et irradians, me sembla veoir issir une splendeur, laquelle plus près la cueur me transperça que ne fist l'aguë sagette de Juppiter Phaeton ... Et pour la recente memoire de l'acerbe douleur où je fuz reduict, mon entendement est si perturbé qu'il me seroit impossible de vous louer et extoller de louenge condigne selon la speciosité de vostre forme . . . (Demats ed., p. 27)

A similar idiom recurs in Jeanne Flore (see below, pp. 238–9); we are still close to the *rhétoriqueurs*: latinisms, epithets, doublets, adverbs in *-ment*, periphrasis (the time of events is nearly always defined by an elaborate mythological periphrasis), chain sequence of sentence structure. In other respects we are in a pre-Petrarchan and pre-Platonic world, and the fairy element reminds one of *Jehan de Paris* or *Le Petit Sainctré*, a fifteenth-century tale first printed in 1517. The cast is small: the triangle of husband, lover, and lady, the treacherous servant, and in the later sections, the faithful friend and the unkind sister-in-law. Helisenne sees love as a disease blind to reason, and she tells her story to secure the sympathy of others and thereby quieten her misery, but also to issue a warning to those who might fall victim to passion. She shows how love has warped her mind which, in its obsession, turns to dissimulation and loss of equanimity, is incapable of rescuing itself, and remains deaf to the call of religion. She attempts to state the truth and to understand the violent reactions of her jealous husband. The first section is not particularly well constructed; the style, which lacks tonal variety, except perhaps in the impish description of ugliness in chapter V, does little to maintain the reader's interest, and there is a certain amount of gratuitous erudition that has lost whatever appeal it may have had. The other two sections move more rapidly, because of the adventures they contain, but they do not open up possibilities of literary development. The first section, in spite of weaknesses mentioned, does look forward. It is the first French novel to describe events from the point of view of the woman, and this has led some critics to trace the work back to *Fiammetta*, though the debt to Caviceo is probably greater. Little attempt is made to idealise the lover, whose character remains unsympathetic in many respects. The inner drama is exposed with insight and the clashes of personality acquire some dramatic vitality; it is a pity that the author's language, sometimes pretentious, is not really an adequate vehicle for the experience she is relating.

Théodose Valentinian[4]

The *Resuscité de la Mort d'Amour* is known by the editions of 1557 and 1558, but earlier printings appear to have existed at one time. Very possibly written by Nicolas Denisot, the novel is interesting for the way in which traditional structures have been modified to develop views on love, marriage, and religion that are in the air in the early 1550s and perhaps earlier. The fictional element is on three levels, the narrative relevant to the 'author', the portrait of the lover on the verge of death through his passion for the beloved, and

Florinde's telling of the story of Aeneas and Dido. Two features are noteworthy in the treatment of a fiction that, initially, owes something to the Spanish novel: on the one hand, the lover is recalled to life and forgetfulness of his passionate experience by the intervention of God. There is thus a religious twist to the end of the story that fits in with the substantial Book II in which M. Meyssour develops her theory of love; according to her, the relationship between the two lovers must be of a spiritual and cultured character (as in Corrozet's *Compte du Rossignol*). Love must be virtuous and indeed the fault of the lover, as is revealed in the final book, is that he puts love of woman before that of God; *folle amour* has taken the place of privilege over *parfaicte amour*. Some of these themes may also be found in the contemporary work of Pasquier, the *Monophile* (1554): the relations between friendship and love, man as an example to his wife, who for her part is seen as inferior on theological grounds (Glaphire). Both works mark, in a sense, a departure from totally Platonic views, but the *Monophile* doubtless seeks to identify passion and friendship more closely in marriage – a theme which was to flourish in a Calvinist climate. The novel, in part a treatise, is divided into five sections, with the unusual feature of the action taking place in England; each level of narration illustrates by thesis or counter-thesis the validity of the conception of love advocated by Margaret Meyssour (?=Seymour) and accepted by all the characters involved. The author has gone beyond the usual formula to introduce a variety of tones and techniques, though his style remains rather conventional.

II. FRANÇOIS RABELAIS (?1494–1553)[5]

Despite his fame and stature, Rabelais remains an enigmatic figure. His life is not well known, much of his work is highly allusive, and the very ambiguity of his laughter has provoked a jostling crowd of irreconcilable views on the 'meaning' of his novel, views that have often been complicated by religious prejudice. Rabelais's own invitation that we should 'sugcer la substantificque moelle' has not helped matters: the relations that exist between the characters and their creator, himself an admirer of Erasmus and Lucian, are not by any means clear, and there may be dangers in associating one *persona* too closely with the inner author. And finally, the authenticity of the major part of the posthumous *Cinquiesme Livre* still remains in some doubt. It is therefore not surprising that his work has been very variously appreciated in time and country. Seventeenth-century France, and Italy at most times, have seen in him essentially a humorist, but the eighteenth century moved towards an allegorical interpretation of his work. After the Romantics who took the fool seriously, there emerges a series of efforts to determine Rabelais's underlying philosophy, whether Stoic (Faguet), naturist (Brunetière, J. C. Powys), indifferentist or rationalist (Lefranc, Lote, Busson). Since Lucien Febvre, an Erasmian approach has predominated, with an increasing tendency to consider Rabelais as remaining, in spite of everything, within the pale of orthodoxy. There is of course nothing incompatible between a serious outlook on life and humorous presentation, but in Rabelais the problem is complicated by his habit of disengaging at critical moments and multiplying his levels of reference.

The increasingly Christian view of Rabelais's writings has led critics to stress his monastic training and late-medieval formation. Rabelais is a product of Franciscan and Benedictine background, and even if he devotes time to satirising monks and their way of life, his categories of thought are conditioned by his formation, and his style of writing owes much to the sermon idiom of the preaching friars. Nevertheless, his attitudes are strongly determined by the intellectual currents stirring in the 1520s and early 1530s. Reference is properly made to his frequenting of humanists at Fontenay-le-Comte (Pierre Amy, Tiraqueau, etc.) and Maillezais. The influence of Greek studies is easily discernible in his work – his Greek books were confiscated in his first monastery – and even in *Pantagruel* the familiars of the hero are endowed with Greek names. Rabelais was also well versed in the study of law: the law is mercilessly ridiculed on many occasions, but much of the humour stems from professional allusions, and the *Tiers Livre* in particular is coloured by the tones of the legal world. It is well known that Rabelais was a doctor of eminence in his time; he may even have made some contribution to anatomical knowledge, at all events medicine is a rich source of humour in his novel. His humanist urge towards polymathy led him to take interest in contemporary cosmography, cryptography, and other fields; but he does not lose touch with what Péguy called his local *país*, and these contacts enrich his handling of language. Finally, his membership of the Du Bellay entourage is valuable, not only for contacts he made there, but also because it facilitated his travels abroad, and chiefly in Italy.

Pantagruel

The first book of the series is in fact *Pantagruel* (1532), written in the main for *délassement* and published under the pseudonym *Alcofribas Nasier*;[6] indeed some contemporaries, including Nicolas Bourbon, thought the work hardly serious enough for so distinguished a humanist. Rabelais took inspiration from the *Grandes et inestimables chronicques de l'enorme géant Gargantua*, published a short while before and prolonging in debased form elements of the Arthurian legend still very popular. Some of the incidents in the *Chronicques* will be developed later in the *Gargantua*, but here direct borrowing is naturally less evident since Rabelais is dealing with the giant's son. Gargantua was likely to attract him in part because the tales were linked with his own region; but there were other literary sources on which he could draw. From abroad, the names of Pulci and Folengo spring to mind (Rabelais is clearly familiar with the drama of his own country – Pantagruel's name occurs in a *mystère*) and with the epic, historical tradition which he burlesques. He is well read in *rhétoriqueur* poetry, and when he does, infrequently, indulge in verse, he belongs very clearly to that school. Finally, he owes a good deal to the techniques of the Franciscan sermon.

Pantagruel himself is nonetheless Rabelais's own creation in great measure; and we are given an account of his birth, upbringing, and education at various universities – especially Paris, where he meets Panurge, who will become an important source of humour. Then the pair set out on their journey and join battle with the King of the Dipsodes. These two characters form the backbone of the book, which is fairly loosely constructed; and only Epistémon, among Pantagruel's familiars, stands out as an identity. Pantagruel does not acquire the importance he will enjoy in the *Tiers Livre*; here he is a source of comic by virtue of his gigantism, but he recedes for a time to allow Panurge to develop his own brand of comic effect: the latter, a cousin of Till Eulenspiegel, provides much of the dynamic verve of the book, a verve that stems not only from his actions, but especially his speech.

Though the work is mainly comic in intention, there are episodes where Rabelais's sympathies with avant-garde humanism come to the surface, on the subjects of warfare and education. Pantagruel's attitude to war, which reflects Erasmian views, may also be seen as part of the formation of the Christian prince, who prefers trust in God to *philautia*: even so, this episode with the King of the Dipsodes forms the conclusion of a book that belongs more to the university world. Rabelais manifests his outlook, both negatively in satire and positively in the famous letter from Gargantua to his son. The satire is directed against the abuses of disputation (though Gargantua does not oppose the exercise when it is properly conducted), and also against the scholastic tradition represented by the Sorbonne in its strict orthodoxy and its suspicion of learning. It should, however, be borne in mind that the burlesque literary catalogue of Saint-Victor was considerably extended in the 1542 edition; and certain enemies of the new learning, such as Noël Beda and Tartaret, receive *mentions déshonorables*. The Gargantua letter has caused much ink to flow: some have considered it heretical, others see in it a fairly straightforward eulogy of the new pedagogy compatible with orthodoxy, yet others have interpreted it, because of its moments of inflated rhetoric, as a burlesque development to bring out Gargantua's rather muddle-headed attitude. It divides up into three main topics: the reason for man's existence upon earth; a comparison between the old learning and the new; and a programme of education for Pantagruel, which is perhaps not as avant-garde as all that.

Yet few of these themes are developed as broadly as in the later books. Rabelais entertains by anecdotes, by use of giant-parallels, by physiological reference, by the comic use of erudition and allusion to sacred texts (monk's humour often consists of 'inside jokes'); but he is learning his trade above all in the combination of satire with verbal proliferation. To a modern reader the most entertaining scenes may well be those in which language is explored and exploited; Rabelais often works by association and amplification, as in Panurge's multilingual virtuosity, but he develops these features particularly in his attacks on fossilised practitioners of language (e.g., disputation and the legal profession, contexts in which *coq-à-l'âne* techniques may also be brought into play). Sometimes it is difficult to draw the line: the Limousin scholar talks like a *rhétoriqueur*, yet Rabelais admired that style of poetry and Lemaire de Belges, and Gargantua's partly Ciceronian prose is not so distantly related. In Rabelais fun and serious purpose are closely mingled; since Erasmus's *Praise of Folly*, both technically and thematically, topsy-turvy elements invade the picture, and the sheer nonsense we associate with the *coq-à-l'âne*, the dramatic monologue, and *fatrasie* becomes an essential part of Rabelais's world. Humour of this kind injects a kaleidoscopic effect into what he is saying; linguistic iridescence allows serious intent to show itself from different angles and different distances, but also affords, at artistic level, the unity and balance that gives shape to his world. In any case truth may not speak with one voice, and in a situation where values and convictions are subject to new pressures, a Lucianic irony becomes the inevitable artistic concomitant. However, there are more general considerations behind the particular, contemporary butts of satire: Rabelais's humour expresses a balanced view of life and is directed therefore against those who insert a screen between themselves and existence either by fossilisation or self-inflation (vanity or more gravely, *philautia*) or by sheer hypocrisy.

Gargantua

Gargantua (1534)[7] was composed after the considerable success of *Pantagruel*; the exact date of its appearance has not been established to everyone's satisfaction, but the contemporary relevance of the *Enigme en Prophetie* would be more pointed if it were written after the *Affaire des Placards* (17–18 October 1534). The work ampli-

fies a series of themes and episodes already treated in the 1532 volume: the origin, birth, and youth of a giant, education, sojourn in
Paris, warfare – all these are common to both. Panurge, for chronological reasons, cannot appear, but Jean des Entommeures helps in
some measure to fill the comic gap. In the prologue, Rabelais, who in
the liminary poem had stated that 'rire est le propre de l'homme',
goes on to stress the 'substantificque moelle' of his book, though the
following paragraphs run counter to this assertion. The reader therefore does not always feel sure where he stands, but a study of tones
and rhythms may sometimes prove useful; it is for instance difficult
not to sense that Rabelais is working at a deeper level of emotion in
the solemn wistfulness that succeeds the *Enigme*.

Gargantua gives an impression of greater balance and unity than
the first book, even if one believes that the Abbaye de Thélème
stands somewhat apart; three *leitmotive* underlie the divers episodes
that unfold in fairly orderly fashion: education, religion, war. At the
same time, they can be redefined as the pegs on which Rabelais
develops his conception of human nature, its place in the world, and
the ethic it should promote. *Gargantua* is a study of behaviour; it
touches on themes that are central to Renaissance humanism at a
time when the religious issue becomes a burning one.

Rabelais's attacks on various accretions in tradition, on the gap
between precept and practice, his irreverent allusions (yet part and
parcel of establishment humour), his call for reform, all these were
current money within the Church; however, his most sustained statement of his religious attitudes here is in the episode of the Abbaye de
Thélème with the *Enigme* that can be related to it thematically. He
spends time on describing the architecture of this anti-monastic
foundation. Precision is often a source of humour with him, but no
doubt less so here: the architecture, not inconsistent with the tradition of medieval allegory, reminds one also of Renaissance castles,
and no divorce is created between the refinements of modern civilisation and the religious community; moreover, care is lavished on the
outlay of the grounds whose hexadic structures prolong the form of
the main building and serve the needs of exercise and sport.[8] The
variations on the number six, it has been suggested, may be inspired
by St Augustine, according to whom 6 is the first perfect number (the
product of its factors), but also the first terrestrial number, being the
product of the male and female (3×2). The centre of the abbey is
explicitly an anti-monastery; in the first place, the name Thelema
(Greek for Will: compare the motto *Fay ce que vouldras*) with its
New Testament associations, may well echo a contemporary theme in
evangelical circles, according to which the exercise of free-will
operates to the benefit of the community. Second, the abbey is
organised both socially and individually on very different lines:

persons of noble birth, including women, are welcome, but not monks, hypocrites, or lawyers; and instead of religious services and ecclesiastical hierarchies, each resident has his own private chapel and should 'annoncer le Sainct Evangile en sens agile'. In addition, the whole text is shot through with biblical allusion or echo. Thirdly, the residents are not bound for life by vows, but may return to the open world as they will. Rabelais, like so many humanists, is interested in the preparation for the active life, and this is one reason why he attacks the monastic principle; he broadened his opposition of principle to include points that were viewed with suspicion by orthodoxy. On other matters too, Rabelais has been suspect: he certainly plays down the role of the saints and of pilgrimages, he takes little interest in the Virgin Mary, and is not willing to accept miracles as they have multiplied down the centuries, though he undoubtedly believes in the veracity of miracles recorded in the Holy Scriptures. For him there is a clear distinction between faith and superstitious credulity, and in any case he is more concerned with the attitude of the believer to miracles than with the miracles themselves.

However, the principles on which Thélème is to be built are closely linked with Rabelais's views on central Christian preoccupations: divine grace, free-will, faith, and charity, all of which affect the problem of action in this world. Rabelais's attitude to free-will seems to be middle-of-the-road: a variant of 1542 shows his hostility to the Calvinist view of predestination, but he was also very aware of man's sinfulness, and this point emerges sharply in the contrast between Gargantua and Picrochole, the 'bad' monarch who gives way to his instincts, becomes self-reliant, and forgets to place his fate in the hands of God – like Claudel's *Tête d'Or*, in fact – whereas Gargantua never fails to pray in moments of crisis. Thélème therefore can only be meaningful within a proper religious framework; earlier Rabelais had written:

Dont j'ay congneu que Dieu eternel l'a laissé au gouvernail de son franc arbitre et propre sens, qui ne peult estre que meschant sy par grace divine n'est continuellement guidé . . . (Grandgousier's letter to his son)

In the Thélème episode, stress is laid rather on man's propensity to good, but it seems that Rabelais offers some form of synergism in which man is the coadjutor of God through Christ, and which avoids the frailty of self-dependence as well as the desperation of Calvinist predestination. One can hardly see how a humanist would attach so much importance to education unless he thought man could play some part in his spiritual progress. In *Pantagruel* Rabelais had already suggested that failure to observe God's commandments would ensure damnation, but that Christian behaviour afforded the chance of grace and salvation. There is here a greater optimism than one would expect to find in Luther or in Calvin and consistent with his *joie de vivre* we find his view of life fuller and more rewarding than for those who turn their faces to the wall. His view of God has little of the Old Testament about it: on the contrary kindness and compassion are His dominant features. Rabelais's conception of synergism is such that man may contribute to achieving a state where God's grace may operate. Like Marguerite de Navarre, he tends to gloss over the themes of eternal damnation, exclusion, punishment, and so forth.

This religious element comes to the fore also in the important section devoted to the education of Gargantua, the *institution du prince très chrétien*, though his pedagogic system is distinct from ecclesiastical supervision. The reading of the Bible is strongly emphasised, and so are prayer and reliance on God. Comparison is of course made with the obscurantist formation of scholastic dye; and Rabelais insists not only on his king having the widest possible culture, but also on the principle *mens sana in corpore sano*, for the prince must set an example to all his subjects. The programme sketched by Rabelais is so all-embracing as to be marathonic, even if we allow for an ambivalent attitude created by the need to cater for a giant; but at the same time it embodies certain principles stressed vigorously by contemporary humanists. The nature of Rabelais's kingship is brought out in greater detail in the episode of the *guerre picrocholine*. Earlier criticism made rather a lot of the local interest of the war (related to the litigious struggles between Rabelais's family and the Sainte-Marthes), but Rabelais lets his satire range over much wider issues, and in this section we have a critique of tyranny (as opposed to equitable monarchy); an attack on Charles V is also introduced, for Rabelais reveals himself throughout his books to be a staunch defender of Francis I and a good example of the chauvinistic patriotism that characterises many humanists in France at that time. Rabelais's conception of kingship belongs to the tradition of divine right: 'Ne croyez qu'y aye aultre gouvernement de l'universel monde que Dieu le createur . . . . ' (*Prognostication*). And the king's qualities are consistent with such a view: he must set a worthy pattern, even if his rights, as representative of God, are unlimited: piety, charity, benevolence. He always governs with the aid of a council, whose functions are nevertheless not specified clearly; he is accessible to his subjects, as in theory the medieval king was. In the special case of war, Rabelais echoes Erasmian and humanist views, using Picrochole to illustrate the anti-king. He categorically condemns aggressive wars, because they are un-Christian, but he does not accept a total pacifism: though every effort must be made to avoid the outbreak of strife, the king's duty is to preserve his country's domain. Grandgousier does in fact have a very efficient army, whereas

Picrochole's mob is as useful as that of the *roi d'Yvetot*; the campaign is waged with the greatest despatch, and the minimum loss of life and property. When victory has been won, mercy will be shown to those who merely obeyed orders, but the main criminals will not go scot-free. Nevertheless Gargantua's magnanimity is stressed in chapter xlviii in such a way that Rabelais is surely attacking Charles for his harsh treatment of Francis I after Pavia. Perhaps the claims of patriotism and erasmianism are not fully compatible: Pantagruel's invasion of the Dipsodes does not fit in very conveniently. On the other hand, Rabelais is opposed to war declared for the purpose of spreading the gospel, though he is not absolutely consistent in his views on religious toleration.

The *Enigme*, with which the book concludes, has baffled many commentators. Superficially the poem, like some *salon* game, may appear to be nothing more than a piece of jollity, a poem perhaps written by Mellin de Saint-Gellais on the *jeu de paume*. But here we have a text written to be understood at different levels; and it is unlikely that this *enigme*, discovered in the foundations of the *abbaye*, described with little humour, should itself be no more than a squib. The 'solution' is given by Frère Jean whose intellect is admitted to be restricted; and, what is more significant, the poem is followed by a statement from Gargantua in a very grave and compassionate tone about the sufferings of the 'genz reduictz à la creance Evangelicque'. If we could be sure that this text was composed after the *Affaire des Placards*, our hesitations about its meaning would be simplified, since it could be seen as an exhortation to comfort the faithful in a world increasingly darkened by error and intolerance.

Taken as a whole, *Gargantua* gives an impression of greater 'body' than does *Pantagruel*. This is partly explained by the fact that the success of 1532 made Rabelais more conscious of an alert public, partly too because the honeymoon of evangelism was nearing its end. In the 1542 edition of the two first books, it is significant that more variants of substance are introduced into the *Gargantua*. At literary level, Rabelais's satire is more highly organised and focused, and he is acquiring a surer mastery of language. Moreover, the full richness of his humanist learning and attitudes is brought into action.

Tiers Livre

Between the publication of *Gargantua* and that of the *Tiers Livre* (1546) there is an interval of twelve years, a period of Rabelais's life on which we are inadequately informed: close associations with Guillaume du Bellay (d. 1543) and his circle, travel in Italy, practice as an eminent doctor, fatherhood, the revised edition of the first two books in 1542. Unfortunately this general framework needs to be filled in with many details that elude us at present. The *Tiers Livre* was put

on the market about January 1546, having been printed by Christian
Wechel, and it was placed on the Sorbonne Index before the end of
April.[9] Rabelais begins by seeming to give the reader the sequel
promised at the end of *Pantagruel*, but not much of this materialises,
and the gigantesque qualities of his characters recede into the background. Moreover, it is Panurge who holds the stage, and a considerably altered Panurge we have: from the merry Parisian student he
was, he has become a victim of indecision, with a touch of cowardice.
Apart from the splendid episode in which he praises debtors, his
character has become less electric, indeed he is rather solemn on
occasion, not all that far removed from the *bien pensant*. Yet this
change of portrait helps him to emerge as a central source of comic
effect, a source that draws frequently for its effect on the repeated
use of a basic situation. Seeking advice as to whether he should
marry or not, he is given counsel, which is commented on by Pantagruel in a manner that does not satisfy him. He then trumps up an
interpretation he finds more congenial but insufficient to lead him to
marriage, and so he has to turn elsewhere for more advice. At the
same time, the book which is perhaps the high-watermark of Rabelais's achievement, taxes the reader's attention very severely, because of the immense range of erudite allusion on which the author
draws and the multiplicity of levels at which this attention on the
part of the reader has to be given. Variety is conferred on a basic
formula somewhat lacking in progression by the dramatic development of dialogue and by an increase in the number of anecdotes
interspersed through the text. Other devices, such as mock-epic
parallel, are pressed into service as before, but it is essentially the
linguistic vitality of the book that has matured and bloomed so
impressively.

The overall structure may appear rather loose, but there is a
pattern. After the initial chapters that link the book with *Pantagruel*, we have three main sections: the praise of debts; Panurge's
marriage quest, with two subsections dealing with divination and
professional consultants respectively; the concluding chapters on the
pantagruélion. One could also see the work as a central section (on
the theme of wedlock) flanked by two varieties of encomium, more
or less satirical; but one may also discern a connecting link in a sentence of the *prologue*:

Je recognoys en eulx tous [i.e. the readers] une forme spécifique et propriété
individuale, laquelle nos majeurs nommoient Pantagruelisme, moiennant
laquelle jamais en maulvaise partie ne prendront choses quelconques ilz
congnoistront sourdre de bon, franc et loyal couraige. Je les ay ordinairement
veuz bon vouloir en payement prendre et en icelluy acquiescer, quand debilité
de puissance y a été associée.

Though the main story in the *Tiers Livre* concerns Panurge's search for a wife, and though several critics have over-eagerly thought of the book as a hostile contribution to the *querelle des femmes*, its importance surely lies elsewhere. The problem of marriage, though certainly topical as a matter of discussion, would serve as a useful point of departure for consideration of yet more fundamental matters pertaining to man's nature and condition. And it is clear that the question of *pantagruélion* and *pantagruélisme*, related antithetically to Panurge, goes a long way beyond the marital problem. This does not diminish Rabelais's opportunities for making the comic most of his material, but the *substantificque moelle* should be sought in another direction.

The persons whom Panurge consults with the help of Pantagruel fall broadly into two main categories: established practitioners of the black-coated professions, and others who resort to irrational means to offer their solutions of Panurge's problem. Among the first we meet are Nezdecabre and Her Trippa, comic indeed and not without thematic significance, but they remain secondary figures, as does Raminagrobis, attractively though he is sketched; but the others are important. Trouillogan (his name is a dialectal word meaning one who 'tourne en rond') claims our attention by a negative attitude; as the chapter heading shows, he represents the pyrrhonic view that can lead nowhere in its dismissing indifference. Rondibilis, the doctor, busies himself with the physiological side of marriage, and medically corroborates the view associated with St Paul, the canalising of concupiscence. In these chapters, we have some satire of doctors; Rondibilis's presentation of his views is fragmented and caught up in verbal gymnastics, but the theme so comically expounded coincides with views expressed in more serious utterances, and this is yet another example of Rabelais's tonal ambivalency. Hippothaddée speaks in a different tone, though he confirms at spiritual level the view taken by Rondibilis: he speaks in the tone one may associate with Rabelais's graver speech and which is so coloured by his reading of the Scriptures. And though critics have differed greatly in their explanation of the character's name, most see in him a spokesman for evangelical ideas. Hippothaddée quotes more than once from *Corinthians* and reinforces the theory of marriage as a lightning-conductor for lust, at any rate for those, the majority, unfitted for the vocation of celibacy. But he goes further, for he has the answer, unheeded of course, to Panurge's fear that he will be cuckolded: it is for him to put his trust in God, a course that will not only profit him, but help him to bring his wife into the paths of righteousness (as Rondibilis had also suggested). This will also aid him to avoid the pitfall of uxoriousness – a theme, incidentally, that has some literary currency in the middle of the century (see Theodose Valentinian and Pasquier's *Monophile*).

For all the help offered, Panurge remains impervious to counsel, either 'rational', or reflecting attitudes less rationally based: dreams, witches, *sors vergilianes*, mutes, jesters, and Judge Bridoye who puts his trust in dice. The importance of these scenes is, once again, not confined to satire and comedy, rich though they may be; they develop in depth the theme we have already noted, the praise of folly and ignorance, the suspicion of knowledge and established reasoning. At bottom, we are offered the principle of humility and trust in forces other than human: a theme of grave import is developed with pyrotechnic erudition in the tradition of Erasmus and Lucian. We are presented with the antithesis of self-sufficiency and *philautia*, of which the *guerre picrocholine* was one form of critique; and Epistémon unfolds this in a style that blends verbal proliferation and evangelical tone:

soy deffiant de son sçavoir et capacité, se recommandant humblement à Dieu . . . le juste juge invocqueroit à son aide la grace celeste, se deporteroit en l'esprit sacrosainct du hazard et perplexité de sentence definitive.

a commentary on human inadequacy, but also on those who would try to fix the future for lack of trust, and those who, too deeply involved and centred in their own preoccupations, lose the sense of proportion that a better-balanced individual would achieve.

In all this Panurge represents the opposite of what Rabelais (through Pantagruel) appears to approve; his failure to solve the problem of marriage is merely a sign of his inability to come to terms with life on a broader front. In the first place, he is exceptionally learned, but endowed with a scholarship that renders his outlook quite useless for the conduct of life, and his polymathic logorrhoea is the outward sign of his spiritual impotence; talk is the denial of action, commitment, and involvement, and Panurge seems to represent 'science sans conscience'. His vast erudition cuts him off from life and no doubt also from God's will; self-delusion and self-love are close enough to one another, for Panurge is striving to fit the world to his scheme of things, and not to adapt himself to that of the divine will ('L'esprit maling vous seduict'). Panurge, in the private sector, is the corollary of Picrochole in the public domain. Over against him stands Pantagruel who has shed most of his giant's characteristics and has ceased to have much comic value; he provides the most sustained commentary on the various episodes. He makes several points clear: we are in a world where we have to act, but we are also the victims of ignorance, therefore we must try to put ourselves in the second place and see things from a point of view other than our limited own. 'Tis folly to be wise, or at any rate learned, and it comes as no surprise that Pantagruel should recommend to Panurge a visit to Triboullet, the court jester ('un fol enseigne bien un sage').

If we see in the marriage theme above all a pretext for a much wider discussion, then it may be easier to establish a proper connection between the central characters and the epilogue on the *pantagruélion*. Here again we have a variation on the enigma, and superficially what we have is a cheerful encomium of hemp. But its name connects it with the figure so close to Rabelais's heart and attitudes – and Rabelais himself stresses the link; he also points to its inner qualities and notes that it was not available to the ancient philosophers. Some earlier critics have interpreted it as a symbol of human industry, but that was hardly absent from the ancient world and this view does not deal satisfactorily with the references to water and wine. It is no doubt closely linked with *pantagruélisme*, defined with more precision in the prologue to the *Quart Livre*, but also mentioned in this book's prologue and quoted above (p. 179). Whether one should go so far as to offer a hesuchist explanation is perhaps doubtful, but one would expect to find an answer, with religious harmonics, that did not conflict with Rabelais's known views: the affirmation of an attitude of mind not bound by sectarian prejudice (cf. Rabelais's hostility to the *larrons* in the *Quart Livre*), steadfast in the face of fire and water, constantly able to distinguish the true from the false, and likely to satisfy the thirst (after the Divine – for throughout the five books, the theme of the *dive bouteille* and the *beuveurs tres illustres* maintains its double face of comic relief and serious intensity).

The opening section, the praise of debtors, has caused much ink to flow: Panurge who enjoys the territory of Salmingondin as a reward for services earlier rendered, has squandered his fortune and, taken to task by Pantagruel, defends debts, which make the world go round and facilitate the working of Christian virtues such as hope, faith, and charity. Pantagruel, with a few well-chosen remarks, deflates Panurge's welfare state. At literary level, the episode is yet another variation on the mock encomium that Lucian developed with such gusto in *De Parasito*, which is a model of comic inflation. Modern critics have sought a deeper meaning under the humorous froth: to see in the episode a Rabelaisian handling of a basically Christian theme (charity) is perhaps going rather too far, except to the extent that Pantagruel is prepared to underwrite it; for after cutting Panurge down to size, he does defend the case for obligation toward one's neighbour in the matter of charity and 'dilection mutuelle', and he also accepts the principle of borrowing as long as it does not promote idleness. If one can agree with some such explanation, it has the advantage of harmonising with the themes underlying the other sections of the book. There exists therefore a real unity of substance in the *Tiers Livre*: Panurge forms the dramatic centre with Pantagruel as the *raisonneur*-in-chief, who knows how to 'vivre dans le vrai', whereas Panurge has not yet unlearned how to live 'dans le faux'. On the other hand, it would be wrong to reduce Pantagruel to the status of an ideological or comic yardstick: he goes beyond such expected terms of reference, but of course he occupies a penumbral position *vis-à-vis* Panurge and his linguistic fireworks. It would be equally misplaced to think of Panurge as unredeemable or unlikeable: otherwise how could we explain the reaction of his friends who are very glad that he should accompany them on their travels? Panurge dominates the scene by his verbal exuberance and the comic elements of his make-up colour the whole texture much more thoroughly than did any character in the previous books. Moreover, he exemplifies that Rabelaisian habit of working at more than one level, for though he can present himself on occasion as a word-spinner of high degree, he serves also to deflate rhetorical inflation which both provides comic outlet and may mark the distance that separates a character from reality. A good example occurs in chapter XXV, when Panurge consults Her Trippa who indulges in an interminable list of means of soothsaying likely to help him:

Voulez-vous (dist Her Trippa) en sçavoir plus amplement la verité par Pyromantie, par Aëromantie, celebrée par Aristophanes en ses Nuées, par Hydromantie, par Lecanomantie et exprovée par Hermolaus Barbarus? Dedans un bassin plein d'eaue je te monstreroy ta femme future, brimballant avecques rustres.

Quand (dist Panurge) tu mettras ton nez en mon cul, soys recors de deschausser tes lunettes.

Par Catoptromantie (dist Her Trippa continuant), moyennant laquelle Didius Julianus, empereur de Rome, praevoyoit tour ceque luy doibvoit advenir? Il ne te fauldra poinct de lunettes. Tu la voyras en un miroir brisgoutant aussi apertement que si je te la monstrois en la fontaine du temple de Minerve près Patras. Par Coscinomantie, jadis tant religieusement observée entre les cerimonies des Romains? Ayant un crible et des forcettes, tu voyras Diables. . . . Par Ichthyomantie, tant jadis celebrée et practiquée par Tiresias et Polydamas, aussi certainement que jadis estoit faict en la fosse Dina on boys sacré à Apollo, en la terre des Lyciens? Par Chœromantie? Ayons force pourceaulx, tu en auras la vescie. Par Cleromantie, comme l'on trouve la febve on guasteau la vigile de l'Epiphanie? Par Anthropomantie, de laquelle usa Heliogabalus, empereur de Rome? Elle est quelque peu fascheuse, mais tu l'endureras assez, puis que tu es destiné coqu. Par Stichomantie Sibylline? Par Onomatomantie? Comment as tu nom?

Maschemerde, respondit Panurge.

Ou bien par Alectryomantie? . . . .

Va (respondit Panurge), fol enraigé, au diable, et te faiz lanterner à quelque Albanoys; si auras un chapeau poinctu. Diable, que ne me conseillez tu aussi bien tenir une esmeraulde, ou la pierre de hyene, soubs ta langue, ou me munir de langues de puputz et de cœurs de ranes verdes, ou manger du cœur et du foye de quelque dracon, pour, à la voix et au chant des cycnes et oizeaulx, entendre mes destinées, comme faisoient jadis les Arabes on pays de Mesopotamie?

The rhythms are inevitably broken by the cuts effected in the passage, but certain features do still emerge. Rabelais has drawn on contemporary knowledge of the arts of divination to form the basis of his comic; and he has enriched it by insertion of allusions to classical erudition (allusions which appeared often in the 1552 text). Her Trippa is a source of comic effect partly because Rabelais is known to be making fun of Cornelius Agrippa, whose works were well known at the time; but more important, he induces laughter because he is yet another example of the gap that can develop between life and learning. Very rapidly, he seems to take flight into a world of spell-binding rhetoric in which the reader is also caught up. This effect is achieved by a series of devices, mostly linguistic: and the most obvious is surely the recurrent impact of *-mantie*. At one time, it was thought that Rabelais had invented some of these variations on divi-nation, but, apart from some rude incursions by Panurge as a means of deflation, these terms are genuine enough; nor does it matter very much, for the incantatory effect shifts the reader from the real world to some surrealistic dimension. The rhythmic development of the *-mantie* is reinforced by the learned additions Her Trippa provides, because this form of erudition makes even more evident his capacity to isolate himself from everyday existence. However, we are not offered a rectilinear, uninterrupted development; at given moments, Panurge breaks in, and by caricature, vulgar statement, or exclam-ation destroys the rhythms and fancy which, however, are taken up again almost immediately by Trippa, well launched on his catalogue, which it should be noted, is presented to a great extent in the interro-gatory mode. There develops therefore a sort of pendulum move-ment between Trippa and Panurge, though of course the former has the lion's share of the 'conversation'. At the same time, Rabelais makes the situation more complex in that Panurge is not simply the mainspring of comic deflation. Shortly before our extract opens, Panurge had already put himself into an ironic situation by calling Trippa a cuckold and applying criticism to him which might seem more pertinent to himself. In the second place, Panurge seems to get caught up in some measure by Trippa's rhetoric, for at the end, though he still maintains his 'realistic' attitude, he lets himself expand linguistically and also adopt the interrogatory mode: a sort of sympathetic incantation has entered the picture – 'Vray Dieu, comment il m'a perfumé de fascherie et diablerie, de charme et de sorcellerie!' this is true in the literal sense, but perhaps there is more to it than that. This passage shows us very well how Rabelais's comic mechanisms acquire enrichment by the interplay of levels and tones. And this is one of the reasons why the *Tiers Livre* is such a rich work; its tonal unity in diversity, its depth of resonance, the linguistic mastery, its breadth of reference, and the sophisticated blend of comedy and erudition put the *Tiers Livre*, in my view, well ahead of the other books by Rabelais; but it is a work that does not yield its secrets easily, partly because of the very range of scholarship that forms the main mechanism of comic reference, partly because of the different levels and tones that Rabelais uses to establish contact with the reader, partly because of contemporary allusion, inevitable in satire, but difficult for readers of another age to grasp and savour. Rabelais demands of his reader a quite exceptional alertness, and much of his comic flavour derives from the speed with which he changes his register. There are still many points that require elucidation, but these areas of darkness cannot hide the degree of artistic control and assurance revealed by the author in his handling of his material; and underlying the whole fabric of the work lies a grave confidence in man's destiny.

Quart Livre

The *Quart Livre* appeared in 1552,[10] very shortly before the author's presumed death; but a partial edition had already come out in 1547 (n.s. 1548), with the text petering out in the middle of a chapter and corresponding roughly to some eleven of the first twenty-five chapters. The problems concerning the reasons prompting this publication have yet to be satisfactorily solved; and further problems await the reader of the whole text whose interpretation is puzzling. Rabelais draws on contemporary geographical accounts to enrich the voyage of his characters; but in recent years, critics have paid increased attention to the allegorical meaning of the episodes, which are even more heavily interspersed with anecdotic material than was the *Tiers Livre*. The prologue continues the definition of *pantagruélisme* that began in the previous book; described as a 'certaine gayeté d'esprit conficte en mespris des choses fortuites', it is also linked with the concept of *mediocritas*. As a whole, the book gives a sharper edge to the satire of both the Catholics and the Protestants – Calvin had already expressed his hostility to Rabelais – and one may feel that the author is calling down a plague on both houses whose attitudes seem to distort the spirit of true religion. Nevertheless, when one gets down to comment on the particular, one realises the difficulty of asserting much with any show of confidence.[11] The travellers are of course bound for the discovery of the *dive bouteille*, and chapter I undoubtedly has strong evangelical overtones – but the opening chapters give a disorganised impression with apparently a host of contemporary allusions. After the brilliantly developed episode of the *moutons de Panurge*, we are faced with two episodes (the *Isle Ennasin* and the island of Cheli with its King Panigon), equally difficult to interpret, but which may, in some measure, be a satire of certain tendencies of fashion at that time. On the other hand, chapters III–XVI can be taken as a further sending-up of the legal world. The famous storm at sea fills chapters

XVIII–XXIV; it is a splendid artistic set-piece, with a skilful juxta-
position of the characters in their reactions to danger (Jean des
Entommeures, Panurge, Pantagruel), but it is more than that, for
essential reactions of these persons in the face of death raise issues of
prime importance. Panurge's character, in particular, has undergone
a change for the worse, in that he has become much more superstitious and *bien pensant*. At the height of danger, he shows great
fear, invokes the saints and the Virgin Mary; he promises all manner
of things should he be saved, hopes for a miracle to occur, and
gabbles through his prayers at top speed. Jean, as ever concerned
with action, remains unmoved by a storm which he considers to
have been raised by devils. Pantagruel's reaction is richer and more
positive: he upbraids Panurge for his fear and for the importance he
attaches to death, and, what is more significant, he attacks him for
his self-centredness and wrongful attitude to God. Here some of the
themes of the *Tiers Livre* are developed with greater urgency, and
this impression is confirmed by certain alterations Rabelais introduced to the text published in 1548, where he shows his divergence
from Calvin on the question of free-will. However, it is not only in
the storm episode that Panurge becomes identified more fully with
religious views for which his creator had little liking. The deeper
meaning of this episode may well be carried on into the following
chapters about the Macraeons, remarkable for their solemn reflections on death and the afterlife of the soul, reflections which are
also inspired by Rabelais's great benefactor, Guillaume du Bellay
(d. 1543).

The rest of the *Quart Livre* gives a greater sense of coherence in
that so much of it is concerned more overtly with the political and
religious issues of the times; Rabelais sharpens his satirical claws
both in direct reference and in the Gaster episode whose interpretation remains uncertain but has been understood as a possible
attack on materialism of one kind or another. The Quaresmeprenant
section is generally agreed to be connected with the struggle between
Catholics and Protestants. Quaresmeprenant himself is seen as the
child of Antiphysis, though some have thought of him as a symbol
of Charles V, already the butt of Rabelais's wit; and in this section,
there is undoubtedly a recurrence of the pacifist strain we detected
earlier. The attack on Catholics and Protestants, at any rate in
their extreme manifestations, is carried over into the *Papefigues/
Papimanes* controversy where Rabelais indulges in highly pungent
satire of the decretalist – a trait that ties up with his gallican sympathies. More important is the episode of the island of Chaneph,
which, in the *Briefve declaration*, is described as 'hypocrisie'; its inhabitants are termed 'cagots' by Panurge, and they seem to be
exactly the people Rabelais banned from the Abbaye de Thélème.

Generally they represent the falsifiers of true religion, though there is difficulty in fixing the meaning of various details. Moreover, the supper of Pantagruel and his *domestiques* has been compared to the Last Supper in the light of certain parallels and for the solemn tone that informs the text. Whatever the truth of the matter, we have one of those passages where Rabelais is speaking at a deeper level, and offering some of the positive principles against which the force of his satire can be felt elsewhere; nor is it a coincidence that this scene should be dominated by Pantagruel. The final episode of the book, the refusal to land on the island of Ganabin, is also very obscure, but has been thought to reflect in some measure Pantagruel's reluctance to have anything to do with, not even settle accounts with, the repressive manifestations of authority.

Taken together, these episodes do not perhaps form so clear a pattern as the *Tiers Livre*, and the allusions are more cryptic. Nevertheless, there is a certain unity in that Rabelais adopts the device of the journey, with its various ports of call, to attack aspects of contemporary political life, the less attractive elements of established religion, sectarianism carried to extremes, and also, it would seem, philosophical positions that tend too far towards materialism or, for that matter, unwarranted idealism. At the same time, some of these episodes, for all their obscurity, carry a graver tone, a more measured expression of attitude, and perhaps more frequently than hitherto, which makes one wonder whether the *Quart Livre* does not bring us nearer than ever to the inner man in Rabelais. We do not have the dramatic unity provided by Panurge in the *Tiers Livre*; the unity is a thematic one, nor has it led to a diminution of the artist in Rabelais. Pantagruel has regained some of his giant's resilience; the old love of words is untarnished, the characterisation remains as shrewd, and the *conteur* shows his paces even more skilfully than previously. A remarkable variety of tone covers the slow-moving dignity of the fundamental tempo. In this respect, as in certain others, Rabelais reminds us of Péguy: on the surface, there are many white horses, froth, and surf, but the groundswell is slow and steady.

The Fifth Book

The *Cinquiesme Livre* poses a further problem – that of authenticity. It came out posthumously in 1562 under the title of *L'Isle sonnante*, and it contained only sixteen of the chapters that form the fifth book as we know it today (descriptions of the *isle sonnante*, outspoken satire of Rome, the *chats-fourrés*, generally understood as a dig at the *Parlement* of Paris, the episodes of the *Apedeftes*, interpreted as a broadside against the *Chambre des Comptes*). Two years later, another edition appeared, *Le cinquiesme et dernier livre . . .* , containing a further thirty-one chapters that continued the voyage of the *Quart Livre* and ended in the initiation of the *dive bouteille*, characterised by a very impressive wealth of descriptive detail. Then a manuscript was discovered in the nineteenth century which reveals significant differences; and this helped to confirm the view that the fifth book was in some measure at least apocryphal. In our century, though most critics agree on the authenticity of the earlier sections, several scholars have argued in favour of the whole work being genuine; the grounds advanced are linguistic (though the vocabulary is strangely deficient in medical and biblical terms), stylistic (somewhat subjective), mathematical, musical, and finally philosophical (continuity of various Platonic themes). On the other hand, the virtual absence of Pantagruel, so essential to the thematic colour of the earlier books, is curious, and the final fate of Panurge is ignored. There is a lessening of dialogue and dramatic presentation in favour of description, often very intricate, and the frequency of anecdote, increasing as far as the *Quart Livre*, has waned. And we require further elucidation of the flattering description of the *Lanterne* (in previous books a symbol for *cagots*, etc.) that takes the travellers to their final destination. In short, the problem is far from resolved, in spite of a reduction of scepticism among many well qualified. However that may be, the fifth book does attempt to bring the whole tale to its conclusion, the search for the *dive bouteille*, and in terms consistent with those used previously.

Modern criticism has busied itself very intensively with the *substantificque moelle*; more recently, however, one may detect a shift of emphasis towards the study of Rabelais's art and the nature of his comic genius.[12] To see in Rabelais nothing but the bearer of a message is as one-sided as presenting him simply as a spinner of splendid word-webs. Laughter is doubtless a form of equilibrium, one means of achieving a balance between involvement and detachment; in the particular forms of comic awareness developed by Rabelais we find the creation of a world of fancy and a linguistic vitality unrivalled elsewhere. Nevertheless, no comic writer of the first rank has earned his fame without this comic sense being closely connected with a lively awareness of a changing world (Cervantes, Molière), and especially of a world in which the gap between illusion and reality becomes more and more visible to him. Rabelais comes to maturity in a rapidly evolving context, where values are being questioned and the gap between the bark and the sap widens steadily. Rabelais's sense of the comic often flowers in the dimension of fantasy in which the reader readily collaborates (the giant episodes, the catalogues developed by linguistic association and proliferation); but there is another source of comic effect, which is linked with the Establishment and a withdrawal from the mainsprings of life. It is no coincidence that the main targets of Rabelais's fun are word-spinners of high degree: *sorbonnicoles*, lawyers, Panurge of the *Tiers Livre*. Rhetoric takes a man into a world of his own and isolates him from existence. And yet, in a world where life is pursued at different levels and where dissimulation in face of danger and a refusal to get excessively caught up in the rhythm of one's own activity allow some distancing from experience, laughter plays its part. This situation, which allows for a certain ambivalence, finds its counterpart in Rabelais: one thinks of the obvious ambiguity of the various *enigmas* that decorate the work, but also of Gargantua's letter to Pantagruel which has been seen both as a serious statement of humanist belief and a burlesque of the humanist idiom. We are faced with the problem of the several *personæ* through which Rabelais works; but he also forbids the reader to settle, breaking his rhythms, shifting his angles, changing his levels – a manifestation of vitality that never becomes clogged. Rabelais's humour is one aspect of his refusal to fossilise, to mistake the husk for the kernel, and of his desire to maintain the open view of life of which we have heard so much since Bergson. And this comic vision is associated in the last analysis with a remarkable serenity, the *Gelassenheit* of which Goethe spoke. Laughter is always *à partir de*, and Rabelais's anchorage reveals a sure awareness of man's place in the Universe, an approval of his wide-ranging activity so long as it fits into a framework of reference that transcends his being. The Renaissance fool is the wise man, always generating fireworks of entertainment, but like Musset's Fantasio a solitary too.

It is difficult to assess just what Rabelais's contribution is to the development of French prose; some have denied him any great part and preferred to give the lion's share of credit to Calvin. This may be true, so far as the treatment of abstract themes in a language moving towards the classical ideal is concerned, but surely Rabelais is doing in prose what his contemporary Marot had achieved in poetry: reintroducing movement and a sense of the natural into a linguistic vehicle that had fossilised and lost momentum. And Rabelais goes further in opening up a whole horizon of linguistic possibilities. He makes his contribution to establishing the claims of the vernacular over Latin, though the character of his fantastic world and vision tends to leave its mark especially in the fields of satire, *conte*, and *nouvelle*; this must not blind us to the fact that his work is a vital expression of what is central to the humanism of the French Renaissance.[13]

THE EMERGENCE OF
THE EPISTOLARY GENRE

The use of the letter as a literary genre is far from uncommon in the Renaissance; though in the vernacular its frequency is still modest, the medium is practised by distinguished humanists. In the Latin field, of course, it plays an important part in the diffusion of scholarship and ideas: the success of the correspondence of both Erasmus and Guillaume Budé bears ample witness to that; and there are humbler practitioners of the genre whose work is well received: Robert Breton (Britannus), Pierre Bunel, and Jean Gélida. To these can be added manuscript collections of letters by Antoine Arlier (preserved at Aix-en-Provence, Méjanes) and of Jean de Boyssonné (preserved at Toulouse, together with his Latin poems); the care with which these manuscripts have been produced suggests that perhaps they were intended for publication, and this goes also for the letters of Jean Binet, the uncle of Ronsard's biographer. In the Calvinist world too, letters were immensely useful for the furthering of the cause. In all the examples so far mentioned, we have been dealing with genuine correspondence, whose aims are not primarily literary – though the literary qualities in many cases are prominent – but form part and parcel of the humanist network. On the other hand, Denys Lambyn composed a number of amatory letters that appear to have been much appreciated by contemporaries. In the vernacular, the more serious type of correspondence, enhanced by a sense of style, is best exemplified in Etienne Pasquier's letters to which we shall return later, because they are an important part of the humanist's activity and shed much light on sixteenth-century attitudes. At the same time, one may well wonder to what extent the epistolary genre has contributed to the development of the literary language. In addition to his 'serious' letters, Pasquier also composed a set of 'lettres amoureuses' which follows on the *Monophile* in the standard Amsterdam edition of the *Œuvres* (1723). As a literary fiction, the epistolary genre deals sometimes with amatory topics, but Pasquier was not in fact the first in the field; the pioneer was seemingly Helisenne de Crenne, whose *Epistres familieres et invectives* appeared in 1539. This work was republished with the *Œuvres* in 1560, and, to that extent, fits in with a literary climate that was more favourable to the genre. For it is in 1568 that Etienne du Tronchet publishes his *Lettres missives et familieres*; such was their success that they went through another twenty-one editions by 1600, and they must therefore have encouraged the author to compose his *Lettres amoureuses* which came out in 1575 and went through six further editions by the end of the century. Another indication of public interest in the genre is the appearance in 1586 of the *Missives de Mesdames des Roches*, so that by the end of the century, the epistolary formula is being used for various ends, fictitious and more 'serious'. The reasons for this growing favour need further investigation: the need for popularisation, a reflection of the development of a new atmosphere of 'society' literature – the Dames des Roches kept a *salon*, and in the seventeenth century the success of the epistolary genre and the *salon* are closely connected – and it may be that the influence of Ovid seeps over into the domain of prose. At all events, the popularity of the genre is reflected too in the number of manuals published on the art of letter-writing: in Lyons, 1566, there appears *Le stile et maniere de composer toute sorte d'epistre*, which is revamped in 1584 under the title: *Nouveau style et maniere de composer toutes sortes d'epistres; plus les lettres amoureuses des amans passionnez*, a title which is very significant in the context. There seem also to have been foreign stimulants: thus Giulio Parabosco's *Lettres amoureuses* were translated into French, and in 1556 C. Gruget, that indefatigable hack, published his rendering of Phalaris's *Epistres*. One may wonder whether, at the 'serious' level, Seneca's example is not important.[14]

NOTES

1. G. Reynier, *Le Roman sentimental avant l'Astrée*, 1908.

2. *Le Roman de Jehan de Paris*, ed. E. Wickersheimer, SATF, 1923.

3. *Les angoisses douloureuses qui procedent d'amours* (1538), Première Partie, éd. critique par Paule Demats, 1968. Copies of first ed. in BM, BN, Besançon; PSG has a copy of 1553 and BM of 1560.

4. Margaret A. Harris, *A Study of Théodose Valentinian's Amant Resuscité de la Mort d'Amour*, Geneva, 1966. The BM holds the 1558 and 1572 editions.

5. *Œuvres* de François Rabelais, éd. critique by Abel Lefranc and collaborators, 5 vols. (unfinished), 1912–31; the *TLF* have up-to-date eds. of the first four books. The bibliography of Rabelais criticism is Gargantuan: the following books should prove useful: J. Plattard, *La Vie et l'œuvre de Rabelais*, 1939; G. Lote, *La Vie et l'œuvre de Rabelais*, 1938; A. Krailsheimer, op. cit., also *Rabelais*, Bruges, 1963; V.-L. Saulnier, *Le Dessein de Rabelais*, 1957; L. Febvre, *Le Problème de l'incroyance au XVIᵉ siècle*, 1942; A. C. Keller, *The Telling of Tales in Rabelais*, Frankfurt, 1963; M. Tetel, *Le Comique de Rabelais*, 1966; W. Kaiser, *Praisers of Folly*, Cambridge, Mass., 1963; D. Coleman, *Rabelais*, 1971; also *Etudes Rabelaisiennes*, Geneva series.

6. The BM and BN hold copies of the first edition. On bibliographical problems see P.-P. Plan, *Bibliographie rabelaisienne*, 1904. On *Pantagruel*, see G. J. Brault, 'The comic design of Rabelais' *Pantagruel*', *SPh*, 1968. Modern ed. V.-L. Saulnier, *TLF*, 1946.

7. The BN holds the only known and slightly imperfect copy of the first edition; it also holds a copy of the 1535 (F. Juste, Lyons) edition. The BM

and O hold the 1542 eds. of *Pantagruel* and *Gargantua*. Modern ed. M. A. Screech, *TLF*, 1970.

8. Attention has also been drawn to the possible significance of Rabelais's journey to Italy in this context. The name *Thélème* has given rise to much speculation: cf., for instance, Per Nykrog, 'Thélème, Panurge et la Dive Bouteille', *RHLF*, 1964.

9. The BN holds a copy of the 1546 (C. Wechel) and of the definitive 1552 (M. Fezendat) editions; the BM has a copy of the Lyons 1546 ed. Modern ed. M. A. Screech, *TLF*, 1964.

10. Copies in BM, BN; modern ed. R. Marichal, 1947, *TLF*.

11. See V.-L. Saulnier, 'Le Festin devant Chaneph, ou la confiance dernière de Rabelais', *Mercure de France*, 1954, and 'Pantagruel au large de Ganabin', *BHR*, 1954.

12. In addition to writings by D. Coleman and G. Josopovici, see A. Glauser, *Rabelais créateur*, 1964. Marxist criticism has also turned its attention to Rabelais: H. Lefebvre, *Rabelais*, 1955; M. Beaujour, *Le Jeu de Rabelais*, 1969; M. Bakhtin, *Rabelais and his World*, Cambridge, Mass., 1968.

13. On Rabelais's reputation and influence see L. Sainéan, *L'Influence et la réputation de Rabelais*, 1930; J. Boulenger, *Rabelais à travers les âges*, 1925; M. de Grève, *L'Interprétation de Rabelais au XVIᵉ siècle, Etudes Rabelaisiennes* III, Geneva, 1961.

14. The genre has been inspected by F. Neubert in various articles (*Rom. Jahrbuch*, 1961; *ZRP*, 1963; *Germ. Roman. Monatsschrift*, 1968; *ZRP*, 1969).

PART III

Chapter 6

THE REIGN OF HENRY II –
POLITICAL AND CULTURAL BACKGROUND

I. POLITICAL OUTLINES

THE accession of Henry II marks a change of attitude in some respects, but in others one notes the persistence of earlier currents. Henry had not been a favourite of his father's; he was a man of limited intellectual ability, and his outlook was that of an anachronistic medieval prince, inspired by the Italian mirage and committed to a bigoted religious policy. Strongly influenced by Diane de Poitiers, his mistress considerably older than himself, he moved rapidly against the protégés of his father, and it is from now on that we notice the presence of the Guise family whose star is markedly in the ascendant during the coming years. One thing Henry II shared with Francis I, a hatred of Charles V, and this will dominate his foreign policy. His wife, Catherine de Medici, certainly did not exercise the power that was to be hers later, but with her presence, court life will undergo strong Italianate influences, coinciding with the explosion of Petrarchism in the early days of the Pléiade. And under Henry II, Paris, which had lost something of its prestige in the last years of Francis I's reign, regains its former authority.

If official attitudes to personalities shifted sharply, Henry continued the policies of his father along two lines: in his opposition to Charles V's imperialism and his persecution of growing Protestant dissent. During his reign, the forces of Calvinism and Catholicism begin to polarise. Calvin, after leaving Geneva for a spell, had returned and was beginning to impose his authority and policies. During the 1550s, the *Institution* was to expand into a much greater work, in which the dogmatic aspects were given more emphasis, partly no doubt as a result of the political context; but it is also the period in which the pastorate is rigidly formed and the Calvinist Church creates its cadres in France. Calvinism will find much support among the bourgeoisie, the artisanate, and in due course the nobility. Some writers have also suggested a link with the economic shift towards the west and to trade across the seas. At all events, Calvinism will make inroads in the west and the south-west, whereas the eastern and southern provinces, east of the Rhône, will be less sensitive to the new religious ideas. Henry II, however, lost no time in asserting himself against the Huguenots; in 1547 the infamous *chambre ardente* was instituted to examine cases of alleged heresy and deviationism, though for various reasons it did not become effective until 1553. At Court, the growing ascendancy of the Guises, originally from Lorraine, was bound to strengthen the hand of the vigilants. Various steps were taken to intensify the persecution; in 1553 – the year in which Servet went to the stake in Geneva – the five scholars of Lausanne were publicly burned in Paris, and four years later Pope Paul IV appointed a commission to eradicate heretical opinion in the country. These measures, as one might expect, did nothing to retard the spread of Calvinism, and in 1559 the first Synod of the Calvinist Church in France met in Paris. Calvin's system of organisation, worked out in great detail, was introduced as an essential part of the Church's strength. The social spread of new adherents was very broad, but among them may also be noted a number of humanists, some the sons of scholars associated with evangelical sympathies (Macrin, Bérault, but also the sons of Budé and Bade), others associated with the printing house of Vascosan and the entourage of Marguerite de France. In more than one case, however, declaration of Calvinist principle was deferred until after the reign of Henry II, when prospects of a liberal compromise had faded – Nicolas de Grouchy, La Ramée, Pierre de Montdoré, or George Buchanan who returned to Scotland in 1560 or so. There was also a substantial Calvinist following among nobles, particularly those families which felt threatened by the growing power of the monarchy (Condé), but others like Odet de Châtillon or Gaspar de Coligny may have been moved more by religious considerations. Nevertheless, it is likely that the severe economic deterioration of the country in the middle of the century, which had ruined certain noble families, accounted also in part for their sympathy with Huguenot dissidence.

Henry II's reign is thus no example of religious enlightenment, nor does it manifest much political perspicacity abroad either. Urged on by his hostility to Charles V, Henry reopened the alliance with the Turks, negotiated with the Protestant princes in Germany (treaty of Chambord, 1552), and after a period of tension brought about by the Vatican decision to call the Council of Trent, also reached an agreement with Pope Julius III, thanks largely to the diplomatic skill of the cardinal de Tournon. He was thus free to declare war on the emperor and invaded Lorraine; Charles V's answer, the siege of Metz (1552), was a failure, celebrated by a number of court poets in France. Henry came out of the campaign with the acquisition of Toul, Verdun, and Metz. In the next few years, hostilities occurred on various fronts: the war of Sienna

(1552–55), the invasion of the Low Countries (1554). More significantly, Charles married his son (later Philip II of Spain) to Mary
Tudor in 1554; having achieved this cherished aim and established
relative order in Germany, he abdicated, but not before the treaty
of Vaucelles was concluded (1556). However, peace did not last long
and the treaty between France and Pope Paul IV (May 1555) was
a strong incentive to the renewal of operations. The war, which
dragged on until 1559, was waged in Italy and then on the north-
eastern marches of France, when Mary Tudor declared war (1557)
on a France that had been somewhat weakened by the Italian
campaign. Things continued to go badly for France, and Paris was
lucky to avoid siege; but the capture of Calais and later Thionville
restored national morale. In any case, everyone was heartily sick of
the fighting, and there were pressing reasons for calling a halt. On
the one hand, the wars had had a catastrophic effect on the economy
of France – no wonder the *Hôtel des Finances* was drastically re-
organised in 1557 – and the religious problem was assuming proportions sufficiently troublesome for Henry to wish to disentangle
himself. Mary Tudor's death in 1558 had simplified matters, and the
different factions of the French Court, for varying reasons, had a
vested interest in the cessation of hostilities. And so the Peace of
Cateau-Cambrésis was signed in 1559. It stands as an important
landmark in the political development of France and indeed of
Europe. The end of the rivalry between France and the Empire
was certainly due to work in favour of the Counter-reformation, and
the separation of Germany from Spain and the Netherlands assured
a more satisfactory balance of power; but from France's standpoint,
the treaty resulted in the establishment, broadly speaking, of political
frontiers consistent with the country's geographical character. She
retreated from Italy and moved nearer the Rhine. Nevertheless, the
treaty was far from welcome at the time in France and the loss of
Savoy and Piedmont was widely resented.

Henry's II's reign, though culturally very impressive, is above all
marked by a great waste of economic and military strength; and his
repressive measures at home augured ill for the future. His legacy
was not a happy one, and he was killed in a jousting accident,
indulging in his anachronistic pastime. Nevertheless, the centralising
process maintained momentum. In 1547 the Secretaries of State
(four in number) were given a clearer status than hitherto and in the
mid-1550s a Comptroller-General was put in indisputable charge of
the Treasury. Moreover, in the judicial field, the *présidiaux* were
established in 1552, to serve as a link between the *parlements* and
the *bailliages*; and the work that had been going on since the
fifteenth century on the *coutumiers* was becoming more effective and
wide-ranging.

II. SOCIAL AND INTELLECTUAL BACKGROUND

It is in the middle of the century that so many of the strands we have mentioned in earlier pages combine to bring about the flowering of the French Renaissance, in spite of a political and religious situation that is too often far from reassuring. The coincidence of various factors is certainly important. To begin with, Paris, which had lost some of its cultural prestige to Lyons and the provinces for a time, now regains its authority as the Athens of the North. This shift under Francis I was due, partly to the tendency for vanguard humanism to move out of the capital, partly because Marguerite de Navarre's patronage was richer in its results than that of the royal Court, partly because Lyons was enjoying a 'moment privilégié' in its own cultural development. In the mid-century, with the polarisation of the religious conflict, we shall find that humanism gradually becomes more closely identified with the 'Establishment', both politically and religiously. The Court also becomes progressively more sympathetic to literary initiative and poets will make a substantial contribution to its life; nor will they be alone, for we are moving into a period when architecture and the visual arts enjoy a heyday, and when music, represented by such figures as Goudimel, Arcadelt, and Orlando di Lasso, imported from abroad, is an important component of the cultural scene. Humanism, whose roots go back to the crucial 1520s, is now attaining its maturity and French scholarship enjoys an international reputation; it is also closely associated with the rising generation of poets, whose impact is determined not only by that connection, but also by two other factors: on the one hand, the concerted presence of an abundance of talent motivated by common ideals, and on the other, the opportuneness of their appearance at a time when the literary potential of the French language can be profitably exploited. Before we turn our attention to the poets themselves, a few words on some of these contributing factors is desirable.

III. THE COURT[1]

It is true that Henry II himself was something of a cultural Philistine and that during his reign poets associated with the Pléiade hardly enjoy the innings to which they feel entitled. Nevertheless, even if Henry II's record cannot be compared in this respect with Charles IX's, Ronsard's favourite monarch, court circles were by no means devoid of cultural preoccupation. Henry II, partly guided by Diane de Poitiers, was aware of the need for a proper architectural presence at Court, and during his reign the Louvre was constantly in the hands of the builders; artists and craftsmen were also employed for the creation of the Château d'Anet, and the names of Goujon, Bullant, De l'Orme, Lescot are coming into prominence. Moreover, court life developed a style in some degree influenced by ideals embodied in books that were known to be read at Court. Henry II himself was fond of novels, and in practice this meant novels that prolonged features of the medieval conception of chivalry. It is not surprising therefore that Maugin should publish in 1554 a novel with the title *Nouveau Tristan*, which corresponded closely to contemporary taste; or that a *rhétoriqueur* like François Habert should enjoy the status of *poète royal*. We also know that the *Amadis* sequence, begun in the early 1540s, was immensely successful, especially at Court. Other literary sources reflect the taste that was developing; Sannazaro's *Arcadia* does much to foster the pastoral style, which will also be reflected in the forthcoming return of the court eclogue. As one would expect, Castiglione's *Courtier* continues to be very popular, and other Italian authors capture interest, including notably Ariosto. Nor is a more austere humanism totally absent from Court: Danès, the scholar we met in the early days of Francis I's reign, and Amyot, the translator of Plutarch, were both royal tutors. The growing interest in allegorical mythology, reflected in *entrées* and other court functions, may owe something to visual arts themselves affected by Italian models, but there are also literary sources for this. In Ronsard's poetic world, we can see the reflection of this courtly world, whose characteristics are beginning to take shape in Henry II's reign.

Nevertheless, the role of the court poet is not what it will become under Charles IX, though we note a very marked increase in encomiastic poetry, both Latin and French, in the last two years of Henry's reign, a phenomenon that is probably linked with the ascent of the Guises, but also with the presence of Michel de l'Hôpital. Cultural patronage, more to the taste of the Pléiade, is found in the circle of Henry's sister, Marguerite de France, whose erudition is sung by all, and who interested herself in many young poets and humanists.[2] Her loss, by marriage to Philippe-Emmanuel of Savoy in 1559, is mourned by the Pléiade.

IV. HUMANISM

French scholarship attains impressive proportions by the mid-1550s. Its links with the 1520s were far from broken: some older scholars had either died very recently (Vatable, Toussaint) or were still alive when the *Deffense* appeared, and they were to be replaced by men who had been their pupils. The system of the *lecteurs royaux*, out of which the Collège de France will grow, is already paying handsome dividends; and the philological studies which are a feature of Renaissance humanism are bearing fruit, not only in textual criticism, but in the approach to all study. One feature of French humanism is the number and quality of classical scholars it produced, and in the middle of the century, students come from far and wide to learn from them. Some outstanding editions of ancient authors appear at this time, Horace and Lucretius (Denys Lambyn), Catullus (Muret), Propertius (Passerat), Greek poets (Henri Estienne II), Sextus Empiricus (Gentien Hervet) – editions of such distinction that they will stand the test of centuries. Nor is classical learning confined to academic circles; as we have seen, translations begin to proliferate, and usually from the hands of highly qualified men (e.g., Leroy for Plato, Amyot for Plutarch).

From the point of view of French literature, the coexistence of such mature scholarship, poetic talent, and vernacular aspirations is an essential factor. Not only are members of the Pléiade deeply versed in the culture of the ancient world, which will affect literature, visual arts, and music; they are in close, personal touch with the most eminent scholars. The links with Dorat are well known, even if some uncertainty hovers over the precise form his teaching took, but Adrien Turnèbe is also on intimate terms with some of the poets; Marc-Antoine Muret, before he has to leave Paris and indeed France, lectures on Catullus and other poets, provides a commentary for the *Amours* of Ronsard, and will soon bring out his edition of Catullus in Venice (1554). George Buchanan, whose *Jephthes* is published in 1554, is teaching at the Collège de Boncourt and is on friendly terms with Du Bellay and, it seems, with Ronsard. Scholars and men of letters (the distinction is often unnecessary) meet in other circles, some in the entourage of Marguerite de France, others in the house of Jean de Brinon (Muret, Jodelle, Le Duchat), and the *salon* of Jean de Morel is becoming well known, though its interests were perhaps more scholarly than literary and it was later to be affected by the Calvinist sympathies of some members of the family.[3]

It would be wrong to identify this humanist fervour solely with classical literature, however important this may be. On the one hand, in a period when polymathy is widespread, science comes to be seriously studied, and though excessive respect for classical authority may impede the emergence of an empirical, scientific spirit, Paris contains many scholars who do much to further various branches of science: mathematics (Oronce Finé, Hamel, La Ramée, Pierre Forcadel, Pierre de Montdoré, Peletier du Mans, Elie Vinet), medicine (Fernel, Paré, Dubois), astronomy (Mizault, Buchanan), biology (Rondelet, Belon), and the boundaries of the known world are being steadily widened. Furthermore, the claims of the vernacular begin to impinge on scientific studies, and we shall find works in this field being translated into French or being written themselves in the vernacular (see below, pp. 224–32). And on the other hand, with the tendency of learning to be more and more associated with the *vita activa*, the human sciences, such as historiography, political theory, and law, assume very considerable proportions; in these fields, of course, the emerging political and religious situation will give an urgency and relevance that increase with the years. We shall return to historiography and political theory, since they affect the literature of the period (see below, ch. 14), but though law has less immediate impact in this context, its academic study is extremely important because the methods and materials can affect other disciplines; and it is in this period, when the magistrature becomes larger and more influential, that we notice the emergence of close links with the world of letters. The study of law had developed impressively in the first half of the century, and particularly at Bourges while Alciat was teaching there; and some study had been made of medieval institutions and frameworks. Several currents emerge in due course: there is, first, essentially scholarly study of Roman law by Cujas and his disciples; but we also find a school of thought which uses the *corpus juris* to defend the claims of central, royal authority, and it is no coincidence that towards the end of the century Poitiers will have among its ranks a number of lawyers aggressively supporting an absolutist view of the monarchy. At the same time, certain lessons of Roman jurisprudence will not be lost on scholars won over to the Calvinist cause (Hotman, Grouchy). Others wondered whether the excessive attention paid to Roman law might not harm France's own common law on which so much work had been done in recent times; and here we have another example of the way in which patriotism and commonsense temper humanist zeal, for it became apparent that Roman law had not got all the solutions for a country which already had its own rich legal heritage. And it is partly through the study of law that historical perspectives, indeed a certain relativism, come on to the horizon and may also affect historiography. The lessons of history had been learned by students of jurisprudence. The achievements of French legal studies at this time must not be ignored, even if, from our point of view, they do not have much direct effect upon the development of literature. On the other hand, it is notable how many of the *modérés* or *politiques* are trained lawyers; and their voice will be heard at literary level, as for instance in the *Satyre Menippée*.

Over and above the emergence of Renaissance attitudes in fairly specialised fields of study, there is a more general intellectual ferment, which not only affects theological debate, but brings to the surface a wide range of views about *la condition humaine*, whose roots are often to be found in classical sources. This philosophical

substratum is important, though one cannot say that the French
Renaissance throws up many original thinkers; it can become an
essential ingredient of much literature, and indeed, since this is the
period in which intellectual discourse is finding its way systematically
into the vernacular, it helps to enrich certain genres up till then not
very prevalent in France.

The presence of these various currents is to be explained in part by
the intense exploration of the classical world, also by the penetration
of foreign influences, but furthermore by the need to find a more
up-to-date answer to the problems facing sixteenth-century man.
For convenience, I shall distinguish various strands of thought
that have currency then, but this is in some measure arbitrary: for
instance, though neo-stoicism becomes important, its relations with
Christianity are not clear-cut. In principle, the two doctrines are
fundamentally incompatible, but there are different brands of
stoicism, St Paul came from Tarsus, a famous Stoic centre, and the
Italian Neoplatonists had succeeded in absorbing elements of Stoic
psychology. Moreover, Christian neo-stoicism will enjoy a considerable vogue in the pre-classical period. In any case, we must take into
account the syncretist tendency of Renaissance humanism, which
often blurs differences. Here, I shall try to emphasise features that
are relevant to literary development.

V. NEOPLATONISM[4]

We have noticed that Neoplatonism was a literary force before
1550, especially in the circle of Marguerite de Navarre, and also, in
adulterated form, in Petrarchism. After the advent of the Pléiade
Neoplatonism still commands a sympathetic audience in Parisian
humanist circles. Some have thought that Plato might benefit from
the challenge offered by Pierre de La Ramée to aristotelianism, but
on the one hand Ramus was opposed to the traditional concept
of Aristotle, not so much to the 'real' Aristotle, and on the other,
most humanists could find room for both philosophers in their
intellectual storehouse. Ficino's translations and commentaries, as
well as his own writings, are reprinted during the 1550s, while Leroy
and others translate various dialogues into French. Turnèbe and
Toussaint had both lectured on Plato; and Platonism, chiefly thanks
to Ficino, was thought to be compatible with Christianity. Very
often, Neoplatonic ideas are diffused by means of dialogues (see
below, pp. 215ff.), but from the literary standpoint, only certain aspects
were of major concern. In the first place, Neoplatonism offered
a dignified conception and justification of poetry. Paramount was
the theory of the four 'fureurs' relevant to man's spiritual ascent;
and Tyard, whose links with Lyons and some members of Mar-

guerite de Navarre's circle are important, writes of them as follows
in *Solitaire* I:

Or, pource que l'ame en descendant, et s'abismant dans le corps, passe par
quatre degrez, il est pareillement necessaire, que par quatre degrez son
elevation de ça bas en haut, soit faite [p. 13] . . . Car la fureur divine,
Pasithée, est l'unique escalier, par lequel l'Ame peut trouver le chemin qui la
conduise à la source de son souverain bien, et félicité dernière . . . En quatre
sortes (poursuivy-je) peut l'homme estre espris de divine fureur. La premiere
est par la fureur Poëtique procedant du don des Muses. La seconde est par
l'intelligence des mysteres, et secrets des religions souz Bacchus. La troisième
par ravissement de prophetie, vaticination, ou divination souz Apollon; et la
quatriesme par la violence de l'amoureuse affection souz Amour et Venus.
(p. 17)[5]

Tyard tends to put emphasis on the relevance of this theory for the
pursuit of knowledge, but most poets took more interest in the first
and the fourth furies. Le Caron, author of some dialogues published
in 1556, discusses a variety of Platonic matters, and in Dialogue III
(*Valton, De la tranquillité d'esprit ou de souverain bien*), goes in
some detail into such matters as the constitution of the soul, the
relation between the passions, and the *âme sensitive*, but in the fourth
Dialogue (*Ronsard ou de la Poesie*) he builds a theory of poetry that
is strongly influenced by Platonic currents. The poet has an essential
role to play in man's redemption, because he makes him aware of
his origins:

. . . leurs chants estoient une vraie doctrine de bien-vivre, ou plustost une
sainte fureur qui inspiroit les hommes à congnoistre le lieu de leur celeste
origine. (fol. 129 v)[6]

The poet also has the duty of ensuring the fame of those he sings,
and of hiding his 'inventions' from the vulgar mob by means of
fables; he is more gifted than the man in the street ('honnore[z] dez
dons de nature & d'art'), and the degree of his inspiration distinguishes the good poet from the bad. For many contemporaries,
the poet is thus making human beings sensitive once again to the
harmony of the Universe; and a similar view is held by the Calvinist
Du Bartas, for whom poetry was a means of keeping fallen man in
touch with eternal truth, and this provides the *raison d'être* for the
Christian epic and indeed for poetry of any value whatsoever. Stress
is also laid on the importance of music in this context. Some of these
ideas, which underpin the Ode to Michel de l'Hôpital, persist in the
principles that lay behind the Academy of Baïf and the Académie
du Palais under Henry III, when poets and musicians, thinking in
Neoplatonic terms, evolve theories about the way in which the arts
could help to calm the passions aroused by the religious wars.
Whatever the individual degree of acceptance of such ideas, Neoplatonism offered both a metaphysical and a social justification for
poetry.

The other *fureur* to catch the poet's eye was Love, so that Neo-platonism adds new harmonics to the treatment of the subject. Woman is understood as the manifestation of Beauty in the heavens; she becomes the path to goodness, truth, and wisdom. In the *Timaeus*, love was posited as the principle of the Universe, and this theory certainly makes its way in Renaissance literature. Beauty in its true sense is not apprehended directly by the senses, but physical beauty will inspire in the lover an awareness of the beauty that lies behind. To this ancillary ideas may be added: the theme of con-templation of beauty of the lovers through one another, or that of the lover accompanying the beloved in the pursuit of this eternal beauty:

Ainsi donc l'amour n'est autre chose, qu'une passion émuë de la beauté, laquelle enflamme à la jouissance & delectation mutuelle, faisant vivre l'amant en la contemplation de l'aimé. (Le Caron, fol. 172 r)

The theme of woman as an incarnation of spiritual perfection ap-pears in Scève and in the Petrarchan activity of the Pléiade, so that beauty and moral elevation are closely entwined. The Platonic theory of the androgyne, though Héroët made much of it, does not have so rich an existence later; the opposition of Eros and Anteros has some currency, especially in Ronsard; but theories of metem-psychosis or reminiscence must be checked by Christian inhibitions, and the idea of the Great Year occurs comparatively infrequently. On the other hand, the Neoplatonic ideas on fable cloaking truth have undoubted influence on contemporary attitudes to classical mythology; but even so, one must realise that poets are not trying always to express Platonic themes in verse, and these will be present at varying levels of involvement. Nevertheless there is evidence that Platonic theories had some currency in cultured society (witness Ronsard's *Sonets pour Hélène*). Concepts such as that of a World Soul are by no means unknown, but usually attempts are made to christianise it; this seems to be the case with Ronsard, and Pontus de Tyard distinguishes clearly between the Creator and His creation, thereby separating what is to be worshipped; Le Caron talks of God as 'la souveraine Idee de toutes choses' (fol. 174 v). In a more general way, Neoplatonism impresses by its optimism and by its offering of what today one might call a 'philosophie de l'épanouisse-ment': Le Caron presents a good illustration when he writes:

Nature, la tres bonne parente, a eu l'homme si cher qu'elle ne luy a reffusé aucun moien pour heureux et content. (fol. 113 v)

but he takes care to sustain the theme in a Christian key:

La fin de l'homme n'est autre, que la pure & vraie congnoissance de Dieu. (fol. 120 r)

and man's existence is seen to be incomplete upon this earth and unable to reach self-sufficiency.

VI. NEO-STOICISM[7]

During the second half of the century, stoicism assumes greater proportions than earlier. Its full development in one direction comes after our period and is to be found in authors like Du Vair, Justus Lipsius, or even Pierre Corneille, where stoicism and Christian outlook have certainly mingled. Its appearance in mid-century is partly to be explained by the time of its infiltration from Italy, a greater understanding of Cicero who acts as one of the Stoic filters during the Renaissance, the accessibility of Plutarch, translated by Amyot, and the emergence of Seneca[8] as the main model for classical drama, but also as a letter-writer. These factors coincide with the atmosphere of the religious wars with their brutality, suffering, and perplexity at the workings of fate. In literature, stoicism reveals itself especially in the Latin epistles of Michel de l'Hôpital, the French dramatists (Garnier and others), and of course Montaigne, but it filters also into the poetry of the Counter-reformation and didactic verse. The Stoic tradition assigns a significant place to reason in the attainment of understanding and truth, it also accepts certain 'innate ideas' on the existence of a god, ethical principle, and the role of providence; but its views on body and soul, on the passions, or on the self-created Universe were hardly compatible with Christianity. On the relations between fate and providence, Stoics appear to have diverged, as they did on the problem of evil and free-will; but they differed radically from the Platonists in their view of psychology. What attracted mid-century humanists was predominantly the Stoic morality, with its stress on virtue based on reason and consisting of four main elements: courage, justice, wisdom, and sobriety, but also emphasising man's role in public life. Though some might not share the Stoics' optimistic belief that sin was curable, this tradition provided an ethic for the times, one that preserved man's dignity in circumstances that overwhelmed him.

VII. SCEPTICISM AND RATIONALISM[9]

It seems unlikely that this period threw up many atheists or total sceptics: perhaps Etienne Dolet for all the lip-service he paid to Christian doctrine in some texts may come nearest to such a state. Nevertheless, we do come across references to the existences of sceptics, and when Guy de Bruès publishes his dialogues in 1557, he will justify his enterprise partly on the grounds that he wishes to refute free-thinkers. A number of contemporaries express concern about the spread of irreligious ideas, but it is not easy to discern how far these fears were justified. In any case, the sources of sceptical thought are not far to seek. The influence of Padua, with its Averroist traditions and its fideist outlook in the discussion of philosophical problems, may well have had some impact in France. Then certan classical authors are becoming well-known: Lucretius's *De rerum natura* goes through a considerable number of editions after 1539, and of these the most distinguished was Denys Lambyn's; and in 1569 Gentien Hervet, with a shake of his orthodox head, published his edition of Sextus Empiricus. Lucian too, known since Erasmian days, contains material in his dialogues which, with its ambiguous presentation, could well act as a solvent. Aristotle is also under fire, at any rate in his medieval garb, and La Ramée, Postel, and especially Vicomercato, the Royal Reader in philosophy (1543–67), lay bare the anti-Christian elements of his thought. One may notice also the presence of rationalist attitudes in theological discussion, though this appears more prominently in certain Protestant areas and releases a certain amount of polemic writing. Such attitudes undoubtedly contribute to the intellectual ferment of the period, and underlie to a greater or lesser degree the preoccupation, widespread in midcentury, with such theological problems as miracles, the immortality of the soul, prophecy, providence. Some of these concerns do penetrate into literature properly speaking: chiefly perhaps in the dialogues (see below, pp. 220–2), where sometimes it is difficult to know to what extent sceptical theses are endorsed by the authors; but they are not always far from the surface in some of Ronsard's poems, and of course they enrich certain passages of Montaigne's essays. Echoes are occasionally found among those writers who are rather termed *conteurs* and whose writings may reflect current intellectual interests.

VIII. OCCULTISM[10]

Over and above the currents described previously, there is an illdefined area of interest that forms an essential part of the Renaissance world-picture. The distinctions between philosophy, science, religion, and para-orthodox thinking (occultism, astrology, alchemy, and so forth) are by no means clear-cut, especially in an age when scientific observation still plays second fiddle to established authority, classical or more recent. This concern with the supernatural has many roots, religious, philosophical, folkloric, and it seems to become even more widespread in the second half of the century. Earlier there had been an increase in students of Hebrew and the Kabbalistic tradition; Jean Thiénaud wrote a *Traicté de Kabale* that appeared in Francis I's reign, and in Rabelais we find some preoccupation with divination. But it is more especially after 1550 that important sources such as Trithemius and the *De occulta philosophia* (1528,

known to Rabelais) by Cornelius Agrippa acquire widespread reputation.[11] Agrippa's work dealt with the powers of magic, it also considered the virtues of numbers and letters, divination, astrology, and it
devoted some space to demonology. There were a number of French
humanists attracted by these matters: Jacques Gohorry, a celebrated doctor, published under the pseudonym *Suauius* his *De usu &
mysteriis notarum liber* in 1550, and in the previous year the lawyer
Auger Ferrier had brought out his *Liber de somniis* at Lyons. The
theory that the Kabbala handed down a world-language accessible
to the initiate was current at this time, and there is speculation on
the ways in which man may foretell the future or seek to affect the
forces of Nature. Astrology was popular at the Court of Catherine
de Medici, who had her own soothsayer, and later Nostradamus
was to enjoy notorious prestige. Various celestial phenomena arouse
intense interest in the 1570s and the passage of comets and important stars is widely discussed. Aratus, whose works were printed
more than once in the 1540s, becomes even more popular in the
second half of the century – for instance, Belleau will translate his
Presages.

These currents were well known in humanist circles around the
Pléiade, and a number of works were also finding their way into the
vernacular: by 1549 François Habert had published his version of
Augurelli's *Chrysopée* and the prolific hack Robert Le Blanc translated some texts by Cardano into French in 1556. A bit later the
works of Paracelsus find French readers, and two *vulgarisateurs*
deserve mention: Denis Zacaire and Blaise de Vigenère. Inevitably,
these occultist currents threaten continually to impinge on orthodox
preserves; in consequence we find that on the one hand Catholic
writers and other vigilants denounce the heretical implications of
such interests – and of course so eminent and influential a figure as
Guillaume Postel,[12] whose disciple Lefèvre de la Boderie will work
occultist themes into his poetry (see below, pp. 384–7), falls foul of
ecclesiastical authority; and on the other hand, attempts will be
made to harmonise these interests with the Christian tradition: obviously the problem of prophecy is uncomfortably close to that of God's
freedom of action.

The reasons for these preoccupations are doubtless many and
various. The widening of intellectual horizons would inevitably involve some attention being paid to these occultist currents; and the
emergence of a certain cosmic awareness, reflected in the renewal of
'scientific' poetry in the 1550s, fits into this pattern. One detects a
growing fascination with the unnatural or exceptional; hence the
number of works dealing with 'prodiges' and 'monstres'. Here,
sensationalism may well play some role, but this is only part of the
story; it does not explain why a serious author like Ambroise Paré

should write his work *Des Monstres et prodiges*, which in fact develops among other things the idea that apparent exceptions to Nature are designed to make us more aware of Universal Harmony and of God's presence.[13] Then, the contemporary interest in Ficinian Platonism (in the Academies especially) may reinforce interest in demonic magic, and the matter of demons is discussed in a series of volumes during the 1580s (e.g., Jean Bodin, Pierre Le Loyer).[14] At a more popular level, one must take into account the growth of superstitious fears in a period of political and social turmoil: soothsayers flourish in such times, portents are taken very seriously, trials for witchcraft are far from uncommon. In these circumstances it is not surprising to find the appearance of many books on various forms of divination: G. de la Taysonnière's *La geomance* (Lyons, 1575) is one example of public interest; but one should not forget Pontus de Tyard's more serious *Mantice*. And Jacques Fontaine published his *Discours de la puissance du ciel sur les corps inférieurs* in 1581; a declared opponent of astrology, he none the less recognises the forces at work in the world.

These interests come to the surface in a somewhat disjointed way in contemporary literature. Discussions on certain topics appear in the discursive works of authors such as Du Fail, and also in the writings of travellers and cosmographers. In the Latin and French poetry of the later decades we come across an interest in numerology – chronograms are composed to reveal the destiny of the person concerned, and something similar occurs in the anagrammatic poem. Jean Dorat, a friend of Gohorry, linked with the Academies, and an admirer of Lycophron, wrote a large number of such poems, and one would be wrong in thinking he was simply indulging in parlour-games. As early as 1557, Charles Toutain, a little-known member of the Poitiers group, introduces occultist themes into his poetry. Traces of interest in prophecy and ghosts appear in the theatre: the theme of the witch of Endor and the ghost of Samuel is dramatised in La Taille's masterpiece *Saül* – it is also discussed at some length in Pierre Le Loyer's *Livre des spectres* (1586). The latter author wrote a comedy in which ghosts supposedly play a role. At more serious level, two points should be made: on the one hand, the occult or supernatural plays a considerable part in the poetry of Ronsard, who touches on demons, prophecy, metempsychosis, dreams and is acutely aware of the forces that are abroad in Nature. And on the other, occultist strands often occur in the 'scientific' poetry, the output of which is sufficiently large to merit separate discussion (see below, pp. 379–94): we shall find them in Du Monin, Isaac Habert, and especially Lefèvre de la Boderie, who was well versed in the Kabbala and other occultist traditions, who tried to harmonise the teachings of the *prisca theologia* with modern Catholic doctrine, and whose views reflect those, not only of Guillaume Postel, but also of the Academies.

There is one other vital current, Calvinism; but as it develops its own aesthetic, so that many works are published carrying its individual stamp, we shall reserve discussion for a separate chapter (see below, pp. 331–63). What emerges from the present survey is already very impressive. It is from the 1550s that philosophical and religious ferment is really widespread; with it goes a growing cosmic awareness which is mirrored in the renewal of epic and scientific poetry, though these adjectives are unsatisfactory terms of description. And though the religious situation will often lead to polarisation of ideas, or watchfulness in the expression of attitudes, we are still left with a powerful sense of intellectual expansion. Moreover, this occurs at a moment when the vernacular is acquiring its proper status, not only in poetry, but also in fields of scientific inquiry where Latin was formerly held to be the proper medium of expression. Resistance will not die out overnight, but it will be gradually eroded. At all events, these various factors, coupled with the restoration of the capital's prestige, mean that we are entering the richest period of the French Renaissance and certainly of its literary manifestations.

NOTES

1. E. Bourciez, *Les mœurs polies et la littérature de cour sous Henri II*, 1886; J. Jacquot (ed.), *Les Fêtes de la Renaissance*, 2 vols., 1955, 1960; *Musique et Poésie au XVIe siècle* (ed. Jacquot), 1953; and works mentioned above, p. 88, n.1.

2. Winifred Stephens, *Margaret of France, Duchess of Savoy, 1523–74*, London–New York, 1912.

3. On the Brinon circle see especially, E. Balmas, *Un Poeta del Rinascimento francese, Etienne Jodelle: la sua vita – il suo tempo*, Florence, 1962; on Jean de Morel, P. de Nolhac, *Ronsard et l'humanisme,* 1921; W. Janssen, *Charles Utenhove, sa vie et son œuvre (1536–1600)*, Maastricht, 1939; S. F. Will, 'Camille de Morel: a Prodigy of the Renaissance', *PMLA,* 1936. Manuscript material in the BN and Munich, Staatsbibliothek, Camerariussammlung.

4. For Bibliography, see above, p. 144, n.39.

5. For the Bibliography of Pontus de Tyard, see below, p. 233, n.4, p. 295, n.4. The modern ed. of *Solitaire I* used, is that by S.-F. Baridon, *TLF*, 1950.

6. On Le Caron, see below, pp. 217–20. See also R. Le Blanc's *Epistre liminaire* to his translation of the *Ion*, 1556, exactly contemporary in this ed. (first ed. appears in 1546, BM).

7. See L. Zanta, *La Renaissance du stoïcisme au XVIe siècle*, 1914; E. V. Arnold, *Roman Stoicism*, Cambridge, 1911.

8. L. Annæus Seneca, son of the rhetorician and a tutor to Nero. An apocryphal correspondence presumed to have been exchanged between Seneca and St Paul lent colour to the widespread belief that the Roman had Christian leanings; and this view was known to Renaissance humanists.

9. See R. H. Popkin, *The History of Scepticism from Erasmus to Descartes*, Leiden, 1968; H. Busson, *Le Rationalisme dans la littérature française de la Renaissance (1533–1600)*, 2nd ed. 1957.

10. See F. Secret, *Les Kabbalistes chrétiens de la Renaissance*, 1964; L. Febvre, *Le Problème de l'incroyance au XVI⁰ siècle*.

11. Charles G. Nauert jnr, *Agrippa and the Crisis of Renaissance Thought*, Urbana, 1965.

12. W. J. Bouwsma, *Concordia Mundi: the Career and Thought of Guillaume Postel, 1500–1581*, Cambridge, Mass., 1955.

13. Modern ed. J. Céard, *THR*, 1971.

14. D. P. Walker, *Spiritual and Demonic Magic from Ficino to Campanella*, 1958.

Chapter 7

THE DEVELOPMENT OF PROSE AND
THE WIDENING OF MAN'S HORIZONS

IN a period when man is reassessing his position, personal, socio-political, and religious, in the world, and when circumstances are working in favour of the vernacular as the medium of expression for an ever-increasing range of subjects, it is hardly surprising that the development of French prose should be associated to a large extent with the renewed interest in what we would now call 'human sciences': history, political theory, philosophy, 'science', to which should be added awareness of a steadily widening world, brought about by the voyages of discovery that have been taking place since the fifteenth century. In this chapter, we shall concern ourselves with developments that emerge during the reign of Henry II, and leave over for later consideration history (including memoirs) and political theory which is understandably more closely connected with the wars of religion. For the present, we shall take a look at two aspects of the humanist's growing interests, the 'philosophical' dialogue and the emergence of a so-called 'scientific' literature in the vernacular.

I. THE DIALOGUE

It is during the 1550s that dialogue literature comes into its own in France, as a selective chronology shows very clearly:

1537   *Cymbalum Mundi* (BN)
1552   P. de Tyard, *Solitaire premier* . . . (BN, Ars)
1554   E. Pasquier, *Le Monophile* (BM, BN have 1555 ed.)
1555   P. de Tyard, *Solitaire second* (BM, BN)
1556   L. Le Caron, *Les Dialogues* (BM)
1556   P. de Tyard, *Discours du temps, de l'an et de ses parties* (MRy, O)
1557   P. de Tyard, *L'Univers* (BM, BN; modern ed. J. C. Lapp, New York, 1950)
1557   G. de Bruès, *Les Dialogues contre les nouveaux academiciens* (BM)
1558   P. de Tyard, *Mantice* (BM, BN, O)
1565   J. Tahureau, *Les Dialogues* (posthumous) (BM)
1578   P. de Tyard, *Deux discours* (BN)
1579   P. de L'Hostal, *Discours philosophiques* (BM)
1587   P. de Tyard, *Discours philosophiques* (BM, BN, NLS, O)

To these one could add the writings of Palissy and Henri Estienne's dialogues on linguistic matters;[1] and there is a rather indeterminate area where dialogue and the framework *devisants* of *nouvelles* overlap in their discussion of serious matters, as in the case of Marguerite de Navarre or Taillemont, though in Noël du Fail the level and tension of debate are reduced. This vogue is undoubtedly encouraged by classical and especially Italian models, but its causes are to be found in the intellectual ferment of the mid-century. In this period of reassessment, many ideas are brought into discussion, often of classical ancestry and ranging from Platonic to sceptical; moreover, interest in these ideas is going beyond strictly scholarly circles at a time when in any case the literate public is increasing rapidly. The dialogue in the vernacular thus offers great advantages: the dramatic form, though not always exploited very intelligently, does try to reduce the formal style of presentation, and helps in the development of techniques of *haute vulgarisation* – and perhaps sufficient attention has not yet been paid to the dialogue as a means of developing French prose in the field of intellectual debate. Equally useful is the fact that the dialogue form allows the author to avoid taking sides, often in areas where discussion verges on the heretical or suspect, and more than one critic has wondered whether authors such as Bruès are not more 'sceptical' than they pretend. At the same time, it seems that for many people a keen interest in fairly uncharted areas of thought was accompanied by a hesitation as to where the truth lay; and this may well explain the popularity of forms of literary discussion which allow the author to sit on the fence, so that the device benefits both the crypto-sceptic and the uncommitted.

The literary models for this type of exercise are not far to seek. There is already in the French mind a predilection for debate form – we see it in the stylised medieval *débat* and also in the *colloques scolaires* that assume such importance in humanist curricula; but the major influences are elsewhere. In the first place, we have the classical writers: Lucian, with his satiric wit, his ambiguity, and his solvent action; Cicero, according to whose formula the genre should not have more than three speakers; and Plato, who overlaps with the Neoplatonic tradition.[2] Second, there is the Erasmian tradition, itself inspired in particular by Lucian, and characterised by urbanity, freshness of speech, and satiric undertone. Finally, and this perhaps the strongest influence in the 1550s, we have the Italian model. An early example was the *Courtier*: the work presented a group, as it were a *salon*, of persons of noble birth, who discussed a series of ideas Neoplatonic in origin and the principles of courtly behaviour, and often introduced the anecdote and the tale in order to illustrate their standpoint. But there were many other works in dialogue form that were known both in the original text and

by translations, works by Ebreo, Bembo, Sperone Speroni, to name
some illustrious examples – but even minor figures such as Agnolo
Firenzuola were read: the latter's *Dialogo della Bellezza delle donne*
was translated by J. Pallet in 1578. Pontus de Tyard, who is one
of the major developers of dialogue in France, starts by translating Leone Ebreo in 1551. The French dialogue often deals particularly with the subject of love; but a more wide-ranging discussion
of ideas occurs in the writings of Bruès and Tahureau. Sometimes the
'characters' are endowed with abstract, classical names that may
embody a quality with which they are in sympathy (*Charite,
Thélème*); in other cases, the names of contemporaries are used
(Ronsard, Aubert), though one cannot assert that the ideas they pro-
pound here correspond automatically to those held by their real
prototypes. Baïf's Academy will attempt to make use of the philosophical dialogue at its sessions; and one might fit into this popularity
of the dialogue form the taste for paradoxical literature, itself encouraged also by Italian models, like the dialogue in that its mode
of presentation allows for a sizeable gap between *persona* and
author.

Cymbalum Mundi (*1537*)

Before we look at some examples of the genre created in the 1550s,
mention must be made of the extraordinary *Cymbalum Mundi* that
appeared without name of author in 1537 and 1538; it has survived
in very rare copies, probably because of the official disapproval its
publication provoked immediately. It is on Henri Estienne's testimony of 1557 that the work has been ascribed to Bonaventure des
Périers.[3] The text is a short one, composed of four dialogues. In the
first, Mercury comes down upon Earth, has the book of Jupiter he is
carrying replaced by one very different by Burphanes and Coutalius.
In the second, Mercury disguised accompanies Trigabus to listen to
three philosophers: each claims to possess the genuine Philosopher's
stone which, broken into small pieces, is scattered among the sands of
this world. The third dialogue has two main episodes, in which
Mercury still figures: the scene between Cupid and Coelia, and that
of the talking horse Phlegon. The final dialogue takes place between
two talking dogs: the one, complaining about the way he is treated
by human beings, thinks of using his powers of speech to improve his
situation, but the other dog warns against this.

Interpretation of this sibylline *plaquette* has varied widely over
the centuries. When it was published, the printer was imprisoned
and both Protestants and Catholics were incensed by it. Later critics
saw in it a pamphlet of sceptical and indeed atheistic tendencies, but
recent opinion has moved in favour of an interpretation that is far
from conflicting with Christian doctrine. The form of the dialogue

is clearly inspired by Lucian; moreover, like certain passages in Rabelais, the material is presented from a variety of angles, so that it is difficult to say when the author is speaking in his own right. In any case, we are dealing with satire, not systematic allegory, otherwise we would be hard put to it to identify the anagrammatic Bucer (*Cubercus*) with the real theologian on many points of detail. On the other hand, two contemporary facts weigh against an irreligious reading of the text: first, the Sorbonne, though it condemned the work as a whole, did assert the 'liber ille non continet errores expressos in Fide', and second, the author, if it was Des Périers, continued to enjoy Marguerite de Navarre's protection.

As Mercury appears in the first three dialogues, but not in the last, where only two dogs take part, critics have been divided on the relative importance of the two parts, as if they were distinct; and some have certainly taken the second dialogue, in which Luther, Bucer, and probably Erasmus figure anagrammatically, as the kernel of the work. Three themes do seem to run through the work generally: first, that of the hidden, eternal grain of truth and the inability of human beings to make much of it; secondly, the theme of speech/silence, which occurs in the second and fourth dialogues more especially and develops in favour of silence, for Minerva is enjoined, on behalf of Mercury, to inform poets

qu'ilz ne s'amusent point tant à la vaine parolle de mensonge, qu'ilz ne prennent garde à l'utile silence de verité. (III)

And finally, there is an unremitting criticism of man's weakness, which shows itself in his greed, his claims to be right, his incapacity to grasp truth, his insensitivity – and the author introduces a comparison with animals, unfavourable to man, a comparison going back to Pliny and the sceptics and taken up by many sixteenth-century humanists. Given the religious controversies of the 1530s and the company which Des Périers was keeping in those years, it is tempting not to see some criticism of these debates and their spokesmen: the two characters in the first dialogue, who have tricked the trickster Mercury, may well both stand for man's cupidity, but they also remind one of those who accept the accretions of authority:

. . . je n'ay point beu de nectar, comme vous dictes qu'avez faict; mais nous croions ce qu'en est escript et ce que l'on en dict.

In the second dialogue, certain details appear to contain a clear reference to Luther, marrying a *Vestale*, but it is surely intellectual pride that is being attacked above all; and in the following dialogue, Coelia, who is often interpreted as a symbol of religious, quasi-Platonic, love, may also be read as a critic of *philautia* and 'folle opinion'. All these interpretations are, in the nature of the case, speculative, but they do fit into the philosophical structures of the 1530s; moreover, the form of expression is also characteristic, with its compound of paradox, enigma, shifting levels of meaning, and ambiguous elusiveness. The shadow of Erasmus lies over the dialogues too, I think, and it certainly recaptures something of the humanist's lightness of touch and deadly seriousness; perhaps too it follows the tradition of righteous ignorance. Whether the theme of silence that occurs here and there is a dominant is less certain, if silence is the expression of fear and persecution or of the hermetic initiate; but it blends in well with the *miseria hominis* for whom truth is not easy to discover in a world of appearances and *tromperie*. The self-confidence so often associated with Renaissance man is hardly present here.

Pontus de Tyard

For Pontus de Tyard[4] the dialogue form does not serve as a means of cloaking attitudes that might otherwise incur suspicion in orthodox quarters, but he does bring in ideas of libertine colour and seems to have gone through a sceptical crisis in the middle 1550s. More central is Pontus's desire to vulgarise current philosophical preoccupations, and what emerges from his dialogues is an intense pursuit of learning on a wide front, which, however, does not impinge upon his Catholic faith. His cultivation of the genre lasts for some thirty years, and it sheds light on the development of his intellectual interests. As we saw, he began by translating the dialogues of Leone Ebreo in 1551; in the following year he published his *Solitaire premier*, which reflects his continuing attention to Neoplatonic thought. The two *Solitaires* scrutinise the *fureurs* of poetry and music, and it seems that originally Pontus intended to pursue the problems of the *fureurs*, but a shift in interests made this plan recede into the background. His next dialogue, *L'Univers*, shows a widening of philosophical range, and *Mantice* attempts to offer a balanced exposition of astrological claims, though Pontus himself is critical of them. As he advances in life, he seems to adopt a more critical and scientific outlook, an interpretation that is supported by the later dialogues and by the variants introduced into the texts of the earlier ones. Undoubtedly, Pontus owes a great deal to earlier polymaths, such as Giorgio, and also to Italian representatives of the Neoplatonic tradition; his aims are more especially of an expository nature and his dialogues do not give an impression of a strong philosophic mind in control of his material. For Pontus, learning is advocated as an essential part of man's activity, something that will further his pursuit of wisdom and virtue; but one may wonder, since Pontus remains firmly within the traditional framework of orthodox reference, whether his very considerable erudition affected his basic outlook in any way, and how, if at all, it became part of his inner life. When he does approach topics that could involve the taking of positions, he seems to prefer remaining at a safe distance. There is urbanity and clarity in his expounding of philosophical matters; too often I feel that a clear gap remains between *vulgarisation* and involvement, and one is not surprised to learn that a later generation of *libertins* took virtually no interest in his work. On the other hand, Pontus claims our attention for a well-presented description of certain contemporary attitudes and for helping in the creation of a prose able to handle matters of some intellectual complexity.

Etienne Pasquier[5] – Le Monophile (*1554*)

Two years after Pontus de Tyard published his first dialogue, a great admirer of his, Etienne Pasquier, tried his hand at the genre by writing *Le Monophile*, which also reflects acquaintance with the Neoplatonic tradition; Pasquier's knowledge of Italian culture was profound, especially since his journey to the peninsula in 1548 and the *Monophile* owes something to Italian dialogues on love, in the way both of themes and of structure. The work is divided into two books; the second is perhaps less interesting for its discussion of love (which includes reflections on the *remèdes d'amour*), but it contains some useful references to contemporary literature:

Desjà voyons-nous nos Poëtes avoir entrepris une ligue contre les ans quasi à l'envi l'un de l'autre: desja gaignent nos historiographes païs; desjà volent parmy le monde une infinité de livres prenans leurs cours de bons esprits. (II, col. 756)

The meat of the *Monophile* is in the first book. There are three chief participants: Monophile, Poliphile, and Glaphire, with Charilée acting partly as co-ordinator, partly as defender of her sex, and Pasquier himself who comes in from the sidelines to join play on occasion. Poliphile, whose name might be translated as the *mondain* (unless Pasquier is also playing on words, since Poliphile in love finds safety in numbers), usually represents a lighter level of discussion, valuable for variation of tone; and Glaphire (from the Greek, meaning 'hollow, polished, subtle, critical') stands for the traditional view of love, against which Monophile speaks. This latter, in love with a married woman, advances the view that love should coincide with marriage, and he suggests that man and woman should be equal in that relationship. Poliphile fears that love for a single woman may become so extreme as to lead us away from the love of God. Glaphire believes that marriage is not based on love – Monophile is bitterly opposed to the money marriage – that love should be controlled by reason, that parental consent should be obtained, that man is superior to woman. Pasquier adds the traditional view that marriage involves procreation and the attainment of immortality through our mortal frame. Monophile himself is very conscious of man's Fall, which makes him unable to appreciate beauty as it really is; but our temperament does incline us towards a proper choice in love. He develops the theme of the androgyne, but sees it as a variation on what is fundamentally a Christian conception. There are indeed a number of Platonic topics discussed here and Monophile's definition of love (II. col. 727-8) is strongly Platonic, as one might expect from one conversant with Italian dialogue literature; but these are Christianised, and one might go so far as to detect themes that are Reformist in tone (the danger of love for woman overcoming love of God, equality of man and woman in marriage), themes that we find also in Theodose Valentinian a few years later (see above, pp. 170–1). Pasquier may have had some sympathy with the Reformation at one time, and these topics do nothing to dispel such a view. At the same time, one must note Pasquier's insistence on woman as a social animal, on the relations between law, *naturel* and *coutume*, which remarks sound a relativist note such as will be heard later in Montaigne. When he develops the argument 'Que l'honneur des Dames ne gist qu'en opinion', the relativist, historical attitude is quite apparent; but one must add that Pasquier has developed a notable maturity of style, urbanity of tone, and variety of mood and level in handling abstract material. Nor must one forget that *Le Monophile* appears before the *Heptaméron*, whose author Pasquier mentions in admiring terms. He also tried his hand at some *lettres amoureuses*; here Pasquier thought he was breaking new ground, at least in prose. There are in fact some precursors in the earlier part of the century (Helisenne de Crenne); but though the genre is already well established in Neo-latin circles, it takes some time for the vernacular to consolidate its claims, and Pasquier may legitimately be seen as an important figure in this process, for he composes not only the 'fictional' letter, but makes the normal one a vehicle for the expression of his own attitudes on all sorts of matters of contemporary concern. His letters occupy twenty-two books and they reveal Pasquier to be an alert and sensitive witness of his times, not only in the fields of politics, political theory, and jurisprudence, but also by his reflections on history, his interest in the development of the French language, and by his pride in the cultural reputation which France was rapidly gaining and to which he fondly imagined he had made some contribution.[6]

Louis Le Caron (?1534–1613)[7]

Le Caron, who hellenised his name into Charondas, is another humanist man of letters who made a name for himself as a lawyer; but in his youth, he was to be found in the circles of the Pléiade and published his own collection of verse (*Poesie*, 1555). From our point of view, it is his *Dialogues*, printed in 1556, that command most attention; the five actually printed were to be followed by others which do not appear to have seen the light of day. Even so, they cover a wide range of topics, and many of the ideas discussed or adumbrated shed light on the intellectual climate of the time. Le Caron appeals frequently to the authority of Plato, and various classical currents of thought are brought into the dialogues, epicurean, peripatetic, Stoic. There is much talk of the 'chemin de la vertu' and of the 'jouissance du souverain bien', but all this is seen in the context of man grappling with the problems of the world around him. The first dialogue, *Le Courtisan*, is concerned chiefly with the ideal, philosopher prince. Here we have a variation on the *institution du roy treschrestien*, who is the mirror of God, who must be guided by reason and justice, who needs to be surrounded by wise counsellors and a properly functioning nobility, as well as by a principled magistrature, in which offices are not sold. A considerable section is devoted to war, and the *topos* distinguishing the king from the tyrant is developed. One or two points, over and above what seems to be a fairly conventional attitude, may be mentioned. Le Caron sketches a 'history' of man since the Golden Age, but what he stresses in particular is man's social nature, and 'la raison' and 'la société humaine' are the yardsticks by which Le Caron sees fit to judge behaviour. Thus laws ought to be changed, when circumstances make change desirable; on the other hand, like so many humanist lawyers he accepts the view that the king is *legibus solutus*, a view which will be contested by the Calvinists. Le Caron's conception of the ideal king is that he should embody *sagesse*, and in his formation he advises the reading of certain classical writers, the study of 'la biendisante oraison', but particularly familiarity with mathematics 'par lesquelles l'esprit se delivre de l'inconstance des choses humaines'. And, finally, Le Caron stresses that wisdom is not only contemplation:

Philosophie . . . c'est de conjoindre l'action avec la contemplation. (fol. 40 r)

The second dialogue entitled *Le Courtisan II* considers 'la vraie sagesse'; and it continues some of the thoughts contained in the first: the stress on man's social nature – hence some anti-Stoic notes – on the importance of action, and a discussion on the nature and ways of achieving wisdom (with a distinction between *sagesse*, more contemplative, and *prudence*, linked with action). Man's position in Nature, the variations in human attainments, the role of reason, come under review, and the problem of judgement, even if man is ignorant, is considered:

Ton esprit doit estre le seul juge de toi, non l'opinion des mortelz, ne l'abondance des possessions. (fol. 74 v)

Dialogue III (*Valton, De la tranquillité d'esprit, ou du souverain bien*) discussed a theme already handled in Latin by Sadoleto and Florentius Volusenus (?Wilson), resident near Lyons, and resumes a conversation between *L'Escorché*, Cottereau, and Rabelais. This is an important, densely packed dialogue: it is agreed that

La fin de l'homme n'est autre que la pure & vraie congnoissance de Dieu. (fol. 120 r)

but attention is focused on how man can attain some 'tranquillité' on earth, which involves the participants in a consideration of man's psychology and of the relationship between the self and the outside world, reason and passions, imagination, memory. The question of *jouissance* is debated, but there are some interesting comments on *entendement*, whose nature anticipates the concept of *jugement* in Montaigne. The role of music, reminding man of his essential harmony, is also touched on:

car elle dresse les mœurs, amollit les courroux, appaise les ennuits, & tempere les afections mal ordonnées. (fol. 126 v)

– a conception that has clear Platonic resonance and reminds one of Baïf's ideas on the subject when he was involved in the creation of the Academies later in the wars of religion. Dialogue IV is the one that has perhaps received most attention: *Ronsard ou de la Poësie*, since it links up very conveniently with poetic theory current in the circles of the Pléiade. It opens with a possibly surprising reference to

. . . les deux, qui sont auiourd'hui à bon droit reputez les premiers poëtes de nostre temps, Ronsard & Jodelle . . . & leurs orateurs Pasquier et Fauchet. (fol. 128 v)

and these four take part in the dialogue, though one cannot uncritically attribute the ideas put forward to the prototypes in real life. Among the topics mentioned are the *sainte fureur*, poetry and fame, the use of fables, the endowment of the poet, poetry and Nature, imitation, the public for which poetry is intended, its edifying value.[8] The fifth dialogue, *Claire ou de la beauté*, develops Platonic themes that will already be familiar, and centres on the problem of where beauty lies – in the Idea or its manifestation – and of man's fitness to apprehend it. In short, the *Dialogues* of Le Caron cover a very broad band of topics; and for all their Platonic direction, they tend to shift the emphasis from contemplation towards man's situation and behaviour in an imperfect world. The speed with which ideas such as those debated here became matters of philosophical concern among many humanists can be measured, not only by the appearance of other sets of dialogues in these years, but by comparison with writings in the vernacular published say a decade earlier, when in fact we draw an almost complete blank. It is a pity

that Le Caron did not complete his set, for not only does he reflect
trends, but his artistic techniques improve visibly as the book progresses, and his final dialogue is much more satisfying from the
literary point of view.

Though Le Caron introduces discussion of certain Stoic and peripatetic principles, the general tone of his work is Platonic or Neoplatonic. There are, however, two other authors, whose dialogues
give more prominence to currents of thought less easily harmonised
with the established world-picture.

Guy de Bruès[9]

Bruès, about whom rather little is known, published his three
Dialogues in 1557; the speakers he puts on stage are Aubert, Ronsard, Nicot, Baïf, but it is not suggested that they are voicing their
own real-life opinions. Bruès, whose links with the Pléiade must have
been fairly close, is very much in touch with the philosophical issues
being debated during the decade. He claims that he published this
work in order to refute the sceptics of his times; but speculation has
sometimes ranged over the possibility of Bruès's own scepticism, so
convincingly does he act as the devil's advocate. In fact, the arguments on the various sides are played with equal skill, and the debate
is conducted with some rigour. Broadly speaking, the dialogues,
which have as their main topics man's condition, ethics, and law,
serve to outline philosophical positions which, in their extreme form,
argue for the rationality or naturalism of man; and though Bruès
might well accept that his dialogues are compatible with a theocentric view of man, they do not in fact impinge on theological territory
in their discussion of the topics mentioned. In Dialogue I, man's condition is asserted to be worse than that of other animate beings, and
values, both of a social and personal character, have no rational
origin and have thereby contributed to a worsening of man's estate.
In the following dialogues, the sceptical view of law and justice is
developed in greater detail; innate ideas are denied, and we are
given a portrait of self-centred man, whose senses cannot be accounted reliable as means of knowledge and whose aim in life should be
more or less hedonistic. (These two themes occur also in Le Caron,
but in a very different *caisse de résonance*.) Much is made of the variation of values and principles throughout the world (the relativist
view is vigorously advanced), and man is seen as motivated chiefly
by self-interest and opportunity. Against these arguments are invoked others that defend absolutes, the ability of man to apprehend
these absolutes through his reason and to harmonise his life with
them by the exercise of his will. Virtue and vice can be differentiated
by man's rational mind, and through his judgement he can assess the
particular conditions of an individual case which accounts for the

variations through which absolutes appear to go in this world. The whole discussion is remarkably taut and well controlled, and one can already detect in this work (which Montaigne must have read) the lineaments of themes and arguments that will be amplified in the *Essais*. The work is above all a precious document on certain aspects of the 1550s, but it is also one of the more successful early ventures in popularisation.

Jacques Tahureau (1565)[10]

   The two dialogues of Tahureau were published posthumously in 1565, but their composition surely goes back some ten years earlier. The friend who writes the preface sees in the dialogues warnings against love, women, flatterers, over-zealous soldiers, ancient philosophers, astrologers, lawyers, and doctors; in other words, he pays special attention to the satirical content, though he also appreciates the author's praise of reason. One of the charms of the book is precisely the manner in which serious and comic elements are mingled. On one occasion, the author stresses the need for comic relief in philosophical discourse; and the use of dialogue is intended to ensure variety of tone and to allow Democritic, by protean approaches, to bring Cosmophile to his way of thinking. Though Democritic admits his sympathy with the classical Democritus, the two names fit in with the prefacer's interpretation: the first shuns society – note his affection for the visitor Monierier, that is the solitary one, reminiscent of Pasquier's Monophile – whereas Cosmophile, a sort of Philinte, is more worldly in his outlook. Le Mondain appears at one stage, but presumably he is to be identified with Cosmophile.

   The dialogues contain a good deal more than satire. Cosmophile, who has the lion's share of the text, is a strong defender of Reason and Nature. Man has suffered because he has failed to follow these two guides, though admittedly human reason needs improvement by further instruction; and the various targets are singled out for their neglect of reason. First, there is an extended passage on the weakness of woman, who follows pleasure, pride, and in whom love is a passion that does not heed sense. Many of the arguments adduced are medieval, reminiscent of Gratien du Pont, in spite of the face-saving admission that exceptions may be found; at the same time, themes such as marriage and dancing are treated along evangelical lines. Democritic attaches more importance to *amitié*, which is there to maintain the species and make it possible for individuals to help one another. The second half of the first dialogue is given over to an attack on those who do not follow Nature, which allows for satire against courtiers, lawyers, and doctors, better advised to let Nature have a greater say in healing the sick. Much of the material in these attacks is traditional, but must be seen against the rationalist background. In the second dialogue, Tahureau inveighs against those who try to wrest the secrets of the Universe, in particular the various soothsayers and the astrologers, but also philosophers and founders of religion. Prediction is not really possible; in philosophy doubt is shed on ancient theories of ideas, the atomic theory, the soul, and founders of non-Christian religions are presented as human in origin, concerned with religion as a social cement and guardian of order. Tahureau thinks that most ancient gods were frauds, but also disapproves of the emergence of new sects in his own time. The dialogues conclude with a resounding vote in favour of Christianity; nevertheless the rationalist thread is a dominant; even laughter is the product of 'raison et bonne grace', something that cannot occur without 'l'esprit fort delié' or without the stripping of ignorance and presumption. In Tahureau, though one cannot perhaps expect a definitive position in a writing belonging roughly to his twentieth year, it seems that the division between faith and reason is already clear-cut. For us, much of the value of these dialogues lies in their literary qualities. Tahureau's masters in this field include Rabelais (some themes, enumerations, word-play), Lucian whom he mentions, and Erasmus in spite of the qualified statements that are made about the humanist. Democritic himself is conceived along Catonian, slightly Stoic lines, but of course he only represents part of the spectrum; Cosmophile, though rather colourless, and admittedly unable to establish any solid position of his own, does tone down the more extreme views of his friend. Tahureau, who quotes Du Bellay on more than one occasion, has a pretty gift for sketching a character, he attaches considerable importance to clarity (cf. his comments on the prolix debates concerning the nature of the soul before the Creation), he likes proverbs and the occasional anecdote, and he develops a pleasantly unpedantic style. What, however, makes Tahureau appear in an ambiguous light is that, though he attacks certain writers popular at the time (Agrippa, Erasmus, Cardan), Democritic does after all put forward theses that are not incompatible with what these humanists had written here and there. The success of these dialogues is illustrated by the fact that the adjective 'tahuréen' is coined by contemporaries.

The dialogue continues to have some success as a genre until the end of our period: Pontus de Tyard's further activity is clear indication of this, and in 1579 we come across a somewhat obscure author, Pierre de L'Hostal (or Lostal), publishing his *Discours philosophiques*, in which he studies how 'le monde est entretenu en une Harmonieuse symmetrie de discordans accords', discusses the immortality of the soul, and also devotes much space to considering political theory.[11] At the same time. the dialogue seems to lose some of the literary value it possessed during the 1550s: at one end of the spectrum, certain elements filter into the looser fabric of the *con-teurs* (e.g. Du Fail, De Cholières), at the other, the dialogue is used in more strictly theological debate (Viret, La Primaudaye). In its heyday, the dialogue reveals the extent to which certain classical authors and Italian humanists were acting as a ferment (Lucretius, Lucian, Cicero, Cardano, Pomponazzi, and others), and how in a sense all questions affecting man's destiny were back in the melting-pot. The fundamental questions of the eternity of matter, linked with the problem of the creation of the Universe, and of the presence of God in or above the Universe, are gingerly surveyed; then man's standing in and relation to the Universe, the world around him, are scrutinised, with thoughts on the animal kingdom. This area of dis-cussion is almost always connected with an analysis of his psycho-logical structures, the relation of mind and body (including the immortality of the soul), the reliability of the senses, the question of absolutes and innate ideas. There often follows – especially as many of the writers have had a legal training – an examination of the social framework in which man is seen to have to live, with special reference to topics such as the authority and code of the monarch, the creation of laws, the exercise of justice, the role of the courtier; and given these wider frameworks of reference, thought is given to the choice of 'faculties' and principles that will help a man to attain his proper aim, in the next world and this, and these are numerous: reason, faith, will, *entendement*, experience, imagination, the passions, custom, social pressures, but also, in the 1550s especially, the question of prophecy (which threads together all manner of motifs, dreams, soothsaying, magic, their relation to free-will and determinism, and also fortune and *fatum*). The study of history, of which Pasquier in particular was aware, will add its perspectives to the debate (see below, pp. 458ff.). At the same time, one notes a deep sense of France's rising prestige in the world of culture and her solid achieve-ments in the field of poetry more especially. With the polarisation of religious issues, it is perhaps difficult to see clearly the direction in which some of the authors we are considering are trying to go; and one can understand how in Ronsard an openly affirmed acceptance of the Catholic Church may be accompanied with an intuition of the world at poetic level that ties up often very closely with some of the points we have mentioned in the dialogues. However, there are cer-tain features which do suggest that a gradual laicisation of attitudes is on the way: an awareness of the issue between acceptance of absolutes and relativism, the emergence of historical perspectives, the increas-ing stress on social, civic pressures in determining human behaviour, the distinction between reason and faith, a growing measure of self-reliance coupled with the need to know oneself better, the consolida-tion of 'human' or 'social' sciences inevitably at some expense to the former queen of faculties, theology, the increasing appeal to experience; these, and doubtless other factors, are symptoms of a changing world-picture. It is for this reason that the 1550s are so important for the development of the French Renaissance and that, in the present, more limited context, the dialogues form so significant a part of the humanist scene at that time.

II. EMERGENCE OF NEW ATTITUDES TO SCIENTIFIC STUDY

The ferment of the 1550s, with its reappraisal of man's condition, was bound to affect the study of natural sciences; it is, however, possible to detect two rather different strands in this domain. On the one hand, the humanist search after universal knowledge prompts the scholar to examine the Universe from a more or less 'scientific' point of view, but his approach is, characteristically, more philosophical (or religious) than empirical; in addition, he tends to see things through the spectacles of such classical authorities as he has read. Thus it is that in the 1550s we note a renewed interest in 'scientific' poetry, both in Latin and in the vernacular; one expression of this interest will be found in Ronsard's *Hymnes*, and towards the end of our period we shall meet Du Bartas and Lefèvre de la Boderie working in this field (see below, pp. 384–90). Yet the point of departure of such humanists is far from that of an experimental science; more visionaries than observers, they do not impart much momentum to scientific discovery, whatever their contribution to literature; indeed, they may have been a positive hindrance, in so far as their work got into the school and colleges: George Buchanan's *De Sphæra*, projected in France in the 1550s and published posthumously in unfinished form, offers a pre-Copernican view of the Universe; a copy of one Paris edition (1597) is extant in the Bibliothèque Nationale, and it is covered with notes by the principal of a Paris college. This is no doubt symptomatic of scientific studies towards the end of the sixteenth century.

On the other hand, a mere 'scientific' spirit will be found in writers whose observation begins with the particular and the pragmatic; they base their statements on the observed and on 'experience'. Impetus here comes from two sources: first, a considerable amount of travel literature is coming on to the market, so that the educated public is becoming aware of a larger world than previously and is learning that each country has its own way of life and history.[21] Second, men who are essentially craftsmen, are writing on their skills in the hope of passing their knowledge on to others who wish to follow in their path. These two currents have an important trait in common over and above their methods of approach: they tend to write more and more in the vernacular, and they attack the prejudice which tries to hide scientific work behind Latin doors. Symphorien Champier, well ahead of his time, had seen no reason for refusing a doctor admission to the profession even if he had no Latin, but resistance from the Establishment was tenacious. Gradually more voices are heard: some object to medicine being based on classical authorities whose *Krankengut* must by definition have been different from what France had to offer centuries later; and it seems that the spread of new infectious diseases necessitated administrative structures in which French must be the language of communication. And the sciences will benefit from the general drift towards the vernacular which becomes marked after 1550. Many of the 'scientific' works in question have little literary merit; what I shall do is to select a handful of these writers, varied in their interests, but all trying to improve scientific method and further their cause in their mother tongue. We shall not be surprised to find that the claims to scientific rigour are not always matched by practice.

André Thevet (?1504-92)[13]
  Thevet, who ultimately was appointed Cosmographer Royal, was a far-travelled man; he had visited Italy, then the Near East, and finally Africa and America. In 1558, his *Singularitez de la France antarctique* were published and enjoyed considerable success. His *magnum opus*, the *Cosmographie universelle*, was to come out in 1575. By the time his first book appeared, interest in travellers' tales was already widespread; since Frenchmen had taken a prominent part in opening up the New World, attention was spurred by patriotism, but foreign books of travel were being translated into French too. In Thevet's writings, we see the co-existence of the traveller, the humanist, the Franciscan, and – as some contemporaries suspected – the charlatan. His *Singularitez* – the title is perhaps more sensational than scientific – purport to be the record of a man who has witnessed exotic life for himself and who wishes to communicate these experiences, in their *singularité*, to his compatriots. Time and again, Thevet stresses that he has seen the marvellous things described, and points out that the classics were at fault, since they were talking of areas then unknown. And yet, where classical authority can be introduced, he does so; thus, the African days of his journey are interlarded with discussions of a humanist colour, and he indulges in fanciful etymologies for the names of places he has visited. He is much struck by the diversity of Nature, identified in his eyes with God, but also by man's insatiable curiosity, which he links with the divine intention that man, through further experience, may be gradually led to 'ce souverain bien'. All things have been

made for man, who must therefore benefit from their presence; and the 'modernes', as Thevet calls them, are to be complimented for having 'faict la recherche'. He opposes certain anthropocentric tendencies among the classics (fol. 2 v) and the hope that men will penetrate *all* the secrets of Nature; the Christian view of the primitive world is preferred to the Vergilian. He is also aware of the differences between cultures, but supports his comments by reference to Galen, and from another, Christian angle, is anxious to detect orthodox religious institutions among the natives, whether it be some innate belief in a form of God or the assertion of the immortality of the soul – a passage which allows him to attack the 'damnables atheistes de nostre temps'. He evinces passing interest in orthodox magic:

... et c'est certain qu'il y a quelque sympathie es choses & antipathie occulte, qui ne se peut congnoistre que par longue experience.

On occasion he reflects, in pre-Montaignian fashion, on certain points that strike him as important (e.g., nudity), and these may be enriched by interesting references to the French life of his times; but above all, he is anxious to tell the truth without shrinking:

Le grand desir que j'ay de ne rien omettre qui soit utile ou necessaire aux lecteurs, ioint qu'il me semble estre l'office d'un escrivain traiter toutes choses, qui appartiennent à son argument, sans en laisser une. (fol. 43 v)

Nevertheless, certain things are omitted, partly because he does not wish to bore his reader, partly also because it is the *singularitez* he is interested in, partly also because his experience is much less extensive than he would have us believe. His knowledge of geography is hazy and very disconcerting to the modern reader, he shows ignorance of scientific instruments and also of certain areas he claims to have visited. His contemporaries were distinctly critical of his testimony, and his claims do seem on occasion designed to cover up important gaps. Even so, his work should not be ignored: his awareness of the 'scientific' approach and also of his contemporaries' interest in the matter is significant; moreover, he raises a host of topics that we have seen to be part and parcel of the intellectual preoccupations current in the 1550s: man's place in Nature, the conflict between 'ancient' and 'modern', appeal to experience, incipient relativism, certain theological matters. And he is, finally, an author who is very conscious that he is writing for a public. He is sensitive to the dangers of prolixity, so that he frequently feels obliged to describe 'sommairement'; but he also wants to be exact, vivid, and civilised, as he states in the preface ('le tout representé vivement au naturel par portraict le plus exquis qu'il m'a esté possible'). Variety of style is essential:

Or sans divertir loin de propos, j'ay esté contrainct de changer souuent & varier de sentences pour la varieté de pourtraicts que j'ay voulu ainsi diversifier d'une matière à l'autre. (fol. 102 v)

and he aims at a certain 'mediocrité' of length so as to avoid excessive brevity or development (fol. 117–18). The picture he gives us sticks to essentials, the country and its flora and fauna, the natives seen in their basic activities, family life, welfare, food-gathering, and religion. Rarely does Thevet refer to his companions, rarely does he allow himself mention of his own feelings – there is one exception that remains in the memory, when he reaches land and finds fresh water. He is precise in his definitions, and like his contemporaries keen to make use of illustrations to aid his text; complex rhetoric is avoided, homely comparisons are employed, but he can write in an alembicated vein, as the liminary letter proves. What emerges from his writing, in spite of the gap between claim and reality, is a man of the golden mean, a firm believer in Christianity, a fervent, though not uncritical, admirer of French achievement, above all one who values 'experience'.

N. de Nicolay

Though Thevet seems to pay lip-service to new ideas and methods, a more genuine example may be found in N. de Nicolay,[14] whose *Quatre premiers livres des navigations* came out in 1568: he opens with an agreeable defence of travel which ought to communicate experience to others and which has many beneficial effects on man:

. . . avec un tant noble exercice se rassasie le desir, s'esveille le jugement [a theme quite common before Montaigne], s'estainct l'oisiveté (qui est la mere de tous les vices), s'esclarcit le cueur, s'occupe le temps & outre le proffit qui en provient, s'y despend la vie vertueusement. (fol.* 2 v)

He is also aware of the advantages of book techniques that allow him to present full-page plates showing men and women in local dress. Above all he emphasises man's need to explore the whole earth, for all things are subject to man, the greatest of God's creatures – a theme we have already seen in Thevet. He wishes to combine 'utilité' and 'plaisir'; and he personalises his account more than Thevet or Belon, by the insertion of dramatic elements, the occasional anecdote, and so forth. He fills out his narrative with the history of towns he has visited, describes carefully the vegetation and produce of each area, but must needs remember classical references to the places he sees. Unlike some contemporaries, he is relentlessly hostile to the Turks and their *mores*. Nicolay shows a lively interest in the religion and the political practice of the countries he visits – sometimes one senses that the comments, though objective enough, are not entirely without contemporary relevance. He also is impressed by the past history of certain countries; and the desolate state of modern Greece prompts in him thoughts of the transience of things and the causes of decline and decay in states that were once famous.

Pierre Belon (1517-64)[15]

Belon, whose books on animals and fish are justly famed for their typographical interest, was sent on a journey in 1546-49 by the cardinal de Tournon, and his account appeared under the title *Les observations de plusieurs singularitez trouvées en Grece & autres pays* in 1553. In Belon, the desire to describe accurately is strongly developed, though he is aware of the dangers of excessive detail, so far as his reader is concerned. Unlike Thevet or even Nicolay, he is not awed by the ancients, whom he does not feel it necessary to quote, except to confirm his own findings, since science has progressed since classical times:

Au surplus apres avoir consideré que les hommes croissent en scavoir de plus en plus par dessus les autres, & que tout ce que nous mettons en evidence n'aiant authorité que de nous mesmes, n'est grandement prisé, il m'a semblé convenable amener quelquesfois les passages des bons autheurs pour donner authorité aux choses que je diray par cy après. (fol. ẽ ii r)

He defends himself from any charges of plagiarism and underlines his own powers of observation – though the reference to the wounded deer eating dittany in Crete has a borrowed air. He notes the decline of modern scholarship in contemporary Greece and the total ignorance of the clergy, though comparative observations are not all that numerous. Belon tries to correct various vulgar errors, such as the belief that chameleons live on air. Furthermore, he seeks no literary embellishment; his style is rather bald, with uncomplicated sentences, in his attempt to be clear and precise. He is, moreover, aware that he is writing in the vernacular:

J'ay traité cette mienne observation en nostre vulgaire Françoyse, & redigé en trois livres, le plus fidelement qu'il m'ha esté possible; n'usant d'autre artifice ou elegance d'oraison, sinon d'une forme simple, narrant les choses au vray ainsi que les ay trouvées es pays estranges: rendant à chascune son appellation Françoise où il m'ha esté possible de luy trouver un nom vulgaire. (fol. q iii v–iv r)

Not all these travellers stand out for their literary value, but they constitute an important phenomenon. One does notice in them the awareness of a difference of experience between themselves and the ancients, the emergence of a scientific spirit, seeking to free itself from authority, though in practice this liberation will be an arduous process: in some, the attitude to the classics remains ambivalent, in others, the scientific 'conscience' is likely to operate only at certain levels. On the other hand, the value of French as the means of communication is accepted, and this will help to promote a style of writing that is quite different from the *rhétoriqueur* tradition (still prevalent in the novel during the 1540s) or from prose using techniques transferred from humanist writing. Many writers link up their travels with matters of contemporary relevance. In a period when, for political reasons, the attitude to the Turks was very mixed, it is interesting to find that the majority of travellers have kind things to say about the Turkish way of life and religion – Belon includes various remarks on certain features of the Koran;[16] and during the religious wars, comparative material may be introduced for the purposes of axe-grinding. One topic that is often mentioned is that of the noble, happy savage, particularly by authors who have visited South America, and it can tie up of course with that of the Golden Age and primitivism.

Ambroise Paré (?1509-90)[17]

Among the writers who develop the language of craftsmanship in the vernacular Ambroise Paré is perhaps the most impressive. He was a professional surgeon – at a time when surgeons were still socially inferior to doctors and not the products of a humanist training – and he spent most of his early life soldiering. His contribution to surgery is important, but so is his literary offering. Had he been a humanist, he would probably have been over-impressed by classical authority and he might have written in Latin. His first book appeared in 1545: *Methode de traicter les playes faictes par hacquesbutes et aultres bastons à feu.* In his later works his defence of the way he writes is significant: he resists the suggestion he publish in Latin, even if this would take his fame across the frontiers:

Pourquoy semblablement ne me sera-il permis d'escrire en ma langue Françoise, laquelle est autant noble que nulle autre estrangere?

This passage shows a national pride in the vernacular, but he also wishes to avoid mumbo-jumbo and refuses to 'cabaliser les arts'. His desire to communicate by the clearest method possible is manifested by his extensive use of plates to illustrate his text; and by his rejection of any style that smacks of inflation or rhetoric:

mes livres sont sans aucun fard de parolles, me suffisant que je parle proprement, & use de mots qui soyent significatifs, & lesquels soyent propres pour le prouffit du François . . .

On a wider front Paré is very refreshing too. He places experience above authority; and tells us that he lost faith in what others said when he ran out of the boiling oil used at the front to disinfect wounds. He evinces a persistent hostility to the *doctes* and asserts that it is not good enough to lecture 'si la main ne besogne', for practice is more effective than theory:

Voilà comme j'ai appris à traiter les plaies faites par arquebuses, non par livres.

His attitude touches on two matters that assume increasing significance: on the one hand, he anticipates Montaigne – though he is not alone in this – in giving experience priority over learning:

. . . bien que le scavoir soit grande chose, si est-ce que l'ame gist en l'experience. . . . Partant, ceux qui ont l'experience, sont plus sages et plus estimez que ceux qui en ont défaut.

And on the other, we discern the dawn of the *querelle des anciens et des modernes*, for Paré deliberately attacks those who refuse to add to the store of knowledge created by the ancients:

Parquoy, ne soyons si simples de nous reposer & endormir sur le labeur des anciens, comme s'ils avoyent tout sçeu ou tout dit, sans rien laisser à excogiter & dire à ceux qui viendront après eux,

and he quotes, in French, the *topos tempus pater veritatis*, in support of his stand. Such an attitude is revealing, for it shows the extent to which humanism could be anti-scientific and therefore liable to hinder progress in the field of experimental activity.

These opinions, important though they are, would not establish Paré's claim to literary status, and it is only towards the end of his life that he publishes his *Apologie et traité concernant les voiages faicts en divers lieux* (1585), which by its non-technical nature allows Paré a greater freedom of expression. The rejection of literary artifice is very obvious here, and the prose is distinguished by a remarkable sobriety and precision, but also by an undoubted ability to 'épouser le mouvement de la vie'. At the same time, the humanity of the man comes through movingly in those passages where he has to depict suffering; but are we right in attributing Paré's stylistic qualities exclusively to his non-humanist formation? After all, he did move to some extent in humanist circles and, later in life, he mingled in elegant society: the mixture of social urbanity and direct vision combats in him the humanist attitude to science, partly because language is felt as a means of communication, not of professional hermeticism.

Even so, there are limits to Paré's empiric outlook. In any case we observe a mixed attitude on his part to the humanism he attacks as an outsider: he does argue on occasion from 'raison, autorités et preuves notables', he is capable of accepting Thevet's authority apropos of 'deux figures de Dragons qui tuent les Elefans', he can write on unicorns and accept their existence to some extent on scriptural evidence. And then, there is that curious work *Des Monstres et prodiges* first published with other writings in 1573: there his main sources include Boaistuau, Jean Wier, Rondelet, Thevet and he appears to have borrowed also from Noël du Fail, not to speak of various biblical reminiscences. He is even willing to appeal to various classical authorities to justify including his freaks in his museum, and the book concludes with a quotation from Psalm CIV. No doubt many strands go to the making of this book: awareness of the contemporary interest in the strange and wonderful, interest in the occult forces in Nature, above all it seems a desire to affirm God's presence behind the universal harmony, of whose existence we become even more conscious by consideration of *monstres* and *prodiges*. And in so doing, Paré has almost completely abandoned his former scientific methods and relies chiefly on bookish authorities; we are back in a near-humanist world, where phenomena are not observed in themselves, but for their relevance to a scheme of things accepted *a priori* on authority.

Bernard Palissy (c. 1510-90)[18]

Like Paré, Palissy is a self-made man from outside the mainstream of humanist activity; he is, moreover, a convinced Calvinist, a feature that colours much of his writing, and his God-fearing nature shows itself time and again:

Or Dieu est sapience: l'on ne peut donc aimer sapience sans aimer Dieu. (P.-A. Cap ed., p. 210)

Like Paré, he is aware of the opposition he will encounter from 'learned' men steeped in the humanities; as Theorique says in one of the Dialogues:

Et toy qui n'est qu'un terracier desnué de toutes langues, sinon de celle que ta mère t'a apris, oses tu bien parler contre un tel personnage, qui a composé plus de cinquante livres de medecine? (ibid., p. 227)

or evenly more pungently a few pages earlier:

veu que tu n'es ny Grec ny Latin, ny gueres bon François. (p. 205)

Palissy's interests are in the applied aspects of natural sciences: the best way of fertilising land, the fabrication of enamel, the mechanism of wells, and so forth; but he is also fascinated by the fundamental principles that underlie the workings of Nature, and here he has put forward impressive theories about the 'salts' that form the basic ingredients of metals, and other elements, the porosity of matter, the importance of water in the Universe, and the possible significance of fossils. What is his real contribution to scientific knowledge is for others to decide; here we are concerned with his method and outlook, and the ways in which he tries to communicate his ideas to others.

What Palissy stresses is first-hand evidence and the ability to extract its significance by rational means. He often shows impatience with the ancients, but the axis of his opposition is not so much *ancien* v. *moderne* as experience (*practique*) v. theory or learning.

The simple phrase 'J'ay aussi plusieurs fois contemplé les sources naturelles' is revealing; he relies on personal observation repeated if necessary. Natural knowledge is more useful than Latin, or theory or simple imagination (pp. 131, 144) and it is significant that Theorique says, 'Je suis de l'opinion des autres'. Palissy does not attack genuine philosophers, but he has harsh things to say about the rest who place learning above experience; he also reproves those for whom knowledge is a means of holding oneself apart from common humanity and believes that knowledge should be common property, as a general rule, though there are situations where widespread diffusion of techniques might not be beneficial and he sees value in the errors that have helped him to progress:

Les fautes que j'ay faites en mettant mes esmaux en doze, m'ont plus apprins que non pas les choses qui se sont bien trouvées. (p. 322)

Equally important from our point of view are the ways in which he imparts his experience. At one time, he gave public lectures in Paris; but his chief medium is the dialogue. He presents Theorique and Practique, in discussions where the latter represents Palissy's standpoint and experience. It seemed to him the clearest means of exposition available to him; though Theorique acts inevitably as a foil, she is less wooden than some of the figures we have met in dialogues and she is endowed with the natural vivacity of Palissy's own personality. But it is Practique who dominates the scene: the lively assertion of hypotheses based on observation, a steady progression from one topic to another, an important and delightful autobiographical element, and a clear, unaffected style to match. What is so attractive in Palissy is the way in which language refuses to stand between him and life; he catches the tone and tempo of conversation with impressive frequency, but his writings are not just gay chatter, they are informed by a deeply moral sense of man's dignity, a spontaneous poetry in the face of Nature, and a cluster of fundamental intuitions concerning the world about him which help to confer a calm and measured unity on what he has to say.

NOTES

1. The formula is of course used beyond the conventional confines of literature: e.g., Eymar de Froydeville, *Dialogues de l'origine de la noblesse*, Lyons, 1574. Neo-latin writers also use the genre.

2. Though the *maïeutique* of Socrates is ousted by the more frequent tutorial lecture to the silent pupil.

3. It is thought that the first ed. appeared at the end of 1537 (?beginning 1538), the second *c*. March 1538. Only one copy of each survives. Modern ed. P. H. Nurse, Manchester, 1957; see also D. Niedhardt, *Das 'Cymbalum Mundi' des Bonaventure des Périers: Forschungslage und Deutung*, Geneva–Paris, 1959, for discussion of theories about its meaning and bibliography.

4. See Kathleen Hall, *Pontus de Tyard and his Discours philosophiques*, Oxford, 1963.

5. Modern ed. E. Balmas, Milan, 1957. See also Irmgard Sturm, *Vorstudien zu einer Neuausgabe des 'Monophile' von Estienne Pasquier*, Würzburg, 1941. See below for bibliography, p. 75, n. 9. Though selections and individual works have been edited in modern times, we still rely mainly on the Amsterdam ed. of 1723 (2 vols.) from which I quote.

6. See various selections by D. Thickett for *TLF*: *Choix de lettres sur la littérature, la langue et la traduction*, 1956; *Ecrits politiques*, 1968; *Lettres historiques pour les années 1556-1594*, 1966.

7. F. Gohin, *De Ludovici Charondae (1534-1613) vita et versibus*, 1901; L. Pinvert, 'Louis le Caron dit Charondas (1536-1613)', *RRen*, 1902.

8. G. Castor, op. cit.

9. Little is known about his life. Modern ed. P. P. Morphos, Baltimore, 1953. See also H. Busson, op. cit., pp. 409-10.

10. The *Dialogues* were very successful: the BN has copies of the following eds.: 1565 (also BM), 1566 (also PSG), 1583, Rouen 1589, Lyons 1602. Modern ed. F. Conscience, 1870; see also London thesis by S. Gouna, and E. Besch, 'Un Moraliste satirique et rationaliste au XVIᵉ siècle, Jacques Tahureau (1527-1555)', *RSS*, 1919. H. Busson has some pages on Tahureau, op. cit., pp. 396-400.

11. H. Busson, op. cit., devotes a few pages to this figure, pp. 393-6.

12. G. Atkinson, *La Littérature géographique française de la Renaissance, répertoire bibliographique*, 1927; and *Les Nouveaux Horizons de la Renaissance française*, 1935; G. Chinard, *L'Exotisme américain dans la littérature française du XVIᵉ siècle*, 1911; F. Dainville, *La Géographie des humanistes*, 1940.

13. In addition to works listed in previous footnote, see J. Adhémar, *Frère André Thevet, voyageur et cosmographe des rois de France au XVIᵉ siècle*, 1948. The BM and BN have copies of the first eds. of the *Cosmographie de Levant*, Lyons, 1554, the *Singularitez*, and the *Cosmographie universelle* (this last also NLS). Interestingly, the *Singularitez* have liminary verse by Jean Bouchet and Belleforest.

14. (1517-83). His work, graced by an elegy from Ronsard's pen, was soon translated into several foreign languages (BM, BN; some other volumes in NLS).

15. *L'histoire de la nature des oyseaux*, 1555 (BM, BN, StA). *Observations* ... (BM, BN, NLS); *La nature et diversité des poissons*, 1555 (BM, BN, NLS, Innerpeffray, MRy). See J. Delaunay, *L'Aventureuse Existence de Pierre Belon du Mans*, 1926.

16. The great orientalist Guillaume Postel (1510-81) was an authority on the Near East. Though much of his work is in Latin, one may consult his *De la republicque des Turcs*, Poitiers, 1560 (BM, which also possesses the ?1566 ed.).

17. See modern ed. of *Des Monstres et prodiges*, by J. Céard, *THR*, 1971; P. Delaunay, *Ambroise Paré naturaliste*, 1923. The *Œuvres* appeared in 1575, reprinted in 1579 (BM, BN), 1585, 1595, and 1607. The *Œuvres complètes* were edited in 1840-41, 3 vols., by J.-F. Malgaigne, but a new ed. is desirable.

18. *Recepte veritable* ..., La Rochelle, 1563 (BN), and 1564 (BM); *Discours admirables de la nature des eaux et fontaines*, 1580 (BM, BN), the latter translated by A. de la Roque, Urbana, 1964. Modern ed. *Œuvres complètes*, ed. P.-A. Cap, reprinted 1961. A new ed. of Palissy is wanted. See L. Audiat, *Bernard Palissy. Etudes sur sa vie et ses travaux*, 1869.

Chapter 8

DEVELOPMENTS IN NARRATIVE
FICTION AFTER 1550[1]

I. GENERAL SURVEY
(INCLUDING EARLIER ACTIVITY)

WE have seen that extended narrative fiction enjoyed some vogue under Francis I; but after the outbreak of the religious wars momentum is not maintained, except perhaps through foreign models and especially the *Amadis*. The shorter tale, whether it is called *conte*, *nouvelle*, *devis*, remains popular throughout our period, but it is after 1550 that it assumes impressive proportions. Before that time, only one or two contemporary writers had published their tales, and the reader's appetite was catered for either by earlier French texts or by foreign works; Des Périers and Marguerite de Navarre were busy on their *nouvelles*, but their works were printed posthumously and only a bit later did much to foster the popularity of the genre. To use the term *genre* is perhaps begging the question, because we shall find that the short story appears in a variety of frameworks: the series of tales or their insertion into a framework of *devisants* are recognised formulae, but when the proportions between the tales and the contribution of the *devisants* are modified in favour of the latter, we have something much more like a spoken *essai*, or conversations that verge on the dialogue genre. During the middle third of the century, the interest in the strange and wonderful will be whetted by experiences purporting to be true (travellers' tales) or illustrative of the marvels of Nature; the distinction between the story and the *exemplum* will be blurred, as in Montaigne's essays, as it was sometimes in Erasmus, and we may also find the epistle serving as a thin pretext for more story-telling. In general, the motive of *délassement* or wonderment lies behind most fiction of this sort, but more serious purposes are sometimes claimed to be present. The result of this vogue for short fictional forms is on the one hand a remarkable widening of thematic range, but also an important contribution to the development of French prose. Some of the techniques will reappear in the genre that develops so rapidly towards the end of the century, the Memoirs: the example of Brantôme springs immediately to mind.

Nevertheless, the *nouvelle* does possess characteristics of a fairly permanent nature, whatever the fluidity of the form. Convention usually demands that the author or his *persona* make claims for authenticity (so often plainly inaccurate, especially with folkloric or archetypal material) and also for edifying intent, but if they do work as more than conventions, it is simply to engage the receptivity of the audience. The *nouvelle* is often well constructed round a central situation – the *conte* will go beyond the single episode – and this may work on the audience by gradation or reversal (e.g., the catcher caught or the *quiproquo*), but it is not unusual for the text to comprise two or three tales forming a fairly coherent pattern, or for the *nouvelle* to assume the guise of a character-study, especially in satiric vein. The tale may be inserted into some larger pattern, as in Rabelais. In the early collections, especially, the satiric intent is prominent and century-old targets recur: the clergy and monks, doctors, lawyers, woman in all her frailty, and the ignorance of louts and rustics furnishes further butts of humour. The *nouvelle* is often therefore a vehicle for the *esprit gaulois*, but this is too narrow a definition: Marguerite de Navarre may draw on medieval romance (e.g., *La Chastelaine de Vergi*), Castiglione's *Courtier* may be used as a source, and after 1550 the thematic range and treatment broaden rapidly. The *nouvelle* in verse is not much exploited, either in French or in Latin, but Marot does use the techniques of prose fiction. Most stories give the impression of being narrated to an audience, which in fact can be present; a suppressed first-person formula is used and in consequence certain dramatic techniques and fruitiness of language can be expected. The *nouvellistes* of talent are masters of language, expressing their vitality linguistically, whether in straight prose, or reproduced speech, dialect, or pastiched Latin. Popular phrases and comparisons are frequent, and a sententious element may appear, though usually at superficial level. The technique of linking, the prototype of which is the *Decameron* but can also be seen with different proportions in the *Courtier*, is effected by the presence of *devisants*: at one end of the scale, the participants comment on the tales as they occur (e.g., the *Heptaméron*), and at the other, the stories are part of a broader portrait of a community, of a wider outlook (Noël du Fail). Language, dramatic presentation, and tempo are vital factors; literary reminiscence is not infrequent, since most writers are humanists with an impressive range of knowledge and interest. Characterisation tends to be rudimentary, since types are often put on stage, but the *nouvelle* can be a school for realism and in the case of Marguerite de Navarre we see the beginnings of acute psychological observation which by its very presence is one example of the way in which she managed to assert her freedom within the framework of an allegedly tradition-bound genre.

Before contemporary writers exploit the *nouvelle* on a large scale, the public relies on traditional and foreign sources. The *Cent Nouvelles Nouvelles*, completed *c.* 1462, were published well before the end of the fifteenth century, enjoyed four reprints before 1520, and were still popular in the following decade.[2] The *Quinze Joyes de Mariage*, finished even earlier, have persistent success[3] and the *Petit Jehan de Sainctré*[4] (followed by the *Histoire de Messire Floridan et de la belle Ellinde* by Rasse de Brinchamel) was printed in 1517. In the same decade the *exempla* tales written in the fourteenth century by La Tour Landry for his daughters were published in 1514 (BN, reprinted 1517), and the ever-popular *Arrests d'Amours* of Martial d'Auvergne were edited again with Benoist Court's ponderous commentary in 1533; Gilles d'Aurigny made slight additions in his reprint, and the work went through some 35 editions by the eighteenth century. No doubt its realism, dramatic movement, and sharp insight into human nature contributed to its success. Finally, among the older traditional sources, mention should be made of the *Légende de Pierre Faifeu*, in verse, published in 1531.[5]

To these works, which do not include the popular lore of the chap-books, difficult to assess at this distance, the foreign purveyors of tales bring strong reinforcements. Italy is the main source, though *Till Eulenspiegel* is known in the 1530s; some tales reach France through Latin versions (e.g., Beroaldo), and the work of Folengo and Pulci has readers this side of the Alps. A little later we shall find some Spanish names to add to the list, but the main impetus clearly comes from Boccaccio's *Decameron*.[6] This work had been translated in the fifteenth century, though it was not printed until 1485 or thereabouts, but it is Le Maçon's version, first printed in 1545, that gains the greatest currency and went through many editions subsequently. Nevertheless, public taste does not confine itself to the shorter type of fiction, even if it relies on foreign models to satisfy the need. The worlds of the extraordinary *Amadis de Gaule* and of *Orlando Furioso* by Ariosto correspond significantly to certain imaginative needs of the French public from the end of the reign of Francis I onwards.[7] Here we are no longer in the domain of the *gaulois* tale; the *Amadis* in particular brings back into favour a wonderland inspired by chivalric ideals, all the more acceptable as this work of Spanish origin was nevertheless considered to have Old French origins. The Spanish author had published his four books of the *Amadis* in 1508, but others had continued the work to the extent of doubling it. Something similar, but on a larger scale, occurred in France: the first eight books were translated by Herberay des Essarts between 1540 and 1548; but ultimately the series comprised twenty-four books by the time it came to end in 1613. Among the contributors who 'translated' the *Amadis* after Herberay des Essarts were Boileau de Buillon,

Jacques Gohorry, G. Aubert, Gabriel Chappuys, and N. de Montreux. The statements of such diverse authors as La Noue, Brantôme,
and Pasquier are often quoted to underline the extraordinary success
of this *roman-fleuve*, which by the end opens the way for the seventeenth-century novel of D'Urfé and his followers; and a perusal of,
say, the *Short-title Catalogue* of the British Museum shows at a
glance, not merely the continuing popularity of the *Amadis*, but also
the frequency with which individual books were reprinted. The
Amadis offered in modern garb the formula of the medieval cycle
of romance, whose popularity at the beginning of our period has
already been noted; it provided a literary correlative of the ideals
which inform the Court of Henry II and his followers – and in this
it has some kinship with the world of Lemaire's *Illustrations de
Gaule* and that of Ronsard's courtly and mythological poetry; it also,
in the eyes of some contemporaries, made an important contribution
to the development of French prose style, at a time when narrative
fiction was still considered to be below the standards expected of
literary endeavour. Though the work enjoyed success far beyond the
confines of the Court, it offered in romance style an ideal of life that
was fed by courtly ideals, Neoplatonic currents to some extent, a
desire to refine social life. It helped to satisfy both the taste for the
merveilleux and fairy-world and the growing tendency to organise
cultural and social life along lines that will take us later to the
threshold of Arthénice's *chambre bleue*.[8]

At yet a different level, the work of Rabelais, which itself shows
sensitivity to emerging fashion (as for instance in the use of the
voyage motif in the *Quart Livre*), will exert a steady influence on
various forms of narrative fiction. This influence will be very diffuse in
certain directions: we shall find Rabelais's impact in comedies at a
rather later date; he will become a model for various forms of satirical
writing, including the *Satire Menippée* and works by Agrippa
d'Aubigné. And his linguistic habits will often be copied, both in
satirical and in other veins. As his books appear, a higher proportion
of tales is to be noted; this may be explained in great measure by the
need for such material to balance other elements, but it may also
reflect Rabelais's awareness of the public's growing taste for the
nouvelle. Attempts to write sizeable works in the Rabelaisian style are
understandably rare, for most would prefer to imitate here and there
to competing with the master; so it is that we find some of Rabelais's
tales making their way into other collections. There is, however, an
early attempt to write in the Rabelaisian vein: the *Mitistoire Barra-
gouyne de Fanfreluche et Gaudichon*, by Guillaume des Autelz.[9] It
seems probable that the work was published as early as 1550-51, but
only the 1574 and 1578 editions have survived. This is the first book
of a work that the author playfully suggested might continue for

another fifteen or so. It is a bizarre blend of Rabelaisian idiom and personal experience. Fanfreluche tells the story of her family and also of Gaudichon's youth up to the time they met: there are thematic echoes of Rabelais (genealogy, feats of strength, reference to giants), but the linguistic influence is the more evident. At the same time, Des Autelz introduces episodes or allusions which shed light on his literary and cultural interests: he makes fun of Petrarchism, he has a curious chapter on contemporary French poets, with it seems favourable views on Scève and Ronsard, and he refers to his days as a law student. To this extent, the fantasy has some anchor in the author's life; it shows his command of French at many levels of linguistic tone and, even if it is a trifle of no great consequence, it is an enjoyable exercise by a cultured and sharp-sighted man.

We must now return to the mainstream of prose fiction. One of the features of the first half of the century is the reluctance of authors to publish, for one reason or another. An early example is Philippe de Vigneulles of Metz, whose tales have only recently engaged critical attention.[10] Then, c. 1531, Nicolas de Troyes wrote his *Parangon*, a title probably influenced by the appearance of the *Parangon des nouvelles* published in 1531 at Lyons, his work, in manuscript until the nineteenth century, is only partly extant – some 184 tales have survived.[11] Two-thirds of these have been traced back to literary sources, but the author does claim, with some justice, to have drawn also on oral tradition and first-hand material: thus the tale about the ghosts fabricated by the Orléans Franciscans is up-to-date, and its veracity is attested by the accounts given in Sleidan and various Neo-latin poets. He attempts to give a sort of 'external' framework to his stories in that he provides different narrators. It is perhaps in the non-literary aspects of his narration that he comes to life; his writing can be clumsy, but he enjoys switching to direct, first-person presentation, which results in some verbal liveliness. His 'moral' attitude is commonplace and not very prominent; what interests him are situations, to which he may try to impart some local flavour. All this hardly adds up to very much, especially as any literary self-consciousness on his part has a most inhibiting effect, but he is after all quite early in the field, and if one may detect some influence of the *Decameron*, he remains squarely in the French tradition and displays an embryonic realism that can be refreshing. What is lacking is the linguistic dynamism that is so cardinal a factor in the work of Des Périers.

Jeanne Flore[12]

One of the first French authors to publish *contes* is Jeanne Flore, only known by her *Comptes amoureux* which appeared in an undated edition (c. 1530?) and enjoyed a modest success until 1574 when the last edition appeared at Lyons. We are offered a collection of seven stories related within a group of eleven ladies. The tales themselves seem to belong to consecrated tradition; and some of the poetic decoration takes us back to the *rhétoriqueurs*, as the following extract shows very plainly:

Finablement la noble matronne excessivement amoureuse, languissante, exagitée en la chaleur des hautes flammes, esguillonnée des illecebres desirs et de prurientz appetitz, de lascive intemperée incrediblement commecie, comme si de Lays Corinthienne fille, elle eust retenu aussi complexion libidineuse, ne pouvant plus supporter telles oppressions, dolente & esperdeue cheut au lit malade. (Jacob ed., p. 84)

Jeanne Flore claims that her style is less 'limé' than one would expect from a male author, but in its use of erudite latinisms and multiple epithets, it shows a disciple of Jean Lemaire. What is perhaps more interesting is that each story, broadly speaking, defends the rights of *amour folle*, and approves retribution against those who refused its call ('touchant la punition de ceux qui contemnent & mesprisent le vray Amour'). There is thus a franker, more pagan atmosphere in the book, which appears to be of Lyonnais origin. Each tale is a case, an *exemplum* designed to illustrate the general thesis of the work. The frame belongs to the Boccaccio convention; the ambiance gives us a foretaste of what we shall find in Yver's tales, and it is a good example of the variety of attitudes represented in these so popular works of fiction.

La Motte Roullant

After Jeanne Flore, there is a gap in publication until the appearance of La Motte Roullant's *Les facetieux deviz des cent et six nouvelles nouvelles*.[13] Most of these are traditional tales centring on marriage; one or two relate pranks that do not concern relations between the sexes, and only a handful count as 'dolentes'. The *epistre exhortative* is entertaining for its open imitation of the Rabelaisian idiom, which is all too rarely carried over into the main text. The author's sole concern, he tells us, is to entertain:

Pour vous exciter à rire & gaudir gallantement, par similitude & faicts modernes escriptz en ce petit traicté pour tousjours augmenter vos creditz & gaillardies . . .

He makes no claims to invent new stories, instead he wishes to bring them up-to-date so far as the language is concerned:

Nous l'auons diligemment veu & leu & totalement immué le langage antique, & remis les nouvelles en leur naturel, brief & succinct, comme vous pourrez veoir par la lecture d'icelles.

He complains about the 'tresrude' and prolix style in which the tales were originally couched. Some are, moreover, omitted, as they seemed to lack point, but he is anxious for the *nouvelles* not to appear 'laides' in the eyes of the Court or the 'gens de sçavoir'; which might suggest that the genre is becoming more highly esteemed than formerly.

Noël du Fail (?1521-91)[14]

In the middle 1540s there are three law students at Poitiers who are on friendly terms with each other and who will make a name for themselves as tellers of tales: Jacques Yver, Guillaume Bouchet, and Noël du Fail. The first to appear in print was Du Fail, whose *Propos rustiques* came out in 1547 and the *Baliverneries d'Eutrapel* in the following year. His *Contes et Discours d'Eutrapel*, which in all probability rework to some extent material from the author's youth, do not come out until 1585. The name *Eutrapel* derives from the Greek equivalent of *facetus* (witty, easily linked with *facétie*); but the originality of Du Fail's writing does not really lie in his handling of time-honoured *nouvelle* material. Indeed his narrative gifts in the genre are somewhat perfunctory, and his tales lack the edge and *brio* we associate with Des Périers. It is the framework into which the tales are fitted and which reveal the author's intimate and shrewd knowledge of village life that sticks in the memory. In the *Propos*, there is not much of a thread, in fact, to hold the chapters together, but we are introduced into the lives of several villagers with whom the author converses. Dialogue thus plays an important part, and the language is often ripe, even if sometimes Du Fail's sentence structure is difficult to grasp and the lawyer lurks near the surface of the story-teller. The telling of the tale is subordinate to the *tableau* of a country way of life in which the author reveals himself as *laudator temporis acti*; he has little sympathy for urban existence, and in two marginal chapters he has something to say on false beggars (a theme we shall find elsewhere, for instance in Ambroise Paré) and also on women and love.

The *Baliverneries* show even less attempt to organise pattern, and the 'story' is little more than a point of departure for wider reflections. Certainly Du Fail has read his Rabelais, of whom clear echoes are audible; but what he is really trying to do is re-create an old-time, stable village world, in which the divers characters have a family air and whose way of life is leisurely and self-contained. This is broadly true too of the 1585 *Contes*, though Du Fail can turn out a polished enough tale, which more often than not steers clear of literary antecedents. The village life he evokes is also a means whereby he offers the reader his own outlook, one that is tolerant, conservative, and moderate in its political aspects. He wants a fairly rigid structure of society with some provincial autonomy (*justice seigneuriale*); he would like to see the nobility better educated and more socially committed, the clergy less obsessed with money, justice better and less cruelly dispensed. Critical of the Court, he is influenced in his expression here by Guevara, but on the other hand does not flatter the countryman or hold his own world up as a variation on the Golden Age. For him the important thing is to be natural:

Il n'y avoit rien laid en nature, pourveu que l'usage en fust legitime (*Contes et discours*, Hippeau ed., II, 14)

and he lays more stress on behaviour than on dogma. He holds views that some think inclined him to Calvinism:

Mais le principal et souverain point sera de regler vostre conscience, vie et mesnage, vertueusement à la mesure de l'Evangile (ibid. II, 283)

and to preserve oneself from passions and learn 'le mespris des choses'; which does not prevent him from accepting the Catholic Church as 'tousjours Eglise'. Du Fail includes many references of a scholarly nature and often mentions notables from the world of law and humanism, but his attitude to the classics is not obsequious. He believes that the moderns have made considerable progress and he attacks pagan threats to Christianity; on the other hand he has a qualified belief in education. He rejects occultist approaches to truth, accepting only a few forms of prophecy. He laughs at the myth of France's Trojan origins, but remains an impenitent admirer of medieval romances which are mentioned time and again. Eutrapel ultimately retires to the country – though not every man can face solitude. In all this, the *nouvelle* has given way to something much broader, closely related to the burning questions of the religious wars, but also maintaining its own independence. One can understand how Du Fail's writings enjoyed their success in the closing years of the century: he may have written that for him literature was essentially *divertissement*:

Mon naturel est follastrer, rire & escrire choses de mesme (Preface to *Baliverneries*)

but the relaxed atmosphere of his books, with their advocacy of the *juste milieu*, hostile to *philautia* and *paraître*, and offering the vision of a way of life different from the hurly-burly of the wars, was bound to appeal to readers eager for peace and disengagement. A minor figure, but an endearing one in whom literature is not just the exploitation of a genre but the expression of an attitude to life.

Claude de Taillemont (?1504-?1558)[15]

In 1553, Taillemont published his *Discours des champs faez* (Lyons); and here again we can see how the *nouvelle* can fit into patterns which themselves have other intentions. There is an overall narrative framework of reference concerning three knights whose journey brings them to the *Champs faez* of which the heroine, accompanied by two damsels, becomes queen. We thus have a variation on the medieval, chivalric romance; but the purpose of the narrative is to develop a Platonic defence of woman, for the work is stated in the full title to be 'à l'honneur et exaltation des dames'. Part of the *querelle des femmes*, then? Perhaps, but also the work of a man who was a close friend of Pontus de Tyard and other writers connected with Lyons. We are not so very far here from the *discours philosophique*; but Taillemont, in addition to the fictional framework, includes a number of illustrative tales, and these, in some measure, are indicative of shift in the public's taste. On the one hand, they are characterised by a more involved plot, and on the other, several of these tales stand out for their brutal elements, thus initiating a trend that will end in the *tragédie irrégulière* or *Titus Andronicus*, and will also receive some impetus from the *Histoires tragiques* of Belleforest (see below, pp. 252–3).

Comptes du monde aventureux (1555)[16]

These *Comptes* have been, understandably, eclipsed by the imminent publication of the tales of Marguerite de Navarre and Des Périers, but they were popular in their day, going through five reprints in the sixteenth century. The identity of their author still remains a mystery, though if he belonged to the entourage of Marguerite at some period, the *raison d'être* of his series becomes clearer. He makes substantial claims to be the first Frenchman to achieve what Boccaccio had done in Italy, if we are to judge by a liminary poem from M.I. to *Ma Damoyselle*; indeed he is very keen that France should soon overtake Italy in the cultural field:

> . . . Là lon veoit des Françoys les escritz surmonter
> Les ans & leurs espris Rome & Grece dompter,
> Si Florence a vanté de son Boccace aymé,
> Les devis amoureux le style bien limé,
> C'est qu'il estoit le premier & seul en ce subject,
> Et que nul n'a ozé imiter son project
> Mais cest autheur hardy a premier en la France
> Imité le discours des comptes de Florence.
> Et en les imitant a vaincu le Boccace
> Et devancé ses pas suyvant mesmes sa trace.

In fact, the writer of these highly derivative tales owes much to Italian sources, notably Masuccio, but he also draws on French tradition.[17] Two features of his presentation are worth mentioning: first, he creates a framework of elementary pattern, compared with the *Heptaméron*, admittedly, but designed to establish some minimal unity. The author meets a nobleman and his wife, whose health has been impaired by her yearning to marry the man she loves; and on the way, the party, bound for Savoy, is entertained by the series of tales, fifty-four in number. The situations range from the risqué and *gaulois* to the sentimental and indeed tragic. Second, the stories are all followed by a moralising epilogue from the author, whatever the level and tone of narration. Love is viewed as having an 'intolerable ardeur' tending to override honour and good sense, even to the extent of making those involved forget God. The tales are situated in different places, and the author takes care to vary tones – hence Tale 7 is introduced to lighten the mood; but generally the gay stories predominate, and there is quite a lot of fun poked at monks and priests, 'combien qu'il ne desire empescher la bonne opinion qu'on doit avoir des bons religieux'; other tales deal with professional or rural characters. Hypocrisy is often attacked, but so is stupidity. The 'moral' conclusions must presumably carry some weight, given the space that is systematically devoted to them, and an undoubted religious concern is present, as for instance in the very strange tale deemed valuable because it describes how a Jew was converted to Christianity; but, like most of his contemporaries, the author is primarily interested in the story. He adopts a pleasing variety of tone, and he avoids the insertion of overmuch learning.

Marguerite de Navarre and her Heptaméron[18]

Marguerite's role in the development of the *nouvelle* is considerable, by the encouragement she gave Le Maçon in his translation of the *Decameron*, by her interest in *nouvellistes* who may be connected with her circle, above all by her own creative work. Her tales were published posthumously, first in an unsatisfactory edition by Boaistuau in 1558, then in the following year by Claude Gruget, whose edition, though much more reliable, removes 'offensive' remarks of a religious character, possibly modified the order of the tales, and probably overlooked material intended for a work whose completion was forestalled by death. Much of the subject-matter may go back quite a long way in Marguerite's life, but it is in the early 1540s that she sets to work: some of the tales carry contemporary allusions and the probable identity of the *devisants* links the composition with Marguerite's later years. A spur was no doubt given by the example of Boccaccio, to whom she refers in the prologue, perhaps also by the popularity of Castiglione's *Courtier*, which may have affected parts of the *Heptaméron* both formally and thematically. After the death of her brother, she probably quickened the pace of composition, and the later tales and days show signs of hasty work and some departure from the structural principles followed in the earlier *journées*.

Originally, the book was to consist of ten *Journées*, spent by five men and five women in enforced company through the hazards of the weather in an apparently 'realistic' setting in the Pyrenees, though this background is invented. The framework of the stories was to allow for systematic variations and linkings: a humorous story to be followed by a serious one, a female narrator to come after a male one, and doubtless some build-up towards an ending in which the full significance of the days would emerge before the *devisants* departed on their several ways. Each Day is bracketed by a prologue and an epilogue, and each tale is followed by a conversation between the participants who discuss the implications of the tale just related; these *devisants* reveal a diversity of attitude extending from the earthly in Hircan (? an anagram of Henric, Marguerite's husband, but also very akin to *hircus*) to the Platonic in Dagoucin; and the women too show a spread of outlook.[19] The work is thus fundamentally serious in nature: we are some distance from the uninhibited enjoyment of Des Périers, and though entertainment is often present, the relation between tale and conduct of life is very much to the fore. To see in the book a sort of *Courtier* and little more narrows its scope unnecessarily; it is informed with a very marked religious and moral aim, and the tales will be seen as *exempla* in a well-established tradition. The group serves as a special technique of presentation, and partly in deference to convention but also because of the moral dimension, the *devisants* will draw attention to the veracity of their stories. In sober truth, a number of them have clear ancestry, but the factual basis of many has been ascertained, and in any case Marguerite has little time for literary embellishment. Her sympathy for Parlemente is very evident:

Il n'y a plus que Parlemente à tenir son ranc, mais, quant il y en auroit cent d'autres, je luy donnerois toujours ma voix d'estre celle de qui nous devons apprendre. (François ed., p. 274)

and Oisille's role, with her reading of the Scriptures, the respect in which she is held by the others, reinforces the serious intent of the work. The fact that some of the tales are bawdy does not affect the issue: variety of tone in the whole structure, expression of different characters present, for one reason or another such tales will find their way into the book; and neither author nor reader in the sixteenth century had quite the inhibitions or repressions of more recent audiences.

The substance of the *Heptaméron* lies in its treatment of love and of its relation to salvation and the good life. Indeed, very few of the tales make no mention of love, whether profane or sacred. Marguerite is closely interested in human relations and character, and the *devisants* sometimes comment on the way love develops according to the quality of the person in question; but her concern with man's spiritual ascent is rarely far removed from the analysis of feelings. These points are much more important than any attempt to see in her a feminist ahead of her time: she accepts both the social and biblical inferiority of woman asserted in her times, though she is careful to underline man's religious obligation to respect law and morality (p. 125); in any case, her focus is on spiritual salvation to be achieved within the social framework that exists, and the state of sin shows up in both sexes in the *Heptaméron*. Many tales describe the break-up of an imperfect personality in the grip of human love, which acts as a corrosive or acid. Love, which sees others not as *toi*, but as instruments, may well undermine reason and will-power, and it is characterised as a form of blindness (p. 94). It also induces in its victim a state of restlessness, a desire for change and mutability, and frequently links are drawn between love and Fortune. Marguerite reveals acute powers of observation here: occasionally, as in xxvii, credibility is overtaxed, but most often the characters are well motivated, and better still, are seen to act from multiple pressures and indeed inconsistent urges; the human condition is contemplated with neither cynicism nor morbid fascination, but with level-headed insight, sympathy often, and a desire to limit the damage.

Marguerite's view of marriage is businesslike and charitable, closely linked with her attitude to human nature and society. The topic is often aired, especially in Days III and IV, and moreover with a remarkable degree of unanimity. She accepts the contemporary interpretation; it is an institution that conforms with natural, social, and divine laws (p. 280) and remains uncoloured by any romantic conception of love. Marriage goes beyond the individuals concerned, connecting property and status and continuing tradition. Social rank, finance, and honour are essential components: and it is significant that the comte de Jossebin's behaviour is considered harsh, but not questioned in its principle. Parental consent is desirable until the age of discretion has been reached and the husband's rights are recognised. Nevertheless, marriage cannot aspire to the name unless its inner meaning is fulfilled; the social conditions already mentioned can lead to the 'fauxbourgs d'enfer' (p. 280), if love provides no counterweight. Yet it is difficult to decide whether Marguerite's views are definitely Pauline or not: she often colours her ideas with Neoplatonic tints (discussion after Tale lxxi), but elsewhere her thinking is more related to Lutheran principles (p. 418). As in other works, it is sometimes easier to grasp the general outlines of her attitude than to pin her down on points of detail; at all events, marriage is seen *sub specie æternitatis*, as a framework within which two beings can influence each other for good, but of course cannot always do so in their fallen state.

Even Hircan accepts the sinfulness of man, who is blind and thus too often impelled by self-reliance, *philautia*, or pride:

Le premier pas que l'homme marche en la confiance de soy-mesmes, s'esloigne
d'autant de la confiance de Dieu. (pp. 233–4)

The answer is to be found in Grace, a theme that recurs time and
time again, though one may find it less easy to discern the terms on
which man can enjoy God's grace. Marguerite of course encourages
humans to proceed from things visible to things invisible and sees the
body as a lowly means of advancement to a higher plane; she is by
no means an ascetic. But man will make himself accessible to grace
by the reading of the Scriptures and by prayer, as well as by throwing
himself on Christ's mercy. It is therefore hardly necessary to stress
here Marguerite's evangelism which informs so many of her writings;
but it is probably more important than her Neoplatonism, if this is
taken in isolation. Parlemente's definition of the 'parfaitz amants'
(pp. 150-1) certainly has a Platonic flavour, and so do remarks by
Dagoucin, who stresses human love as a path to higher things and
also refers to the doctrine of the Androgyne. Yet, Marguerite's ideas
normally concern the development of spiritual awareness in love
already properly constituted, whereas Platonic ideas of the soul in
its prenatal state conflict with Christian doctrine; furthermore, her
attention is concentrated on virtue rather than on beauty or on
knowledge; nor is woman very frequently put on a Platonic pedestal.
In any case, her view of human nature is gloomier than the Neoplatonists': she has more doubts of man being able to find salvation
through his own efforts:

Sans la grace de Dieu, il n'y a homme où l'on doive croire nul bien

hence the greater role of Christ in her thought. Marguerite of
course does not carry these considerations explicitly to their conclusion, but the tone of her writing hardly shares the serenity or
optimism of a Ficino. The *Heptaméron*, in its own way, is a serious
call to a devout and holy life; and like the *Tiers Livre*, it goes beyond
the obvious *leitmotive* (marriage, love) to contemplate the wider
issues of the human condition. Nor can one think that Dagoucin the
Platonist, for all his charm and kindness, acts as a *persona* for Marguerite as faithfully as Oisille and Parlemente.

On the other hand, Marguerite's orthodoxy was suspect to some
contemporaries, and Gruget felt constrained to temper the text to the
winds of religious polarisation. Her evangelism is certainly not in
doubt: the reading of the Scriptures, the stress on justification by
faith, the disapproval of Christianity by gesture, the almost total
absence of the Virgin Mary; but there is no evidence that she sought
to transcend the frontiers of orthodoxy. She accepts justification by
works properly inspired, and though the tone of her attacks on the
Franciscans is strangely virulent, such references as there are to
priests and the sacraments are unexceptionable. Her failure to make

much of the doctrine of Hell and a somewhat inconsistent, turbid attitude to the problem of Grace do not add up to much; indeed in 1545 she writes a poem expressing the hope that 'la foy nous fasse en toute guise/En triomphant triompher Saincte Eglise'. Inner reform of the Church, yes; schism, no. She belongs to the sentimental wing of the Church, the wing in which Madame Guyon and churchmen like Fénelon were to live, and thus she has earned the suspicion of those who favour a more dogmatic approach. But this is not sufficient to brand her as a heretic, and in any case the moral preoccupation remains uppermost:

Et, quant à moy, je me arreste à la religion que dict Sainct Jacques: avoir le cueur envers Dieu, pur et nect, et se exercer de tout son pouvoir à faire charité à son prochain. (p. 317)

Given the edifying intent and content of the tales, one can hardly expect Marguerite to pay much attention to artistic matters, as she herself admits. Classical decoration is signally absent, both in the way of mythological allusion and of the language. She does not seek unduly lively realism, she pays rather little attention to description of milieu or characters; some glimpses of persons from various social classes may be noted (e.g., *la muletière d'Amboise*), but these hardly add up to serious social portraiture, they are usually asides, and serve rarely to build up the situation artistically. There is nonetheless a marked difference between the realism of the framework and that of the *nouvelles* themselves. Marguerite devotes much care to the presentation of the *devisants*, to the circumstances attending their sojourn in the monastery, to differentiation by speech, and the art of the dramatist is put to good use, especially in the handling of dialogue. Yet, in the tales, these features are less prominent: the milieu may be described in the vaguest of terms, as in a fairy-tale; the characters are not all that clearly distinguished; many persons of noble birth are rapidly portrayed as paragons of social graces and dismissed with eulogious superlatives; no use is made of the short-story device of the recurrent trait allowing us to conjure up a character effortlessly. The nature of Marguerite's interests means in addition that little room is granted to eternal action: some events that appear marginal to the author are sketched with perfunctory vagueness (p. 165). What is curious is that she tends to avoid realism in the speech of her protagonists: characters not in love are described by their actions, those who are in love talk in an elevated style, though it is not consciously literary. Marguerite's comparative indifference to language is curious at this period, when so many humanists, often in her entourage, concern themselves with this problem. This may lead to incongruity, such as when the old sea-captain sees fit to write a verse epistle to his lady. Perhaps she is more interested in character than in characters as such. In consequence we find several tales ending abruptly or almost indifferently (p. 40), and Tale xl comes to a rather unlikely conclusion. Generally speaking, the longer tales rather than the shorter ones are open to criticism of this kind; Marguerite has more control over internal than external form. After reading the *Heptaméron*, one comes away with a clear impression of the sensibility that lies behind, but the individual tale makes less impression. This derives in part from a lack of colour as well as from a relative absence of realism; the vocabulary is not as rich as that of contemporary *nouvellistes*; the infrequency of image, comparison, and metaphor may be due, as she claims, to a reluctance to adorn truth, but there is also a loose use of superlative that becomes a habit: she often employs the formula 'si . . . qu'il n'estoit possible depuis', and the introductory lines of a tale contain imprecise hyperbole (e.g., Tales xvi and xxxvii). The sentence may thus give an impression of dilution and spread; but when she does introduce colour and comparison, she can be most effective:

. . . et, sur le poinct qu'il attendoit ce qu'il avoit tant desiré, bruslant d'un feu non cler comme celuy de genevre, mais comme un gros charbon de forge . . .

This anchors the feeling in reality, and possibly in legend too, since the juniper is a symbol of fidelity.

However, the tempo of description does quicken when she passes from jealousy and love to satire: an excellent example occurs at the beginning of Tale xxii, where the *prieur*'s personality comes through in sharp outline. Not that stylistic laxity is absent, the meaningless repetition of some words and instances of vague phrasing are common, but closeness of observation, moral rather than physical, and the sprightliness of the sentence stand out to provide a revealing and suggestive portrait of the old satyr. Marguerite is not averse from the witty thumbnail sketch (p. 210), but it is in her analysis of the mind's workings that she excels, questions of style apart. She possesses a sure sense of motives, sometimes conflicting, that lead to action; she is well aware of the *intermittences du cœur* and of the instability of human feelings. Here, her religious outlook, so far from obscuring her vision, lends added shrewdness, and we are given as revealing a tableau of human behaviour as we can expect before Montaigne. It is Marguerite the moralist who claims us today: she can tell a story, she has a gift of dialogue, she treats herself to some humour and a wry irony, but her view of art and an acceptance of a language that still has its roots in the past reduce the aesthetic appeal of her tales. Nor can her Platonism mask her dispassionate view of human nature, rarely cruel, but fully conscious that human relations carry within themselves the seeds of their own destruction.

Bonaventure des Périers (1510-44)[20]

The *Joyeux Devis* appeared fourteen years after the presumed author's death, and the debate about their authorship has continued since. Though the tales added to the 1558 edition are in all likelihood apocryphal, opinion has tended to follow Pasquier's statement that Des Périers indeed wrote the *Devis*. Internal evidence, once the posthumous details and allusions are removed, remains inconclusive; the author's personality does not come through in overt or explicit fashion.

The *Devis* claim to be nothing more than entertainment: 'les personnages tristes et angoissés s'y pourront aussi heureusement recreer', and the reader would be wasting his time looking for any 'sens allegorique, mystique, fantastique'. The tales will eschew the giving of advice, apart from exhorting the public to 'bien vivre et se resjouir'. In addition, it is made clear that the stories are essentially French in origin:

Je ne suis point allé chercher mes comptes à Constantinople, à Florence, ny à Venise, ni si loing que cela.

This is an overstatement: reference is made to Boccaccio and the *Celestina*, and many of the Italian *conteurs* were already common currency in France. Still, the claim is not without foundation: many of the tales have been traced back to French sources, *fabliaux*, *nouvelles*, and *facéties*, and others have their roots in contemporary reality. Occasionally, Rabelais's stamp is to be found.

Even so, what strikes one is the manner in which Des Périers tempers the tradition of the *nouvelle*: his satire, such as it is, is distinctly muted ('je n'y songe ny mal ny malice'), and the conventional targets such as the Church, the professions, women, rustics, come out of his tales with few bruises. When the priests are mocked, it is for ill-fitting learning, gluttony, but there are none of Marguerite's bitter thrusts at the *Cordeliers*, and high-ranking ecclesiastics like René du Bellay are mentioned in glowing terms. Perhaps only the alchemists are attacked with more edge, and in those instances it is noteworthy that the language takes on a markedly Rabelaisian character with strings of enumerations. This may give us a slight clue to the author's attitude: he doubts whether they should waste their time trying to penetrate secrets likely to elude them for ever. Throughout the tales, there is pleasure taken in the linguistic and comic possibilities of learning, genuine or otherwise, but often we are informed that wisdom of that kind does not lead to happiness; fortune will help those who trust their natural initiative, 'car l'homme sçavant est de trop grand discours', and an apocryphal tale strikes a genuine note when it relates the regret for Triboulet's passing, 'car il estoit plus heureux que sage'. Nature is more important: such is the burden of the linguistic joust between the pedant and the fishwife, for learning inhibits spontaneous response. The author may think little of avarice and ambition, but he is normally content to observe rather than to comment, and his comments can be as platitudinous as folk-wisdom. The tales will therefore impress by a certain natural dynamism without concern for moral reflection, and this is what comes through strongly. There may be an area of melancholy behind the façade, as some critics have suggested, but detachment appears to be the more frequent, and Des Périers' mood is more akin to La Fontaine's than to Marguerite's; in any case, tone is more in evidence than structure. Though, particularly at the beginning of the series, the tales show a sense of narrative pattern, the formal characteristics are often missing: we may be offered a series (two or even three) of stories on a similar subject or character, sometimes within the framework of one so-called *nouvelle*; others are little more than character-sketches illustrated by various incidents, embryonic denizens of La Bruyère's world; yet others are studies in linguistic virtuosity. The tales are often embroidery on the theme of the trickster tricked – 'les gaudisseries retournent quelquefois sur les gaudisseurs' (xxvi), but elsewhere we may find little more than anecdote, and two *nouvelles* are about monkeys. Only one tale, certainly genuine, is starkly cruel: the husband who punishes his wife's infidelity by drowning her, a situation made all the more repugnant by the fact that he and his manservant watch her agony.

Dividing tales into categories has only a minor usefulness; what emerges is a remarkable ability in Des Périers for maintaining the reader's interest. Like Marot at his best, he has a shrewd feeling for what the audience is thinking, and he not only varies his thematic fare, but rings changes on his introductions, his endings, and above all, he knows when to break a rhythm into which the tale is falling. We are switched from one level of attention to another, the angles are changed, and the feeling of vitality is thus preserved. At the same time, Des Périers's mastery of language forces itself upon the reader's imagination; he has a natural gift for dialogue, which he uses to full effect, and he draws fruitfully on dialectal idiom; he converts some tales into linguistic exercises, and many of these are built on verbal situations: if he thinks that learning is not the only, or the best, path to happiness, he would be sorry not to have the chance of making fun of pedantry. And over and above the comic resources of the vocabulary on which he can draw, we note his very keen sense of sentence structure. Marguerite de Navarre can become involved and colourless. Des Périers is always in command of the direction his sentence is taking. It is this quality of style that lifts him above the contemporary *nouvellistes*; for all the banter, we see the lineaments of classical French prose, and the refusal to follow Rabelais more often than he does is perhaps an indication of this. Also, one senses behind the story-telling an outlook which is remarkably stable, and, I am inclined to think, not entirely devoid of serenity. At any rate, there is an acceptance of the natural and a refusal to be too emotionally involved; all Des Périers's tales move this way, neither acrid satire nor spiritual elevation break the line of a certain human contemplation. This is what likens him to La Fontaine; what he might have accomplished, had he lived longer, is obviously a matter of speculation, but there was much promise cut off in its prime.

Henri Estienne (1531-98)[21]

The name of Estienne is often associated with that of Des Périers because of the overlap of tales that can be found in the *Joyeux Devis* and the *Apologie pour Herodote*. This latter work is something of a hotch-potch: its main theme purports to be the comparison between the *mores* of the ancient world and those of the author's times, a theme which brings Estienne down against the moderns in what is already a *querelle des anciens et des modernes* (see pp. 230, 460); the original title was *L'Introduction au traité de la conformité des merveilles anciennes avec les modernes, ou traité préparatif à l'apologie pour Herodote*. Estienne's Calvinist convictions no doubt reinforce his views on the frailty and corruption of human nature, irrespective of time, but he also takes every opportunity to attack the Catholic Church in its priests and monks, and there are vigorous observations against the atheists and free-thinkers of his times: he attacks Des Périers as 'ce mechant Lucrece' and asks the rhetorical question:

Qui ne sçait que nostre siècle a faict revivre un Lucian et un François Rabelais en matiere d'escrits brocardans toute sorte de religion. (Ristelhuber ed., I, 189)

Euhemerists also come in for punishment, as does Postel. What is rather curious is the large gap between the standards of accuracy he puts forward to underpin his case methodologically and the reliance he places on *nouvellistes*, gossip, and fancy when he comes to select his material. His anti-Italianism is very much to the fore, but more than particular topics it is perhaps his alert awareness of what is going on in the human scene that remains in the memory. The structure of the work is frankly chaotic, and Estienne is very aware of his tendency to digress massively and often; but the 'varieté des propos' can be fascinating. He has interesting things to say on what, if more fully developed, could be called the sociology of crime; he is conscious of the differences between countries in their ways of life and introduces a sense of historical relativity; he comes back frequently to the subject of language as a social index and to proverbs

as capsules of popular wisdom and attitudes. He is concerned with
the evolution of the French language in his time, telling us of the
need not to *pindarizer* but also warning us not to take advice of those
who 'suyvent l'ancienne'. Then we come on some pages that point
out the anomalies in medical practice: why should physicians and
surgeons live in separate compartments, why are doctors so ignorant, why do they prescribe without giving thought to the particular
case:

Les autres se servent des receptes des anciens medecins sans avoir esgard à la
region et à la manière de vivre totalement différentes. (I, 317)

What we have here is the breakdown of any genre-structure so that
a text becomes the expression of a wide range of an author's attitude
to life; and this feature is particularly to be observed among certain-
so-called *conteurs* or *nouvellistes*. Estienne, in fact, introduces a considerable number of tales, whose provenance he often mentions
(Marguerite de Navarre, Des Périers, Bandello, and so forth) and
which serve to illustrate the numerous points he wishes to make; but
of course some, alleged to be first-hand, belong just as much to the
tradition. Estienne has a lively gift of dramatic presentation, his dialogue is alert, and he maintains a brisk tempo; but there is none of
the serenity we saw in Des Périers, for all Estienne's writings reflect
the fully committed humanist. Hence the satire is fiercer, and he will
also seek to play upon our emotions by introducing pathetic or cruel
tales.

P. Boaistuau and F. de Belleforest

These two men, close friends, form an important link in literary
developments during the middle of the century. They were curious
hack polymaths, Jacks-of-all-trades who did a vast amount of translation, adaptation, and vulgarisation. Boaistuau wrote on the dignity
and the misery of man in two successive works, but essentially he is a
humanist who gives wider currency to trends established by more
original minds, and that is also true of Belleforest whose taste for
philosophising is, however, more developed. These two men are
responsible for the 'translation' of Bandello's *Histoires tragiques*
(1559).[22] These tales were immensely successful, and though each
translator adapts his text in rather different fashion, the significance
of the work probably lies elsewhere. In the first place, there is the
tendency to write the tales in one vein, instead of varying tones and
situations; and in the second, the taste is shifting towards the cruel
and the gruesome. The Grand Guignol elements of Bandello's fiction
undoubtedly found a ready public, and whatever moral considerations may have affected the translators in their work, it is the playing
upon emotions, the *recherche de la sensation*, that remains the dominant feature. It is believed that some of the events really occurred,

but they indicate in any case a move towards melodrama, illustrations of 'la condition humaine' destroyed by its unleashed passions.

The search for emotionalism or thrills of some sort is reflected in the *Histoires prodigieuses* which also enjoyed an immense vogue.[23] Here there are several strands at work: the passion for collecting instances, such as one may already find in Erasmus and is developed particularly in Mexia's *Diverses leçons* translated from the Spanish by Claude Gruget, the second editor of the *Heptaméron*. There is also the desire by various humanists to spread knowledge for the benefit of a wider public. And in a period when an awareness of Nature is becoming more widespread and when people show interest in questions of prophecy, sorcery, monsters, and other phenomena that appear to go against Nature, one can understand the rapidity with which the taste for the unusual developed. We have mentioned Ambroise Paré (see above, pp. 229–31); he and Boaistuau, who launches the *Histoires prodigieuses*, are very anxious to insert their collections of curiosities into a clearly orthodox framework of reference. The vogue is reinforced by the accounts of travellers and cosmographers which are beginning to multiply. All this goes beyond the normal boundaries of the *nouvelles*, but once story and sensationalism combine, it is very difficult to draw the line, and we are still in an area where veracity and fantasy overlap. These cases of *monstres*, in which Boaistuau sees 'le plus souvent ung secret jugement & fleau de l'ire de Dieu', indicate how long it will be before a genuinely scientific approach to evidence emerges. Boaistuau, giving a list of many sources, deals with monstrous births, strange animals, but also 'histoires prodigieuses de cruauté', ghosts, and astrologers, though he takes the greatest pains not to be involved in theological difficulty; he also shows marked signs of anti-semitism. He echoes contemporary focus upon precious stones:

Il ne se trouve aucune chose plus admirable . . . que l'excellence & propriété de pierres precieuses. (1594 ed., in BM, p. 77)

His *Histoires prodigieuses* were expanded from edition to edition, and were imitated, perhaps amplified, by Jean de Marconville, and with the help of collaborators who included Belleforest and Claude de Tesserand. The success of the work must also be seen against the background of the wars of religion, when superstition and wonders assume importance in a world that has lost its bearings. But it is not the only work in which the short story tends to degenerate into anecdote.

Jacques Yver's Printemps[24]

Closer to the example set by Marguerite de Navarre is Jacques Yver's *Printemps*, first published in 1572 and reprinted frequently before the end of the century. Here we have a framework which is represented in much detail and introduces us to the manorial life of a noble society, no doubt slightly embellished, but still anchored in this world and enlivened by varied reference to matters of contemporary import. The group is 'led' by the *châtelaine* whose conception of love is spiritual indeed. The five days are spent in relating five stories predominantly tragic in character, though Yver is capable of adapting, with some slackening of tempo, the Rabelaisian idiom to the more *gaulois* strands of his fiction. Love is portrayed, in the tales themselves, along traditional lines: it is inevitable, 'desreglée', and usually fraught with tragic consequences; much of the author's effort is put into eliciting pathetic response from his reader, as well as from the fictitious audience in the book itself. The theme of Fortune is all-pervading, but religious tones are discernible in the commentary. Yver's style is an expansive one, and he is not afraid to load his prose with much erudition, particularly when comparisons are utilised; this may weigh down a style which is already rather alembicated and self-conscious. Yver does not vary his speech much from one narrator to another, or within the character when the crisis looms, so that dramatic tension is not boosted when it is most required. The *devisants* all have *rhétoriqueur*-sounding names and the realism of which critics speak is without question tempered by a pronounced stylisation, which may of course have filtered in from the pastoral mode as well. Human nature is not seen in a particularly favourable light ('il n'y a rien si malicieux et desnaturé qui ne trouve lieu au cœur de l'homme'), but the world in which these tales are recounted seems far removed from contemporary strife, highly civilised, perhaps a trifle self-contained.

Bénigne Poissenot – L'Esté (*1583*)[25]

The unifying tale acting as a substantial framework to a series of stories is found in the translation from the Italian published in 1570 of the *Histoire pitoyable du prince Erastus fils de Diocletien*, where the threatened execution of the hero is delayed (rather as in the *Arabian Nights*) by a series of tales. A similar technique is employed by Bénigne Poissenot, who in his *Esté* (1583) admits that he has modelled his book on that of Jacques Yver, though the social milieu of the *devisants*, all students from Toulouse spending their holidays in and about Narbonne, is quite different. Poissenot, who was to publish his *Nouvelles histoires tragiques* three years later, informs us that he wrote the book to cheer himself up after three years' buffetings from Fortune. His own *Sommaire* gives a clear idea of the subjects round which the stories gravitate:

La premiere [i.e. *journée*] parle de ceux qui par un babil indiscret, ont encouru peine, honte, blasme, ou reproche, où sont trois histoires à ce propos.

La seconde est divisée en deux membres; au premier est reprouvée la com-
mune erreur des vindicatifs, qui pensent reparer leur honneur se vengeant,
avec plusieurs histoires de ceux, qui se sont laissez transporter à ceste maudite
passion. Au second, est traité de la loiauté des Courtisans envers leur Prince,
& y sont trois histoires sur ce propos. La tierce contient un avant-propos
d'amour & trois histoires, non moins belles que plaisantes, de ceux qui en
amour, ont esté hazardeux & fortunez.

There is thus some attempt to vary tone and ending of the tales,
which are drawn from earlier sources; most of them deal with
persons of noble rank, but the *conte salé* of the *clerc* is also represented. Yet Poissenot does not have as much talent as Yver; his style
in the tales is rather colourless and sluggish, except perhaps in the
most racy. On the other hand, he achieves better results when he is
dealing with the 'real' world of the students, and the *propos* element,
so much more developed in Du Fail or Cholières, is within its limits
spirited and sometimes interesting. Poissenot sees a connection between the medieval romances and the popularity of the *Amadis*,
which he praises for its 'langage, pur, net & fluide' and for the way
in which love and arms are so skilfully blended. Though he criticises
love-poetry for its distance from reality, he defends Ronsard stoutly
against Bèze who attacked the poet for his lasciviousness after his own
shabby performance in his Latin poems. However, Poissenot's inferiority to Yver was recognised by his contemporaries, for whereas
his *Esté* was reprinted once, the *Printemps* enjoyed continuous popularity for some forty years.

*Developments at end of period: E. Tabourot, Gabriel Chappuys,
Guillaume Bouchet, N. de Cholières*
  Towards the end of our period, the short story continues to find a
welcome audience, but does little more than expand the trends to
which reference has already been made. Du Fail's last book appears
in 1585; a few others deserve brief mention. The first in time is
Etienne Tabourot who published his *Bigarrures* and other works
under the pseudonym of the Seigneur des Accords.[26] His *Bigarrures*
appear in instalments from 1583: this fairly well-known book is a
farrago of magpie lore collected by the author from *contes*, poets,
local legend, but also showing his interest in certain aspects of poetry,
particularly parlour-game verse (*Contrepeterie, allusion, equivocque*).
In this he overlaps with chapters of Pasquier's *Recherches*; he knows
Des Périers's tales which he is convinced were written by Peletier
du Mans, he has browsed through Utenhove's *Allusiones*; in his
hands, the *nouvelle* becomes a fragmented part of a loosely organised anthology. Gabriel Chappuys, an assiduous adapter of foreign
material, publishes his *Facetieuses journées* (with the title based on
Straparola's popular work) in 1583.[27] He sets down a series of a
hundred tales, some claiming to be 'advenues de nostre temps', the

others deriving from the best authors. Chappuys's originality is nothing to worry about, since he has none, but his choice of material is indicative of contemporary taste. He informs us that he is following the *Decameron* framework, but the moralising element is inconspicuous. There is an occasional story in romance style, also two or three 'tragic' and brutal ones; the traditional *nouvelle* against the monk is much reduced, and there are virtually no satires of the black-coated professions. Most tales are variations on deceptions in love:

Il n'y a chose plus agreeable & plaisante à raconter & ouir que tromperie,

so that many of them are of the backfiring type or turn out unexpectedly. The jealous husband is almost always duped; but there is also a sequence of stories built round the priest Arlotte which rarely treat erotic material and are essentially about worldly pranks. One detects a strongly Anglophobe tone; more seriously, there is some social criticism, of the way in which girls may be forced into convents, of the Court, of those discontented with their lot, of astrologers. But, like others at this time, Chappuys plays on the extremes of emotion, from the pathetic to the bawdy (e.g., 'L'accident de Suzanne esmeut, un peu à pitié, les tendres cœurs des jeunes Dames de la compagnie').

Guillaume Bouchet's *Serées* (three books spread over 1584–98)[28] set the reader in a bourgeois milieu of Poitiers; the *devisants* meet of an evening to discuss or illustrate some particular topic. In his work we see the fusion of various currents, the *nouvelle*, the collection of 'interesting phenomena', the discursive comment on a variety of subjects. A similar pattern is worked out in the *Matinées* (1585) and *Après Disnées* of Nicolas de Cholières,[29] and indeed the reappearance of material among these writers makes one wonder who is indebted to whom. Cholières, a lawyer of Grenoble, says he wrote these works for *délassement* in a period of turbulence. He recognises their disorganised character, and offers a different view of the Frenchman from the traditional one:

Il y a plus – que Nature se plaist en la variété et nouveauté; . . . Nous sommes François, nos humeurs sont françoises, nos *Apres-disnées* ont esté basties à la françoise.

The members of the group are drawn from reality but endowed with pseudonyms; various topics are discussed: some are traditional, as for instance marriage; others touch on contemporary matters such as astrology, and many references are made to men of letters (Rabelais, Scaliger, Ronsard, Du Bartas). The author attempts to be lively in his language, by reproducing the spoken word, but also because he considers himself a disciple of Rabelais. When a serious note creeps in, we find a convinced Christian attacking stoicism and astrology. In his *Guerre des masles contre les femelles* (1588), the dialogue or debate rejoins the *conte* in the framework of friendly discussion, but also reflects the pastime of a lawyer who is conservative in outlook, but is prepared to be liberal when fundamental attitudes do not come under fire.

The *nouvelle* is not only a popular genre, it is one which is extremely flexible and blends easily with other literary forms to accommodate itself to current fashion. The old *gaulois* vein persists, but it is not always dominant; and as the century grows older, we find the short story associated with the emerging taste for more powerful emotion, with the passion for collecting information, with a move into a more discursive consideration of topics that interest contemporary sensibility, though a distance is maintained from the more unsettling issues of the troubled times. In some so-called *conteurs* it is as if the formula of Montaigne's *Essais* had been taken over by inferior hands, transferred to the oral mode, and fragmented into different *personæ* whose varying attitudes to contemporary problems and interests are reproduced in a leisurely atmosphere. Certain formulae allow for a more realistic awareness of the world around, also for a gradually sharper observation of human behaviour; and in their own way, these different books, with their group patterns, mirror the tendency that will grow into the classical view of literature as a social activity; but at the same time, the notion of genre is somewhat eroded. Of all the writers we have mentioned, three perhaps stand out for their literary qualities: Bonaventure des Périers, Noël du Fail, and especially Marguerite de Navarre.[30]

NOTES

1. See General Bibliography.
2. Modern ed. F. P. Sweetser, *TLF*, 1966; also in *Conteurs français du XVIᵉ siècle*, ed. P. Jourda (Pléiade), 1965.
3. Modern ed. J. Rychner, *TLF*, 1967.
4. Modern ed. (from an earlier, reliable MS.), by Misrah and Knudson, *TLF*, 1965.
5. Modern ed. D. Jouaust, 1880; and F. Vallette, *TLF*, 1972. Original ed. in BN.
6. L. Sozzi, *Boccaccio in Francia nel Cinquecento*, Florence, 1971.
7. A. Cioranescu, *L'Arioste en France, des origines à la fin du XVIIIᵉ siècle*, 2 vols., 1939.
8. The first book of the *Amadis de Gaule* was ed. by H. Vaganay, 2 vols., *STFM*, 1918. See also E. Baret, *De l'Amadis de Gaule et de son influence sur les mœurs et la littérature au XVIᵉ et au XVIIᵉ siècle*, 1873; H. Vaganay, *Amadis en français (livres I–XII). Essai de bibliographie*, Florence, 1906; J. J. O'Connor, *The Amadis de Gaule and its Influence on Elizabethan Literature*, New Brunswick, 1970.
9. See above-mentioned biography of Des Autelz by M. L. M. Young. There is a photographic reprint of the 1578 ed. by M. Françon, Cambridge, Mass., 1962.

10. C. H. Livingston, 'Les Cent Nouvelles de Philippe de Vigneulles', *RSS*, 1923 (with further stories published in the *Mélanges Abel Lefranc* and *Alfred Jeanroy*, and also *PMLA*, 1925). The full text of these tales has just been published by Livingston and collaborators in *THR*, 1972.

11. K. Kasprzyk, *Nicolas de Troyes et le genre narratif en France au XVIe siècle*, 1964; also ed. by same critic, *Le Grand Parangon des Nouvelles Nouvelles (Choix)*, STFM, 1970.

12. Various later eds in BN. Modern ed. Jacob, Turin, 1870.

13. First published in 1550, with three reprints in same year (BM, BN) and later in 1570 and 1574. The main source is the *Cent Nouvelles Nouvelles*, and in its turn it becomes a principal source for *Les joyeuses adventures* (1555, reprinted several times till 1602). See L. Loviot, 'Les *Cent Nouvelles Nouvelles* adaptées par La Motte Roullant', *Auteurs et livres anciens*, 1917; J. Bolte, 'Les *Joyeuses Aventures*, ein französisches Schwankbuch des sechzehnten Jahrhunderts', *ASNS*, 1926.

14. *Propos rustiques*, Lyons, 1547 (BN), also 1548, 1549, 1573; modern ed. A. de La Borderie, 1878; *Baliverneries*, 1548 (BN), modern ed. E. Courbet, 2 vols., 1894; *Contes et discours*, Rennes, 1585 (BM, BN, O), Rennes, 1586 (EUL), Rennes, 1598 (BM, BN); modern ed. E. Hippeau, 2 vols., 1875. See E. Philipot, *La Vie et l'œuvre littéraire de Noël du Fail* and *Essai sur le style et la langue de Noël du Fail*, both 1914; C. Dédéyan, 'Noël du Fail et la structure des *Propos rustiques*', *FS*, 1950.

15. The BM and PSG have copies of the 1553 ed., the BN one of the 1571; Taillemont also published some poems, *La Tricarite*, Lyons, 1556 (BN).

16. Cioranescu mentions two eds. for 1555; the BM holds copies of the Paris 1555, Lyons 1572, Paris 1582, and Lyons 1595 eds. Modern ed. F. Franck, 2 vols., 1878.

17. G.-A. Pérouse, 'Les *Comptes du monde aventureux* et le *Roman de Jehan de Saintré*', *BHR*, 1968.

18. The BN holds the 1558 and 1559 eds., the BM, O, and MRy the second. Modern ed. M. François, 1943 (also lists the manuscripts) and Y. Le Hir, 1967. See P. Jourda, *Marguerite d'Angoulême, duchesse d'Alençon, reine de Navarre*, 2 vols., 1930; L. Febvre, *Autour de l'Heptaméron. Amour sacré, amour profane*, 1944; J. Gelernt, *World of Many Loves: The Heptameron of Marguerite de Navarre*, Chapel Hill, 1966; E.-V. Telle, op cit.

19. A. J. Krailsheimer, 'The *Heptaméron* reconsidered', Boase *Festschrift*, 1968.

20. First ed. 1558 (BM, BN), some dozen eds. till 1615. Modern ed. in *Contes* ... ed. P. Jourda (Pléiade). See P.-A. Becker, *Bonaventure des Périers als Dichter und Erzähler*, Vienna-Leipzig, 1924; J. W. Hassell jnr, *Sources and Analogues of the Nouvelles Recréations et Joyeux Devis of Bonaventure des Périers*, I, Chapel Hill, 1957; II, Athens, 1970; L. Sozzi, *Les Contes de Bonaventure des Périers*, Turin, 1965.

21. Modern ed. P. Ristelhuber, 2 vols., 1879. See L. Clément, *Henri Estienne et son œuvre française*, 1899; P. Toldo, 'L'Apologie pour Hérodote von Henri Estienne', *ZFSL*, 1907.

22. Copies in BM, BN, StA (later eds. NLS). See R. Sturel, *Bandello en France au XVIe siècle*, Bordeaux-Paris, 1918.

23. For the various, augmented eds., see R. Schenda, *Die französische Prodigienliteratur in der zweiten Hälfte des sechzehnten Jahrhunderts*, Munich, 1961. The *Diverses leçons* were extremely popular (BM has 1552 ed., and four others, apart from Du Verdier's *suite*).

24. Yver lived from *c.* 1520 to *c.* 1571. His *Printemps*, according to P. Jourda, went through seventeen eds. till 1618. The BM holds 1572, 1575, 1588, Lyons 1589, Niort 1598, Lyons 1600; PSG the 1585 ed.; EUL the Lyons 1578; and O the 1588 and Rouen 1599 eds. See H. Clouzot, 'Le *Printemps* d'Yver', RSS, 1931.

25. His dates of birth (?? 1558) and death are unknown. The BM and BN hold copies of the 1583 ed., the BN one of the *Nouvelles Histoires tragiques*, 1586. See L. Loviot, 'Le conteur Bénigne Poissenot', *Revue des livres anciens*, 1913.

26. G. Choptrayanovitch, *Etienne Tabourot des Accords (1549–1590)*:

Etude sur sa vie et son œuvre littéraire, Dijon, 1935. Modern ed. of *Bigarrures*, 3 vols., Brussels, 1866.

27. Copy of first ed. in BM.

28. Modern ed. C.-E. Roybet, 6 vols., 1873–82. See S. Rabinowitz, *Guillaume Bouchet. Ein Beitrag zur Geschichte der französischen Novelle*, Leipzig, 1910.

29. The BM has the first ed. of the *Matinées*, and the 1587 of the *Après Disnées*, the first ed. of which appeared *c.* 1585. Modern ed. E. Tricotel and D. Jouaust, 2 vols., 1879.

30. The reader may well find it worthwhile examining the treatment of one story or theme in different authors: such analysis will bring out not only traits special to each author, but also shifts of values in successive generations.

Chapter 9

THE PLÉIADE[1]

I. INTRODUCTION

THE term Pléiade has come to refer to the poets who, by a more or less concerted effort, brought French poetry to a pitch of distinction that it had not known before 1550. However, the term itself becomes current sometime after the early successes of Ronsard, Du Bellay, and their friends; and when Ronsard draws up lists of the members, they vary from poem to poem, nor is the matter of great consequence. In the first years, the group was known as the Brigade, but with the passing of time we find new names associated with it. And though important stimulus is given by the poets and humanists associated with the Collège de Coqueret – Baïf, Ronsard, Du Bellay, Dorat – there are other groupings which help to swell the current. In Lyons, the cousins Pontus de Tyard and Guillaume des Autelz are already active, but Des Autelz will have reservations to make about the *Deffense* and his links with the Pléiade occur rather later. In Poitiers, too, before the *Deffense*, a number of poets including Du Bellay were to be found, and there will continue to be a poetic connection with that university town. When Marguerite de Navarre dies, a *tombeau* will be organised by Nicolas Denisot and followed by a more substantial one; and the contributors, who include Neo-latin writers and transitional figures, show another pattern of literary interest. In Paris, the Collège de Boncourt houses some poets who will be associated more especially with neo-classical drama (Buchanan, Grévin, Jodelle), and it is only after the success of *Cléopâtre* that Jodelle joins forces with the Pléiade; even so, his association will always maintain a certain reticence.

What is impressive, therefore, at this time is not merely the inner circle which admittedly contains Ronsard and Du Bellay, poets of outstanding gifts endowed with powers of leadership, but the simultaneous presence of so many worthwhile *poetæ minores* ready to contribute to a new approach. As I have suggested above, this factor blends fruitfully with others – the renewed prestige of Paris, the full flowering of French humanism, the tipping of the scales in favour of the vernacular.

The movement opens with a number of love-sequences that owe much to the Petrarchan tradition: 1549, *L'Olive* and the *Erreurs amoureuses* of Pontus de Tyard; 1550, the second edition of *L'Olive*; 1551, the second edition of the *Erreurs amoureuses*; 1552, the *Amours* of Ronsard; and other sequences are appearing or in the making. This massive invasion of Petrarchism is significant. In some degree, Ronsard and his friends were bringing together strands already present in French poetry, and Scève had pointed the way by his sequence in *dizain* form. The Petrarchan conception of love is discernible in various pre-Pléiade writers; it is acceptable to a society where the influence of women is increasing, and especially at a Court where an Italian princess, Catherine de Medici, is queen; and it blends or overlaps with aspects of the Neoplatonic tradition that had already become acclimatised. And since the renaissance of French poetry is not merely a thematic, but a stylistic and linguistic, matter, Petrarchism affords the French poet a ready-made store of formal structures (sonnets and sequence), poetic conventions, and rhetorical devices; all these properties will serve, as it were, as a springboard for each poet's own invention. In so highly stylised and aristocratic a form of poetry, there is always a danger that it become the victim of preciosity, and this is what sometimes happens later, especially during the second wave of Petrarchism. On the other hand, Petrarchism at its best has much to impart. To the French poet, suspicious of a frivolous home tradition, it offers dignity and serious purpose; and the formality of the convention is far from being incompatible with deep underlying emotions or imaginative involvement. The Petrarchan tradition probably intensifies awareness of the function of imagery and the interrelationship of images; and the presence of a basically rigid poetic structure allows the poets to weave fascinating counterpoint through their own development of sentence and rhythmic patterns against a so-called structural norm. And, since the French poet is working in his own vernacular, the very strength of the poetic conventions he is using will allow him to experiment widely at linguistic level. Petrarchism, which forms firm roots in French Neo-latin poetry during the 1530s, is also the means whereby the vernacular can establish its poetic claims.

Petrarchism is, however, only one feature of the Pléiade's early achievement. Soon a reaction sets in – Du Bellay writes wittily against the vogue he had helped to create – and the poets explore other genres and incur obligations to other writers. When they turn to a less exalted form of love-poetry, they will explore Catullus and the Roman elegists, Greek anacreontic poets, Jean Second's *Basia*; but they experiment in other genres where amatory themes are absent or less prominent. Ronsard's publication of the *Odes* in 1550 is an important event, because it introduces a genre that is capable of the greatest flexibility, ranging from highflown stylisation (Pindaric) to the most personal of lyric trifles. The influence of Horace will, in one domain, be enriched by that of the pastoral poets (such as Sannazaro), and this genre will allow not only for great variation of inspiration from poet to poet, but also for rewarding experiment in metrical pattern. The Pléiade's achievement lies not only in its more up-to-date conception of poetry, or in the themes and genres it helped to naturalise, but also in the metrical and stylistic originality it introduced into French verse. And the humanistic and social conditions of its existence mean that it will extend its innovations into the fields of 'scientific' verse and also court poetry. Scientific poetry begins to attract interest in the 1550s, but it is not until the accession of Charles IX that court poetry really gets under way again. Classical models will fertilise these experiments as they did other genres; and it is in this period that allegory becomes again a vital aspect of poetry. Under the pressures of classical writers, Neoplatonic currents, court ritual, perhaps also attitudes taking shape among earlier French humanists, the classical gods, for a short, fruitful spell, will become dynamic symbols of themes and attitudes that are close to these humanist poets' hearts. This process is especially visible in Ronsard's work, where the gods of poetry and the Muses seem to occupy a privileged place in the eyes of a writer who like French poets of a later century – Mallarmé, Baudelaire, Valéry – saw poetry as a fitting subject for its own activity.

II. NEO-LATIN POETRY

Though the Pléiade will increasingly validate the claims of vernacular poetry, one must not assume that Ronsard and his friends showed any animosity to their humanist friends who preferred to stick to Latin verse composition. The opposite is in fact true; moreover, only Ronsard of these poets remained faithful to the programme of the *Deffense* and to his own decision to forsake Latin pastures; all the others took out an insurance policy with posterity in Latin poetry. And in the early 1550s, we shall find humanists such as Muret and Le Duchat affirming their belief that Latin poetry could still contribute significantly to the prestige of France. The truth of the matter is that the mature humanism of the 1545–55 period, which does so much to nourish the Pléiade, also brings French Neolatin poetry to its highest peak of distinction. Various factors have hidden the importance of this Latin Pléiade, so clearly linked with its vernacular colleagues: Théodore de Bèze, whose *Poemata*, published in 1548, ran rapidly through five editions; Marc-Antoine Muret, whose *Juvenilia* are published in 1552 and quickly reprinted; George Buchanan, who is back in Paris and actively teaching; François le Duchat who prints his *Prœludia* in 1554 and is a member of the Brinon circle; Gervais Sepin, of Saumur, whose *Erotopœgnion* appears in 1553 and may well have caught the eye of Ronsard; Du Bellay, whose *Poemata* appear in 1558; and finally Michel de l'Hôpital, whose competence in Latin poetry is already well known, and Jean Dorat, who will become *poeta regius* in 1567 and believed that higher forms of poetry should still be couched in Latin. There are in fact a great number of lesser authors too, but most of these major poets will be read for their Latin verse until the eighteenth century at a time when Ronsard is very much under an eclipse. This period is a privileged one; linguistically it comes after contemporary Neo-latinity has reached a suitably correct standard, but before a growing Ciceronianism stifles its creative ability. Most of the poets I have mentioned knew one another, but they were unable to maintain any group cohesion for long: to begin with, Bèze's Calvinist faith made him move to Geneva in 1548 and Muret, for very different reasons, soon left for Italy (1553). Others, like Gervais Sepin and Le Duchat, appear to have died young, as is also the case with Joachim du Bellay. Furthermore, neither George Buchanan nor Michel de l'Hôpital were to publish much for some years, and indeed the most complete editions of their works are posthumous; but their writings often circulated in manuscript and were highly esteemed. In these poets we see a close thematic parallelism with vernacular poetry – amatory verse, drama (in the case of Buchanan and Muret), scientific poetry (Buchanan and Sepin), nature inspiration, and later, court and encomiastic verse (Buchanan, Dorat, L'Hôpital). One may also see the interaction of specific texts: Bèze and Muret leave traces in the works of many vernacular poets, Buchanan affected Du Bellay and, in some measure, the dramatists; and in Du Bellay we can see a theme being worked out in both Latin and French. Later, during the religious wars, we shall also notice texts being translated from one language into another, and occasionally as a bilingual work.[2] In other words, Neo-latin verse is in an extremely healthy position, and is being written by poets some of whom will enjoy high posthumous fame on that account. Latin goes hand in hand with French for a while, and on occasion it is capable of giving the lead.

Though the work of the Pléiade goes on well into Henry III's reign, it will be more convenient to consider the individual poets now; even so, it will be possible to discuss certain aspects of their work under special rubrics at a later stage. Since the prestige of the Pléiade is so great, we shall select only a few disciples in the provinces to show how that impact spread through the country.[3]

III. PONTUS DE TYARD (1521–1605)[4]

The first book of the *Erreurs amoureuses* appeared in 1549, the other two coming out in 1551 and 1555 respectively. Overt influence of the Pléiade is not visible until the second book, for obvious reasons, and there is indeed evidence to suggest that Pontus was writing some of the poems as early as 1543. He remains faithful to the earlier generation of Marot, Saint-Gellais, and Salel, so that he may be seen partly as a precursor of the Pléiade and as a link between two poetic movements. He is, by composition rather than by publication, a pioneer in meditating a Petrarchan sonnet sequence – his copy of the Italian poet is still extant. In the sequence he sings of Pasithée, one of the Graces, who becomes a paragon of otherworldly virtue and inspiration.

Pontus follows certain features of the Petrarchan canon very closely: the *blason* techniques, the range of emotions undergone by the lover – fear, hope, solitude, secrecy, frustration, envy – and there is some psychological dialectic present; also various themes connected with love: tears, rings, music, dancing, painting. And, as one might expect, much play is made with antithesis. In this first book, Pontus is walking in the shadow of his master Scève, not so much in the choice he makes of Petrarchan themes as in matters of structure and rhetoric. He affects the argument form, creates similar sentence structures, and shows a decided liking for *incise*, certain forms of repetition, the holding-off of the main verb, *correctio*, *anaphora*, and on occasion he employs the conceit in the final line in company with an image so that an effect of reverberation is achieved. On the other hand, Pontus does not explore the resources of the language so fully, his use of the image is less sure, less successful, and his feeling for poetic structure is less mature; a surprising number of sonnets end in a sag.

These weaknesses do not prevent his poems from having their own ring, and this is in part due to his more sustained Platonism, which appears frequently and determines to some extent his choice of Petrarchan themes and images: the sun, the contrast between light and shade, the hand, music. Some Platonic subjects, such as the androgyne and palingenesis, are introduced as well. Pontus does not confine himself to the sonnet; he includes some epigrams and *chants non mesurés*, in which he is often successful, probably because the tautness of the sonnet does not cramp him and allows an elegiac vein to appear. A useful example of his sonnet writing is I, lii.

> Fortune enfin piteuse à mon tourment,
> Me fit revoir le Soleil de mes yeux,
> Alors qu'Amour me traittant encor mieux,
> Me feit jouir de mon contentement.

O Jour heureux esclarci clerement,
De mon Soleil! O Soleil gracieux,
Saint, et luisant plus que celuy des cieux!
Digne de luire en tout le firmament.

Le grand plaisir, que j'euz de toy jouir,
Feit tellement mes deux yeux esblouir,
Au flamboyer de tes vives ardeurs,

Que prenant peur de trop me contenter,
Content je fuz loing de toy m'absenter,
Dont maintenant, hélas, hélas, je meurs.

Here we have some characteristic themes: the identification of the
beloved with the Sun, symbol of happiness but also of spiritual good.
The theme of delight is flanked by that of sadness from which the
poet emerges, only to re-enter it; and secondary themes of Fortune
and war are inserted. Certain Scevian habits and echoes may be detected: line 1 is reminiscent of *Délie*, in its control of stress; the clear
syntactical articulation of the sonnet as a whole likewise, and the use
of repetition, both of the same word and of the same root; and we
may add the substantivised infinitive in line 11 as well as the *incise* of
the final line. Nevertheless, for all its careful construction, the sonnet
makes an uneven impact, which stems, I suspect, from an inability to
sustain where sustained tone is essential. This shows up for instance
in the second half of the first quatrain which fails to maintain the
quality of the opening lines, and also in the nondescript use of
grand in line 9. The sonnet tends to flag in the centre, and tone does
not always keep in step with structure.

Book II shows that the Pléiade has come on the scene; tribute is
paid to Ronsard and Du Bellay, but it seems that the latter has influenced Pontus the more.[5] One notes the increased presence of
mythology (though such material is also to be found in the *Délie*),
early Pléiade themes such as the *fureur poétique*, the importance of
posthumous fame, contempt for the madding crowd. Certain tricks
of rhetoric, such as *antonomasia*, enumeration, and *anaphora* appear
to be more frequent and may owe something to Du Bellay's example
but Pontus remains independent in other ways. He rarely sets
Pasithée against a natural background, though some nature themes
are developed in due course; he tends to avoid the anecdotic aspect of
the Petrarchan tradition, but one may feel that this second book is a
trifle more consciously erudite. Rhetorically, the habits of Scève
persist throughout the series, but in the later poems composed in
and for the entourage of the maréchale de Retz (1573), some changes
have occurred. This comes in part from a new literary climate, to
which Pontus makes reference in *A une docte et vertueuse Damoiselle*,
and which encourages the greater prominence of urbanity and indeed of preciosity; the Platonic currents still flow, but through a

salon. The mythology is more discreet (and flattering), the theme of fidelity is emphasised, and though certain familiar figures (e.g., repetition) persist, the sentence as a whole tends to run with a greater classic ease; for instance, the *incise* of earlier poems has faded into the background. The sonnets give an impression of greater facility and spaciousness, partly because they are in alexandrines, as one might expect at this period. At the same time, subjects barely adumbrated in the second book come to the fore, notably the passage of time and the mutability of fortune and fate. The sun shines rather less brightly in Pontus's poetic sky, and his muse has adopted an elegiac tone that becomes her well. This does not mean that he cannot write vigorously, as is evident from Sonnet xvii of the *Nouvell'œuvres poétiques*. The intellectual content is not diminished: philosophical themes may be worked and his interest in astronomy affords him further material.

Pontus rarely tries his hand at the longer composition – two elegies, one in dejection, are the most ambitious; but he seeks commendable variety in metre, not only in the *chants mesurés* already mentioned, but in *terza rima*, and in the odes that were brought together in the *vers lyriques*, printed not so long after Ronsard and Du Bellay had popularised the genre. Here Pontus reveals more suppleness and lightness of touch than one might have anticipated from his handling of the sonnet; and his Ode v (on the demise of a dog) possesses a verbal vitality and indeed poetic exuberance that foreshadows developments later in the century. All this does not add up to make a major poet of Pontus, and he has suffered by coming between Scève and Ronsard, a timing that could have encouraged him to persist in a poetic form for which his meditative turn of mind was not best suited; but he has left a handful of poems that make him something more than just an important historical link. He is endowed with a sense of rhythm and sentence structure; what weakens him is a certain lack of linguistic control.

IV. JOACHIM DU BELLAY (1523–60)[6]

Du Bellay's achievement tends to be eclipsed by that of Ronsard who, in addition to having genius, lived long enough to develop his full powers; even so, Du Bellay's attempts to write, in rivalry, on so wide a range may not have been to his advantage. Within the limits of his own sensibility he has built his niche, and it is possible that a longer life might have brought out in him gifts that were beginning to show themselves: one wonders, for instance, how Du Bellay might have shaped as a poet of the Counter-reformation.

L'Olive (1549), though a landmark in literary history and a practical example of some of the things the *Deffense* advocated, does not really show Du Bellay at his most typical. He is importing to some extent themes and styles, and many of the sonnets are exercises in linguistic adaptation; and Du Bellay will explore more fruitful avenues than love-poetry in due course. The preface to the first edition affirms a Petrarchan view of woman 'voyre quasi une Deesse entre les Femmes'; the poet admits to following the master, and like the Petrarchans disclaims any attempt to please a wide audience. He hopes to meet the approval of writers like Saint-Gellais (!), Héroët, Carle, Scève, and Martin. The sequence orchestrates a vast number of themes of the tradition and Du Bellay draws heavily on the armoury of classical rhetoric. He creates interesting patterns between Olive and various aspects of Nature, as in Sonnet xlv:

> Ores qu'en l'air le grand Dieu du tonnerre
> Se rue au sein de son épouse aimée,
> Et que de fleurs la nature semée
> A fait le ciel amoureux de la terre:
>
> Or que des vents le gouverneur desserre
> Le doux Zephire, et la forêt armée
> Voit par l'espais de sa neuve ramée
> Maint libre oiseau qui de tous côtés erre:
>
> Je vais faisant un cri non entendu,
> Entre les fleurs du sang amoureux nées,
> Pâle, dessous l'arbre pasle estendu:
>
> Et de son fruit amer me repaissant,
> Aux plus beaux jours de mes vertes années
> Un triste hiver sens en moi renaissant.

The basic antithesis, Petrarchan in source and frequency worked throughout the sequence, develops the contrast between the erotic symbolism of Nature and the poet's solitude which causes him to see only winter in spring. The antithesis is carefully balanced between quatrains and tercets and the description of springtime Nature is effected by mythological periphrasis, a device we find often in Petrarch and also in Scève, whom Du Bellay may be recalling here. The periphrases suggest violence, exuberance, but also harmony, liberty, peace; whatever the mood, the poet himself feels apart from the marriage of heaven and earth, and this is expressed both by direct statement and by the symbolism of a tree whose pallor evokes the draining of all vitality in the poet himself. The fruit turns bitter in his mouth and in the final line winter, the season of death, is ironically described as *renaissant*. The *fleurs* in line 10 are doubtless a sign of Adonis and therefore of love lying dead – an image also employed by Scève – and the poet represents himself as crying unheard. The sonnet, however derivative in its theme, is most satisfying in its balance, control of sentence structure, and the complex emotions conjured up by epithet and periphrasis. Du Bellay indeed makes a powerful and regular use of the epithet here (*armée* applied to the forest is a vigorous twist of the normal meaning); he draws on mythology, but not pedantically, and achieves balance, not only between the two sections, but also by chiasmatic effects, sometimes on a considerable scale, as in the placing of the two main verbs in the tercets. The sonnet is in decasyllabic lines; only a few years later will the alexandrine begin to take over among the Pléiade, but Du Bellay does succeed in conferring *ampleur* on the shorter line. He is already a master of rhetoric.

The first edition of *L'Olive* consisted of fifty sonnets; the second edition (1550), with a preface aimed at critics such as the *Quintil Horatien*, was considerably enlarged by the addition of 65 sonnets, which introduce the theme of the rival and therefore variations on jealousy, and also relate the death of Olive. More important, these sonnets are coloured by what might loosely be described as Platonic-Christian elements. Olive is 'l'idée de la beauté que j'adore', but there are some poems addressed to God. At the other end of the tonal scale, the appearance of the rival allows Du Bellay to reveal a satiric gift of vituperation.

Though *L'Olive* naturally predominates in any assessment of the early Du Bellay, right from the start he shows a broad range of inspiration. There is of course the aspiring court poet, as the poems of 1549 reveal, but there is also the Horatian, the experimenter in verse patterns, the anti-aulic writer, the poet of suffering, the lover of Nature. Already certain themes that will acquire maturity during the sojourn in Rome have made their appearance: the Ulysses motif and an admiration for ancient Rome. Du Bellay's acquaintance with Italian poets is already very wide; and the elegiac already emerges, for instance, in the translation of Buchanan's Elegy I (*Adieu aux Muses*) or in the *Plainte du Désespéré* which belongs to an Italian genre. The humanist armed against Ignorance, the bard of 'honnête amour', the translator, the satirist of Petrarchism, all these aspects are manifest before Du Bellay leaves for Rome to become a fully fledged poet.

When Jean du Bellay was charged by Henry II with a delicate mission in Rome, Joachim accepted the chance of joining his retinue. His motives were clear enough: he had not made much headway at Court, he wanted to undertake the humanist's *voyage d'Italie*, though Rome had perhaps less to offer *prima facie* than Padua, Florence, or Venice, and his precarious health may have encouraged him to seek sunnier climes. The convoy left in April 1553, reaching Rome two months later. Du Bellay's duties as a sort of *intendant* were light enough, though barely congenial, and he complains that they often interrupted poetic composition. On the other hand, he did have interminable correspondence in connection with long-drawn-out litigation at home and he gives the impression that Rome was a great disappointment. This is all somewhat exaggerated: he found time to make friends with a number of cultured Italians, he met interesting men in French diplomatic entourages (e.g., Magny), above all he did in fact enjoy the leisure to write a lot – the *Antiquitez* and most of the *Regretz*, the *Jeux Rustiques* and the four books of the *Poemata*, for he goes back on the message of the *Deffense*. He claims that Latin was an easier form of communication for him with the Italians, but he may have wondered whether post-humous fame did not still lie with Latin; and above all, this was a field in which Ronsard had refused to compete. Ronsard's shadow lies heavy over the last years of Du Bellay, in 'exile' when his friend is ever more *persona grata* in high quarters. The *Poemata* are often interesting for the parallels they contain with texts in the *Antiquitez* and the *Regretz*, though we have no safe means of ascertaining priority of composition.

The *Antiquitez* form an impressive collection of 32 sonnets, fol-lowed by the *Songe* sequence of 15 sonnets. Though the date of composition is not known, and the second book was never written, they were stimulated by Du Bellay's own reactions to Rome and also perhaps by a literary source, Lucio Mauro's *De Antiquitatibus urbis Romæ* (1549, abridged edition 1552). The series of alternating sonnets (decasyllables and alexandrines) is built round the motif of Rome's decadence, often enriched by the more personal one of *regret*. Such a description is nonetheless oversimple, as a perusal of Sonnet iii indicates:

> Nouveau venu, qui cherches Rome en Rome
> Et rien de Rome en Rome n'apperçois,
> Ces vieux palais, ces vieux arcz que tu vois,
> Et ces vieux murs, c'est ce que Rome on nomme.
>
> Voy quel orgueil, quelle ruine, & comme
> Celle qui mist le monde sous ses loix,
> Pour donter tout, se donta quelquefois,
> Et devint proye au temps, qui tout consomme.
>
> Rome de Rome est le seul moment,
> Et Rome Rome a vaincu seulement.
> Le Tybre seul, qui vers la mer s'enfuit,
>
> Reste de Rome. O mondaine circonstance!
> Ce qui est ferme est par le temps destruit,
> Et ce qui fuit, au temps fait resistance.

The poet wishes to impress upon the reader the obsessive force of his meditation; Du Bellay's best poems often carry this element of insistent flow. It is for this reason that the word *Rome* occurs so frequently – as in the poem by which it is inspired – appearing at different stress-points in the line, and doubly effective for its ambiguity: *Rome* stands for the city of the past and for the city today. The theme is developed by the contrast of past and present, the sense of time flowing (with the Tiber skilfully introduced as an image of flight), the motif 'how are the mighty fallen' and its harmonics of Fortune's wheel, the sense of *hubris*. Here Rome is the object of contemplation by a poet belonging to the Christian tradition. However, the poem is much more than a wistful reflection on the glory that is past; at all times, I suspect, Du Bellay was sensitive to what remained of Rome (cf. *Romæ descriptio* in the *Poemata*). In this poem of metamorphosis (a *leitmotiv* of the sequence), the paradoxical ending makes it clear that he is fully aware of Rome today and that it has its own lasting quality; the theme of fluidity, of *passage*, has melted into one of permanence, without the self-centred attention that intrudes on some of the *Regretz*, and without reliance on classical periphrasis, mythology, or decoration.

What is remarkable about the sequence as a whole is the quickening of the poet's imagination and the vigour of his language; this derives in great measure from a denser use of imagery, a skilful use of literary tradition (Bible, Petrarch), and a daring exploiting of the *dream*, which by convention, allows the poet a very obvious freedom without annihilating aesthetic distance by excessive 'realism' less assimilable outside the dream-formula. Nevertheless, one can see in some of the sonnets of *Les Antiquitez* a heralding of Counter-reformation poetry, with its violence, its stress on transformation, its recourse to apocalyptic themes, its treatment of the *topos* 'all is vanity'. Sonnet viii is a particularly good example, and gives cause for regret that the second book never reached paper.

The *Regretz* show us other facets of Du Bellay's reactions to Rome, though they also provide a 'journal' of his return journey and include courtier verse of Parisian reference; moreover, the preamble (Sonnets i–xxiv) gives us thoughts on poetic inspiration, and Sonnets xvi–xxiv are messages to friends left behind in Paris. After the valedictory poems, Du Bellay develops the topic of the journey and the absent homeland. Life in Rome, with its manifold disillusionments, evokes at first a Stoic response, then attempts to *amuser le temps*, and finally satire in which he moves from lighter mood to a sharper portrait of the city. All this suggests that the collection is more varied than the title (taken from Ovid) might imply. In his hands, the sonnet is much more than a vehicle for the feelings of love and it confirms what Ronsard was discovering, the suitability of the alexandrine as its metre. In Sonnets i and iv, Du Bellay informs us that he is forsaking the conception of highflown, divine poetry in favour of a 'style plus bas', which means among other things the avoidance of epic and philosophic poetry. He fears that his Muse has lost some of her vitality (*ardeur*), and since his poetry is unlikely to bring him patronage in Rome, he makes it a source of consolation and *délassement* (Sonnets xi and xiv). He will, it seems, try to narrow the gap between literature and reality, the sonnet will embody everyday experience. Though Du Bellay will not in fact reject all fidelity to literary tradition, there is here no submission to a model as was the case of *L'Olive*; on the other hand, his indulgence in the *style bas* will in no wise reduce the presence of classical rhetoric, but it is the full flowering of his sensibility that will give the *Regretz* their peculiar flavour.

The *Regretz* embody in sonnet form a variety of genres popular at this time: the satiric epigram, the epitaph, the *blason*, even the letter, sometimes personal and autobiographical, at others meditative. Though the encomiastic and patronage poems take up considerable space, it is the satiric and elegiac sonnets that reveal Du Bellay's stature; the distinction is slightly artificial, since satire is often directed at what impedes *épanchement* or genuine feeling. In the satirical sonnet, Du Bellay is pioneering to the extent that he is introducing into French poetry the genre developed by Piccolomini, Berni, and others – but he uses, with one exception (Sonnet clxxii), the French tercet rhyme-scheme. Du Bellay takes delight in showing up the gap between *paraître* and *être*:

> Marcher d'un pas grave et d'un grave sourci,
> Et d'un grave soubriz à chascun faire feste,
> Balancer tous ses motz, respondre de la teste,
> Avec un *Messer non*, ou bien un *Messer si*:
>
> Entremesler souvent un petit *Et cosi*,
> Et d'un *son Servitor'* contrefaire l'honneste,
> Et, comme si lon eust sa part en la conqueste,
> Discourir sur Florence, et sur Naples aussi:
>
> Seigneuriser chascun d'un baisement de main,
> Et suivant la façon du courtisan Romain,
> Cacher sa pauvreté d'une brave apparence:
>
> Voilà de ceste Court la plus grande Vertu,
> Dont souvent mal monté, mal sain et mal vestu,
> Sans barbe et sans argent on s'en retourne en France.
>
> (Sonnet lxxxvi)

This sonnet may be compared with lxxxii which deals with a similar topic and exploits thoroughly the techniques of enumeration and repetition. Sonnet lxxxvi is perhaps more successful, partly because it is better organised. The use of 'realistic' detail, added to sure control of tempo and repetitive effects, conveys the mask- and marionette-like nature of the courtier. In addition, the final tercet comes off so much better: here the emptiness of the Court is revealed, and the sense of waste is all the more powerfully communicated in that Du

Bellay allows us to identify the courtier to some extent with himself. Nevertheless, one may ask whether the best of these sonnets are essentially satiric: Du Bellay, following perhaps Horace, uses elements of satire, striking detail, movement, caricature, but we do not find here the strong moral indignation we associate with Dryden or Juvenal, nor does Du Bellay impart so much full-blooded vitality to the targets of his attack. I am sometimes inclined to think that, at his best, he draws on satiric elements to express what is surely an elegiac mood: he is the spectator rather than the 'committed' writer. Some sonnets, like lxxxii, lack the structure one would expect to underlie concerted satire; on the other hand Du Bellay often impresses where he conveys his sense of waste, of fruitless endeavour, and of the passage of time. He is a poet of *absence*, whether temporal or spatial, and his observation of the present is more especially effective in the evocation of the past; this is not to deny his attraction to life and the present, but the same fullness of tone is not always forthcoming.

This sense of absence appeared in the *leitmotiv* of the *Antiquitez*; it also shows itself as the unfulfilment of one's destiny, to which is added on occasion the awareness of hurrying time; and finally it occurs as uprooting and nostalgia. It is often expressed through the Ulysses myth (Sonnets xl, lxxxviii, xciv, and the Latin poems), but above all in the most famous poem of the sequence:

> Heureux qui, comme Ulysse, a fait un beau voyage,
> Ou comme cestuy là qui conquit la toison,
> Et puis est retourné, plein d'usage et de raison,
> Vivre entre ses parents le reste de son aage!
>
> Quand revoiray-je, hélas, de mon petit village
> Fumer la cheminée, & en quelle saison
> Revoiray-je le clos de ma pauvre maison,
> Qui m'est une province, & beaucoup davantage?
>
> Plus me plaist le sejour qu'ont basty mes ayeux,
> Que des palais Romains le front audacieux:
> Plus que le marbre dur me plaist l'ardoise fine,
>
> Plus mon Loyre Gaulois que le Tybre Latin,
> Plus mon petit Lyré que le mont Palatin,
> Et plus que l'air marin la doulceur Angevine.
>   (Sonnet xxxi)

The theme of absence dominates: comparisons are established between the homestead and the so-called greatness of historical destiny, and to these are added the thought of the journey that has disappointed. In the first quatrain, Du Bellay introduces two images of classical colour: Ulysses and Jason, but Jason is not mentioned by name, perhaps in part to avoid the stylistic parallel with line 1, but mainly to bury any unhappy associations (Jason did not return home 'plein de raison', nor were his relations with Medea exemplary or satisfying), so that the stress of the line is brought on to *toison*, the symbol of success and fulfilment. One may compare this quatrain, patently joyful, with the opening one of Sonnet xxxviii. Here, the major key is confined to the quatrain, and replaced by very different tones. Du Bellay picks out a few everyday details to evoke his *pays*, but they are selected not for realistic, but sentimental, effect, and, moreover, in opposition to the fallen splendour of Rome, so that the themes of Rome and *patria* are cleverly brought together. The emotions are heightened by the poet's use of adjectives and by his stress on *mon*, so that Rome is made to appear foreign, alien, distant. This sonnet is constructed on several of the stylistic devices favoured by Du Bellay: enumeration linked with repetition; but these are not guarantees of success, for there are quite a lot of sonnets where these techniques miss their target, partly perhaps because Du Bellay does not possess that logocentric vitality we associate with Rabelais or D'Aubigné. Nor does he innovate significantly in matters of vocabulary or imagery. Where he often comes off best is in the evocation of states of mind of a lingering, almost obsessive nature, that will reverberate like a *point d'orgue*; and in the sonnet just quoted, this effect is obtained in part by the induction of rhythms by the repetition of rhetorical patterns subtly reversed in the final line with its delayed and therefore more emphatic reference to home. Du Bellay is rarely memorable for the definitive, solitary line (e.g., 'Le tardif repentir d'une esperance vaine', Sonnet xxvi), for he achieves his poetic effects more often by the creation of a rhythmic and imagic flow embracing more than the line, by the diffusion of his *persona* through the texture of the whole poem, and by a certain undulatory movement. This sonnet is in a sense a lullaby, and in many of his fine sonnets he avoids a dense pattern of imagery or the conceit in favour of the more diffuse sense of flow.

The conditions of success in such poetry are therefore very delicate, and Du Bellay is often at his best in the tone-poems where the *persona* is blurred and which do not have the pressures of intellectual structure such as we saw in the *Délie*. When he does experiment in the 'argument' poem, as in Sonnet lii, admittedly an adaptation from Navagero, the dialectical bones stick out through rather emaciated poetic flesh, and the final effect is one of dullness and rigidity. Moreover, there are sonnets where one wonders whether Du Bellay is not simply composing an exercise on some rhetorical device, with the result that the sonnet seems to lack inner organisation.

The *Jeux Rustiques*, also written in Rome, are diversions; they may consist of elegant trifles, or translations from Italian poets; some are *vœux*, and Du Bellay, like other members of the Pléiade, is attracted to the rustic mode; and he returns to his satiric vein (as in *La Vieille Courtisane*). However, though these poems give us a broader idea of the range of his sensibility, I doubt if they add markedly to his poetic stature. Above all, Du Bellay's art is one of quiet refinement at its best; he is happier in half-tones, his register is that of the *mezzo*, and he rarely gives an impression of radiance or blood-red vitality. He is at home when meditating on absence, time past, and time passing; and here he also reveals a very fine feeling for the music of the French language. It is a measure of his art that he manages nearly always to avoid the suspicion of sentimentality; at its best he gives an impression of limpidity and simplicity, such as one finds also in Lamartine or Verlaine, though this limpidity is without question the product of mature craftsmanship. There is a gift of classical line about his poetry that few sixteenth-century poets were to acquire, and one may see in his work certain virtues that will go to the making of French classical art.

And yet one has misgivings about leaving Du Bellay's achievement there. His contemporaries clearly thought highly of his satiric gifts, and traces of his influence may be found in the satires of the next generation. And though he did not perhaps have time to develop fully as a religious poet, his work in this vein was sufficiently well thought of for it to appear in some anthologies in the 1580s. But it is especially a re-reading of the *Antiquitez* that makes one see another, important aspect of his writing, which does not fit into the assessment just offered, and which, by its violence, its rhetorical mastery, and its thematic appeal announces the poetry of the *monde cassé* that makes its appearance in the last decades of the century. I have touched on this point already, but a sample of Du Bellay's writing in this vein deserves quoting:

> Je vis un fier torrent, dont les flots escumeux
> Rongeoient les fondements d'une vieille ruine:
> Je le vy tout couvert d'une obscure bruine,
> Qui s'eslevoit par l'air en tourbillons fumeux:
>
> Dont se formoit un corps à sept chefz merveilleux,
> Qui villes & chasteaux couvoit sous sa poitrine,
> Et sembloit devorer d'une esgale rapine
> Les plus doulx animaux & les plus orgueilleux.
>
> J'estois esmerveillé de voir ce monstre enorme
> Changer en cent façons son effroyable forme,
> Lors que je vis sortir d'un antre Scythien
>
> Ce vent impetueux, qui souffle la froidure,
> Dissiper ces nuaux,, & en si peu que rien
> S'esvanouir par l'air ceste horrible figure.
>
> *(Songe, viii)*

The impression of this nightmare is conveyed by a very dynamic and powerful use of language, heightened by the presentation through personal witness (as we often see in Sponde); the visual element is predominant, and phenomena are described in terms of movement, destruction, and metamorphosis, though as usual Du Bellay makes impressive use of the epithet to heighten emotion. Great care is taken with the interplay of sounds (especially *f*s and *v*s) and the control of sentence throughout is admirable. Another remarkable poem is Sonnet xvi of the *Antiquitez*:

> Comme lon void de loing sur la mer courroucée
> Une montagne d'eau d'un grand branle ondoyant,
> Puis trainant mille flotz, d'un gros chos abboyant
> Se crever contre un roc, où le vent l'a poussée:
>
> Comme on void la fureur par l'Aquilon chassée
> D'un sifflement aigu l'orage tournoyant,
> Puis d'une aile plus large en l'air s'esbanoyant
> Arrester tout à coup sa carrière lassée:
>
> Et comme on void la flamme ondoyant en cent lieux
> Se rassembler en un, s'aguiser vers les cieux,
> Puis tumber languissante: ainsi parmy le monde
>
> Erra la Monarchie: & croissant tout ainsi
> Qu'un flot, qu'un vent, qu'un feu, sa course vagabonde
> Par un arrest fatal s'est venue perdre icy.

The basic theme is of course the ephemeral nature of glory; but it is developed in rich complexity. Du Bellay takes three comparisons from Nature, all of which show how elemental forces come to a sudden end, and then he introduces the second limb of the comparison, cutting across the tercet structure (ainsi parmy le monde/ Erra la Monarchie), with its slightly ironic presentation. The whole theme is brought closer together by the repetition of certain words or verbal roots: *arrester, ondoyant, aguiser*. The momentum is also determined by the restless vocabulary (a high proportion of verbs, and the use of the durative present participle, at the rhyme), the fact that the sonnet is really one sentence beautifully balanced in its parts and discarding the 'normal' structure of the sonnet, which also lacks *pointe*, and finally the recapitulation technique that will become fairly common in later poets. What is also impressive is the vital way in which destruction and evanescence are conveyed to the reader, a feature that recurs in Sponde and Chassignet. A sense of immediacy is created, often with magnification of certain elements, and a liking for numeral hyperbole; and Du Bellay anticipates later poets by his use of visual, emotional illustration of a didactic point. A concomitant feature is the occurrence of rhetorical figures that will be pressed into service by Counter-reformation poets: enumeration, repetition, alliteration, *traductio, anaphora*, antithesis, *compar, prosopopœia*, a penchant for binary and ternary structures that impart balance, flow, and emphasis to the text.

Inevitably, Du Bellay was overshadowed by Ronsard in his impact upon the younger generation; nevertheless, poems such as I have just quoted show Du Bellay, towards the end of his existence, to be ahead of his times in certain respects; and one wonders what he might have achieved had he been granted a greater span of life. As it is, his achievement is impressive, and he has created a music in areas where even Ronsard was rarely able to match him.

V. RÉMY BELLEAU (1528–77)[7]

Belleau is surely a *poeta minor* of the Pléiade and, given the limited range of his sensibility and his heavy dependence on models, it is understandable that his work should have received less than its due. There is none the less a genuine sensibility at work, and Belleau emerges as a fine, though undemonstrative, craftsman of metre and language; besides, his poetry serves as a useful mirror of contemporary trends. His first publication, the translation of Anacreon and the *Nouvelles inventions*, reveals the delicate worker in the field of *émaux et camées*, master of the timely detail and able to maintain the tempo of the original:

L'Arondelle

Ha vrayment je vous puniray
Babillarde, & vous rogneray
De mes cizeaux l'une & l'autre aelle:
Ou bien, comme la main cruelle
De Teree a fait autrefois,
Vous tondray la langue & la vois,
Qui tousjours, las! quand je sommeille
Devant le point du jour m'esveille,
Et de son importun babil,
M'arrache du sein mon Bathyl.
(Marty-Laveaux ed., I, p. 15)

It is, however, in his *Bergerie* that we see the different facets of his art in play. This collection, published in part in 1565, and in augmented form in 1572, is so called on account of its pastoral element, but also because Belleau is rendering the Latin term *sylva*, that is a varied selection of poetry. The *Bergerie* brings together a number of poems belonging to the whole of his career and set in a framework which, when not loose, is highly artificial: Belleau is aware of this in the preface of *Journée* II, when he promises his protector the cardinal de Lorraine 'un ouvrage mieux tissu & ourdy de meilleure main'. The work was conceived during the years 1563–66 at Joinville, when he was tutor to the son of the marquis d'Elbeuf, that is after his years of study in Paris and a year's soldiering in Italy. The first *Journée* provides as its framework a stylised description of the castle of Joinville; the poet either 'notes down' poems on the borders of tapestries, or records the songs of shepherds and nymphs. Thus, the poems are encased in a matrix of prose, rich, indeed alembicated, in its Renaissance wealth, but also reminding one of an earlier prose, that of the *rhétoriqueurs*, though Belleau fondly imagined himself to be pioneering. In the second *Journée* (1572), the poet describes a day at the castle, in the company of a friend, but this framework is even flimsier than that of the first part.

Predominant is the pastoral character of the collection. During the 1550s and 1560s, pastoral comes into favour. There were signs of it under Francis I and among the Neo-latins; the eclogue, though its uses can be varied, flourishes with the Court. On the one hand, through Italian influence especially, it serves as an allegorical mask to celebrate court events, military happenings, and on the other, by its semi-dramatic character, it fits in easily with the fashion for court masks and *cartels*, in which the pastoral element has its place. During the middle third of the century, Belleau is not the only one to experiment in this field: Dorat sets an example in both Latin and French, and Ronsard, whom Belleau often follows, is also active. In practice, therefore, the genre may overlap with the Genethliacon, the Epithalamium, and the *Déploration* or *tombeau*; Belleau will in addition contract a debt to Sannazaro, in his development of the marine eclogue, for fishermen appear in the *Bergerie*. As a rule, Vergil's influence is all-pervasive, but Belleau departs from the model to the extent that he prefers Greek models. In his own 'original' creations, Belleau translates as often as in his acknowledged renderings; nevertheless his nice feeling for language imparts movement to the scene, and on occasion he evokes a sense of spaciousness; in *April*, one of his better-known pieces, he shows a delicate control of lyric metre, introduces synaesthetic effects, and expresses a pleasing harmony of natural existence. In *L'Esté*, he modulates the theme of love in the key of sensual Pan, but also in that of music and peace:

> Voy les boutons eclos en poignant s'avancer,
> Au bord de ce ruisseau voy ces deux colombelles
> Qui sont bec contre bec, & tremoussant les ailes
> Se baisent tour à tour, & vont faisant l'amour,
> C'est presage certain de voir quelque beau jour:
> Voy l'esmail bigarré de ces fleurs nouvelettes
> Encore non touché des paillardes avettes:
> Escoutte parmy l'air les petits oisillons,
> Voy le sable menu qui sautelle à bouillons
> Et tramblotte au dedans de cette pierre vive:
> Voy ces bords couronnez d'une mousse naïve
> Qui feutre tout le creux, & à la veoir rouler
> On diroit que son eau s'efforce de parler . . .
> (I, 187)

The theme of love is often combined with this pastoral element. Here Belleau can be seen, as he is in other respects, as a bridge between the Petrarchan tradition of the early Pléiade and the *salon*

love-poetry of Henry III's reign. In the *Bergerie*, there are some
Petrarchan sonnets, but Belleau does not seem to be really at home in
them: as in his Nature poetry, everything is domesticated, losing
something of its refinement and elevation in favour of greater *mignardise* and sensuality. He draws not only on his Alexandrian Greeks,
but on Italian Neo-latins and more especially Jean Second, whose
Basia, already popular in France, were reprinted by Wechel in 1561.
In the *Basium* genre, we find some debased Petrarchan themes, a
refurbishing of Catullus, an unmistakable sensuality, but also a series
of stylistic devices. Belleau has imitated Second in his own *Baisers*
(expanded from 19 to 49 in the second edition of the *Bergerie*). The
following sonnet shows how he exploits the *poncif*:

> Si tu veux que je meure entre tes bras, m'amie,
> Trousse l'escarlatin de ton beau pelisson,
> Puis me baise & me presse, & nous entrelasson,
> Comme autour des ormeaux le lierre se plie.
>
> Degraffe ce collet, m'amour, que je manie
> De ton sein blanchissant le petit mont besson:
> Puis me baise & me presse, & me tien de façon
> Que le plaisir commun nous enyvre, ma vie.
>
> L'un va cerchant la mort aux flancs d'une muraille,
> En escarmouche, en guarde, en assaut, en bataille,
> Pour acheter un nom, qu'on surnomme l'honneur:
>
> Mais moy je veux mourir sur tes levres, maistresse,
> C'est ma gloire, mon heur, mon thresor, ma richesse,
> Car j'ay logé ma vie en ta bouche, mon cœur.
>
> (II, 98–9)

The repeated addressing of the beloved in familiar terms, the recurrence of certain formulae at intervals, the military comparison,
the simile of the ivy, enumeration, all these belong to the convention.
Belleau is perhaps happier in the shorter metre, where he makes play
with the diminutive:

> O doux baiser colombin
> Poupin, sucrin, tourterin,
> Qui sur ces levres descloses
> Vas pressottant, fleurottant,
> Mignotant, & suçottant,
> L'œillet, le lys, & les roses.
> Ces menus souspirs larrons,
> Ont tiré sur les fleurons
> De sa bouche tendre & molle
> Mon âme qui de plaisir
> Soule, ne voudroit choisir
> Autre lieu tant elle est folle.
> Mais Baiser si tu voulois
> M'arroser une autre fois

> De cette humeur familiere,
> Je suis seur qu'au gré d'Amour,
> Bien tost seroit de retour
> En sa demeure premiere.
>
> (II, 101–2)

There is another field in which Belleau seems to announce more interesting developments: religious poetry. As a rule, the Pléiade, though they supported orthodoxy, sometimes after initial vacillation, did not make their mark as religious poets. Belleau's contribution, if not very great in bulk, is significant, provided we leave aside the tasteless poem on David's love for Bathsheba. There is little doubt that about 1563 the poet went through a Huguenot phase: this is reflected in three poems published in 1566 in honour of Condé, and marginally in *La Reconnue*, where the central character leaves her convent because of Calvinist sympathies. In the *Bergerie* (second edition), the Condé poems are substantially altered – in many cases Belleau removes almost all trace of the circumstances in which the poems were originally composed and published – but the themes and treatment do seem to anticipate later writing in this field. The second *Journée* opens with some paraphrases from Job; this Old Testament book, which is widely read during the religious wars, is already catching the attention of humanists in the 1560s: Patrick Adamson's Latin paraphrase was circulating in manuscript then; not so long after Orlando di Lasso set portions of Job to music, and in 1587 De Thou's version (in Latin) appeared. Some of the passages rendered by Belleau show a preoccupation with decay, suffering, and physical repulsiveness:

> Ha! tu me tiens trop de rudesse,
> Seigneur, & sous ta main maistresse
> Je souffre trop de passions,
> Trop de maux, trop d'afflictions,
> Et rigoureux de chaisne dure
> Tu tends mes pieds à la torture,
> Et aux ceps qui sont imprimez
> Dessus mes talons descharnez:
> Et comme le bois mort se mine,
> Pourry & mangé de vermine,
> Tout ainsi je vis en langueur:
> Ou comme le drap d'une robe,
> Où la tigne ronge & desrobe
> Le fil, la grace & la couleur . . .
>
> (II, 7–8)

Belleau shows in many poems a gift for choosing the telling detail, but into his religious verse there may enter emotive tones that do not always come through in his parnassian writing. In the *Chant de Triomphe*, his descriptive powers verge on the caricatural and give an inkling of what D'Aubigné will manage in the way of allegorical portrayal. Belleau of course is not devoid of satiric talent, as one may see in his macaronic *De bello huguenotico*, and in the following passage there is sustained vigour and sense of movement:

> Là les Fureurs, les tourments, les orages
> Pendoient au char, comme mortes images:
> Là souspiroit la pallissante Mort,
> Riche despouille à si vaillant effort:
> Là l'imposture en signe de conqueste
> La bouche close, & couverte la teste
> D'une grand'nuë alloit à pas contez:
> Là les malheurs renversez & dontez
> L'accompagnoient d'une fort longue suite
> D'hommes masquez au visage hypocrite,
> Tous revestuz de grandz robes de dueil,
> De couleur perse, ayant la larme à l'œil.
> Là descouvroit cent testes monstrueuses
> L'Opinion aux langues venimeuses,
> L'Opinion qui n'eut jamais de bout,
> Qui croit en tout, & qui doute de tout,
> Qui n'a cerveau que de cire aussi molle,
> Que ce qui naist du vent de sa parolle:
> L'Opinion qui n'a rien de certain,
> Qui tousjours bruit, & se travaille en vain
> De se bastir une ferme asseurance
> Sur le sablon de legiere inconstance. . . .
>
> (II, 34)

The poem ends with the theme of 'la France esplorée' which is common in Latin and French verse at that time, and no doubt owes something to Ronsard's development of the topic. Belleau has also written poems inspired by the Song of Songs, the *Discours de la Vanité*, and the sacred eclogues, where he can agreeably blend pastoral idiom and religious allegories.

Belleau's talent for objective description appears at its most mature in his last major publication: *Les amours et nouveaux eschanges des pierres precieuses*.[8] In one sense, this work develops a particular branch of the traditional *blason*: it describes a series of jewels and stones, using material from classical sources such as Dioscorides, so that we are given not merely a physical presentation, but are told much about the properties these stones were believed to possess: aesthetic pleasure and instruction go hand in hand. But Belleau may go further, by introducing an imaginary mythology about the stones in their earlier manifestations; the example of Ovid's *Metamorphoses* has not been lost on him, but his imagination can let itself go well beyond sober realism to create a world of its own:

> Comme un chancre malin, s'avançant insensible
> Rampe de nerf en nerf d'une alleure invisible:
> D'Opalle tout ainsi une froide rigueur
> Rendurcit peu à peu les tendons & le cueur.
> Un Hyver eternel entre dans les jointures,

Dedans le creux des os & de leurs emboitures,
Une glace, une horreur jusqu'aux ongles s'estend,
Un long sommeil ferré jusqu'au foye descend,
Qui luy bouche soudain le chemin de la vie
Transi plus ne souspire, & son ame ravie
Recherche sa maistresse, & son corps bigarré
Sur le gravier Indois se retrouve empierré:
N'ayant de ses Amours, pour memoire eternelle
D'avoir baisé, mortel, une dame immortelle,
Que les couleurs qu'il porte . . .

(II, 205)

His plastic imagination, on occasion, senses forces behind the visible
that appear disturbing; and one wonders how Belleau might have
developed had he lived longer. In spite of his subservience to many
models, and an over-enthusiastic fidelity to Ronsard, not to speak of
a certain lack of inner life, Chamard has perhaps done Belleau less
than justice in calling him the Théophile Gautier of the sixteenth
century.

VI. JEAN-ANTOINE DE BAÏF (1532–89)[9]

Baïf tends to appear as the also-ran of the Pléiade and this is
surely unfair. He is one of the most learned of the band – he was the
natural son of the author of various works including the *De re navali*
and numbered Jean Dorat and George Buchanan among his tutors.
He shows in his writings a vast range of subject-matter and metrical
experiment, indeed he is a kind of walking *Deffense*; but over-hasty
composition (the poems to Francine were written in under a year), a
rather cramping view of poetry as translation, *imitatio*, and versified
didacticism, all this serves to reduce his poetic stature, though his
excursions into theory, which extend from ideas on spelling to his
role in the Academies under Charles IX and Henry III, are often
exciting.

After the fashion of his friends, he embarks on love-poetry, first
the poems to Méline (1552) and then those to Francine (1555), whom
some have identified as the sister of Jacques Tahureau's *Admirée*.
In these collections Baïf remains very close to the trends of his time:
the sonnets are for the most part strongly indebted to Petrarchism
and echo textually many Italian models in such a way that his poems
often appear more derivative than do those of his friends. Sometimes
he can achieve a delicate independence:

Comme le simple oyseau, qui cherche sa pasture,
Lors qu'il n'est jour ne nuit (quand le veillant berger
Si c'est ou chien ou loup ne peut au vray juger)
Ne pensant au danger, mais à sa nourriture,

S'empestre en la pantiere: ainsi moy qui m'assure,
Libre de tout lien, sans soupçon de danger,
En passant mon chemin droit je me vin ranger
Dans un si doux filet qu'en sortir je n'ay cure:

N'y n'en sçay le moyen: le moi devant Avril
J'entray à l'impourveu dedans ce doux peril.
Sur le soir j'entrevy tant seulement la belle.

Ce fut devant son huis: si tost que je la vy,
Aussi tost me perdant, de moy je fus ravy,
Et de me recouvrer il n'est plus de nouvelle.
                    (*Francine*, I, Caldarini ed., p. 13)

The moment of the Petrarchan *morsure*, evidently, but with its own
tonality: the extended comparison (though the shepherd image inter-
feres with rather than reinforces it), the antithetical movements of
the last lines, the suddenness of the poet's capture, all this belongs to
a tradition. Yet the general flow of the line, with frequent *enjambement*, the early use of the alexandrine in the sonnet, the development
of the solitude theme, and the more familiar tone of the final line,
these features give the poem a more personal quality. Nevertheless,
Baïf never manages to catch up with Ronsard in this collection: he
shows a careful sense of metrical values, a nice mastery of classical
rhetoric, and refuses to flaunt aggressive erudition; the sense of
Nature – Francine belongs to Anjou – appears frequently, and generally speaking, the Petrarchan character of the *innamorata* is rendered
more homely and familiar. This is of course far more true of the
chansons, which form the second pair of books – whereas in the
Méline sequence sonnets and lyric poems were not separated. Here
the Neo-catullan and elegiac traditions mix with the franker approach
we associate with Ronsard in his post-Petrarchan moods; but above
all, Baïf is exploiting new metrical schemes, perhaps with more
enthusiasm than discretion and taste. The poet who was to make such
attractive translations in the anacreontic tradition is already at home
in this idiom, just about the time that Henri Estienne II was publishing his edition and renderings into Latin of these Greek lyric poets.

In 1567 Baïf appears again on the scene with his adaptation of
Plautus's *Miles gloriosus* and his own *Premier Livre des Meteores*,
the sequels of which never saw the light of day. In this work, he
follows very closely the *Urania* of Pontano, but presumably he was
aware of his French predecessors in the field of scientific literature:
Peletier du Mans tentatively and more closely Pontus de Tyard in
his *L'Univers* (1557). In Baïf's work the didactic concern is often to
the fore, and this recurs in the *Mimes, Enseignemens et Proverbes*,
first published in 1576, but reprinted posthumously in expanded
form. Here, the poet uses verse as the vehicle for *sententiæ* and
potted wisdom such as one may find in Erasmus, or in Pibrac's
immensely successful *Quatrains* (1574), which may conceivably have

lent some impetus to Baïf's work, on the stocks for many years before it came out. Here, as in the *Meteores*, poetic imagination is expected to give way to scientific or moral truth and though the book contains some metrical felicities, there is a limit to the enjoyment of so many thousands of concentrated adages.

Baïf's main achievement is to be found in the massive *Euvres en rimes*, published in four volumes in 1573.[10] The edition contains works previously published and is interesting for the variants introduced into the poems to Méline and Francine. There are the usual *billets de circonstance* to friends, many poems rendering Greek and other poets, five books of *Passetems*, a real farrago of epigrams. Where Baïf displays the greatest originality is in his series of eclogues, some of which must count among the earliest composed by the Pléiade. He contributes to the genre more especially in the greater stress he lays on the pastoral, natural elements, which in some contemporary eclogues are reduced to the bare necessities of the convention. There is a nature poet in Baïf, stimulated by links with the west country, his fairly sharp eye, and his acquaintance with the Greek bucolic tradition. Sometimes he makes quite a lot of the amatory themes, but the dramatic techniques he acquired in translating the Roman comedians and Sophocles do not brush off on to his eclogues.

Baïf's work gives an immense impression of conscientious effort. He tried his hand at every type of poetry preconised by the *Deffense*, and in that sense he is the all-rounder of the Pléiade, for Ronsard never chanced his luck in drama, through lack of enthusiasm and perhaps an innate sense of inadequacy. In Baïf too, the Greek tradition, particularly in its later Alexandrian manifestations, has coloured his output pervasively. He corresponds here to Henri Estienne in Latin poetry. Moreover, he is the most systematic experimenter of his time in metrical patterns and he possessed a sensitive feeling for language over many bands of the spectrum. Though we came upon sporadic attempts before him (Boteauville, De la Farge, Jodelle), Baïf is the most serious exponent of *vers mesurés à l'antique*, a failure, it is said, because they were alien to the 'spirit of the language'; but in any case, his own verse in the medium is rugged, which did not prevent others, notably among the *politiques* (Rapin in particular), from following his example. Baïf also, through the Academies, deepened the study of the relations between music and poetry. Though a convinced orthodox believer, he never developed into a committed poet in the sense that Ronsard was, for instance. He was a man of many ideas and well attuned to the poetic needs of his time; but there are defects of sensibility that mark him down: a lack of stamina, an inadequate control of imagery, perhaps too narrow a view of the relations between art and truth, and in the last analysis a lack of touch with his material, so that either he loses his sense of artistic proportion or he allows himself to lapse into solemnity and even pedantry, for much of his work is soaked in learning and mythology. His lack of recognition hurt him and his *Carmina* (1577), heavily indebted to the *Greek Anthology*, appear to be the last bid of a poet whom success had eluded in the vernacular. 'Inventif et laborieux' was the description he gave of himself, slightly harsh, but understandable. If his technical sense and ingenuity had been accompanied by a matching imagination, he would have been a poet indeed. Perhaps his best work emerges in those poems where Nature appears in the stylised idiom of the Alexandrian tradition and forms a background to sentiments, not deep, but delicately etched, or where Baïf is able to confer movement, too often absent, on its denizens.

VII. ÉTIENNE JODELLE (1532–73)[11]

Jodelle's claims to fame have traditionally rested on his dramatic achievement, so that his other poetry has lurked in the penumbra. Recently, a new look has been taken at his writings, and substantial manuscript material has been added to the corpus. Jodelle's output is written in both Latin and French; he does not seem to have suffered any of the inhibitions that attacked the Pléiade in their early days about Latin poetry; indeed his associations with the Pléiade seem to belong properly to the days that followed his first dramatic success. His poetic roots go back to earlier currents: he makes graceful reference to Hugues Salel, he composes several epitaphs on Marot, his more scabrous verse has Rabelaisian harmonics, and when he is in Paris, we find him frequenting the circle of Jean de Brinon. Moreover, he was on friendly terms with Nicolas Denisot; a poem to this humanist suggests that, to begin with at any rate, he did not share the Ronsardian conception of poetry and that he sympathised with a Christian rather than a 'pagan' treatment of theme.

His poems were published posthumously, and we have no record of the order in which Jodelle might have arranged them had he lived. This does not exclude the possibility of detecting some evolution in his composition. In the years 1552–53 or so, he comes to share views more in sympathy with the Pléiade, and he is conscious of the difficult and erudite character of some of his own poems; he attacks 'l'impudente ignorance' and one may also notice some Platonic themes fairly early on, even if more usually he displays an anti-Platonic temperament. He is adept at handling 'abstract' subjects and reveals an undoubted stamina and 'sweep' in some courtly poems (e.g., *Sur la mort de la reine d'Espagne*, ed. E. Balmas, I, 208). From the outset he shows a persistent search for technical variety and originality; we have *vers mesurés, terza rima,* sonnets in *vers rapportés;* some poems he hoped would be set to music by Orlando di Lasso, others reveal a complexity of structure that would have gladdened the hearts of the *rhétoriqueurs.* Throughout the corpus one discerns a notable preference for ternary structures; and Jodelle takes delight in composing a series of variations on a chosen theme.

The court poet in Jodelle reveals some interesting lines, usually of a reflective nature, but he comes more alive in his 'committed' verse. There is adequate evidence to indicate that Jodelle was seriously attracted by Calvinism at one time, but he soon reverted to orthodoxy. In the poems inspired by the wars of religion, a vigorous visual imagination is at work, though the feeling behind it is perhaps more political than spiritual. If we take the following sonnet:

> Que de ce siecle horrible on me peigne un tableau,
> Par ordre y ordonnant l'estrange mommerie
> Où tout vice, tout crime, erreur, peste, furie,
> De son contraire ait pris le masque et le manteau:
>
> Aux peuples et aux Rois dessous maint faux flambeau
> Qui les yeux esblouit et les cœurs enfurie,
> Soit de ces masques faux l'énorme tromperie
> Conduite, et pour moumon porte à tous un bandeau:
>
> L'injustice prendra le beau masque d'Astrée,
> En science sera l'ignorance accoustrée,
> Sous le masque de CHRIST; d'humblesse et charité,
>
> Satan, ambition, sedition felonne
> Marcheront, et n'estoit la chance que Dieu donne,
> Leurs faux dez piperoyent tout heur et verité.
> (*Contre les Ministres de la nouvelle opinion,* I, 276)

we can see that Jodelle stands between the Du Bellay of the *Regretz* and *Les Tragiques,* whose author found much to admire in him. There is of course the theme of *paraître/être* which will become a major one in the last decades of the century, but it is also in the ways he develops it that Jodelle foreshadows the future. The dramatising of the forces, seen in a series of visual images, emphasised by enumeration, repetition (note the *leitmotiv faux* recurring at suitable intervals), the relentless movement of the whole sonnet, helped by skilful *enjambement,* and the whole tone shot through with moral indignation. Here Jodelle may not be in the highways of the Pléiade, but he is exploiting veins that will soon come into their own; but may one not ask whether some of this linguistic vitality does not also derive from pre-Pléiade sources too? – Rabelais, Marot, poetry in which movement and a sharp eye for the visual trait are strongly developed? This is very much in evidence in the hate poem of the same sequence (xxiv), where the dynamic quality of the line is determined by the proportion of verbs as well as by the obsessive line-openings (I, 278–9). In such compositions the poet often reaches a pitch of intensity that brings out exceptional satirical gifts.

Jodelle has written a considerable amount of love-poetry. Its first characteristic is perhaps a great search for technical variety; the metres may attain a high degree of complexity and his handling of language is matched by a keen sense of tempo. In some ways, these poems often show little sympathy with certain Pléiade trends; Jodelle has harsh things to say about Petrarchan conventions, and in one *chanson* he sings the relations between love and marriage. He seems more at home in the *contr'amour*, he does not situate love so often in Nature surroundings as do other Pléiade poets – his Muse in any case is more urban, though pastoral elements are not absent – and many poems seek no display of erudition. In this more sparse atmosphere, he develops with marked success the themes of absence, solitude, silence, and love lost. Towards the end of his life, he appears to have returned to a more spiritual, indeed Platonic, love, not only in the three *Chapitres d'Amour*, but also in the sonnets devoted to the *amour obscur* (another dark lady of the sonnets). One may also have to take into account a general influence of the maréchale de Retz's *salon* and of course the literary climate was shifting towards a form of neo-petrarchism in the 1570s. Even so, Jodelle is able to maintain a certain independence of fashion and his love-poetry reveals a very wide range of mood and tone. Sometimes too his handling of language becomes very sophisticated and dense, as in the well-known *sonnet à vers rapportés*:

> Des astres, des forests, et d'Acheron l'honneur,
> Diane, au Monde hault, moyen et bas preside,
> Et ses chevaulx, ses chiens, ses Eumenides guide,
> Pour eclairer, chasser, donner mort et horreur.
>
> Tel est le lustre grand, la chasse, et la frayeur
> Qu'on sent sous ta beauté claire, prompte, homicide,
> Que là haut Jupiter, Phebus, et Pluton cuide,
> Son foudre moins pouvoir, son arc et sa terreur.
>
> Ta beauté par ses rais, par son retz, par la craincte
> Rend l'ame esprise, prise, et au martyre estreinte:
> Luy moy, pren moy, tien moy, mais hélas ne me pers.
>
> Des flambans forts et griefs, eux, filez, et encombres,
> Lune, Diane, Hecate, aux cieux, terre et enfers
> Ornant, questant, genant, nos Dieux, nous et nos ombres.
>
> (I, 393–4)

At first blush, a study in or play with words, something rather precious, with the relentless pursuit of the triad. Yet the blend of verbal density and remarkable rhythmic vigour that underpins the poet's appeal takes the poem beyond the *salon amusette* and beyond the musky grace of Desportes. It is a poem of fright, not alembicated flirting, and the final effect is a disturbing one.

Jodelle's poetry, then, deserves a fresh look; he does not fit tidily into pigeon-holes, and indeed he traverses several stages of poetic development in France without becoming totally identified with any single one. At the same time, his work suggests that the Pléiade did not achieve its expected break with the past and that in the poetry of a man like Jodelle the continuity of a poetic tradition is maintained.

The impact of the Pléiade upon younger, less talented writers was rapid, powerful, and varied. In a period when the writing of poetry becomes even more widespread than before, it is impossible, and probably supererogatory, to present even a sketch of the poetic panorama studded as it is with so many minor figures. Some poets of talent do show promise like Jean Tagaut, but he soon turns to Geneva and his works have to wait almost four centuries before seeing print;[12] and Olivier de Magny, though a conscientious craftsman, is too much of a pale mirror of Ronsard and Du Bellay to warrant serious consideration.[13] However, it might be worth while to mention one or two poets, coming from different parts of the country and able to suggest by their 'spread' the change in poetic outlook brought about by the entry on stage of the Pléiade.

VIII. THE PLÉIADE AND THE PROVINCES

Etienne Forcadel (c. 1518–73)[14]

Etienne, the brother of the celebrated mathematician Pierre, is a useful example to take, partly because his verse has some agreeable qualities, but also because his literary career starts before the *Deffense* and the later edition of his poems (1579) contains both poems which were composed late in life and some which were modified in the light of the Pléiade's advent. His roots lie therefore in the Marotic tradition, to some extent, but he is also a Neo-latin poet who publishes his *Epigrammata* in 1554, a collection that links him loosely with the humanist currents of the 1530s. Some of his poems celebrate persons who died in the 1540s, others show *blason* techniques at work; Forcadel makes use of traditional genres such as the *complainte* or the *chant royal* and he writes elegies and epistles. His love-poetry usually reminds one of the Bèze idiom, but he has also read Petrarch and Jean Second as well as the Roman elegists, though he maintains the rather colourless style we find in various pre-Pléiade poets:

> Il ne te faut aller au sacré mont
> Qui va dressant deux testes contremont,
> Pour devenir Poëte promptement
> Tu en seras, suy l'amour seulement.
> C'est le chemin que Properce a tenu,

> Et le Tuscan de Laure retenu.
> Taire d'Amour le plaisir et la plainte,
> Seroit chastrer la Poésie sainte.
>
> (*Œuvres poétiques*, p. 116)

But many epigrams (such as *A Ysabeau*) remind one of Neo-latin models and, on occasion, of Martial. Forcadel works in the encomiastic vein and the eclogue; he is very fond of the prosopopœic formula; and though there is mention of various members of the Pléiade (Baïf, Jodelle, Du Bellay; and in the *Epigrammata*, Ronsard) and certain compositions have been affected by his reading of their works, Forcadel remains a good illustration of the persistence of an earlier poetic breed, wearing new clothes but without essential change of personality. His verse is pleasant and well constructed; but the language lacks vigour and in spite of a search for metrical variety, his range of inspiration is limited. In consequence, he tends to be more successful when he is dealing with a homely topic and does not seek to inflate his modest talent. He attaches little importance to posthumous fame; for him poetry was entertainment, he was suspicious of excessive learning in poetry, and he liked his precursors:

> Louons les vieux, & usons de nos ans,
> Puis que les vieux furent jadis enfans.

In other words, his enthusiasm for the Pléiade, quite genuine, was tempered by his own formation and his sense of the golden mean.

Marc-Claude Buttet (1530–86)[15]

Buttet was introduced to Marguerite de France when he was a young man in Paris; and after her marriage to Philibert-Emmanuel, he returned to his native Savoy. His sojourn in Paris coincided with the formative years of the Pléiade and his whole output reflects this experience. His most substantial work is the sequence to Amalthée, which develops the Petrarchan idiom in the erudite fashion of the early Pléiade, but often remains a trifle angular and short-winded:

> Si plus tu vas pleignant apres ta belle Sainte,
> Mon Desautels (pour qui doux me seroit l'exil
> Aux Scythes, aux Indois, aux sept gorges du Nil)
> Escoute comme Amour a ma force contreinte.
>
> Quand je vis Dubellai premier faire sa pleinte,
> Puis ton docte Tyard, pris d'un oeil si gentil:
> Je me mocquai d'Amour, & de son trait subtil,
> Et vous estimai tous ne gemir que par feinte.
>
> Amour rouge devint de si jeune constance:
> Son petit arc il bande, & d'un trait de vengeance
> Tout colere il m'abat, trop foible à son effort.
>
> Depuis plus que tous vous je langui miserable:
> Car vous avés encor' quelque trait favorable,
> Et je n'ai autre bien, que le seul déconfort.
>
> (p. 280)

An honest development of a *topos*, but not really coherent at imaginative level. Buttet probably achieves more success in some of his short odes, but he follows Ronsard faithfully in a series of different genres. He wished very much to become a court poet to Marguerite, and a goodly number of his compositions celebrate military events, court happenings, and in particular matters concerning the princess. In various ways he reflects the literary interests of the 1550s: he was involved in attempts to reform spelling and his own orthography betrays his reading of Meigret. He tries to develop the possibilities of the poetic language as had been suggested in the *Deffense*: he invents compound words, introduces latinisms, and makes up new words as well as using a profusion of epithets. He is also absorbed in the technical problems of metre and his work reveals a remarkable range of experimentation, including some *vers mesurés à l'antique*, which he enriched with rhyme. Essentially he is a craftsman, and though occasionally a poetic personality peeps through, he has given us the materials for poetry rather than poetry itself. An engaging character, rarely indulging in hostile verse, he remains the provincial amateur.

IX. POETS ASSOCIATED WITH POITIERS

Poitiers was connected in some measure with the formation of the Pléiade in that Du Bellay, La Péruse, and others had studied there before the appearance of the *Deffense*. There is a second period, in the middle 1550s, which brings together a number of young poets who had mostly been students at Paris and were already converted to Pléiade poetics: Baïf, Roland Bétholaud, also known as a lawyer and a Neo-latin versifier, Scévole de Sainte-Marthe, Jacques Tahureau, Charles Toutain, and Vauquelin de la Fresnaye.

Vauquelin de la Fresnaye (c. 1535–1606)[16]

Of this group perhaps Vauquelin possesses the greatest local interest, whereas Sainte-Marthe's later fame is much more widely based. Vauquelin is remembered in part for his *Art poétique*, which though published in 1605, reflects attitudes current at the time of its composition requested by Henry III; but he published his *Foresteries* in 1555, and these poems are in the vanguard of the pastoral revival that characterises these post-Petrarchan years of the Pléiade; they also promote the vogue for the pastoral eclogue. Vauquelin had studied under Turnèbe and Muret before leaving Paris to take his legal course at Poitiers, and his allegiance to Ronsard, Du Bellay, and Baïf is affirmed in various poems where he mentions them by name. The *Foresteries*, however, mark a return to classical and Italian sources to express a feeling for Nature that only rarely seems to draw on visual awareness:

> Pour lui plaire il verroit mille connils courants
>   Aux guarennes fuiants:
> Mille ecureuls courroient par les branches des chênes
> Pour rongeoter l'erable ou la graine des fresnes,
> Et pour lui plaire encor l'un sur l'autre d'un saut
>   Culbuteroient d'en haut.
>
> (Bensimon ed., I, 2)

Vauquelin's conception of pastoral is fairly loose; love constitutes a major theme of course, but he ranges over different genres, *silve*, *folastries*, eclogue, and idyll. He has returned to the Theocritean formula, with some attention paid to Vergil, and among modern authors he owes quite a lot to Sannazaro, whose *Arcadia* was translated in 1546 by Jean Martin. His Muse is very derivative, and rarely does he muster enough imaginative fire to fuse his material into some organic unity. Where he does show some originality is in the variety of metres and stanza forms utilised; indeed for the size of the volume, this variety is exceptional, but the relation of metrical structure to sentence is rarely mastered and Vauquelin's poems often give an impression of clumsiness. Inoffensive, agreeable, glucotic poetry, but of little more than technical and historical moment.

Jacques Tahureau (1527–55)[17]

The poet who seems to have enjoyed the greatest standing with his local friends was Tahureau, perhaps better known for his *Dialogues* published posthumously in 1556 (see above, pp. 221–2); but before his untimely death he brought out in 1554 two volumes of verse, the *Premieres poésies* and the *Sonnets, odes, et mignardises amoureuses de l'Admirée*. Tahureau gives the appearance in his dialogues of having acquired a precocious polymathy, though some of his learning is decidedly second-hand; in his poetry he shows himself very sensitive to the various poetic fashions. He composes his own Petrarchan sequence, writes a goodly number of *baisers* and *mignardises*, so popular then, and like his friends, is particularly interested in metrical exploration; he attacks critics of those who write in French, particularly odes, and is ready to introduce cautiously some neologisms. Too often, his work seems to suffer from over-hasty composition, but had he lived he might have produced works of genuine originality. Even so, when one reads these poems, so derivative on occasion, one is regularly brought up with a start: a line here, a thought there, makes us aware of a sensibility that was not always the slave of convention. This is perhaps the reflection of his graver imagination – his dialogues have a sombre streak in them – but in his love-poetry his feelings seem to push beyond the Petrarchan convention. His poems have quite a strong intellectual framework, and at its best one might, without undue exaggeration, see in his poetry an intermediate talent between the *Délie* and Jean de Sponde; but this impression occurs only fleetingly and his works rarely divest themselves of a certain immaturity. The following sonnet shows none the less how a commonplace can be developed with dignified vigour:

> Je ne veux point, pour me vanger de toy,
> D'ongles pointus te deschirer la face,
> Et si ne veux par une folle audace
> Dessus ton corps faire aucun desarroy.
>
> Je n'entreprens pour ta parjure foy
> Cruellement te traisner par la place,
> Quelque villain de trop mauvaise grace
> Ces lourds debats recerche, & non pas moy:
>
> Mais je peindray d'une plume immortelle
> Une trop fiere et dure Tourangelle
> Qui se nourrit de me veoir en douleur.
>
> Et si bien que peu te soit mon escriture
> Si t'en pourra quelquefois la lecture
> Faire changer de honte la couleur.
>
> (*Les Poésies*, 1574, 72 r)

Charles Toutain[18]

Toutain's version of the *Agamemnon* and his *Chants de Philosophie et d'Amour* came out in 1557. Broadly speaking, he shares the outlook of the Pléiade; he considers himself lucky to be living in so fine a century, opposed to *Ignorance*, and to be a Frenchman with roots in the west country. His friends are chiefly in the Poitiers group, but he also expresses great admiration for his teacher Pierre de La Ramée. He prefers the longer poem, in which he tries out a variety of metres, including a few *vers mesurés à l'antique*. His philosophical poems, though they contain some cosmological themes – he appears later as a friend of Lefèvre de la Boderie – and warn against Epicureans and the new Stoics, are more moralising than strictly philosophical. His amatory verse to Clorine is situated against a background of Nature and expressed in the minor, diluted mode of the Petrarchan tradition: the loved one is portrayed in the key of silence, absence, and rejection. Sometimes affecting high style, he likes classical comparison and allusion, and experiments modestly with language, but more often than not, his poetry is near to prose and the proportion of direct to oblique statement is substantial. Toutain follows in the paths of the Pléiade, but in more abstract language and with a restricted range of mood and theme.

Scévole de Sainte-Marthe (1533–1623)[19]

Though Sainte-Marthe leaves the interesting *Elogia* (1600) and some Latin poetry of distinction, he also belonged in his youth to the Poitiers circle. His first publication, the *Premieres œuvres poétiques*

(1564), does not in fact show to any great extent what he may have derived from his friendship with his fellow-poets, for it contains chiefly imitations and adaptations of Latin and Greek models, including some bucolic poets and the more recent Palingenius. He stresses the value of vernacular composition, but his taste for *salon* verse is already discernible:

... puisque les hommes ignorans se mocquent de tout, & que les hommes sçavans ont de quoy trouver leur contentement ailleurs qu'en nostre vulgaire, le Poëte François, qui desire estre leu, doit tellement composer les œuvres, qu'à tout le moins il y mesle quelque chose qui soit propre & convenable aux yeux des gentiles & vertueuses Dames auxquelles principallement j'estime appartenir la lecture de tels escriptz ...

which is also a commentary on the evolution of the public for which poets were writing. Sainte-Marthe's renderings are graceful and urbane, and they also display the command of metrical variety we have seen in other Poitiers authors. Still, Sainte-Marthe no more than others is putting all his poetic eggs into the vernacular basket, for there are a number of Latin pieces, often connected with his Poitiers or west country friends, including Salmon Macrin for whom he writes a French poem in commemoration. However, he took care with his French poetry and in the fuller editions of 1569 and 1579 he inserted pieces of a more original nature as well as correcting the text of earlier poems. These later volumes are characteristic of the verse that is then fashionable, especially among members of the legal fraternity: occasional pieces inspired by friendships, translations from Ariosto, moralising verse, Christian poems (translation of Job), adaptations from Ovid (*Metamorphoses chrestiennes*), humanist epigrams, a certain precious love-poetry, in which Bèze's influence, among others, is visible:

O bien heureux Collet, qui vas couvrir le sein
D'une qui m'est cent fois plus chere que ma vie,
Je ne me puis tenir de te porter envie
Pour l'aise dont sans moy tu t'en vas estre plein.

Pleust à la volonté du grand Dieu souverain
Qui ne borne de rien sa puissance infinie,
Que pour jouir ainsi du beau sein de m'amie
Ie devinsse collet d'un changement soubdain.

Mais au moins, beau Collet, si je suis le moyen
Qui te fay recevoir un si doux & grand bien
Pour user envers moy de quelque recompense,

Entr'ouvre toy par foys, & fay place à ma main
Afin qu'au moins il puisse un peu toucher ce sein
Duquel tu as ainsi parfaitte jouissance.
(*Les Œuvres*, 1579, fol. 133 r, *L'Amour* xxvii)

Poetry now finds matter everywhere in life; but if Christian sentiment finds its way into Sainte-Marthe's verse, it is also true to say that poetry is also becoming more domesticated, trained to be the suitable activity of the *salon* and the *cénacle*.

This survey of the Pléiade requires some concluding remarks, even if certain aspects of its work will be considered a bit later (court poetry, committed verse, drama). Its claims to originality, so far as theory and intention were concerned, were doubtless overstated in the interests of propaganda; but its success was due, as we have seen, to a happy conjuncture of circumstances: the maturing of French humanism, the increasing efforts by royalty to bring culture to reflect national aspirations, the restored prestige of Paris, the presence of a dynamic poetic group headed by a man of genius, and the ripeness of the vernacular to take over as the recognised vehicle of poetic sensibility. The Pléiade not only gave French poetry a dignity and status which, in the eyes of many contemporaries, it did not fully enjoy; it widened its thematic range and social involvement in a way that had not been previously possible. Poetry may have become rather more 'literary' in its nourishment – this is a criticism voiced by more than one critic, and certain contemporaries such as La Ramée and the Calvinists had misgivings about so 'aristocratic' a conception of poetry, but the fact remains that poetry becomes part of the lives of more educated people than ever before, a point to which Ronsard grudgingly alluded:

> Non, je ne me deulx pas qu'une telle abondance
> D'escrivains aujourd'huy fourmille en ceste France,
> Mais certes je me deulx que tous n'escrivent bien,
> Sans gaster ainsi l'ancre, & la lampe pour rien.
> (*Elegie à Chrétophle de Choiseul*, 1556)

There are, to be sure, areas in which the Pléiade did not fulfil its promises – I think more especially of religious poetry and drama, which was never seriously tackled by the Brigade, and the epic also missed its target. Yet it produced the linguistic vitality and the technical versatility that brought French poetry to one of the summits of its history. The *poetæ minores* tended to succeed fleetingly and in the slighter genres; but their very quantity and exuberance helped to forge the necessary instruments for use by a later generation and also to prolong the momentum generated by Ronsard and in a lesser measure his friends. They provided the poetic foundations on which both classical and 'Baroque' could build their mansions.

APPENDIX

Space does not allow for the scrutiny of many minor poets of this period, nearly all indebted in greater or lesser measure to Ronsard. I give a selected list of the figures who, of course, spill over into the later part of our period. Where poets have received recent critical treatment – over and above M. Raymond's masterly work on *L'Influence de Ronsard sur la poésie française 1550–1585*, 2 vols., 1927 – a bibliographical reference is given.

1553　Guillaume des Autelz: *Amoureux repos*, Lyons (BN, O) (see monograph by M. L. M. Young, *THR*, 1961).

1555　E. Pasquier: *Recueil des Rymes et proses* (BM, BN).
　　　G. de la Taysonnière: *Les Amoureuses occupations*, Lyons (BM).

1556　C. de Taillemont: *La Tricarite*, Lyons (BN).

1557　P. Bugnyon: *Erotasmes de Phidie et Gelasine* . . . , Lyons. (see F. Brunot, *De Philiberti Bugnoni vita et eroticis versibus*, Lyons, 1891).
　　　L. des Masures: *Œuvres poétiques*, Lyons.

1559　C. d'Espinay: *Premier Livre des Amours* (see H. Busson, *Charles d'Espinay, evêque de Dol et son œuvre poétique*, 1922).

1560　N. Filleul: *Discours* (BN) (see under 1566).
　　　J. Grévin: *L'Olimpe, ensemble les autres œuvres poétiques* (BM, BN). (see thesis mentioned p. 456, n.9, by L. Pinvert).

1561　N. Ellain: *Œuvres poétiques françois*, ed. A. Genty, 1861. *Les Sonnets* . . . (BN).

1565　J. Béreau: *Eglogues et autres œuvres poétiques* (Niort) (modern ed. J. H. de Tranchère and R. Guyet, 1884).

1566　N. Filleul: *Les Théâtres de Gaillon* (BN) (modern ed. F. Joukovsky, *TLF*, 1971).

1568　F. d'Amboise: *Odes lamentables*.

1572　C. Turin: *Œuvres poétiques*.

1573　C. Binet: *Diverses poésies* (follow works of La Péruse) (BM, BN).

1574　F. Perrin: *Pourtraict de la vie humaine*.

1575　G. du Faur de Pibrac: *Plaisirs de la vie rustique* (BM) (see thesis mentioned below by A. Cabos).

1576　F. Breton: *Poésies amoureuses*, Lyons.
　　　P. de Brach: *Poèmes*, Bordeaux (BN, 1580 ed. BM). (ed. R. Dezeimeris, 1861; ed. *Les Amours d'Aymée*, *TLF*, J. Dawkins, 1971).

1578　J. de Boyssières: *Premieres Œuvres* (BN).
　　　　　　　Les Secondes Œuvres (BN).

1579　　　　　*Les Troisièmes Œuvres*, Lyons (BN).
　　　C. de Pontoux: *Les Œuvres*, Lyons (BM, BN).

1580　J. Le Masle: *Nouvelles recréation poétiques*.

1582　I. Habert: *Œuvres poétiques* (BN, NLS).
　　　J. E. du Monin: *Nouvelles Œuvres* (BM, BN).

1583　C. Gauchet: *Le Plaisir des champs* (BM, BN).
　　　Jean de la Gessée: *Premieres œuvres françaises* (BM, BN).

1584　J. de Romieu: *Meslanges*.

Certain poets, such as Jean Passerat, Nicolas Rapin, or Jean Vatel, are already active, but their works are not published in anything like substantial fashion until the seventeenth century.

Closely related with the Pléiade, though not a poet himself or a humanist inclined to writing in French, stands *Pierre de La Ramée*, a controversial figure who later in life declared himself in favour of Calvinism. He plays a prominent, though not always clear, role in the aristotelian dispute, the reformation of the syllabus, the reclassification of traditional discipline (e.g., the place of rhetoric), the role of poetry. There is still much disagreement among scholars on important points, e.g., his influence, if any, on Pléiade poetics, though it is pretty certain that Ramism was more powerful in Great Britain. See the following works:

C. Waddington, *Ramus (Pierre de la Ramée) sa vie, ses écrits, ses opinions*, 1855.
R. Tuve, *Elizabethan and metaphysical imagery*, Chicago, 1947.
W. J. Ong, *Ramus, Method and the Decay of Dialogue*, Cambridge, Mass., 1958.
J. J. Verdonk, *Petrus Ramus en de Wiskunde*, Assen, 1966.
P. Sharratt, Durham thesis on Ramus's literary ideas.
R. Hoykaas, *Humanisme, Science et Réforme. Pierre de la Ramée 1515–1572*, Leiden, 1958.

NOTES

1. H. Chamard, *Histoire de la Pléiade*, 4 vols., 1939–40; H. Weber, *La Création poétique au XVIᵉ siècle*, 2 vols., 1956; R. J. Clements, *Critical Theory and Practice of the Pléiade*; G. Castor, op. cit.; H. W. Wittschier, *Die Lyrik der Pleiade*, Frankfurt, 1971.
2. There are earlier examples too: the Ronsard-Dorat tandem in the *Tombeau* of Marguerite de Navarre; and the bilingual edition of *Hymne de Bacchus* as an appendix to the 1555 ed. of the *Hymnes*. Under Louis XII certain Neo-latin poems are rendered into French verse by *rhétoriqueurs*.
3. For a detailed treatment of the question, see Marcel Raymond's thesis listed above, p. 294.
4. *Erreurs Amoureuses*, Lyons, 1549 (Ars); *Continuation des Erreurs Amoureuses*, Lyons, 1551 (BN, Ars); *Solitaire Premier . . . Plus Quelques Vers Lyriques*, Lyons, 1552 (BN, Ars); *Erreurs Amoureuses, augmentées d'une tierce partie*, Lyons, 1555 (BM, BN); *Les Œuvres Poëtiques*, 1573 (BM, BN). Modern eds.: *Œuvres poétiques complètes*, ed. J. C. Lapp, *STFM*, 1966; *Les Erreurs amoureuses*, ed. J. A. McClelland, *TLF*, 1967. See S.-F. Baridon, *Pontus de Tyard (1521–1605)*, Milan, 1959, and *Inventaire de la bibliothèque de Pontus de Tyard*, Geneva, 1950.
5. Ronsard's *Amours* will not appear for another year.
6. See H. Chamard, 'Bibliographie des éditions de Joachim du Bellay', *Bulletin du Bibliophile*, 1949. The BN and O hold many first eds., and the BM is also very rich; occasional early eds. in NLS, MRy, EUL, PSG. See H. Chamard, *Joachim du Bellay*, Lille, 1900; V.-L. Saulnier, *Du Bellay l'homme et l'œuvre*, 1951; G. Saba, *La Poesia di Joachim du Bellay*, Messina–Florence, 1962; R. Griffin, *Coronation of the Poet: Joachim du Bellay's Debt to the Trivium*, Berkeley and Los Angeles, 1969; R. V. Merrill, *The Platonism of Joachim du Bellay*, Chicago, 1925; R. Schwaderer, *Das Verhältnis des Lyrikers Joachim du Bellay zu seinen Vorbildern*, Würzburg, 1968; G. Dickinson, *Du Bellay in Rome*, Leiden, 1960; A. W. Satterthwaite, *Spenser, Ronsard and Du Bellay, A Renaissance Comparison*, Princeton, 1960; V.-L. Saulnier, '*Les Antiquitez de Rome' de Joachim du Bellay*, CDU, 1961. The standard modern ed. is by H. Chamard, *STFM*, 6 vols., 1908–31, to which should be added H. Chamard's ed. of *La Deffence et illustration de la langue française*, STFM, 1948, and that of the *Regretz et autres œuvres* by M. A. Screech and J. W. Jolliffe, *TLF*, 1966.
7. *Les œuvres poétiques*, 1578 (BM, PSG); 1585 (BM, BN, PSG, O); 1592 (BM BN); *Les Odes d'Anacreon Teien*, 1556 (BM, BN); *La Bergerie*, 1565 (BN), 1572 (BM, BN, EUL). Modern ed. Marty-Laveaux, 2 vols., 1878; and

of 1565 ed. by D. Delacourcelle, *TLF*, 1954. A. Eckhardt, *Rémy Belleau, sa vie, sa Bergerie, étude historique et critique,* Budapest, 1917; D. Delacourcelle, *Le Sentiment de l'art dans la Bergerie de Rémy Belleau,* Oxford, 1945; M. Jeanneret, 'Les œuvres d'art dans la *Bergerie* de Belleau', *RHLF*, 1970.

8. Hilda Dale, 'Rémy Belleau et la science lapidaire', *Lumières de la Pléiade*, 1966; copy of 1576 ed. in O.

9. *Euvres en rime,* 1572–73 (BN, MRy). Modern ed. Marty-Laveaux, 5 vols., 1881–90. *Les Amours,* 1552 (BN, EUL); *Quatre livres d'Amours,* 1555 (BM, BN); *Le premier livre des meteores,* 1567 (BN); *Le Brave,* 1567 (BM, BN); *Mimes, enseignemens et prouerbes,* 1576 (BN), 1581 (BM). Modern eds. of certain works: *Les Amours de Francine,* ed. E. Caldarini, I *Sonnets,* 1966, II *Chansons,* 1967, *TLF; Chansonnettes,* ed. G. C. Bird, Vancouver, 1964; *Poems,* sel. M. Quainton, Oxford, 1970. See M. Augé-Chiquet, *La Vie, Les idées et l'œuvre de Jean-Antoine de Baïf,* Paris–Toulouse, 1909.

10. Mention should, however, be made of Baïf's unpublished psalm paraphrases, preserved in BN. Ms. fr. 19140 in three *états:* Pss. 1–68 (vers mesurés) completed by November 1569; Pss. 1–150 (vers mesurés), completed towards end of 1573; the whole series (vers rimés) finished beginning 1587. This last version has been ed. by Y. Le Hir, 1963. See also M. Jeanneret, op. cit.

11. *Les œuvres & meslanges poétiques,* 1574 (BM, BN, NLS), modern ed. *Œuvres complètes,* ed. E. Balmas, 2 vols., 1965–67. See E. Balmas, *Un Poeta del Rinascimento francese, Étienne Jodelle.*

12. M. Raymond, 'Jean Tagaut, poète français et bourgeois de Genève', *RSS,* 1925.

13. *Les Amours et quelques odes,* 1553 (BM, BN), enlarged ed. 1572 (BN); *Les Gayetez,* 1554 (BM), modern ed. Alistair R. Mackay, *TLF,* 1968; *Les souspirs,* 1557 (BM, BN); *Les odes,* 1559 (BM, BN). Modern eds. *Les Odes amoureuses de 1559,* ed. M. S. Whitney, *TLF,* 1964; *Les Cent deux sonnets des Amours de 1553,* ed. M. S. Whitney, *TLF,* 1970. See also J. Favre, *Olivier de Magny (1529–?1561),* 1885.

14. *Poésie,* 1551 (BN); *Œuvres poétiques,* 1579 (BM, BN). See C. Oulmont, *Un juriste, historien et poète vers 1550. Etienne Forcadel,* Toulouse, 1907.

15. *Le premier livre de vers . . . le second, ensemble l'Amalthée,* 1561 (BN); enlarged ed., Lyons, 1575 (BN); *Deux livres des œuvres poétiques,* 1588 (Ars). Modern ed.: *Œuvres poétiques,* ed. P. Lacroix, 2 vols., 1880; and that of A. Philibert-Soupé, Lyons, 1877. See F. Mugnier, *Marc-Claude de Buttet, poète savoisien (XVIe siècle),* 1896.

16. *Les deux premiers livres des Foresteries,* Poitiers, 1555 (BN), modern ed. M. Bensimon, *TLF,* 1956; *Diverses poesies,* Caen, 1605 (BN).

17. *Les premieres poésies,* Poitiers, 1554 (BM, BN); *Les Poésies,* 1574 (BM, BN). Modern ed. P. Blanchemain, 2 vols., 1870. See above under dialogues, pp. 221–2.

18. *La Tragedie d'Agamemnon, avec des livres de Chants de Philosophie & d'Amour,* 1557 (BM, BN). Not much is known about his life.

19. *Les premieres œuvres,* 1569 (BM, BN); *Les œuvres,* 1579 (BM, BN), and 1600 (BN). See J. Plattard, *La Vie et l'œuvre de Scévole de Sainte-Marthe, Bull Soc. I'Ouest,* 1922–41; A. J. Farmer, *Les Œuvres françaises de Scévole de Sainte-Marthe (1536–1623),* Toulouse, 1920.

Chapter 10

PIERRE DE RONSARD (1524–85)[1]

W ITH Ronsard, French poetry attains its majority; he may well be France's greatest poet, if like Goethe we link quantity and quality in our assessment. He arrives on the scene at a moment when the issues between Latin and the vernacular have become clear-cut – though the debate will continue yet awhile – he is able to create his poetic world, as it were, on the crest of Renaissance humanism's wave, and he sets to work when social conditions are also highly favourable. It is true that, for some centuries after his death, Ronsard's star was on the wane, largely as the result of poetic criteria which he helped to bring to fruition; but since Sainte-Beuve his fortunes have improved and in the last half-century his genius has come to be recognised for what it is. The fact still remains that for many he is essentially the poet of rosebuds and love, and that, though much fundamental research on his life and world has been undertaken in his native land, we still await the full-scale literary assessment to which he is entitled.[2]

Ronsard's débuts, ill known biographically, are also rather vague at the level of literary composition. We know, however, from his own pen, that he made a beginning in Latin verse – under the influence of Macrin perhaps? – but quickly changed his mind; he was in fact the only member of the Pléiade not to go back on the vernacular programme of the *Deffense*:

> Si autrefois sous l'ombre de Gâtine
> Avons joué quelque chanson Latine,
> D'Amarille enamouré,
> Sus, maintenant, Luc doré, . . .
> Change ton style, & me sois
> Sonnant un chant en François. . . .
>   (*Bocage*, ɪɪ, Laumonier ed., II, 155–6)

But he may have learned to appreciate the Horatian idiom through Neo-latin models as well as through the original text, for the aims of the Pléiade are sometimes anticipated in the Neo-latin world. In the same poem, however, Ronsard stresses his intention to become a court poet, points to his love of painting and music, both of which will affect his poetry, and, already developing the concept of the *vates* or *voyant*, sees the arts as forming a link between this imperfect world and the other. Nevertheless, only a handful of poems are published before 1550, an Ode to J. Peletier, and two encomiastic compositions in 1549, where the patriotic element is already evident.

I. THE ODES

Ronsard's public appearance really begins with the first four books of *Odes* (February–March 1550, BN) : 94 odes followed by 13 'irregular' odes grouped under title *Bocage* (= the Latin *silva*). This constitutes his first contribution to the Pléiade programme, with Du Bellay launching the theory and more especially the love-poetry. Here we have the return to classical models, emphasis on the public role of poetry, claims to be the first French poet in the field of the ode – overstated to be sure, but substantially correct so far as scale of achievement is concerned. Ronsard is seeking a model in the grand style: Pindar's poems were associated with the Olympic games and belonged to a tradition of ritual, so that there was a link with the *res publica* and religion. Ronsard was fully aware that a complete adaptation of the idiom was out of the question, but he felt it offered a better vehicle of expression than anything proposed by the older school of French poetry. The odes are therefore used to praise famous people of the realm, but they also offer the author a chance of developing his ideas on the nature and function of poetry: like so many other French poets of stature, Ronsard finds in poetry its own substance. His ideas come to the fore especially in the ode to Madame Marguerite and in a poem published two years later (Book V of the *Odes*), the *Ode à Michel de L'Hospital*, who played some part in the reconciliation between Ronsard and Mellin de Saint-Gellais. The second of these odes is constructed in Chinese-box fashion, themes within themes, the most important being that of the *fureurs* or divine inspiration, and the relations between the arts, morality, and wisdom, themes which reflect some acquaintance with the Neoplatonic tradition. The poem is a splendid piece of Olympic running; and though it is over-long and too loaded with classical decoration, it is not without its fine moments. Ronsard's enthusiasm for the Pindaric idiom wanes rapidly. That he had not successfully adapted the genre would not in itself prevent Ronsard from writing fine poetry – in any case the structure of the Pindaric ode has been appreciated only in fairly recent times: but he may have felt that the exceptionally elaborate external structure was not always matched by a correspondingly satisfying internal structure. In his early work there are a number of poems where the internal structure is defective – abrupt endings, fragmented sections, and so forth – and the Pindaric mode was particularly exposed to these dangers. In any case, Ronsard's search for imaginative complexity will look elsewhere than to metrical patterns of this type. However that may be, the Pindaric ode was not doomed to immediate extinction: several of Ronsard's followers, notably Sainte-Marthe, worked happily enough in the medium, and among Latin and Greek poets of the period, under the stimulus of Jean Dorat, its career is quite prosperous.

So Ronsard concentrated on the Horatian ode, to which he had turned long before the Pindaric experiment, though of course there are elements in the Horatian formula which are not all that remote from the Greek model. On the other hand, Ronsard is adding Jean Second's *Basia* (from the other end of the spectrum) to his sources of inspiration. In general, the Horatian formula allows a greater flexibility in rhythmic experimentation as well as a wider thematic range. The ode and the *odelette* rapidly become a favourite vehicle for his sensibility, and the successive editions of the *Odes* reflect the new preoccupations taking shape in his mind – the fifth book was added in 1552, with a revised edition in 1553, and the whole series appeared in a new edition in 1555. This is also the period in which he publishes his *Amours* and the sequels as well as the *Meslanges* and *Bocage*. All in all, a time of intense activity, in which the genre as such becomes less important, since Ronsard's sensibility seems at home in all these collections of 'familiar' and love-poems, though the later volumes will show a modification of taste brought about by acquaintance with poets such as Marullus, Catullus, Theocritus, and Anacreon.

In the first four books of odes, Ronsard has not yet attained full range of expression, and love themes are more often left to the *Amours*; but the poetry shows almost an *embarras de richesses*. In what is in a sense a polemic collection, the claims of learning are paraded against the *monstre Ignorance*; court poetry is not forgotten, and Ronsard develops the theme that poetry confers glory on the great; and there are other compositions, more personal, more reflective. What emerges among other things is a complex feeling for Nature – which becomes a dominant theme in contemporary poets, especially the Poitiers group. There are the traditional commonplaces, *rus* compared with *urbs*, anti-aulic sentiments, Nature as a source of solace and refreshment, and to all this will be added the harmonics of local patriotism. But there is also the poet who sees Nature peopled with the figures of classical antiquity and nymphs who help to express the various meanings he reads into Nature. His imagination tends to see Nature in terms of certain patterns and forces, and to these we shall return; his attitude is ambivalent, for at times he presents Nature as a sympathetic presence – so that the pathetic fallacy can come into play; but at others, he evinces a malaise, sometimes amounting to fear in the face of Nature in its more sinister workings (*A Denyse sorciere*). Though a fully matured attitude has yet to take form, several poems stand out: *A la fontaine Bellerie*, with its skilful blends of the themes of Nature and Glory; and more especially *De l'election de son sepulcre*, which is a technical *tour de force*. Created by a happy *contaminatio* of reminiscences from Propertius, Vergil, Theocritus, Horace, and Sannazaro, it expresses a steady flame of confidence in the conquest of time. The thematic lay-out is classical in its symmetry, the erudition is contained within poetic bounds, and the tricky metre does not impair the strangely dignified tone. This exquisite sense of balance and rhythm is also present in *A sa Muse*, where Ronsard's touch is sure in establishing the right relationship between metre and sentence structure and creating a satisfying pattern of stresses and flows. There is more than a hint of a gift for pictorial pattern, and poetic energy is often discharged strongly when two themes are developed side by side. In this early collection, then, the merits immeasurably outweigh the defects (over-ambitious metrical schemes, superabundant learning, structural weaknesses); there is a range and richness here, with a promise of the maturity that time will bring.

II. THE AMOURS

We have noted some of the causes of Petrarchan penetration into France about this time; Ronsard, ever a sensitive *écho sonore*, was bound to respond to its challenge, and all the more so as it offered such excellent formal incentives – though it is highly probable that a good number of love sonnets were written well before the publication of the *Odes*.[3] The Petrarchan mode also presented interesting problems in the relation between stylisation and emotion and the prospect of stimulating linguistic experiments within that style. There appears to be some emotional origin in Ronsard's meeting with Cassandre Salviati in 1545 or 1546 at Blois; but it is not overcynical to suggest that the potentialities of the sonnet became clearer after the success of *L'Olive*. Moreover, a fair number of the Cassandra poems have little or nothing to do with the lady, nor would many sixteenth-century poets make an issue of personal affection in lovepoetry. The personality of Cassandra does not emerge from the cycle, and she is often more a peg on which Ronsard can hang themes, attitudes, and emotions. A further preoccupation, as in the *Odes*, is the desire to shine at Court, and this may be one reason why Ronsard arranged for musical settings to accompany the poems at the end of the volume, for the sung poem was then popular at Court.[4]

The sequence opens with a rather disappointing sonnet that compares unfavourably with the opening *dizain* of the *Délie*, and more's the pity as LI would have served very well; here some of Ronsard's major qualities are already present: a fine gift of organising imagery, a mastery of rhythms, with timely *enjambements* and an acute sense of the links between metrical and sentence structure, an ability to communicate a feeling of vital force. Ronsard often sets his lady in a framework of Nature, as in this sonnet, and the imagic associations can be striking. As in the *Odes*, Ronsard's imagination tends to catch fire by the blend of two main themes: LVII and LXXVI offer good examples of this complex treatment.

Sonnet CXXVII also develops the love theme in terms of Nature classically conceived. The beloved's effect on surrounding Nature is of course a *topos*, but Ronsard makes fine use of it to express indirectly his attitude to the lady:

> Or que Juppin espoint de sa semence,
> Hume à longs traictz les feux accoustumez
> Et que du chault de ses reins allumez
> L'humide sein de Junon ensemence:
> Or que la mer, or que la vehemence
> Des ventz fait place aux grandz vaisseaux armez;
> Et que l'oyseau parmy les bois ramez
> Du Thracien les tançons recommence:
> Or que les prez, & ore que les fleurs,
> De mille & mille & de mille couleurs,
> Peignent le sein de la terre si gaye,
> Seul, et pensif, aux rochers plus segretz,
> D'un cœur muet je conte mes regretz,
> Et par les boys je voys celant ma playe.
>
> (Laumonier ed., IV, 123–4)

The final tercet is an obvious echo of a Petrarchan theme (*Solo e pensoso*) and one will easily notice rhetorical devices spread across the fabric of the sonnet. Moreover, the basic structure is an antithesis between the final tercet and the rest of the text. But Ronsard is not simply developing a Petrarchan contrast in which two statements are placed in opposition; the force of the antithesis is achieved by its very porosity: in other words, the final tercet is fed by the images and themes of the rest of the poem. It is obvious that the sonnet describes something far removed from Petrarchan love, and indeed many of Ronsard's sonnets take us beyond the traditions from which they have, at one level of composition, sprung. Here we have as powerful an expression of frustration in love as we are likely to find. Four themes are worked: Jupiter in one of his well-known mythological roles, the sea and wind in all their violence, the lurid motif of Philomela transformed into a nightingale after having been violated by Tereus, and finally the smiling countryside, a symbol of happiness and fulfilment. The Philomela image, which some critics have disliked, is precisely the expression of violent and unprincipled desire (cf. also *Thracien, grandz vaisseaux armez*); and Ronsard has quite deliberately recognised the destructive element of his urges and introduced it by antithetical image to complete the description of his *playe* which is thereby stripped of its conventional tarnish. The unleashing of Nature in the first section is contrasted with the muting of the poet's emotions in the final tercet. The sonnet in fact reveals in striking fashion two features of Ronsard's poetry, a vein of powerful sensuality that breaks through the Petrarchan veneer, and a consummate mastery in the selection and ordering of his images. This is a disturbing poem, intended to shock and jostle the reader's sensibility. These features explain in part the impression of greater immediacy conveyed by the young Ronsard's verse; but imagery, exploration of language, and exploitation of the dream also contribute their share. Ronsard no doubt follows many precepts of the *Deffense*; but he has a linguistic talent that is peculiarly able to reproduce movement, ensured by the persistent use of verbs, as well as through his command of rhythmic pattern. It has to be noted that the older Ronsard reduced the violence of many of the verbs he had earlier selected: thus, *pousser* is substituted for *darder*, *tomber* or *voler* take the place of *culbuter*.

One should not, on the other hand, suggest that a satyr is for ever lurking beneath the Petrarchan fleece; a sense of physical vitality is often present, but this can appear without sensual or sexual tones, and Ronsard is also capable of writing an impressive poem where Neoplatonic harmonics dominate: such as CLXXIV, which without perhaps showing Ronsard at his vintage best, is very far from negligible:

> Comme on souloit si plus on me blasme,
> > D'estre tousjours lentement ocieux,
> > Je t'en rends grace, heureux trait de ces yeulx,
> > Qui m'ont parfait l'imparfait de mon ame.
> Ore l'esclair de leur divine flamme,
> > Dressant en l'air mon vol audacieux
> > Pour voir le Tout, m'esleve jusqu'aux Cieux,
> > Dont ici bas la partie m'enflamme.
> Par le moins beau, qui mon penser aila,
> > Au sein du beau mon penser s'envola,
> > Epoinçonné d'une manie extreme:
> Là, du vray beau j'adore le parfait,
> > Là, d'otieux actif je me suis fait,
> > Là, je congneu ma maistresse et moi-même. (ibid., 164–5)

The poet has taken a well-known Neoplatonic theme, in which the loved one acts as a medium for the gradual dematerialisation of the lover; and this helps him to free his soul in part from the torpor of matter. Nevertheless, no specific source appears to have been followed, but once again what Ronsard has brought out is movement, the urge of the lover's soul towards the heavenly regions. Nearly all the imagery is connected with motion (*lentement ocieux*, *esclair* – later weakened to *rayon*, *Dressant mon vol*, *aila*, *Epoinçonné*). The pattern is thus one of accelerated, spiralling movement that ends in exultation.

The *Amours*, impressive collection though they are, do not give us a structured presentation of a spiritual journey under the aegis of love; many poems are in a sense autonomous and less concerned with values that take us beyond this world. They allow the poet to express his apprehension of beauty in ever widening circles of sensuous exuberance, an experience in which Cassandra herself becomes a pretext rather than a presence. The success of the collection was very great, and further poems followed (augmented edition, 1553; *Continuation*, 1555; *Nouvelle Continuation*, 1556).[5] One of the new subjects treated is Marie, but one must not overstress the differences in tone and style between the Cassandra cycle and the Marie sequence: both the *style élevé* and the *style bas et naïf* are conventions, with their own rhetorical norm; and though Ronsard, like some of his friends, reacts against the Petrarchan vogue, there is relatively little 'Nature' in the Marie sonnets, and simplicity creeps into those concerned with Cassandra, while just as many poems of the *Continuation* and *Nouvelle Continuation* are erudite and elaborate. Nevertheless, Ronsard is affected by fresh trends: the Neocatullan idiom enriched with the style of the Roman elegists and Marullus is fairly marked; more familiar and homely than the Petrarchan formula, it is reinforced by the vogue of Jean Second's *Basia*, nor should one forget that Marc-Antoine Muret, a close friend of the Pléiade, was at work on his edition of Catullus before he had to leave Paris in 1553. The presence of what are loosely known as the Greek anacreontic and pastoral poets is also of significance; and Ronsard has perhaps not forgotten his acquaintance with the traditional French *chanson*. In all this, the arrival of motifs such as time passing, of certain stylistic devices (diminutives, repetitions, *mignardise*) reveals some shift in taste; and at the same time, Ronsard is developing his treatment of the epitaph (*Bocage*) and also of descriptive poetry. Similar trends may be observed among contemporaries (e.g., the Poitiers poets' interest in pastoral, Belleau's exploring of *blason* poetry, and the anacreontic vein). Among Ronsard's recent compositions is the celebrated *Ode* to Cassandre:

> Mignonne, allon voir si la rose
> Qui ce matin avoit desclose
> Sa robe de pourpre au soleil,
> A point perdu, cette vesprée,
> Les plis de sa robe pourprée,
> Et son teint au vostre pareil.
> Las, voiés comme en peu d'espace,
> Mignonne, elle a dessus la place
> Las, las, ses beautés laissé cheoir!
> O vraiment maratre Nature,
> Puisqu'une telle fleur ne dure
> Que du matin jusques au soir.
> Donc, si vous me croiés, mignonne:

> Tandis que vostre aage fleuronne
> En sa plus verte nouveauté,
> Cueillés, cueillés, vostre jeunesse
> Comme à cette fleur, la vieillesse
> Fera ternir vostre beauté.
>   (Laumonier ed., v, 196–7)

The theme of time passing can first be found in *A Jeanne* (*Odes*), but here it reaches definitive form. Its mastery lies in a few simple elements, so much more difficult to fuse together than the complex. Ronsard takes a familiar *topos* (deriving from Ausonius and the *Greek Anthology*); and a comparison with Ausonius shows just what Ronsard has made of it. He takes the greatest care to identify the loved one with the rose, and the images associated with the flower are thereby determined (*robe, plis*); and in the third stanza the images are switched to the lady. This is an important feature, because it illustrates Ronsard's mastery of symmetry by inversion, which is only one of the ways in which he seeks a classical balance. Two other methods are: first, the discreet, but unmistakable, dialectical backbone: invitation, interjection of regret, explanation, conclusion; and second, the way in which the poem is made to rise and fall, the centre being a *fortissimo* flanked by a *crescendo* and a *diminuendo*. Some critics have thought line 10 damaging to the evenness of tone, but surely Ronsard is climbing from suggestion to irritation and regret, released by the broken rhythm of lines 7-8, and then he descends on a note of supplication. If weakness there is in line 10, it is perhaps that *vraiment* fails to generate the power demanded of it. In line 13 'si vous me croiés', taken by some as a *cheville*, serves both to show the lack of confidence in the poet and to guide the tone back to the quieter note on which the poem began. Breaking, it seems, with tradition, Ronsard has renovated the theme by conferring a greater immediacy through the use of direct speech addressed to the beloved.[6] This allows for a more subtle interplay of past, present, and future; and the persistent repetition of various words gives the text insistency, appeal, and incantation.

The shorter poems of this period are so rich and varied that it is difficult here to convey a fair idea of Ronsard's creative urge. There is, for instance, the volume of *Folastries*, where humour and learning often marry happily and where a more shaped attitude to Nature comes into view: a Nature whose permanence stands out against the transient character of mortal life.[7] The theme of old age is present, and sometimes casts a grey shadow. Nevertheless, this is essentially a period of love-poetry. Once we go beyond the screen of the Petrarchan tradition, we become more aware of the poet's irrepressible vitality; this, with the rapid maturing of his aesthetic sense, reaches definitive expression thanks to a sure awareness of pattern and organisation, though this does not necessarily mean a classical sense of form: Ronsard has often reflected the contemporary feeling for diversity in unity – the image of the *prées diaprées* recurs more than once in this context. Coherence of imagery; a gift of melodic control; blending of erotic themes with Nature, death, movement; an acute sense of rhythm; and a widening *vision du monde* – all this underlies a remarkable poetic achievement. This superabundant vitality may sometimes lead to lapses of taste, literary and linguistic, or to an incomplete fusion of the constituent elements, but they are not as numerous as the variants of the ageing Ronsard may incline us to believe.

III. THE PHILOSOPHICAL POET

Ronsard's poetic range is now about to extend very considerably; he becomes fledged as a philosophic poet or at any rate as a poet of philosophic intuitions, and this will also involve him in the exploration of new technical avenues. No doubt his reading of Marullus, whose *Hymni* were well known to him, played some part, but there is more to the matter. In Paris there is considerable philosophical and scientific ferment in the 1550s, and a number of poets, often working in Latin, try their hand at the scientific poem. In any case Ronsard had from the beginning accepted that Science and Poetry were sisters. His imaginative intuition of the world was growing rapidly; in consequence, any attempt to imprison Ronsard within the limits of 'lyric' poetry must make a fair assessment of his poetry impossible. Marullus's example was nonetheless important, and if his outlook was pantheistic, even perhaps pagan, Ronsard would be impressed both by the hieratic tone (which he had not brought off entirely in the Pindaric ode) and by the imaginative apprehension of the Universe which went beyond dogma. Critics have sometimes wondered whether Ronsard's intuitions do not verge on the unorthodox – he seems on occasion to have a Lucretian view of the relations between matter and form, he returns more than once to the question of metempsychosis, he is fascinated by dreams, astrology, prophecy; but at conscious level, Ronsard never seems to have found orthodox Christianity constricting philosophically, and indeed, impressed as he was with the fluidity and evanescence of things, a religion of tradition and firm doctrine may have offered him comfort and assurance. At all events, the *Hymnes* of 1555 are a milestone in his evolution, though one must add that many so-called elegies and epistles raise analogous questions.[8]

Ronsard's general ideas about the world remain broadly traditional and Christian with some enrichment from classical or neoclassical sources. He accepts the division into the sublunar world, the Universe beyond, and the intermediate region where the 'astres' have their influence. The eternal Universe, being beyond death, is also beyond movement:

> Tout ce qui est là haut, outre la Lune,
> Vit seurement, sans desfiance aucune
> De veoir son estre ou dissoubs ou mué
> *(Epitaphe d'André Blondet, Laumonier ed., X, 308–9,*
> see also *Hymne de l'Eternité)*

The source of the Universe, which also informs it continually, is God, the *primum mobile*, as Ronsard stated in the exordium to *Le Chat* or in the *Hymne du Ciel*, a poem which expresses his marvelling at the *ronde perfection* of the cosmos. Elsewhere he interests himself in the series of creatures that act as links between God and the sublunar world – spirits that live in His presence, or in 'les airs', and also the 'astres'. The subordinate gods appear to embody specific qualities (Eternity, etc.), whereas the Demons have functions to perform rather than incarnate a specific principle or force.[9] It seems that since man's soul retains some awareness of the divine soul and is capable of transcending its mortal frame, the Demons are present to initiate the soul into higher mysteries, which brings them into close association with the Muses. There is some imprecision in Ronsard's conception of the Demons, but at the very least one can say they are agents of communication and form an indispensable link in the Chain of Being.

In the sublunar world, Ronsard believes that our planet, subject to movement and time, but also to various forces that exist beyond (*Puissance, Discord, Paix,* etc.), has emerged from chaos, but is perpetually threatened with a relapse into that state. In the *Hymne de l'Eternité,* Ronsard dramatises this constant predicament of unstable equilibrium by means of two allegorical figures, Eternity and Discord. With this theme, he may develop those of the *monde cassé* in which France was living, and also of the Golden Age, though his concept of this era differs in a number of respects from traditional views. Man's fallen state is rarely evoked in terms of original sin; for Ronsard, the world is a place where man, in spite of everything, can develop his potential and which to that extent is made for him. However, he appears to accept considerable limitations on man's freedom by the forces exerted by various gods, such as Nature and Destiny, but he is careful to avoid impinging on the freedom of the divine will; later he defines cautiously the relations between God and Nature:

> Qui blasme ma Nature il blasme Dieu supreme
> Car la Nature et Dieu est presque chose mesme :
> Dieu commande partout comme prince absolu ;
> Elle execute et fait cela qu'il a voulu,
> Son ordre est une chesne aimantine et ferrée.
> *(Tombeau de Marguerite de Savoie,*
> variant published posthumously)

Like other Renaissance poets, Ronsard executes variations on the theme of Nature: sometimes he develops the idea of 'marastre Nature' which has favoured animals rather than humans and which opposes its own permanence to man's ephemeral being. At others, he seems to identify Nature and Venus, in so far as she is concerned with the continuation of the human species (*Hymne de la Mort*). But the 'astres' also play a substantial role:

> Chante moy du Ciel la puissance,
> Et des Estoiles la valeur,
> D'où le bon-heur et le mal-heur
> Vient aux mortels dés la naissance.
>> Soit qu'il faille dés lors
>> Regarder que nos corps,
>> Des mottes animées
>> Et des arbres crevez
>> Nasquirent elevez
>> Comme plantes semées,
> Soit qu'on regarde au long espace
> De tant de siècles empanez
> Qui, legers de pieds, retournez,
> Se suivent d'une mesme trace,
>> On congnoistra que tout
>> Prend son estre et son bout
>> Des celestes chandelles,
>> Que le Soleil ne voit
>> Rien ça-bas qui ne soit
>> En servage sous elles. . . .
>
> (*Hymne des Estoiles*, *1574*,
> Laumonier ed., XVII, 38)

This passage indeed shows that Ronsard's views on this topic had become firmer with age, for in 1555 he did not go further than claim the stars watched over the destinies of the eminent. At all times, though, he is concerned with the problem of determinism: now he thinks we can know so little of God's way, now he hopes that some indication may be given through astrology or some occult means. There is a superstitious vein in Ronsard, fascinated by divinatory practices, witches, magicians; and we find ambivalent attitudes in his poetry to the Universe: he may be enraptured by the one-ness of the creation, or he may express sharp anguish about human destiny. There might seem therefore to be a danger of his falling into a heretically deterministic view of phenomena or alternatively into some form of pantheism, and precisely at a time when Stoic doctrines were enjoying some currency in France. In practice, Ronsard resisted any determinist temptation, and all the more so after his brush with the Huguenots; and clearly much depended on his conception of the human soul. From the first Ronsard eschewed the Neoplatonic theory of pre-existence, and he establishes a clear distinction between body and soul, a distinction that becomes meaningful in his discussion of the demons whose power is limited to the body only. In one poem he asserts that man should do all in his power to circumscribe the influence which stars may have upon our temperament. At the same time he is aware that consciousness and feeling only occur when the soul can manifest itself through a body.

One may also wonder whether Ronsard's views on the soul and free-will did not vary as he aged. In *Le Chat* he appears to come close to suggesting that God's presence in everything makes the soul just part of the *grand tout*. With the passage of time, he develops more and more the theme that the form of things is unstable, but that matter persists beneath the forms it must inevitably take. In an epistle to Chauveau, Ronsard refers to the doctrine of metempsychosis, and though he does so in order to deny it, one gains an impression that he remains preoccupied with the theory. In the probably late *Elegie aux Bucherons de la forêt de Gastine*, he introduces a Lucretian coda:

> O Dieu, que veritable est la philosophie
> Qui dit que toute chose à la fin perira,
> Et qu'en changeant de forme une autre vestira . . .

and the 1587 edition of the *Hymne du Ciel* added the following lines (Laumonier ed., VIII, 147):

> Du grand et large tour de ta celeste voute
> Une ame, une vertu, une vigueur degoutte
> Tousjours dessur la terre, en l'air, et dans la mer,
> Pour fertiles les rendre et les faire germer:
> Car sans ta douce humeur qui distille sans cesse
> La terre par le temps deviendroit en vieillesse.

What is clear at all events is Ronsard's awareness of the interpenetration of things and the all-embracing force that irradiates everything. He gives the impression of experiencing a growing intuition of the world as something essentially vitalist, so that we may ask at times whether he is not straying into the no-man's land between firm doctrine and heterodoxy. We are of course in a period of syncretism, when humanists are endeavouring to harmonise varying philosophical strands, and in any case one must not blandly identify poetic statement with philosophical belief. Nevertheless, it may well be that Ronsard's maturing imagination fashioned for him an outlook which seems to loosen the philosophical structures he had taken for granted at the outset of his career, and yet without leading to any crisis of belief.

The *Hymnes* (1555) mark the first serious and massive attempt on Ronsard's part to widen his poetic range in the philosophical direction: instead of presenting experience as a series of more or less isolated moments, he sees it as part of a cosmic pattern. The *Hymnes* express these intuitions in the sustained style of a genre that ranked as one of the highest forms of poetry; and we must not forget that in these poems Ronsard is exploring the potentialities of the alexandrine. Nevertheless, these *Hymnes* are perhaps not an unqualified success. On the one hand, there is an evident difficulty in maintaining the dithyrambic tone over any distance, and on the other, whatever his intuitive powers, has he really got a philosophical turn of mind that is at ease in abstract discourse? In any case, his imagination is more inclined to develop organically proliferating structures than classical schemes of exposition. It does not therefore surprise me that Ronsard soon prefers the less exalted *poème* or the more homely epistle or elegy whose rhetorical norm is more congenial and tractable. Yet, limited though the poetic quality of the *Hymnes* may be, poetic quality there is; his imagination is fired in its apprehension of the unity of the cosmos (*Hymne du Ciel*) and he shines when he dwells on movement, on man's endeavour, or even on the role of death in the Universe. When he talks of the gods, he willingly draws on the armoury of allegory, to personify and therefore to dramatise; not that all these figures spring to life, but some like *Discord* stand out. Once again it is the forces coursing in the world that stimulate his imagination, whether they manifest themselves through the gods, or through the animals he is so good at portraying when he goes beyond the idiom of the bestiary or the *blason*. With his growing awareness of man's destiny comes also a certain historical dimension which allows him to move away from the present-day, shop-soiled world (*Isles Fortunées*, 1553). The *Hymnes* help to release some of the potential present in the *Odes*, give him the opportunity to develop his techniques on a broader front, and deepen his awareness of man's destiny.

IV. THE COURT POET

Not of course that the *Hymnes* are exclusively philosophical poetry; many of them are addressed to persons of high rank and authority and often contain a eulogy of the living that is more or less effectively hitched on to the main theme of the poem; and the composition on Justice (for the cardinal de Lorraine) is essentially a piece of high-flown court poetry. In fact, the court element, here and elsewhere, is so extensive that we must accord it some consideration.

Right from the start, Ronsard had stressed the courtly functions of the poet, no less than his predecessors the *rhétoriqueurs* had done, and his own literary activity is partly determined by this view. He shares, like other French humanists, the patriotic aspirations of culture and sees himself as under some obligation to praise famous men. Quite early on, he lauds the French Court with the help of mythological structures, a technique which, without being novel, serves to enhance its permanent significance and will in due course be richly elaborated by him. Under Henry II, it seems that Ronsard's own financial position was precarious; and this colours his views when he discusses the relations between king and poet. Some of his work (commissioned) conforms, on his own admission, to standards other than his own. Nevertheless, one notices an ambivalent attitude to the Court which cannot be conveniently explained by simple reference to the anti-aulic tradition in poetry which certainly flourishes in the sixteenth century.[7] After all, Ronsard received nothing from Henry II, and Henry III, whose Court Ronsard will sometimes satirise fiercely, did not take a very marked interest in the *prince des poètes*. On the positive side, Ronsard sees the poet, who is after all a seeker after truth, as one concerned with proper government; and he understands himself as forming part of the court machinery which helps the king and his entourage to cut a figure before a wider public.

Henry II's reign covers the period of Ronsard's formation and ripening. From the outset, the poet sought favour and patronage (e.g., *Avant-entrée, Ode de la Paix*, 1549); the *Franciade* is perennially dangled as bait; the *Amours* as well as the *Odes* serve to present his claims for consideration, and this is also true of the *Hymnes*, one of which is a paean of the king. But all in vain, as were his endeavours to gain the support of the cardinal de Lorraine. His approaches to Odet de Châtillon were rendered nugatory by the latter's conversion to Calvinism. In some *Hymnes* of this period, and also among the epitaphs,[11] we shall find tones of dejection and discouragement. Nevertheless, Ronsard is one of the poets, writing in Latin as well as in French, who contribute to the extraordinary outcrop of *plaquettes* celebrating the military events of 1558-59, the marriage of Mary queen of Scots to the Dauphin François, and other matters of concern to the Court. What he has to say suggests that his ear was 'close to the ground' and that he was, with others, a sort of spokesman for official policy. Some of the themes he develops in these poems (see Laumonier ed., vols. IX–XI) will find their way into a good deal of the committed poetry of the wars of religion.

Under Charles IX, things take a different turn; Ronsard's financial situation improves and the young king soon becomes, what he was always to remain, the poet's favourite monarch. It is not surprising therefore that Ronsard's court poetry will increase greatly in output, and all the more as the outbreak of the civil wars will provide a further stimulus. In addition to the politically 'committed' poetry (see below, pp. 313–16), Ronsard supplies commissioned verse, triumphal entries (though here his role is small), masquerades, and *cartels*, not major compositions of course, but developing gracefully the commonplaces of love, transience of life, the stages of man, and accompanied by music.[12] More important is the revival of the eclogue in this context, not only in pastoral form, but adapted to the needs of the political situation. The formal characteristics, fairly numerous, have to be observed rather strictly: limited number of characters, absence of female roles, presence of the judge to settle the issue, unity of theme on which all the participants discourse, pastoral setting. Very often the characters are thinly disguised presentations of royal personages (as in the Italian eclogue), so that the poem becomes a dramatised allegory of events connected with the Court. Now the *Deffense* had asserted the need for a revival of the genre, but without immediate response. Opinions are divided as to whether Baïf or Ronsard was first in the field; whatever the truth of the matter, Ronsard, who had introduced pastoral material into many of his *Odes*, first composed a full-blown eclogue in 1559, in connection with the double marriages settled *inter alia* by the Peace of Cateau-Cambrésis, so that the poem is essentially a form of epithalamium with pastoral trappings. Metrically and in matters of tone, one can see in the eclogue a rather formalised composition, the prolongation of the sustained style we found in the *Hymnes*. In 1563, Ronsard published two bucolic poems and a *Bergerie* for the celebrations of the carnival at Fontainebleau, so-called no doubt because it did not respect the conventions of the eclogues, but rather puzzling in that there is no record of the work being performed at Court. What is interesting in some of this court poetry is the way in which Ronsard's poetic world, the world in which he embodies certain values and attitudes, begins to take shape. Compounded of many sources, it creates a sort of intermediate existence between the harsh realities of everyday life and the next world, and we shall find its lineaments not only here, but in the *Franciade* and other poems (see below, p. 324).

One remarkable portion of Ronsard's activity, small in bulk, is that composed for the benefit of some other person. Some of these poems appear in the *Trois Livres des nouvelles poesies* (1563), though the finest will not be composed until Henry III's reign. It is almost certain that a number of these love-poems were written for the use of Condé; and there are court poems, scarcely involving the poet's feelings at first hand, which are outstanding for their literary worth – a fine example is the *Elegie* to Mary queen of Scots embarking for Scotland. In this poem the three chief elements, the queen herself, the castle, and the sea over which she is to sail, are brought together in a beautiful pattern of movement. More substantial in intention than in achievement is the *Franciade* (1572); the fact that Ronsard left it to drag on so long – it was never completed – suggests that his heart was not fully in it, and he was also hampered by Charles IX's wish that it be composed in decasyllables, after the poet had come to terms with the alexandrine. Only rarely does the poem come to life; the Vergilian machinery creaks ominously from the start, repetitions occur, and with the Chinese-box system of episodes, we find ourselves, like the Trojan vessel, taking an unconscionable time a-launching. The failure need not be explained by the argument that the epic was a worn-out genre; in fact, it had regained a certain popularity in Europe and for three centuries it will attract French poets, including Voltaire whose *Henriade* was his *violon d'Ingres*. Ronsard, however, does not have a gift for large-scale architecture, he has problems with the construction of his cantos, he does not make very much of his central symbol, and the thing simply peters out in shapelessness. And yet, there are some fine passages, when his imagination catches fire; indeed the poem provides us with a lot of insight into the workings of his poetic mind, but the fruit grows elsewhere.

During Charles IX's reign, Ronsard's notable activity appears in yet another genre: of the 84 elegies he wrote, 49 were composed during six years of the young monarch's rule. That many were written to order is clear not only from the context, but from a statement in his preface to the 1587 edition to the effect that if he had been a free agent, he would have composed shorter poems. Nevertheless, the elegy constitutes an important feature of his output, even though it is difficult to define the genre outside the Latin formula, where metrical considerations are relevant too. Ronsard himself remarks somewhere that the elegy has become a very free mode of expression, and he sometimes alters the title Elegy to *discours*. In his hands, therefore, it is not surprising that it becomes a loose formula giving him scope to say what he feels and thinks. There may be love elegies in a familiar tradition, he may also give vent to sad, 'elegiac' sentiments, but many are poems in which autobiographical and meditative elements loom large. Sometimes it allows us to see the emergence of Ronsard's satiric gifts; in short, the genre permits a very wide range of style, tone, and theme, and with its indeterminate length, it can be suited to a variety of moods.

Under Henry III, that is for the last twelve years of Ronsard's life, we note less court poetry flowing from his pen. In any case, he is ageing and less prolific than before; but his stock in high quarters is poorer and he adopts a sharp satiric tone against court life in a way that he had not done previously, even in poems of an anti-aulic flavour. Nevertheless, he is still active in court circles: quite apart from the rivalry with Desportes, he is involved with Baïf in the creation of the Academy founded in the hope of exercising cultural influence upon the course of events, though we are ill-informed on the details of Ronsard's participation.[13] Then, we know that he wrote for Henry III a number of love-poems, when the latter had fallen violently in love with Marie de Clèves. The 1578 collection contains poems on this princess, both quick and dead. Some of Ronsard's finest love-poetry is thus composed on behalf of another, though perhaps it is tinged with Ronsard's recaptured memories of another Marie. The most famous of the set is the following sonnet (*Sur la mort de Marie*, IV, Laumonier ed., XVII, 125):

Comme on voit sur la branche au moys de may la rose,
  En sa belle jeunesse, en sa premiere fleur,
  Rendre le ciel jaloux de sa vive couleur,
  Quand l'Aube de ses pleurs au poinct du jour l'arrose;
La grace dans sa fueille, et l'amour se repose,
  Embasmant les jardins et les arbres d'odeur;
  Mais batue ou de pluye, ou d'excessive ardeur,
  Languissante elle meurt, fueille à fueille desclose.
Ainsi en ta premiere et jeune nouveauté,
  Quand la Terre et le Ciel honoraient ta beauté,
  La Parque t'a tuée, et cendre tu reposes.
Pour obsèques reçoy mes larmes et mes pleurs,
  Ce vase plein de laict, ce panier plein de fleurs,
  Afin que vif et mort ton corps ne soit que roses.

Not for the first time does Ronsard develop the theme of the rose; but here it is linked with actual death, not an anticipated one. Yet this does not prevent him from investing the text with an ever greater density of imagery to evoke the richness of natural beauty. These images do not serve to contrast past and present, for the poet deliberately repeats them, now as real objects in a votive offering, to make the theme come full circle. The persistence of essence after death is strongly affirmed, and we are far from the valley of tears. Ritual and aesthetic distance have combined to remove us from any display of mourning, any emphasis on personal loss, and paradoxically the poem works less as an epitaph than as a lullaby. As so often in Ronsard, much of the poem's impact stems from an exceptional mastery of rhythm and sound: the *carmen* has become a *charme*, partly through subtle balance of clause, but also by intentional repetition of key words (slightly varied), often at the rhyme, and the cycle of life and death is consciously underscored by the final line where the votive offering serves as a link, thus blurring in some measure the distinction between the two.

V. THE COMMITTED POET

Clearly, Ronsard's courtly activity helped him to widen his range, formally, perhaps also in his outlook, certainly in a satiric direction. This broadening of his thematic horizon was brought about in large measure by the outbreak of the religious troubles, and he published several 'committed' poems of some length in the early years of Charles IX's reign.[14] The first work to appear was the *Institution du roy chrestien* (c. 1561);[15] developing a series of generalities, it alludes only fleetingly to the Huguenots, perhaps to some extent to avoid exacerbating a delicate political situation. We are given a portrait of the ideal ruler, drawn in part from the humanist current of Erasmus, Guillaume Budé, and Michel de l'Hôpital, but also prompted by

Ronsard's awareness of the fierce ambitions of families such as the Condés or the Guises. The poet presents himself as the upholder of traditional virtues, with the principle of kingship never in question, and with orthodox religion bringing spiritual unity into harmony with the political unity of the country.

Between the appearance of that work (1562) and the *Discours des misères de ce temps* (composed ? May, 1562), events had taken a nasty turn (massacre of Vassy) and Ronsard advocated a strong line against the Huguenots; his arguments were developed in more strident tones in the *Continuation* and the *Remonstrance au peuple de Paris*, texts which soon drew Calvinist fire. Stung by their rejoinders, he felt obliged to reply in his *Response aux injures* (1563). His defence reiterates the basic principles of the *Institution*; Ronsard's deep distrust of the people is reflected not only in his acceptance of divine right, but in his élitist view of culture, though in these pamphlets he will have to adopt a view of poetry that reaches a much wider public. He doubts the value of individual reason, which leads to a multiplicity of sects and of gospels spreading to all and sundry. He views with dismay the threat of intervention from outside, and points gleefully to the discrepancy between Huguenot precept and practice. At the same time, Ronsard has to clarify somewhat his religious position, though he spends little time on doctrine: as a Catholic he would prefer to leave dogmatic matters to those better qualified, the theologians, but his imagination tends to move away from the abstract towards a more concrete, dramatic utterance. He admits that not all is right in the Catholic camp, but he opposes root-and-branch standpoints that destroy tradition, both good and indifferent. Ronsard, like so many humanists of his generation, is an eager partisan of orthodoxy and conservatism.

We must therefore not expect too much from Ronsard's contribution to the ideological debate, and we should look elsewhere for his artistic achievement in the field of committed poetry. It is not negligible, though we can hardly expect him to express the tortured vision of a D'Aubigné. There is a poet of death, dissolution, and even putrefaction in Ronsard, but he does not give us so intense a tableau of the *monde cassé* as does the author of *Les Tragiques*, who nevertheless owes so much to his predecessor. There is still something of the optimist in him, the world does not seem to him to be beyond repair, and France appears to him, as it does to Michelet, as a person. His imagination, for all its Christian elements, is richly coloured by the classical world; and it is significant that at the beginning of the *Remonstrance* he admits that, were he not certain of his faith, he might well have become a pagan. This poem, above all, gives an impression of far greater personal involvement: Ronsard is reacting to slights upon his person from the Calvinists, he is also defending a policy that belongs to a monarch for whom he felt a great deal of affection, but he is also upholding, in addition to religion, a certain conception of humanism. Finally, it seems, in a situation where he is being taunted by the Calvinists for an attitude to literature which is too 'aristocratic', he is only too keen to show his paces as a 'committed' poet. In consequence, we are not surprised to find a powerful imaginative urge welling up in this poem and parts of the others that belong to this group. Of course, the student of Vergil has not forgotten his lessons: thus he makes much play of the extended comparison, but as happens in other aspects of his work, the imaginative vitality of the second element of the comparison often leads the poet to stress the point of departure less than the immediate context might require, and on the way sheds much light on certain 'constants' of Ronsard's imaginative apprehension of the world. A good example occurs in a passage where he is counselling more repressive action against the Huguenots; he introduces a comparison by way of illustration, but here one may well feel that his imagination is caught up in the element of comparison for its own sake:

> Comme ces laboureurs dont les mains inutiles
> Laissent pendre l'hyver un toufeau de chenilles
> Dans une fueille seiche au feste d'un pommier:
> Si tost que le soleil de son rayon premier
> A la fueille eschauffée, & qu'elle est arrosée
> Par deux ou trois fois d'une tendre rosée,
> Le venin qui sembloit par l'hyver consumé,
> En chenilles soudain apparoist animé,
> Qui tombent de la fueille, & rempent à grand peine
> D'un dos entrecassé au milieu de la plaine:
> L'un monte en un chesne & l'autre en un ormeau,
> Et tousjours en mangeant se trainent au coupeau,
> Puis descendent à terre, & tellement se paissent
> Qu'une seule verdure en la terre ne laissent.
> Alors le laboureur voyant son champ gasté,
> Lamente pour néant qu'il ne s'estoit hasté
> D'étoufer de bonne heure une telle semence:
> Il voit que c'est sa faute, & s'en donne l'offense.
>
> (*Continuation du Discours*,
> lines 351–67, Laumonier ed., XI, 55–6)

For the comparison to hitch into its proper context (the Calvinists seen as a plague allowed to prosper through untimely carelessness), these caterpillars ought to be presented in a more loathsome light; in fact, Ronsard the lover and observer of Nature has caught their progress in a splendid vignette. We know from other passages that he was fascinated by the caterpillar, as by the serpent, which reproduce a form of movement he also found so fundamental in water – undulation. Given the context in which he was writing, one might have expected the presence of rather more biblical elements – though it is fair to add that the *Continuation* contains some apocalyptic features. From the epic tradition, Ronsard also learns about the use of direct speech, *prosopopœia*, and invocation *Prosopopœia* forms part of Ronsard's technique of the allegorical portrait, in which he may pull off an impressive success, as in the descriptions of *Opinion*, when he is trying to convey his distrust of human reason. In his sketches of Calvinists, whom he sees, dramatises, and caricatures, he seizes on the vital detail, the revealing gesture, the automatism of the character; and behind his portrait there lurks his own moral conviction or indignation that imparts tone and movement. Ronsard's imagination is always pulling him away from the abstract and the 'logical' towards the concrete and the living; moreover, his mastery of classical rhetoric and of the alexandrine is now very sure, as one may grasp from the following brief extract:

> Hà, qui voudroit, cafard informer de ta vie,
> On verroit que l'honneur, l'ambition, l'envie,
> L'orgueil, la cruauté se paissent de ton cœur,
> Et s'yvrent de ton sang, comme l'Aigle vainqueur,
> Dont l'immortelle faim, par nulle chair domptée,
> Se paist safre et goulu du cœur de Prométhée.
> Tu n'as pas, en changeant d'habits et de sermons
> Changé de sang, de cœur, de foye, et de poumons,
> Et tu monstres assez par ton orde escriture
> Que, pour changer de loy, n'as changé de nature,
> Ny ne feras jamais, bien que d'un habit saint
> Tu caches ta pensée et ton courage feint.
> (*Response*, lines 647–58, Laumonier ed., XI, 150)

Behind the manifest use of enumeration and the judicious presence of the epithet, one soon notices the close relationship between rhythms and the repetition of certain words at various places in the line (e.g., *cœur, changé*); the careful symmetries, or the real *coupe* of the line cutting across the hemistich, the prominence given to the important word at the caesura (e.g., *jamais*), and so forth. The strength of the passage derives here not so much from imagic development (so often the case in Ronsard) as from movement. Ronsard's success may be judged both from the reactions sparked off in the Huguenot camp and from the way in which his style influenced Catholic poetry of committed character. From another standpoint, one can see how Ronsard in the field of satiric poetry forms the link between Marot and D'Aubigné.

VI. THE LATER POETRY

In the last years of his life, Ronsard produces only one major collection of poems, the *Sonets pour Hélène*[16] – the *Franciade*, as we have seen, earned him no more than a nominal success; on the other hand, he devotes much energy to revising the complete works, and we shall also find impressive poems, often satiric, in the *Bocage royal.* The Hélène cycle, which in some editions contains poems that did not originally belong, was published in 1578, but Ronsard had embarked on some of the sonnets ten years earlier, and one can detect a general difference of tone between the two books. The emotional source seems thin enough, Hélène being a rather dreary blue-stocking, but there is also the literary rivalry with Desportes, whose star was then in the ascendant and who was one of the leaders in the revival of Italianate taste at Court. The sonnets to Hélène reveal a more mature Petrarchism: some of the elements have been more thoroughly assimilated, but tempered by an explicitly stated anti-Petrarchan attitude, by the evolution of his own taste and temperament, and no doubt by the urbanity of *salon* life. Ronsard's attitude towards Hélène is a mixed one, often detached and sometimes critical; and the Petrarchan conventions have been widened to include some rather different sentiments, indeed the collection is distinguished by an unusually extensive range of tone and theme. Ronsard also shows his mastery of the alexandrine of which he is now in complete control. Of course, quite a lot is made of the parallel between Hélène and Troy, though this association does not often occur in the finest sonnets, and Ronsard may show some of his essential qualities in poems where the classical decoration is at its most discreet:

> Le soir qu'Amour vous fist en la salle descendre
> Pour danser d'artifice un beau ballet d'Amour,
> Vos yeux, bien qu'il fust nuit, ramenerent le jour,
> Tant ils sceurent d'esclairs par la place respandre.
> Le ballet fut divin, qui se souloit reprendre,
> Se rompre, se refaire, et tour dessus tour,
> Se mesler, s'escarter, se tourner à l'entour,
> Contre-imitant le cours du fleuve de Meandre.
> Ores il estoit rond, ores long, or'estroit,
> Or' en pointe, en triangle, en la façon qu'on voit
> L'escadron de la Grue evitant sa froidure.
> Je faux, tu ne dansois, mais ton pied voletoit
> Sur le haut de la terre; aussi ton corps s'estoit
> Transformé pour ce soir en divine nature.
>
> (II, 1)

We are in a more urban world here than in that of Cassandra; the *salon* has replaced Nature, and a fair sprinkling of sonnets contain a firm element of wit. The sonnet, to be sure, gets off to a somewhat trite start: the first two lines are straightforward statement, the next two try, not very successfully, to refurbish a Petrarchan conceit. Then, in the second quatrain, things come to life, violently, and the momentum is maintained until the end; in the second tercet, the movement turns upward, and the whirl of the dance has literally and metaphorically taken the loved one into another dimension, so that the poet, though fascinated by the movement of the tableau, opens his mind to something more than kinetic delight; movement implies transformation. This movement, that recurs so often in Ronsard's poetry, whatever the period to which it belongs, is grasped here in the most accomplished fashion; it is also found, with a very different tempo and tone, in one of the most famous of his sonnets:

> Quand vous serez bien vieille, au soir, à la chandelle,
>   Assise aupres du feu, devidant et filant,
>   Direz, chantant mes vers, en vous esmerveillant,
>   Ronsard me celebroit du temps que j'estois belle.
> Lors vous n'aurez servante oyant telle nouvelle,
>   Desjà sous le labeur à demy sommeillant,
>   Qui au bruit de Ronsard ne s'aille resveillant,
>   Benissant vostre nom de louange immortelle.
> Je seray sous la terre, et fantaume sans os:
>   Par les ombres Myrteux je prendray mon repos:
>   Vous serez au fouyer une vieille accroupie,
> Regrettant mon amour, et vostre fier desdain.
>   Vivez, si m'en croyez, n'attendez à demain:
>   Cueillez dès aujourd'huy les roses de la vie.
>
> (II, xxiv)

Here the themes of love, glory, and death blend together. Ronsard thinks of the passage of time (*carpe diem*), but he also realises how poetry may conquer time. He is not unmindful of his own passing, as the first tercet makes splendidly clear; but he is caught up in the vision of old age in which he presents Hélène and her maidservant in a fine garland of images, but also in cadences and rhythms that associate themselves easily with the lethargy of old age. Beneath it all there lies desire, yes, but without the angry frustration we have seen in some poems; instead we have an unmistakable serenity ending on a note of confident persuasion rather than of peremptory command. The sense of distance is maintained, not only by the device of the vision, but by the removal of all familiar address to the loved one herself; and in any case, the poet is more conscious of old age than in the earlier love sequences. With this awareness there creep in other motifs which concern the reality or otherwise of love. In the previous sonnet Ronsard had remarked that 'S'abuser en amour n'est pas mauvaise chose', and elsewhere he seems to sense that the relations between dream and reality are falling apart, and he will resign himself to the failure of the enterprise. The final deliverance is expressed in a memorable *Elegie*, which also shows Ronsard's preoccupation with Nature, stronger than even earlier. If in these poems the sensation of failure peeps through – failure in love, failure at Court, failure of the *Franciade*, failure of certain values in a France rent by civil war – we have in this poem themes and insights whose utterance seems ahead of its time: the detailed descriptions,

freed from the more obvious stylisation of a literary tradition, the
satisfaction afforded by solitude, homely *tableaux* in which the
colouring of classical legend has passed quietly into the penumbra.
But, of course, we still have organised observation, for Nature is seen
as both picture and movement. This sensitivity to Nature persists in
other late poems, such as the well-known *Contre les bucherons de la
forêt de Gastine*, in which feeling for the countryside and plant life,
satiric shafts, classical allusion, and finally Lucretian meditation
combine to form a finely controlled pattern. The last few lines repeat
that awareness of the flux of things, of which the poet had apparently
become increasingly conscious:

> Que l'homme est malheureux qui au monde se fie!
> O Dieux que veritable est la Philosophie,
> Qui dit que toute chose à la fin perira,
> Et qu'en changeant de forme une autre vestira:
> De Tempé la vallée un jour sera montagne,
> Et la cime d'Athos une large campagne,
> Neptune quelquefois de blé sera couvert.
> La matiere demeure, et la forme se perd.
>   (Laumonier ed., XVIII, 146–7)

And in his later poetry, urbanity and poetic control go hand in hand
with a subtler use of language whose referential quality becomes even
more complex and iridescent.

VII. RONSARD'S POETIC WORLD

So far we have given some account of the different aspects of
Ronsard's poetry as they fit into a career whose course is determined
not only by inner creative urges, but by court requirements and the
intrusion of the civil wars upon the scene. There is undoubtedly an
evolution in Ronsard's poetry and in his taste; but even so, there are
also elements of his poetic vision which, when allowance is made for
fluctuations and the divers conditions that apply to each genre or
style in which he was writing, can reasonably be called 'constants'.
It is indeed rather important to be aware of the special qualities of
Ronsard's imagination, for it is these that set him apart from his
contemporaries and indeed above them. He is not merely the poet
of love, or a court functionary or a patriot speaking out in troubled
times; over and above all this there is a poet whose imagination has
explored areas on which any outlook on life must be built.[17]

Ronsard seems to have been aware of his imaginative activity
from early on: he refers to his youthful habit of peopling Nature
with satyrs and nymphs, and if he did not go so far as William Blake
who saw angels on a tree at Peckham Rye, he considered his imagination to be 'saturnine' and 'fantastique'. We shall see that this

imagination does try to create a world that is, as it were, between everyday existence and pure fantasy – he was suspicious of Ariosto's 'excesses' in this field; but at the same time, Ronsard tends to apprehend reality in certain dimensions and registers, which seem often to be what certain critics would term 'archetypal' but which also take us to the confines of reality and dream. There is in Ronsard a poet who is always trying to go beyond himself, to break through the normal categories by which we intuit existence, and who apprehends things imaginatively in a richer way than in the intellectual formulations (often contradictory) which stud some of his writing.

If we examine Ronsard's imaginative grasp of Nature, leaving aside his explicit utterances on *natura naturans* or *naturata*, and so forth, we shall soon notice that it manifests itself especially along three axes. If we take them in inverse order of importance, relatively speaking, the first is sound. For Ronsard, one sign of death or limbo is silence: he talks somewhere of 'sombres silences' and he describes Chaos as void of sound. In any case, for the Poet *la Parole* must be a central preoccupation, and Ronsard considers that a man incapable of music must be inaccessible to higher truths. And when he gives an impression of some natural phenomenon, he stresses where it is possible its acoustic qualities: birds sing, but so does water, and fame is a sound across Time.

Perhaps even more important is light, with warmth as its concomitant. There is a poet of the Sun in Ronsard, and he was aware of it himself. One can of course find literary and philosophical antecedents for solar themes in Renaissance poetry – Petrarchism and Neoplatonism both contribute – but in Ronsard the sun, in particular, enjoys a place of privilege that cannot be accounted for solely by contemporary fashion or concern. It is not merely that the sun itself inspires Ronsard to speak in a special tone:

> Soleil, source de feu, haute merveille ronde,
> Soleil, l'Ame, l'Esprit, l'Œil, la beauté du Monde
> (Laumonier ed., XIII, 110)

He goes rather further: on the one hand, he associates sun and light with other themes which mean much to him: love, peace, immortality, the absence of fear, the opposite of darkness and ignorance; it often occurs in connection with the motif of gold which appears in the love-poetry, in praise of youth and of course in visions of the Golden Age. And on the other hand, Ronsard's linguistic inventiveness can be fired by the solar theme, and such an occurrence is surely a touchstone in the matter.

Most prominent, however, is Ronsard's inclination to observe phenomena in terms of movement. This feature has caught the attention of a number of critics in recent years, and very rightly.

At primary level, we notice the pure delight taken in movement for its own sake; time and again, Ronsard will linger over some scene in which movement predominates, the departure of a vessel, the prancing of a horse, the pleasures of swimming. Nevertheless, he has a marked preference for certain kinds of movement: thus, though context compels him on occasion to describe the sea in considerable detail, he is not always reassured by the forces it can unleash, and on the other hand, he rarely has time to portray lakes or pools, for he likes movement that steers a middle course between violence and stagnation. This fascination with unhurried movement is very often expressed in his descriptions of water: for him, as he remarked once, water and fire are the two elements that appeal to him. But water and movement often have a further character which increases their appeal: they are apprehended in terms of undulation, and here we come to another feature of Ronsard's imagination which is his interest in the curve, perhaps even more than in the circle. The circle, in harmony with traditional ideas, represents perfection, immutability, and eternity; but the uncompleted circle, the curve, appears more persistently in Ronsard's poetry. The curve appears usually associated with another feature or concept: thus it may be symbolic, when seen in the form of the bowl, urn, or goblet, of fertility – whereas the bottomless pit, the *gouffre*, signifies the *néant*; but as we shall see shortly, the 'inflated curve' may be associated also with less desirable concepts, so that Ronsard is bringing into use a valuable ambivalent symbol. The other feature that often appears is movement with the curve, so that an undulatory quality is evoked. This characteristic is present in a great number of Ronsard's descriptions of water; but it underlies his fascination with billowing smoke, clouds, serpents, even caterpillars. What we have here, in the last analysis, is an intuition of life (through various Nature phenomena) which is felt as movement of a certain type and tempo. Water naturally becomes a pervasive symbol of life in its continuity, but also in its fluidity and its changeability, in other words of the contradictory and ambiguous character of existence. And this attitude on Ronsard's part finds its way also into his love-poetry, as may be seen in a sonnet from the Cassandra cycle (LXXVI).

This central interest in movement, which can often be enriched by the light and sound motifs, is also closely allied to other principal concerns in Ronsard's poetry. In the first place, the poet is fascinated by phenomena that are connected with assimilation or osmosis; this is reflected, for instance, in his frequent use of imagery suggesting flow, melting, distillation, and which serves to express communication, coming to life, going beyond the individual. These images, which to some extent belong to traditional sources (e.g., Petrarchism), occur with an expected frequency in love-poetry and in descriptions of Nature; but they form part of a rather larger complex of imagery that penetrates into other areas of experience. Images of absorption and of envelopment occur in *De l'election de son sepulcre* (Laumonier ed., II, 101ff.); and others, involving hunger, eating, devouring, recur at different periods of Ronsard's development too. What is interesting about them is not only their persistence and their appearance with cognate imagery, but also their capacity for verging on the ambiguous: images of enveloping suggest fusion and togetherness by assimilation (frequent in love-poetry), but they are very close to images of devouring which occur in passages where destruction is the theme. Similarly, the process of melting can be understood as a stage towards rebirth or fusion, it can also signify 'melting away' and the image moves then in the direction of dissolution. But whatever way may be taken by these images, they point to an awareness in Ronsard that life involves movement and change, and preferably the blending with something beyond.

It is therefore understandable that Ronsard should have been obsessed with the matter of metamorphosis. Matter may be continuous in principle, but it seems unable to maintain one particular form for any length of time:

> Rien ne peut estre
> Longuement durable en son estre
> Sans se changer incontinent
> (Laumonier ed., I, 209)

otherwise it would become dead and lacking in sense. His interest in the subject cannot be adequately explained in terms of the contemporary vogue for the *Metamorphoses*; we have already noted a passage on the subject from a very late poem, and Ronsard shows an interest here and there in metempsychosis. He likes to introduce Ovidian themes of metamorphosis into his poems, and he very often expresses the wish, in his love verse, that he could be transformed into some person or object, again a motif that has literary ancestry, but is developed with greater insistency than a conscientious fidelity to models would require. When he refers to 'Mon desir/Qui en vivant en cent formes me mue' (Laumonier ed., XV, 198), he is going beyond cliché, and some of the shapes he would like to assume can be very revealing (water, cloud, etc.). In this love-poetry, he is thereby attempting to go beyond his personality which is by definition ephemeral and also incapable, it seems, of satisfying the *innamorata*. Metamorphosis, or the desire for it, suggests some discontent with present reality. The chain: desire – metamorphosis – illusion is a perfectly logical one; and it brings us precisely to the third *leitmotiv*, the whole problem of the relations between illusion and reality, *paraître* and *être*.

Ronsard adopts different approaches to the fluid, mutable quality of life. He may accept it in the anacreontic poems and dwell on the reality of the instant; more usually, he may prefer to insert some principle of continuity into life: hence the importance of the theme of glory which transcends time, but this is not a conviction that supports Ronsard at all times. Another course open to him is to harness man's power to create illusion in order to solace himself: no more than the previous technique will it guarantee success, but it is worth trying, and Ronsard experiments at different levels. We find it in the love-poetry, when Ronsard, 'heureusement de [s]oymesmes trompeur', tries to create a mirage or illusion as a substitute for reality: the technique is essayed in the Cassandra cycle, but it recurs in the sonnets for Hélène, where he appears to be resigned to the fact that illusion will be more meaningful than the reality of Hélène's feelings. And even if the counter-theme is sometimes developed, what is significant is the fact that Ronsard is working along these lines at all. But there are some interesting poems, whose value Ronsard himself, sharing perhaps contemporary suspicion of the imagination, was apt to play down, but which bring out very clearly his temptation to enter the no-man's-land between dream and reality. The motif of the cloud recurs more than once in his poetry: in the Hymn on the Demons, he uses clouds as one element in a comparison with them: admiring their intermediate state between Heaven and Earth, and their capacity for assuming different shapes constantly, but also for their movement without metaphorical implication. Moreover, there are two poems, from different periods of his life, in which the clouds assume the major role: the earlier one, a *folastrie* (*Le Nuage ou l'Ivrogne*), allows for imaginative scope because the *persona* viewing them is a drunk man; but a drunk man can be understood as one who, through stimulus, has gone beyond his normal self and entered a fantastic world. In *Les Nues ou nouvelles*, the fascination exerted by their shapes and motion is still present, but they are also connected with falsehood and rumour: the clouds are insubstantial and on the point of evaporating, but they can produce rain, and like the news, affect people. Elsewhere the cloud is associated, in the context of the Titans, with *hubris* and *enflure*. If one brings all this evidence together, one can see that the cloud, an intermediate phenomenon physically speaking, becomes an ambivalent symbol for self-expansion, but also inflated importance and illusion or error. Nor is it the only central symbol that bears on this area of experience. We have seen that water, for very evident reasons, has a great flexibility or polyvalency; and wind is another. Very often, of course, the wind serves to illustrate the vanity of this world, and Ronsard also associates it with the misfortunes of war and anger; but it appears in conjunction with water to induce the undulating movement that Ronsard finds so attractive:

the wind breathes vitality into the water which otherwise would be stagnant. Here the symbolism can verge on the domain of plenitude and expansiveness (curves of fertility), but even so the margin between plenitude, evaporation, and dissipation is perilously thin. *Enflure*, as the trite phrase 'enflé d'orgueil' has it, can be linked easily with over-inflation, and therefore pride, ambition, and illusion. In the Hélène cycle, it is no coincidence that the fable of Ixion infatuated with Juno should be symbolised by the cloud, which combines the ideas of presumption and illusion.

This ambivalency is reflected equally in the allegorical portraits Ronsard traces of *Renommée* (about whose permanence the poet often entertained doubts) and two others who resemble *Renommée* very closely, Victory and Fortune: the themes of appearance, iridescence, wind, and illusion come very close in these contexts. But there are other very suggestive passages, where Ronsard introduces the theme of what one might call the 'inflated curve', and which bear on the nature of creative art. There is a memorable *Elegie du verre* in which he offers on the one hand an impression of glass associated with light, love, wine, joy, and on the other a description of glass being created 'du seul vent de son haleine ouvriere' by a great Cyclops. The relations of wind and form that constitute so important an aspect of Ronsard's imagination reappear here in the specific context of artistic creation; and the theme is present in his descriptions of bagpipes and of the lyre, a musical instrument that frequently symbolises poetry for him. Significantly on one occasion, he refers to the instrument's 'ventre orgueilleux', the source of its splendid sounds; and yet are we all that far from the symbolism of *Renommée*? No, all the more so as poetry and fame are closely linked in the Renaissance poet's mind. One gains the impression that Ronsard, without perhaps achieving anything like a conscious formulation along these lines of what art is about, may have had intuitions about poetry, whose 'illusion' is a means of creating an order which the everyday world does not provide and which can 'perpétuer', as Mallarmé says, the valued experiences relating to that world. Nor is my reference to Mallarmé fortuitous: in the Symbolist poet, there is also a poetry of the fruitful, inflated curve (the 'mandore', the grapeskins of the *Faune*), and moreover these symbols are linked with poetry that uses itself as a subject of its verse. A great deal of Ronsard's poetry is concerned with the Muses, the act of poetry; and in the imaginary world he has created and peopled with demigods, demons, nymphs, heroes, and gods, it is not surprising to find that among the gods represented, those associated with the arts (Orpheus, Mercury, Bacchus) enjoy a privileged role.

In this poetic world, Ronsard has expressed intuitions on life which run deeper than his explicit statements; at intellectual level it is easy to pick out the contradictions and hesitations, and critics have also pointed to Ronsard's preoccupation with problems that lie at the limits of orthodoxy (dreams, astrology, prophecy, for instance). In his imaginative apprehension of reality he is able, by means of archetypal symbolism, to express and embrace life in all its contradictions. His world is characterised by an immense vitality in the first place: Ronsard loves to portray its diversity and iridescence (the *prées diaprées*). But he is also concerned to express man's attempts to enter into fruitful communication with that world; he is a poet increasingly aware of the richness and complexity of his responses to life, which in his eyes is change, diversity, discontinuity too, expansion and going beyond oneself, sunlight, dream, but also the source of poetry.

Historically, Ronsard's role is fairly plain to see. The Pléiade succeeded in restoring to a position of dignity the role of poetry in contemporary society, and this by a concerted programme, based on fidelity to valid traditions, and by a poetic activity on a very broad front. But when all is said and done, the achievement of the Pléiade is primarily that of Ronsard himself; no other poet of the group has his stature, range, or stamina. His imagination is fashioned on a far larger scale than some assessments of his work would lead us to believe; and what is equally important, he had the gift of poetic language in a measure unrivalled by any contemporary. In his earlier works his intuitions are often accompanied by remarkable powers of linguistic vitality, not only in the choice of imagery, but in the handling of syntax's articulate energy and also in the invention of new words. As time wore on, Ronsard took increasing pains to polish and revise his poetry, and the different editions of the *Œuvres* published in his lifetime are a precious sign of his evolving taste. Opinions have varied on the poetic value of the innumerable variants, the late omission of youthful poems, the various orders into which the poems may be put. His late corrections do at times suggest a prudish solicitude, sometimes a preference for the cliché, but they also remove the roughness and the over-erudite initiative of the Pléiade enthusiast; so that the later variants, though they may tame too fiercely the exuberance of youth, do at their best enrich Ronsard's exquisite sense of harmony and line in the structure of his poems. A notable example is the well-known 'Marie, levez-vous, vous estes paresseuse' (*Continuation des amours*, 1555, Laumonier ed., VII, 140). The 1584 version, leaving aside intermediate *états*, is substantially different, so much so that one can talk of a new poem. Both texts are impressive, but the shifts of emphasis are noteworthy. In the first tercet, the essential alteration seems to stem from the poet's wish for orthodox *alternance* and also for a different rhyme scheme – the early version gave the impression of a $4+4+4+2$ structure; even so *jurastes, jurastes vos yeux* is stronger than the original, though line 11 introduces, possibly, an air of slight preciosity. *Marie* replaces *Mignonne*, *doucement* is substituted for *frisquement*, the latter change reflecting the desire to reduce angularity of tone. The starts of certain lines are, on the other hand, more vigorous in the 1584 text: *Sus debout* is more striking than *Debout doncq*. *Harsoir* may have appeared a trifle archaic to Ronsard towards the end of his life, and he may also have felt that the repetition of *hier* did not carry any real weight. In this sonnet, there has been both profit and loss, but the sonnet to Cassandra 'Franc de raison . . .' (*Amours*, Laumonier ed., IV, 89) seems to me to have suffered by the undoubted dilution of vigour in the revision: the more powerful images tend to vanish, and the final lines are weakened by the substitution of a thoroughly trite maxim for the original *pointe*. This particular poem, though not vintage Ronsard, is instructive in showing how sensitive the poet was to the consequential alterations necessitated by some variant. Generally, these latter-day changes show Ronsard concerned with the attainment of *legato*, preferring urbanity, polish, and understatement to violence and becoming ever more interested in the temper and tone of the line.

Nevertheless, very few poets can claim to possess the vitality that was his at the height of his powers. The range of his imaginative insights, his mastery of so many moods and genres, his daring and sensitive exploration of language, and his quite exceptional sense of verbal music and pattern, all these qualities place Ronsard in a privileged position, not only in Renaissance France, but in the broader course of French poetry.

NOTES

1. Editions: the *STFM* ed. prepared by P. Laumonier, and completed by R. Lebègue and I. Silver, 18 vols., 1914–70 (reproduces text of first editions); Pléiade ed. in 2 vols. by G. Cohen, 1950 (gives 1584 ed.); *Œuvres* of 1587, ed. in 4 vols. by I. Silver, Paris and St Louis, 1966–68. On the life see, *La Vie de Pierre de Ronsard*, éd. crit. by P. Laumonier, 1909; and P. Champion, *Ronsard et son temps*, 1925. M. Dassonville's *Ronsard. Etude historique et littéraire*, Geneva, I, 1968 and II, 1970, is still in course of publication. P. de Nolhac, *Ronsard et l'humanisme*, 1921, is still useful. On other aspects, see I. Silver, *The Intellectual Evolution of Ronsard*, vol. I, St Louis, 1969 (three vols. to follow); G. Gadoffre, *Ronsard par lui-même*, 1960; M. Raymond, *Baroque et Renaissance poétique*, 1955; D. B. Wilson, *Ronsard Poet of Nature*, Manchester, 1961; L. Terreaux, *Ronsard correcteur de ses œuvres*, Geneva, 1968; Elizabeth Armstrong, *Ronsard and the Age of Gold*, 1968; R. E. Hallowell, *Ronsard and the Conventional Roman Elegy*, Urbana, 1954; A. L. Gordon, *Ronsard et la Rhétorique*, Geneva, 1970.

2. Though the lineaments of such an assessment appear in the fine insights of G. Gadoffre, op. cit., and H. Weber, op. cit.

3. On Ronsard's love-poetry see: F. Desonay, *Ronsard, Poète de l'amour*, 3 vols., Brussels, 1951–59; H. Weber, op. cit.; D. Stone, *Ronsard's Sonnet Cycles*, New Haven and London, 1966; A. Gendre, *Ronsard poète de la*

conquête amoureuse, Geneva, 1969. The first ed. of the *Amours* appeared in 1552, with the fifth book of Odes (Orléans, BM); see ed. by H. and M. Weber (Garnier), 1954.

4. On Ronsard's connections with music, see *Ronsard et la musique*, special issue of the *Revue musicale*, 1924; J. Tiersot, *Ronsard et la musique de son temps*, Leipzig and Paris, 1903; H. Prunières, 'Ronsard et les fêtes de cour', *Revue musicale*, 1924; N. C. Carpenter, 'Ronsard's *Préface sur la musique*'; *MLN*, 1960.

5. *Amours*, 1553 (BM, BN), *Continuation* (BN), *Nouvelle Continuation* (Ars).

6. In the poem by Ausonius, direct address occurs in the last couplet of a poem that is much longer than Ronsard's.

7. The Ars has a copy of this exceedingly rare volume.

8. The *Hymnes* appeared in three parts (BM, BN). In addition to A.-M. Schmidt's thesis on scientific poetry and H. Weber, *La Création poétique*, see two articles by I. Silver: 'Ronsard's Reflections on Cosmogony and Nature', *PMLA*, 1964, and 'Ronsard's Reflections on the heavens and time', *PMLA*, 1965. Recently the seasonal Hymns have been engaging critical attention, and very rightly: the reader is advised to peruse these texts that tell us so much about Ronsard's imagination.

9. See A.-M. Schmidt's ed. of the *Hymne des Daimons*, 1939.

10. See P. M. Smith, *The Anti-courtier Trend*.

11. M. de Schweinitz, *Les Épitaphes de Ronsard*, 1937.

12. M. C. Smith, 'Ronsard and Queen Elizabeth', *BHR*, 1967.

13. See F. A. Yates, *The French Academies of the Sixteenth Century*, 1947.

14. P. Perdrizet, *Ronsard et la Réforme*, 1902; F. Charbonnier, *Pamphlets protestants contre Ronsard (1560–1577)*, 1923; and H. Weber, *La Création poétique*; *J. Pineau, *La Polémique protestante contre Ronsard*, STFM, 2 vols., 1973.

15. Original ed. in Ars.

16. Modern ed. M. C. Smith, *TLF*, 1970. The sequence first appeared in the *Œuvres* of 1578. On Ronsard's relationship with Desportes, see articles by Mary Morrison and C. Faisant in *BHR*, 1966; see also G. Castor, 'The theme of illusion in Ronsard's *Sonets pour Helene* and the variants of the 1552 *Amours*', *FMLS*, 1971.

17. The following observations are developed in a chapter contributed to a volume edited by Dr Terence Cave on Ronsard and published in 1973 by Methuen.

PART IV

PART IX.

Chapter 11

THE WARS OF RELIGION

I. HISTORICAL OUTLINES FROM 1559[1]

WITH the death of Henry II, we enter a period of French history which, for all its turmoil and disruption, has a certain unity. It is the period when Henry II's children reign successively until the assassination of Henry III; it is also the period in which everything is dominated by the emergence of Calvinism as a political force in France; and this is reflected in the literary activity of these decades, when the crisis of Renaissance humanism is deepened by the polarisation of religious and political attitudes, which also help to promote literary activity beyond the already very broad areas cultivated in the 1550s. It is finally a crisis of central government, whose outcome will foreshadow the absolutist monarchy of the seventeenth century.

When Henry II died prematurely, he left France in a parlous condition. Weakened by economic depression and the financial consequences of an over-ambitious foreign policy, threatened by religious dissension within and potential enemies abroad, the country had yet other difficulties to face. Henry II left a family of sons all under age, so that Catherine de Medici, his widow, was bound to assume more authority than would otherwise have been the case; moreover, there were several factions at Court. More powerful with the passing of time were the Guises (Lorraine), ambitious, fanatically religious, and eager to meddle in foreign policy; then there were those associated with Anne de Montmorency, who served the royal family well over the years and who, for all his faults, was more prudent and moderate than the Guises. He himself was unambiguously orthodox, but some of his nephews had espoused the Calvinist cause, and a number of nobles had also declared their sympathies. Some of these were no doubt actuated by other motives too, at a time when the economic and political authority of the local nobleman was being progressively eroded; and the ambitious prince de Condé's flirting with Calvinism was not innocent of political opportunism, quite apart from the Bourbons' animosity against the upstart Guises. When the wars of religion broke out, these tensions were bound to come to the surface. In due course, Catherine made strenuous efforts to maintain some *via media*, as is symbolised by her appointment of Michel de l'Hôpital to the Chancellorship; he was a humanist of distinction, with a moderate political outlook, but his wife was a Huguenot. Catherine's own position was not enviable, and all the more so because of her Italian origins. Her task, in principle, was clear enough; she must maintain the authority of the monarchy and ensure some balance between the various forces threatening it, a task which she performed with varying success. However, her day was not yet come, for when Francis II succeeded to the throne, the Guises, whose niece Mary queen of Scots had married the king when he was still the dauphin, took matters into their own hands, and the harsh policies on the home front were continued from the previous reign. Their severity, as revealed by the suppression of the *conjuration d'Amboise* (1560) in which Condé played some part, provoked a reaction in favour of greater toleration; but in any case, matters were altered by the death of Francis II towards the end of 1560. Catherine was appointed regent for two years, during which time she sought to counter the Guises by the recall of Montmorency, and to grant some measure of official recognition to the Huguenots, whose first Synod had taken place in 1559 (*Colloque de Poissy*, 1561; and Edict of Toleration, January 1562). This softening of attitude precipitated the hostility of the Guises, but also of Montmorency and other members of the Court, some of whom formed a triumvirate to defend the interests of the Catholic religion; moreover, the massacre of Vassy (1562), probably sparked off unintentionally, envenomed relations between the partisans of the two religions. Guise then seized Charles IX who was joined by his mother; and within a short time the wars of religion had officially begun.

Space does not allow for a proper description of the intricacies of a religious and political situation that was constantly being modified by the personal interests of the individuals and parties involved, but the wars can be broadly divided into major phases. The first covers the years 1562–70, during which three of the wars took place (August 1562–March 1563; September 1567–March 1568; September 1568–Peace of Saint-Germain, August 1570). During this period some important protagonists are killed: Montmorency in action (November 1567), Condé murdered at Jarnac (March 1569). The fortunes of the Huguenots fluctuate; beginning well, they lose ground, then latterly Coligny, in many ways the spiritual leader of the Huguenots, comes to exert considerable ascendancy over Charles IX. Catherine persists in her moderating policies, but playing from a position of weakness, such moves as she made elicited sharp reaction from the party most affected; it was therefore no surprise that Michel de l'Hôpital had to demit office as Chancellor in 1567, when attitudes became irretrievably polarised; only very much later will the middle-of-the-road outlook of the *politiques* command effective support (see below, p. 335). Towards the end of the decade, a more restrained attitude on the Catholic side, fostered by Catherine, does inspire the Peace of Saint-Germain which grants the Protestants the best deal they had so far enjoyed: but the diehard Catholics felt that appeasement had gone far enough, and given the privileges accorded to the Calvinists in various parts of France, others too might think that the political consequences of such religious independence were very risky.

Then intervened another factor, in that Charles IX, anxious to be rid of his mother's apron-strings, sought further military action by planning an attack through the Netherlands against Philip II whose growing power was causing anxiety. Charles was supported in this by encouraging noises from the Low Countries, but chiefly by Coligny, now a firm favourite with the king. This situation inevitably aroused violent opposition from the Catholics and the Regent Catherine, but Coligny managed to keep the initiative. However, he had made too many enemies and his death was plotted. An attempt on his life (22 August 1572) failed, but it probably unleashed the reactions that led to the massacre of Saint-Barthélemy (24 August), which spread in due course to the main regional towns. The Protestants stiffened their opposition in the south-west during what became the fourth war: its most signal event was the fruitless siege of La Rochelle, the Calvinist stronghold, and it ended with the Peace of La Rochelle (June 1573); the Edict of Boulogne (July) granted freedom of conscience to the Huguenots and also gave them the right of worship in specified towns. Charles IX, whose final days were disturbed by the military posturing and intrigue of the duc d'Alençon, died at the end of May 1574, partly, it was believed, through remorse at his conniving at the Saint-Barthélemy.

Charles was succeeded by Henry III, at that time king of Poland and unpopularly so. When the latter returned in September 1574, there was plenty of trouble in store for him: the Huguenots were already in ferment in the Midi, furthermore they had the growing support of the *politiques* led by Danville, one of the sons of Anne de Montmorency and an opponent of the Guises; and this support was ratified, as it were, by the agreement of Milhaud. In addition, reinforcements were forthcoming from John Casimir, Elector Palatine, whose troops joined up with the Huguenots; Henry III, in no position to offer effective resistance, agreed to the *Paix de Monsieur* (1576), which gave the Huguenots terms even more favourable than had the Peace of La Rochelle and restored to the *politiques* some of the power and prestige they had lost towards the end of Charles IX's reign.

This victory carried the seeds of further trouble, for the Catholics, bitterly resenting the extension of freedom of Huguenot worship, set about forming the *Ligue* under the leadership of the Guises. The *Ligue*, though paying lip-service to popular representation as well as accepting the patronage of the king, was nevertheless an expression of loss of confidence in the monarchy; in addition it came to be seen as a means of furthering the fortunes of the Guises; and finally, it reinforced a tendency, already evident in earlier wars, to call upon foreign aid, which the *politiques* viewed as a serious threat to national unity and identity. The *Ligue* enjoyed the backing of Pope Gregory XIII and Philip of Spain; and its ideology was strengthened by the principles of the Counter-reformation. With the emergence of the *Ligue*, war breaks out sporadically in what are known as the sixth war (ending in the Peace of Bergerac, September 1577) and the seventh war (April–November 1580), after which the Peace of Fleix reaffirms the terms agreed at Bergerac. The interests and aims of the parties involved were far from clear-cut, and religious labels often masked personal ambition; one prominent maverick is the duc d'Anjou (formerly the duc d'Alençon) whose ambition leads him to join and then to defect from the *politiques* and whose scatter-brained hopes in the Netherlands were terminated by a haemoptysis in 1584. His death was perhaps more important than his existence, for the heir presumptive to the throne was now Henry of Navarre, a Huguenot. This change of situation kindled the embering activities of the *Ligue* into something more dynamic; and this in turn sharpened the conflict between Henry III and the Guises. By the treaty of Joinville (1585), the *Ligueurs* negotiated with Philip II who agreed to support their cause and the claims to the throne of the cardinal de Bourbon; they then launched their manifesto in March 1586 which asserted the rights of the Catholic monarchy, but also appealed to popular feeling by its statements on taxation and the States General. Henry III, in spite of his fierce distrust of the *Ligue*, felt it prudent to subscribe to its positions (treaty of Nemours, July 1586) and to annul the various measures of toleration hitherto enjoyed by the Huguenots; his decision was also motivated by his opposition to Henry of Navarre. In these circumstances, the outbreak of the eighth war was inevitable, and two main aspects of this stage can be noted: on the one hand, some indecisive fighting in which Joyeuse is defeated by Henry of Navarre at Coutras, and in which later German troops sent to help Navarre are worsted (Vimory, Auneau); and on the other, the flare-up of the conflict between Henry III and the Guises. The duc de Guise, in spite of royal injunction, enters Paris (*Journée des Barricades*, 12 May 1588), and then the king, retreating to Chartres, plots the duke's death (23 December). In consequence the *Ligue* takes up arms against Henry III, with Paris in their full support; Henry is forced to seek alliance with Henry of Navarre, and acting in concert, they improve their military position, but before Paris is seriously threatened, Henry III dies of a stab wound inflicted by Jacques Clément, a *Ligueur* Dominican (2 August 1589).

Henry IV's reign lies beyond the scope of this volume, but it is he who brings the wars of religion to an end and rebuilds the unity of France. His conversion to Catholicism, the military defeat of the *Ligue*, the diplomatic handling of various powerful noblemen, the settling of accounts with Spain, and also a careful oversight of the country's economy (thanks in great part to Sully), all these factors help to restore the fortunes and prestige of France; but it took years for the heir to Henry III to assert his authority fully throughout the country; in a sense he never overcame all opposition, nor did the full consequences of his husbandry emerge until after his death by assassination.

Henry III's reign was a major disaster, in which the unity of France was threatened more than ever before and the kingship suffered an immense loss of authority. The country was, inevitably, in a state of great economic distress and disruption; the Court, in spite of moments of brilliance, was viewed with suspicion, partly because of the *mores* of the king and his minions, on which D'Aubigné has left us a brilliant, biased, but first-hand account in *Les Tragiques* and the *Histoire Universelle*. The maelstrom brought into its orbit interested foreign parties who further endangered the unity of the country. In spite of all this, certain currents noted earlier were not destroyed and indeed they come to the surface again by the end of our period. In the *Satire Ménippée* (see below, pp. 472–4) we have the work of several humanists deeply concerned about the destiny and tradition of their country; for them order is more important than extreme principle, and their xenophobia is the inevitable concomitant of their patriotism. They represent the true *politiques* or *modérés* and carry on the ideals of Michel de l'Hôpital and his friends; it is perhaps no coincidence that the Chancellor's *sermones*, in six books, were published in 1585 and again in 1592. The very state of chaos, by reaction, will soon accelerate the process towards absolutism: lawyers in universities, the closer ramifications of the administrative network, the pressures of the Counter-reformation (including the emphasis on divine right), the evolution of the magistracy, all these elements will work in favour of centralisation.

Not that the Counter-reformation gets under way in France as rapidly as elsewhere. The decrees of the Council of Trent which had wound up its proceedings in 1563 were not accepted in France until 1615, though other countries had shown greater alacrity; and the expulsion of the Jesuits for a period under Henry IV no doubt reduced the growing momentum of the Society. Nevertheless, the impact of Jesuit colleges – not only the Collège de Clermont (1564), but those founded on the periphery of France (Douai, Pont-à-Mousson) – was far from negligible, and the University of Paris took umbrage at the Jesuits' thrusting policy in the early 1570s. More significant at the time was the general spread of devotional literature, renewed interest in the Church Fathers, the attention paid by the Court, and especially Henry III, to religious matters, closer links with Italy, where piety had taken on a new and more sincere look, through the efforts in part of Cardinal Borromeo; and also no doubt, the very reaction engendered by the fervour of the Huguenots. The Counter-reformation probably sets up, in some degree, cultural barriers with the Protestant countries and the classical spirit, manifesting itself in literature as a desire for order, will be reinforced by connections with the meridional countries. But all this is still very much *in posse* while the turmoil of Henry III's reign rages. The Valois, with their last sickly representatives, go out in violence and disruption, and the pieces cannot be put together again overnight.

If we go back to the 1560s and consider the intellectual and cultural background, we shall note that the currents already flowing under Henry II continue to exert their pressures; and in surveying the activity of the Pléiade, we have up to a point described aspects of the reigns of Charles IX and Henry III. Nevertheless, there are still two cardinal factors that give further dimensions to the cultural scene: on the one hand, the role of the Court becomes very much more important than it was under Henry II, and on the other, the outbreak of the wars of religion will not only introduce new themes into genres already flourishing, but will promote the growth of new areas of literary activity, in which the sense of contemporary relevance is naturally developed to a high degree. We shall consider the implications of the Court for poetic evolution in particular in a later chapter, but it may be suitable to say something immediately about the entry of Calvinist values.

II. CALVINISM AND ITS RELEVANCE
TO LITERARY DEVELOPMENTS

It is difficult to know where to draw the line in discussing the relevance of Calvinism to French literature: some Huguenots left France in the mid-stream of their literary career, certain works seem to be more important than others, from the *French* standpoint, and there are prominent authors who, in spite of their Protestant outlook, remained more obviously within the French literary purview (e.g., in the field of neo-classical tragedy) or continued to reside in France during our period. Some writers shifted their religious allegiance, in others it would be over-ambitious to equate their Calvinism with their literary practice, though a Huguenot of profound conviction would surely wish to subordinate literary flourish to his religion. At the same time, we must not try to draw too many Swiss currents into the French orbit;[2] what we shall attempt here is to sketch out, first, Calvin's work in so far as it comes into the realm of literature; second, outline the Protestant view of literary activity; and finally mention the areas in which the Calvinists contributed to genres, themes, or techniques, mentioning as we go along practitioners whose merits should not be ignored. Authors who belong clearly to the mainstream of French literature are mentioned elsewhere. Broadly speaking, the Calvinist presence becomes significant after 1559 or so: Calvin's *Institution* goes back earlier, of course, but it is with the firm establishment of the Calvinist Church in France (Synod of Paris, 1559), the final edition of the *Institution* revised by the author (1560), the outbreak of the wars of religion, and the consolidation of structures in Geneva that Calvinism really gains momentum at literary level.

III. JEAN CALVIN (1509–64)[3]

This is not the place to describe Calvin's theological outlook, which has been competently expounded by many theologians; he earns his niche here first because he is the pioneer in shaping a Calvinist conception of literary activity, and second, because his own vernacular writings constitute a landmark in the development of French prose. Calvin's energy was prodigious: in addition to his *magnum opus*, the *Institution chrestienne*, he published commentaries on the sacred texts, polemical treatises and tracts for the times, letters and sermons, though these were handed down by scribal transcription and therefore have rather less value as primary texts, so far as their literary value is concerned. Certain tracts, like the *Traité des reliques* or the *Excuse aux Nicodémites*, in which Calvin inveighs bitterly against those who temporise and sit on the fence, are excellent illustrations of his range of writing, but the *Institution* remains his life work. Before he had abandoned his Catholic faith and turned to the writing of this book, Calvin had enjoyed the humanist training of the 1520s: he had studied at Montaigu which left the mark of scholastic thinking on him, though he did not follow Ignatius de Loyola in the latter's migration to Sainte-Barbe, he had known the Paris of Erasmian humanism, and he had studied at Orléans and Bourges, where he had not only undergone a full legal training, but had come under the influence of Melchior Wolmar who was soon to exert an influence on Théodore de Bèze, his close collaborator in later Genevan days. Calvin's humanist formation is reflected in his edition of Seneca's *Libri duo de clementia* (1532). The stages of Calvin's conversion are obscure, but must be sought in the humanist circles of Orléans, Bourges, and Paris, in those crucial years *c.* 1530 which so affected the religious evolution of countless humanists. By the end of 1535, Calvin had completed the first, Latin version of his *Christianæ religionis Institutio*, as it was first called, and in the following year it appeared in Basel. Three years later, a much enlarged edition, embodying a wider doctrinal range, was published in Strasbourg; but the text was still in Latin, and it was in 1541 that the work appeared in French. No doubt Calvin, like many reformers, was aware of the need to bring religious discussion to a wider public by the use of the vernacular; but he also reflects the shift in attitude towards the vernacular that we have detected in the early 1540s in such different persons as Etienne Dolet and Scève. At the same time, the fact that Frenchmen were very conscious of the rapid evolution of their mother tongue – which involves the problem of intelligibility – has not escaped Calvin; but the consequence of his act was to bring theology down into the arena of discussion, and the Catholics will in due course have to follow suit, to some extent at least.

The *Institution* will be continually revised by its author until the last edition he personally supervised (1560); it will also be very substantially increased over those twenty years or so, and though controversy has raged over the extent to which later editions were the work of Calvin or his collaborators, recent opinion tends to accept Calvin's dominant role. Whatever the precise truth of the matter, the edition of 1541 is from our point of view the most important, both as a landmark in the emergence of French literary prose and as an organic structure.

In Calvin's eyes, the importance of an authoritative statement of position could hardly be underestimated: he was in the process of setting up a new Church and his rejection of Catholic tradition meant that he must supply the foundations of a new authority. Certain tenets were crucial: God's will and predestination, the role of Christ the redeemer, justification by faith, man's fallen nature and the problem of evil, the divine choice of the few for salvation; in addition, these and other articles of belief were to be affirmed on the evidence of the Scriptures, taken in their entirety. Theologians have pointed to the difficulties raised both by the doctrines themselves and by the total acceptance of Scripture; these need not concern us here. What is clear is that the *Institution*, in Calvin's eyes, is a work devoted to explaining the meaning of the Bible – he does not see himself as the creator of theology – and of making it acceptable to as many people as possible. These assumptions naturally have considerable bearing on Calvin's views about literature and the techniques that should be employed in the pursuit of his aims. He combines artistic humility, in that he is convinced that the author should not come between God and the reader, and an awareness that the reader needs to be persuaded. Calvin's main position may appear monolithic and uncompromising, but there is in him a man very sensitive to the workings of human psychology; for instance, he did not have so cut and dried a hostility to the theatre as some of his followers, he took rather the view that plays could be both beneficial and harmful and was prepared to judge according to circumstances. A similar sensitivity to realities is found in his practical reaction to specific problems: it was later Calvinists, not himself, who moved firmly against the presence of bishops in the structure of the Church.

For Calvin, therefore, art has a place in human existence, but one must be very clear about its functions: the author acts as a vessel of communication between God and mortals, and not as a screen, and Calvin would be horrified to think otherwise:

Il n'est pas icy question de leur opinion ou de la mienne. Je montre ce que j'en trouve en l'Escriture. Et ne me suis pas hasté d'en faire une resolution sans y bien penser plus de troys foys. Qui plus est, ce que je dis estant notoire, nul ne peut dire le contraire sans nier pleinement la Parole de Dieu. Car je ne dis rien de moi, mais je parle par la bouche du Maistre, alléguant tesmoignages esprès pour approuver ma doctrine depuis un bout jusqu'à l'autre. (*Excuse aux Nicodémites*, in *Three French Treatises*, ed. F. M. Higman, 1970, p. 141)

What he is developing therefore is a Calvinist rhetoric, in so far as the word retains its original meaning of the 'art of persuasion'. Though he will owe more than he might consciously concede to classical rhetoric, Calvin makes the Bible the main source of his style, or more properly, styles. Self-conscious ornamentation, diverting classical harmonics, undue elegance, all these must be avoided; as he is reported to have declared on another occasion:

Et cependant notons ce qui est écrit en sainct Pierre, c'est à savoir que notre ornement est intérieur.

His whole effort will therefore be put into making God's message accessible to as many as possible and to denouncing, by contrast, those in whom he sees the enemy of the Gospel.

Calvin's first problem is therefore one of intelligibility. He is dealing with a wide range of philosophical or abstract concepts, often hitherto confined to theological circles, he is using a vernacular within which the linguistic equivalents have, in many cases, to be stabilised at a time when the language appears to be developing so fast that contemporaries feared they might not be understood by their children. To handle this problem a number of techniques have to be employed, of which the first perhaps is definition. In any case, Calvin conceives his task as one of linguistic elucidation ('What does this word or phrase in the Bible really mean?'), and the philologist in him is well equipped to cope: of course, where he can he likes to

stress the clear nature of the original text, which may be reinforced
by further testimony:

Tout ceci se voit encores plus clairement aux autres Prophètes (I, 105)

or various reasons adduced will make recognition of some point 'aisé'
(I,121). But if problems do arise, then Calvin may use one or more
devices: definition of a word or of a doctrine, and he may introduce
further affective guidance towards the suitability of a particular
definition:

Or afin que cecy ne soit dit à la vollée, il nous faut définir le péché originel.
Toutesfois, mon intention n'est point d'examiner toutes les définitions de ceux
qui en ont escrit; mais seulement j'en donneray une, laquelle me semble
conforme à la verité. (II, 16)

and here Calvin inserts the contrast: plurality of definitions (therefore erroneous) × the single (true) definition. He may then go on to
break the definition into its parts and analyse them separately: so
that he employs the techniques of reduction to identifiable and
comprehensible parts and of logical pattern. No doubt here his rhetorical and legal training has stood him in good stead, and examples
abound:

Il nous faut maintenant expliquer le troisième article: c'est que nous avons
dit que la penitence consiste en deux parties, en la mortification de la chair
et la vivifaction de l'Esprit. (III, 72)

And his analysis will be conducted in a series of points that are made
to flow one from another and to lead to a conclusion that is seen to
be evident and theologically right. Calvin's technique thus stresses
clarity and order, which are either obvious from the start or become
so as a result of the points being analysed and classified.

There is thus a strong intellectual structure to Calvin's writing,
and critics have been quick to seize on this feature; from there it is
but one step to point to a certain lack of warmth as a corollary. It is
true that Calvin resists the outpouring of emotion, and in any case he
prefers to let the Scriptures speak for themselves as far as this is
possible; but this does not mean that he avoids ways and means of
gaining the reader's sympathy by techniques that are not exclusively
'intellectual'. He takes as his norm the average man in the street,
and he watches his probable reactions very closely. To begin with,
plain speaking on a footing of equality, so that a bond is established
with the reader, while the others are placed in a different perspective.
This device, exploited frequently in the 'polemic' texts, is used to
good effect also in the *Institution*, when Calvin is attacking philosophers or Catholics; and if we are all sinners, nevertheless we are
better placed to hear unvarnished truth than thinkers who embellish their ideas and therefore warp them:

Or selon que l'Escriture, se conformant à la rudesse et infirmité des hommes, parle grossièrement, quand elle veut discerner le vray Dieu d'avec ceux qui ont esté faussement controuvez, elle l'oppose specialement aux idoles; non pas qu'elle approuve ce que les Philosophes ont inventé avec belle couleur, mais pour mieux descouvrir la sottise du monde, mesmes pour monstrer que tous pendant qu'ils s'arrestent à leurs spéculations sont hors du sens. (I, 120)

Pejorative language will be used to characterise the enemy:

Mais je laisse pour cette heure ces pourceaux en leurs estableries. (I, 72)

And the simplicity of the divine message will be affirmed, with the contrasting complications introduced by the false thinking of opponents:

Cest argument seroit desja assez amplement deduit, n'estoit que les Papistes nous barbouillent.... (I, 137)

But in order to ram home a point, an appeal will be made to homely experience and illustration; the reader is identified with certain virtues of commonsense and native intelligence which are contrasted with the intellectual convolutions of blunt-minded adversaries. At the same time, care must be taken to avoid two pitfalls: on the one hand, variety of tones and rhythms is essential, if an alert interest is to be ensured, and this is no doubt the reason why Calvin makes considerable play with questioning and exclamation; and on the other, the reader is not simply a target to be bombarded passively, he must have room for come-back, and here Calvin adroitly uses the technique of inserting objections which may be made, perhaps by some opponent, but no less frequently by someone very similar to the reader or listener. This not only breaks the rectilinear development of the argument, but takes into account the imagined reactions of the audience.

Calvin's use of some of these points will be seen better in an extended passage, where we shall note how his intentions are translated into grammatical and stylistic means:

Par ce moyen la defense frivole que plusieurs prétendent pour couvrir leurs superstitions. Car il leur semble, quand on s'adonne à servir Dieu, que toute affection, quelque desreiglée qu'elle soit, suffit. Mais ils ne notent pas que la vraye religion doit estre du tout conforme à la volonté de Dieu, comme une reigle qui ne fleschit point, cependant que Dieu demeure tousjours semblable à soy, et qu'il n'est pas un fantosme qui se transfigure à l'appetit d'un chacun. Et de fait, on peut voir à l'œil, quand la superstition veut gratifier à Dieu, en combien de follies elle s'enveloppe comme en se jouant. Car en retenant soigneusement les choses dont Dieu prononce qu'il ne luy chaut, elle rejette ouvertement ou mesprise celles qu'il recommande comme précieuses. Parquoy tous ceux qui dressent des services à Dieu à leur poste adorent leurs resveries seulement, pource qu'ils n'oseroyent ainsi apporter à Dieu des menus fatras, sinon que desjà ils l'eussent forgé en leur moule semblable à eux pour approuver leurs inventions. Parquoy S. Paul prononce qu'une telle conception qu'on a de Dieu, vagabonde et erronée, est ignorance de Dieu; 'Pource que vous ne cognoissiez point Dieu, dit-il, vous serviez à ceux qui n'estoyent point Dieu de nature' (Galat. 4, 8). Et en l'autre passage il dit que les Ephésiens estoyent du tout sans Dieu, du temps qu'ils estoyent esgarez de celuy qui l'est à la verité luy seul (Ephés. 2, 12). Et n'y a pas ici grande distance entre les deux, pour le moins en ce poinct, c'est de concevoir un dieu ou plusieurs, pource que tousiours on se destourne du vray Dieu, et quand on l'a délaissé il ne reste plus qu'une idole exécrable. Par ainsi nous avons à conclure avec Lactance qu'il n'y a nulle religion si elle n'est conjoincte avec la verité. (I, 65)

This passage from Book I, iv, 3 is based on the contrast between the believers in false gods or superstition and true religion; and it shows how Calvin develops in tandem the techniques of the 'intellectually manifest' and various emotive effects. One of the first things to strike the reader will probably be the sentence structure. To begin with, there is variety in length, some sentences being fairly short, others quite complex. However long the sentence, one feels that Calvin, like Proust, has complete control and that he will not, like some loose writers of the French Renaissance, let the syntax peter out in chaos; and by giving the reader this impression of direction, he increases the logical acceptability of what he has to say. This impression is reinforced by other means: the high proportion of causal conjunctions, the care with which every main sentence is introduced by a conjunction or linking part of speech (*Car ... Mais ... Et ... Car ... Parquoy ... Parquoy ... Et ... Et ... Par ainsi*): Calvin takes trouble to let the paragraph 'breathe', but at no point is its demonstrative power allowed to flag; an impressive momentum has been generated. And in some sentences the architecture is very skilfully ensured: the second, with its two inserted subordinates, allows the final word *suffit* to develop its full force. Elsewhere a *point d'orgue* is created ('comme en se jouant ... idole exécrable'). The structure and rhythms of the whole paragraph have been worked out in great detail. In this, the quotations count for much: Calvin often quotes from the Bible, as one would expect in an author for whom the Scriptures are at the root of his work, and here two biblical quotations are introduced to reinforce one another at a relevant juncture, but Calvin goes on to 'conclure' with the help of Lactantius, so that his case is given added strength by an appeal to impeccable authority. Finally, the logical acceptability of his thesis is promoted, in some measure, by his frequent reference to the 'obvious': 'on peut veoir à l'œil ...'

This structure is enriched by a number of devices of a more affective or intensive character. Calvin's style has a stark architectonic quality; he does not seek undue variety, he relies a great deal on biblical material, he avoids rhetorical flourishes, and his metaphoric language remains within clear limits. Such variety as he allows himself – and this must not be underestimated – is concentrated on a single-minded vision, and serves to focus the reader's mind on essentials; this is the conclusion that seems to arise from an analysis of this passage. Calvin likes using adverbial phrases that leave little room for doubt: *du tout, de fait, tousiours, ne . . . plus,* and indeed the negative presentation can reinforce this impression, as for instance in the final sentence. Calvin's use of epithets is not self-indulgent, but he finds them useful to strengthen the impression already given by the noun to which he has attached them (*menus fatras, idole exécrable*), and once he uses them in binary structure: *vagabonde et erronée.* Calvin is much given to this formula, whether it concerns adjectives, nouns, or verbs; in this he resembles other sixteenth-century writers – Montaigne makes much play with the device. Some have seen in it a legacy from legal language (cf. English 'without let or hindrance'), but whatever its origins, it serves both to define more closely and to emphasise. The word *Dieu* recurs time and again in the passage; this is no cause for surprise, but note how further emphasis is lent by concentrated repetition round the quotation from Galatians and by a discreet symmetry of structure: 'conception qu'on a de Dieu . . . . ignorance de Dieu'. Calvin also makes some use of comparison and image, often at the end of a sentence but without showmanship, and by this means he can combine clarification and some emotive enrichment. The final sentence, as we have seen, is strengthened by a reference to an authority (Lactantius), but here again other elements are brought to bear on the reader's attention: a sense of inevitable logic is provided by 'nous *avons à* conclure', and the whole paragraph ends on the all-important word *verité*.

This passage does not give as wide a range of stylistic effect as some, but even so it is a good example of the way in which Calvin combines a firm intellectual structure with devices designed to play on the emotions of his audience. In his wish to be completely understood by his readers, he has anticipated developments of the French language, so that some critics have seen in him an early paragon of classical control: precision in the use of words, the use of personal pronouns before the verb at a time when their presence was far from obligatory – a cursory look at Rabelais will show that – a firmer handling of negatives, a highly developed sense of the relations of parts of speech and of sentences one to another, all this and more underlines the importance of his *Institution* in the emergence of the French language as a sophisticated instrument especially in the realm of intellectual discourse.

IV. THE CALVINIST CONCEPTION OF LITERATURE[4]

Calvin promoted a Calvinist view of art not only through his own example but by firmly expounding views which found their way to

talented collaborators and disciples. The prime concern of the
Calvinist was edifying and in no wise 'aesthetic'; embellishment
was not sought, unless it helped to clarify and illustrate, for *parure*
and *paraître* are too closely related. Moreover, the Calvinist was addressing himself to the man in the street and not exclusively to the
scholar; thus it comes about that many Calvinist writings are models
of *haute vulgarisation* embodying the classical principles of simplicity, clarity, precision, and order. The genres to be exploited will
therefore be those in which God's will can be sung and His enemies
confounded; and much literary endeavour will be powerfully influenced by the Bible. When Théodore de Bèze writes his *Abraham
sacrifiant*, he tells us that biblical examples were of great value and
that their dramatisation served two aims in particular: 'pour les
mieux considerer et retenir', and, more broadly, 'pour louer Dieu
en toutes sortes à moy possibles'. Similar attitudes lie behind Des
Masures's trilogy on David; and thus from quite early on we have
the statement of an aesthetic totally opposed to that propounded by
the Pléiade in their *Deffense*. The Calvinists in any case disapproved
of what we should now call an élitist conception of art, but they also
attacked the profane, indeed pagan inspiration of Ronsard and his
friends; they viewed with suspicion aspects of classical rhetoric, they
saw no reason to discard peremptorily the older, well-tried genres,
and they were unfavourable to artistic 'invention'. Des Masures, in
his preliminary *Epistre*, makes a number of points about his literary
standpoint which measure his distance from the Pléiade:

> . . . Mais l'action presente
>   J'ay cependant rendue entierement exempte
> Des mensonges forgez, et des termes nouveaux
> Qui plaisent volontiers aux humides cerveaux
> Des delicates gens, voulans qu'on s'estudie
> De rendre au naturel l'antique Tragedie.
>   (lines 169–74)

For him as for others, art must be subordinated to Scripture:

> Aussi l'ay-je [i.e., David] voulu ici representer
>   Pour servir à instruire, et non pour plaisanter,
> Ni de Dieu le mystere, et la saincte Parole
> Destourner, par abus, à chose vaine et fole,
> Comme pour quelquesfois les yeux rendre contens,
> Sont les publiques jeux produits à passe-temps.
> Non, non. Que du vray Dieu la Parole tant saincte
> Jamais prise ne soit qu'en reverence et crainte.
>   (lines 119–26)

The Calvinist seeks therefore to narrow artistic activity so as to
make it a weapon for religious advance. The choice of subject will be
restricted, the artist will be seen as a medium, not someone whose
philautia interposes his personality between God and man, and all

stylistic efforts will be directed to the engraving of the Word in the mind of the reader. At the same time, in a world peopled with enemies, a militant literature is bound to come to the fore, and consideration will have to be given not only to man the penitent in the sight of God but also to man placed in a certain social and political predicament. These principles determine in great measure the genres in which the Calvinists will deploy their activities.

V. FIELDS OF CALVINIST LITERARY ACTIVITY

The Theatre

Perhaps the first genre in which the Huguenots make their mark is drama. We saw that Calvin's view of the theatre was not as rigid as some of his contemporaries', and in the early days certainly, the propaganda value of the drama was quickly appreciated by the Calvinists, much quicker indeed than by the Catholics who enter the scene distinctly late. Though we shall meet several neo-classical tragedians who belonged to 'la religion', the dramatists who had left France before composing their works were broadly opposed to the Pléiade outlook and favoured loyalty to the older genres; thus farces, suitably angled, continue to be performed in Geneva, and Conrad Badius's satire on the *Pape malade* belongs to the 1560s. A similar attitude is found in the prefaces to 'tragedies', and here two examples spring to mind – Bèze and Des Masures.

Théodore de Bèze – Abraham sacrifiant[15] (1550)

Bèze's tragedy is structurally a transitional work, as is shown by his hesitations as to whether he should call it one or not. Written in 1550 at the request of the Academy of Lausanne, it treats a theme already dramatised on several occasions. Bèze has used the *mystère* tradition, in choice of subject, style, attitude to time and place, introduction of Satan and the angel. In his preface he is hostile to contemporary trends, attacking Petrarchism, an over-sophisticated return to the classics, and pagan inspiration. Though Bèze claimed to have written the play 'leviter', this is disproved by the way in which he identifies himself with the protagonist. He had trodden the road to Damascus and when Abraham talks of those who have left their country and come through adversity to faith in God, surely we hear the voice of Bèze himself. Though characterisation is not something on which the sixteenth century laid a great deal of stress, the impact of the play derives from the way in which Abraham dominates the scene; his vigorous faith, Calvinist in its stress on obedience, grace, belief, constitutes the backbone of his character, but one must also stress his humanity. Humanity is an ambiguous word, for it can mean human weakness, represented here by Sarah through whom Satan works, but it is also the awareness of suffering, and the play depends much on the use of pathos. The figure of Satan, who not only echoes the others in recognising God, but is almost overwhelmed by the sadness of the situation, is firmly and shrewdly drawn, and all the more so as he is presented in homely, familiar gesture and speech. Bèze was at pains to underline the 'simple' tone of the play: he has removed the irritating features of the mysteries (the cruder Satan, the donkey, too violent contrasts of tone) and of course overheated classical rhetoric has no place here. Yet the 'simplicity' also has classical kinship: the removal of all inessentials, the central place of Abraham, the unity of tone. Nor is art absent, else the risk of monotony would be great. Bèze achieves considerable range of tone within discreet bounds: some attempt is made at differentiation of character and therefore of style, and Bèze has also exploited the possibilities of the chorus. In addition to uttering various 'moral' sentiments, the chorus acts marginally as confidant and introduces a lyric dimension, coloured greatly by the Psalms; it also gives information about Abraham's early life and conjures up the world as a background to the events enacted. The style, shorn of obtrusive rhetoric, still relies much on certain figures: repetition, interrogation, invocation, antithesis, stichomythia, and isocolon, and above all Bèze makes powerful use of dramatic irony on occasion. And finally, the conditions in which the play came into being impose a brevity that reinforces the classical simplicity of outline and tone.

Louis des Masures – Tragédies saintes[6] (*1566*)

Des Masures is, like Bèze, a humanist deeply steeped in classical culture, and like him he wrote in both Latin and French. His trilogy, first printed in 1566, lacks the literary qualities of *Abraham sacrifiant* – indeed I find much of his writing unnecessarily long and flat – but it does illustrate very clearly the Calvinist conception of tragedy; and in this respect, the proemial *Epistre* is a valuable statement of principle. The Scriptures furnish Des Masures with his material, and David serves as an excellent example to later believers:

> Ceste saincte Parole (à cause que ne puis
> Me repentir encor' de l'estude où me suis
> Quelquesfois adonné; et qu'encor ne m'amuse
> Ou la lire Latine, ou la Françoise Muse)
> M'a donné argument, pour en nombres divers
> Escrire et t'adresser quelques tragiques vers:
> Afin qu'en escrivant je laisse aumoins les feinctes,
> Pour ma plume reigler sur les histoires sainctes ...
> De Dieu donc, et des siens en son nom, les victoires
> Me font escrire en vers ces tragiques histoires,
> Qui serviront aussi pour instruire et former
> A craindre le Seigneur, et de vertu s'armer
> Mon petit Masurim.... (lines 63–93)

The action will also allow him to portray the wicked courtier, against whom all princes must learn to defend themselves – a theme which recurs in most tragedies of the period, and also in moralising satire; but Des Masures is keen to stress the interval between himself and the 'profanes autheurs', a proof of which is offered by his adherence to the older non-classical genre:

> J'ay donc suivi de pres, et tousjours je suivray
> Ce qui est en ceci de naturel et vray ...
> Afin donc qu'au théâtre icelle [Scripture] j'accommode,
> Ici je represente, à l'ancienne mode,
>   Quelques tragiques traits, lesquels je forme, autant
> Que la chose de soy me le va permettant ...
> Seulement ay voulu (laissant la marche à part
> Du brodequin tragique, et des termes le fard)
> Retenir, pour enseigne aux passans rencontrée,
> Le nom de Tragedie, et l'escrire à l'entrée.
>   (lines 187–210)

So Des Masures takes three episodes in the life of David (I Samuel, xvii; xviii; xxvi); the Calvinist inspiration lies not only in the choice of theme but in the portions that contain religious discussion and psalmic inspiration. At the same time, the author uses the framework of the *mystère* to embody the action, with a loose view of time and place, the presence of Satan, and a very numerous supporting cast. One does not expect 'action' in the modern sense from a sixteenth-century tragedy, but though critics have discerned in Des Masures an acute observer of human nature, the canvas of these plays is shapeless, and the dramatic effects of the occasional scene are not sufficient to redeem a very slow-moving text. Des Masures may well see in David's predicament a useful illustration of the doctrine of Grace; his severe Calvinist anti-rhetoric imparts to the text a flatness and barren simplicity that depresses, but one must ask whether this effect is merely the consequence of making practice fit aesthetic precept or of a painful lack of poetic feeling in the author, irrespective of his religious belief.

Non-dramatic poetry. Meditations

These two plays give us a representative idea of Calvinist aesthetic, but it is in other fields of poetry that we shall find a greater activity. I do not propose to enter into detailed discussion of individual poets here, but shall confine myself to general remarks about the trends; in any case, certain poets are discussed under other rubrics. Though, obviously, doctrinal attitudes separate Protestant and Catholic, there are areas where some overlap in genre and theme does occur, since both religions manifest the desire to return to a more inward form of devotion, may draw on similar earlier sources, and sometimes have common concerns that are not inhibited by dogmatic issues. And from another angle, when two sides are involved in a long-drawn-out struggle, it is not uncommon for a certain osmosis to occur in that each side is affected by and seeks to affect the attitudes of the other: this tends to occur, for instance, in the realm of satire and polemic poetry. Nevertheless, certain features by definition cannot be shared, and serve therefore as distinguishing marks.

One genre that comes to the fore in the wars of religion is the paraphrase of sacred texts: the practice is not confined to one religion, nor indeed is it restricted to one language, for Latin paraphrases will be published throughout our period. In the early days, however, the Calvinists do stand apart by their stress on the Psalms and also on the importance they attach to the vernacular; but as the decades pass by, the Catholics also begin to take an interest, and the linguistic veto of former days dies out, as can be seen by the work of Rémy Belleau or Philippe Desportes. Other sacred texts also attract religionaries, Job and Jeremiah in particular. So far as paraphrases of the Psalms in Latin are concerned, it is once again the Protestants who take the lead, but significantly Buchanan's paraphrases, published towards the beginning of 1566, very soon obtain the Catholic *imprimatur* in the Netherlands. In another field, the Protestants took the initiative, that of the anthology intended to be a tract for the times. The first of these is the *Recueil de plusieurs chansons spirituelles* which in its essentially original form or with certain additions (e.g., the edition of 1569) has six editions up till 1601. As has been recently shown, this anthology owed much to publications of the 1530s and also to the volume prepared by Guéroult (and others) in 1554.[7] If we add to these the anthologies that appeared in the last quarter of the century (Montméja, Maisonfleur, and Valagre), and were very successful, we can see that the anthology, as a formula, is an important aspect of religious literature at this time, and that the Protestants were the first to understand this. Their success is proved, not only by the frequency of reprints, but by the fact that the Catholics felt impelled to provide their own counterparts, such as the *Muse chrestienne* which appeared in 1582. On the other hand, a genre (in prose) which remains the preserve of the Calvinist is the meditation: in our period, the genre is exploited by four authors, three of whom have in common the fact that they were closely connected with Calvinist circles in the Midi: Sponde, D'Aubigné, Duplessis-Mornay, and Théodore de Bèze. Though all owe much to the penitential psalms and to cognate biblical texts, the formula allows for considerable personal development of the basic themes, with varying stress on the logical structure of the argument, the amount of colour allowed in the style, the balance between edification and personal involvement; on the other hand, all have a family air in the emphasis laid on contemporary issues and also on the high level of stylistic tone sought. The style which may be often broken and jagged, eager to jostle the reader, possesses many of the features we detect in late-century poetry of a religious character, a style for the times, but also one that reflects in many ways the literary sources of the genre, both biblical and 'spiritual'. Of all these, perhaps the texts written by Sponde are the most impressive from a literary point of view;[8] his four *Méditations* on Psalms XIV, XLVIII, L, LXIII are of considerable interest, for they enlarge the scope of the genre as we see it in Théodore de Bèze or Duplessis-Mornay, from whom Sponde may have indeed learned something. Sponde seems to have enriched the meditation through a more coherent infusion of his own religious attitudes, though critics have detected hollow rhetoric here and there; he has intensified the relevance of the genre to make it more of a tract for the times, though writings of this nature are perforce affected by the conditions in which they take shape; and he has, surely, pressed a greater stylistic abundance into service in order to express his variations on the theme of man's *miseria* in the face of the Almighty's abiding greatness. Certain influences have been detected in the creation of this style: Ramist ideas on rhetoric, a Senecan tradition that also plays its part in the stylistic qualities associated with Lipsius, also no doubt techniques developed in the Calvinist sermon, techniques which undoubtedly assume a substantial role in the creation of devotional prose; other elements could be isolated, in all likelihood, but even a short extract will show how self-conscious an artistry is at work:

Nous sommes toute mauvaistié, mais tu es toute bonté, Seigneur: Nous sommes toute ordure, et tu es toute pureté: nous ne sommes que mort, et tu n'es que vie. Qu'attens-tu donc de nous, que tout le contraire de ce que nous attendons de toy? Hé! si tu desployois ta fureur sur nos crimes, qui soustiendroit? Y a-il rien de juste au monde, au prix de ta Justice? la lumière est-ce pas ténèbres en comparaison de ta Lumière? L'innocence mesme des hommes, est-ce pas coulpe devant ton siege? O Déité infinie, ces morceaux d'argile se parangonneront-ils à toy? Ces charongnes empuanties d'iniquité entreront-elles dans le flairant pourpris de ton héritage? Ouy, Seigneur, car le bien que tu nous fais, tu le nous fais pour l'amour de toy, et le vice qui nous engloutist, est englouti de ta misericorde. C'est pourquoy jadis incessamment, et de nouveau avec plus de curiosité,
Nous avons considéré ta misericorde au milieu de ton temple.
Nous l'avons méditée, Seigneur, nous y avons bandé tous les nerfs de noz esprits, nostre force s'y est roidie, nostre entendement s'y est occupé, et attentivement. (Boase ed., pp. 67—8)

All those writing in this genre must by definition remain in a state of dependence on the original text; but Sponde is able to confer a greater resonance, movement, and apparent autonomy than most. Here we are far from the measured prose of the Ciceronian tradition; instead, we are offered a hurried, insistent rhythm, but still one that has patterns of repetition and symmetry, related to the central antithesis between man and his Creator. The opening lapidary contrast repeated several times is followed by a series of interrogations, and these are reinforced by images of decay and putrefaction which we have noted in other writers of this period. But even such images are characterised by a notable vitality which shows itself to an even greater extent in the final sentence, where mental reactions are given, as it were, a physical presence; and this physical presence is heightened by the quaternary movement of the phrases, which are brought to a dramatic close by the isolation of the adverb *attentivement*. Patterns of symmetry are to be found not only at the beginning, as we saw, but also in the sentence 'Ouy, Seigneur . . . ' Even so short an extract gives some idea of the linguistic energy that Sponde is capable of generating, in a genre that is essentially a Calvinist preserve. In Catholic circles, the prose meditation does not appear to flourish, though a verse equivalent is practised;[9] but in these genres, no less than in religious verse such as that of Jacques de Billy, we find poets, irrespective of sectarian attitudes, familiar with earlier currents of Christian spirituality.

Over and above the poetry of lyric effusion[10] and sombre introspection, we find a very large output of militant and polemic verse; much of it is ephemeral and often fails to attain a respectable literary level, but it inevitably constitutes an important aspect of poetry at the end of the century. Much of it too is published abroad or circulates in manuscript, and here I shall mention the main themes. With the advent of the religious wars, the criticism of the Church and its high representatives is less and less developed by Catholics, for one would hardly expect them to help their opponents in this way; but the Calvinists devote much activity to attacks on the Church of Rome, on the Pope, and various high ecclesiastics. A certain amount of this verse is in Latin, contrary to one's immediate expectation, but the vernacular is naturally more exploited. So far as France is concerned, the monarchy comes in for a lot of hostile poetry, partly because of the official attitude to the Calvinist minority, partly because of Henry III's mode of life, partly because of the way in which the Court – naturally a focus for anti-aulic poetry – was involved with the Guises. When the Guises become more closely linked with the *Ligue*, there will develop a bitter current of satire and invective directed against their ambitions, and here animosity will go beyond sectarian boundaries, as for instance in the *Satyre Menippée*. The Guises, with their fanatical hatred of the Calvinists, and also their ill-disguised ambitions at the highest level, become a special target.

Political theory

In a sense, the Calvinists represent one attitude by French Renaissance man to the recent developments of 'la condition humaine'; and it is therefore not surprising that they should feel it necessary to define their views in the field of 'human sciences', that is in the field of studies that seek to define man's position in time and place on this globe. We shall see how the Calvinists take an interest in so-called 'scientific' poetry, with Du Bartas and D'Aubigné offering a panorama of man through the centuries. Similarly, we find a number of Calvinists active in the field of historiography: the element of sectarian bias may vary considerably, from La Popelinière who makes a serious attempt to base his work on serious and impartial research to Agrippa d'Aubigné, whose *Histoire Universelle* often reads like a prose correlative of the *Tragiques*. Equally, perhaps more important are the Calvinist excursions into political theory: and here the contribution by Calvinists interested in the French situation is notable among other things for its difference from the Genevan outlook. Though a decently coherent doctrine is hardly evolved in those turbulent years, the theocratic conception of the State envisaged in Geneva was not really relevant to France;[11] moreover, Calvin had insisted on strict obedience to the government of the day, however brutal and tyrannical it might be, and had condemned rebellion out of hand. Such an attitude was hardly congenial to Huguenots after the Saint-Barthélemy. No doubt ideas on the limitations of royal authority had circulated for some time; they had a medieval pedigree, and in the 1550s the study of jurisprudence had brought such ideas again to the notice of humanists. With the development of Calvinism and then the traumatic effect of the Saint-Barthélemy, a much more radical attitude makes its appearance. All, it seems, accept the principle of monarchy and of its divine justification, in the sense that ideas of Natural law are hazy, if they are distinct in any way from Divine law; but the Calvinists came to believe that absolute monarchy is an abuse, and that though the king may wield power, the principle of that power lies with the people; therefore the king is the servant of the people and subject to their control. Thus a series of theses are advanced: that kings were originally elected, and not determined by hereditary right; that magistrates, elected by the people, are designed to keep watch over the king's exercise of power; and that the people does have the right of rebellion; one or two theoreticians go so far as to advocate tyrannicide as a solution in desperate cases.[12] After the Saint-Barthélemy, a number of works appear in print, often by Frenchmen, but also by foreigners whose sympathies were Calvinist and whose works were sometimes translated from Latin to French; many of them were connected by ties of friendship or interest. These works vary in tone from the polemic to the more academic, and make a varying use of history to bolster their theses; some of these texts preserved their relevance until the following century. They furnish a counter-thesis

to the ever-growing sympathy in Establishment circles for the absolutist view of monarchy. Here are some titles and dates:

1573   F. Hotman, *Franco-gallia*
1574   Translation of the *Franco-gallia* into French *Reveille-Matin*
1576   Simon Goulart, *Mémoirs de l'estat de France sous Charles neufviesme*
        (including full text of La Boétie, *Contr'un*)
        T. de Bèze, *De jure magistratum*
1579   G. Buchanan, *De Jure Regni*
        Vindiciæ contra tyrannos
1581   Translation *De la puissance legitime du prince sur le peuple et du
        peuple sur le prince* ...

All these writings came out against the theory that the king was
'legibus solutus'; a number of authors base their case on historical
'fact' (Hotman, Buchanan) and sometimes on classical authority.
One can understand how, in these circumstances, the youthful dissertation of La Boétie was eagerly seized on by the Calvinists and
also how Bodin saw fit to combat the theory of tyrannicide in his
De la Republique. However, once peace is slowly restored under
Henry IV, 'democratic' views fade in France, though they enjoy
currency abroad.

The Calvinist presence in the cultural, religious, and political
history of the second half of the century is an important one. The
Calvinists show a pioneering spirit in certain 'literary' genres and
they develop political theories of substance. Their presence, however,
is circumscribed in time and in effect: some Calvinist writers who
remain in France are absorbed into currents that do not mark a
break with new humanist trends (La Taille, Du Bartas); in other
cases, the migration to Geneva will finally take authors out of the
French mainstream; elsewhere, the Counter-reformation will harness
forces that underlie Calvinist endeavour, as in the field of devotional
poetry. But Calvinism presents France with one major masterpiece:
Les Tragiques.

VI. AGRIPPA D'AUBIGNÉ – LES TRAGIQUES[13]

The first edition of *Les Tragiques* came out in 1616, the second, in
enlarged text, *c.* 1623; but by inspiration and theme the work belongs
to the end of the sixteenth century. The *Tragiques* not only form a
summa of D'Aubigné's career, they bring to fruition many of the
germs of the Pléiade, and by their subject-matter and poetic range
they offer a fusion of the main concerns of the poets active during
the last quarter of the century. Finally, they constitute one of the
summits of French poetry through the ages, and their comparative
neglect until quite recently has not been to the credit of critic or
reader.

The roots of the poem go back to the late 1570s when D'Aubigné was involved in the religious wars, fighting on the side of Henry of Navarre; wounded at Castel-Jaloux and at death's door, he 'traça pour testament cet ouvrage, lequel encores quelques années après il a peu polir et emplir' (*Aux Lecteurs*). From the outset the composition is designed in a spirit of militant commitment, and it becomes a work that accompanies the author until his last years. A very sizeable part of the poem must have been completed by 1589, as we know that Henry of Navarre was able to read the manuscript before he succeeded to the throne; but there is also evidence to show that much of this original version was modified, often amplified, and from internal signs we can determine the *terminus a quo* of various passages such as those criticising Henry IV's later attitude to religion or the praise accorded to Queen Elizabeth. Once D'Aubigné's own position had crystallised – and he admits that in his younger days he had strayed from the narrow path, succumbing to the charms of the Court, and even fighting for the Catholic cause – it forms a rigid backbone to the whole poem; it also underlies his somewhat complex attitude to Henry IV.

The *Tragiques* are made up of a foreword to the reader, a *Preface* in octosyllables, and seven books composed in alexandrines, the number seven being determined in some measure by religious considerations. Though D'Aubigné refers several times to the rather untidy and unplanned character of the work, its structure is perfectly clear in its general outlines. In Book I (*Misères*), which serves as a sort of prelude and was in all probability composed at an early stage, the poet laments the state of France, disrupted by religious strife and loss of principle; the range of tone is very wide, varying from passages of pathetic description to strident and sustained invective against the two figures whom D'Aubigné holds mainly responsible for France's plight: Catherine de Medici and the cardinal de Lorraine. The next two books are bound together in the sense that they constitute attacks on two aspects of the Establishment that persecutes the faithful Huguenots: *Princes* (Book II), as the title makes clear, is an onslaught on the Valois, but its invective is coloured by D'Aubigné's remorse at the way in which he had succumbed to the lures of the Court; and *La Chambre dorée* (Book III) is directed against the Law, which has become the instrument of Injustice in a world where all is topsy-turvy. The next two books are also linked (IV, *Fers*, and V, *Feux*) in so far as they develop the subject of the suffering faithful through the centuries. *Les Feux*, to my mind, is less interesting poetically than *Les Fers*, which opens with a scene in heaven, where we are shown Satan in the presence of God, and is devoted in great measure to the religious wars and more especially the Night of the Saint-Barthélemy which we know to be one of the main emotive sources of the poem taken as a whole. D'Aubigné escaped the slaughter by a dubious piece of good fortune, as he had to flee the capital after killing someone in a duel; but the Night, a traumatic experience for all the Huguenots who escaped, becomes one of the fundamental sections in *Les Tragiques*; it is presented as the handiwork of Catherine de Medici and the cardinal, who appear as the agents of Satan upon Earth. *Vengeances* (Book VI), whose composition seems to belong to the earlier years, is concerned with the persecutors of the true Church down the ages, and their punishments are often described in gruesome detail. Stress is placed on three different epochs, that of the Old Testament, the Roman Empire, and finally the Popes and princes of the Middle Ages, when the Church had moved away from its pristine purity. In this book another central episode is introduced, that of Abel and Cain, which symbolises from the earliest time on the struggle between good and evil, between the persecuted and the persecutor, between the false and the true Church, in short between *avoir* and *être*. In *Jugement* (Book VII), the end of the struggle is in sight, and the true Church comes into its own in heaven, so that the poem ends on a note of peace.

The main thread of the poem can thus be seen to be the struggle and final victory of the Church after centuries of oppression, persecution, but also sin. Though the faithful children of the Lord ultimately attain peace and blessed happiness, they have been human and therefore tainted by sin, so that their journey through the world is a perpetual symbiosis with the forces of evil, who are essential to their salvation and who must live on in eternity to purge their own wickedness. The poem, conceived on a cosmic scale, is one of breathtaking grandeur; with all its faults and lapses, it is a remarkable work of sustained fervour and poetic achievement, whose riches are never exhausted by renewed reading. The total effect is created from a number of elements, of which the first, obviously, is the simple structure of the sequence of books. We move from *Misères* to *Jugement* in a gradual ascent from suffering to spiritual peace and reward, a process which D'Aubigné himself claimed is reflected in the various 'styles' that characterise the several books. Thus *Misères* is written in 'un style bas et tragique, n'excedant que fort peu les loix de la narration', whereas *Jugement* is endowed with 'un style eslevé, tragicque'. The term *style* must not be taken in too narrow a connotation, because D'Aubigné's literary style in the modern sense is immediately recognisable, irrespective of the book under contemplation: it doubtless involves considerations of tone, but it also concerns matters of poetic invention, seemingly: when the poet refers to the 'style tragicque eslevé, plus poëtic et plus hardi que les autres' in *Les Fers*, he proceeds to discuss the use of the *tableaux celestes* in which the martyrs of the faith see in Heaven the suffering they will later undergo upon Earth; and the device of the *tableau* is certainly

more poetic or fanciful than the description of *Misères* which, for all
its vivid quality, is relatively down-to-earth.

Though D'Aubigné claims to avoid undue planning, the work
must reflect in its own direction the main theme of God's will; and
this comes through at all points, even if the poet makes no effort to
stick to anything resembling chronological sequence – as is seen in
the episode of Cain and Abel which comes nearer the end than
the beginning of the work and is introduced after the full-scale
picture of the Saint-Barthélemy. Indeed time, at certain levels,
counts for nothing; one notices this, for instance, in the unconcerned
manner in which D'Aubigné blends the *merveilleux chrétien* and the
merveilleux païen. Though spiritual regeneration occurs in function
of time, the presentation of this in temporal sequence, as opposed to
form, is not essential (see below, pp. 356–7).

The *Tragiques* are built on a massive antithesis between God and
Satan, good and evil, and this antithesis is presented in dramatic
form through the evolution of human history. However, D'Aubigné
does not confine himself to the temporal dimension here upon earth:
for instance, when he inserts the *tableaux celestes*, we are not only
made aware of the heavenly world, but time is shown simply in a
finalist sense, and as we shall see, symbolism is employed to bring
together different sections of time. Even so, the basic contrasts are
maintained throughout, either by means of key episodes, like that of
Abel and Cain or of God and Satan, or by the *leitmotiv* of the
persecutors and persecuted. One way in which the ground theme is
enriched is the treatment of Nature: as a result of man's original sin,
vice has entered the world and Nature has ceased to coincide with
herself. This may be expressed in a variety of ways: for instance,
since Nature is *desvoyée*, D'Aubigné will show the human condition
is a state of contradiction with itself, in which the true has been
replaced by the false. Linguistically, this state of affairs is often
expressed by statements followed by an immediate denial (*ces loix,
non-loix*); and in *La Chambre dorée*, the figures of Justice are replaced by the vices attendant upon Injustice. The world is thus
portrayed as a parody of itself, and the poet presses into service the
armoury of caricature in order to make the fullest impact upon the
reader. One of his more usual weapons is to animalise human beings:
they may be presented as such in an extended simile – this is the case
with Catherine de Medici or the cardinal de Lorraine – but the
image may often be introduced more discreetly, as when some person
is defined as 'allouvi'. The animals recruited by D'Aubigné to symbolise fallen humanity are often biblical in origin, but he uses them to
portray not only morally but visually, and it is here that his powers
of caricature come into play. When he describes Nature as Non-
Nature, he may present phenomena in the mode of truth/untruth,

but he is also much given to treating the theme in the key of *paraître/être*. A good example of this occurs in the description of the Court: D'Aubigné harnesses the anti-aulic tradition, whereby the Court is displayed as show without substance, to a more vital purpose. Frequently he brings in the words *paroistre* or *masque*, and the motif of the actor, or disguise, or simply clothes, may be developed in this context. This feature is used by some critics to bring him within the Baroque orbit; at all events, the presence of the theme is hardly a matter for surprise in a poet belonging to a generation that had observed so great a gap between principle and practice, the value laid on ostentation, and, at a deeper level, a sense that the unity of an apparently well established world was threatened, possibly damaged beyond repair. This withdrawal from truth and reality is expressed not simply by means of the mask, but also by the symbol of pallor; figures who stand for false values, a spiritual death, are shown to turn pale, to appear ashen-grey, and so forth, for true life has ebbed away from within. This symbol may be further associated with the idea of flight; thus, after Cain has committed his crime, he is presented both as pale and as fleeing in fear. One might go so far as to say that movement is often an indication of an unnatural state, contrasted with the peace that will descend upon the chosen at the end of things. D'Aubigné has an exceptional sense of things in movement, and his presentation of the world-conflict is chiefly a dramatic one. Sometimes he describes an action through its repercussions, and we are shown some sort of chain reaction; on other occasions, he develops the 'catcher caught' motif. This is particularly so in *Vengeances* where enemies of the true Church reap the punishment they inflicted on the martyrs: they die a death that, at symbolic level at least, is a *correspondance* of the martyrs' agony. The fallen world is thus a caricature in motion.

This world has further characteristics that reinforce its identity and unity: one of these is the role played by time in the drama. In one sense, of course, the cosmic process of regeneration can only be considered in terms of passage and time, but D'Aubigné often cuts across the barriers of ages to show the close interdependence of phenomena, partly because this device strengthens the reader's awareness of God's plan, partly because the conflict between good and evil is, in the fallen world, permanent and manifested through different embodiments. In modern times, D'Aubigné, as we have mentioned, sees Catherine de Medici as the *suppôt de Satan*, but she is likened to previous incarnations of that state, such as Jezebel or the Greek Furies; the different enemies of the Church, Old Testament figures, the Herods, the Roman emperors, various Popes and other medieval persons, all represent the same forces of evil; and by the insertion of divers symbolic devices, the reader will recognise their essential identity. Of particular interest is the episode of the *tableaux celestes*, which D'Aubigné introduced only after much thought and conferring with friends, such as Sainte-Marthe and Rapin, and at a more modest level, the poet likes to present events that have already happened to his knowledge as prophecies, which he jokingly referred to as *apopheties*.

Symbolism plays some part in establishing the correspondences across the centuries; it is also used to create other 'figures in the carpet', to borrow Henry James's phrase. In D'Aubigné's world everything is closely interrelated, both on theological grounds, but also by virtue of the cast of his imagination, which belongs to that cosmic type that reappears in authors like Hugo or Claudel. And in the worlds created by such imaginations, symbolism is one of the main devices used to bind the poetic fabric together. In such minds, the forces behind figures acquire more significance than the figures themselves, however vividly they may be portrayed. The characters do not live in their own right, but are defined by reference to other phenomena, and it may happen in consequence that symbolism and caricature overlap. D'Aubigné's symbols are not as a rule sophisticated or far-fetched; he contents himself with straightforward signs, sometimes taken from the Bible, or drawn from the arsenal of Calvinist propaganda. Thus, the identification of Rome with Babel is common practice; but when the poet wishes to organise a pattern on a more ambitious scale, he seeks symbols that, by their polyvalency, will bring various phenomena into relationship. The most obvious symbol of this class is the colour red, which naturally stands for the blood of the martyrs, suffering, persecution, but also signifies purging, purification ('washed in the blood of the Lamb'). Such a symbol thus brings together persecutor and persecuted, who are in any case essential to one another. D'Aubigné will extend the symbol in various fashions: he will make some play with the fact that the arch-enemy, the cardinal de Lorraine, wears purple as a sign of his status, and that colour thus effects a link between the Church of Rome and the idea of persecution. Alternatively, the poet will draw on the negative possibilities of the symbol and develop, as we saw above, the implications of the withdrawal or draining of blood.

By touching upon symbolism we have also considered one vital aspect of D'Aubigné's handling of language. What is remarkable is the extraordinary dynamism of his style. Though he eschews in principle undue search after literary effect – the Calvinists had after all misgivings about art and aesthetics – he does remain a polymath steeped in the classics and moreover, since he admits that the *Tragiques* are intended to communicate a view of the world that will affect the emotions of his readers in a way that he thought other works of his might not, he will make abundant use of rhetoric, which is the art of persuasion, of playing upon the emotions of the audience. D'Aubigné possesses several traits that confer an impressive dynamic quality on his verse: dramatic symbolism, representation of movement, enumeration; but he also uses devices that will achieve emotive, pathetic effects. In addition to reproducing scenes designed to move the reader by their subject, he will bring in the abundant use of epithets, chiasmus, and zeugma – the two latter being recognised from classical times on as powerful emotive agents – and frequent use of repetition. D'Aubigné aims at a high norm of tension and sustained emotion, but he is also capable of many moods other than the highly dramatic: the appeal to pity, the satirical, the lyric, and towards the end of the work, an almost mystic tone. And just occasionally there peeps through a face that is able to laugh without abrasive scorn. One of his masters was Rabelais, who sharpened in him a rich sense of the vitality of words. Attention is often called to D'Aubigné's talents for satire, and very rightly so: the telling shaft, the ability to degrade by symbolism, the moral involvement that carries with it the urge to destroy, the sense of caricature that can border on the obsessive, all these traits are present, but without their linguistic means of expression, the satire would be still-born. Many of the qualities of his language are naturally to be found in the verse of his contemporaries: the devices conveying deep concern, invocation, interrogation, *anaphora*, repetition, images of decay; and some of his techniques of presentation make one think of the latter-day preacher. But he is writing on a vaster scale, and his powers of sustained dramatic vision have greater opportunities therefore to show themselves. There is indeed a volcanic quality about D'Aubigné's writing, which expresses itself in his capacity for distorting reality, his headlong rush of language, but also accounts for his reluctance to stop at the right moment, his occasional failure to control language whose syntax may vanish in smoke, a certain insensitivity to what the reader can tolerate; it is these weaknesses that make the *Feux* a disappointment, and though D'Aubigné always has his eye on the reader, he sometimes loses touch with his likely reactions.

It will be appropriate to exemplify some of these generalisations by a scrutiny of a substantial passage, part of the section in which Catherine de Medici is castigated for her role in contemporary events: D'Aubigné's powers of rhetoric are understandably to be found in passages where he stigmatises the enemies of the Church:

> Ainsi, en embrazant la France miserable,
> Cett' Hydra renaissant ne s'abbat, ne s'accable
> Par veilles, par labeurs, par chemins, par ennuis;
> La chaleur des grands jours ni les plus froides nuits
> N'arrestent sa fureur, ne brident le courage
> De ce monstre porté sur des aisles de sa rage;
> La peste ne l'arreste, ains la peste la craint,

Parce qu'un moindre mal un pire mal n'esteint. . . .
Mais quand l'embrazement de la mi-morte France
A souffler tous les coins requiert sa diligence,
La diligente au mal, paresseuse à tout bien,
Pour bien faire craint tout, pour nuire ne craint rien.
C'est la peste de l'air, l'Erynne envenimée,
Elle infecte le ciel par la noire fumée
Qui sort de ses nareaux; ell' haleine les fleurs:
Les fleurs perdent d'un coup la vie & les couleurs;
Son toucher est mortel, la pestifere tue
Les païs tout entiers de basilique veue;
Elle change en discord l'accord des elemens.
En paisible minuict on oit ses hurlements,
Ses sifflements, ses cris, alors que l'enragée
Tourne la terre en cendre, & en sang l'eau changée
Elle s'ameute avec les sorciers enchanteurs,
Compagne des demons compagnons imposteurs,
Murmurant l'exorcisme & les noires prieres,
La nuict elle se veautre aux hideux cimetieres,
Elle trouble le ciel, elle arreste les eaux,
Ayant sacrifié tourtres et pigonneaux
Et desrobé le temps que la lune obscurcie
Souffre de son murmure: elle attir' et convie
Les serpens en un rond sur les fosses des morts,
Desterre sans effroi les effroyables corps,
Puis remplissant les os de la force des diables,
Les fait saillir en pieds, terreux, espouvantables,
Oit leur voix enrouée, & des obscurs propos
Des demons imagine un travail sans repos;
Idolatrant Sathan et sa theologie,
Interrogue en tremblant sur le fil de sa vie
Ces organes hideux; lors mesle de leurs tais
La poudre avec du lait, pour les conduire en paix.
Les enfans innocens ont presté leurs möelles,
Leurs graisses & leur suc à fournir des chandelles,
Et, pour faire trotter les esprits aux tombeaux,
On offre à Belzebub leurs innocentes peaux.

(*Misères*, lines 853–920)

The diatribe against the queen-mother goes on for some two hundred
lines without flagging, but this section brings out various techniques
used by D'Aubigné to create his effects. Catherine is represented as
the agent and accomplice of the devil; elsewhere the poet associates
her with Jezebel, as do many Huguenot writers of the time, but
here he adds the references to the Hydra and the Furies, to increase
her symbolic range. He stresses Catherine's league with devilry and
sorcery and thus plays on a contemporary obsession with witchcraft;
but – and this is more germane to the work as a whole – he sees her,
as he sees Satan in relation to God, as a principle of change, movement, and therefore human wickedness ('change en discord l'accord
des elemens'). The portrait is carried beyond the bounds of verisimilitude, and it is this type of writing that makes us think of the
term 'fantastic realism'; we are indeed in a sort of surrealist world,

real in one sense but bearing little resemblance to our conventional existence. This impression is brought about partly by the symbolism to which we have alluded, partly by the speed of the passage – an exceptionally high number of verbs are woven into its fabric – but in great measure by the affective devices of rhetoric selected by the poet. D'Aubigné devotes much space to a fusion of the gruesome with the pathetic, when Catherine is indulging in witchcraft involving the sacrifice of innocent children. This preoccupation with the violent and indeed the morbid is not confined to D'Aubigné by any means, but it is a key element in the texture of the *Tragiques*. Catherine is shown not merely as a figure of revulsion, she is portrayed as one whose presence blights all that surrounds her. The air and flowers are sullied by her passage, her touch and sight have lethal effect; she transforms life into death. The portrait is intensified by the series of epithets scattered over the text, often placed before the noun they qualify: *envenimée, pestifere, basilique, enragée*; and with the aid of certain verbs the similarity between Catherine and the beasts is brought out, developing the initial description of her as a *monstre*: *Elle s'ameute, elle se veautre*. These elements are reinforced by the spate of accumulation and enumeration that characterises the passage; D'Aubigné is trying to impart to the picture a breathtaking movement, in itself a criticism of Catherine in so far as movement is the contrary of peace ('Des demons imagine un travail sans repos'). These repetitions may be straightforward, they may also form part of a binary motion which either extends over two hemistiches of a line (sometimes in negative presentation) or over a couplet in the pattern $6+18$ syllables. The binary movement within the line is often created by reinforcement of chiasmus or antithesis. And there is one feature that recurs everywhere in the *Tragiques*: the intense repetition of a single word, perhaps in a variety of forms. There may be insistent exploiting of the preposition which lends added force to an enumeration; or a word employed some way back may recur in another part of speech (*embrazant, embrazement*). D'Aubigné will also insert repetition into a chain movement: *Compagne des demons compagnons imposteurs*, a device that is all the more useful as it is a simple way of conveying a sense of relationship. In a world where Nature has ceased to be herself (*nature desnaturée*, as he calls it, or *le monde à l'envers*), repetition occurs with a negative to show the differences of level at which life goes on, as in the phrase *Desterre sans effroi les effroyables corps*. Repetition at a distance serves obviously to underline some important feature, such as the *innocens* of the last lines of the passage. Occasionally, D'Aubigné uses a word twice in an antithetical context (VII, 893), and, though not here, he is much given to *anaphora*. Reinforcement may be obtained in another manner: *La diligente au mal, paresseuse à tout bien*; and among other features which recur elsewhere should be mentioned D'Aubigné's exploiting of participial clauses which, at their best, help to maintain the tempo of the sentence as a whole, and his considerable use of the abstract noun (*l'embrazement de la mi-morte France*), a device whose merits he may have observed in Ronsard.

From all this we can see how a diversity of recurrent features is created: the extraordinary vitality of the phrase, the dramatic presentation of events – D'Aubigné's mastery of visual effects is impressive, but one must not forget the role of auditive techniques – the curiously obsessive quality of his writing, and in consequence of these features and his use of symbol and allegory, an exaggeration of detail that makes us enter a world totally different from the one we know, violent, twisted, exaggerated, macabre sometimes, often claustrophobic. Like so many poets of this period, D'Aubigné is unusually able to portray the dynamism of a world whose wickedness appals him at moral level. Nevertheless, one does him injustice by stressing these characteristics of his world to the exclusion of others: there is, for instance, in him a lyric poet of a high order whose presence not only helps to vary the tones of the poem as it advances, but is called up to express D'Aubigné's glimpses of immortality and the peace lying beyond this life. A number of the cantos end in a sort of lyrical coda, where the inspiration of the psalms introduces rich harmonics, or where some spiritual figure pronounces an imaginary discourse, or, as in the final book, where the poet is absorbed in the contemplation of the divine presence. And there are curious passages where the symbiosis of the persecutors and the persecuted is expressed in moving, elegiac tones. There is one such passage, unexpectedly perhaps, in *La Chambre dorée*:

> Les cendres des bruslez sont precieuses graines
> Qui, après les hyvers noirs d'orage et de pleurs,
> Ouvrent au doux printemps d'un million de fleurs
> Le baume salutaire, & sont nouvelles plantes
> Au milieu des parvis de Sion fleurissantes.
> Tant de sang que les Rois espanchent a ruisseaux
> S'exhale en douce pluie & en fontaines d'eaux,
> Qui, coulantes aux pieds de ces plantes divines,
> Donnent de prendre vie & de croistre aux racines;
> Des obscures prisons les plus amers souspirs
> Servent à ces beautez de gracieux Zephirs.
> L'ouvrier parfaict de tous, cet artisan supreme
> Tire de mort la vie, & du mal le bien mesme,
> Il resserre nos pleurs en ses vases plus beaux,
> Escrit en son registre eternel tous nos maux:
> D'Italie, d'Espagne, Albion, France & Flandres
> Les Anges diligents vont ramasser nos cendres;
> Les quatre parts du monde & la terre & la mer
> Rendront compte des morts qu'il lui plaira nommer.
> (*La Chambre dorée*, lines 654–722)

In a world where the sound of fury and violence bursts on us so frequently, these passages of quiet lyricism and *recueillement* produce a very striking effect, and rightly so, for the poem is after all the search at both personal and cosmic level for a return to the peace that passeth all understanding:

> Chetif, je ne plus approcher de mon œil
> L'Œil du Ciel; je ne puis supporter le Soleil.
> (*Jugement*, lines 1209–10)

Les Tragiques constitute a poem whose greatness is becoming apparent only now, after centuries of neglect. It is a remarkable expression of the impact of the Renaissance on a Christian mind of unusual vigour and integrity; it is also a poem in which so many of the characteristics and trends present in other poets of the last thirty years of the century come together to form an artistic composition successful on a scale which is very unusual in French Renaissance poetry or indeed in later periods. It is also the product of an imagination that rarely shows itself in French literature: it reminds us of Hugo, Balzac, and Claudel, and though it may resemble a volcano in the way it produces scoriae and rubble as well as unparalleled vigour, brilliance, and scale of activity, it is an imagination capable, in its highest moments of control and thrust, of taking D'Aubigné into the company of those French authors whose significance transcends national boundaries.

NOTES

1. In addition to works in the General Bibliography, see J. E. Neale, *The Age of Catherine de Medici*, 1943; L. Romier, *Les Origines politiques des guerres de religion*, 1913–14; and *Le Royaume de Catherine de Médici*, 1922.

2. See J. Pineaux, *La Poésie des Protestants de langue française (1559–1598)*, 1971.

3. E. Doumergue, *Jean Calvin, les hommes et les choses de son temps*, 8 vols., Lausanne, 1899–27; A. M. Hunter, *The Teaching of Calvin*, 1921; R. N. C. Hunt, *John Calvin*, 1933; F. Wendel, *Calvin, the Origins and Development of his Religious Thought*, 1963; A.-M. Schmidt, *Jean Calvin et la tradition calvinienne*, 1957; J. Pannier, *Calvin écrivain*, 1930; L. Wencelius, *L'Esthétique de Calvin*, 1937; F. M. Higman, *The Style of John Calvin in his French Polemical Treatises*, Oxford, 1967.
    The standard ed. of Calvin's works is *Opera quæ supersunt omnia*, ed. J. W. Baum, E. Cunitz, etc., Brunswick, 1863–1900, 59 vols. The 1541 ed. of the *Institution* has been published by J. Pannier, 4 vols., 1936–39, AGB; see also ed. by J. Benoît, 5 vols., 1957–63, which gives the 1560 text, with variants, and from which we quote.

4. In addition to L. Wencelius, op. cit., see M. Jeanneret, op. cit.; T. C. Cave, *Devotional Poetry in France, c. 1570–1613*, Cambridge, 1969; two articles by M. Richter, 'La poetica di Théodore de Bèze e le *Chrestiennes Méditations*', *Aevum*, 1964, and 'Aspetti e orientamenti della poetica protestante francese nel secolo XVI', *SF*, 1967; also his ed. of the *Chrestiennes Méditations*, *TLF*, 1964.

5. See P. F. Geisendorf, *Théodore de Bèze*, Geneva, 1949; G. D. Jonker, *Le Protestantisme et le théâtre de langue française au seizième siècle*,

Groningen, 1939; P. Keegstra, *Abraham Sacrifiant de Théodore de Bèze et le théâtre calviniste de 1550 à 1566*, The Hague, 1928; and R. Lebègue, *La Tragédie religieuse* ... Modern ed. of *Abraham sacrifiant*, K. Cameron, K. H. Hall, and F. M. Higman, *TLF*, 1967.

6. See R. Lebègue, op. cit.; modern ed. C. Comte, *STFM*, 1907. (The BN has the 1588 ed., the BM the 1595.)

7. G. Guéroult also published *Le premier livre des chansons spirituelles,* Lyons, 1548 (the BN has the 1550 ed.), and *Chansons spirituelles*, 1559 (BN); see E. Balmas, 'Guillaume Guéroult traducteur des "Psaumes"', *RHLF*, 1967.

8. *Méditations avec un Essai de Poèmes chrestiens*, introd. Alan Boase, 1954; F. Higman, 'The *Méditations* of Jean de Sponde: A Book for the times', *BHR,* 1966.

9. Catholic spirituality is, however, often nourished by translations of the Church Fathers, medieval texts, and Spanish works, see below, p. 395.

10. Brief mention should be made of Pierre Poupo, an interesting transitional figure who moves from a Pléiade point of departure to a style developed by the pressures resulting from a clash between Calvinism and a mind that is not content with a Genevan aesthetic or indeed always a harsh doctrinal standpoint. *La Muse chrestienne* appeared in 1585 (Geneva, copy in Ars), the 2nd ed. in 1590–92 (Ars, BN). Incomplete anthology, ed. E. Roy, 1886. See R. M. Hester, *A Protestant Baroque poet. Pierre Poupo*, The Hague–Paris, 1970; M. Jeanneret, 'Pierre Poupo: recherches sur le sacré et le profane dans la poésie religieuse du XVIe siècle', *Bull. ann. Fondation suisse de la cité internationale, 1965*, 1966.

11. See General Bibliography.

12. The States General would appear to some as more representative of the common will than the *parlements*.

13. A. Garnier, *Agrippa d'Aubigné et le parti protestant*, 3 vols., 1928; I. Buffum, *Agrippa d'Aubigné's 'Les Tragiques': a study of the Baroque style in poetry*, New Haven, 1951; H. A. Sauerwein, *Agrippa d'Aubigné's 'Les Tragiques'. A Study in structure and poetic method*, Baltimore, 1953; J. Bailbé, *D'Aubigné poète des Tragiques*, Caen, 1968; G. Fasano, *'Les Tragiques', un' epopea della Morte*, 2 vols., Bari, 1970–71. See also H. Weber, *La Création poétique*. Copies of 1616 ed. in BM, BN, PSG; of 2nd ed. in BM, Ars, Geneva. Modern ed. A. Garnier and J. Plattard, 4 vols., *STFM*, 1932. See also Pléiade ed. of *Œuvres*, by H. Weber, J. Bailbé, and M. Soulié, 1969, containing the *Tragiques,* and among other things, several important prose works.

Chapter 12

POETRY UNDER CHARLES IX
AND HENRY III[1]

I. GENERAL SURVEY

AFTER 1560, to give a rough date, poetry develops on a very large scale indeed; there seem to be many more competent rhymesters than ever before, and we find a great number of humanist groups whose identity is often best reflected in its enjoyment of poetic composition. Ronsard, in many respects, gives an impressive lead, and his example is followed as much in the provinces as in the capital; the wars of religion encourage poetry of a committed character as well as of escape through the writing of verse; and much activity will be found in Paris colleges, but also in the humanist, especially legal, circles of the main provincial towns. To begin with, we shall glance rapidly at the kinds of poetry being written and the *milieux* with which they were connected; and then examine more closely worthwhile examples of the main currents of poetic endeavour.

The Court

In this period, the Court plays an important role. We have seen how through the whole of the period up to 1550, the Court was gradually acquiring more prestige, particularly thanks to Francis I. The momentum is maintained through Henry II's reign, especially in court ritual and in the development of the visual arts to suit the royal purposes; but under Charles IX, literature, which was less catered for under Henry II, comes into its own. The young king himself liked to read poetry well into the night, and Brantôme tells us that Catherine de Medici

. . . ne fut jamais chiche à l'endroit des sçavants et qui escrivoient quelque chose.

And if the literary contribution to court life is not always of great intrinsic merit, it is necessary to understand in general outline the interaction of Court and letters at this time. Earlier, the court poet might, as was the case with the young Marot, send news of events back to his patron, and the *rhétoriqueurs* often accompanied the royal entourage in the Italian wars; in mid-century, there is less of this, but there were plenty of other poetic occasions. Catherine, who had been brought up in Italy, expected the Court to exist on a lavish scale; moreover, she came to believe that certain activities might help to reduce political tensions during the troubles. Over and above this, parade and ostentation becomes a means whereby the monarchy, in its centralising process, can impress itself on the Frenchman, whatever his station; and if protocol and ritual do not reach the formalism of the seventeenth century, a certain style and identity are created, partly through architectural improvements, artistic developments which are inspired by classical models, but also late-medieval, chivalric ideals (cf. the popularity of the *Amadis*), and no doubt Italian example; nor should we forget the importance assumed by costume, jewellery, gold and silverwork, and tapestries. A certain artificial world is being fashioned, of which reflections can be found in the work of Ronsard or Caron; and in it music will also play its part. There are many state occasions on which the whole machinery of *paraître* may be brought into action to assert the prestige of the monarchy. In the first places, th*e entrées* which the king might make into his 'bonnes villes' were events which were not only very splendid, but also involved a substantial section of the local population.[2] The 1548 entry into Lyons was organised by Maurice Scève and included a mock battle on the water, *tableaux vivants*, a performance of Bibbiena's *La Calandria*, and many other features. These festivities reflected both humanist and Italian ideas, for the dramatic performance introduced settings in which classical features and techniques of perspective were hitherto unknown, apparently, in France;[3] and the technical sophistication of the machinery in the creation of effects was an augur of things to come. Other entries, such as those into Paris in 1549 and 1572, were also on a very lavish scale, and assembled the talents of poets, musicians, and men distinguished in the visual arts. Sometimes, the contribution of men of letters, so far as texts were concerned, might be relatively modest, as for instance in the 1559 ceremonies when Jodelle was involved; on other occasions, a much greater effort might be made, as when Filleul composed his *Théâtres de Gaillon* for the royal entry into Rouen in 1566.

Then there were entertainments which were more narrowly confined to the Court.[4] First may be mentioned the *cartels* and *mascarades*; the *cartels*, connected with jousting, no doubt had a medieval flavour about them, but the *mascarades* also allowed the playing of parts by members of the royal family and nobility; the texts of these were provided by the court poets and could be quite extensive. During the middle 1560s, they might have the express purpose of quietening the passions aroused by the wars of religion:

this appears to have been the case with Ronsard's *Bergerie,* and it is curious to note that the formula was also used, in Latin, for court purposes by George Buchanan when Mary queen of Scots had returned to Scotland. A more sophisticated theory of the social functions of the arts was developed by Jean-Antoine de Baïf, in the 1570s during the existence of the Academies: part of his effort goes into attempts to acclimatise classical phenomena, such as elegiac verse, in France, but he also believed in the value of associating music and poetry and in the efficacy of music as a social calmant, a view in which he was seconded by Thibault de Courville and the more famous Claude Le Jeune. The *Académie de poésie et de musique* was founded in 1570, the *Académie du Palais* about four years later; broadly speaking, these projects sought to transplant the spirit and activity of the Florentine Academy with its Neoplatonic harmonics, but they appear to have had some political backing as well. We are imperfectly informed about the activities of the courtiers, poets, and musicians who assembled from time to time, but we know that poets such as Desportes, D'Aubigné, and Jamyn were to be found in the company of Ronsard and Baïf.[5]

The traditional singing of births, marriages, and deaths continues, both in French and in Latin, and so does the celebration of military events. In the process, some genres come into favour: the paean is one example, a more striking one perhaps is the court eclogue which in the hands of Dorat, Belleau, and Ronsard manages to assimilate new elements. Though Vergilian and classical models still count, the influence of Italian sources such as Sannazaro is also important, and we have eclogues that are not only pastoral in character, but may become 'forestieres' (Belleau, 1572) or introduce hunting features, very welcome to kings devoted to the sport.

As time went on, other elements come into the picture, though tragedy, originally performed at Court (e.g., *Sophonisbe,* 1559), was discontinued by Catherine, whose superstitious nature found representation of royal disaster uncongenial. The interest taken at Court in astrology and soothsaying probably has something to do with Jean Dorat's development of anagrammatic and chronogrammatic epigram: the name of the person concerned may be worked, as an anagram, into a short poem, revealing qualities or the destiny hidden in the original. These look very much like parlour games, were it not for the fact that Dorat believed passionately in their significance. The mechanical complexities of certain court entertainments assume startling proportions – and no doubt introduce techniques that will be put to good use in the tragicomedy and tragedy of the next century. Moreover, it is towards the end of our period that the *ballet de cour* makes its appearance in France (1581). Finally, so far as genres are concerned, it is perhaps chiefly in and around the Court that love-poetry continues to flourish: in certain circles it will be less welcome, given the religious temper of the age; which will not prevent a number of Petrarchan techniques finding their way into devotional verse.

The prominence achieved by the Court helps to revive the anti-aulic strain in French poetry that goes back a long way. In the first place, it benefits from the xenophobia so current during the religious wars; and even before, the Court of Henry II came under fire for its Italian orientation, owing to the presence of Catherine de Medici. The reaction from Petrarchism owes something to this feeling; and anti-Petrarchan sentiments are voiced by Du Bellay, later by Nicolas Le Digne and also Noël du Fail who lets off squibs at this ultra-refined view of love. But Henri Estienne, campaigning for a vigorous, middle-of-the-road French, equidistant from Court and dialect and marrying the claims of 'raison' and 'usage', builds up an amusing portrait of the courtier affecting Italianisms:

... je trouvai par la strade un mien ami, nommé Celtophile. Or voyant qu'il se monstret estre tout sbigotit de mon langage (qui est toutesfois le langage courtisanesque, dont usent aujourd'huy les gentils-hommes Francés, qui ont quelque garbe, & aussi desirent ne parler point sgarbatement) je me mis à ragionner avec luy touchant iceluy, en la soustenant le mieux qu'il m'estet possible. Et voyant que nonobstant tout ce que je luy pouues alleguer, ce langage italianizé luy semblet fort strane, voire avoir de la gofferie & balorderie, je pris beaucoup de fatigue pour luy caver cela de la fantasie.
(*Deux Dialogues du nouveau langage françois, italianizé . . .*, 1578,
Ristelhuber ed., 1885, Vol. I, 3–4)

On a broader front, the Court attracts a good deal of criticism, especially that of Henry III, who with his *mignons* had introduced *mores* that scandalised the Calvinists and were looked at askance by others of less puritanical outlook. In *Les Tragiques*, the Court becomes a symbol of moral decadence, peopled by the enemies of God, true religion, and Justice; but the themes, even if they are orchestrated on less grand scale, do recur in other writers. Also, at a time when the king's stature is diminished in the presence of so many powerful forces around him, it is no surprise to find the old *topos* of flatterers and evil counsellors having a good run for its money; but it can overspill into another theme, which occurs in the extended meditative poem often, namely that of the proper role that ought to be adopted by nobles in disrupted France. Here again, we have a revamped theme present in the *rhétoriqueurs* of the late fifteenth century, but its treatment fits in tonally with the times. Closely related is the commonplace of *rus* v. *urbs*, which acquires added value towards the end of the religious wars and humanists, out of sheer weariness, leave the capital to cultivate their garden, but in Horatian rather than in Voltairean spirit. To the extent that the capital and the Court are identified, the *topos* enriches the anti-aulic current. And finally, the Court, which in principle is the symbol of parade, ostentation, show, *paraître*, becomes a convenient sign of the denial of *être*; particularly strongly developed in D'Aubigné, it is extensively used elsewhere. In Ronsard already, one may see in close company the themes of dynamism, exuberance, and illusion; later, a more vital contrast between appearance and reality is asserted by poets of religious complexion.

One more point about the Court: though its separate identity is obvious, it is not isolated from other circles: on the one hand, the world of humanism and scholarship (especially the *lecteurs royaux* and the Paris colleges) has a firm footing at Court, with Ronsard as *poète royal* and Jean Dorat as *poeta regius*, and also through the close links between the legal *milieux* and the Court; and on the other, we have the beginnings of the aristocratic *salon* which we normally associate with the seventeenth century.[6] The important example here is the circle of the maréchale de Retz, in whose *salon* we find Jamyn, Sainte-Marthe, and Etienne Pasquier, but also a significant number of musicians. For a while too, the house of the marquis de Villeroy and his wife attracted men of letters, but Villeroy's fall from grace had repercussions on the *salon*; and mention should be made of the circle that formed round the duc d'Anjou and included Jean de la Gessée, Lefèvre de la Boderie, Jean Bodin, and Hesteau de Nuysement. The *salon* of Jean de Morel was more scholarly in character, but the early death of his wife, Antoinette de Loynes, and the Calvinist tendencies of the family probably reduced its appeal as the years progressed.

Literary salons and groups. Types of poetry composed

The social, group character of literary activity constitutes a notable feature of the period; not that such groups are new – we have seen important examples earlier – but they seem to be much more numerous and more widespread. This emerges clearly from the greater liking for the publication of collective verse, often commemorative in theme, but not always;[7] the *tombeaux*, usually written in at least two languages, become very common, and reveal the personality of a group or sometimes of a section of some profession. Moreover, there are many circles flourishing in the provinces, and especially in towns where the *parlements* are established: the link between the magistrature and letters is once again illustrated. Dijon has quite a marked literary activity, with Jacques de Vintimille, Bounyn, and others, who maintain links with Lyons; Poitiers has the *salon* of the Dames des Roches, whom eminent lawyers visited on the occasion of the *Grands Jours*;[8] Rouen also appears to be quite active, as does the south-west (Du Bartas, Pierre de Brach, Florimond de Raemond); and, a bit later, Aix-en-Provence will harbour Malherbe among other poets. In the provinces, we shall find the influence of Ronsard and the Pléiade rippling out, so that quite late in the day Pierre de Brach will compose a love-sequence in honour of his *Aymée*;[9] but it is also in the provinces that we shall find new stirrings, for instance in the field of religious poetry; and Neo-latin verse will have its enthusiastic adepts there as well as in the capital. This group-conditioned writing does sometimes produce the less satisfactory verse of a closed society: form becomes more important than content, and when poets are busy executing variations on a given theme (as in *La Main* or *La Puce*),[10] preciosity soon takes over, but at the same time, we do note a willingness to explore new metrical and stanzaic patterns. Enigmas are popular, though they may sometimes serve a more serious purpose, and anagrams and word-play, whose earlier devotees Pasquier and Etienne Tabourot study with evident relish, find much favour. The taste for extempore writing remains as lively as ever; Brantôme recounts how once when he was dining at Court, with Ronsard, D'Aubigné, Baïf, and Desportes, the guests talked of love and were invited to extemporise quatrains.

A high proportion of such literary activity was by definition entertainment when people sought relief from the pressures of the troubles; and one must not expect a deeper exploration of poetry from people for whom such activity helps to confirm a social identity. But this does not mean that there is no great amount of serious poetry at this time: on the contrary, several categories can be easily discerned. There is a large bulk of committed verse, often written by humanists who take an important part in these *salons* and provincial groups, and this verse employs both Latin and the vernacular as its vehicle of expression. There is also a significant amount of what, for lack of a better term, one may call meditative or moralising poetry; in Latin we have the impressive *Sermones* of Michel de l'Hôpital, in the vernacular, a series of *satires* or 'discours' on the evils of the times, on man's nature, on the role of different sections of society, on the cultivation of the simple life, in short serious poetry that remains this side of the religious, but may incorporate Horatian, Stoic, golden-mean values. On either side of this current we have two other important streams: on the one hand, the persistence of a didactic poetry. Old favourites continue to be popular, such as the moral distichs of Cato or Faustus Andrelinus; and Alciat's Emblems seem to increase their appeal. Such texts will be read in Latin, but there are also potted versions of classical wisdom (e.g., *Les sentences graves et belles authoritez de plusieurs sages Grecs & Latins*, 1570) and the boiled-down commonplaces of the Bible find a ready market. We have noted Lyons's role as a publishing centre for much verse of this type, but the outstanding success of the century was surely Pibrac's *Quatrains* which went through innumerable editions.[11] And on the other hand, we have the resurgence of religious poetry. Even if we leave aside Calvinist poetry, most of which is printed beyond the frontiers of France, we shall still find a rich output within the country: there is the vogue for paraphrases of the Psalms and of certain books of the Bible (especially Job and Jeremiah); then there is the poetry of a more personal, intense nature which owes much to the impact of the Counter-reformation; and religious themes will naturally make their way into the 'committed' verse of the wars, but also into certain strands of more extended compositions concerned with man's fate upon this Earth, compositions which reach their high-watermark in *Les Tragiques*.

Among more extended genres, two stand out: on the one hand the scientific poem which may deal with man's destiny, or may confine itself to some more technical subject, such as hunting. And on the other hand, the development of neo-classical tragedy. In short, we are dealing with a period of intense poetic energy, ranging from the sublime to the trivial, but consolidating the work achieved by the Pléiade and laying the foundations for future development. Some genres have only made a tentative appearance: this is the case with the pastoral, in spite of the popularity of Sannazaro and of the appeal one might have thought the mode would have for a war-weary generation; but we come across only sporadic ventures such as *La Camille de Pierre Boton* (1573) or François de Belleforest's *La Pyrenée et Pastorale* (1571), which owes rather more to Spanish models.[12] Works such as these, beyond what encomiastic ends they may serve, are highly stylised and written in an over-alembicated language. One might, with a little goodwill, see glimmerings of an attempt to analyse feelings; but their leisurely longwindedness and monochrome presentation of the characters pall rapidly.

Neo-latin poetry

There remains one general point of substance: the persistence of Neo-latin poetry. Though, from a literary point of view, one might think that the 1550s had brought Neo-latin verse to its highest pitch of achievement, there is no doubt that it continued to thrive under Charles IX and Henry III, and much of its activity runs parallel with what is going on in the vernacular. The wars of religion, far from weakening its prestige, appear to have strengthened it; and when poets begin to regain their position at Court *c.* 1558, this recognition works to the benefit of both vernacular and Latin verse composition. Some writers of encomiastic verse celebrating the events of 1558–59 may write in both Latin and French, others may have their work translated into the other language, and some poems are sufficiently well thought of to be reprinted, either separately or in anthology. Most of these writings tend to be by Establishment figures, but occasionally Calvinist poems appear in print, though inevitably the bulk of Huguenot composition will be published abroad or remain manuscript. At the same time, when the wars of religion break out, there will be texts written earlier which will acquire relevance, such as A. Frusius's epigrams against heretics or Buchanan's *Franciscanus* (printed 1566). After the encomiastic verse of the years 1558–1560, we find that college humanists continue to compose Latin verse, ranging from drama (Roillet) to more didactic verse (Gilmer); but inevitably attention will be focused on events. Until 1563, committed poetry is modest in scope, but the assassination of the duc de Guise elicits response from both Catholic writers and Calvinist sources—indeed the *Poltrotus Merœus*, variously attributed to Adrien Turnèbe and Pierre de Montdoré, is a poem of very considerable merit. Between the second and third wars, we notice a hardening of attitudes and this is expressed in a number of texts; on the other hand, the Saint-Barthélemy does not produce much in the way of printed verse. During the reign of Henry III, things are rather confused and though the *Ligue* stimulates a certain amount of Latin verse, it is the occasional event (the death of Joyeuse, the murder of the duc de Guise, the execution of Mary queen of Scots) that inspires humanists. Normally, a higher standard of performance is to be found in poems which, possibly prompted by particular events, prefer to develop general themes concerning the plight of France (e.g., Malvyn's *Gallia gemens*); here the author tries to play on the feelings of his readers, by graphic scenes often using Vergilian techniques, by pathetic effects (the plight of mothers and children) in which *prosopopœia* plays a large part, and by emphasis on France's cultural tradition, and the value of orthodox religion in maintaining her identity and structures.

As one might expect in a period of turmoil, the epic note is struck from time to time, but less than one might have expected: some epics remain manuscript, such as Des Masures's *Borbonias*, others do not seem to have gone beyond the planning stage, one completed work has vanished from our ken, but there is some attempt to revive the mock-epic tone in macaronic verse. Another genre, in which the influence of Vergil is often strong, is the eclogue; but though, in the hands of Dorat mainly, it is used for court encomium, it appears less frequently as a fully committed form; much more fruitfully developed is the *tumulus* already mentioned above, since it straddles more than one language (see p. 368). There is also a respectable current of religious poetry in which contemporary reference gives way to more general considerations: thus the paraphrase of sacred texts (especially the Psalms, but also other books of the Old Testament) is common, and occasionally we note a curious blend of Ovid (*Heroides*) and portraiture of biblical heroines. In addition, Sainte-Marthe's *Paidotrophia* contains an interesting section on the Fall, and Du Bartas is translated into Latin verse. There is a vigorous development of religious poetry by poets associated with Douai and St Omer (Simon Ogier, Toussaint Sailly, and Robert Obrizius), but within France we find nothing so clearly concerted. More interesting in many ways are the *Sermones* or epistles of Michel de l'Hôpital, printed sporadically or incompletely during his lifetime: these poems, greatly valued towards the end of the century, are interesting not only for their literary qualities in an essentially meditative key, but because they express at political level the outlook we associate with that of the *politiques* whose influence grows towards the end of the troubles, and at more philosophical level a view of life that obviously owes a great deal to Stoic sources, at a time when the so-called Christian stoicism is in the process of taking shape. We must get to know ourselves and remove the various screens, *amour propre* and passions, that stand between us and ourselves, so that proper self-control and the exercise of reason can prevail. As he grows older, L'Hôpital for all his involvement in a most active life, meditates more and more on death for which existence is seen as a preparation. At the same time, his reflections go beyond personal destiny to consider political behaviour and proper ways of governing a country; but his presentation is that of an observer of the human scene, not of a satirist.

Latin poetry, however, reflects the polarisation we shall find in the vernacular: it serves both to express committed attitudes in a *monde cassé* and to offer a means of recreation and diversion. The latter tendency will be found frequently in the group literary activities to which attention has already been drawn; it occurs also in the parody (of which Florent Chrétien was a master), and in the *xenia*, sometimes very elaborate in the case of Jean Passerat, as well as in the enigma and in epigrams that depend much on word-play. For Etienne Pasquier, who in his youth had defended the vernacular against the claims made for Latin by Adrien Turnèbe, Latin verse composition seems to have been essentially a pastime; his more serious thoughts about contemporary events are expressed in French. Love-poetry is not particularly cultivated, with the notable exception of Jean Bonefons's *Pancharis* (1587), a cycle on the Petrarchan-Neocatullan model which enjoyed a continued success down to the eighteenth century and indeed beyond. The didactic strain, fashionable in the vernacular, is equally successful in Latin; and the provincial centres of letters often take a marked interest in Latin verse. Where group activity flourishes, lyrical modes tend to make way for something more frivolous and ephemeral. Nevertheless, Latin poetry is far from moribund, and there are still humanists who believe that

their posthumous fame is more likely to rest in the Latin idiom.
And that belief will still be shared by humanists active in the seventeenth century.

It is important to remember that this is a period in which poetry
diversifies very considerably and in which stylistic, linguistic, and
metrical possibilities are explored on a wide front. The different
milieux where poetic composition is carried on determine in some
measure the styles that will prevail, ranging from high encomium
through elegant *salon* verse to the reflective, the didactic, and the
more emotively tortured: we must therefore not be surprised to find
both the lineaments of a classical urbanity and the emergence of a
more violently imaginative idiom whose worth has only come to be
recognised in recent times.

II. LOVE-POETRY

It is not easy to isolate strands of poetic activity in this domain,
and all the more so as love-poetry is so frequently found in the far-
raginous volumes produced by court and society rhymesters catering
at different levels for their friends and patrons. This is true of a poet
like Flaminio de Birague, who writes odes, *stances*, epistles, and
sonnets on love, or a series of *Chansons*, such as the following:

> La nuë qui par l'air s'en va pirouettant,
> Ne demeure iamais ferme & constante une heure,
> Obeyssant au vent contrairement ventant
> Tant que sans nul pouuoir fracassée elle meure
> Ainsi mon pauvre cœur, qui sans cesse souspire,
> Depuis que de l'amour ie suys les estendars,
> Vogue à tout vent d'ennuy produit d'amoureux dards,
> Si que vaincu de dueil à sa fin ià il tire.
> (*Premieres œuvres poëtiques*, 1581, fol. 10 v)

Hesteau de Nuysement prints his *Œuvres poétiques* three years
earlier,[13] and includes a book of *Amours* – but also various poems on
fortune, peace, or 'Les gemissemens de la France'.

Amadis Jamyn (?1540–93)

A bit more substantial are the works of Amadis Jamyn, who was
at one time secretary to Ronsard[14]: considered as one of the master's
most representative disciples, he falls more easily into the ranks of
court poets under Henry III, though he was already active during
the previous reign. His muse is indeed a civilised and polished one;
the Petrarchan tradition has been thoroughly assimilated in his
love-poetry, indeed one might say domesticated. His series of sonnets,
in which the traditional themes harmonise with a certain moralising
tone, are expressed in the measured terms of refined rhetoric, with

the help of a classical culture readily adaptable to a courtly audience; only rarely does Jamyn make an excursion into the grand manner, and then without conspicuous success. Agreeable verse, but hardly compelling, nearer surely to Desportes than to Ronsard; Jamyn is sensitive to the winds of fashion and his links with the Retz circle accelerate this evolution. In this choice of genres, he reflects the trends of the last third of the century: love-poetry, various compositions of an encomiastic character, reflective and moralising verse, also a mild satiric composition. The fashion for the metamorphosis poem is reflected in several texts; he also exploits, like contemporaries, the figure of *prosopopœia*, and tries his hand at pastoral and eclogue. Jamyn writes one piscatory eclogue in the style of Sannazaro and a curious work entitled *De la chasse*, where three different blends of inspiration are brought together: the technical hunting poem, the fusion of this theme with a political one concerning the Huguenots, and a more strictly pastoral element:

> Carlin est nostre Dieu, c'est l'heur de nos herbages,
> Il preserve nos Bœufs de ces bestes sauvages:
> C'est luy qui maintenant redonne au Pastoureau
> La grace de jouer du tendre chalumeau.
> Pource nous souvenant d'un si grand benefice
> Nous teindrons son autel (annuel sacrifice)
> Du sang d'un aignelet: et monts, vaux et buissons
> Resonneront tousjours de rurales chansons
> Prises de ses vertus. . . .
>
> (*Premières Poésies* . . . , Carrington ed., p. 309)

One can hardly claim that Jamyn has enriched the tradition; he has a refined poetic instrument which plays delicately on stock responses. His concept of love is a very tame one:

> Car l'amour n'est sinon qu'un certain doux plaisir
> Dont l'esprit en aimant se sent du tout saisir,
> Se plaisant en la choze où telle bonne grace
> Pour se faire admirer aura choisi sa place.

Only perhaps in his religious poems, published rather later, does he display something more original.

Philippe Desportes (1546–1606)[15]

The love sequence is by no means defunct, and we shall find practitioners in both capital and provinces. I shall choose two, one because he sets a certain tone, the other because he offers the promise of further poetic development. The first is Philippe Desportes, and at this distance we may find it difficult to accept that in the 1570s he was an arbiter of literary fashion, so much so that Ronsard had to take notice of his presence. We find him at Court, and in the Villeroy and Retz circles. Though he is a quite prolific author, he does not reveal much stylistic variety, except in his religious poetry which falls mostly outside our period. He is associated with the wave of Neo-petrarchism that appears at Court shortly before Charles IX's death and persists into Henry III's reign; and though Malherbe cut his classical teeth on Desportes's poetry, his work should be seen as a transitional form of writing that foreshadows in some degree the classical idiom of the seventeenth century. His *Premieres Œuvres* appear in 1573, the 'Dernière edition' dates from 1607, that is a year after the poet's demise.

In the 1573 edition were included the *Amours de Diane*, which give an idea of the change in taste since Pléiade days. These poems, mostly sonnets, but interspersed with *complaintes, chansons, épigrammes, stances*, and dialogue, may in the words of the poet be 'naiz de ta flamme et des tourmens divins/Dont tu me fis present, quand je vins à ta suite' (II, i), but they draw heavily on Italian models – as one might expect from a poet well conversant with Italian culture and translator of texts from Ariosto; but he has benefited from his rivalry with Ronsard, whose influence has been noted in later poems. The following sonnet will give some impression of Desportes's style:

> La Foy, qui pour mon temple a choisi ma poitrine
> Jamais n'en partira, quoy qui puisse arriver;
> L'effort du temps vainqueur ne l'en sçauroit priver:
> Contre tous ses assauts plus ferme elle s'obstine.
>
> Que le ciel courroucé contre moy se mutine,
> Il ne sçauroit pourtant une escaille enlever;
> Les tourments plus cruels ne font que l'esprouver:
> Comme l'Or en la flamme, aux maux elle s'affine.
>
> Elle arrête mon cœur à cloux de diamant,
> Et, pour tout artifice, elle fait qu'en aimant
> Je me serve d'Amour et de perseverance.
>
> Mon feu brusle tousjours et n'est point evident:
> Aussi l'amour en moy n'est point par accident;
> Il est de ma nature et ma propre substance.
>
> (*Amours de Diane*, Graham ed., II, lxiii)

The opening lines owe something to Ariosto, but in any case they are not untypical of French sensibility then, which carries further than the older Petrarchan canon the mingling of religious and amatory themes. There is a very careful symmetry in the arrangement of the motifs, and the last two lines echo the first two. Desportes's handling of sonnet structure is often firm and he has nothing to learn in the way of rhetorical technique. Nevertheless, the poem is not entirely satisfactory. It gives perhaps a feeling of *déjà vu*, though too much need not be made of that; but there is a certain languor in the emotions portrayed, and with Desportes love has become the inmate of the *salon*, tamed, sophisticated, and rather self-conscious. There is furthermore a self-centred quality – the poet is in love with *une Dame*, not more precisely specified – and this narcissistic melancholy verges on the insipid; indeed this is the danger that threatens Desportes's technical competence all too often. The poetic structures are not always in a relation of sufficient tension with the substance of the text, and in this sonnet there are lines which, lacking vitality, tend to become passengers (line 11 is particularly weak). Once a certain asthenia is noticed, then the almost mechanical repetition of rhetorical devices (exclamation above all) becomes obvious. Even Desportes's frequent attempt at surprise comes as no surprise, and we have entered a world of comfortable convention. This is perhaps a harsh way of singling out his deficiencies, for there are compensations: Desportes has a definite feeling for the music of a line, he is not far off the classical alexandrine, and his erudition is never obtrusive, assimilated as it is for a well-bred audience. His attitude is that of the tireless craftsman. Nevertheless, the cultured *abbé* pirouettes his way through the *salon* of delicate admirers, but surely we have here poetry that has moved from the sphere of innovation to that of convention, poetry in which the dynamic is fading and which is becoming the apanage of a closed society. He reduces poetry to an over-alembicated and anaemic *galanterie* which tries to hide its vapidity beneath the virtuosity of his tailor-made facility. In many ways the strength of late-century poetry lies in the provinces.

D'Aubigné – Le Printemps[16]

Though *Le Printemps* was published posthumously, it belongs in the main to the years 1571-73; some of the *Stances* and a few other texts were written later. The work is made up of the *Hecatombe à Diane* and the *Stances*, but other poems (odes) are closely related. The poems owe their origin in part to D'Aubigné's infatuation for Diane de Talcy, a niece of Ronsard's Cassandre, but some other ladies lurk in the penumbra of inspiration, and it may be that the Neoplatonic strands, more marked in the *Stances*, derive to some extent from a stay at Nérac (the Court of Marguerite de Valois), though such elements form part and parcel of the literary climate at that time. And indeed, these poems are much affected by literary fashion: there is an overall debt to Ronsard, D'Aubigné's acknowledged master, but the Petrarchan character of the work mirrors the shift in taste of the 1570s. It is possible that the sombre political situation colours the sequences in their imagery, often military, in the violence of the language, and perhaps in a certain morbid tendency – features which of course will recur in the different context of *Les Tragiques*. On the other hand, the pastoral fashion affected by so many court poets is reflected in D'Aubigné's extensive use of nature themes; this feature belongs to the Petrarchan canon, but

D'Aubigné has altered the proportions of its role as an expression of mood. The sonnets form a sequence of one hundred, linking the motif of Hecate (a manifestation of Diana) and the hecatomb (the Greek word for a hundred):

> Je brusle avecq' mon ame et mon sang rougissant
> Cent amoureux sonnets donnez pour mon martire,
> Si peu de mes langueurs qu'il m'est permis d'escrire
> Souspirant un' Hecate, et mon mal gemissant.
>
> Pour ces justes raisons, j'ay observé les cent:
> A moins de cent taureaux on ne fait cesser l'ire
> De Diane en courroux, et Diane retire
> Cent ans hors de l'enfer des corps sans monument.
>
> Mais quoy? puis-je congnoistre au creux de mes hosties,
> A leurs boyaux fumans, à leurs rouges parties
> Ou l'ire, ou la pitié de ma divinité?
>
> Ma vie est à sa vie, et mon âme à la sienne,
> Mon cœur souffre en son cœur. La Tauroscytienne
> Eust son desir de sang de mon sang contenté.
>
> (Sonnet 96)

This poem conveniently illustrates some of the qualities of D'Aubigné's love-poetry. Its dependence on tradition is evident: there is, first, a fairly heavy element of classical reference, both explicit and periphrastic; the relation of the poet to the beloved is couched in Petrarchan tones – languishing, fire, cruelty of the *innamorata*, identification of his spirit with hers; then there are the stylistic correlatives of these themes – repetition of key words, antithesis, logical disposition of the argument between quatrains and tercets, symmetry between the two parts of the line. On the other hand, D'Aubigné does stand somewhat apart from the Petrarchan vogue of the 1570s: his imagery is undoubtedly more violent and his command of movement more dynamic, sometimes to the point of being uncompromising. As a general rule, he does not seek to impress by erudition, though, as he states in the prefatory poem, he is far from wanting his verse to be in the mouth of 'chamberieres'; and, in spite of some exceptions, he avoids undue verbal preciosity, the straining towards a final conceit or too rigid antithesis. In his imagery, he draws extensively on the tradition, but shows a special liking for Nature imagery, military terms, legal phraseology on occasion, and discreet mythological allusion. Though he expresses great admiration for Scève, whom he may imitate, he does not go in for the 'abstract', theorem-like discussion of amatory matters, nor does he seek such startling linguistic effects. He may certainly have learned from his predecessor's handling of the image, but his temperament leads the reader into a very different atmosphere: violence and macabre tones affect his use of Nature imagery, and if we exclude one or two poems (such as *Stances* 19 and 21) which are strongly Platonic, he moves away from the abstract towards the dramatic, and it is his ability to bring visual imagery to life and his refusal to achieve too polished, too smooth an effect that places him at a distance from poets like Desportes. Sometimes auditive effects are brought in to support the visual; indeed much of his strength stems from his accumulation of imagery which is not, at first blush, all that coherent. This gift of imparting a sort of harsh descant to a refined tradition is visible for instance in Sonnet 3:

> Misericorde, ô cieux, ô dieux impitoyables,
> Espouvantables flots, ô vous palles frayeurs
> Qui mesme avant la mort faites mourir les cœurs,
> En horreur, en pitié voyez ces miserables!
>
> Ce navire se perd, desgarny de ses cables,
> Ces cables, ses moyens, de ses espoirs menteurs:
> La voile est mise à bas, les plus fermes rigueurs
> D'une fiere beauté sont les rocs impitoyables;
>
> Les mortelz changemens sont les sables mouvantz,
> Les sanglotz sont esclairs, les souspirs sont les ventz,
> Les attentes sans fruict sont escumeuses rives,
>
> Où, aux bords de la mer, les esplorés amours,
> Vogans de petitz bras, las et foible secours,
> Aspirent en nageant à faces demivives.

We also see a handling of language that will be put to valuable use in religious poetry in the near future: an obsessive repetition, either of important words or of parts of speech (*ces*) or syntactic structures, emphatic use of affective epithet, invocation, above all an appeal to the sight and to feeling. The *Stances* lend themselves less easily to brief comment here: generally speaking, they are less sustained in quality, and their very length is not always an advantage: D'Aubigné has yet to master the stamina that will characterise the *Tragiques*. Nevertheless, *Stances* 1, 5, 6, and possibly 13 have much to offer, with interesting imagery patterns in 3, where the theme of red seems to spread through the text, and the sense of mobility, unlike the *sables mouvants* of the sonnet just quoted, is identified with the warmth of Nature in contrast to the frozen chill of the *innamorata*. In the *Stances*, which by definition are metrically variable, we can see D'Aubigné experimenting with the movement of the line and sometimes achieving impressive results, but at the same time, his imagination takes the opportunity to explore in greater complexity certain Petrarchan *topoi* in the direction of the macabre, the distorted, and the cruel. In all these poems, comparison with Desportes is inevitable; D'Aubigné is writing them when Ronsard and his young rival are working in the Petrarchan idiom, and there seem to be clear textual echoes of Desportes in some of the *Hecatombe* sonnets; but this only serves to bring out the essential differences of their imaginations, and to suggest that D'Aubigné, rather than Desportes, is capable of adding something worthwhile to the canon.

III. 'SCIENTIFIC' POETRY[17]

The term 'scientific' is unsatisfactory in this context, because the poetry thus designated is often more and also less than one might expect: at one end of the spectrum it does have technical qualities, because it is either descriptive (along *blason* lines) or aims at the formal didactic treatise (hunting, medicine, etc.), and at the other end, it becomes philosophical or religious in tone and aim, so that it may develop into poetry about man's destiny through the ages.

In the 1550s, various forces combine to encourage the writing of this type of poetry. There is in any case a central urge in humanism towards polymathy and sciences should attract the scholar as much as philology and other branches of learning. Moreover, a number of distinguished scientists – doctors, biologists, travellers – begin to publish their works, many of which are in the vernacular. Attempts to write scientific poetry in Latin verse, with a pedagogic view in mind, are far from uncommon (Lygæus or Lyège, Mizault, George Buchanan). The poets of the vernacular also take an active interest: after all, the poet is the rounded man of culture, in whose eyes philosophy is close to the Muses. We have seen how Neoplatonic and occultist currents come into view at this time; and the cosmic schemata of the Church Fathers and Doctors doubtless play some part. In the 1550s one comes across examples of the blend of religious and scientific interests in works such as Pierre Duval, *De la grandeur de Dieu, et de la congnoissance qu'on peult avoir de luy par ses œuvres* (1555, reprinted 1557) or, by the same author, *De la puissance et bonté de Dieu* (1558). Both these works were published by Michel Vascosan, from whose house a number of scientific works appear towards this time. Then, a widespread awareness of the classical *visions du monde*, often at variance with Christian orthodoxy, was bound to quicken interest in these matters; Lucretius, so handsomely edited by Denys Lambyn, made a deep impression on many a humanist mind, however firm Christian resistance might be to his doctrine. It is in this period of intellectual ferment that Ronsard turns his attention to philosophical poetry (*Hymnes*).

Peletier du Mans – Amour des Amours (*1554*)[18]

In the realm of scientific poetry, Jacques Peletier du Mans, as elsewhere, emerges as a notable pioneer. We have already met him in the vanguard of poetic reform, acting as a mentor to a younger generation and trying his hand in new modes, particularly in love-poetry. After the first productions of Ronsard and Du Bellay, he comes to the front again with his *Amour des Amours*. Admittedly this is a mixed bag, divided very loosely into three sections, composed, he tells us, partly as recreation from an over-studious life – a love cycle, the *Uranie*, and the *vers lyriques* already known. The first section, it seems, was conceived much earlier, but revised for this volume: it has many features of the Petrarchan cycle, but it is more than that: Peletier has on various occasions expressed disquiet at the Petrarchan vogue, and in his own poetry he was hoping to combine the arts and the sciences. The cycle develops a number of themes which on his own admission were *Platonis imitatione scripta*, and he introduces more 'scientific' elements: the zodiac, the relations between love and Nature's contraries, and also with the cosmos and eternity – for love takes man beyond himself and is the principle of harmony in the Universe. Other themes, such as hope, Nature, death, man's intellectual yearning, find space. *L'Uranie*, the title of which is reminiscent of Pontano, a source of several themes, is a series of poems opening with *L'er* (i.e., air; Peletier was concerned with spelling reform); in this poem he traces the passage from chaos to the ordering of the elements, but sees in the air the vehicle of the earth aspiring to the skies. A number of poems deal with climatic phenomena, dew, rain, hail – and Peletier has an observant eye for the details of Nature; then there follow five planetary poems. The one to the Moon begins thus:

> Sœur de Phebus, la plus proche des Terres,
> Ornant la nuit de noir emmantelée,
> Plus que les sis legerement tu erres
> L'oblique tour de la voie etelée [i.e., estoilée].
> Tu reluis la plus evidente
> Du ciel, apres la lampe ardente
> De ton frere, qui te renflamme,
> Tous tes mois, de nouvelle flamme.
>
> (1555 ed., p. 91)

In this type of writing we have a craftsman very conscious of his art; Peletier takes care to vary his stanzaic forms, and prides himself on using the vernacular. He also tries to marry an elevated tone (can one detect a muted Pindaric note sometimes?) and richer imagery with a didactic element, to which end *blason* techniques are sometimes directed. Erudition is expected to play a significant role, and Peletier shows that deeper interest in mythology which characterises the middle of the century, but his hopes of composing an *Hercule chrétien* were never fulfilled. In *Venus* we see the return of themes developed in other poems:

> C'est Deesse, par ton secours,
> Que la Nature s'esvertue,
> Et qu'en filant de cours en cours
> Ses siècles elle perpetue:

Quand du grand Monde les vivans
De tes plaisirs ne degenerent,
Et tousjours ton instinct suivans,
Ne peut qu'ils ne se regenerent . . .

Bien heureux qui point ne suis
A la geniale liesse:
En terre on ne veut que les nuiz,
Pour l'effet de sa hardiesse.
Peur, soupçon, deulh et malheurté
Sentent leur Amour Terrienne:
Foi, honneur, joyeuse surté
Sont de l'Amour venerienne . . .
(1555 ed., pp. 96, 99)

But they are worked out in a pastoral and sometimes more sensual
tone – deriving in part from Jean Second and the Greek lyric poets? –
so that Peletier's rather dry line assumes a greater roundness and
vitality than is often the case; here he seems to have allowed
emotion a greater share and the stanzas acquire thereby a finer resonance and vigour. Peletier thus plays an important part in the development of scientific poetry: he makes us aware of the forces at
work in Nature, but though he expatiates on the links between
macrocosm and microcosm, he communicates to the reader a lesson
rather than an intuition. But he confers dignity on the role of the
poet, whom he sees as a *conscience élargie* of the human condition;
and he is a writer whose interests never cease to widen. Later in his
life he publishes his *Savoye* (1572):[19] the result of two years' sojourn
in that region, it reflects the author's sensitivity to the wars of religion, but it is essentially a descriptive poem. It fits into the tradition
of the extended *blason*, which is also exploited in Neo-latin (Germain
Audebert), but the scientific and descriptive elements are more prominent here. Peletier can still be dry on occasion, as for instance in his
catalogue of medicinal herbs; he does not interest himself in the
history of Savoy, and tends to extract poetry from many of the things
he observes, though he recognises that there are dangers in too detailed, full descriptions. He will tell us of the vegetable kingdom:

Je chantere la naïve structure
Des Montz ornez de moyenne culture,

then of the animals, the trees, the beneficial waters of Annecy. These
descriptions are accompanied by other themes: Peletier reflects on
man in Nature, especially in Book I, at the end of which there is an
invocation to Nature that for once does take poetic wing. There is
also a passage worth remembering on the snow. Peletier's final poetic
work was the *Louenges* published in 1581: thematically they do not
show marked progress, but he finds a happy outlet for his talents in a
framework less grandiose than that of the *Savoye*.

Maurice Scève – Microcosme (*1562*)[20]

Maurice Scève was a friend of Peletier du Mans, and he published his *Microcosme* in 1562, nearly twenty years after the *Délie*, though it was probably completed, in spite of its uneven polish, towards 1559, as the last three lines of the poem suggest. It is divided into three books of a thousand lines apiece, and the author has taken much care with the overall structure and symmetries of the poem. It opens with the narrative of Adam from his creation to the crime of Cain. In Books II and III Adam sees, through the device of the dream, the evolution of man's achievement in the world up to the appearance of Christ the Redeemer in whose image man has been fashioned. The poem concludes, as it began, with the praise of God, and man's destiny is thus bracketed within the divine presence and will. Nevertheless, it seems to strike a more anthropocentric note, partly because God gives man a very great measure of freedom to shape his own destiny, partly because the theme of the Fall is played down through the greater emphasis laid on Cain's sin which, contrasted with Adam's fate, is shown to lead to nothingness, partly because of the tones and proportions that colour Scève's presentation of man's inventiveness and accomplishment. It is not that the materials on which he draws are in any sense new, for the sources are often medieval or early humanist, though one may wonder whether he has not been affected by the works of Charles de Bouelles (see above, pp. 76–7). There are long passages, especially those in which Scève describes the content of the *trivium* and *quadrivium*, such as the mathematical elements, which strike us as distinctly arid from the poetic standpoint, because of their highly technical language which is used in a 'flat' manner, dictated by intellectual rather than imaginative needs, and decorated occasionally by rhetorical devices of repetition and ternary pattern. The interest of the poem lies elsewhere.

Scève stresses man's privileged position in the Universe ('seul sur tous animaux capable de raison'); of course man's character may lead him towards God or to brutality in his relations with other humans, 'Selon qu'il se reçoit spirituel en soy,/Ou sort dehors charnel'; but though his passage through his world was determined by his fall, that passage is often presented as triumph, the triumph of his own initiative:

> Par là, seigneuriant en air, eau, terre, aussi,
> Non sans solicitude, esmoy, cure et souci
> Soulagea son travail, et sa melancolie
> Par recreation d'honneste eutrapelie
>   [Greek for wit, liveliness]
> Après avoir trouvé mille et mille beautés . . .
>   (Guégan ed., p. 271)

a passage that dominates the following lines where the other 'postulation' is described. Though man's first fashioning of clothes is shown as the consequence of his fall (the sense of shame), this mood does not last. Man's progress in agriculture and later in knowledge, and above all in craftsmanship (architecture, painting, metalwork, coal-mining), is related in forceful lines that press on urgently; and the long section in which Scève portrays man's journeying on horseback through all the known world is important for its tone, even if, as some critics have noted, man does not actually achieve anything by these peregrinations. In fact, this passage serves to conjure up the personality of the Earth which is peculiarly man's own: it forms thus a sharp contrast with the picture of Paradise in Book I, and one may feel that man's role as a microcosm has swollen somewhat in stature. Yet even in Book I, there are passages which reveal the humanity of man: the scenes from Nature, though they owe something to a liter-ary tradition, are very much more dynamic than their medieval counterparts, and the lines evoking Adam's relations with his wife have lost their biblical tones. At one time one may think that Adam has been reading Petrarch (or *Délie*), at others, his awareness of his wife is startlingly sensual. There peeps through an enjoyment of life in its own right than links up vigorously with Scève's enthusiastic pronouncements on man's cultural achievements; in this context the scenes where Adam or his wife is shown eating are noteworthy, and indeed the special note of excitement is often that of hunger, natural or intellectual ('De curieux desir tousjours insatiable/Et en inven-tion subtile esmerveillable'). So it comes about that, however sincere the religious framework of the poem – and I see no reason to doubt Scève's feelings on that score – the emotive weight of the text lies elsewhere; optimism and confidence replace any preoccupation with original sin, and here Cain acts, as it were, as a sort of lightning con-ductor. A sense of vital apprehension comes through also in the pas-sage dealing with architecture; it is a pity that the musician in Scève was unable to make the section on music come to life in the same way. There is delight in the 'futur bien du monde' and in passing the humanist salutes Greece and Paris. The dividing line between vanity and pride is a narrow one, but Adam remains this side of Cain.

Stylistically, the *Microcosme* reflects the antinomies of the sub-stance: passages of linguistic aridity (technical vocabulary, enumer-ation) alternate with others where a dynamic rhythm finds itself at home in the ampler dimensions of the alexandrine; but the innovator of syntax, imagery, and vocabulary is less to the fore than when the *Délie* was on the stocks. An occasional word, the successful inversion, the appropriate *incise*, these sometimes occur, but the effects are obtained not by concentration so much as by a sensitive control of the broader phrase. The *Microcosme* is certainly a heterogeneous composition, aesthetically speaking, and execution sometimes appears less accomplished than the plan. Nevertheless, Scève's poem gives timely utterance to a certain conception of Renaissance man, and here and there, he shows what can be achieved in poetic quality in the realm of 'scientific' poetry.

Guy Lefèvre de la Boderie (1541-98)[21]

It is after 1570 that the taste for the extended philosophical composition becomes more noticeable; and among the first authors to work in this vein is Guy Lefèvre de la Boderie. We saw him earlier in the company of Vauquelin de la Fresnaye and Charles Toutain; in his poetry he follows in the tradition of Peletier, Pontus de Tyard, and Scève whom he mentions in respectful terms. He reveals a very wide culture coloured by religious and philosophic preoccupations that show an interesting awareness of the Hebraic as well as of the classical traditions. He was a friend of Guillaume Postel, to whom he owes much; he translated F. Giorgio's *De harmonia Mundi* and a work by Marsilio Ficino; his interests extend to *prisca theologia*, patristics, and indeed all forms of learning to which he can gain access. He is convinced that poetry and *sapientia* go hand in hand:

> Les poetes allechans ont usé mon enfance
> Et la Mathematique a eu l'adolescence,
> De la Filosofie ay senti devancer
> L'age qui vient apres puis les langues diverses
> La Jeunesse restant ont comblé de traverses,
> Et ores, mon Toustain, c'est a recommencer.

We find him in the circle of the duc d'Anjou; he is on friendly terms with Jean Dorat with whom he shares a belief in the efficacy of anagrams:

> Tourne NOBLE ou rebours, tu trouveras LE BON.
> Voy combien ce beau nom convient bien à la chose!
> Sous le voile du mot l'essence se repose.
> Vrayment les Noms certains ne sont point composés
> Par opinion d'homme, & par homme imposés;
> Mais Nature a caché dessous leurs caractères
> Ne sçay quelle vigueur pleine de grans Mystères.
>
> (*L'Encyclie*, p. 73)

However, his syncretist enthusiasms do not impede him in his passionate desire to defend the Catholic religion; he refers to the great number of 'atheistes' springing up everywhere, he believes that the study of philosophy should reveal 'la preuve naturelle des articles de nostre Foy', and he composes a number of religious poems, some of which are biblical paraphrases, others inspired by the Church Fathers (cf. Jacques de Billy towards the same period), yet others utilising the old *rhétoriqueur* form of the *chant royal*, and rather impressively too. His first work, the *Encyclie*, was published in 1571, though it was more than planned some years earlier, for at the age of fifteen he became convinced that there are 'de tels monstrueux esprits qui osoyent pleinement denier & Dieu & sa Providence'. The work is primarily a discussion in verse of various central problems of philosophy bearing on 'les secrets de l'Eternité', and coloured obviously by the Neoplatonic tradition. The following extract shows how a philosophic theme can be developed by descriptive techniques and the use of an elevated tone we have seen in similar compositions:

> Aussy l'Ame qui fait & croistre & bourjonner
> Les arbres verdoyans, veut vivre & sejourner
> En la racine creuse, & tire sous l'escorce
> Et la sefve & le suc, leur nourriture et force:
> Qui les fait pulluler, & aus branches conduit
> Du pied jusqu'au coupeau & feuille & fleur & fruit:
> Mesme au centre du fruit Nature esmerveillable
> Recele la Vertu d'engendrer son semblable.
> Elle hume l'humeur, & sa fertilité
> Poind les greffes au tronc plein de sterilité.
> C'est elle qui produit la Poésie sur l'Espine,
> Dessus le Merisier l'Agrioche poupine:
> Fait sur les Sauvageaus les Pommes d'or meurir,
> Et dedans le Prunier les Abricots fleurir . . .
>
> (*L'Encyclie*, pp. 76-7)

In his other major work, the *Galliade ou la Revolution des arts et sciences* (1578), many of the preoccupations that go to the making of the *Encyclie* are accompanied by a vigorous cultural nationalism. The author shows his awareness of the relationship of the poem to the epic, but distinguishes it carefully from what is 'pour la pluspart tissue de fables, & contes plaisans', whereas he is writing for 'l'utilité & la verité'. Here, as in Baïf and others, a narrower view of the links between art and truth (or science) is being developed. The work is divided into five books: the first deals with 'le department de la Terre habitable', which does not seek to repeat the formula of the hexameric poem, however often La Boderie emphasises the religious perspective in which his work is conceived, but it gives a rapid account of the origins of French culture. We are offered the myth of the *Hercule gaulois*.[22] Gaul, through Gomer, develops the arts that can be traced in their spread through the Hebrew and Greek worlds on to Rome – incidentally the duc d'Anjou, to whom the poem is dedicated, is referred to as Alcide. Pluto, taught by Janus, had conquered France and inaugurated the reign of letters and arts. These various myths, whose origins we have mentioned (see above, p. 49), serve above all to underline France's cultural supremacy and priority. La Boderie is willing to praise the Italians for their cultural achievements, but attributes them to the pioneer work of Gomer:

> Je vous salue Esprits, bonne posterité,
> Qui avez de Gomer nostre pere herité
> La science encerclée, & remis en lumiere

Du bon siècle doré l'excellence premiere:
Politian poly, subtil & fin Ficin,
Grand-Prestre, Philosophe, & docte Medecin,
Et toy restaurateur de la faconde rare
Qui n'a jamais rien eu sinon le nom Barbare: . . .

But La Boderie soon goes on to praise famous Frenchmen, after a respectful bow to Francis I:

Je vous salue, Esprits clairs, & divins flambeaux,
Qui aurez esclairé dans les mortels tombeaux
Des corps grossiers obscurs, & chassé de la France
Le monstre tenebreux de l'aveugle Ignorance.
(fol. 19 v, 31 v)

There follows a list which includes Lefèvre d'Etaples, Oronce Finé, Guillaume Budé, Erasmus ('qui t'es dict Gaulois', writes the patriotic opportunist), Vatable, Amyot, Lazare de Baïf, Postel, Pierre de La Ramée, Fernel 'Archidruide heroïque & divin,/Mathematicien ensemble & Medecin', Peletier du Mans, and Forcadel. La Boderie clearly attaches great importance to French mathematicians, all the more significant as in the first half of the century, the science of mathematics was hardly at the top of the humanist league table. The second book treats of architecture and once again pays particular attention to French masters; the third sings of the 'sçavoir admirable de noz Druides en la connoissance de toutes disciplines' and works its way through all aspects of national distinction:

Mais qui pourroit parler de Gaule maintenant,
Qui enferme en son sein, & qui va comprenant
Toutes lettres, tous arts, tous autheurs, toutes langues,
Toutes loix, toutes meurs, tous discours & harangues?
(fol. 69 r)

Universities, magistrature, and *parlements* are lauded, but actors condemned; and special mention is made of French saints and theologians. Book IV concerns itself with music and harmony (celestial and human), and the last book discusses poetry, which La Boderie considers to stand apart on account of its 'saincte fureur & elevation d'esprit', but deserving of praise on its return to France after several centuries of neglect. Poetry and music are sisters and La Boderie, who praises Dante for writing in the vernacular, suggests that these arts restore our sense of the primitive harmony that existed before the fall of man. He pays tribute to those poets who have made this cultural renewal possible, above all Ronsard whose name has anagrammatic value:

Vive le grand *Ronsard*, qui d'esprit haut & rare
A fait en son nom clair *Se redorer Pindare*.
(fol. 124 v)

Héroët obtains a *mention honorable*, but what is more interesting is that this declared admirer of the Pléiade is very favourable to Marot:

> Marot, l'un des premiers d'un vers doux et facile
> De la muse se feist auditeur fort docile,
> Et chanta l'epigramme, & l'Eglogue bien joint
> Tant après Martial, que Vergile plus coint:
> Puis son stile elima de façon plus heureuse
> En la Metamorphose heroique et nombreuse,
> Et aux chants de David, qu'en vers il a rendus
> Assez bien agencez, & non pas entendus.
>
> (fol. 123 r–v)

La Boderie's work is thus an extension of the scientific poem strictly interpreted; in addition to technical descriptions and an account of origins, where myths, religion, and knowledge intermingle, he has created a work that is a paean to French culture. Poetically, the moments of elevation are few and far between, but La Boderie prolongs the Pléiade endeavour and gives abundant expression to a cultural attitude of which we saw early affirmation in the Neo-latin poets of the 1530s, but which reaches maturity in the vernacular with the Pléiade.

Saluste du Bartas (1544–90)[23]

Du Bartas's aims were very ambitious, but an early death prevented him from realising them; the *Seconde Sepmaine* remained unfinished. It is the *Premiere Sepmaine* which established his fame, for it went through more than 25 editions before the death of Henry IV, was immediately translated into several European languages, and was the subject of a learned commentary by Simon Goulart. A meridional, Du Bartas was the friend of Etienne Forcadel and Pierre de Brach; he may have met Peletier du Mans when the latter was principal of the Collège de Guyenne and he knew D'Aubigné about 1577 – their conceptions of epic poetry in the service of the Huguenot cause overlap slightly, but Du Bartas has none of D'Aubigné's acrid militancy. He lived happily in his province, where there were quite a number of humanists with kindred literary interests. In 1574 he published his *Triomphe de la Foi*, the *Uranie*, and *Judit*,[24] whose themes were apparently suggested by Jeanne d'Albret, and in 1578 there came out the *Premiere Sepmaine*.

The poem's structure is determined by its hexameric theme, which became popular in the sixteenth century, no doubt in part through renewed interest in early Christian writers, some of whom had devoted their energies to this type of composition. At the same time, Du Bartas's work has the polymathic aspirations we have noted in La Boderie and others. It must be conceded that Du Bartas's sense of large-scale form is frail: sometimes the poem gives the impression of a vast Parnassian and humanist junk-shop, and the clumsiness that betrays itself in language and in presentation has put off readers of later generations. Much of Du Bartas's information is perforce second-hand and bookish; and there is a didactic tone that pervades much of the text. The author is less interested in science than in preaching the doctrine, though he deliberately avoids too partisan an approach:

> Sage, n'aille jamais cingler en haute mer;
> Ains costoye la rive, ayant la Foy pour voile,
> L'Esprit sainct pour nocher, la Bible pour estoile
> (I, lines 82 ff.)

and his further aim is to lead man into the paths of righteous behaviour. He attacks court poets who devote their time to singing of love, when poetry has a much higher mission (Canto II, opening lines). Digressions, inevitably, abound: passages on the character of the good king, or the virtues of astrology and numerology, over-extended sections on controversial scientific or philosophical matters; and if, as Du Bartas seems to have believed, everything in the world is worthy to be sung as it has been created by God, then we have another reason for rarely invoking the principle of artistic selection. The great variety of subject-matter calls for a similar range of poetic genre and tone within the overall structure, as the poet himself was perfectly aware. It is easy to single out his weaknesses, lapses of taste, stylistic obsessions, linguistic infelicities, passages of unending aridity; nevertheless, his defects have blinded critics to other, more admirable qualities. What makes him difficult to quote pleasurably is that his failure to sustain tone introduces an unhappy contrast of levels, as in the following extract where a certain sensitivity to natural beauty is swamped by didactic intent:

> Jà la vigne amoureuse accole en mainte sorte
> D'un bras entortillé son mary qui la porte –
> Vigne qui cede autant à tout arbre en beauté,
> Comme tout arbre cede à la vigne en bonté.
> Son fruict, pris par compas, les esprits vivifie,
> Enhardit un cœur mol, les cerveaux purifie,
> Resveille l'appetit, redonne la couleur,
> Les conduicts desopile, augmente la chaleur,
> Engendre le pur sang, la trouble subtilize,
> Chasse les excremens, l'entendement aiguise,
> Espierre la vessie et preserve nos corps
> Du Lethé jà voisins de cent sortes de morts.
> (III, lines 509 ff.)

The inability to shorten the inventory, linked with a monotony of stylistic resource, destroys the poetic promise of the first lines. How-ever, Du Bartas does on occasion reveal a genuine response to the world around him, there are passages in which his Gascon patriotism brings out a fresher fervour, and he does have a sense of the majesty of the Universe. Here and there, too, he shows a *fin-de-siècle* awareness of the crumbling nature of the world, which theologically he does not allow to pass into permanence:

> Un jour de comble-en-fond les rochers crouleront,
> Les monts plus sourcilleux de peur se dissoudront,
> Le Ciel se crevera, les plus basses campagnes,
> Boursouflées, croistront en superbes montagnes;
> Les fleuves tariront, et si dans quelque estang
> Reste encor quelque flot, ce ne sera que sang;
> La mer deviendra flamme, et les seches balenes,
> Horribles, mugleront sur les cuites arenes;
> En son midy plus clair le jour s'espaissira,
> Le ciel d'un fer rouillé sa face voilera.
> Sur les astres plus clairs courra le bleu Neptune,
> Phoebus s'emparera du noir char de la lune;
> Les estoiles cherront. Le desordre, la nuit,
> La frayeur, le trespas, la tempeste, le bruit,
> Entreront en quartier; et l'ire vengeresse
> Du Juge criminel, qui jà desjà nous presse,
> Ne fera de ce Tout qu'un bucher flamboyant,
> Comme il n'en fit jadis qu'un marez ondoyant.
>   (I, lines 353 ff.)

The linguistic tricks – compound words, dialectalisms or technical terms, overheated comparisons – are not pressed into service here, nor is the momentum impaired, so that we have a prophetic tone-poem that reminds us of Sponde or D'Aubigné expressing their sense of awesome disintegration. Unfortunately Du Bartas achieves only rarely that unity of vision, that density of tone, or the linguistic vitality that characterises so much of D'Aubigné's finest writing; his success remains patchy, and there is probably at bottom a lack of originality that becomes only too evident in poems of the scale he hoped to compose, where dithyramb and vacuum too often are synonymous.

After Du Bartas, the scientific poem continues to enjoy success, but none of its practitioners is very notable. Edouard du Monin, that eccentric and disorganised polymath who died too young to show more than longwinded promise, ventures into the field with, on the one hand, a Latin translation of Du Bartas's *Premiere Sepmaine*, and on the other, a translation or adaptation of part of George Buchanan's *De Sphœra*, the loss of the original manuscript of which poses some intriguing problems. Like other poets of that generation, Du Monin is fascinated by the spread of alchemy, to which he pays more attention than to the Copernican theory. Joseph du Chesne's *Grand Miroir du Monde* was published in 1587 and reprinted some eight years later; he is yet another example of polymathic ambition that overspills into alchemy, but betrays some inkling of what the empiric method is about. Two other authors may be mentioned in rather more detail: Beroalde de Verville and Isaac Habert.

Beroalde de Verville (1556–?1629)[25]

Verville's career goes beyond our period and also moves into the field of devotional poetry and anti-aulic satire; but the early work of this extraordinary polymath, who dabbled in alchemy and astrology and abjured his Huguenot upbringing to become a Roman Catholic, compels our attention. His *Apprehensions spirituelles* (1583) show that his main concerns are philosophical, with the poetic trailing behind. In the preface to Du Gast he mentions his long passion for philosophy on which he is now writing,

usant d'un style que j'ay esleu pour delecter, diversifiant mes discours, ores en prose, ores en vers, suyvant en cela la liberté que j'ay eu & ay avec vous & celle de mon esprit.

The *Cognoissances necessaires* form a lengthy, shambling poem which claims to resolve various philosophical points and discusses among other things the creation of prime matter, the four elements, fortune (linked with God's will and sent to punish us), Nature (which is not 'subjette à l'abus d'un destin casuel'), the creation of man and woman, the 'premieres forces d'amour', and the androgyne, also marriage:

> Le mariage aussi commence par destin,
> Se forme par amour, par honneur prend sa fin:
> Car nulle n'est jamais à sa moitié donnée,
> Si tout premier au ciel elle n'est ordonnée,
> Et si d'un saint amour on n'eschauffe son cœur,
> Ainsi que n'estant rien, il n'y a point d'ardeur . . .
> (fol. 20 r–v)

Verville's mind loosely embraces a vast array of knowledge, which leads him into the need to guard his orthodoxy at this corner and the next. The volume contains dialogues, the 'rechercher de la pierre philosophale', and the *Poeme de l'ame et de ses facultés*, which is strictly a didactic poem, as may appear from the following passage on the imagination:

> Mais il seroit bien peu si ne luy survenoit
> Ce qui en son estat entretenir le doit.
> Et le plaisir soudain delairroit nostre vie,
> Si cette ame n'avoit en soy la fantasie,
> Qui est un mouvement que par son action
> Le sens fait naistre estant en quelque passion:
> C'est le divin tableau où se peint sans peinture
> Tout cela qui n'est point, ou qui est en nature,
> Le principal outil de cette faculté
> Estant dans le cerveau, en la concavité,
> Qui moins que la premiere humide & vaporeuse,

Reçoit l'impression d'une image douteuse,
Ayant pour son object ce qui est delaissé
Apres que le cachet de la chose a pressé
Son simulachre au sens, & qui diverse essence
Retient tout freschement du senti la semblance,
Ayant son action egalement au trait
Du senti absenté, qui laissant son portraict
Comme tout relevé, encores le releve,
En la matiere proche en sa forme il reserve.

                              (fol. 38 v–39 r)

His portrait of the Golden Age has rather more to commend it, and is a good example of the way in which the legend continues to grip the Renaissance imagination:

L'aage estoit simple, & saint, & innocens encor
Nos ancestres estoient, regnans en l'aage d'or,
Tant d'estats n'estoient point & de tant de trafiques,
On ne s'alloit trompant parmi les republiques,
Et l'homme ne tiroit mesmes du font d'enfer,
L'or, le cuyvre, l'argent, l'estain, le plomb, le fer,
On n'estoit different par mestier, ny estude,
Il n'y avoit grandeur, estat, ni servitude,
Les nobles ne pressoient dessous leur joug contraint
Le pauvre roturier qui n'a le cœur atteint
Des delices d'honneur, & par tant d'artifices
On ne faisoit sembler les vertus estre vices:
La difference encor, les degrés, ni l'honneur,
Ne pressoient de dedain, de gloire, de fureur
Les hommes qui ne sont maintenant que l'ombrage
De la perfection qui fut au premier aage.
Le grand n'estoit pour lors pour autant qu'il eut plus
Que le moindre que soy de force ou de vertus,
Et le sage n'estoit distingué par personne:
Car en un tout estoit d'une ordonnance bonne,
On ne recherchoit point par sa vacation
La richesse ou grandeur: & cette ambition
Qui mesme touche au cœur le philosophe sage,
N'avoit encor saisi de l'homme le courage,
Et l'esprit remuant ne faisoit rechercher
Les secrets où ne faut prophanément toucher,
On ne mesloit aussi au Mercure volage
Le Mercure fixe, pour de leur alliage
Une poudre non poudre, & liqueur non liqueur
Former . . .

                              (fol. 21 r–v)

But too often Verville fails to use his imagination to clothe the bones of his argument, and we have little more than arid versification of abstract prose. In his scientific poetry he rarely manages to inject any sense of cosmic wonder, his detachment is so great as to suggest indifference to the subject treated. Perhaps he feels more at home in restricted genres, where he is able to infuse feeling and imagination, as for instance in some sonnets of the *Muse celeste ou l'Amour divin*:

Source de verité, lumiere de ce monde,
Mets en moy les desirs d'un amour eternel,
Et que t'adorant seul mon cœur soit immortel,
Prenant par ta bonté une essence seconde,

Jà desjà transmué, dans l'abysme profonde
Je voy mille tourmens menacer le mortel,
Je voy mille regrets d'un soin perpetuel
Faire autour de son cœur incessamment la ronde.

Ton Amour sur les Cieux m'esleve d'icy bas,
Où loin du desplaisir des journaliers debats,
Travaillans les meschans je voy sauvé ma vie.

Garde moy en ton sein & fais que dans le mien
Je tienne si cher qu'au monde il n'y ait rien
Qui d'oublier tel bien me face avoir envie.

(Sonnet xi)

The tone of supplication, the use of contemporary rhetorical devices, the visual element, all these help to give the poem a sense of urgent appeal. Verville's use of rhetoric may lead to alembication, he does not always seem to know when enough is enough; as a result the combination of abstraction and verbal insensitivity hinders him from achieving poetic success as often as he might. His lack of organisation and firmness constitutes a major weakness, so that he comes off best in the shorter form or in some isolated passage of an extended composition. His religious poetry, however, acquires an individual tone in that his themes are enriched by his awareness of other philosophical traditions.

Isaac Habert (?1560–   ?)[26]

Habert printed his *Trois Livres des Meteores* in 1585, that is three years after his *Œuvres poétiques*. His work mirrors faithfully certain contemporary trends: the pervading influence of Ronsard – he writes love-poetry, Pindaric odes, ventures into the pastoral mode – interest in the scientific poem, and excursions into Christian verse. Habert informs us that he aims to describe 'les corps qui peignent leur naissance/Aus regions de l'air, la pluie ou le frimas', dew, lightning, and whirlwinds; but he will also write on 'le premier principe' (God), the elements, the sun and stars. The third book is devoted to lapidaries; so that we have a blend of cosmic vision and the *blason* techniques used for the description of precise objects. Classical mythology and a perusal of the Pléiade poets, especially Du Bartas, colour Habert's style, but the work as a whole is lopsided, as we move from the wider horizons to the minute object. Here is a sample of his verse, *Du tremblement de la terre*:

La Terre eut autrefois du tenebreux Tartare,
Un fils nommé Typhon, geant fier & barbare,
D'excessive hauteur, qui fort & furieux
Fut l'effroi des humains, & la terreur des Dieus . . .

Il touchoit de son chef aus estoiles luisantes,
Aus coins de l'Univers, son grand corps se vestoit
De plumes par le haut, par le bas il estoit
Espouvantable à veoir, ses jambes écaillées
En forme de serpens estoient entortillées,
Du bas jusques au chef des viperes pressoient
Son effroiable corps, & rampans s'enlassoient
En noeuds & en replis, sa longue chevelure
Du poil rude & retors sur son espaule dure
Flottoit au gré du vent, dessus son sein velu
Pendoit de son menton un long touffeau pelu:
Ses yeux estinceloient comme ardantes chandelles,
Et vomissoit le feu de ses levres jumelles.
                              (fol. 37 r–v)

What weakens this passage is the unskilful use of the epithet which is over-exploited and often tautological, but some sense of movement and atmosphere is achieved. Habert's love sonnets, inspired by a dilute Petrarchism, can be passed over; more interesting is his pastoral vein, where we have the *Louange de la vie rustique*, eclogues, adaptations of Ovid, horticultural verse, some *pescheries* showing the influence of Sannazaro, and here and there an interest in the occult (*Aeromancie*, *Hydromancie*) against a bucolic background. Habert reflects the fashion for rustic poetry which is characteristic of the last years of the wars of religion, and his Christian verse, thoroughly orthodox, also echoes contemporary concerns: the greatness of God, man's sinful nature, the intercession of Christ and the saints:

> . . . Rien ne demeure icy ferme, stable, & constant,
> Tout s'altere, & corrompt, tout change en un instant,
> L'acier, l'airain, le fer, le marbre, & le Porphire,
> Cedent en fin au temps qui va tout consumant,
> Fol donc qui les tresors du Monde ayme & desire,
> C'est en Dieu seul qu'il faut mettre contentement. (fol. 7 v)

A somewhat servile fidelity to Pléiade practice and an inordinate fondness for enumeration give Habert's verse a sense of superficial inevitability; he follows literary fashion, as one might expect from this minor court poet and friend of Desportes, and only in the smaller poem where he can describe the outer world does he rise above himself.

The poetic harvest of this scientific poetry is patchy and not very abundant, but the genre constitutes a sizeable aspect of the literary scene in the last three decades or so of the century. It reflects the humanist desire for man to master universal knowledge; it also expresses his search for his position in the cosmos, and this aspect is given a greater urgency in the context of the religious wars, an urgency which is often accompanied by a clear profession of faith. More often than not, the 'scientific' element belongs to the philosophic rather than to the experimental world, and we may find some overlap of interest with the subject-matter of the dialogues which are also so characteristic of this phase of intellectual ferment. At the same time, humanists are encouraged to write these large-scale works because they are convinced that poetry and higher wisdom should go hand in hand, and many of the compositions develop the older theme of God's glory reflected in the world He created. The attitudes we might associate with Pico della Mirandola and Charles de Bouelles, with their anthropocentric tendencies, are not as prominent as one might have expected *prima facie*, but after all most of these works are conceived fairly late on during the wars. In spite of their many imperfections, they shed much light on the humanist mind during these troubled decades.

IV. RELIGIOUS POETRY[27]

Though several members of the Pléiade wrote religious poems of high quality, one can hardly say that as a group they made their mark in this field, however fanatical they might be in their orthodoxy; and the Calvinists reproached them for their allegiance to pagan models. During the 1550s, if we keep Calvinist activity on one side, there is not a great deal of religious poetry being published. One interesting work deserves mention: Nicolas Denisot's *Cantique du premier advenement de Jesu-Christ* (1553), with introductory verse by Belleau, Jodelle, and Muret.[28] This series of poems reveals a determined attempt to forsake classical Pléiade inspiration for Christian verse. The fourteen *cantiques*, written in different short ode forms, include themes such as the 'grand' charité de Dieu', but also that of the Immaculate Conception. What is interesting is precisely the transference of Pléiade preoccupations to Christian ends: the tone of the poems, wide in range, is often dithyrambic and elevated, reminiscent of the tone Ronsard was seeking in his Pindaric experiments; a considerable amount of space is given over to pastoral elements, and Denisot's poetry comes to life especially when he sings of the sun and the night: indeed the theme of light is a dominant and vigorously handled. The canticles, which are addressed to the wife of Jean de Morel, are set to music, of a solo kind, so that they can be sung in solitude. In this musical concern, Denisot is looking for the Christian counterpart to Ronsard's *Amours*: Muret, who composed one of the Ronsard settings, invites poets in his liminary verse to forsake love themes and follow Denisot in singing Christ.

Otherwise, it is the Calvinists who set the pace, as can be seen more especially in drama and in psalm paraphrase, though Lancelot de Carle publishes his numerous paraphrases of sacred texts between 1558 and 1562.[29] Inevitably the deliberations of the Council of Trent

and the outbreak of the religious wars in France will give powerful
impetus to the composition of religious verse. The tendency to paraphrase biblical texts will persist, both in Latin and in the vernacular,
and these may sometimes be on an impressive scale (De Thou). The
comparative rigidity of the Counter-reformation in doctrinal matters
was a blow to those who hoped for some compromise in the interests
of avoiding schism; but, as many agreed, the views described as
'evangelical' reflected the conviction that religion had lost its way
and that inwardness had given way to gesture and even commercial-
ism. There are of course link figures, such as Claude d'Espence who
was studying in Paris in the late 1520s and who enjoys some prestige
at the beginning of the 1560s.[30] Nor is it surprising that works belonging to the *devotio moderna*, such as the *Imitation of Christ*,
enjoy a genuine vogue, or that foreign writings, like Loyola's *Spiritual
Exercises* or Granada's *Le Vray chemin et adresse pour acquerir et
parvenir à la grace de Dieu . . .* and *Devotes contemplations et
spirituelles instructions sur la Vie, Passion, Mort, Resurrection et
glorieuse Ascension de nostre Sauveur Jesus Christ*, translated by
Belleforest in 1579 and 1585 respectively, should be widely read.
The titles in fact underline evangelical themes: spirituality, the need
for grace, the meditation on the life of Christ; and Loyola was in
Paris (Montaigu and Sainte-Barbe) in the critical years *c.* 1530.
Apart from the written word, various centres encouraged a greater
religious concern: in the first rank no doubt were the Jesuits, in spite
of their stormy passage in France. It seems too that the *puys* played
some role: I have referred to the *chants royaux* composed by Lefèvre
de la Boderie, and in 1575 and 1583 that very popular composer
Orlando di Lasso was a prizewinner at Evreux. Then there are the
currents of devotion: Henry III's mystical excesses were often interpreted as a reaction to other forms of excess, but he was truly
interested in spirituality, he encouraged the founding of new orders,
and he had around him men devoted to a religious renewal: Baïf's
Academy, for all its Neoplatonic flavour, also had a spiritual orientation.

In addition to impetus from Calvinist sources (see above, pp. 347–8),
there is one further source of devotional attitudes: neo-stoicism.
Stoicism and Christianity form an alliance in the works of Justus
Lipsius and Du Vair, and these authors were certainly read by contemporary poets; but so were the classical sources, Seneca, Epictetus,
and Cicero, and it is not only the ethic that holds attraction for
inhabitants of a world turned upside down, but the stylistic devices
used by these authors to communicate their thoughts.[31] Senecan
attitudes find their way into neo-classical tragedy, but also into the
Latin epistles of Michel de l'Hôpital. There are of course limits to
the encroachment of stoicism on Christian attitudes: there is a world

of difference between the self-sufficiency of the Stoic and the penitent seeking grace through Jesus Christ, and the place accorded to reason is hardly the same; even so, the spirit of the age admits a noticeable Stoic colouring of Christian outlook.

One consequence of these developments is that religious poets will move away from their previous dependence on classical and Petrarchan models – though up to a point spiritual ecstasy may draw on similar stylistic and thematic material as profane adoration; the Italian poets they cultivate will be of a different order: sometimes Dante will come into the picture as will the Neo-latins Vida and Sannazaro; more important, writers turn to the direct study of the Church Fathers. The choice of literary genre is naturally affected by these new sentiments: we have already mentioned, as it were, the ends of the spectrum: on the one hand, the didactic, gnomic verse (Pibrac), and on the other, the extended composition, with scientific and epic elements. In between, we have various meditative genres, where the techniques of spiritual devotion and also of the sermon come to the fore: the *stance* and the sonnet, which is no longer used exclusively for love-poetry or inserted into sequence form in the Petrarchan style. In this poetry, where inwardness is emphasised so much, and where the sources underline the importance of emotional involvement as well as of an intellectual approach to the penitent's problems, a much more conscious effort is made to play upon the feelings of the reader: first by developing themes such as the suffering of Christ, the nullity of the world, the imagining of a world without God, the presence of death, the worthlessness of the individual, and so forth. The poet seeks a wider audience than did the Pléiade in their early days, he will intensify the dramatic effects of his verse, and he will make use of a vigorous and indeed obsessive rhetorical structure. It is probably less in the realm of vocabulary than in the development of imagery (with increased comparison and simile) that the originality of these poets stands out. The training in rhetoric at school no doubt plays its part, but many of the favourite stylistic devices derive from philosophical and religious sources – the Bible, the Stoic tradition, the Counter-reformation meditational literature, Calvinist sermons. We shall frequently come across images of instability, *paraître*, decay, deflation, but also those drawn from accessible reality. The importance of imagery stems in part from the stress laid in introspective literature on the visualising of certain themes, such as Christ's passion. It is common practice to illustrate a point by some imagic device, and one may wonder to what extent the popularity of the emblem book contributes to this 'picturing' technique. In spite of some fundamental opposition, one cannot pretend that the ancient world is neglected as a source of imagery, but there is understandably less search after the erudite, abstruse, and exclusive,

which would militate against successful emotional impact. Much use
is made of accumulation and enumeration, also of repetition in its
various forms; and in a world where things are not what they seem,
antithesis, paradox, and negation (*ces loix, non-loix*) flourish. There
is of course a well-established literature of paradox, which may also
have played some part here. Many poets develop binary, ternary, or
even quaternary patterns in their sentence-building, and powerful
effects are obtained by a proper control of sentence structure, frequently reinforced by *enjambement*. Certain devices come into play
in poetry which is addressed directly to the reader or, one feels sometimes, to an imaginary audience on a larger scale: apostrophe, exclamation, frequent interrogation (including the rhetorical question),
the hidden conditional, and of course the counter-effect of the
staccato, brief sentence. There are many sources for these tropes: the
sermon, Seneca, but also the *tombeau* rhetoric where an imaginary
traveller is addressed (the *Viator* technique of the *Greek Anthology*).
Adunaton is often employed, and hyperbole of one sort or another;
and in D'Aubigné more especially, zeugma, a source of emotional
effect in classical treatises, is much favoured. In all this, one notices
a refurbishing of various devices in the direction of more movement,
often of a turbulent character, and above all of greater emotional
urgency. Other figures and devices that are pressed into service
include alliteration, chiasmus, *sententia*, high frequency of verbs,
demonstratives, and abstract nouns; and the epithet of course maintains its popularity and efficacy.

One further point before we look at some of these poets individually: although there was much interest in religious poetry at the
Court of Henry III, there is a marked tendency for it to develop in
the provinces, where we have seen literary activity continues to
flourish: the south-west, Rouen, and later Aix are perhaps more
significant in the present context, but centres such as Dijon and
Poitiers should not be forgotten.

Anne des Marquets (?   −1588)[32]

The beginnings of these religious currents are not very inspiring.
I am thinking, for instance, of Anne des Marquets, a minor pioneer
figure. Her talent, as she recognised herself, was meagre, and a great
number of her poems were not published until the seventeenth
century; but she interests us, partly for her translations of the *Carmina
sacra* of Marcantonio Flaminio, and partly for her *Sonets, prieres et
devises en forme de Pasquins*, inspired by the Colloque de Poissy
(1561) and printed in the following year. Strictly orthodox, fearful
of Calvinist advance, and seeing in poetry something essentially
didactic, she has nevertheless let some of the Pléiade's practice rub
off on her. The *pasquins* are biblical texts selected to be applied to

various ecclesiastical celebrities; she is early in the field in her use of the sonnet for religious purposes, at that time, infrequent. Though she talks of her 'Muse tant ignorante', classical reference is not entirely absent, even if her main spiritual fare is Church Fathers and medieval authors. In the sonnets that follow the Flaminio texts, she develops Counter-reformation themes, the seeking after union with God, the Passion, the deep-rooted nature of sin. An earlier sonnet shows her occasional ability to visualise what she is trying to say:

> Lors je vis une mur espoisse et bien obscure,
> Qu'un brouillas pestifere & puant conduisoit,
> Qui soubdain obscurcit le beau jour qui luisoit,
> Donnant crainte et terreur à toute creature:
>
> Cependant la pluspart marchoient à l'adventure,
> Et à peine un d'entre eux le chemin avisoit:
> L'un tomboit en la fosse, & l'autre se brisoit
> Contre quelque rocher ou autre pierre dure.
>
> Mais quelque temps apres je vei au firmament
> Les celestes flambeaux luire si clairement
> Qu'ils feirent escarter ceste tant noire masse.
>
> Puis je vei le soleil en son luysant sejour,
> Qui l'obscur effaça, & ramena le jour
> Par les divins rayons de sa tant claire face.
>
> (fol. b 2 v – b 3 r)

There is a rather self-conscious use of repetition which, however, does not prevent the impression that stressed words may fail to pull their weight; but normally this Dominican nun, with her puritanical hatred of profane poetry, is almost as rigid as Calvinist theorists in eschewing literary effect.

Georgette de Montenay (1540– ?)[33]

Another poetess who ventures into the religious field is Georgette de Montenay, whose *Emblesmes ou Devises chrestiennes* came out in 1571, though the *privilège* is dated 18 October 1566. The poems themselves are brittle and dry, but they illustrate a significant tendency. We have noted that the emblem flourished especially in Lyons (Scève, Alciat, Aneau, Girard), and that illustrated poetry of a sort was frequently published there. The adaptation of the emblem to religious rather than to moral ends is perhaps not quite as original as the poetess claims ('Lesquels ie croy estre premier chrestiens'), but her enterprise is timely, and all the more so as the illustrations are of very satisfactory artistic quality. Georgette de Montenay, who has clear Calvinist sympathies and dedicates the book to Jeanne d'Albret, is characteristic of the Huguenot awareness of what visual aids can achieve: Bèze makes much use of the Icon, as do Boissard and others. Her themes concentrate on the unique role of Christ, faith, grace, mercy, the mighty fall of those who set value on temporal things or show pride, Job as the symbol of patience in suffering, God's choice of those to be saved. The poems are all *huitains* in decasyllables (*ababbcbc*) without regular *alternance*; they explain the emblem and the motto (always in Latin). They have few artistic pretensions, though one notices a trait that recurs in D'Aubigné and other religious poets, the denial of what has just been described:

> Ce feu, non feu, fondé dessus un songe
> Soufflé de loups d'habits simples couvers,
> Où ces corbeaux aportent leur mensonge,
> S'en va estainct. Car par tout l'univers
> Les abus sont presque tous descouvers.
> Le sang coulant pur de l'arbre de vie
> Suffit pour tous purger & mettre à vie,
> Et rendre mort ce feu feinct des pervers.
>
> (*Emblesme* 7)

The didactic purpose is not accompanied here by great religious feeling; or if it is, the poetic utterance is unequal to the task. The use of illustrations, though less systematic, may also be found in the unvarnished and rather prosaic *Decades de l'Esperant* composed by Guillaume le Saunyer *c.* 1580.[34] The poetic value of this collection is negligible: the poems are really paraphrases or commentaries on sacred texts, but they are often in *chant royal* form, and given that the author resided in Rouen, show the persistent influence of the *puys*.

Jacques de Billy (1535–81)[35]

More significant and more interesting is Jacques de Billy, who wrote in both Latin and French and whose brother Jean plays a useful role in translating German books of devotion. Jacques de Billy's *Sonnets spirituels* first appeared in 1573; they went through a second edition in 1577, and a further book of sonnets came out in the following year. The didactic purpose is still to the forefront: the author explains that he is trying to embellish his themes, taken in great measure from early Christian sources (St Augustine, St John Chrysostom, Cyprian, etc.): 'il me prit fantasie d'y ajouster comme par maniere de saulce la doulceur de la poesie', though he does repeat the *topos* of the 'rudesse & dureté de mes vers'. He uses the sonnet mainly, because of its brevity, for he had been ill and was composing in a period of convalescence. At the end of the 1573 volume, the didactic element is displayed in the 'table des similitudes' (where the comparisons and images serve pedagogic rather than lyric ends) and in the 'table des principales matieres & sentences'. The stress on patristic sources is significant at this time, as is the gloomy, self-abasing tone of the themes selected: the inability of the soul to find satisfaction here upon earth, the 'amertume' of everything, the mortification of the flesh 'souverain remede en tribulation'. In one

commentary Billy expatiates on *tristesse* which comes from confession
and penitence, *devotion*, and what is even better, compassion; but he
adds a fourth category:

C'est quand l'homme par une vie de meditation de la beatitude eternelle
commence à deplorer sa presente peregrination, & ardemment appeter sa
vraye patrie, la celeste Hierusalem, & pour comble de ses souhaits desire la
dissolution de son corps, pour estre avec son Dieu. (1577 ed., p. 107)

The themes harmonise with a number of those in Georgette de
Montenay's book, emphasising the lack of sectarian distinction so
often found in the religious literature of the time. Billy draws on the
imagery of death and putrefaction, but does not 'realise' poetically
with so much force as will occur a while later. Many of the poems are
didactic developments, but a personal note does creep in here and
there. One interesting sonnet develops the theme of tears in a manner
that foreshadows the metaphysical:

> *De la tristesse spirituelle*
> Qui me donra de l'eau pour mon chef miserable,
> De larmes pour mes yeux un ruisseau tout entier?
> Qui un lieu me donra secret & à cartier,
> Pour pleurer jour et nuit mon offense execrable?
>
> Pour deplorer en l'estat piteux & lamentable
> Auquel nous nous voyons, pour nous estre au bourbier,
> Plongez de tous pechez, en quittant le sentier,
> Qui droict guide l'esprit au sejour perdurable.
>
> Pour aussi pleurer ceux qui sont hors de l'Eglise,
> Et les enfans pervers, qui font qu'on la mesprise,
> Qu'on s'en rit, qu'on luy donne à present maint assaut.
>
> Outre ces pleurs encor, hélas, hélas, que n'ay-je
> Pour me baigner le cœur, un torrent d'eau de neige,
> Au penser de Sion, & des biens de là haut.
>   (Sonnet 33, p. 104)

Here we have the lineaments of a good poem: Billy handles quite
successfully the technique of repeated syntactical devices for opening
sentences (*Qui . . . qui, Pour . . . pour*); he achieves a lilting balance
of sentence in the quatrains; and the tear-motif is married well to
images relating to the journey. There is a forceful use of ternary
rhythms in the first tercet, but the second, though thematically it
makes sense, with thoughts of a higher life, falls away poetically, and
this split between theme and expression mars what otherwise might
have been a very fine poem. Another sonnet of quality is instructive
by its exploiting of devices that will become common practice in
devotional poetry and also by its dialectical structure; in poetry of
this kind, we shall find that writers introduce a strong intellectual
framework which may combine very well at poetic level with the
more emotive elements, but at the same time illustrate the principle

that 'intellectual apprehension' is part of the spiritual process involved:

> *Complaincte spirituelle*
> Ha quel piteux estat! Que doy je desirer
> De vivre ou de mourir? Plus je vy, plus j'offence,
> Plus croist de mes pechez le thresor, plus j'avance
> D'aller tousjours en pis, & ma peine attirer.
>
> Mais quoy? Si de mon corps Dieu vient à separer
> L'esprit, c'est fait de moy: car de toute esperance
> Je me verray forclos de faire penitence,
> Et par tristes regrets mes fautes reparer.
>
> Que feray-je pauvret, puisque je m'apperçoy
> Serré des deux costez de si pres que ne voy
> Lequel m'est de ces deux le plus utile à prendre?
>
> O mon Dieu! je voy bien qu'en un si grand esmoy
> Rien trouver je ne puis plus utile pour moy,
> Qu'en toy me rejecter, & ton vouloir attendre.
>
> (Sonnet 9, p. 22)

The sonnet is based on a binary movement, expressing the poet's hesitation, and this movement is given further impetus by the rhetorical devices employed: the *plus . . . plus* formula, very frequent in these poets, exclamation, interrogation. Note also the skilful command of *enjambement*, the subtle insertion of the diminutive and in the second tercet, not only the proper climax of the poem, but the sharp and sudden shift from the first person singular to the *tu* and *ton* addressed to God. The effect of the poem does not depend as much as is often the case with these religious writers on imagery; another sonnet based on Proverbs, v, is richer in this respect:

> *Que les plaisirs mondains finissent par amertume*
> Fy de monstre marin, si divers de nature,
> Qu'en haut avoit de vierge en soy l'impression,
> De vierge tous les traits, beaux en perfection,
> Mais par en bas avoit d'un serpent la figure.
>
> Fy de l'amy fardé, qui d'accomplir n'a cure,
> Ce qu'il promect de bouche en fraude & fiction!
> Qui s'envole arrivant le temps d'affliction,
> Comme fait l'arondelle, approchant la froidure.
>
> Fy du morceau friand, qui plaisant au gosier,
> Amer à l'estomac se trouve estre au dernier.
> Fy de l'or qui en fin en charbon degenere.
>
> Fy du serpent qui pique en queu[*sic*], & de l'appas
> Qui pres de l'ameçon donne un mortel repas.
> Fy du plaisir mondain dont la fin est amere.
>
> (Sonnet 83, p. 344)

The main structure here is rather different; indeed it reminds one of certain sonnets in *Les Regretz*, where the same rhetorical opening formula is repeated, and here *accelerando*, throughout the poem, without development of argument from one section to another. It is an enumeration without marked movement towards a climax; but from another angle one can already detect in this sonnet the presence of two motifs that critics have labelled as 'baroque' in the works of Sponde or Chassignet: *paraître* and metamorphosis, and which in devotional poetry are basically amplification of the prophet's cry that all is vanity. Billy's verse tends usually to be more skeletonic than the examples quoted; and yet here we have a monk ensconced in his monastery, absorbed in early Christian literature, usually shunning the Court and literary circles, but who at his best turns out to be in tune with the spiritual needs of his time; he is a precursor of a 'moment' when religious poetry comes into its own, combining a strong didactic or intellectual vein with intense spiritual emotion, and even his stylistic devices are ones that will be exploited by others.

During the 1570s and 1580s the current of religious poetry swells rapidly; from 1575 Desportes begins to work in this field, the Song of Solomon inspires not only Belleau but Marin Le Saulx in his *Theanthropogamie* (1577; BN); Du Bartas and Boyssières also make substantial contributions. A number of anthologies of Christian verse are published and often enjoy a considerable success. The earliest is the *Poèmes chrestiens* of Montméja and others, which is essentially Calvinist in spirit; it is followed by the *Cantiques* of Etienne de Maisonfleur, whose sympathies are also Calvinist: this work, apparently first published in 1580 (according to older authorities), reappears in 1581, 1584, 1586, 1587 (with the *Cantiques* of Valagre), 1591, 1592, and 1602, with successive additions and sometimes removals. Though the main texts are the work of Huguenots, the anthology also includes works by Pléiade members and others whose orthodoxy is recognised: Ronsard, Belleau, Du Bellay, one of whose texts (*Cantique* I, ed. 1587) is divided irregularly into stanzas. In the preface, a statement of aesthetic attitude shows the Calvinist orientation:

Telles meditations de la puissance de Dieu (m'a-t-il dit) luy ayant particulieres, qu'il a trétées non d'un stille empoullé, ainçois commun: le plus conforme . . . qu'il luy a esté possible . . . n'ayant esté son dessein de trouver leur gloire, ne la sienne, ains de cercher celle de Dieu, & se consoler avec luy de quelques infirmitez de nostre vie. (ed. 1587, fol. a iiij)

Other anthologies came from the Catholic side, such as the *Muse chrestienne* (1582), and *L'œuvre Chrestienne de tous les Poëtes François* (1581) which, though orthodox in its selections, was perhaps rather less aggressively so than the other one. Such anthologies no doubt correspond to the taste of the times, but they also reflect a polemic intent in the context of the religious wars. Space forbids a detailed examination of the many poets who contribute to the output of these

decades, and I shall confine myself to two outstanding religious poets,
Jean de Sponde and Chassignet.

Jean de Sponde (1557–94)[36]

In some ways, Sponde reminds us of D'Aubigné: like him, he has
the makings of a polymath, dabbling in textual editions, astrological
science, philosophy; like D'Aubigné too, he was a man of action.
On the other hand, he never writes on the grand scale, and the fact
that he was constantly assailed by illness explains to some extent the
central role of sickness and death in his writings. We do not know
as much as we would like about his life, and his poetry is comparatively barren of personal reference, unlike D'Aubigné's. It seems
probable that the greater part of his religious verse was composed
before his conversion to Catholicism, but his outlook is not, in poetic
terms, sectarian. He also wrote some love-poetry: again, we are unable to date its genesis, though it may belong to the poet's early years.
One example of his amatory verse is worth quoting:

> Je contemplois un jour le dormant de ce fleuve
> Qui traine lentement les ondes dans la mer,
> Sans que les Aquilons le facent escumer,
> Ni bondir, ravageur, sur les bords qu'il abreuve.
>
> Et contemplant le cours de ces maux que j'espreuve
> Ce fleuve, dis-je alors, sçait que c'est d'aimer,
> Si quelque flamme eust peu ses glaces allumer,
> Il trouveroit l'amour ainsi que je le treuve.
>
> S'il le sentoit si bien, il auroit plus de flots.
> L'Amour est de la peine et non point du repos,
> Mais ceste peine en fin est du repos suivie,
>
> Si son esprit constant la deffend du trespas,
> Mais qui meurt en la peine il ne merite pas
> Que le repos jamais luy redonne la vie.
>
> *(Sonnets d'Amour*, xix,
> Boase and Ruchon ed., p. 191)

The mechanism of the sonnet is quite simple: the picture of a river
flowing down to the sea, evoking in the poet's mind parallel thoughts
of love, interwoven with the contrasted theme of *peine/repos*. The
second quatrain is perhaps a bit self-conscious and does not quite
come off, though its sense is essential for the further progress of the
poem. Two features stand out: first, the opening quatrain which is a
remarkable piece of compressed writing. The *dormant* strikes an
attractive note, a neuter present participle in substantival meaning
stressing the abstract quality rather than the object in which it is
embodied. The second line evokes beautifully the sluggish flow of the
water, whereas the fourth line with its *incise* at the caesura contrasts
forcibly with the second hemistich. Such a natural description, shorn
of obvious literary reminiscence, may be relatively rare then, but it

owes much to the dynamic quality of the verbs. And on the other hand, note the balanced movement of the tercets with the interplay of 'repos' and 'peine'. It is as if the poet's thoughts are influenced by the rhythm of the river, which introduces a happy contrast with the forthright nature of their content. More generally, this sonnet shows how Sponde's love-poetry combines features of the Petrarchan tradition that will recur in his religious verse: the extended comparison, the use of antithesis, the search for the *sententia*, *pointe* and *incise*, and what is more characteristic, the use of the demonstrative. However, when he comes to write on death, he will also draw on the rhetorical armoury of the devotional tradition; and when Sponde was in Switzerland, he moved in literary circles where knowledge of meditational texts and of sermon technique was extensive and deep.

In his twelve *Sonnets sur la mort* Sponde reached heights rarely attained by his contemporaries in this field. Take for instance Sonnet ii (ibid., p. 234):

> Mais si faut-il mourir, et la vie orgueilleuse,
> Qui brave de la mort, sentira ses fureurs,
> Les soleils haleront ces journalieres fleurs,
> Et le temps crevera ceste ampoule venteuse.
>
> Ce beau flambeau, qui lance une flamme fumeuse,
> Sur le verd de la cire esteindra ses ardeurs;
> L'huile de ce Tableau ternira ses couleurs,
> Et ces flots se rompront à la rive escumeuse.
>
> J'ay veu ces clairs esclairs passer devant mes yeux,
> Et le tonnerre encor qui gronde dans les cieux,
> Où d'une, ou d'autre part, esclatera l'orage.
>
> J'ay veu fondre la neige, et ses torrents tarir,
> Ces lyons rugissans, je les ay veus sans rage,
> Vivez, hommes, vivez, mais si faut-il mourir.

We have here what seems an anacreontic poem in reverse: let us live and be merry, but death comes at the end. As in Chassignet, the themes of death and life are thoroughly interwoven; Sponde uses images and symbols of vigour and freshness to evoke the thought of death, by a blend of affirmation and denial. One notable feature is the force of the verbs, bringing about a feeling not only of destruction, but also of restless tempo which derives at the same time from other elements – enumeration, visual images of light and violence. These images are organised into a fairly stern pattern; note among other things the repetition of the first hemistich to conclude the poem, symbolic of the process of life and death coming full circle and strengthening the sense of inevitability aroused by other means; its force is increased by its placing after the repeated *Vivez*. Note also the presentation of the quatrains in prophetic form (use of the future), stating the inescapable decay that inhabits all beauty; the shift of focus in the tercets, where we are, first, thrown back into the past seen from another angle (*J'ay veu*), second, given another series of examples which are quite dissimilar from those in the quatrains, examples reinforced by the sense of personal experience; and finally the shift to the imperative addressed not only to the reader but to men at large. Sponde's handling of the *topos* is very fine; we have already noted the taut structure which controls his material, but he also possesses an unusual gift for the single, definitive line (as Chassignet rarely does), and above all the way in which he conveys the sense of immediacy and urgency. This is brought about partly by rapid enumeration, *anaphora*, repetition of certain words and sounds, persistent alliteration, recurrent demonstratives (*ces*, strengthened by homophonic *ses*). The poem is not faultless – the first tercet gives an impression of padding – but the vitality of the whole structure is sufficient to carry the passenger phrase.

This gift for structure shows itself again in Sonnet ix (ibid., p. 241):

> Qui sont, qui sont ceux là, dont le cœur idolâtre
> Se jette aux pieds du Monde, et flatte ses honneurs,
> Et qui sont ces Valets, et qui sont ces Seigneurs?
> Et ces ames d'Ebene, et ces faces d'Albastre?
>
> Ces masques desguisez, dont la troupe folastre
> S'amuse à caresser je ne sçay quels donneurs
> De fumées de Court, et ces entrepreneurs
> De vaincre encor le Ciel qu'ils ne peuvent combattre?
>
> Qui sont ces louayeurs qui s'esloignent du Port,
> Hommagers à la vie, et felons à la Mort,
> Dont l'estoile est leur bien, le Vent leur fantasie?
>
> Je vogue en mesme mer, et craindrois de perir
> Si ce n'est que je sçay que ceste mesme vie
> N'est rien que le fanal qui me guide au mourir.

Once more, the theme of death coming at the end, but this time it is developed through that of the *paraître* of this world, with the false values most people give it. Yet we are nearer the Chassignet view in that *paraître* is the prelude to *être*, spiritual existence for which this world is the preparation. Sponde opens with a device common at this time and much affected by him, the interrogation, which here queries less the identity than the worth of the folk in question. The world is a court and the crowd which throngs it is alike in heart; no one can tell who is servant or master. The fourth line not only suggests similarity but announces the theme of appearance, so that the motif of the actor, also a common one, may develop in the second quatrain. The verb *s'amuse* may have a double meaning, 'to seek amusement' and 'to waste time', possibly with the further nuance of deception ('donner la muse'). The fourth line of this quatrain is a characteristic one, with its concentrated point, and shows the density

Sponde can attain. The first tercet carries the questioning of the first part, but the poet switches to the ship-image, which itself acts as a transition to the second tercet where he brings the focus on to himself and to the second part of the antithesis, *être* rather than *paraître*; the meaning of the poem is gathered up here by the introduction of the paradox of death as the aim of life. This sonnet is colourful and endowed with a brisk tempo, features which derive not merely from the accumulation of images but also from the skilled use of *rejet* on three occasions.

Sponde's output, though modest in quantity, is impressive by the range of poetic effects it achieves. His basic themes are limited, but they are presented with intellectual force and a sequence of images that impart speed and density to the structures. The intellectual framework prevents the imaginative urge from getting out of hand or losing coherence. Sponde's view is one in which life and death are intermingled; as in D'Aubigné, the poor estimate of this life upon earth is accompanied by a rich feeling of the vitality that none the less informs our existence. Some critics would see in this a feature of metaphysical poetry, in which the affirmation or denial of an element simultaneously evokes its opposite. This is not always the case in Sponde, but it is a frequent occurrence. His handling of language naturally calls for comment. Its originality does not lie so much in its vocabulary: we do not come across many archaisms, neologisms, or technical terms, nor is there the sophistication we associate with Scève, whereby a twist is given to syntax and vocabulary. It is said that Sponde was an admirer of Jodelle, but I doubt if the latter's impact was as great as on D'Aubigné's poetry. In any case, Sponde's attitude to language is not as wilful; we do not get the same sense of rugged effort. His artistry is to be found rather in the selection of image and terms of comparison and in the rhythms he develops by their placing in the line. Sponde has a number of tricks of style which form the stock-in-trade of this poetic area: repetition of key words, rapid series of questions or exclamations, assonant patterns, antithesis, direct address; but when all is said and done, the main effects come very often from a combination of tempo, sensitively controlled and varied, and a delicate awareness of the relations that can be extracted from the succeeding images. In Sponde the poetic relation between intellect and emotion is of high quality; vitality and discipline go hand in hand; only when the emotive element is below par (as for instance in Sonnet iii) do the bones seem to stick through the flesh. At his best, Sponde represents richly the flowering of lyric poetry in the last decade of the century.

Jean-Baptiste Chassignet (?1578–?1635)[37]
Chassignet's main work, *Le Mespris de la Vie et Consolation*

contre la mort, appeared in 1594; he had been engaged on it, he claims, for some six months. It consists of a series of 434 numbered sonnets interspersed at intervals by various poems (unnumbered sonnets, odes, *stances*, and *Syndereses*, some extended compositions) and one or two prose passages. The *leitmotiv* of the sequence is clearly stated in the title: life can only be seen in the proper perspective of death which is something to be accepted, welcomed when it comes. Some of the poems are addressed to the reader, others are prayers to the Lord, yet others appear in a more sententious vein, but all seek to turn the reader from the values of this world to those of the next. A very high proportion of the sonnets may be traced back to Stoic or neo-stoic sources, but Chassignet also owes much to Montaigne and to a Huguenot, Duplessis-Mornay. His major debts, however, are to the Bible, and more particularly the Psalms, the Book of Job, and the Song of Songs, all texts which he either translated or paraphrased at some time in his life. Though he asserts he did not seek to 'polir le visaige maigre et descharné de ces escrits', these poems, however hasty their composition may have been, show evidence of high competence in rhetoric and poetic structure; and sometimes a comparison with the obvious source will reveal the measure of Chassignet's originality. Moreover, the range of technique and matter is impressive.

> Nostre vie est semblable à la lampe enfumée,
> Aus uns le vent la fait couler soudainement,
> Aus autres il l'esteint d'un subit soufflement
> Quand elle est seulement à demi allumée.
>
> Aus autres elle luit jusqu'au bout consumée
> Mais en fin, sa clarté cause son bruslement:
> Plus longuement elle art, plus se va consumant
> Et sa foible lueur ressemble à sa fumée;
>
> Mesme son dernier feu est son dernier cotton
> Et sa dernière humeur que le trespas glouton
> Par divers intervalle ou tost ou tard consume.
>
> Ainsi naistre et mourir aus hommes ce n'est qu'un
> Et le flambeau vital qui tout le monde allume,
> Ou plustost ou plus tard, s'eslogne d'un chacun.
>
> (Sonnet xl)

Here Chassignet has taken a commonplace simile – the source of his imagery, often determined by biblical reminiscence, is usually homely, readily accessible to the reader – and develops it in some detail to illustrate the inextricable nature of life and death (cf. Sonnet ccii). In itself the comparison is not treated in startling fashion; what is less expected are the tone and tempo in which the development takes place. The tempo is a slow one, stressed by the long words often at the rhyme; there is an oscillating movement (*Aus uns ... Aus autres*; *Plus . . . plus*; *tost ou tard*) which is reinforced by the common device of repetition; and *naistre* and *mourir* help this associative rhythm to strengthen what is stated at intellectual level. Sonnet v also displays various features of the poet's style:

> Assies toy sur le bort d'une ondante riviere,
> Tu la verras fluer d'un perpetuel cours,
> Et flots sur flots roulant en mille et mille tours
> Descharger par les prez son humide carriere;
>
> Mais tu ne verras rien de ceste onde premiere
> Qui n'aguiere couloit; l'eau change tous les jours,
> Tous les jours, elle passe et la nommons tousjours
> Mesme fleuve et mesme eau, d'une mesme maniere.
>
> Ainsi l'homme varie et ne sera demain
> Telle comme aujourd'huy du pauvre corps humain
> La force que le tems abbrevie et consomme.
>
> Le nom sans varier nous suit jusqu'au trespas
> Et combien qu'aujourd'huy celuy ne sois-je pas
> Qui vivois hier passé, tousjours mesme on me nomme.

A poem of this sort, with its water imagery, may be used to illustrate the Baroque theme of change; but note that Chassignet, following a biblical stimulus, does what he did in the first sonnet, he links two contradictory themes together: (apparent) change/sameness. Note too that the language is, as far as vocabulary is concerned, uncomplicated, almost homely. As in the previous sonnet, we have a developed simile – though Chassignet uses other techniques too in his poetry: a series, one might say, a clash of successive images, or, what is less noticed, an absence of imagery, to illustrate instability. The theme here is further expressed by two characteristic devices: first, the obsessive repetition of key words, and second, a strongly articulated logical structure. This last feature we have already observed in Scève, but it becomes very frequent in devotional poetry towards the end of our period. Here, the structure is very clear: statement, followed by counter (*Mais*), conclusion (*Ainsi*). The last line rarely ends in a *pointe*, more usually in a *point d'orgue*. In this sonnet, Chassignet makes telling use of epithet, but also of *enjambement*, of which he seems to me to be a master. His feeling for sentence-control is very acute, and it is this quality that imparts so often to his verse a dignity which, at its best, verges on the majestic. His linguistic sophistication lies not in the range of vocabulary so much as in the command of a very rich rhetorical arsenal which exploits to the full his imagery, often familiar as I have said, but inclined to verge on the medical, the morbid, the abhorrent. Nevertheless, he is capable of a more anguished tempo, as in cclxiii:

> Est il rien de plus vain qu'un songe mensonger,
> Un songe passager, vagabond et muable?

La vie est toutefois au songe comparable,
Au songe vagabond, muable et passager.

Est il rien de plus vain que l'ombrage leger,
L'ombrage remuant, inconstant, et peu stable?
La vie est toutefois à l'ombrage semblable,
A l'ombrage tremblant sous l'arbre d'un verger.

Aussi, pour nous laisser une preuve asseurée
Que ceste vie estoit seulement une entrée
Et depart de ce lieu, entra soudainement

Le sage Pythagore en sa chambre secrette
Et n'y fust point si tost, ô preuve bien tost faite,
Comme il en ressortist encor plus vistement.

The vanity of all things underlies this sonnet, which is clearly articulated in its two parts. The quatrains work on the reader by accumulation and repetition; the repetition is varied and use is made of *anaphora*; in addition, Chassignet employs the interrogative form to introduce the quatrains, but these devices increase both the sense of oscillating rhythm and also the obsessive tone. The tercets, less dense, but quickened by *enjambement* and the exclamatory *incise*, maintain the tempo of a shimmering poem. If I stress the rhetorical fabric, it is deliberately to show that it is as important to the effect of such poetry as is the imagery woven into the texture; and indeed some of the successful poems of this era owe much to the judicious use of rhetoric, more indeed than to the imagery that is fairly generalised.

In his poetry – in which perhaps the sonnet is only an apparent unit, in that a cumulative force is acquired from sustained reading – Chassignet goes far beyond the mere suggestion that all is vanity; on the one hand, paradoxically perhaps, there is a very marked response to the vitality that informs this world below, and often the poet apprehends the world in the vitality and not in the vanity that informs its *paraître*. And on the other, behind the instability of the world, there is the very solid reality of the *port celeste*, as Chassignet calls it somewhere. The whole sequence is based on a substratum of spiritual confidence and serenity; even the recurrent awareness of human imperfection and repulsiveness (e.g., Sonnet ccciiii) fails to shake this steadfastness.

V. COMMITTED, SATIRICAL, AND MORALISTE POETRY[38]

The dominant concerns of the Pléiade may tend to obscure the presence of a large volume of satirical and moralising verse written in the second half of the century, sometimes by poets associated with the Pléiade, more often by members of the legal profession and those involved to a greater or lesser degree in the wars of religion. Much of this poetry is, by definition, ephemeral, but it constitutes an important feature of poetic activity and here and there heralds the appearance of D'Aubigné on one hand and of Régnier on the other.

The traditional satire of *mœurs* and *caractères*, which was strongly developed in the Neo-latin verse of the 1530s, is maintained in part; it owes something to the influence of Martial, and often the poems are little more than epigrams, short and sharp. As the century progresses, there is a shift to longer poems, the extended satire which reflects other classical sources such as Juvenal and Horace; the influence of Italian satirists, notably Berni, Ariosto, and Aretino, is discernible, though these writers were not yet translated into French. At the same time, social conditions call for a shift in the type of satire and commitment expressed in literature. Of course, the older, more general form of character-satire persists (the doctor, the lawyer, the flighty woman); it occurs in the *nouvelle* and farce as well as in non-dramatic poetry. Du Bellay, among others, attacks the courtesan and the *entremetteuse*, and Ronsard composes a curious poem against *Denise sorcière*; but among the minor poets, J. Doubert writes an entertaining satire (though he calls it an *Elegie*) on the former courtesan who advises a younger woman to marry money. F. de Birague in *La mère Cardine* develops the *lais* theme in mock-epic dimensions with Hell as the scene of the action; and Jean de Boyssières continues the anti-feminist current:

> Furie des Enfers, des horreurs allumée,
> Serpent encolleré, couleuvre envenimée,
> Crapaut villain, infect, herbe de puanteur,
> Retrait d'infections, senteur pestifferée,
> Sur la froide cicuë en poison preferée,
> De la perdition des hommes seul auteur.
> ('Des humeurs de la femme',
> Fleuret and Perceau, I, 246)

Towards the end of the century authors like Hesteau de Nuysement and Joffrey de Calignan also exploit the genre, though at the same time pastoral and the romanesque novel are getting off the ground. From time to time, marriage is satirised from an anti-feminist angle (Jamyn, Desportes), but one may wonder whether some authors are not also making fun of the Calvinist defence of marriage. These themes are developed in contrary motion by Desportes and Boyssières, so that one thinks of a minor 'querelle des amyes mariées', since the topic was taken up by a number of poets at that time.

At the beginning of the Pléiade period, there were still vestiges of the anti-sorbonnic poem so beloved by Neo-latin poets. Pierre Lizet, the bugbear of all humanists, was notorious for the length of his nose, and Buchanan and other Latinists made satiric capital out of this, but so did Bèze in his *Passavant*:

> Messire Pierre, estonné
> De voir son nez boutonné
> Prest à tomber, par fortune,
> De la verole importune,
> De grand colère qu'il eut,
> Print son grand verre, et y beut,
> Puis, d'une musique ivrogne,
> Contournant sa rouge trongne,
> Jettant son œil chassieux
> Vers son royaume des Cieux,
> (C'est à dire ses bouteilles,
> Belles, grandes, nompareilles,
> De son buffet l'ornement,
> Et son seul vray sauvement,
> Acoudé dessus sa table,
> Rota ce cry lamentable:
> 'Ha, pauvre nez, tu t'en vas,
> Et je demeure icy bas!
> Nez né seulement pour boire;
> Nez, mon honneur et ma gloire . . .
>
> (Fleuret and Perceau, I, 13–14)

What we have here is a development of the satiric *blason* by a
relative contemporary of Rabelais whose general influence on satire
is inevitably very great. The traditional attacks on Popes, cardinals,
and the abuses of the Church, very vigorous during the early half of
the century, persist in Du Bellay's *Regretz* – and Du Bellay's satiric
sonnet serves as a model for criticism of political and military leaders
during the troubles; there are also French variants on the Italian
pasquil or *pasquinade*, and in the middle third of the century a fair
number of anti-papal pamphlets. However, during the last third,
when religious schism is beyond recall, when the Church is seen by
many as part of the French tradition, and when French humanism
rallies to orthodoxy generally, satire of this type tends to be confined
to the Calvinists who are often writing from Geneva and abroad.
Protestant satire continues to attack the Pope, the monastic orders,
and the Mass. There is, it is true, some vigorous poetry directed
against the Jesuits while they were establishing themselves in France,
partly because they constituted a threat to the academic world by
their teaching methods. Of the older traditions still current, one may
mention the satiric epigrams against the *zoilus* (or *médisant*), anti-
petrarchan poetry; and sometimes older stylistic features live on, as
for instance in the curious poem by Du Verdier who makes *rime
équivoquée* its main feature, though the writings of Pasquier and
Tabourot suggest a revival of interest in older poetic forms.

However, this tradition of satire tends to make way for either
committed writing or satire of a more extended, generalised nature
which reflects on the unhappy state into which the country has

fallen; a few titles will suffice to indicate the matter treated –
A. du Verdier, *Satire des mœurs corrompues de ce siècle*; Jean Vatel,
Discours sur les corruptions de ce temps (c. 1570); Balthazar Bailly,
L'importunité et malheurs de nos ans (c. 1570). The dosage of satiric
comment or moralising thought will vary with the writer; but certain
themes tend to predominate. One of the most important strands is the
anti-aulic; attacks on courtiers and Court have a long history in
France and may be enriched by classical antecedents, but after 1550
presentation and tone change. There are, it is true, recent literary
influences, such as the famous work by Guevara, the *Menosprecio de
Corte* translated into French in 1542 and frequently reprinted;[39]
there is also a certain reaction to the Neoplatonic tradition fostered
by Castiglione and his French admirers; and Lucian no doubt has
some relevance to the development of techniques. The popularity of
the genre is tied up with social evolution, the rapid development of
the Court in a period when royalty is trying to assert its authority
throughout the realm, and often against the interests of the nobles.
The drift of the nobility towards the Court gathers momentum
during the last third of the century. In the religious wars the courtier
theme is complicated by others, such as the danger of flattery – an
idea that recurs in books of political theory and is often symbolised
by the legend of Actæon – and by xenophobia; Catherine de Medici
had many enemies, and anti-Italian satire figures prominently in
Henri Estienne (see *Epistre de Monsieur Celtophile aus Ausoniens,*
1578). Later, the behaviour of Henry III's *mignons* will provide
ready ammunition for the satirists, but one must also remember that
anti-aulic poetry may be cultivated by writers who are essentially
court poets (Jamyn). Anti-Italian satire will also find its way into the
drama, through the presence of the braggart (Pantaleone). The Court
was criticised for its insincerity, for the idle nobles, for *paraître* as
opposed to *être*, and in a period when economic difficulties were
multiplying, for extravagance and self-indulgence in the matter of
fashion; often in the last instances, the tone was sharpened in the
writing of a Calvinist mind. Clothes are of course a form of disguise
and show, and this theme is handled as early as 1563 by the somewhat obscure Nicolas de Margues:

> Que le monde est en ses habits muable!
> Qu'il est soigneux de se rendre admirable
> Par un habit qui le peult desguiser!
> or' le verrés, pour trop mieux courtiser,
> Tout affeublé d'un chapeau sus sa teste
> Levant le bec tout ainsi qu'une creste,
> Ore abaissé, et tout ainsi qu'un plat,
> Il vous applane et contrefait le fat . . .
> L'homme n'est plus cogneu en sa chaussure,
> Par trop souvent desguiser sa nature:

> Il semble, à voir, que les vens d'Aeolus
> Soient maintenant dans les chausses perclus;
> De toute part, il se fait regarder
> Chausses bouffants, pour se mieux bragarder,
> Aiant le cul plus gros et plus enflé
> Qu'un tabourin, ou qu'un bœuf boursouflé . . .
> (Fleuret and Perceau, I, 98–9)[40]

Margues also exhibits anti-Italian sentiments, but a strong religious vein runs through his poetry. Here he develops his material chiefly by a combination of moral reflection, caricatural portrait, and comparisons of a ridiculous nature, sometimes derived from the classical domain. Margues lacks real verbal invention and control of the extended passage, and yet he stands, in a modest way, between the Ronsard of the late 1550s (to whom he owes something) and the D'Aubigné of the *Tragiques*. In Guillaume du Buys,[41] active rather later, the alexandrine is preferred to the decasyllable, and the moralising is inspired partly by Stoic sources:

> Ceste force d'esprit, ou magnanimité,
> Pour se rendre asseurée a le sens indomté,
> Le mespris de soymesme, avec l'experience
> De destendre les las de la concupiscence,
> Tant qu'ainsi, se rendant de soy l'homme vainqueur,
> La colere jamais ne luy trouble le cueur;
> De toute ambition le pourchas il dechasse
> D'un accident mauvais il ne craint la disgrace,
> Il ne s'enorgueillit, ayant le vent à gré,
> Et pour trop s'eslever ne change de degré,
> Sinon lorsqu'on le juge avoir la suffisance
> Pour servir aux estats de plus grande importance:
> De chacun les honneurs souvent il n'aymera,
> Et de jouyr de ceux, sur tout, luy suffira,
> Qui peuvent seulement apporter tesmoignage
> Combien est deu d'honneur à un grand personnage.
> (Fleuret and Perceau, II, 112–13)

The anti-aulic line can be expanded in various ways. For instance, some poets address their poem to the nobility, pointing out where the path of duty lies in these troubled times and reproaching those who substitute self-seeking for their traditional role: thus Jean le Masle composes a *Discours traitant de la noblesse et de son origine* (Fleuret and Perceau, II, 133ff.), and Guillaume du Buys does something similar in *La Noblesse. Aux Seigneurs et Gentilshommes de vertu* (ibid., II, 101ff.). Then, the anti-aulic strand may be blended with the Horatian motif that acquires particular relevance towards the end of the wars, the contrast between *rus* and *urbs*: a well-known example of this is Jean de la Taille's *Courtisan retiré*, which owes something to the work already mentioned by Guevara.[42] A relatively early example of the *rus* v. *urbs* theme will be found in Etienne du Tronchet's *Contentement d'un homme de village* (1568):[43] probably affected by Claudian, it develops the *topos* of the old man, which occurs in prose in Noël du Fail and later finds its way into André Chenier; but it is chiefly an attack upon the Court and what it stands for – ambition and striving beyond the golden mean. The virtues of the country life are also celebrated: the old man is not a scholar, he has not gone far from his parish pump, he has kept his station; he loves God and his neighbour. La Taille's poem of course differs structurally in that the *persona* knows the Court; moreover, he developed the thesis that Christians should cease to fight among themselves and unite against the heathen; in other respects, though with more skill, he ranges over ground similar to Du Tronchet.

In this period, of course, satire is exploited in the service of political commitment; much of this writing is ephemeral and of scant literary value, but a few remarks are necessary. The popular *chanson* with militant overtones and seeking a large audience flourishes apace, though most are anonymous and have often remained manuscript; at the same time, a sense of commitment leads to a revitalisation of older genres (e.g., the *complainte*), and there is a marked symbiosis between Latin and vernacular composition, so that some poems are found in bilingual form, being either translated at a later date or published simultaneously in the two versions. Many of the authors belong to the legal profession, and there is the court poet who represents the *vox imperii*.

Pamphlets in both languages seem to increase with the assassination of the duc de Guise at the hands of Poltrot de Méré (1563). On the Protestant side, stress is laid on Poltrot's heroism and the infamy of the house of Guise, and on the Catholic side, praise of the duke was expressed more in Latin than in the vernacular. A theme that constantly recurs is that of 'la France éplorée': authors play on the feelings of their public both by a satiric portrait of their enemies and by a pathetic description of the state of the country. Frequently this second theme is presented by means of *prosopopœia*, France herself speaking. Examples of this in Latin are poems by Geoffroy de Malvyn and Jean Passerat: in French one can mention Jean Béreau's *Complainte de France sur la guerre civile.... (*1562):

> Je qui, brave, soulois me faire renommer
> Sur toutes nations, que l'oceane mer
> De ses longs bras enserre, entre la blanche Aurore
> Et le brun Occident, sur toutes je suis ore
> Miserable et ploreuse, et preste de sentir
> Que le tems, quelquefois, doit en rien convertir
> Empires, nations, et toute chose née. . . .
> Onze cens ans y a qu'en la Gaule planta
> Mon beau nom Pharamond, suivy de trouppes belles
> De gens, qui, desireux de conquestes nouvelles,
> Cerchans honneur, avoyent delaissé leur païs,
> Les Mœtides Palus et le froid Tanaïs . . .

> (Fleuret and Perceau, I, 105)

This short passage is useful for showing some stock themes: France is sketched as superior to all nations and in particular as a result of her culture – we have already noted the chauvinistic colour of French humanism; moreover, this point is developed by an evocation of France down the centuries of her history, and the myths we associate with the *Franciade* are abundantly present in the militant poetry of the times. Certain 'moral' commonplaces are introduced: the change of Fortune, sometimes linked with the idea of hubris, but also the hope that the Golden Age will, with Justice, return to the devastated country; France's troubles are due to her 'discorde intestine', she would do better to unite her forces against the infidel. Poetry of this sort, often using themes exploited by Ronsard after 1558, tends to be extended and to develop a variety of tones, satiric, deploratory, moralising, and near-epic, for descriptions of contemporary battles as well as historical evocation are part of the stock-in-trade of these writers. Many of them, with their humanist formation, incline to moderation, stressing the need for unity and the maintenance of a glorious tradition. The Passerat who composed his poem on the death of Guise in 1563 will, some twenty-five years later, collaborate in the *Satire Menippée*. With the theme of national pride goes a hate of the foreigner fighting on native soil and playing the role of the dangerous parasite. Pleas for peace and solidarity are fairly general at this stage, but on the Catholic side two further arguments will be emphasised, the need for the restoration of royal authority and the fear that individual liberty, unless controlled by reason and conscience, will lead to anarchy. However, counsels of moderation were not to last for ever: the change of climate can be found in the exchanges between Ronsard and his Calvinist critics or in the hostility to Coligny, and after the second war, which leaves few traces in contemporary literature, the humanist Michel de l'Hôpital ceased to be Chancellor, sharper voices are heard (as in Jodelle's polemic poetry), and Royal Readers such as Dorat and Léger Duchesne allow themselves extremist views. After 1570 further tones of moderation emerged (Passerat, Pasquier), and the official poets seem to turn their attention to other matters of public concern. The Saint-Barthélemy, oddly enough, evoked little response immediately among the Huguenots, but Catholic humanists, with the honourable exception of Ronsard, tended to speak out strongly in favour of the massacre. The fourth civil war does not cause much stir among the poets.

With the death of Charles IX, more interest is taken in the return of Henry III from Poland; but the reign of the new monarch does not show a very clear pattern of committed poetry. There may be reasons for this: central authority is even less secure for a time, and though the Academies provide a centre of stimulus for literary effort,

Henry III's curious character does not elicit a great amount of favourable poetry. Moreover, a number of the older humanists leave the stage in these years. This does not mean a dearth of militant composition, far from it: but literary activity gives the impression of being rather more fragmented, though of course there is a rather different picture of Calvinist poetry beyond the frontiers. At home, extended satire of the Calvinists, encomiastic poems celebrating Catholic victories or the death of orthodox heroes are common enough, and the emergence of the *Ligue* stimulates writing both in defence of and against the leaders, and in this context the Huguenot hatred of the Guises reaches new heights. Later on the *Ligue* will inspire one masterpiece of satiric writing, the *Satire Menippée* (see below, pp. 72–4). The theme of 'la France éplorée' continues to enjoy some currency: for instance, Hesteau de Nuysement in his *Gemisse-mens de la France* (1578) uses a number of the techniques we have associated with the genre and develops some Ronsardian views, notably on man's senseless search for material, including sulphur, to make arms. The poem is coloured by the author's cosmological interests, but the remarks directed against the rebellious are more spiteful than in earlier compositions. As the end of Henry III's reign draws near and the claims of Henry of Navarre are being laboriously established, the voice of the moderates is heard more and more clearly. The fatigue of these years is reflected in a desire for peace and unity. The themes we saw present in the heyday of the Pléiade, such as the Golden Age and the return of Astrea (Justice), recur frequently and indeed the allegorical formula is still vigorous (as it will also be in the *Tragiques*), not only in the generalised *complainte*, but also in the eclogue, which enjoys some renewal of favour in the last twenty years or so. Certain features come into the picture: the relative fading of the religious element in favour of the political and simply human, and also, where humanist poets are active, the reappearance of the more elaborate genres with their sustained rhetoric, often rich in classical overtones; the meditative strain enriched by praise for the country life, far from the madding crowd – at the other end of the scale, one notes the persistence of the partisan *chanson*, often adapting the themes and idiom of the Psalms. Sometimes the compensations are of a collective nature, and it is during this period that the bilingual or polyglot *tumulus*, expressing the attitudes of some group, humanist or political, assumes impressive proportions. As I have mentioned before, the full-scale militant satire in verse is rather less frequent – an early example was Gabriel Bounyn's *Satyre au Roy contre les républicains* (1565) when he was still in the entourage of the duc d'Anjou; satire also finds expression in macaronic verse, as for instance in Belleau's well-known *De bello huguenotico*. It is the generalised satire that returns towards the end of our period, such as will culminate in the works of Mathurin Régnier. Here we shall find the traditional attacks on nobles, but also on other classes of society: Jean Passerat, the librarian of Henri de Mesmes and a distinguished editor of Propertius, composed an entertaining *Divinité des Procès*:

> Ce qui est ja passé et une fois est faict,
> Par tous les dieux ensemble estre ne peut desfaict:
> Les Procès en ce poinct ont sur eux l'avantage,
> Pource qu'un alibi, avec un tesmoignage
> Presté en charité, desfaict tout le passé,
> Fait un vif estre mort et un vif trespassé.
> On recongnoist les Dieux, ainsi que dit Homère,
> Au mouvement des pieds qu'ils tournent en arriere:
> Mon Procès prend plaisir à tousjours reculer.
> Les Dieux sont recongneuz souvent à leur parler,
> Car toute autre est leur voix que n'est nostre langage
> Les Procès, vrais Bretons, ont à part un ramage.
> Aux Dieux, francs de la mort, on dresse des autels:
> Qu'il en dresse aux Procès puis qu'ils sont immortels!
> Mon Procureur Guillot en sçauroit bien que dire,
> Qui mon Procès jugé tire encore, et retire,
> Et, depuis seize mois, m'a, tant villonnisé
> Que je le tiens desjà pour immortalizé.
>   (Fleuret and Perceau, II, 197–8)

Lawyers have always been game for satire, but the increase in their professional and social role during the century, the fondness for litigation, the immense dragging-out of lawsuits, all these favoured a renewal of legal satire, often by poets trained as lawyers, who enrich their verse by classical allusion, sophisticated rhetoric, and more developed structures. Satire of the soldier, of which one finds samples in the comedies, occurs also in poets such as Hubert-Philippe de Villiers whose *Cinq livres de l'Erynne française* reflect on the lethal consequences of war: the author blends satiric and pathetic elements, and occasionally gives us a foretaste of what D'Aubigné will offer in much more accomplished form in the *Tragiques*:

> Tandis, je poursuivray, d'un metre pitoyable,
> Tous les embrassements, et l'horreur effroyable
> De tant de sang versé, le pays fourragé,
> De mille indignitez le bas peuple outragé,
> Des vefves sans confort les plaintes desolées,
> Les durs gemissements des vierges violées,
> Les freres regrettez et les peres aussi,
> Des parents et amyz le remordant soucy,
> D'un et d'autre costé le destin miserable,
> Et du royaume entier la perte irreparable.
>   (Fleuret and Perceau, II, 128)

Balthazar Bailly, mentioned earlier, certainly attacks the nobles, but he lays blame for the troubles at the door of all the Estates, criticising lawyers and making a digression on the evils of borrowing; and Du

Verdier in his *Omonimes*[44] hits out at all the professions for their vicious ways that have brought on the plagues now assailing the country.

There is also a rejuvenation of the reflective satire on the human condition, Nicolas Rapin translates Horace's satires and often writes in a similar vein himself; as does Vauquelin de la Fresnaye, with a strong moralising tone:

> Heureux aussi n'est pas celuy qu'on voit reluire
> Par Estats, par Thresors, ou par grandeur d'Empire;
> Mais celuy qui sçait bien commander à propos
> Aux apres passions qui troublent le repos,
> Et qui ne laisse point, d'un cœur pusilanime,
> Emporter aux fureurs la raison magnanime;
> Qui preudent, se deffend du convoiteux desir
> Qui vient un homme avare en ses liens saisir . . .
> (Fleuret and Perceau, II, 214)

The Horatian formula harmonises of course with a number of other strands, the developing neo-stoicism which appears in the gnomic verse of the period, the flight away from the *paraître* of Court and urban life, expressed in works like Claude Gauchet's *Les plaisirs des champs* (1583) as much as in Noël du Fail's hostility to Petrarchan love; it is no coincidence that Rapin the Horatian and Pibrac the author of neo-stoic quatrains should figure in the anthology *Les plaisirs de la vie rustique* (1583); nor that satire will include among its targets any forms of excess or irrational behaviour (e.g., Sainte-Marthe's *Contre la gourmandise* or Marc Papillon's *Fléau feminin*). All this is consonant with a climate of opinion emerging in the aftermath of the civil wars and seeking new structures of order, security, and peace at both political and moral levels. In the pages of these *moralistes* – among whom we must include Michel de l'Hôpital – we detect the beginnings of classicism, literary and ethical, and though many of the authors I have mentioned are not well known or of great artistic merit, they form an indispensable link in the development of taste between Renaissance and the *grand siècle*.

VI. CONCLUSION

The chapters devoted to a survey of French poetry since the advent of the Pléiade could not fail to bring out two obvious points: first, the immense increase in poetic endeavour and achievement, even at a purely quantitative level, and second, the marked shift in sensibility since the *Deffense et illustration*, or more fairly, since the appearance of Scève's *Délie* in 1544. During this period, the widening of the poetic spectrum corresponds to a variety of phenomena that all make their contribution to the literary situation: the return to Paris as the centre of cultural stimulus; certain important social shifts, including the rapid emergence of the magistrature as a social and cultural force; the political involvement of the wars of religion; and in a more general fashion, the complex feelings aroused in a period marked by an impressive revitalisation of culture as well as by a sense that the known world is entering a period of change and instability. What is striking, though natural, is the way in which so much of this climate of sensibility expresses itself through poetry, precisely at a moment when the claims of the vernacular are making themselves powerfully felt. But, massive though this poetic revival is, one must not assume that confidence in the Pléiade conception of poetry in the vernacular overcomes all resistance or hesitation: on the one hand, the devotees of Marot and his disciples do not vanish overnight, and Marot remains with Ronsard the most popular poet until the end of the century; and on the other, poets are reluctant to accept that Latin has ceased to be a viable means of poetic utterance. Some indication of contemporary hedging of bets may be seen in the *Art poétique* of Vauquelin de la Fresnaye, published at the beginning of the seventeenth century, but conceived very much earlier: here the self-professed admirer and disciple of Ronsard still owes much to Thomas Sebillet and Peletier du Mans, nor does he object to including some technical advice on the composition of *chants royaux*, *ballades*, or *rondeaux*. This is a period of experiment and muscle-flexing, but it reflects also the deeper responses of a sensibility faced with a rapidly changing world. The more obvious features, at technical level, need little more than a brief reminder; all sorts of new genres (at any rate in name) come over the horizon, the lessons of classical rhetoric have been relearned in the context of Renaissance humanism; theories of poetry (imitation, tradition, formal structures) allow the poet to devote much of his attention to refashioning poetic idiom, and this does not only mean widening of vocabulary or syntactical shifts, but also concerns an awareness of linguistic rhythms developed often against the so-called norm of the line or genre.

All this would bear little interest, if it were not closely related to a deepening and broadening of sensibility, the inevitable concomitant of the intellectual ferment we have witnessed. The first feature to strike one, no doubt, is the immense vitality, indeed exuberance, that seems to be released; nor is this just a matter of tempo and simple movement, for Marot had already introduced these qualities into a poetic idiom that had become too static: the framework in which this sensibility can reverberate becomes more spacious and is felt in greater depth, and one technical sign of this change is no doubt manifest in the richer functions conferred upon the image – though this shift is not necessarily expressed consciously in the *arts poétiques* of the period. Ronsard's world, even if its distinction sets it apart from that of lesser poets, is marked by this greater resonance and 'body', by its richness and diversity, by its ability to see reality in different perspectives and levels. Moreover, this sensibility reflects a sharp awareness of a changing world, its fluidity and mobility, its elusive quality, seen so often in the register of *paraître/être*, its vitality that paradoxically stems from its imperfection. As the period progresses, different ways of apprehending this fluctuating, slippery reality come to the surface: the imagination may assert itself increasingly and subject the apprehended world to its own pressures and urges; at the other end of the spectrum, the need to organise experience may declare itself and the lineaments of a pre-classical spirit enter the scene. Without giving theoretic expression to certain workings of the mind, some poets begin to treat language, whose vitality they sense shrewdly, not only as a means of exploring the world, but of creating a world in which their values may be held in poetic suspension; nor is it surprising that in some poets of distinction, the claims of imaginative impulse *and* of organisation should reveal themselves (Ronsard, but also Malherbe). In any case, the coexistence of heightened awareness and artistic stylisation carried to a high point of refinement is present in the major poets of our period, in Scève before the threat of the 'monde à l'envers', in Ronsard who creates his own world of stylised value, later in Sponde and D'Aubigné. But there are other levels at which poetic utterance develops: there is a poetry of the *salon* and also one of recollection and retreat, which is contemporary with the cult of the garden and its welcome peace. As in the intellectual debates, we are dealing with a period in which a final solution, however much sought, is not found, and we have the opening-up of avenues whose exploration will be continued through the next century.[45]

NOTES

1. M. Raymond, *L'Influence de Ronsard sur la poésie française* (*1550–1585*), 2 vols., 1927; R. Lebègue, *La Poésie française de 1560 à 1630*, 2 vols., 1951; Odette de Mourgues, *Metaphysical, Baroque and Précieux Poetry*, Oxford, 1953; J. Rousset, *La Littérature de l'âge baroque en France*, 1953.

2. For a convenient list of *entrées* see F. Joukovsky, *La Gloire dans la poésie française . . .*, *THR*, 1969, pp. 610–11; see also *Les Fêtes de la Renaissance*, I, ed. J. Jacquot; J. Chartrou, *Les Entrées solennelles et triomphales à la Renaissance*, 1928.

3. T. E. Lawrenson, *The French Stage in the Seventeenth Century*, Manchester, 1957.

4. See E. Bourciez, op. cit., Margaret McGowan, op. cit., P. M. Smith, *The Anti-courtier Trend*.

5. F. A. Yates, op. cit.

6. L. Clark Keating, *Studies on the Literary Salon in France, 1550–1615*.

7. F. Lachèvre, *Bibliographie des recueils collectifs de poésies du XVIe siècle*, 1922.

8. G. E. Diller, *Les Dames Des Roches. Etude sur la vie littéraire à Poitiers dans la deuxième moitié du XVIe siècle*, 1936.

9. Modern ed. of *Les Amours d'Aymée*, TLF, 1971, by Jasmine Dawkins, who has also completed a Nottingham thesis on Pierre de Brach.

10. *La Puce* appeared in 1582 (Besançon has the only known copy; 2nd ed. 1583, in BN); *La Main* came out in 1584 (BM, BN).

11. A Cabos, *Guy Faur de Pibrac. Un Magistrat poète au XVIe siècle (1529–1584)*, 1922. The *Quatrains* appeared in 1574, were reprinted twice in the following year, and reached their complete form in 1576.

12. Both these works are in the BM.

13. These works of Birague and Nuysement are available in BM and BN; little is known about the first; the second has also a niche in the development of scientific poetry.

14. *Les Œuvres poétiques*, 1575 (BM, BN), 1577 (BM, BN, MRy), 1579 (BM, BN, PSG), modern ed. by S. Carrington, TLF, 1973; *Le second volume des Œuvres*, 1584 (PSG). See T. Graur, *Un Disciple de Ronsard, Amadis Jamyn (?1540–1593)*, 1929.

15. *Les Premieres Œuvres*, 1573 (BM, BN). Both BM and BN have many editions until the end of the century; EUL has a copy of the Antwerp ed. 1582. Modern ed. by V. E. Graham, TLF: *Cartels et masquerades*, 1958; *Les Amours de Diane*, I and II, 1959; *Les Amours d'Hippolyte* 1960; *Elegies*, 1960; *Cleonice, Dernières Amours*, 1962; *Les Diverses Amours*, 1963. See J. Lavaud, *Un Poète de cour au temps des derniers Valois. Philippe Desportes (1546–1606)*, 1936.

16. Modern ed. H. Weber, 1962.

17. A.-M. Schmidt, *La Poésie scientifique en France au XVIe siècle*, 1939; A. K. Varga, 'Poésie et cosmologie au XVIe siècle'; D. B. Wilson, *Descriptive Poetry in France from Blason to Baroque*, Manchester, 1967.

18. To references given above, p. 145, n.51, add A.-M. Schmidt, *La Poésie scientifique* and D. B. Wilson, op. cit.; also H. Staub, *Le Curieux Désir*, THR, 1967.

19. See also H. Guy, 'La *Savoye* de Jacques Peletier', *Miscellany . . . L. E. Kastner*, Cambridge, 1932.

20. In addition to A.-M. Schmidt, *La Poésie scientifique*, and Staub, op. cit., see V.-L. Saulnier, *Maurice Scève*, and H. Weber, *La Création poétique*. Modern eds. of *Microcosme* (original ed. in BN), by Valery Larbaud, 1928, B. Guégan, *Œuvres complètes de Maurice Scève*, 1928, and H. Staub, *Œuvres complètes . . .*, 1969.

21. *L'Encyclie des secrets de l'Eternité*, Antwerp, 1570 (BM, BN); *La Galliade*, 1578 (BM, BN, PSG); *Les hymnes ecclesiastiques . . .*, 1578 (BN), 1582 (BM). In addition to works by H. Busson, A.-M. Schmidt, and D. B. Wilson, see F. Secret, *L'Esotérisme de Guy Le Fèvre de la Boderie*, Geneva, 1969.

22. See M. R. Jung, *Hercule dans la littérature française du XVIe siècle*, THR, 1966.

23. *Les Œuvres*, 1579 (BN), 1580 (BN), 1583 (BN, PSG); *La Sepmaine*, 1578 (BM), 1579 (PSG), 1582 (BM), 1584 (BN), Louvain, 1585, n.p., 1593 (BN); *La seconde Semaine*, 1584 (BM, BN, O). Modern ed. U. T. Holmes, J. C. Lyons, R. W. Linker, 3 vols., Chapel Hill, 1935–40. See K. Reichenberger, *Du Bartas und sein Schöpfungsepos*, Munich, 1962, and 'Das epische Proömium bei Ronsard, Scève, Du Bartas . . .', ZRP, 1962; H. Ashton, *Du Bartas en Angleterre*, 1908; A. E. Creore on Du Bartas's vocabulary in articles, BHR, 1953 and 1959.

24. Cf. recent edition by A. Baiche, 1971.

25. The *Apprehensions* appear in 1583 (BN) and 1584 (BM, BN); I quote from the second ed. See V.-L. Saulnier, 'Etude sur Béroalde de Verville. Introduction à la lecture du *Moyen de Parvenir*', BHR, 1944; J. L. Pallister, *The World of Béroalde de Verville*, Paris, 1971.

26. The *Œuvres poétiques* (1582) are preserved in BN and NLS, the *Meteores* in BM and BN. See A.-M. Schmidt, *La Poésie scientifique*.

27. To T. C. Cave, *Devotional Poetry in France*, M. Jeanneret, *Poésie et tradition biblique*, J. Pineau, *La Poésie des Protestants*, and R. Lebègue, *La Tragédie religieuse*, add A. Muller, *La Poésie religieuse catholique de Marot à Malherbe*, 1950.

28. This work is held by BM and O. See C. Jugé, *Nicolas Denisot du Mans (1515–1589)*, Le Mans-Paris, 1907; an up-to-date study is needed on this rather mysterious figure, who is found in the company of the Pléiade and also of humanists sensitive to evangelical currents. Denisot also organised the 1551 *Tombeau* of Marguerite de Navarre (BM, BN, O, PSG).

29. See L. C. Harmer, 'Lancelot de Carle, sa vie', *BHR*, 1939, 'Lancelot de Carle et les hommes de lettres de son temps', *BHR*, 1945, and his Cambridge thesis on this humanist.

30. His *Opera omnia* were printed in 1619 (BM, BN, O, Worcester Cathedral), and include the 1566 essay *De Divina Poesi*. He publishes a number of *plaquettes* during the 1560s. See H. O. Evennett, 'Claude d'Espence et son *Discours du colloque de Poissy*', *Revue historique*, 1930.

31. One may wonder to what extent early Christian writers had a stylistic impact too; St Augustine had been at one time a teacher of rhetoric.

32. The BM has a copy of the 1576 ed. See M. H. Seiler, *Anne des Marquets poétesse religieuse du XVIᵉ siècle*, Washington, 1931.

33. Copies of the *Emblesmes* (1571) in BM, BN. See J. Zezala and R. J. Clements, 'La troisième Lyonnaise – Georgette de Montenay', *ECr*, 1965. A polyglot edition of the *Emblesmes* appeared in Frankfurt in 1619. The title shows that the theoretical distinction between the emblem and the *devise* could be less rigid in practice.

34. Copy in BM. Some date the volume earlier.

35. *Sonnets spirituels*, 1573 (BN), 1577 (BM, BN); *Sonnets spirituels – livre second*, 1578 (BN, NLS). See T. C. Cave, *Devotional Poetry in France*.

36. The *Essay de Poemes chrestiens* followed the *Quatre Méditations sur les Psaumes*, 1588 (BN); the love-poetry came out in 1599 at Rouen, A. Boase and F. Ruchon, life and ed. of *Œuvres poétiques*, Geneva, 1949; ed. of *Meditations* by A. Boase, 1954. See also T. C. Cave, 'The Love-sonnets of Jean de Sponde: a reconsideration', *FMLS*, 1967; M. Richter, 'Lettura dei Sonnets de la mort di Jean de Sponde', *BHR*, 1968.

37. Copy of first ed. in BN; modern ed. H.-J. Lope, *TLF*, 1967; see A. Müller, *Un Poète religieux du XVIᵉ siècle: Jean-Baptiste Chassignet, 1578?–1635?*, 1951; R. Ortali, *Jean-Baptiste Chassignet, THR*, 1968; R. E. Leake, 'Jean-Baptiste Chassignet and Montaigne', *BHR*, 1961; M. Richter, 'Une fonte calvinista di Chassignet', *BHR*, 1964.

38. C. Lenient, *La Satire en France ou la littérature militante au XVIᵉ siècle*, 1877; Fleuret and Perceau, *Les Satires françaises, XVIᵉ siècle*, 2 vols. (Garnier; used here as this anthology contains poems otherwise not easily accessible); F. Charbonnier, *La Poésie française et les guerres de religion*, 1919; H. Weber, 'Poésie polémique et satirique de la Réforme sous les règnes de Henri II, François II et Charles IX', *CAIEF*, 1958. On non-committed satire, see O. Rossettini, *Les Influences anciennes et italiennes sur la satire en France au XVIᵉ siècle*, Florence, 1958, and P. M. Smith, *The Anti-courtier Trend*.

39. This work, translated into English in 1547 from Alaigre's French version, develops themes that will be exploited, not only marginally at the time of the *querelle des amyes*, but under Charles IX and Henry III: the mutability of life, the world as stage, the charms and authenticity of country life, the difference between words and deeds at Court, the procession of parasites and bogus figures at Court. Guevara also owes something to Plutarch.

40. N. de Margues published in 1563 his *Description du monde desguisé* and *A la noblesse de France* (both BN).

41. *Les Œuvres*, 1583 (BM), 1585 (BN); see L. Bergounioux, *Guillaume du Buys, poète satirique du XVIᵉ siècle, 1520?–1594*, 1936.

42. Published with *La Famine* in 1573 (BN); see P. M. Smith, *The Anti-courtier Trend*, and Cambridge thesis by Christopher Smith on La Taille.

43. Sister M. Sullivan, *Etienne du Tronchet, auteur forézien du XVIᵉ siècle*, Washington, 1931.

44. Lyons, 1572 (BM, BN).

45. An interesting anthology of French poetry since the *Délie* has recently appeared and is very relevant to the issues raised in our survey: *La Poésie française et le Maniérisme 1546–1610?*, *TLF*, 1971, with an Introduction by Marcel Raymond and notes by Alan Steele.

Chapter 13

THE THEATRE AFTER THE ADVENT OF THE PLÉIADE[1]

WITH the arrival of the Pléiade, the urge to renew dramatic forms is as strong as in other genres, though the Brigade did not number among its ranks anyone sufficiently gifted as a dramatist to make the necessary breakthrough; Jodelle, who makes his mark in both tragedy and comedy, comes into the orbit of the Brigade a few years later, and it will take time for new attitudes to establish themselves on the stage. The older forms of drama, though they had lost momentum and were affected by royal decree, did not die out overnight:[2] they maintained some popularity in the provinces and the Calvinists saw virtue in preserving genres that still held more popular audiences.[3] Nevertheless, new developments emerge in the main from ideas that were circulating in humanist *milieux* towards the middle of the century; we have already considered Calvinist experiments (see above, pp. 345–7).

I. TRAGEDY

Though neo-classical tragedy does not get under way until *c.* 1552, its theory is already well known. Translations of Greek dramatists, especially Euripides, were already current: Erasmus's versions of the *Hecuba* and the *Iphigenia* had appeared in the first decade of the century and were reprinted from time to time; Buchanan's *Medea* (1544) and *Alcestis* (1556) were also on the market; Gentien Hervet's rendering of the *Antigone* had appeared in 1541. Humanists had themselves experimented in Latin tragedy: Buchanan's *Jephthes* and *Baptistes* had been performed at the Collège de Guyenne in Bordeaux *c.* 1540, and Muret had followed up with his *Julius Cæsar*, published in his *Juvenilia*, 1552, but composed some years earlier. Translations into French are beginning to appear: Lazare de Baïf's *Electra*, 1537; Sebillet's *Iphigénie*, 1549; in 1557 Lalemant will publish his translation of Sophocles. The plays of Seneca are easily available and are no doubt being studied in the colleges. Writers such as Josse Bade, Charles Estienne, and later Peletier du Mans had added their comments to the classical theorists; and Jules-César Scaliger was at work on his *Poetice,* which was published posthumously in 1561, though one may wonder whether some of his ideas were not finding their way through humanist friends at a rather earlier date. Horace's views enjoy considerable currency, but aristotelian theories will begin to make some progress in the 1550s. Finally, there are two practitioners of dramatic art who are teaching in Paris colleges at the beginning of the decade and who are closely connected with the Pléiade – George Buchanan and Marc-Antoine Muret. In these circumstances the theory of tragedy was being shaped without undue difficulty, and dramatic practice was soon to follow.

Tragedy – Theory

Tragedy is seen to differ from comedy by the social status of the protagonists, the loftiness of the theme, and the evolution of the action from relative happiness to catastrophe. The hero, of noble birth and attested historically or mythologically, is caught up in some dire situation (though his responsibility or otherwise is not always stipulated, nor do all dramatists agree on the degree of culpability involved); and the theme of Fortune's wheel often occurs, with which may be associated the counselling of kings, who must follow virtue rather than worldly lures.

Certain formal conventions are mentioned by most theoreticians. Though the rule of the three unities is not yet established, there is agreement on the need for unity of action, and for the author to plunge *in medias res,* so that interest is aroused from the start; but playwrights do pay attention to time and place, though more towards the century's decline (when a form of 'irregular' tragedy emerges too). The play is to be divided into five acts (earlier commentators allowed six, but Horace prevails), and there may be a prologue and an epilogue, though practice varies in the matter of protatic characters. The divisions are shown, partly by the place at which the indispensable monologues occur (usually at the beginning of each act), and partly by the presence of the chorus, whose functions are various: it should be 'du parti de l'auteur' (Peletier) and make explicit the sense of the action, it will also moralise and it often plays the role of confidant. In several ways, classical simplicity and decorum are achieved; the presence of characters on stage is generally limited by the 'rule of three', and violent action is relegated to the wings, so that the messenger's role acquires increasing importance. In any case, the cast tends to become more limited than in earlier French theatre. The style, which owes much to the obvious classical model, Seneca, is highly rhetorical and certain figures and tropes occur regularly: the use of *sententiæ,* stichomythia in key passages, invocation is particularly important for tone, but other devices crowd the text. So far as metre is concerned, there is considerable latitude in the schemes used by the chorus, affording variety that may correspond to the different motifs; in the main text, two different metres may be employed in the earlier days, but there is a gradual move towards standardisation in favour of the alexandrine, which in any case is expected in the more elevated genres with the passage of time. There is less tendency to favour any criterion of length, and some plays are very much longer than one is accustomed to in the works of Corneille or Racine.

In such a conception of tragedy, where fate and a certain Stoic resignation (which Seneca also communicates) predominate, characterisation is neither subtle nor of overriding importance; the heroes are involved in inextricable situations, so that the atmosphere of the play is much determined by effects of pathos, dramatic irony, sometimes claustrophobia, but also by the presentation of different attitudes to the central crisis; rhetoric is pressed into the service of debate and the characters may therefore often seem little more than vehicles of such views. A theatre of this type is necessarily more static than at certain other periods, but this does not mean that it was unacceptable; it clearly was not, and moreover it was believed that the chief model, Seneca, wrote as he did for performance. It is certain that many of these tragedies were acted, mostly in colleges or at Court[5] – though Catherine de Medici came to exclude them out of superstitious fear – and perhaps occasionally in the provinces, but details are too often lacking, and it may well be that the borderline between recitation and acting proper was commonly blurred; in any case more needs to be learned about the development of staging which owes a good deal, it seems, to the writings of Serlio and Vitruvius in the long run.[6] The plays, during the wars of religion, often reflect obliquely contemporary preoccupations, both political and religious, though humanists tended to view with disapproval the overt propaganda of certain Huguenot writers who for their part were divided on the propriety of the theatre, after their initial pioneer work; it is only in the last quarter of the century that a Catholic tragedy as such appears. Nevertheless, classically conceived tragedy hardly dominates the scene decisively; as we saw, medieval traditions persist in the provinces, and 'irregular' tragedy, with its violence and indifference to classical rules, acquires undoubted popularity. At Court, more sumptuous spectacles are in demand; and yet, here as in so many other domains, we find the coexistence of the two trends, expansion and restraint.

In the development of neo-classical tragedy, Seneca inevitably plays a dominant role: on the one hand, he is the incarnation of various conventions formulated in the *arts poétiques*, and on the other, he affords a model of rhetorical utterance; Greek dramatists, though far from unknown, play a lesser part: Æschylus seems to remain in the penumbra, and the fact that Greek texts continue to be rendered so often into Latin as well as into French, makes one wonder just how much humanists outside the smaller circle of distinguished Hellenists were at home in Greek literature. Moreover, Seneca appealed by his themes and the philosophical undertones of his plays: in a period of civil turmoil and disrupted values his treatment of fortune and fate, of Stoic resignation and human dignity, was bound to reinforce his formal attractions. The static quality of Renaissance tragedy is often laid at his door, but after all his prestige is accounted for to a marked extent by his relevance to the times; and the strong streak of cruelty in his drama would appeal to a public that eagerly read the *Histoires tragiques* of Bandello, adapted by Belleforest and Boaistuau. Furthermore, the doctrine of imitation applies to Seneca no less than it does to Petrarch, its application still allows the poet to show his originality, and dramatists vary not a little in the importance they attach to this or that aspect of Senecan example: Garnier and La Taille, both greatly indebted to the Latin author, can still reveal their own unmistakable identities within a common tradition. Nor does relative independence from Seneca constitute *a priori* proof of originality or quality; the Roman playwright tends to be underestimated, particularly in his handling of dramatic irony. In any case, a strong model was required to fill the vacuum created by the regression of the medieval tradition which had hardly renewed itself for a very long time. Seneca's impact was unequal, and some of the Renaissance tragedians are endowed with only moderate talent; but three names stand out: Grévin, La Taille, and Garnier, though individual plays by other writers may be interesting, and Jodelle deserves recognition for his pioneering role.

Jodelle[7]

Jodelle's *Cléopatre* indeed marks the beginning of French neo-classical tragedy; and it is after its appearance that its author becomes closely involved with the Pléiade – before that time he had been a member of the Brinon circle. The play was performed twice in the spring of 1553, in all probability. It stimulated interest in humanist circles – La Péruse is said to have taken part in the second performance – and helps to set a pattern in a field where the leaders of the Brigade felt ill-equipped to give an example. Based on Plutarch's life of Antony, it is carefully constructed even if it is scarcely dramatic by modern standards: division into five acts (though they are not indicated as such) after a prologue, 'tragic subject', chorus, *confidents*, stichomythia, dream and portent (though Senecan influence is not emphasised by critics), development of *topoi* such as fortune's caprice, behaviour of princes, but also awareness of unity of time, however ill-defined that of place may be.

Jodelle alternates the use of alexandrine and decasyllable from act to act; for a time this practice will be common, though some dramatists will vary the metre within a given act, according to the speaker or sometimes for other reasons. Apart from structural features, several points deserve mention: for instance, Jodelle does not offer progress from 'happy' opening to tragic outcome, but remains tonally monochrome; the central character dominates the whole action, whereas in later dramatists this will not automatically be the case (e.g., Bounyn). Cléopâtre is given considerable stature, through her singlemindedness and her regal bearing, and the removal of Antony to the next world reinforces her central position, as do the presence of the chorus, her behaviour towards Seleucus in Act III, and the attitude of her enemy Proclus; moreover, she is flanked by two *confidentes*. The chorus assumes an interesting role, for it not only closes each act, with the exception of III, but also comments on the characters in the course of various acts, without actually affecting the action. In the first two acts, its part is extensive, it expresses itself in a variety of metres (including a Pindaric ode) and develops in great measure the lyric tones of the play – by its use of isometric trisyllable lines it takes us back to the days of Marot. For Jodelle, as for later writers, a tragedy is more elegiac than dramatic, though his emphasis on this quality comes dangerously near tedium. There are some very fine passages of poetry, notably Eras's invocation to death and some utterances by the chorus. Jodelle has enlarged upon Plutarch's data, no doubt in order to enhance sympathy for the protagonist, by his treatment of Octavien who appears in an unsympathetic light; in any case, Jodelle, as he states in the prologue which is chiefly a eulogy of Henry II, plays on national pride: he points out that his play is composed in French and that it owes little to classical playwrights. The general atmosphere is gloomily elegiac; Jodelle develops the themes of death, vicissitudes of fortune, treachery, dissimulation, dark future, and he makes little effort to relieve the murkiness.

In some ways *Didon se sacrifiant*, whose date of composition is unknown and a copy of which was destroyed by Ronsard's dogs, reminds one of *Cléopâtre*: there is no real dramatic conflict, the protagonist is a woman, rare for those days, and moreover a woman in whom public office and violent passion are opposed, and her death is linked with an emerging dignity of self. There are equally important differences, quite apart from the increased maturity of outlook and self-analysis that characterise the heroine. Formally, the play, though longer than *Cléopâtre* by some 600 lines, shows a greater sobriety in its recourse to varying metres and an almost consistent use of the alexandrine throughout the main text, but two choruses are put on stage. Though Jodelle has kept his classical models in mind, he makes little use of dramatic irony, and the edifying elements are not such as to be easily extracted from their context; the dramatist is more concerned with psychological interest and the poetic atmosphere that pervades the text.

Æneas, who Dido and Anne are convinced has deceived them, in spite of his protestations, suffers in some degree like Octavien from the fact that the sympathy is directed towards Dido, and he fades out after Act III. He is sure that the gods have decided the course of events; there is some discussion about 'fresle congnoissance' and the difficulty of discerning the right path, but he does not believe that even reason can alter the will of the gods. His view is opposed by Achates and others with their outbursts against *anagke* (in more sombre tones than anything on fortune in *Cléopâtre*). A further thread in his make-up is his patriotism, but he is not presented as a monster of righteous inflexibility and Jodelle has tried to humanise him up to a point. Dido is kept constantly in focus, but Jodelle does not let sympathy impinge upon the credibility of her portrait: she is acutely conscious of her guilty behaviour towards her husband, who figures prominently in her thoughts – indeed the Trojan past and Sichee are powerful factors in the creation of atmosphere. The chorus and Barce point out that her love is a form of madness for which she is not responsible: this no doubt serves to mitigate her unethical actions, it also lets Jodelle dwell on the Stoic theme 'happy is the man bereft of passions'. Dramatically speaking, there are no conflicts, rather meditations on various topics, and above all the growing awareness within Dido of her predicament. Jodelle shows some subtlety in the way he feeds in psychological motifs; moreover, he delays her appearance until Act II, using the first act to build up a picture of her in the spectator's mind. Her hope of settling things, the arguments on which she draws in order to sway Æneas, her reactions after his departure, the memory of her husband, all these things are managed with commendable care. The secondary figures are very thin; Palinure means little, Achates like Anne is a supporting character for the protagonists; and Barce helps to develop the witchcraft theme, to act as a messenger at the end, and to put into words a reaction to Dido's fate. The two choruses sometimes develop arguments supporting their 'side', on other occasions they express commonplaces; they indulge in stichomythia which is less frequent than in the previous play and never between the main characters. The sombre mood of the text is reinforced by the themes they develop: the changeless will of the gods, however different their faces may show themselves to humans, the way in which they prevail against reason, the brutality of Nature, the ease with which the wicked get away with their evil acts. Such dramatic elements as are present find their way into the messenger's speech and into the references to the past; Jodelle has attempted a sort of elegiac tone poem, in which he makes use of traditional rhetoric (repetition, invocation, enumeration, Vergilian comparisons, the theme of the sea). As theatre, the play is less taut than *Cléopâtre* – though that does not amount to much – but in its attitudes it shows more 'body' and greater poetic range.

Jacques Grévin – Jules César (*1561*)[9]

Before the appearance of Grévin, several authors try their hand at tragedy, in which the element of adaptation is sizeable: La Péruse's *Médée*, published posthumously, shows a greater tightness of structure by an author whose poetic gifts were snuffed out by an early death;[8] Charles Toutain included an *Agamemnon* in the poems he published in 1557; and the *Sophonisbe* which Saint-Gellais had adapted from Trissino in 1556, was performed posthumously at Court in 1559. A more important play is Jacques Grévin's *Jules César* (1561); in his preliminary *Brief discours*, the author claims some priority in the field of tragedy, with the exception of Jodelle: he interprets the genre as 'une imitation de quelque faict illustre et grand de soymesme', and as something to be constructed in accordance with Horace and Aristotle. He pays tribute to the Greek tragedians, then to Seneca, and admits his debt to Muret's *Julius Cæsar*, though without prejudice to his own originality. Grévin, a convinced Huguenot, does not follow the pattern of biblical inspiration but sticks to a classical theme, the day of Cæsar's death. Though many of the *topoi* of princedom are trotted out – Fortune's wheel, the happiness of the humble citizen, the falsity of courtiers and so-called best friends – the play turns on the problem of tyrannicide in the name of liberty, of which Brutus is the spokesman and agent. The play was subsequently understood to favour tyrannicide – a theme that emerges often in Calvinist writings during the wars (e.g., Buchanan's *De Iure Regni*) – but it is doubtful whether such an interpretation can be substantiated: Cæsar is presented in human terms, capable of doubt and unheroic feelings. Calpurnia plays an important part, affectively, in the scheme of things, a part which supports Cæsar in the eyes of the spectator, and the play ends not with a flourish but with Mark Antony's passionate plea that Cæsar's death be avenged, and the view of the soldier who concludes: 'Ceste mort est fatale/Aux nouveaux inventeurs de puissance Royale'. Generally speaking, the chorus (of soldiers, whom Grévin considers more 'vraisemblables', though he does not use the term) acts as a background of opinion for Cæsar, whose achievement it praises, and not for Brutus; in so far as the chorus is normally understood to support the main character and themes, it is on Cæsar's side. However, in the tradition of dramatic debate, both viewpoints are given adequate ventilation. The structure of the play is carefully conceived, though not 'dramatic' in a modern sense: classical conventions of time, action, and place are observed, and violence on the stage is eschewed, so that Cæsar's death is reported by a messenger in the fourth act. The 'acts' are separated by chorus interludes (in one of these, a soldier develops a curious poem to the sun and Nature after the manner of Ronsard), and the first three open with substantial monologues. Cæsar appears in Acts I and III, when Brutus makes him change his mind and spurn Calpurnia's advice to defer decision for a day. The acts become progressively shorter; Grévin makes little or no use of stichomythia or dramatic irony, and introduces fewer *sententiæ* than do many playwrights. On the other hand, he devotes much space to dream and presentiment – hence the scope of Calpurnia's role – and the sun theme may, by its association with Cæsar, enhance artistically his prestige. There are no protatic characters, and the play is in alexandrines, except for the choruses which are in octosyllables; *alternance des rimes* is respected, and though Grévin employs a number of obvious rhetorical devices, his verse has a rounded dignity, surprisingly mature in a poet who was barely eighteen when he wrote the play. Like Jodelle, he will also make an excursion into comedy (see below, pp. 445–6), but in the realm of tragedy he marks a considerable advance on his predecessor.

Gabriel Bounyn – La Soltane *(1561)*[10]

La Soltane is the first French classical tragedy to treat a contemporary and exotic subject, one which may make us think of Racine's *Bajazet*: Rose (Roxane) plans, with Rustan, her son-in-law, to destroy Moustapha whom the sultan has chosen as his successor over the head of Roxane's children. The first three acts show the two plotting Moustapha's death, the other acts (where the latter appears) present his betrayal, though he refuses to flee or otherwise go against his fate. The play thus revolves round three main characters, the others having little definition or presence: Act I, for instance, is really one scene between Rose and Rustan. Since Moustapha does not appear until well on in the second half, his point of view is represented at first by the chorus and the strange 'génies de Moustapha'. The chorus, which does not take a direct part in the action, ends the first act with an attack on Rose; the nature of the 'génies', who are winged but apparently mortal, is difficult to interpret, except as a picturesque reinforcement of the chorus in its supporting role. One cannot claim that there is much in the way of local colour; indeed classical overtones, such as Moustapha's dream in which Mahomet takes him through *Æneid* IV, tend to obscure the oriental character of the action. Bounyn, for all his acquaintance with Greek literature – he translated a work of Aristotle's in 1554 –

does not emerge as an impressive disciple; the hero bears little tragic stature and seems more Senecan, the unities of time and place are not observed, and the chorus creates problems, as its identity is not clear and the absence of unity of place makes one wonder whether more than one chorus is not in fact required. Stylistically the play leaves a good deal to be desired: Bounyn is very fond of certain figures, *sententiæ, adunaton, reprise,* doubling of word or phrase, binary and ternary rhythms, but no stichomythia. The vocabulary can be alembicated, for he affects the Pléiade compound word ('le nuit-chantant hibou', 'soing triste-songeard', 'léger-ailé', 'j'avantvoi'), classically derived words, newfangled epithets (*cielin, chienine, gaimentable*); he introduces numerous references to classical mythology that clash with oriental ambience. And he lacks skill as a versifier; metre and the needs of rhyme often twist sound and syntax, and the text does not read very happily. Like contemporaries, Bounyn employs both the decasyllable and the alexandrine, but he also brings four 14-syllable lines into play; here and there we come across independent half-lines, and once a quarter-line that is left hanging. Once the chorus indulges in a pattern poem; but it usually remains at a low poetic level, developing *topoi* with predictable banality. The lack of overall structure – Rose and Rustan disappear after Act III and Act V does not exploit the crisis properly – and the limits of tonal range make this play a disappointing one, in spite of its thematic originality.

A. de Rivaudeau – Aman (1566)[11]

Rather more interesting is Rivaudeau's one play *Aman,* published in 1566 but written perhaps some six years earlier, and certainly after the appearance of La Péruse's *Médée* and Claude Roillet's Latin *Aman* (1556). It is the first 'regular' French tragedy on a Christian theme – for the plays of Bèze and Des Masures belong to another tradition – and it broadly justifies its claim to well-thought-out construction. In his preface, Rivaudeau emphasises the unity of time on the grounds of verisimilitude:

. . . Ceux qui font des tragedies ou comedies de plus d'un jour ou d'un tour de soleil (comme je parle Aristote) faillent lourdement . . . Mais ces tragedies sont bien bonnes et artificielles, qui ne traitent rien plus que ce qui peut estre advenu en autant de temps que les spectateurs considerent l'ebat . . . Mais je ne mesle point de groec parmi le françois.

This leads him to reduce the Esther episode to the events immediately preceding Aman's death (as is clear from the title which refers to Esther vii). The exposition of the situation is therefore made by means of retrospects in speeches spread over the first three acts; dramatically this may have its weaknesses, but tonally it fits in with the important theme of the destiny of the Jewish people (as in

Garnier's *Juifves*, of which we are reminded in other ways too. In the interests of credibility, Rivaudeau condemns the *deus ex machina*; though Scaliger's *Poetice* had appeared in 1561, he does not seem to have used it, but he does show some knowledge of Greek tragedy:

Pour le reste je me suis rangé le plus reservement et estroitement que j'ay peu en escrivant ceste tragedie à l'art et au modelle des anciens Grecs, et n'ay esté ny trop superstitieux, ni trop licencieux, ni en la rime, ni ès autres parties de la poésie.

Rivaudeau also prepared an unpublished commentary on the *Electra* c. 1559. At all events, care is taken with the external structure, and unity of place is ensured. The central crisis, which lasts a few hours, is properly organised round the opposition of Aman and the Jewish people; the outcome of this conflict depends on the relations between Assuere and Esther, resolution being delayed until the final scene. Aman is presented as a character obsessed with the desire for vengeance, more so perhaps than in the biblical account; he appears in every act and has by far the longest part. Two other features develop his *persona*: on the one hand he is the enemy of God, self-centred and dubious of the force of destiny:

> Je n'ay que faire aux Dieux, car ma grande puissance
> Me promet à part moy la fin de ma vengeance.

And on the other, no doubt in memory of Seneca (*Hercules furens*), but also to maintain as far as possible the dramatic momentum of his character, Aman verges on the demented in his later appearances: he sees himself haunted by the furies and he trembles for his future. This forms part of a dramatic tradition perhaps, but one may also see in his instability a symptom of the man who has forsaken God. For the play is a deeply religious one and is, moreover, coloured by Rivaudeau's Calvinist sympathies. That Rivaudeau was a Calvinist is suggested by his friendship with Babinot, author of the *Christiade* (1559), La Noue, and others, the choice of the name Deborah for his daughter, the clear allusions in the text to the present predicament of the Huguenots (as in the themes: how long must the wicked prosper? will God come to the rescue of His chosen ones?) and in the characters who may well have some personal reference to contemporaries. Over and against Aman there stand a series of Jewish figures who represent what one might call a neo-stoic ethic – it will be recalled that Rivaudeau published a commentary and translation of Epictetus in 1567. Aman's viewpoint is questioned by the eunuch, and also by his wife who counsels the moderation of his anger and reminds him that God succours the faithful. At a more important level, Mardochée represents the conscience of the Jews and is bent on keeping Esther on the strait and narrow path; Aman rightly recognises him as his most dangerous enemy. Syméon is introduced briefly to present an example of the fate of the Jews over recent generations; and in various speeches the earlier history of the people is emphasised. The chorus plays an interesting and valuable part: though it participates modestly in the action by direct address to various characters, it resembles the *Juifves* in Garnier's play in that it develops themes associated with the destiny of Israel. At the end of the first two acts, the stanzas of these 'servantes de la Royne Esther' are followed by the voice of 'une de la troupe' who presents a slightly different motif. Among other things, the chorus stresses the inability of man to escape his destiny ('Car nul ne peut eviter son destin'); the single voice affirms that kings are the instruments of God ('Les Roys sont verges de Dieu') and that the wicked form part of the divine plan ('Car Dieu se sert du meschant'). The chorus also serves to put a more vigorous point of view to Esther at a critical moment, and this is the one passage in the play in which stichomythia is employed. The pivotal characters Assuere and Esther have relatively short parts; Esther does not stand out particularly, though she is taken as an example of the power of beauty in Harbone's speech, V, i; Assuere could have been portrayed in rather grotesque fashion, but in fact, though he appears as weak-willed and as a latter-day Petrarchan suitor, he maintains some dignity and reinforces the Christian view of destiny by recognising that, whatever his power and the might of his ancestors, he too must follow the 'ordonnance des Dieux'. Nevertheless, the final decision, acceptance of Esther's request, is rushed, not exploited to proper dramatic effect. An ironic touch is created by Aman being hanged on the gibbet he had had prepared for Mardochée; but the play takes a long time to get under way, owing to the great length of the prologue and also of Aman's speech in Act I. In spite of its faults, *Aman* is worth reading: it shows some structural progress on earlier tragedies, it achieves some impressive lyrical effects – Rivaudeau varies the strophic patterns of the chorus well – and he has written a sort of tract for the times, a poem of exhortation and comfort for the Huguenots.

Jean de la Taille (?1533–?1617)[12]

The four tragedies of the La Taille brothers, of whom Jacques had died in 1569(?), appeared in 1572–73, and an *art de la tragédie* that constitutes one of the most valuable statements by a French Renaissance tragedian on his genre. Jean develops certain ideas already accepted, such as the division into five acts, the role of the chorus, the absence of stage violence, but he reveals some originality and precision in his formulations. He defines tragedy as the portrait of

piteuses ruines de grands seigneurs . . . inconstances de fortunes . . . bannissemens, guerres, pestes, famines, captivitéz, execrables cruautés des Tyrans but he goes on to advance a conception of the hero which recalls Aristotle, in that he should be neither excessively good nor excessively bad:

Que le Subject aussi ne soit de Seigneurs extremement meschants, et que pour leurs crimes horribles ils meritassent punition; n'aussi, par mesme raison, de ceulx qui sont du tout bons, gens de bien et de saincte vie, comme d'un Socrates, bien qu'à tort empoisonné.

La Taille does not stress as much as his contemporaries the progression of the hero's fate from happiness to misfortune, nor does he seem very interested in the relevance of a play to its own times. What he does insist on is the need of a break with medieval tradition, a point developed in connection with his remarks on the audience. He scorns college performances and would wish to have his plays acted in a classical theatre in front of an aristocratic audience, with proper respect given to 'débit'; at the same time he considers pleasure and entertainment more relevant than edification and wants 'd'esmouvoir et de poindre merveilleusement les affections d'un chascun'. This attitude might explain La Taille's more sparing use of *sententiæ*; it also fits in with his seeing a play as drama rather than literature, and of course his verse does not have the poetic quality of a Jodelle, a Grévin, or a Garnier. It is generally believed that La Taille has given us the first clear statement on the rule of the three unities, but recently doubt has been cast on the meaning of 'temps' in the formula:

Il faut tousjours représenter l'histoire ou le jeu en un mesme jour, en un mesme temps, et en un mesme lieu.[13]

Of the four plays, *Saül le furieux* is without question the most impressive and the most original. La Taille follows in broad outline the biblical narrative, taking some details from Josephus, but also contracts a special debt to Seneca's *Hercules furens*. His Saul is aristotelian in conception and he tries to reduce the tyrannical aspect of his character, by evoking his past sympathetically, by dealing harshly with the theme of the Amalekite's tyrannicide, and by playing down David who ends by stating that Saul did not persecute him; and the stress is on the *furieux* which has warped his character and is the direct consequence of his having sinned against God through his wrongheaded act of clemency. By reducing David's stature, La Taille increases Saul's centricity; his audience's sympathy is induced to some extent by his wrongheaded sparing of Agag's life, by his honourable death, and by the creation of the first equerry who acts as a sort of conscience to the king. Great care is taken with the dramatic structure ('Or, c'est le principal point d'une Tragedie de la sçavoir bien disposer, bien bastir'); we are plunged *in medias res* and La

Taille maintains a certain dramatic ambiguity throughout: the contrast of Saul mad and normal, the attitude of David reported in two different ways, the rumours about David and the Amalekites, the two reports of Saul's death. On the other hand, no serious use is made of dramatic irony; but care is taken with the injection of new information at well-timed intervals (messenger's speeches, etc.). The secondary characters are allowed time to assert themselves – one has only to compare their treatment here with the wasted opportunities in *Didon se sacrifiant*. Jonathe's functions are straightforward, he stands for youth and action in the early debates, but also represents Saul's son, and by his death heightens the pathetic element. The witch of Endor – the only 'female' figure – is the centre of one of the most extraordinary scenes in French Renaissance tragedy and contributes powerfully to the atmosphere of the play. She enhances the consolatory and touching elements of the scene, whereas Samuel's ghost symbolises part of Saul's guilt – once again La Taille's dramatic sense is well shown here in the emotive balance of the scene. The Amalekite soldier represents the more sordid aspects of war, acts partly as a messenger, brings out an attitude to tyrannicide, and by his false report enriches the build-up of sympathy for the protagonist. David, who, like Alexandre in *Daire*, appears only in the final act, is kept as far as possible in the penumbra and acts as an epilogue character with his dirge. The chorus is perhaps not exploited as fully as by some other playwrights: La Taille's talents do not lie in lyric poetry, but he does use the chorus to emphasise ideas that concern the main figures: fighting the good fight, condemnation of necromancy, kings as *exempla*, Fortune's wheel. The play is written for the most part in alexandrines, apart from the chorus sections, but the last act is in decasyllables.

La Taille stands out as one of the few dramatists of the period to possess a vivid sense of the stage, all the more striking for the fact that his conception of the ideal audience was bound to cut him off from the stage life of his times. He has an acute sense of structure and timing, and he is one of the first dramatists to bring primary and secondary characters into a productive relationship. Though La Taille was a Huguenot, his plays do not display any partisan commitment (only his choice of biblical subjects may be noted), nor does he give the impression of being deeply involved politically. In *Saül* I gain the feeling that his move towards a more aristotelian view of the hero also involved a shift towards a deepening of psychological insight; Saul undoubtedly dominates the play, but not so much by conflict and assertion as by centricity and ambiguity. The potential force of David as a counter-hero has been suppressed. In a sense, La Taille is trying to achieve in the field of the drama what Du Bellay preached in the *Deffense*, a break with the national past and a return to the valid models of antiquity:

Et voudrois bien qu'on eust banny de France telles ameres espiceries qui gastent le goust de nostre langue, et qu'au lieu on y eust adopté et naturalisé la vraye Tragedie et Comedie, qui n'y sont point encor à grand'peine parvenues, et qui toutesfois auroyent aussi bonne grace en nostre langue françoyse qu'en la grecque et latine.

Robert Garnier (c. 1545–90)[14]

Garnier's theatrical career stretches over nearly twenty years, from the *Porcie*, published in 1568 but probably composed four years earlier, to *Les Juifves* (1583). He acquires his poetic training at a time when the Pléiade has come fully into its own; his own professional links are legal and he numbers many lawyers among his friends. He trained at Toulouse and his theatre, among other things, shows concern with questions of political theory, questions that are also often present, inevitably, in the main model, Seneca. In his prefaces Garnier points to the relevance of the subjects he treats, and indeed his emphasis on political matters shows a certain difference, proportionately, from Seneca. By later standards, his plays are structurally far from flawless, characterisation may be loose, and the main theme is not always clear (e.g., *Porcie*); but, with the exception of La Taille in *Saül furieux*, he stands head and shoulders above his contemporaries, partly through his gradually widening awareness of dramatic possibilities, partly because his poetic gifts harmonise with his dramatic sense, in a way, for instance, that does not happen with Jodelle.

Garnier wrote seven plays, of which one, *Bradamante*, a late experiment in tragicomedy, will be examined below (pp. 452–3); in subject-matter his tragedies fall into three stages, Roman, Greek, biblical. The Senecan pattern tends to predominate, but Garnier also draws on Lucan, thematically so congenial to authors active during the wars of religion, Greek drama, and the plays are often suffused with poetry that links Garnier with the finer inspirations of the Pléiade. Here only brief consideration may be given to one play in each section.

Marc-Antoine (1578) follows *Porcie* and *Cornélie*; it also treats the same subject as Jodelle's first tragedy. Structurally, it carries the main body in the three middle acts, the first and the fifth being shorter and consisting mostly of monologue. The action is limited: Marc-Antoine, militarily at the end of his tether, seeks an honourable solution in suicide, and Cléopâtre, who has meanwhile shut herself up in 'ce sépulchre morne' to avoid capture by Cæsar, dies over her lover's body. Though foreshortening of events allows the unity of time to be respected, dramatic openings are barely sought: there is some misunderstanding between Marc-Antoine and Cléopâtre in the interpretation of her actions *vis-à-vis* Cæsar, whose personality can be felt from behind the stage; also Cléopâtre and her *confidente* Charmian debate whether an appeal should be made to Cæsar, but this does not add up to much. Garnier works in other ways to obtain his effects: he introduces a group of themes which, in their development, not only help to give dimension to the main characters – though one can hardly talk of psychology – but also bring the protagonists together in a network of issues. Marc-Antoine is naturally associated with the power of love, which overwhelms his reason and is the instrument of his downfall. However, when the theme is taken up by Cléopâtre, it is connected with the problem of the gods, fatality, free-will, in which Philostrate, present only in Act II, takes the totally determinist view that refuses freedom of action even to Jupiter. This problem of human liberty and therefore of moral initiative is one to which Garnier returns elsewhere and his plays are often variations on a cluster of themes. When Cæsar and Agrippe discuss Marc-Antoine's fate, they talk in terms of his hubris (*outre-cuidance*), but psychologically the theme is somewhat warped without, I think, dramatic irony, in that Cæsar himself seeks un-shared power, which he defends partly on grounds of political expediency. Cæsar, indeed, in his first speech, sounds like a precursor of Nebuchadnezzar (*Les Juifves*) by his assertion of power, but later he becomes a mouthpiece for feelings of sympathy after Marc-Antoine's collapse. Cléopâtre herself stands for the claims of passion and fidelity to Marc-Antoine, which she links with the cause of human freedom, even if it entails danger and destruction. These central issues are enriched by ancillary ones: friendship, which explains the presence of Lucile and gives another dimension to Marc-Antoine; Rome, whose power is affirmed, but whose possible decline is also foreseen; Fortune, especially of kings; the dignity of the prince's end; the defence of suicide, a theme which recurs elsewhere. Compared with some plays, the political aspects are not stressed overmuch, though the soldiers who form the chorus in Act V attack civil war, but also refer to the advantages of unified government and the preference for warlike activities to work outside one's own country.

In *Marc-Antoine*, as in many of Garnier's plays and unlike those of some contemporaries, women play a front-rank role, and this determines in some measure the atmosphere of the action. At the same time, Garnier's plays impart a sense of abundant vitality and cosmic range. This derives in part from the role the playwright assigns to Nature: the choruses often develop motifs from Nature, and sometimes the characters, as they take leave of life, sing a moving hymn in its honour (Antigone), or they may make use of solar imagery (Cæsar, Nebuchadnezzar). Moreover, Garnier's protagonists, though the private aspects of their drama are not hidden from view, make explicit their links with their country and their family through time – Marc-Antoine does not forget his descent from Hercules, also tamed by love – and their exploits are described as ranging over the whole earth (Antoine, Nebuchadnezzar). All this, coupled with Garnier's slowly and often majestically undulant rhythms, confers upon the plays a spaciousness and richness of tone which help us to forget the narrower 'dramatic' effects that have been neglected. There is no sense of hurry in his world, and in this context his messenger's speeches can take on a tonal role that is often impressive (*Antigone*). Temporally, as it were, Garnier leaves his plays in an open-ended state, and it is by his power of reverberation that he strikes our imagination. No doubt his predilection for special figures of rhetoric – repetition, chiasmus, *anaphora*, Vergilian comparison – contribute to this effect, but he also seems to me to have a far greater control of imagery than other dramatists at this time.

In *Antigone* (1580), Garnier allows himself a much broader canvas, for the play runs to some 3,000 lines. The themes, more closely knit together perhaps than in *Marc-Antoine*, are developed through a series of characters who are all losers in the predicament in which they find themselves, whereas in the earlier play we were left to think that Cæsar and therefore Rome emerged victors. The dramatic node of the play is clear: Antigone versus Créon; and the issues that divide them are brought out in stark antithesis. Basically they gravitate round that of the individual conscience (guided by religious feeling) against the laws of the state excessively asserted. In this play, Antigone is much more central: she is presented, first in relation to her father Edipe, then to her brother Polynice, then to Créon, but also to Ismène. At the same time, the action ends in the destruction of the whole family, as Créon comes to understand. The characters emerge by the attitudes they adopt to problems arising from their situation: the individual and fate, principle and greed, the rights of the individual and those of the state, the degree (or otherwise) of compromise. Antigone stands out in firm contrast to all those around her; all the members of the family, we are made to feel immediately or by the end of the play, live by values she denies, even though this means her own elimination. She also expresses the rights of life in extremely moving verse. Though the destiny of Thebes is involved, the family drama is emphasised more, relatively speaking. The *leitmotive* of the tragedy are manifested up to a point through political issues, but Antigone also stresses moral principles, and there is in her behaviour a religious sense that perhaps foreshadows *Les Juifves*. One may notice some progression or variation in Garnier on key topics through his plays: fate or free-will, the relation of the individual to the gods. His plays do not always end on a clear-cut note, whatever the explicit statement made in the final lines (as in *Antigone*); the political affirmation there hardly obliterates the values for which Antigone stands and dies.

Les Juifves (1583) is rightly considered to be Garnier's masterpiece, though one may carp at certain structural defects. Here Garnier moved into religious drama and he is, it seems, the first orthodox playwright of real stature to do so (a tragedy of Catholic inspiration is recorded in 1576) within the framework of neo-classical convention; and the relevance of some of the matter to contemporary affairs is not far to seek. The shadow of Seneca is still cast over the text and there is a greater measure of dramatic irony than in the two plays so far examined. Nevertheless, the structure is reasonably coherent: in the first place, the predicament of the Jews is seen clearly as part of God's plan, so that, though Nebuchadnezzar appears as the sovereign who has power of life or death over rebellious subjects – and Garnier has no sympathy for rebellion – he is in no less certain terms presented as the instrument of God's wrath, however little he may be aware of it. This sense of claustrophobia is heightened by the way in which *all* characters are shown to be dependent on Nebuchadnezzar, not excluding his wife. At the same time, the chorus, from one point of view, becomes the chief character and thus helps to impart unity and tone to the tragedy. It develops themes suitable to the play as a whole: sin as the fundamental trait of human nature, man's tendency to wanton destruction, Israel's hubris and consequent downfall, farewell to Jordan and to the former glories of Sion, the mutability of Fortune. Garnier's mastery of style allows him to confer a high lyrical quality on the utterances of the chorus, which acts as a confidant to various main characters and represents Jewry through time. By these themes and the final remarks of the Prophet, the destiny of the Jewish nation goes beyond its present predicament to embrace both its past and its future. In these circumstances, though there are some dramatically effective scenes, the elegiac tone must assume great importance. Garnier takes us *in medias res* and of course much depends on Nebuchadnezzar's decision in Act III, but there is no great explosion, and though the play is divided into five acts, they look very much like three central acts flanked by a prologue and epilogue. The characters make rather sporadic appearances, Sédécie does not appear until Act IV, of the main figures Amital is by far the most constantly on stage; but they seem to stand between God and the chorus of *Juifves*. The main theme of the play is well stated in lines 67–70:

> Helas! voylà que c'est d'offenser l'Eternel,
> Qui te portoit, Sion, un amour paternel:
> Tu as laissé sa voye, et d'une ame rebelle
> Préféré les faux Dieux qu'adore l'Infidelle.

This is enriched by political harmonics, the emotions associated with the present predicament of the Israelites, but also curiously by reminiscences from an earlier play by Garnier, the *Troade* (1578), in spite of its pagan context.

Act I is carried by the Prophet and the chorus whose functions have already been outlined. The Prophet, though a protatic character, is none the less indispensable to the structure: he acts as God's mouthpiece, states the issues of the action, the reasons for the Jews' present plight, and warns against self-centredness. In all this he helps to set the tone and the tempo of the play: he also prophesies the time when tribulation will end and takes us beyond the claustrophobic action of the present; he acts as a messenger in Act V and as elsewhere does much to determine the emotive colour of the text. Act II really divides up into three sections: first, the entry of Nebuchadnezzar, whose role upon earth is made clear and whose presence will allow for discussion of a Renaissance commonplace, the tyrant; Amital, who says of herself 'Je suis la douleur même', but also represents human dignity in suffering, adds to our knowledge of the earlier history of the Jews, and, by her prayers, maintains the divine dimension in the spectator's mind; and finally the presence of the queen who reinforces the sense of claustrophobia by stressing her dependence on her husband, introduces the sense of foreboding discreetly, and gives an impression of dramatic relief by her wish to intercede on behalf of the Jews. The following act also breaks into three sections with the dialogue between Nebuchadnezzar and his wife; the most dramatically effective scene of the tragedy, the confrontation between the king and Amital; and the chorus with its warnings against forgetting the Lord. Act IV allows Sédécie to take shape before the spectators' eyes, and here we have a blend of Christian and Stoic themes in the presence of death; through the creation of the Prévost, who orders the children to be killed before Sédécie's eyes, other emotions are introduced: the sense of sadism (though off stage), brutal dramatic irony, further foreboding. The final act, in which the Prophet recounts the death of Sédécie, is more of an epilogue; it introduces, even more than before, the note of pathos, but it also offers a silver lining to the cloud, with the promise that Nebuchadnezzar will have to be brought to book and that the Jews will ultimately know a happiness denied to this generation. In this play, where Garnier reaches the height of his poetic powers, we have a tonal rather than a dramatic structure, with the contrast between God and the *Juifves*, the *huis clos* of the present set against the wider horizons of past and future, the man-centred and the god-centred, an antithesis that is also expressed by the different rhetorical levels, biblical and classical; and all this enriched by harmonics (political and Stoic) that would find eager response in that troubled period. Here Garnier has created a dramatic atmosphere of finer scope and quality than in any previous play.

Within the space of thirty years, neo-classical tragedy makes impressive progress, and in spite of many difficulties. In the provinces the medieval tradition had not died out, no doubt Italian troupes introduced material from their native country, and in addition the Court preferred comedies, tragicomedies, and in due course the *ballet de cour*:

Elle [says Brantôme of Catherine de Medici] aimoit fort à veoir jouer des comedies et tragedies: mais depuis *Sophonisbe*, composée par M. de Sainct-Gelais et tresbien representée par mesdames ses filles et autres dames et damoiselles et gentilshommes de sa cour, qu'elle fit jouer à Blois aux nopces de M. de Cyprière et du marquis d'Elbeuf, elle eut opinion qu'elle avoit porté malheur aux affaires du royaume, ainsy qu'il succeda, elle n'en fit plus jouer, mais ouy bien des comedies et tragi-comedies, et mesmes celles de Zané et *Pantalons*, y prenant grand plaisir.

Ariosto's *Ginevra* was performed at Fontainebleau during one of the three great court *fêtes* in Catherine's lifetime, but tragedy was at a great disadvantage. On the other hand, Filleul's *Lucrèce*, more interesting for the choice than for the treatment of its subject, was performed during the Rouen *entrée* in 1566.[15] A tragicomedy on Job was performed at Poitiers before 1579; Sainte-Marthe wrote the prologue, but the play has not come down to us. Classical tragedy required a sophisticated, humanist audience more often than not; but there are occasional tragedies that take an episode in French history for their plot. Humanists in the provinces compose tragedies, like Beaubreuil's *Regulus*, 1582, published at Limoges: in this play, where Regulus is always called Attilie and the action is of the loosest, the author asserts his right not to comply with the so-called unity of time.[16] The relative lack of audience to determine structure may have been a hindrance; nevertheless, it is important not to view Renaissance tragedy simply as an early abortive form of the classical drama we associate with Corneille and Racine.

II. COMEDY

Survey and Theory

Like tragedy, comedy develops in a complex set of circumstances: the medieval is seen as played out, though elements will persist in the provinces, inspiration is sought from classical sources, but also from abroad, especially Italy, and Italian-style comedies are popular at Court. Brantôme informs us that

La feue royne mere fit une fois jouer une fort belle comedie en italien pour un mardy gras, à Paris à l'hostel de Reims, que Cornelio Fiasco, capitaine des galleres, avoit inventé[e].

There are also Italian troupes about; but at the same time many authors wish to develop a new, genuinely French comedy. Before the Pléiade, scholars like Estienne were showing the way; in his translation of the *Andria* (1542), he describes the classical type of comedy:

[la comedie]ne touchoit qu'en general toutes personnes par manieres d'esbat: et ne parloit que d'amours, et n'introduysoit que personnaiges de basse condition. En icelle y avoit motz pour rire, sentences joyeuses, argument bien disposé et conduyt reformations de mœurs corrumpues et lascives.[17]

From the classical tradition and Donatus comes the practice of prologue, epilogue, and division into five acts, between which there are *intermèdes* or musical intervals; though Paris often serves as the scene of the action and contemporary reference may be introduced, the intrigue is normally invented or taken from literary sources, and attacks on particular persons are frowned upon. Plautus and Terence were of course abundantly studied in the colleges and, once humanist comedy becomes acceptable, will provide certain conventions; Aristophanes' *Plutus* was also well known about the time of the *Deffense*: it was latinised by the Portuguese humanist Cabedius (Paris, 1547), two years later by C. Girard, and performed in French at the Collège de Coqueret in 1549. However, writers do not let themselves be constricted by classical models: for instance, by the end of the century, the plot may become very involved, and Roman comedy is not the only source for a number of character types that tend to recur from play to play. Medieval characters do not die out overnight – the farce element persists, as does the old octosyllabic line – and the *commedia erudita* plays an important part, developing the valet into a positive, though less often pleasant, character, and in making something more of the confidant. It is still rare for a play to be built round a single character; the situation or a complex of themes affords a clearer structural design, and in any case realism and social observation remain at best partial, overshadowed by the stereotypes. We do not know a lot about the performance of these plays: some were doubtless staged at colleges, and though some comedies were performed for court entertainment or during *entrées* – Bibbiena's *La Calandria*, Plautine in inspiration, was performed for Henry II's entry into Lyons (1548) and is associated with the introduction of neoclassical scenery and perspective – it is not certain that the Court showed any continuous interest in the genre so that bourgeois audiences were more likely. As strolling troupes developed, actors tended to specialise in the types recurring in comedy. The language is naturally more 'realistic' than in tragedy, not merely because of the conventions concerning the social status of the characters but also because verse was not indispensable. Sometimes patois elements are introduced and racy, popular phrases and vocabulary may well be represented. The edifying element is not prominent: Jodelle and

Grévin verge on the cynical, and if Larivey, a churchman, emphasises the moral value of comedy:

> . . . j'ay mis, comme en bloc, divers enseignemens fort profitables, blasmant les vitieuses actions et louant les honnestes affin de faire cognoistre combien le mal est à eviter, et avec quel courage et affection la vertu doibt estre embrassée, pour meriter louange, acquerir vertu en ceste vie et esperer non seulement une gloire eternelle entre les hommes, mais une celeste recompense après le trespas.

his statement hardly embraces his cheerfully immoral *Les Espirits*. D'Amboise's comedy is rather good-natured with no particular attempt to moralise. Nevertheless, the achievement of French comedy at this time is distinctly modest: though a goodly number may well have been performed, only a portion of them have come down in print or manuscript, and less than a dozen are extant for the period ending with Charles IX's death. Some, like Larivey's, are pretty close to their Italian originals; and generally, the adherence to various literary conventions meant that comedy was less the mirror of *mœurs* than was commonly claimed. The sense of construction is often rudimentary, and the range of social observation narrow. Some other points will emerge in the discussion of individual authors or plays; but first we shall look at authors more or less connected with the Pléiade.

Etienne Jodelle – L'Eugène[18]

In his *Elégie à J. Grévin* (Laumonier ed., XIV, 198), Ronsard recognises Jodelle's contribution to the development of both tragedy and comedy:

> Jodelle le premier, d'une plainte hardie
> Françoisement chanta la Grecque Tragedie,
> Puis, en changeant de ton, chanta devant nos Rois,
> La jeune Comedie en langage François . . .

His *Eugène*, probably written in autumn 1552, shows him rather to be a transitional figure between the medieval and Renaissance worlds. The prologue, formally an innovation and decasyllabic in verse, states the author's intention: avoid old-style farce and *sottie*, and write something worthwhile in a genre which 'des yeux François se retire', but which does not simply imitate classical comedy:

> Le style est nostre, et chacun personnage
> Se dit aussi estre de ce langage.

The characters have clear French identities and the language, though admitted to rise sometimes above the popular, is nevertheless racy and well rooted in the vernacular.

Written very possibly for a college audience sensitive to contemporary events on the war front, the play centres on a frankly amoral plot, with the main character Eugène, an *abbé*, in a crisis. He has managed to maintain his mistress, Alix, as he thinks, safe by arranging her marriage with Guillaume, an apparently simple fellow. This situation is threatened, in a small way, by certain debts contracted by Guillaume, and more important, by the return of Florimond from the German front, a man who had formerly been in love with Hélène, sister of Eugène, but had consoled himself with Alix whom he looks forward eagerly to seeing again. The gaff is inevitably blown by Florimond who threatens fire and brimstone against Eugène; the latter saves his bacon by finding an ecclesiastical benefice for Matthieu, the creditor, and getting Hélène to agree to marry Florimond. Guillaume, whom Eugène brutally informs about Alix's way of life, cynically accepts the situation and all the loose ends are tied up.

One is immediately struck by the unprincipled nature of the plot and more particularly by the immorality of Eugène and his 'chapelain', Messire Jean; the two represent the irreligious aspect of the contemporary Church. On the other hand, the two women, in spite of Alix's unconcern with ethics, are shown as human and sympathetic persons. They take no active part in the plot, which is essentially the settling of accounts between Eugène and Florimond; the *confidents*, of inferior status, Messire Jean and Arnault, make little more than suitable gestures. Florimond is perhaps the most interesting figure: doubtless, he owes something to the traditional soldier and also to the matamore (for he has his moments of boasting), but he is nationalised by his references to his *gasconnades*. His range is also broadened beyond the stereotype by his criticism of aspects of warfare, and in addition of Parisian life, especially war profiteers, and here and there of the Court. He is the vehicle of Jodelle's satirical talents which right from the beginning are sharp and give considerable edge to the tone of the play. The comedy has its roots in traditional farce – *apartes*, certain situations, octosyllabic metre, popular saws; but from time to time the language smacks of the humanist on holiday, the plot in spite of some dragging is more central, tauter, and better balanced in its distribution of characters. There is no attempt at edification, only satire. Though the average Renaissance dramatist was not much concerned with psychological finesse, Jodelle does reveal an embryonic talent for characterisation; and yet the two persons one might expect to emerge vigorously, Eugène and Alix, lack sap and nuance. Nevertheless, there is enough novelty in the structure to justify the historical importance that has been given to the play, which appears to have made some noise.

Jacques Grévin

Grévin has left us two comedies,[19] both of which were performed at the Collège de Beauvais after the *jeux satiriques*; the *Esbahis*, according to his statement, were put on at the same time as *Jules César*. He does not develop his views on comedy: he eschews the farce and the morality, preferring a return to 'antiquité', though the *Trésorière* hardly carries this into practice, and he accepts a certain realism in the freedom of language he uses. The *Trésorière* (1558), concerned with the amorous intrigues of a lady then living near the Place Maubert, is built on the fondness for money (*gain*) on which Loys expatiates towards the middle of the play. The comic elements derive from misunderstandings – *aparte* is much practised – and parallel developments between master and servant. Constante, ironically so called, is the hub of the action, but Marie her servant remains outside, furnishing reflections on the love that has not come her way: generally in the play love is portrayed as a mirage. There may be some parody in the dilute Petrarchism by means of which the soldier Loys expresses his love. The characters are not well differentiated, and all the more so as they are, one and all, self-interested; the language is lively with a sprinkling of popular wisdom; and once the intrigue is laid bare, the play comes to a patched-up end.

Les Esbahis (1561) is a more extended affair, the course of true amoral love being fostered by two devices, a disguise and the return of a wife believed dead. The action progresses slowly, with a fair number of soliloquies, but the basic pattern of three main characters and three servants is preserved. The old man, Josse, who hopes to marry Madeleine, in love with a young lawyer, is given rather more depth of portrayal – though types, not characters, are on stage – and the marked anti-Italianism of the comedy is brought out by Pantaleone, who is a mixture of the traditional braggart (inherited in part from the French poltroon of the dramatic monologue) and of the Petrarchan lover who quotes from Ariosto (in Italian). The contrasted French view is conveyed in part by Julien, the *homme moyen sensuel* whose monologue concludes the play. Earlier monologues develop anti-aulic sentiments, also anti-feminist views, and the bawd has an amusing excursion on fall in trade; but of dramatic action there is comparatively little, except perhaps when the two old men nearly come to blows in a scene that works *accelerando* with fair success. Grévin is writing for a college audience, so that literary allusion joins forces with some freedom of language and thinly veiled allusion. Grévin has an undoubted linguistic vitality, and it is a pity we have no later samples of his comic writing.

Rémy Belleau – La Reconnue[20]

La Reconnue was published posthumously and in need of some revision; it stands apart from contemporary comedies. In the first place, it eschews all acerbity of psychological comment, though a lot of space is given over to a satirical portrayal of Justice and the legal profession, which furnishes many of Belleau's characters. Second, the so-called protagonist herself has some unusual features: like a heroine of J.-J. Bernard's theatre she is conspicuous by her absence, for she appears in one scene only (IV, i), and she is singled out for having left her nunnery out of sympathy for the Huguenot cause, a trait which is left hanging in the air at the end. The play moves slowly in the first four acts and depends on misunderstandings, overheards, and deception for the action; in the final scene two characters appear unexpectedly, sort out the marriage of convenience planned for the elderly lawyer's benefit, and bring the two lovers together; Anthoinette would otherwise have been married off to the lawyer's clerk. Two conventional figures stand out: the aged lover and the braggart captain, whose name (and other echoes) suggests acquaintance with Ariosto and Italian sources; on the other hand, the valet Potiron hardly lives up to his claims as a schemer in the Figaro mould, and the maidservant of the lawyer's household, far from assuming the role of bawd, confines herself to servant talk, cooking, and complaints about her lot in life. To these are added a sour wife and a clerk who shows no interest in the other sex. The mixture of characters is thus slightly different; monologue plays a substantial part, and in addition to the satire of the courts, we have lengthy love soliloquies, fadedly Petrarchan in linguistic tone. A few contemporary references, Huguenot sympathies, anglophobia (on the subject of Le Havre), some digs at Parisian life, nothing more; no moralising, little attempt at comic effect. All this adds up to a pleasant play lacking edge, but fairly coherent, though the structure is loose enough. The satirical set pieces reveal a modestly dynamic verbal realism, and one may detect an effort to reproduce the colour of everyday life here and there; but the comedy as a whole gives the impression of staying agreeably at one remove from reality.

Jean de la Taille – Les Corrivaus (1573)

The only other member of the Pléiade who tried his hand in this field is Baïf, through his translations;[21] but Jean de la Taille belongs in spirit and training to the neo-classical outlook and thus differs from later comedy-writers mentioned below.[22] Though the plot is claimed in the prologue to derive from an incident during the troubles in Toul – La Taille tickles the appetite of the audience by telling part of the action only – his main source is the *Decameron*, with possible support from Ariosto and distinct echoes from Terence. Like Jodelle he marks his distance from earlier French comedy:

Une Comedie pour certain vous y verrez, non point une farce ny une moralité . . . Vous y verrez jouer une Comedie faite au patron, à la mode et au pourtrait des anciens Grecs, Latins, et quelques nouveaux Italiens . . .

and after remarks that show his national pride in what the French language can do, he aims at 'Une Comedie toute entière, naïve, et faite à l'antique'. The nub of the plot rests on the hidden identities of the lovers: Filadelfe, who has put Restitue in the family way, is pursuing Fleurdelys who is also being courted by Euvertre. When it becomes known that Fleurdelys and Filadelfe are sister and brother, a fact that troubled times and *déplacements* have hitherto hidden, Fleurdelys is to be married off to Euvertre, while Filadelfe takes to wife Restitue, just delivered. Fleurdelys, following the tradition of the maiden in comedy, does not appear on stage, and indeed the other lovers take a decreasingly active part in the play. The language is well handled, owes some comic effect to traditional puns, and maintains a brisk tempo; the comic elements occur in mother Jacqueline's *inconscience* about her daughter so near term, in the valets or servants, of whom Gillet furnishes a pale sketch of the braggart and Felix is reduced to the feature of hunger, and in the *aparte* techniques employed between Claude and Alizon in Act III. There is some kindly laughter at miserly fathers, doctors, and lawyers, but the play is characterised by a genial benevolence, in which certain effects are exploited in the register of sentiment – the condition of Restitue in the first act, the theme of friendship between Fremin and Benard, in the tone with which the recognitions are brought about. The domestics have little opportunity to develop active parts; but some attempt is made to give the play a French atmosphere – the references to contemporary wars, the stress on Fremin's Picard character, the Parisian framework. It would not take much alteration to make the play resemble late eighteenth-century comedy.

In the later part of our period, the pattern changes somewhat in that playwrights owe more to Italian sources and tend to make the plots more intricate. Many of these authors appear fairly closely connected with one another, though Larivey and D'Amboise may be linked with Jodelle through the circle of Gilles Bourdin.

Pierre de Larivey (?1540–1619)[23]

Larivey is perhaps the most prolific of this generation; his first plays come out in 1579. A canon of Troyes, he emphasises the moral purpose of his work: comedy is the 'mirouer de nostre vie', and like La Bruyère he feels that 'tout est dit' and that we cannot help owing a great deal to our classical masters, but he does value other features:

. . . ainsi belle est la comedie, si premierement la fable est embellie par industrieuses tromperies et gaillardz et improuvez evenemens, puis tissue de graves et plaisans discours, plains de sentences, comparaisons, metafores, railleries et promptes et aiguës responses non d'inepties qui, comme choses goffes et peu honnestes, font rire les ignorans, mais d'une modeste gayeté et soigneuse prudence qui emeuvent encores les plus doctes. (Prologue to *La Vefve*)

Which does not prevent later readers from finding his plays less edifying than he claims. *La Vefve* is a very complicated imbroglio, inspired by Buonaparte's *La Vedova*; the intended matches do not correspond to the final arrangements in which every woman is mistaken for another by the men concerned. As in *Les Esprits* the young *amantes* do not appear on stage, and therefore much depends on reported narrative. The false identities are often arranged by Gourdin and Guillemette, both characters being filled out by their love of food or the bottle. Bonaventure is nearly tricked by the false Clémence concerning the 'widow' Clémence who turns out to be his long-lost wife. M. Ancelme, a priest, plays a somewhat dubious role as a go-between with curious views on unconscious adultery. There is hardly a main character, though Bonaventure and Madame Clémence remain fairly likeable; the others are either variations on the lover or domestics. The symmetrical relations of the characters preserve the balance of the plot through *paraître* and *être*, and the *homme moyen sensuel* enjoys a protracted innings.

In *Les Espirits* (deriving in part from a play by L. de Medici), the characters of the title make a very small appearance, but there is something approaching a central character in Severin the miser. The women are either absent (Apoline, pregnant in her convent) or totally episodic (like Elizabet, who appears as a sort of *confidente* in I, i). The atmosphere is characterised by a gay immorality, and the play ends with three marriages, but no grand finale because of the inevitable absence of some of the parties concerned. The plot is centred on Fortuné's attempts to marry Apoline, but the other two weddings are worked out as the play proceeds. The momentum is maintained first by Frontin, then in greater measure by Hilaire, Severin's brother. Farce is introduced into the ghost scene (with M. Josse as the practitioner); monologue plays little part, but much use is made of *aparte* and overheards, and Larivey is capable of brisk dialogue. The obligations of the author to Italian comedy have been variously assessed; he himself was quite happy to recognise his debt:

. . . nos devanciers ont esté tant ingenieux en leurs estudes, et sceu si bien dire et faire, qu'il nous est impossible pouvoir parfaictement faire ou dire aucune chose, sinon ce qui a esté dit ou faict par eux. (Prologue to *Les Esprits*)

What he has done usually is to remain fairly faithful to the original, but suppress or amplify parts of the model, introduce where necessary some local references, and above all pay attention to the language of his plays which combine workmanlike dialogue and a wide range of vocabulary.

François d'Amboise[24]

These linguistic concerns are also apparent in François d'Amboise, only one of whose plays has come down to us. In the preface to his *Neapolitaines*, published in 1584 though written earlier, the author says:

Aux autres qui la liront elle apportera aussi un grand proffict et contentement, autant ou plus que pas une de celles qui ont esté divulgées jusques à présent, d'autant qu'en ceste-cy on y trouvera un françois aussi pur et correct qu'il s'en soit veu depuis que nostre langue est montée à ce comble . . .

and he refers to

la gentillesse de l'invention, le bel ordre, la diversité du subjet, les sages discours, les bons enseignemens, sentences, exemples et proverbes, les faceties et sornettes dont elle est semée de toutes parts.

It is indeed a pity that more of this industrious dramatist's work has not survived, for this is a play of considerable merit. The intrigue, though it has elements of imbroglio, is less important than in Larivey; the main action is not unduly complicated and the loose ends are tied up conveniently by two characters that arrive from Italy (Marcaurèle lapidaire, and Louppes). Augustin will marry the pseudo-widow Angélique while Camille will marry Virginie whom he has raped, and in this latter instance good luck allows him to marry without after-thought, since the requisite 'noblesse' is found to adorn the bride. Nevertheless, such an attitude is exceptional in a play where the char-acters are much more attractive than in Larivey; though Angélique appears only briefly in Acts III and IV, her kindness and humanity make of her more than a stock figure, and this also goes for Augustin who had been a fellow-student of Camille. There is a marked differ-ence linguistically between the lovers, who have obviously read Petrarch and Ariosto, and the servants. Another reason why the characters seem more filled out is that the monologue is more com-mon here than in Larivey (e.g., Act IV comprises four scenes, three of which are devoted to soliloquies). The humorous figures have acquired more 'body'; Gaster is not only the 'valet remuant' and parasite, but like Gourdin he makes much play of his gastronomic penchant. Diegos is Spanish – some attempt is made to differentiate the characters nationally – but he is also the braggart, both in feats of arms and in amatory prowess. Generally the tempo of the action is slower than in Larivey, and the atmosphere is more genial, verging sometimes on the idyllic; even the braggart is properly suited at the end, and moments of tenderness creep in from time to time. In short, humanity predominates over action, at the expense of movement perhaps, but to the great advantage of other values.

Odet de Turnèbe – Les Contens[25]

Two other dramatists deserve brief mention – Turnèbe and Le Loyer. Odet de Turnèbe, son of the famous scholar who died in 1565,

had himself a very short life, and his comedy was published posthumously in 1584. In it, he comes nearer to Larivey than to
D'Amboise. We have an extremely complex plot with disguises and
quiproquos; three suitors are courting Geneviève; eventually it is
Basile whose hand is accepted after the inevitable *fait accompli*. The
cast is a large one, with a number of stock characters over and above
the lovers, Alix the woman of pleasure, Françoise the bawd, Rodo-
mont whose name defines his personality. What is particularly
striking about the play is its verbal dynamism: this not only ensures
a remarkable tempo sustained throughout, but serves to bring out the
individual characters more than one normally expects. Many of the
cast are dubious – especially the slippery mother Louise – and the
impression left at the end is slightly sour after all these exhibitions of
meanness; but some figures are impressive, notably Françoise who is
almost, but not quite, the *carrefour* of the action (?shades of La
Celestina). Clearly Turnèbe owes something to Italian comedy, but
no less than others of this period, he blends his models with the
tradition of French farce.

Pierre Le Loyer – Nephelococugie[26]
Pierre Le Loyer's *Nephelococugie* (1578) stands apart from the
comic tradition established in this period. Its obligations to Aristophanes' *Birds* are obvious enough, and in any case the author claims
that he is the first in France to revive the *vieille comédie*. Two elderly
brothers wish to leave Toulouse for the *pays des cocus*, of which Jean
Cocu is king; here the birds agree to build the city for cuckolds. We
are offered character sketches of humans who wish to become members of the city; and there is the major episode in which the builders
seek to prevent the gods from crossing their city. News of a god
attempting to 'passer outre' arrives, it is Iris warning the cuckolds
not to try a *cocumachie* against Jupiter. We are then told that the
gods are willing to make peace; Hercules and Neptune appear as
ambassadors, Genin's condition that Coquart marry Zelotypie,
daughter of Zeus, is accepted and the play ends on a Pindaric
epithalamium. The action is, as one can see, sketchy in the extreme;
we have none of the complicated intrigue that is prevalent at the
time. Moreover, the stock characters do not put in an appearance;
and it is also difficult to detect any clear major figure, except possibly
one of the old men (Genin). For the rest, the intrigue is a sort of trellis
on which satire of *mœurs* and character can grow; episodic figures
such as a soldier, a lawyer influenced by Rabelais, a group of astrologers, alchemist, and sophist are pressed into dramatic service. All in
all, the play possesses liveliness and momentum; Le Loyer seeks
originality by the introduction of his metrical *système entrecoupé*,
which allows for prosodic variation. There are no clear divisions by

acts, and a number of the poetic sections retain the Greek names that were used by Aristophanes. The play remains an isolated phenomenon, for it had no followers; presumably it met with indifferent success, and it is indeed rather difficult to say just what the play is about over and above the 'story'.

III. TRAGICOMEDY

R. Garnier – Bradamante (*1582*)[27]

We have had occasion to mention other dramatic trends in the period: some survival of medieval forms, genres associated with court life, of which the *ballet de cour*, apart from the 1581 performance, really develops after the wars of religion. 'Irregular' tragedy is in a similar position; and in the provinces, there is also dramatic activity in local dialect. Tragicomedy is a late starter too, but it would be wrong to leave aside Garnier's excursion into this field.

This, his last play, was defined by himself as a *tragecomédie*, and it possesses several distinguishing features. First, the chorus associated with tragedy is lacking, but Garnier suggested that the intervals between the acts might be shown by a series of 'entremets'; then, the play differs from tragedy by its happy ending, though the characters are of noble descent; on the other hand, there are some less than 'noble' elements worked into the fabric of the play. The intrigue, in its essentials, is simple enough: Bradamante, who will marry only the man capable of defeating her in combat, really loves Roger, but he, who owes his life to Leon when they were younger, assumes Leon's colours and defeats Bradamante for the benefit of another. In the end, all sorts itself out: Bradamante marries Roger, and Charlemagne's daughter, unheard of until the very end, is palmed off on Leon. The intrigue is concentrated on Acts II–IV, the others being void of action, and Ariosto has left his mark on it, both in incident and even in textual echoes. The sense of time and place is very much less evident than in genuine tragedy, and we are almost into a fairy-tale world. The *liaison des scènes* is distinctly loose, a number of characters appear in one or two scenes only, and inconsistency of behaviour is to be noted in several cases. The play opens on a grandiloquent tone, with Charlemagne uttering thoughts on kingship, God's role, and patriotism in a manner not unworthy of *Les Juifves* – the imagery of the sun is similarly present; but in Act II, the tone changes completely, for we are presented with Aymon and Beatrix who haggle over the marriage of their daughter; Aymon cuts a comic figure of greedy meanness. Elsewhere the tone may flag; sometimes marginally, as in the case of comments made by subordinate characters, but in a different category stands the role of Leon as an anti-hero; he resorts to extremely odd means to win Bradamante's hand and constitutes a fanciful variation on the braggart, though it is fair to say that his final renunciation of Bradamante has a magnanimous touch about it. Above all, love plays a part such as it never enjoyed in any other play of Garnier's; and this has a number of consequences. The poetry of the play expresses itself often in the amatory lines which show a rich afterbloom of the Petrarchan idiom and whose presence contributes greatly to the lyric atmosphere of the text as a whole. Then, we have a foretaste of Cornelian debate and conflict between love and duty, carried to a very high pitch of rhetoric, and a scene between Leon and Roger in which each strives to outdo the other in generosity. The rhetoric is also provided by a sort of *récit de Théramène* uttered by a minor character recounting the defeat of Bradamante. Stichomythia is frequent in scenes where themes of substance are debated (e.g., the relations of love and marriage). The action as such is not particularly well knit, and the *peripetiæ* could have been introduced with greater skill. Garnier devotes a good deal of space to eliciting the pathetic, but what is rather curious is the virtual failure of Bradamante and Roger to meet throughout the play, except in the final act where they do not speak to each other. The first act does little to announce the central situation of the play, though it serves, through Charlemagne's lengthy monologue, to develop a motif that runs through the action, the praise of Christianity closely linked with convinced patriotism, which leads among other things to disparaging remarks about Greece. The action has some of the looseness and complexity of certain comedies we have mentioned, but we have not yet reached the stage of melodramatic imbroglio that will form so marked a feature of the theatre of Alexandre Hardy. One notes considerable variety of tone, emotion, and style, and all this is spread over a multiplicity of characters; nevertheless one or two of the protagonists stand out with a measure of individuality. We are in a wonderland which robs the characters of a certain reality, and the play achieves *divertissement* rather than any form of cathartic effect.

IV. CONCLUSION

One must be careful not to end this section on too *simpliste* a note. Of course, the medieval formulae are being gradually phased out, and to some extent replaced by neo-classical ideas; but, they still retain a measure of popularity in the provinces and some of their features are seen to be compatible with a Calvinist conception of the theatre. Neo-classical ideals still have some way to go, whether in tragedy or in comedy: it is towards the end of the century that the 'tragédie irrégulière' with its taste for violence begins to attract audiences; comedy becomes more indebted to Italian models, and the fashion for complicated stage-machinery, in great part of Italian origin, grows apace. The visual element in drama appeals to audiences in a way that classical theatre does not. Nevertheless, the way is being prepared for the classical theatre that will reach its climax in the seventeenth century; and if progress is slow, it is in part because people realise, with more or less clarity, that the theatre reflects social pressures, and the various conceptions of dramatic art reflect the different outlooks of a country in crisis and transition. Moreover, the conditions under which actors can perform their work have yet to stabilise – permanent stages, professional troupes, regular patronage, and public. We are still in a period of interesting experiment, from which emerge a handful of plays that can command critical respect today.

CHRONOLOGICAL TABLE OF PLAYS

	Tragedy	Comedy	Others	Translations
1506				Erasmus, *Hecuba* and *Iphigenia*
1537				L. de Baïf, *Electra*
1544				Buchanan, *Medea*
1548				C. Estienne, *Abusez*
1549				J.-P. de Mesmes, *Les Supposez*
1550	Bèze, *Abraham sacrifiant*			Baïf, *Hecuba* Sebillet, *Iphigenia*
1551			Coignac, *Desconfiture de Goliath*	
1552	Muret, *Julius Caesar*			
1553	(Jodelle)			
1554	Buchanan, *Jephthes* publ.			
1556	Roillet, Latin plays			Buchanan, *Alcestis*
1557				Toutain, *Agamemnon* Lallemant, Latin Sophocles
1559				St-Gellais, *Sophonisbe*
1561	Bounyn, *Soltane*	Grévin, *La Trésorière* *Les Esbahis*		Le Duchat, *Agamemnon*
1562	Grévin, *Jules César*			
1566	Rivaudeau, *Aman* Filleul, *Lucrèce*			

	Tragedy	Comedy	Others	Translations
1567	Dubledier, *Philoxène*			Baïf, *Le Brave*
1568	Garnier, *Porcie*			
1571	Guersens, *Panthée*		Bretog, *Tragédie à huit personnages*	
1572	La Taille, *Saül*			Baïf, *L'Eunuque*
1573	La Taille, *La Famine*	La Taille, *Les Corrivaus*		La Taille, *Le Negromant* Baïf, *Antigone*
1574	Jodelle, *Cléopatre* (1553) and *Didon se sacrifiant*	Jodelle, *L'Eugène* (1552)		
1575	Chantelouve, *Coligny* Garnier, *Hippolyte*			
1576	Chantelouve, *Pharaon*	Le Loyer, *Le Muet insensé*	L. le Jars, *Lucelle*	
1577		De Vivre, *Theseus et Dianira* De Vivre, *Com. de la fidélité nuptiale*		
1578	Garnier, *Marc-Antoine*	Belleau, *La Reconnue*		Lavardin, *La Celestine*
1579	Garnier, *La Troade* Le Breton, *Adonis* and *Pompée*	Larivey, first six comedies	Le Coq, *Caïn*	
1580	Garnier, *Antigone* A. d'Amboise, *Holoferne*			
1581	F. du Duc, *Histoire trag. de la Pucelle*			
1582	Beaubreuil, *Regulus* Bousy, *Meleagre* La Grange, *Didon*		Garnier, *Bradamante*	
1583	Garnier, *Les Juifves*			
1584	Mermet, *Sophonisbe* Robelin, *Thébaïde*	F. d'Amboise, *Les Néapolitaines* O. de Turnèbe, *Les Contens*		
1585	Du Monin, *Orbée/Oronte* Matthieu, *Esther*			Chrestien, *Sept contre Thèbes*
1586			B. Voron, *Comédie françoise*	
1589	R. Brissot, 4 plays A. Favre, *Les Gordiens et Maximins* Matthieu, *Aman*, etc.	F. Perrin, *Les Escoliers*		
1594		J. Godard, *Les Desguisez*		
1596	Montchrestien, *Sophonisbe*			

	Tragedy	Comedy	Others	Translations
1597			Papillon, *La Nouvelle tragi-comique*	
1598	Behourt, *Esaü*			
1599	De Virey, *La Machabée*	Larivey, *Angelique*		

NOTES

1. See General Bibliography for main works of reference.

2. J. Bretog's *Tragedie françoise à huit personnages* . . . ., Lyons, 1571, is in fact a morality.

3. See above, p. 345. Contemporary events, however, are dealt with in *La Tragédie du sac de Cabriere*, preserved in manuscript in the Vatican (modern eds. by F. Benoît and J. Vianey, Marseilles, 1927, and K. Christ, Halle, 1928).

4. The *Poetics* were available in Greek in a Paris edition in 1541; and in the following year A. Paccius's Latin version was printed by J. Bogard.

5. G. Le Breton's *Adonis*, published 1579, was seemingly performed before Charles IX ten years earlier.

6. Jean Martin published his translation of Vitruvius in 1547; Serlio's *Livre extraordinaire de architecture* came out at Lyons in 1551, but he had been invited by Francis I *c.* 1540–41 to come to France and supervise matters at Fontainebleau, and the first book of his work on architecture appeared as early as 1545.

7. See bibliographical references above, p. 296, n.11.

8. *Les Œuvres*, 1573 (BM, BN); 1577, Lyons (BM). See N. Banachevitch, *Jean Bastier de la Péruse (1509–1554)*, 1923.

9. *Le theatre,* 1562 (BM, BN), modern ed. L. Pinvert, 1922; ed. of *Jules César* by E. Ginsberg, *TLF*, 1971. See L. Pinvert, *Jacques Grévin (1528–1570), sa vie, ses écrits, ses amis*, Fontemoing, 1898.

10. Copy of original ed. in BN; modern ed. E. Stengel and J. Venema, Marburg, 1888. Bounyn lived from *c.* 1520 to *c.* 1604; at one time he was associated with the circle of the duc d'Anjou.

11. *Les Œuvres*, Poitiers, 1566 (Ars); modern ed. K. Cameron, *TLF*, 1969 (see also review article of ed. in *BHR*, 1970). See also R. Lebègue, *La Tragédie religieuse*.

12. La Taille's plays were probably written by 1562, though revised before publication: *Saül le Furieux*, 1572 (BN, MRy); *La Famine*, 1573 (BN), 1574 (MRy). Modern ed. of these two plays by E. Forsyth, *STFM*, 1968 (see review, *BHR*, 1970), also in *Dramatic Works*, ed. Kathleen M. Hall and C. N. Smith, 1972. See T. A. Daley, *Jean de la Taille (1533–1608), étude historique et littéraire*, 1934; and Cambridge thesis by C. N. Smith.

13. Modern ed. of *De l'art de la tragédie*, by F. West, Manchester, 1939.

14. *Porcie*, 1568 (BM, BN); *Hippolyte*, 1573 (BM, BN); *Cornélie*, 1574 (BM); *Marc-Antoine,* 1578 (BM); *La Troade*, 1579 (BM, BN); *Antigone*, 1580 (BN); *Les Juifves*, 1583 (BN); *Les Tragedies*, 1580 (BM), 1585 (BM, BN), Toulouse, 1588 (EUL). Modern ed. *Œuvres complètes*, L. Pinvert, 1923; W. Forster, reprint of 1585 ed. of tragedies, Heilbronn, 1883. See M. M. Mouflard, *Robert Garnier 1545–1590. La vie, L'œuvre, Les sources*, 3 vols., 1958–64; R. Lebègue, *Robert Garnier. Les Juifves*, CDU, 1958; M. Gros, *Robert Garnier – son art et sa méthode*, *THR,* 1965; Dora Frick, *Robert Garnier als barocker Dichter*, Zurich, 1951; G. Jondorf, *Robert Garnier and the Themes of Political Tragedy in the Sixteenth Century*, Cambridge, 1969.

15. Modern ed. of *Les Théâtres de Gaillon*, *TLF*, 1971, by F. Joukovsky.

16. Copy in BM.

17. See also H. W. Lawton, 'Charles Estienne et le théâtre', *RSS*, 1927.

18. Modern ed. E. Balmas, Milan, 1955.

19. Both printed in the *Théâtre* of 1562 (BM): see above for bibliographical references.

20. Published 1577; reprinted Viollet-le-Duc, op. cit.

21. *Le Brave*, 1567 (BM); *L'Eunuque*.

22. See *Dramatic Works*, ed. Kathleen M. Hall and C. N. Smith.

23. *Les comedies*, n.p., 1579 (BM); *Les comedies facecieuses*, Lyons, 1597 (BM, BN), Rouen, 1601 (EUL). See M. Apollonio, *La Comédie italienne dans le théâtre de Larivey*, Lyons, 1909.

24. Two copies of his comedy in Ars; modern eds. by Viollet-le-Duc and E. Fournier.

25. Modern ed. N. Spector, *TLF*, 1964.

26. Le Loyer also wrote the *Comedie du Muet insensé*, published in his *Erotopegnie*, 1576 (BM). The *Nephelococugie* appeared in the *Œuvres et meslanges poétiques*, 1579 (BM, O). See W. Süss, *Aristophanes und die Nachwelt*, Leipzig, 1911, and 'Die Néphelococugie des Pierre Le Loyer', *ZFSL*, 1910.

27. See H. Carrington Lancaster, *The French Tragi-comedy, its Origins and Development from 1552 to 1628*, 1907; the genre is relatively loose, injects a comic element into an essentially serious structure, but ends happily. Lancaster sees in it, not only a channel for some foreign plays (*La Celestine*), but an intermediate stage between medieval forms (*mystères* and *moralités*) and Hardy's theatre. Only L. le Jars's *Lucelle* (1576) is worth mentioning in addition to *Bradamante* – it is reprinted more than once.

Chapter 14

PROSE WRITERS AND THE STUDY OF MAN IN HIS HISTORICAL AND POLITICAL CONTEXTS

W E have already taken a look at the development of philosophical and 'scientific' prose, which begins to take shape rather earlier than it does in the fields of historiography and political theory – that is to say in the vernacular. These latter areas of human sciences naturally form part of the Renaissance scene, but in France much of the groundwork is still being prepared in Latin; in the last third of the century more especially humanist and political pressures encourage the use of the vernacular. At certain levels the contribution to the development of French prose remains modest – Etienne Pasquier is probably the most impressive historian, but much of his work appears late in and beyond our period, and one of the most original minds of the century, Jean Bodin, usually prefers Latin as a means of expression. To neglect the work going on in Latin would be wrong, but detailed examination here is precluded by the limits of space; on the other hand, many humanist attitudes find their way into the militant writing of the civil wars, and it is during this period that the composition of more 'personal' memoirs makes its appearance.

I. THE STUDY OF HISTORY[1]

The development of historiography in sixteenth-century France is a rather slow, halting affair, for though there is clearly a very great interest taken in history and many historiographical works are printed in France, older traditions seem to persist tenaciously, the prestige of foreign authors remains strong, and certain historiographical advances appear to benefit in the first place from work in other fields of study. During the reign of Francis I, there were printed in Paris the works of Boethius (Boece), author of the history of Scotland; of Polydore Vergil, whose writings mark some methodological progress; and Paolo Giovio, who had been historiographer royal and whose *De rebus gestis Francorum libri IIII* was reprinted many times through the century, with later editions containing the supplement by Arnould Ferron. Gaguin's work was rather less successful, but it still went through a number of editions up to the 1530s and is mentioned later with respect. The historiographers royal, originally *rhétoriqueurs*, do not make a substantial contribution, and Pierre Paschal in the reign of Henry II was so dilatory in his writing that his enemies accused him of charlatanism. What is particularly notable is the continued reprinting of earlier historians (Commynes, Froissart, Monstrelet); perhaps the most striking success is the *Annales* of Nicolas Gilles, which are constantly brought up to date: Denys Sauvage augments the text in 1553, and further instalments are provided by Belleforest in 1573 and Chappuys in 1585. One can hardly talk here of methodological advance, and an author like Belleforest, though he will dispute the Francus myth, takes the opportunity to assert certain principles relevant to contemporary political theory – the value of the Salic law, the view that the king's 'volonté est par-dessus les loix'. In these circumstances, it is not surprising that the late *rhétoriqueur* Jean Bouchet should have some success with his *Annales d'Aquitaine* and his *Anciennes et modernes Genealogies des roys de France*.[2] He does stress the suitability of writing in the vernacular (. . . 'en gros langaige, & non pas curial'), but for the rest he prolongs traditional attitudes – the chronological approach by years, history as a reservoir of useful examples (which he hopes might serve to reduce the cruelty of wars), a marked patriotism which reinforces his belief in the Trojan legend, the attempt to 'concorder la diversité des cronicques'. On the other hand, he eschews rhetorical display in the writing of history and prizes truth above classical decoration.

After 1550, these traditions are by no means worn out; and important historical works are still being written in Latin. However, new stirrings are abroad: in the first place, there is a continuing stimulus from Italy, for Guicciardini will be translated into French (in the last third of the century) and the work of Machiavelli, which stirs up considerable resentment in certain humanist circles, provides food for thought for the historian as well as for the political theorists.[3] There are, however, native forces at work: in a general way Guillaume Budé's work, by its philological and comparative methods, had done a good deal to train the French humanist mind and sharpen critical examination of evidence. However, it seems that we must look especially to the world of jurisprudence and legal history to find stimulus. One of France's great contributions to the Renaissance world lies in her legal studies: here many strands are at work, the study of Roman law, the renewed interest in national, common law, a fresh look at medieval jurisprudence. Broadly speaking, legal studies help greatly to provide a theoretical basis for the emerging absolutist view of the monarchy, but in the short term they stimulate inquiry on a wider front. Historiography's debt to these legal studies has still to be fully assessed, but it does seem that certain aspects of historical

study are brought into prominence as a consequence: a more favourable attitude to the Middle Ages, more interest in the comparative
approach, a more sophisticated application of historical studies to
politics, a move against the dominance of classical law in favour of
national institutions and customs, the importance of the study of law
for historiography.[4]

At all events, under the reigns of Henry II and Charles IX one
notes a growing interest in the methodology of history; this appears
even in Henri Estienne's *Apologie pour Herodote* (1566), where a
curious blend of uncritical acceptance of biblical authority and of
sober relativism is to be found. More important, of course, is Jean
Bodin's landmark, the *Methodus* (1566),[5] which among other things
rejects the old scheme of the four empires, sees history as a gradually
emerging process, thinks of history as a critical record of all human
knowledge, and stresses the need for rigorous methods in establishing
chronologies of various nations in the field of comparative or 'universal' history. What was also very valuable were his remarks on the
proper training of a budding historian and his critical assessment of
earlier writers. One other name deserves mention here: Louis Le
Roy, whose *De la Vicissitude* came out in 1576 but had been a long
time in the making.[6] In these various writings we find a growing
stress on critical assessment, classification, and synthesis; but these
studies are not simply scholarly in their spirit, for when these humanists do venture into the field of political theory, they emerge as sup-
porters of traditional monarchy, though they stress variously the
extent to which royal authority should or can be 'limited'. From
another angle, one may note a growing interest in primary sources
and documents, which was rarely apparent in the chroniclers except
in so far as they claimed to provide first-hand evidence for contemporary happenings: Bouchet, for instance, does sometimes give the
impression of keeping a journal, but when he refers to events of previous generations, he depends much on sources such as Trithemius.

In our period, several interesting historians appear on the scene,
though few would claim to achieve literary distinction. A number
have Calvinist sympathies: but whereas D'Aubigné's *Histoire universelle*, essentially a record of his times, is aggressively partisan, a
much more balanced and impartial attitude is revealed in La Popelinière, *Histoire de la France* (1581).[7] This author is anxious to
search out possible sources of error ('l'ignorance, la haine, l'avarice &
l'ambition', and the hope that you will not be found out!); and one
thing which emerges from this discussion is a refusal to maintain a
blind confidence in the ancients. It is indeed in the field of historiography that we detect the beginnings of the *querelle des anciens et
des modernes*. La Popelinière also sees in the writing of history a field
where the French language can develop properly – this ties up with

the previous point – and he is generally a staunch supporter of the vernacular. He shows a critical awareness of cause, context, and consequence when he considers the course of events, and he is anxious to defend the high place of history in the hierarchy of knowledge; he considers it superior to philosophy and to all other sciences. He is very aware of the dangers of emotional involvement in the historian, or of trying to woo the reader, but his defence of his discipline in an impassioned one: 'Mais l'histoire ne mourra jamais'.

Etienne Pasquier

The pattern of French humanism at this stage encourages the study of French origins and institutions: this can be seen very clearly in the work of Claude Fauchet, but this scholar, for all his worthiness, remains a dull dog with little stylistic control;[8] very different is Etienne Pasquier,[9] whose interest in contemporary events is splendidly manifested in his letters, but who has also made a more panoramic contribution to historical studies in his *Recherches de la France*, which came out by instalments until the beginning of the seventeenth century. In his approach to earlier history, Pasquier reveals not only a sensitive awareness of the value of source material, he appreciates the cultural achievement of the past with less prejudice than many contemporaries. His training as a lawyer has probably helped him to see in history something more than military events and court politics; he is keenly conscious of social and political structures, for him history is also cultural history, and above all it is not plain panegyric. He is especially interested in political structures ('le faict de nostre police'), but he does not approach their study with a predetermined political attitude; in fact, as he writes, he seems to become more sensitive to the existential as opposed to the normative, and in his shift in emphasis from Roman law to custom law as a valid structure for his own times he is probably reflecting a general trend in legal studies, but no doubt patriotism and the prevalent anti-Italianism play some part. His study of history leads him, as it led Montaigne, to a less absolute view of the human condition; and he is not the only historian to combat a common humanist view that life in this world is a progressive distancing from the original ideal. For Pasquier, history is not just a series of *exempla* culled from the past, though his own moderate monarchist outlook will gladly find support in history; moreover, history is something to be written with clarity and elegance, but without high-sounding bombast. By its range, scholarship, and judgement, I see no work to compare with it beforehand in France. Pasquier is one of the great all-rounders of a remarkable humanist generation, one whose reputation needs a more generous reappraisal.

We are therefore witnessing a considerable change in attitudes to history: the humanist antinomy of the dignity and misery of man is reconsidered in a historical perspective; the problem of determinism and emerging knowledge comes under scrutiny; nationalism and a growing confidence in the value of cumulative experience leads to a challenging of classical authority and of the view, so eloquently expressed in Du Bellay, that civilisation was crumbling; and more closely than before, history is associated with the search for valid political structures in a world where the desire for security and stability becomes more and more urgent.[10]

II. WRITERS OF MEMOIRS

It is in the final decades of the century that the urge to write memoirs becomes noticeable. Earlier, a few sporadic texts hardly constitute a current: the biography of the chevalier Bayart, the interesting but objective *Journal d'un bourgeois de Paris*,[11] or the valuable, though unfinished, memoirs of Guillaume du Bellay[12] which offer first-hand material for the diplomatic history of his times. In the memoirs we are now considering, the tone changes: the authors do not seek to exclude themselves from their narrative, far from it. No doubt there are factors of a more general order to account for this phenomenon: the greater interest in history, the consequent stress on first-hand testimony, the increasing need to 'se manifester' in a world of war and disruption; but there is also, it seems, a compulsion to write one's *apologia*. People are anxious to fashion their own image in the eyes of posterity: we have seen this stimulus in the writings of 'scientific' authors such as Ambroise Paré, but the memorialists are more often to be found among people closely involved in the political or military history of their times. These authors often lack real historical perspective; their awareness of the significance of the events in which they were enmeshed may be rudimentary, and for a man like Brantôme literary creation is more particularly 'à la recherche du paradis perdu'. Many of these authors are not deeply educated in the classics, and of this they may be proudly or pathetically conscious; but this may affect the nature of their style. I shall confine myself to three authors who represent widely differing parts of the spectrum.

Blaise de Montluc (1502–77)[13]

Montluc's *Commentaires* were published posthumously in 1592. Ostensibly they were written, first to provide a military manual based on experience, second to offer a defence of his own life, in the face of various accusations brought against him. Like some other memorialists he shows that suspicion entertained by the man of action towards the humanist, though he will succumb on occasion to the temptation to imitate him:

Ce n'est pas un livre pour les gens de sçauoir, ils ont assez d'hystoriens, mais pour un soldat, capitaine, et il peut estre qu'un lieutenant de roy y pourra trouver de quoy apprendre.

In this type of writing, the autobiography, the *apologia*, and the *exemplum* are brought together. Montluc left his home at the age of fifteen and for the next sixty years led an adventurous existence on military service until an appalling injury to his face forced him to retire. His book is thus both an apology and a recapturing of time past; he boasts of rejecting the evidence of others and of relying on his own memory for everything. Like many memorialists he is very well endowed with visual memory and can reveal the act and the gesture of his contemporaries with startling precision. The portrait that comes through is that of a man of intense patriotism; service to the king seems more important than the values for which kings stand. In a period of religious turmoil one sees little inner conflict, little metaphysical preoccupation; the broader issues escape Montluc. And within his own professional competence, there is a similar limitation; he is more master of individual enterprise and tactics than of overall strategy. In many ways, the *Commentaires* are a study in the proper development of the self within a professional framework. Of course we have the portrait of the Gascon, exuberant, dynamic, but at the same time canny and cold as the Meridional can be, and Montluc is never totally unaware of the effect his self-description should make. Nevertheless, his comments on discipline, on close relations with the troops, on the need to strive to 'montrer ce que vous valez' in action, all these developments are exciting; there is a Stoic in action, avoiding gambling, 'avarice', women, wine – factors which would otherwise prevent him from becoming one of the 'grands hommes'. Montluc is a sort of sixteenth-century Rastignac in his self-control and desire to dominate; but he is also someone much concerned with honour and reputation, so that if he is willing to recognise his Gascon temperament ('fascheux et collere'), he will suppress events and features that might harm the portrait of himself as the incarnation of the ideals proper to a soldier.

All this is interesting in its reference to contemporary principles, but where, without his literary gifts, would he be? Montluc has a splendid capacity for making even the distant past relive in the present; his visual imagination is highly developed; he has a wide command of language, with various dialectal elements picturesquely introduced; he normally maintains good control of his sentence, though a self-conscious moment or a multiplicity of associations may prolong the structure beyond its useful dimensions. His writing is rectilinear; there is little subtlety of psychological insight – though he has traced the portrait of the soldier with impressive fidelity and contour; he lives in the concrete detail; reflection is rapid and not too welcome; but his communication of movement and first-hand experience is more developed than in any other memorialist of his time. It is only when self-consciousness leads him to divorce language from life that he moves into pretentious rhetoric, and where the sentence, inadequately controlled, loses character that he falls below his best. Like Brantôme he relives the past with intensity and electric vividness; but whereas Brantôme re-creates a past in which he would wish to live, Montluc is making his own past the substance of his work. The theory that saw in the Renaissance the affirmation of the individual is now seen to be an overstatement, but the presence of Montluc does give colour to such an interpretation.

Pierre de Bourdeille (Brantôme) (c. 1534–1614)[14]

Brantôme forbade the publication of his memoirs until after his death; in any case, much of his work does not concern the immediate contemporary situation. For the first forty years or so of his life, his activity was military and courtly, but two events in particular threw him back on his own resources: the loss of Henry III's favour and a riding accident which kept him on a bed of sickness for most of his later years. The memoirs reflect, therefore, a desire to recapture time past and to find there compensation for an existence often marked by frustration and remoteness. For him memory replaces life ('resjouir ma memoire de ce que j'ay veu'), and digressions are often excused on the grounds that memories crowd up *calamo currente* and should be noted before they fall back into limbo. Not all he tells us – and he was a voluminous writer – is based on first-hand experience, though his information is often personal, and when not, reliable: he expresses a special debt to his aunt Madame de Dampierre, whom he calls 'un vray registre de la cour'. Though his writing often comes properly into the category of memoirs, much space is devoted to biographical sketches, including portraits of people he could not have known himself, and his world is not far removed from that of the *conte* or *nouvelle*, with its polarisation into the beautiful fairyworld of the Court and the more *gaulois* aspects of life. Significantly, Brantôme often refers to Boccaccio (in whose steps he follows in the *Dames illustres*), and also to Ariosto and the *Amadis de Gaule*; his presentation of court life reminds us of, say *Jehan de Paris*, where everything is perfect and worthy of all hyperbole, and where the characters are splendid models of chivalric ideals. Then suddenly we find ourselves in another world where sexual prowess and virtuosity have become the yardstick. In both these worlds we have the viewpoint of a man on the sidelines, possessing the accurate eye of the bystander, but also giving the impression of being an outsider; he creates a dream-world and would wish to be a denizen. Though he is not a psychologist of developed powers, he often seizes upon the significant detail or trait – and this ability seems to increase with the years. Thus Anne de Bretagne is presented as a woman of immense qualities – in his eyes, she established court life as it was to flower throughout the sixteenth century – but he makes it clear that she was also very ambitious, eager to remain queen and letting her behaviour be guided by this obsession. Brantôme is undoubtedly attracted to characters whose personality and ability to assert themselves are their chief merits, but he is not a *moraliste*; he does not inveigh against *philautia* or the courtier, he admires individualism and he tries to set it in the framework of a fairy-tale atmosphere richly gilded by distant memory ('un vrai paradis du monde'). *Male fortune*, dreams, portents, astrology, these are contemporary themes, but they serve to reinforce his ambience.

These polarised elements of his world picture are reflected in his style: Brantôme is capable of the sustained, oratorical sentence, not as alembicated as in some contemporaries perhaps, but none the less aiming at a *style noble* – and hyperbolic enumeration is a marked feature of this level of his writing; but there is also the visual reporter, with a keen eye for the dramatic and flamboyant, who prefers the shorter construction and tries to reproduce the rhythm of life, a life that is often violent. He does not build up his main sections particularly well; each chapter may well have a main theme, but his memories are always breaking in and there may be a local reason for inserting a substantial paragraph that takes us away from the mainstream; chapters sometimes end on an irrelevance or a short-cut comment. He himself said 'je ne scay nul de bien escrire' – perhaps like Montaigne he felt a certain contempt at the thought of being considered a writer; he has not bothered to take lessons in sophisticated rhetoric, otherwise the lay-out of his material would leave less to be desired, but his material may become organised along different associative principles, which allow him to recapture an experience in its freshness as it emerges into his conscious memory. He has a wide linguistic range, he shows a resourceful use of imagery (often gastronomic or military in origin), and his interplay of different stylistic levels may be rich in effect. Though he can get tied up in an involved sentence, his style is usually a clear one. No metaphysical complications, little coherent outlook on life, no message, but for all that the creator of a literary world.

Marguerite de Valois (1553–1615)[15]

Marguerite's *Mémoires*, in their published form, go no further than 1582, and only part of her life is recorded in this work, though her letters, well worth reading, help to take the story further. The *Mé-*

moires are addressed to someone whose identity is not revealed, but is believed by many to be Brantôme, who devotes a whole book to her in his *Dames*. She claims to tell nothing but the truth:

Je tracerai mes mémoires, à qui je donnerai plus glorieux nom, bien qu'ils meritassent celui d'histoire, pour la verité qui y est contenue nûment, et sans ornement aucun, ne m'en estimant pas capable, et n'en ayant aussi maintenant le loysir.

and later she confirms that it is not 'mon intention d'orner des mémoires, ains seulement narrer la verité'; when she introduces an anecdote, she is careful to show its different nature from the main tenor of her work. She weaves into her narrative the theme of God's will – at every turn she proclaims her ardent Catholicism and there is a curious passage on God's warning illustrious persons of impending events; but she also talks of Fortune 'qui ne laisse jamais une félicité entière aux humains' and which she sees in dramatic conflict with Nature. Nevertheless, the *Mémoires* are also a skilful *apologia pro vita sua* which is worked out over a fairly simple ground scheme. On the one hand, we are presented with the personal relationships that determine in great measure the course of her life – Catherine de Medici, her mother, to whom she always shows respect, but whose scheming comes through the text very clearly; her brother the duc d'Anjou, to whom she is greatly attached; Henry III, whose growing hostility is underlined. Then we have her marriage to Henry of Navarre, whom she portrays with some objectivity and not without kindness. She describes events in the perspective of Henry III's enmity to both the duc d'Anjou and to Henry of Navarre, and the two monarchs are shown frequently as acting under the evil influence of those who surround them (the word *possédait* is constantly used in this connection) – Dugast in Henry III's entourage, La Fosseuse in Navarre's. We thus have an evident pattern of relationships that are worked out in the main events of Marguerite's life, such as her adolescence, when Henry III's feelings against her begin to take shape; her marriage, which is very well portrayed in its political machinations; the Saint-Barthélemy, in which she appears as the unknowing victim of circumstance; Dugast's efforts to get rid of Bussy; the sojourn in the Low Countries and especially Spa; the five happy years at Nérac, in spite of contretemps such as La Fosseuse's pregnancy; and finally the return to Paris. On the other hand, historical events tend to be explained in terms of personal motives and patterns, and these form the setting to her own personality. Her material is presented in a fairly quick-moving narrative, in which dramatic techniques are exploited, though the set speeches tend, as in earlier historiography, to become stylised. There is a liking for superlatives that fail to describe with precision, and the characters in her drama are roughly separated into sheep and goats. One or two passages stand out for other qualities: the intrigues surrounding her marriage; the tale of Mlle de Thorigny (which has a fairy-world quality); the strangely emotive section on Nature in God's scheme of things, unique in the book. Here and there she displays shrewd insight into behaviour, and she is able to catch the movement of a scene, though with little colour or depth; for instance, neither the duc d'Anjou nor Henry III come through with any marked personality. Her style shows how the former, rather involved prose of the historian is becoming more limpid, more characteristic of the *salon*; there is some classical reference, but it does not obtrude; imagery is rather sparse; on the other hand, she has a delicate sense of sentence structure, apart from a few lapses, and generally remains in control of her material. She does not resort to a wide range of rhetorical devices, but points the lesson to be drawn from some historical event by means of the *sententia*. Her memoirs are the work of an intelligent, alert woman, but not of a profound mind; and so far from reflecting in any depth on the course of history, she uses events to create an image of herself in the eyes of posterity.[16]

III. MID-CENTURY POLITICAL THOUGHT[17]

Throughout the century the current of political theory acquires breadth and momentum, and though little of this attains a high level of literary expression – much theory in any case is still couched in Latin – no understanding of the period is complete without some awareness of the lines along which political theory was evolving, for in a troubled age, when literature is often militant, we shall find these attitudes underpinning combative and satiric literature and making their way into discursive works (essays, letters, opinions of *devisants* in collections of *contes*) and also into the neo-classical drama. Beneath the surface and in spite of the obstacles and threats, the history of France in the sixteenth century concerns the extension of royal power and the gradual centralisation of administration; and these trends are echoed in the writings of political thinkers. Early in the century, the defenders of the monarchy are found among the court chroniclers and men who had served royal masters (Lemaire de Belges, Seyssel). With the development of humanism, other elements enter the picture: on the one hand, the concept of the benevolent despot, such as we saw in Erasmus and Rabelais, will persist, partly through the intermediary of Guillaume Budé, in Ronsard's views, and on the other, the study of Roman law will provide grist to the monarchist mill, though it must be added that the partisans of a more limited constitutional monarchy also found material to suit their thesis in the *corpus juris*. Debate will be sharpened also by the views associated with Machiavelli – as, for instance, in the works of

Innocent Gentillet.[18] Under Francis I, Antoine du Moulin had made an impressive contribution towards monarchist theories, and the religious wars accelerate the process, though Counter-reformation thinking in Europe does not automatically support an absolutist view of the monarchy: there are some similarities between the Calvinist Buchanan and the Catholic Suárez in their conception of limited monarchy, but in France, absolutism will be supported by many towards the end of the century. Theoretical discussion tends to concern itself with the manifestations of royal power, and to some extent, with its limits; but all thinkers will agree on the divine origin of authority.

This theocentric outlook inevitably involves writers in the problem of the relations between Church and state; and the debate is complicated by the disputes between France and the Vatican, with gallican sympathies often to the fore. Later on, the emergence of Calvinism raises the problems of religious minorities, toleration, the legality of war undertaken on religious grounds, and so forth. Finally, the accounts of travellers in distant lands gradually make Europeans more aware of different political structures and systems, a sense of relativity creeps in, and in Bodin's work for instance, the relevance of time, climate, and milieu to structure is taken seriously. However, the majority of thinkers gear their ideas to the specific problems of France, and in these troubled times, the dividing line between theory and propaganda is often blurred.

Jean Bodin – De la Republique (*1580*)[19]

During the religious wars, three main currents may be discerned, reflecting the three main elements involved in the fighting. In the first place, there are the supporters of central monarchy, in its traditional, integral form; then there are the Huguenots; and finally the partisans of the *Ligue*. The traditionalist view of the monarchy, which appeals to many humanists and finds literary expression in Michel de l'Hôpital and Ronsard, is based in part on patriotic as well as on religious grounds; it tends to moderation and accepts a measure of compromise, so that toleration is acceptable, though some distinguished scholars who ought to have known better, like Dorat and Léger du Chesne, warmly welcomed the Saint-Barthélemy. Among the moderate traditionalists stands Jean Bodin, one of the most remarkable minds of French humanism. In his *De la Republique*, translated in due course into Latin (1586), Bodin is concerned to offer a definition of the state which bears some resemblance to reality; he soon realises that the state is not something fixed and immutable, but a body subject to pressures of differing sorts, and, moreover, an entity more and other than the sum of the individuals who compose it:

Republique est un droit gouvernement de plusieurs mesnages, et de ce qui leur est commun, avec puissance souveraine.

His book then attempts to analyse the conditions under which states exist and develop, but also to discover the form of government most likely to suit France. Sovereign power, which cannot be alienated, comes to be accepted by the individual (often by force), but is subject to several *de facto* limitations. Bodin makes a fundamental distinction between the type of sovereignty and the means by which that sovereignty is exercised; he lists monarchy, aristocracy, and democracy, but suggests that, for instance, a monarch may exercise his sovereignty through the medium of an aristocracy or even of a democracy. Much of the work is devoted to studying the nature of each type of sovereignty, and to describing the causes of its transformation into some other type. Nevertheless, Bodin's sympathies lie with monarchy, whose disadvantages are outweighed by its merits; he thinks it is probably the only form of government in which sovereignty is properly exercised and the one most suitable to countries that have attained a certain territorial magnitude. Bodin draws a number of conclusions relevant to his time, for instance that the nobles and the States General are instruments of government and not partners in sovereignty. In these respects and others, kingship is portrayed as the most satisfactory form of government for France in an imperfect world.

The middle-of-the-way view of monarchy comes through towards the end of the religious wars in the activities of the *politiques* or *modérés*, some of whom collaborate in the famous *Satyre Menippée* (see below, pp. 472–4). They prolong the humanist tradition (Rapin, Chrétien, etc.), but they also represent the emergence of bourgeois stability. They accept that the king rules by divine consent, but do not follow the absolutists (whose voices will become louder in the near future): they feel that the States General should meet regularly, that the king will make laws in which reason is active, and that toleration must be granted to religious minorities. The other elements were less moderate in outlook. First, the Huguenots. They did not draw up any clear-cut doctrine, but tended to work *ad hoc* partly because of the divergent tendencies in their ranks.[20] Many of the ideas that appealed to the Huguenots were hardly new; there is a current of 'democratic' thought that goes back to the Middle Ages, and in the 1520s writers such as Almain and John Major were advancing such views in print. The study of Roman law furthered discussion of these theories, as for instance in the works of Nicolas de Grouchy, whose *De comitiis Romanorum libri III* appeared in 1554 and who in due course went over to Calvinism. One of the basic divergences between absolutist and democratic attitudes is seen in the debate whether the king is bound by the laws of the realm or not.

Secondly, there was the *Ligue*, which came into being as the result of various political forces and therefore also suffers from *ad hoc* thinking which often smacked of ambiguity and downright opportunism. Generally, the *Ligueurs* upheld the claims of the Roman Catholic Church to be the sole religion of France, and though they loudly asserted the authority of the king, they sought to restore more power to the States General[21] – a thesis that rallied the supporters of federalism and decentralisation; and the involvement of the Guises was viewed with suspicion by many.

Etienne de la Boétie (1530–63)[22]

Important though these currents are, they do not often reach a high level of literary expression in the vernacular, and Protestant views are either incoherent (Hotman's *Franco-Gallia*), are published abroad, or are written in Latin. In the field of straight political thinking, perhaps only one text acquires literary stature in its own right: La Boétie's *De la servitude volontaire*. The work raises many questions; there is doubt about its date of composition, and if it was written before La Boétie was twenty, that is *c.* 1549, it must have been revised here and there, as for instance in the passage praising the endeavour of the Pléiade and referring to Ronsard's *Franciade*. And does the text, as it stands, come down to us without revision by another hand? Was La Boétie inspired by specific current events or is the tract essentially a rhetorical exercise? Its publication (1574) gave it an unfairly partisan colour, since it was taken over by the Huguenots, who saw in it powerful grist to their mill.

In fact, the essay does not provide a positive answer to the questions it raises; no political solution is offered, and the question of principle – government by one, that is monarchy – is shelved for another occasion. On the other hand, the work is more than a pupil's overheated exercise: there runs through the prose a glowing affirmation of liberty. La Boétie believes that, in our natural state, we are free, but have come to accept various forms of tyranny, imposed by 'democratic' election, force of arms, or hereditary succession. Whereas reason and Nature would have us free, habit has induced us to think otherwise:

La nature de l'homme est bien d'estre franc & de le vouloir estre, mais aussi sa nature est telle que naturellement il tient le pli que la nourriture lui donne (Bonnefon ed., p. 29)

Many educated people preserve their awareness of freedom, but society encourages the *status quo*, and interest and ambition help to maintain the tyrant, though by definition he can neither be loved nor love. La Boétie shows how the social hierarchy proliferates *à la* Parkinson so that it is in the interest of those fitting into the structure to keep it going ('la tyrannie semble profitable . . . ils veulent servir

and sophistication, especially in a relatively closed society, will promote moves to the involved and labyrinthine in style. In the last
decades of our period, all these currents are near or on the surface;
but we must regard this stage as one of experiment and of prose-
writers finding their feet in genres for which they often had no
immediate examples in their vernacular predecessors. Foreign and
classical models may give some guidance, but this is only part of the
story, and when the history of this phase comes to be written, it may
be that men such as Etienne Pasquier will emerge as much more
significant figures than has been previously assumed.

NOTES

1. J. W. Thompson, *A History of Historical Writing*, 2 vols., New York,
1942.
2. Both available in BM and O.
3. As for instance in I. Gentillet, *Discours sur les moyens de bien gouverner . . . contre Nicolas Machiavel*, 1576 (BN).
4. See J. H. Franklin, *Jean Bodin and the Sixteenth-century Revolution in
the Methodology of History*, New York, 1963; D. R. Kelley, *Foundations of
Modern Historical Scholarship: Language, Law and History in the French
Renaissance*, New York, 1970.
5. Copy in BM; translated by P. Mesnard, *La Méthode de l'histoire*, 1941.
6. W. L. Gundersheimer, *The Life and Works of Louis Le Roy*, *TRH*,
1966. The full title is *De la Vicissitude ou variété des choses en l'univers*.
7. Published at La Rochelle, available in BM, BN, O.
8. *Œuvres*, 1610 (BN); *Recueil de l'origine de la langue et poésie françoise*, 1581 (BM, BN, NLS). See J. G. Espiner-Scott, *Claude Fauchet, sa vie,
son œuvre*, 1938.
9. *Des Recherches de la France. Livre premier,* 1560 (BM, BN), 2nd Book,
1567 (BN); the final book appeared in 1621. See Margaret J. Moore,
Etienne Pasquier, historien de la poésie et de la langue française, Poitiers,
1934; P. Bouteiller, 'Un historien du XVIᵉ siècle – Etienne Pasquier', *BHR*,
1945; L. Clark Keating, *Etienne Pasquier*, New York, 1972. The standard
ed. of the *Œuvres* is still the Amsterdam ed. of 1723 (2 vols.).
10. Among other historians may be mentioned B. du Haillan, *De l'estat et
succez des affaires de France,* 1570 (BN).
11. Ed. V.-L. Bourrilly, 1910. Covers the years 1515–36.
12. *Les memoires: trois livres des Ogdoades de Guillaume du Bellay*,
1569 (BM, BN), often reprinted. See V.-L. Bourrilly, *Guillaume du Bellay,
seigneur de Langey (1491–1543)*, 1905.
13. *Commentaires*, Bordeaux, 2 tomes, 1592 (BM, BN, StA), modern eds.
by P. Courteault, 3 vols., 1911–25, and recent Pléiade ed. 1961. See P.
Courteault, *Blaise de Montluc, historien*, 1908.
14. The *Mémoires* came out in 1665; the BN now possesses the Bour-
deille MSS. Modern ed. by L. Lalanne, 11 vols., 1864–82. See L. Lalanne,
Brantôme, sa vie et ses écrits, 1896; R. D. Cottrell, *Brantôme – The Writer
as Portraitist of his Age*, Geneva, 1970.
15. Modern ed. P. Bonnefon, 1920. See J. Mariéjol, *La Vie de Marguerite
de Valois, reine de Navarre et de France (1553–1615)*, 1928.
16. There are, of course, many other writers of memoirs whose accounts
are interesting to the literary mind as well as to the historian: R. de la Marck,
seigneur de Fleurange; Vieilleville; Saulx-Tavannes (whose memoirs were
noted down by his son); and for the later part of our period the indispensable
Journal of Pierre de L'Estoile.

17. See General Bibliography.

18. *Discours sur les moyens de bien gouverner un royaume, contre N. Machiavel*, 1576 (Geneva) (BM, BN); 1577 (?Geneva) (NLS); 1579 (?Geneva) (NLS). Modern ed. of 1576 ed. C. Edward Rathé, Geneva, 1968; see P. D. Stewart, *Innocent Gentillet e la sua polemica antimachiavellica*, Florence, 1969.

19. The work was published at Lyons (BM, BN). Over and above the general introductions to political theory (see General Bibliography), the best introduction is still R. Chauviré, *Jean Bodin, auteur de la République*, 1914.

20. The political theories of the Calvinists have been outlined above, pp. 350–2.

21. Who seek at this time to assert themselves, especially on the principles of taxation.

22. The work first appeared in its complete text, but anonymously, in S. Goulart, *Mémoires de l'Estat de France sous Charles neufiesme*, Geneva, 1576. Modern ed. of his works by P. Bonnefon, Bordeaux, 1892.

23. Definitive ed. 1594 (BM); modern ed. Charles Read, 1876.

Chapter 15

MICHEL DE MONTAIGNE (1533–92)[1]

IN 1580 the famous Bordeaux printer Simon Millanges brought
out the first two books of Montaigne's *Essais*; they were the work
of a local gentleman who had seen service on behalf of Henry of
Navarre, had witnessed at first hand the ravages of the religious wars,
but had also found time to read widely, especially among classical
authors. With the encouragement of his father he had translated the
work of Raimond Sebond on natural theology; and he had enjoyed the unforgettable experience of a perfect, though short-lived,
friendship with Etienne de la Boétie. Towards 1571, he decided to
retire to his *château* in order to read and to meditate:

Dernierement que je me retiray chez moy, deliberé autant que je pourroy,
ne me mesler d'autre chose que de passer en repos, et à part, ce peu qui me
reste de vie: il me sembloit ne pouvoir faire plus grande faveur à mon esprit,
que de le laisser en pleine oysiveté, s'entretenir soy mesmes, et s'arrester et
rasseoir en soy . . . et m'enfante tant de chimeres et monstres fantasques les
uns sur les autres, sans ordre, et sans propos, que pour en contempler à mon
aise l'ineptie et l'estrangeté, j'ay commencé de les mettre en rolle, esperant
avec luy en faire honte à luy mesmes. (I, viii)

He was hardly aware that, in so doing, he was setting down a work of
world class; or, even more modestly, that the *Essais* would be so
instantly successful. He continued to write and, encouraged by his
reception, published an enlarged edition in 1588, which included the
third book and various additions, additions that were to be further
amplified in the posthumous edition of 1595. These later insertions
had been enriched by travel in Italy, by Montaigne's two periods of
office as mayor of Bordeaux, and also by the onset of illness which
sharpened his mind wonderfully on several themes central to the
Essais.

Montaigne is the first author to use the term *essai*; and as he
explains, they are the written expressions of essays or exercises of his
judgement on the various topics it occurs to him to consider. The
term judgement itself requires definition; and in a sense its meaning
becomes clear only when we have read the whole of the *Essais*, which
are in essence a search for the identity of the self undertaken for the
better conduct of his life. What emerges is not a lesson but a mind
and a personality *se faisant*, expression by *devis* rather than by *advis*.
reflections and also a self-portrait without mask or palliation; and at

477

the same time, a mirror of many end-of-century attitudes which show how the lessons of the Renaissance are assimilated but also tempered by a mind that is far from being just a mirror of its time. Historically the essays can be seen, in some measure, as a means of coming to terms with a human situation in which the high hopes of the early Renaissance had foundered on the disrupted world of the later Valois, before political absolutism and 'classical' minds of the seventeenth century had tried to reconstruct a world after the breakdown of the medieval pattern of life. This partly explains Montaigne's relevance today for readers seeking a *modus vivendi* with themselves and a world whose values are crumbling. He will not appeal to the extremist, to those who polarise problems or who deny that 'l'intérêt commun ne doibt pas tout requerir de nous contre l'intérêt privé'; on the other hand, he will not offer tidy, comfortable solutions to those for whom order is more important than probity. Nevertheless, intellectual integrity compels a coming to grips with the attitudes that underlie Montaigne's *vision du monde*.

For indeed what is important in Montaigne is his general approach rather than any attempt to adopt a clear-cut position on some particular problem. Montaigne induces in the attentive reader a move from the normative towards the existentiality of his situation. His general ideas do not, of course, preclude development in his thinking or in the conception of the essays which at first are short and markedly anecdotal, compared with, say, those of Book III: the several editions reveal a constant transcending of what has already been written by Montaigne, and further experience enriches the fabric of his meditation. Nevertheless, the traditional division of his intellectual biography into recognisable stages commands less respect than formerly, and one characteristic feature of his mind is precisely the ability to embrace contraries. In a chapter such as this, any detailed study of variation of attitude is impossible; in any case, Montaigne is less easy to pin down than almost any other author, and a critical portrait of the essayist probably says more about the critic than about his subject. I shall therefore not pretend to do more than to offer a model of what Montaigne means for one reader, though I naturally hope that it may incite others to create their own model. The French phrase 'Pour un Montaigne' is very helpful, as it avoids excessive claims of definition. Still, there may be some agreement on the main *foci* of Montaigne's meditations, once he attained maturity. Perhaps in his first gropings, he had thought of composing essays on various *exempla* within the traditional framework of morality and psychology: at all events, the early essays are rather balder in substance than the final one where the author himself recognises a fuller length and development of theme. If such was his starting-point, it was not in any way new; Erasmus, Italian humanists had paved the way, as had his constant bedside book, Plutarch. Montaigne had in common with the tradition a concern with the moral development of man, an interest in a cluster of Stoic themes, notably the importance of death in the pattern of life. But Montaigne's scepticism, strengthened it seems by his study of Sextus Empiricus and Pyrrhonism, and his exploration of his own mental workings in a troubled world, must have encouraged him to question some familiar assumptions: *exempla* are the events of other people, and may have only a limited value beyond the individual concerned, the construction of a corpus of rules of conduct may conflict with experience, and doctrines of too finalist or too rationalist a nature may also lend themselves to criticism.

'Nous sommes nés à quester la verité' (III, viii); but what truth and by what means? Montaigne rejects man's search for certain truths, as they are beyond his powers or authority; the concern of his *essais* is with the nature of man, his place in society, state, and Universe, and what he may make of himself. To answer these questions – though they are not advanced as the preconditions of his journey through life, since this would narrow inquiry in a field where question so often determines answer – he examines man in himself and in his relations with others, but at the same time he is forced to scrutinise his epistemological powers. Man's ability to acquire knowledge is clearly limited; Montaigne is convinced that man cannot communicate with *être* (II, xii) and is not qualified to examine what is the concern of God, but even in his human domain, he is restricted. To begin with, he cannot be sure of the validity of his own sense data, though these are the only means whereby he can get in touch with something beyond himself. They are conditioned by his physical character, they appear to vary from one individual to another, and they may be seriously warped by passions, imagination, reason, or 'présomption'. Our view of the world is determined by the categories through which we apprehend it and we project ourselves into a reality whose essence eludes us. Montaigne conducts a full-scale campaign against the urge to put reason on a pedestal in the *Apologie de Raymond Sebond*, by far the longest of the *essais*; reason, so prized by the schoolmen and philosophers, is exposed as a weak and wavering reed. In addition, he attacks reason on the ground that no one part of the human mind should be isolated, and therefore favoured, at the expense of the other elements. This is not the same thing as doing away with reason, any more than one would wish to rid oneself of the 'passions', whatever their disadvantages; in this, as in other respects, Montaigne rejects stoicism. At the same time, having read widely and noted the experience of travellers (including himself), he wonders whether reason has the universal validity that is sometimes accorded to it.

Doubtful about the reliability of the self in its links with reality beyond itself, Montaigne is also sceptical of various assumptions about that self. The theory of the *dignitas hominis* loses some feathers in the course of the essays: man is seen as a mixed bag of good and evil, of contrary passions and desires, varying in his behaviour successively and indeed simultaneously. He is a restless character incapable of *repos*; he rarely follows the dictates of reason, his motives often conflict with his conduct and its consequences. Incapable of proper insight into himself, does he compare so favourably after all with the animals? He is indeed 'onloyant et divers', a creature conditioned by time and mobility. Two characteristics are singled out for criticism, and they are not unconnected. First, there is *curiosité*, the desire for knowledge, in spite of the limits imposed on man's chances of success. In so far as *curiosité* involves the desire to know things beyond our own existence, it involves precisely a flight from the present with which we ought to be getting to grips. More generally, the search for knowledge is attacked because of the questionable value of the knowledge so acquired. Montaigne mounts a vigorous onslaught on learning, both in education and in later life. The taxing of memory may impair other areas of the mind whose usefulness is more evident; moreover, knowledge that is by definition second-hand may stand in the way of one's own capacity for experience. If knowledge is associated with the search for a code of behaviour, we may find that the experience of others can have only a limited validity for ourselves ('Qui suit un autre, il ne suit rien'). Finally avidity for learning has a close kinship with the other sin, pride. Pride, with its anthropocentric sense of superiority, is the vice most damaging to proper living: it may set impossible ideals, and, since it is linked with *paraître* and therefore the values of others, it introduces a screen between self and existence. In any case, it threatens to encourage a rigidity of attitude which yields a similar result. In the *Apologie*, depreciation of human pride is one of the *leitmotive*:

... froisser et fouler aux pieds l'orgueil et l'humaine fierté; leur faire sentir l'inanité, la vanité et deneantise de l'homme; leur arracher des points les chetives armes de leur raison ... Abbatons ce cuider, premier fondement de la tyrannie du maling esprit. (II, xii)

Those, briefly, are the arguments invoked by Montaigne to undermine undue confidence in man's powers. Some of these also explain his suspicion of codes of behaviour that have been laid down to help man on his way. Montaigne always insists on the need for 'doctrine' and living to coincide; he detests the gap between *être* and *paraître*; and he disapproves of any scheme of things that does not take the individual fully into account. He rejects too rigid a code, or one that is too exalted, or one that fails to acknowledge the mutability of human nature. The *vertu excessive* of classical *exempla* is a case in point; and Montaigne will also come to doubt the value of organising one's life in terms of one's death, though in an early stage the thought of death appears to be obsessively present. Life and death form an indissoluble whole and it is to be hoped that one's death would harmonise with one's way of existence, but a narrow finalist view of life can only impose upon us a rigidity that will defraud our existence of its potential and preclude the possibility of experience carrying the weight to which it is entitled. Ethics should not divorce the body from the mind, nor should it place too great a stress on *coutume* or habit, which are signs either of fossilisation or living in accordance with other people and the past: *exempla* are thus criticised for being a *vérité empruntée*, and the dangerous interference of pride is warned against. In all this, we have the refusal to let the self be imposed upon by others, the past, or the paralysing stiffness of a code; otherwise it will be unable to achieve its fullest realisation, to 'épouser le mouvement de la vie', as the Bergsonian formula expresses it. Anything that, intentionally or not, restricts or suppresses parts of the self is to be cast aside, though we shall see that Montaigne is far from advocating a Gidian attitude or a complete moral *laissez-faire*.

Though Montaigne's assault on man's pride and other limitations has been set out in a fairly orderly way, it must not be thought that he presents his case in systematic fashion, apart perhaps from the *Apologie* which is a special case. Nor is it his intention to leave the matter there; Montaigne is no enemy of the human race, but he is very anxious to understand what the fundamental facts of the situation are, so that he can build fruitfully on acceptable foundations. What he has set out to do is to destroy theories of man that simply do not correspond to reality and at the same time to move, in the field of behaviour, from a normative to an existential standpoint.

As he examines man's psychology, he is compelled to transform parts of the traditional hierarchy of man's faculties. In any case, it is very difficult to differentiate these 'faculties': quite apart from the problems involved in trying to explore 'les profondeurs opaques de ses replis internes' (II, vi), the faculties tend to run into one another: 'nous ne sçavons plus distinguer les facultés des hommes' (III, ix). An obvious case is that of the reason whose operations are often affected by the passions; moreover, the arbitrary separation of body and mind must go by the board. A cardinal principle in Montaigne is the indivisible unity of the human being, warts and all; man forms a living organism in which the noble and the base, the virtuous and vicious, all play their part; and unless we respect this basic principle, we shall be unfaithful to our being. For instance, even though according to the established belief we should pay no attention to

dreams or the imagination, these do in fact contribute to our knowledge of ourselves. Besides, since less good causes may have beneficial
results, these workings of our mind can further positive action. The
'songe' can be useful, the imagination can put up 'false images' in
the mind capable of siphoning off undesirable passions; and the
passions themselves, which after all provide some of the mind's
energy, have an important role to fulfil. Nor must we seek to suppress
or streamline the contradictions in our nature; they are essential
ingredients and we must accept them as such. To do otherwise is to
render self-knowledge impossible and to stultify further development:

Qui auroit à faire son faict, verroit que sa première leçon, c'est congnoistre
ce qu'il est et ce qui luy est propre. (I, iii)

In this connection, Montaigne has interesting things to say on neighbouring topics. By adopting an 'open' attitude to our being, we shall
come to know more about it; we shall let 'hasard' and 'fortune' play
their rightful role – this is a theme to which the essayist returns
time and again. Any attempt to provide a 'closed' outlook and keep
fortune at bay will limit our self-awareness; in any case, the process
of self-knowledge involves the action of time. Time may be the
symbol of man's imperfection, it is also the medium within which he
becomes conscious of his nature. As he evolves, by his contact with
the outside world and himself – a process in which he is both actor
and spectator – he becomes gradually aware of what makes him what
he is: this is the *maistresse forme* on which Montaigne expatiates
from time to time. Not as simple as Taine's *faculté maîtresse*, not the
product or the principle of a fixed structure, it is something whose
identity emerges with the unfolding of one's life. No doubt, it was
present *in posse* from the beginning – for man's individual nature can
hardly be altered – but only through existence, the play of fortune,
and a heightened awareness that interacts with the life process, does
this pattern – and Montaigne uses the imagery of pattern to explain
his view – attain full realisation and identifiable character:

Regardez un peu comment s'en porte nostre experience: il n'est personne, s'il
s'escoute, qui ne descouvre en soy une forme sienne, une forme maistresse, qui
luicte contre l'institution, et contre la tempeste des passions qui luy sont
contraires. (III, ii)

At the start of the passage, Montaigne uses the word *experience*, and
it is a critical one in his view of life.[2] The word, of course, has some
meanings that are easily defined: *an* experience, an experiment, the
act of experiencing, and also the harvest of such experience. However, for Montaigne, experience is also an attitude of mind in which
judgement and other mental factors have their part. This attitude
derives from a refusal to prejudge or to think in terms of categories
imported, imposed from outside; it is something that develops in the

light of the events that go to form one's existence, and above all it entails a judicious balance between involvement and detachment, the art of combining awareness with the act, the achievement of a proper relation between self and others, an awareness of what is possible and what is not in the interplay between desire and reality. It is something more than reason or knowledge; it may require the collaboration of intuition or 'feel'; it is perhaps the widest category on which we can draw to apprehend life in all its plenitude:

> Il n'est desir plus naturel que le desir de connoissance, Nous essayons tous les moyens qui nous y peuvent amener. Quand la raison nous faut, nous y employons l'experience . . . qui est un moyen plus foible et moins digne; mais la verité est chose si grande, que nousne devons desdaigner aucune entremise qui nous y conduise. (III, xiii)

Montaigne's slightly deprecatory phrase should not mislead us: the whole of the last, essential essay is entitled *De l'experience*. It is the attitude of mind which allows for the greatest fidelity between the self and its own nature, as well as with Nature in a broader sense, which Montaigne never defines closely but which remains for all that another key concept in his scheme of things.

In this context, the concept of judgement is very relevant. Montaigne alludes to it frequently, and sometimes attempts a definition:

> Le jugement est un util à tous subjects, et se mesle partout. A ceste cause, aux essais que j'en fais ici, j'y emploie toute sorte d'occasion. (I, 1)

It is the instrument whereby the faculties of the mind can be brought into *free* play in connection with any subject under the sun. It is related to experience, but also to liberty, and even if, like all other elements of our mental life, it remains subject to error and disproportion, it is the best means of affirmation of our being in relation to the world: 'L'avantage du jugement, nous ne le cedons à personne' (II, xvii). The ideal of proper detachment in the exercise of judgement is doubtless a distant one, as Montaigne recognises:

> It est peu de choses ausquelles nous puissions donner le jugement syncere, parce qu'il en est peu ausquelles, en quelque façon nous n'ayons particulier interest. (III, vii)

In any case, such 'interferences' are bound to occur since we are in this world to act and can only become ourselves, in some measure, through action; nevertheless, it is one of the ways in which our mental equilibrium may be achieved:

> Il s'en prend à soy, et se condamne, ou de s'arrester à l'escorce, ne pouvant penetrer jusques au fons, ou de regarder la chose par quelque faux lustre. Il se contente de se garantir seulement du trouble et du desreiglement; quant à sa foiblesse, il la reconnoit et advoue volontiers. Il pense donner juste interpretation aux apparences que sa conception luy presente. (II, x)

For all its faults, judgement remains the surest guarantee of our authenticity and of our keeping in touch with Nature. It will be associated with tranquillity, but also with humour, and a certain open-mindedness, a refusal to be bogged down in habit and routine, an acuity kept alert by the changing nature of things:

afin qu'ayant en l'imagination cette continuelle variation des choses humaines, nous en ayons le jugement plus esclaircy et plus ferme. (I, xlix)

Montaigne does not pretend that knowledge of so fluid and layered a phenomenon as the self can be easily attained. The revelation of self depends, like all other things, on the play of hazard, but there are other interferences too: as soon as we become aware of describing ourselves to an audience (whether others or indeed ourselves), self-consciousness, even a certain modesty, may limit the insight of our gaze. *Amour-propre* may intervene, and with it the desire not to be so open as to become vulnerable. The awareness of self may stem from a wish to know ourselves better, but it also involves the maintenance of an identity not to be dominated from outside. Montaigne's attitudes to the self are as complex as they are towards phenomena outwith himself.

Montaigne's ideas on liberty, judgement, and experience mean that he entertains only a qualified belief in the benefits of any education that seeks to do more than translate the potential of a person into reality. Education must not constrain the individual, on the other hand it cannot claim to modify the essential fibres of his being, though it should do what it can to discipline judgement and 'mœurs'. To attempt to alter nature is futile, and one will spend one's time better in preparing the individual for the life that lies ahead of him. In this context, Montaigne's strictures on learning become doubly significant. Other people's knowledge and experience are valuable only in so far as they can be assimilated: like Barrès, Montaigne is deeply suspicious of the *barbares*. Learning too is suspect: what he extols rather is ignorance, which for him is also the antithesis of curiosity and desire, so that we come once again very close to the concepts of experience and judgement:

Qui veut guerir de l'ignorance, il faut la confesser. Iris est fille de Thaumantis. L'admiration est fondement de toute philosophie, l'inquisition le progrez, l'ignorance le bout. Voire dea, il y a quelque ignorance forte et genereuse qui ne doit rien en honneur et en courage à la science, ignorance pour laquelle concevoir il n'y a pas moins de science que pour concevoir la science. (III, xi)

Ignorance is opposed to 'doctrine' which, like glory, *noblesse*, dignity, riches, and beauty, may be indispensable features of life, but should be held at a distance (II, xii). Ignorance keeps us on a level with reality, and thus the average peasant or man in the street may well enjoy a more normal, healthy approach to life than those screened from it by various impediments such as those just mentioned:

C'est par mon experience que j'accuse l'humaine ignorance qui est, à mon advis, le plus seur party de l'escole du monde. Ceux qui ne la veulent conclurre en eux par un si vain exemple que le mien ou que le leur, qu'ils la recongnoissent par Socrates, le maistre des maistres. (III, xiii)

Knowledge must therefore be valued not for itself but by its relevance to living; and so the specialist, often represented by the doctor, is given short shrift in the *Essais*. Montaigne does not usually hold up other men as models for reasons that will be obvious from what has gone before; sometimes he mentions Seneca, though with reservations, Plutarch (for his judgement rather than for his ethical ideas), Democritus (for his well-balanced laughter), and one contemporary, Adrien Turnèbe, for whom he has a quite exceptional admiration; Etienne de la Boétie of course remains unique. Of the ancients it is Socrates who stands out, perhaps not in fact a classical Socrates, but one who comes to resemble the essayist himself. This Socrates is admired for his 'simplesse naturelle', for his maturity of experience grounded in everyday life:

Certes la veneration en quoy j'ay les perfections de ce personage merite que sa fortune fournisse à l'excuse de mes principales imperfections un si magnifique exemple. (III, ix)

Socrates corresponds to his idea of the great mind which he described in that highly autobiographical essay *De la présomption*:

Mais les belles âmes, ce sont les âmes universelles, ouvertes et prestes à tout, si non instruites, au moins instruisables. (II, xvii)

In his own style. Montaigne is continuing a theme that we have already seen in Erasmus and Rabelais; it is characteristic of the Renaissance in France that a major theme is so often accompanied by its counter-theme, the praise of folly balancing the praise of learning.

It would of course be a betrayal of Montaigne's outlook to search for anything in his essays that resembled a firm code of behaviour in a narrow sense. Nevertheless, certain mental attitudes do appear to him to be the indispensable prerequisites of a genuine and full mode of living. One must avoid any line of conduct that is directed to some finalist aim; no behaviour should result in an inadequate or an over-affirmed relationship between the self and the rest of the world. The self must be apprehended and respected in all its variety and its contradictions; it must not seek to 'possess' either in the present or in the future – thus learning and 'gloire' are played down – but it must evolve in the right context of action. The mind must not be divorced from life in its flow, for man must accept that he is a creature of time and cannot realise himself through any attempt to withdraw therefrom. *Etre* for the human being cannot be achieved otherwise; and, if one may risk using the slightly anachronistic categories of Gabriel Marcel, most of the caveats Montaigne enters against certain codes and principles of conduct are determined by his fear of the freezing of the self into the mode of *avoir*. When he talks of his own temperament, Montaigne tends, especially in old age, to favour forms of behaviour that appear to add up to a golden mean and to a refusal to be drawn too far into any single path. He talks of an 'âme bien réglée', and elsewhere he defines *sagesse* as 'un maniement réglé de nostre âme' (II, ii). Man should be in control of his passions, but he should not strive to suppress them; Montaigne admits that he is not given to 'violentes passions', but sees nothing wrong in indulging his whims and appetites. He does not therefore emerge as a Stoic, and one of the themes of the *Essais* is the playing down of 'art' as opposed to 'nature', however difficult the latter may prove to define and however much it may differ from the savage and untutored. Man must also avoid falling into the rut of dreary routine, just as much as he should eschew straining towards goals that are beyond the scope of his being. Montaigne talks of the value of 'repos', but this does not mean inertia or sloth. He sees little chance of our being undergoing radical change, though we may induce modifications of detail (our attitude to pain or death, for instance). We must indeed remain ourselves and not seek to ape others, any more than Montaigne expects his behavioural model to be imposed on his readers:

Or, comme dit Pline, chacun est à soy-mesmes une très-bonne discipline, pourveu qu'il ait la suffisance de s'espier de pres. Ce n'est pas ici ma doctrine, c'est mon estude; et n'est pas la leçon d'autruy, c'est la mienne.
Et ne me doibt on sçavoir mauvais gré pour tant, si je la communique. Ce qui me sert, peut aussi par accident servir à un autre. (II, vi)

Though Montaigne's attitude to life has seemed, in the eyes of some critics, to be rather tepid and even negative, it is important to note the positive aspects of the matter. In the first place, he is in no wise passive about the emergence of his self: in spite of its *maistresse forme*, it is something which is up to a point constructed, and does not merely grow like Topsy; we must indeed 'composer nos meurs':

Quel que je soye, je le veux estre ailleurs qu'en papier. Mon art et mon industrie ont esté employez à me faire valoir moy-mesme; mes estudes, à m'apprendre à faire, non pas à escrire. J'ay mis tous mes efforts à former ma vie. Voilà mon mestier et mon ouvrage. (II, xxxvii)

and elsewhere he adds that his book has made him as much as he had made it. Secondly, freedom is not simply freedom *from* . . . , it is closely connected with *resjouyssance*, often presented as the opposite of possession and *avoir*, and more richly in company of plenitude. Life is the search for enjoyment, one must seek to 'estendre la joye', and gaiety is an essential part of our make-up. Thirdly, Montaigne's ethical attitude is not exclusively self-centred in a selfish way. Of course, he always stressed the need for reserve, for the safeguarding of one's 'arrière-boutique'; and one is told to give oneself to oneself alone, only to 'se prester à autruy'. These statements must nevertheless be seen in their proper context: the danger of neglecting one's inner being is that one becomes the prisoner of things alien to one's essential nature (and *gloire*, i.e., what other people think, must be understood as an example of this). Moreover, all men no doubt operate some shuttlecock between themselves and others as part of the way in which they ensure their inner equilibrium. At the same time, Montaigne has never shunned the world: 'je suis sociable à l'exces' (III, ix), and in his view neglect of what the world has to offer can only impoverish one's human substance. The world in fact may contribute richly to our self-knowledge:

Ce grand monde, que les uns multiplient encore comme especes soubs un genre, c'est le mirouer où il nous faut regarder pour nous connoistre de bon biais. Somme, je veux que ce soit le livre de mon escholier. Tant d'humeurs, de sectes, de jugements, d'opinions, de loix et de coustumes nous apprennent à juger sainement des nostres; et apprennent nostre jugement à reconnoistre son imperfection et sa naturelle foiblesse: qui n'est pas un legier apprentissage. (I, xxvi)

The world may be accessible through books, for literature is also a powerful means of self-revelation – Montaigne's comments on the art of reading have lost none of their salt or edge; but if the impact of books goes so far as to destroy our gaiety and our health, then they are best left aside (I, xxxix). We can also learn much from travel and the 'commerce des autres' – as Montaigne's own *Journal du voyage* makes abundantly clear. Our neighbours teach us a lot, not only because of the differences that may separate them from us, but through their similarities, arising from the fact we all participate in 'l'humaine condition'. If Montaigne at one time saw in his self-portraiture the opportunity of underlining his 'différence essentielle', by the time he came to write Book III, he was very much more conscious of his solidarity with his fellow-men. He does not want us to take over lock, stock, and barrel values and codes that will allow us to live solely in order to acquire value in the sight of others, for the 'approbation d'autruy' is too fragile a foundation on which to build the purpose of our existence; nevertheless, it is a proper relationship to others that some of Montaigne's most intimate utterances come to stress:

Le plus fructueux et naturel exercice de nostre esprit, c'est à mon gré la conférence. J'en trouve l'usage plus doux que d'aucune autre action de nostre vie; et c'est la raison pourquoy, si j'estois asteure forcé de choisir, je consentirois plustost, ce crois-je, de perdre la veue que l'ouir ou le parler. (III, viii)

Far greater, though, is friendship. In Montaigne's view, marriage comes out as inferior to friendship: it is connected with the fortunes of one's family, and feminine psychology may in any case preclude the possibility of friendship. At this point, the relationship with La Boétie assumes crucial importance: La Boétie, whose political views may have brushed off in some details on to his friend, died young, and the memory of this experience colours the texture of the *Essais*: friendship is one of the things Nature has sought to induce in us (I, xxviii) and La Boétie appears to have fulfilled the ideal beyond expectation. Rarely does Montaigne give the impression that his style has been taken in hand by his feelings, but in the essay just referred to there are paragraphs where the self has been obliterated in the awareness of a transcendent relationship:

> Ce n'est pas une speciale consideration, ny deux, ny trois, ny quatre, ni mille: c'est je ne sçay quelle quinte essence de tout ce meslange, qui, ayant saisi toute ma volonté, l'amena se plonger et se perdre dans la sienne; qui, ayant saisi toute sa volonté, l'amena se plonger et se perdre en la mienne, d'une faim, d'une concurrence pareille. Je dis perdre, à la verité, ne nous reservant rien qui nous fut propre, ny qui fut ou sien ou mien.

A major portion of the paragraph from which this extract comes belongs to the additions of the 1595 edition, and thus confirms the permanent significance of friendship in Montaigne's outlook on life. For him, clearly the self without possibility of communication is a contradiction in terms. At a lower level, he once wrote 'Nul plaisir n'a goust pour moy sans communication' (III, ix); but at the highest pitch of intensity, communication merges into communion, and such a relationship, though of the rarest, is a necessary part of one's existence. It is the medium in which two selves, equally open, but also fully matured, may bring about that osmosis that crowns the values Montaigne attaches to life, a medium where *être* takes over from *avoir* as much as it does from *paraître*. To interpret Montaigne's outlook without proper regard to the theme of friendship is to impair his scale of values.

Friendship is a special relationship with another person; but there are others with the outside world that command the essayist's attention and on which some comment is required. To begin with, the problem of the individual and society. Some critics have regretted Montaigne's refusal to commit himself in the political sense, but this is to overstate and simplify the position. Undoubtedly Montaigne would have rejected any tendency to politicise the individual completely; and he spoke with the experience of a man who had been a mayor and a successful one. He was quite aware of the possible conflict between private and public claims, and he has made some remarks on the extent to which the individual can warp his conscience to suit the pressures of the common weal (III, i). He is inclined to establish a sharp distinction between the two sectors, which allows him to comment on the public interest in such a way as to appear

Machiavellian in the eyes of some readers. On the other hand, he has things to say about princes that reveal high standards of expectation: he demands a strict sense of duty from them, insists that they are not *legibus soluti*, that their main function is the dispensing of justice, without hindthoughts of liberality smacking of self-interest. His view of government is probably more reserved than that of an earlier generation of humanists for whom the king was the benevolent despot. However, Montaigne prefers to keep his distance, fully conscious of the dangers of self-involvement. For him the structure of the state is a necessary evil; aware of the fluidity of man's destiny and of the *bransle des choses*, he offers a traditionalist, conservative view of polity. He is suspicious of political instability, he is positively afraid of 'la domination populaire', he doubts whether reforms do more than affect the shadow and leave the substance intact; alternatively he wonders whether we know enough about the body politic to judge how reforms will work. In any case, the political reformer is one whose individual judgement is subject to 'présomption' and error as much as is the religious rebel; and finally, 'l'excellente et meilleure police est à chacune nation celle soubz laquelle elle s'est maintenue' (III, ix), for whatever the weaknesses of this or that law, one is on balance wisest to respect 'l'usage'.[3]

In all this, we may discern the standpoint of a man whose experience of the religious wars has induced in him a yearning for order, national security, and peace; and to some extent this is true of a man who detested violence and torture. More fundamental, surely, is his wish to maintain a social structure such as will allow the individual to develop his own being without undue pressure from outside. Up to a point, too, he may have seen in the political fabric one aspect of divine providence, something that was not to be questioned lightly.

A similar impression may be gained of Montaigne's attitude towards religion, a matter on which a great deal of ink has been spilled.[4] There appears to be a sort of dichotomy between the Montaigne of the *Essais* and Montaigne the citizen. By all accounts, the man was scrupulously attentive to the ritual of his religion; and in many ways he proved the genuineness of his belief in circumstances that were uncomfortable and could have become dangerous. Yet, if we turn to the *Essais*, the religious dimension becomes very much more modest. It is true that from time to time Montaigne inveighs against the Huguenots: he is hostile to their rationalist defence of religion – the *Apologie*, in which he refers to the Huguenots as *docteurs*, has been read in this sense; he doubts the value of religious popularisation and he questions whether religion, in the form they advocate, could show any improvement on what tradition has to offer. Yet, a positive view of the Catholic faith can hardly be said to emerge: critics have noted Montaigne's lack of reference to dogma, to Christ, to the Scriptures which are quoted with some reticence. He appears unconcerned with the afterlife, and where his religion could bring grist to the mill of his essays, he fails to seize the opportunity. Death, for instance, may be understood as an essential complement to life, but the problem is not tackled *sub specie æternitatis*. Moreover, since the whole cast of his mind, as it is revealed in the *Essais*, hardly suggests a man of fervent religious emotions, one is tempted to ask what religion could mean for him in any deep existential sense. There is clear evidence here and there that he affirms his acceptance of Christianity: and since all human presuppositions 'se valent' (II, xii), we must agree with the need of a divine starting-point. True reason – not the weak tool that functions in the human mind – 'loge dans le sein de Dieu' (ibid.); what is more, the power of God is beyond our knowledge and human span, and this is one reason why we should not question miracles. These may, on the one hand, appear as such because we imperfectly understand the workings of Nature, and on the other, they are 'real' because they come within the purview of God, not of human comprehension. Elsewhere, Montaigne affirms the need for grace without which man can never raise himself above his station (II, xii). He also makes it clear that there can be no half-way attitude to the problem of ecclesiastical authority and he comes down on the side of the Ayes; here he takes the same view as he does on politics, namely that the matter is to be accepted or rejected in its entirety, for nibbling or piecemeal acceptance is totally unjustified.

Yet when all is said and done, the reader may well feel some dissatisfaction and wonder whether the *Essais*, deprived of their religious references, would not yield the same resonance. By putting the emphasis on what comes within the range of man, Montaigne inevitably makes religion fade into the penumbra, so that at the end of the day, its very discretion becomes the sign of a possible dispensability, and all the more so because Montaigne, after having reduced man's pretentions to their essential nothingness, is able to build on the ground thus cleared a positive ethic for man's journey through life, which rarely, if ever, is tinged by thought of the afterlife. Somewhere the essayist points out that we are responsible for the good and the evil that inform our being. It is, on the other hand, open to question whether Montaigne himself would be happy with such an interpretation of his outlook; no doubt, in religion as in politics, he considered the external framework essential for the individual to make any sense of his 'humaine condition'; and this is suggested by the hostility Montaigne shows towards those who threaten the fabric of religion (both atheists and Huguenots). Yet, one can understand with hindsight why the *Essais* were placed on the Index in the mid-seventeenth century, and also appreciate the appeal his writings have had for agnostics of distinction: Bayle, Sainte-Beuve, Gide. The substance of the *Essais* has grown precisely because of the difference the author establishes between the human and the divine dimension, and also, in all probability, because Montaigne appears to emphasise action rather than belief:

Je propose les fantasies humaines et miennes, simplement comme humaines fantasies, et séparément considérées, non comme arrestées et reglées par l'ordonnance celeste, incapables de doubte et d'altercation: matiere d'opinion, non matiere de foy; ce que je discours selon moy, non ce que je croy selon Dieu, comme les enfans proposent leurs essais: instruisables, non instruisans; d'une maniere laïcque, non clericale, mais tres-religieuse tousjours. (I, lvi)

For after all, the *Essais* constitute a unique exploration of identity of the self; and Montaigne was very well aware of this special feature. Up to a point, their origins stem from an effort to while away the time, but they soon assumed a more important role:

C'est une humeur melancolique, et une humeur par consequent très ennemie de ma complexion naturelle, produite par le chagrin de la solitude en laquelle il y a quelques années que je m'estoy jetté, qui m'a mis premierement en teste ceste resverie de me mesler d'escrire. Et puis, me trovant entierement despourveu et vuide de toute autre matiere, je me suis presenté moy-mesmes à moy, pour argument et pour subject. C'est le seul livre au monde de son espece, d'un dessein farouche et extravagant. (II, viii) (cf. also I, viii)

Success of the first edition helped to make him realise the value of such a book for others, though not in any didactic spirit, for the *raison d'être* of the *Essais* goes deeper. He is trying to record the 'essais de ma vie', something that so few people have ever thought of undertaking (II, xxxvii). This standpoint accounts for certain characteristics: on the one hand, no topic is too trivial or base to be excluded, no *fantasie* is too weird to be dismissed as of small consequence, for all these things may light up some dark corner of the mind. On the other hand, the essays will not follow the model of the *dissertation française*; time and again, Montaigne stresses the disorderly, fragmentary, arbitrary nature of his writing, he talks of *fagotage* and *lopins*, he will often enlarge on some passage, but to remove anything would be to mask a facet of his inner life. And so it is that there are very few erasures of earlier texts; in any case, the reader may be able on his own to take some hint further:

Elles [i.e., mes allegations] portent, souvent, hors de mon propos, la semence d'une matiere plus riche et plus hardie, et sonnent à gauche un ton plus delicat, et pour moy qui n'en veux exprimer d'avantage, et pour ceux qui rencontreront mon air. (I, xl)

However, Montaigne's assertions about the disorderly presentation of his essays must be taken with a pinch of salt; even if they do not conform to certain norms of tidy structure, they have an undoubted organic unity, in which the themes may be developed sometimes in rectilinear fashion, sometimes in recurrent form, at others in a relationship between two neighbouring essays. As Montaigne continued with the setting-down of his thoughts, he discovered that a two-way relationship began to develop between himself and his book; hence his statement that his work had formed him as much as he had been responsible for its existence. The regular keeping-in-touch with himself by means of the pen had by its very nature modified his life; and by *c.* 1577–78, he appears to have attained clarity on a fundamental issue of the *essais*: self-portraiture.

The novelty of Montaigne's undertaking is also apparent in the form and style of the *Essais*. The fundamental problem is: what is the best form to provide the artistic correlative for an inner life whose *maistresse forme* is not to be categorised and docketed in tidy pigeon-holes? Montaigne has on occasion indicated his distaste for extended narrative (I, xxi); he also returns frequently to his condemnation of formal structures and rhetoric:

J'ay naturellement un stile comique et privé, mais c'est d'une forme mienne, inepte aux negotiations publiques, comme en toutes façons est mon langage; trop serré, desordonné couppé, particulier; et ne m'entens pas en lettres ceremonieuses, qui n'ont autre substance que d'une belle enfileure de paroles courtoises. (I, xl)

Rigid structures formalise a content that cannot be so formalised; moreover, too stiff a presentation implies a rigid relationship with a reader who probably, by definition, would belong to too narrow a band of the public whom Montaigne wishes to reach. Montaigne emphasises the need for greater spontaneity and for accepting the unexpected appearance of thoughts which might well not emerge under more stylised conditions. He recognises that digressions will introduce 'bulges' into the pattern of his text, though he warns his readers that there *is* some order, shape, some logic in the presentation of his thoughts (III, ix), and he asserts confidently that 'mon livre est tousjours un' (ibid.). He does not abdicate control of his material, and patterns of structure within his essays have been detected by critics willing to make the effort, though the title of an essay may not always correspond to its content, as the author himself was quick to point out (ibid.).

At stylistic level, the problem is equally acute: how to find the language suitable for reproducing what one might call broadly, in William James's term, the stream of consciousness? The language must also establish the right means of communication with the reader. To begin with, there is the problem of the tongue in which the essays should be written. Montaigne, though more at home in Latin than in French in his youth and liable to break into Latin under stress, mentions that the aims of the essays do not require so exalted a language as Latin; moreover, his venture was allegedly so ephemeral that it did not matter composing in French at a time when the vernacular was evolving so rapidly. This must not be taken to mean that Montaigne was insensitive to the potential of the French tongue or to what a writer of standing can do to enrich his native idiom:

Le maniement et emploite des beaux esprits donne pris à la langue, non pas l'innovant tant comme la remplissant de plus vigoreux et divers services, l'estirant et ployant. Ils n'y apportent point de mots, mais ils enrichissent les leurs, appesantissent et enfoncent leur signification et leur usage, luy aprenent des mouvements inaccoustumés, mais prudemment et ingenieusement . . . En nostre langage je trouve assez d'etoffe, mais un peu faute de façon: car il n'est rien qu'on ne fit du jargon de nos chasses et de nostre guerre, qui est un genereux terrain à emprunter; et les formes de parler, comme les herbes, s'amendent et fortifient en les transplantant. Je le trouve suffisamment abondant, mais non pas maniant et vigoreux suffisamment. Il succombe ordinairement à une puissante conception. Si vous allez tendu, vous sentez souvent qu'il languit soubs vous et fleschit, et qu'à son deffaut, le Latin se presente au secours, et le Grec à d'autres. (III, v)

The author must bring out the possibilities of the language, but should not, in moments of deficiency, go too far beyond its confines, otherwise the style will don a borrowed air. Montaigne's vocabulary is therefore not unduly scholarly or pedantic, and when it does draw on special areas, the words it uses are often dialectal – as befits an author from the south-west – or professional, but the matter may be complicated by the demands of imagery. In later editions, Montaigne tended to reduce his latinisms and archaisms, but was not averse from introducing neologisms. Generally speaking, he prefers his style to show kinship with the spoken rather than with the written word:

Au demeurant, mon langage n'a rien de facile et poly; il est aspre et dedaigneux, ayant ses dispositions libres et desreglées; et me plaist ainsi, si non par mon jugement, par mon inclination. . . . Comme à faire, à dire aussi je suy tout simplement ma forme naturelle: d'où c'est à l'adventure que je puis plus à parler qu'à escrire. Le mouvement et action animent les parolles, notamment à ceux qui se remuent brusquement, comme je fay, et qui s'eschauffent. (II, xvii)

Throughout the *Essais*, Montaigne expresses marked hostility to rhetoric, to which he opposes his own 'parler simple et naïf'; he affects some scorn for the Ciceronian period, and this may be one reason why his admiration for the Roman orator is qualified. One can see why rhetoric should be a target for suspicion: a style, based on codified practice, could hardly be spontaneous or individual enough to produce the tone so desired by Montaigne, and it would remain a *style emprunté*; but there is worse to come, the style is not only borrowed, it is inflated and a style that belongs to the world of *paroistre* can scarcely be the right vehicle for the communication of Montaigne's experience. Nevertheless, his strictures on rhetoric do not prevent him from using its resources on more than one occasion; in any case, he will require styles of different levels to express the several registers of feeling, thought, and attitude.

When Montaigne is recounting an episode or tale, or when he is discussing a book or some matter of public concern, he is in a sense treading familiar ground: authors such as Tahureau and Pasquier had preceded him. Where a new note has to be struck is in those areas where such subjects stimulate in Montaigne a flow of thought, whose tone and mobility must not be lost, and also where he is communicating to his reader the inner workings of his mind: not a schematic psychology but an individual continuum. Montaigne has, in some measure, to create his own mental geography, and all the more so as we have seen how he tends to break down the traditional categories. The language must therefore be faithful to the movement of the mind, and also be intelligible to the reader. This will affect the rhythms of the sentence, the length of the paragraph, the digression; there will also be the groping, *calamo currente*, for the right word that clinches the character of some process of thought or experience. And it is here that Montaigne's imagery has a vital role to play, for he is always moving towards the concrete, in the realm of what is common to writer and reader. Montaigne often associates the progression of his thought with the idea of a journey along roads more or less well-trodden; he also makes extensive use of the imagery of structure and pattern. Time and again, he refers to his existence as fragments of some fabric or tissue, and he may sometimes introduce metaphors from the world of building. Where experience involves exchange or assimilation, we are offered organic images of osmosis, digestion, absorption. But more often than not, these various images belong to the domestic way of life; the recondite literary comparison is comparatively infrequent, for imagery should not serve as embellishment, but as the necessary concomitant to the exploration of experience.

For all that, Montaigne does not in fact scorn figures of rhetoric: the *sententia* occurs regularly, though perhaps less as the pithy summary of accepted wisdom than as the bringing-together of his reflections or experience. More complex, no doubt, is the matter of the quotations; Montaigne had little time for the cullers of commonplaces, who thereby display their inability to write a book of their own making (III, xiii); but he quotes richly and frequently throughout the *Essais*. In his early days, no doubt, he shared contemporary liking for drawing on the potted wisdom of others – quotation is an essential feature of Renaissance writing – but, as his essays become more concerned with his own portrait, he will quote others, as he says, to reflect himself. It is also noteworthy that in the third book he quotes especially from the poets; perhaps in poetic utterance he sensed a more faithful communication of personal experience, but whatever the truth of the matter, quotations are used not so much to give authority to the point he is wishing to make as to illuminate and colour the passage – the substance is his.

Perhaps some of Montaigne's stylistic character will emerge more naturally from a reading of a short extract, taken from an essay which is all the richer for touching upon a key motif of the book:

Le jugement est un util à tous sujets et se mesle partout; à cette cause, aux *Essais* que j'en fais ici, j'y emploie toute sorte d'occasion. Si c'est un subjet que je n'entende point, à cela mesme je l'essaye, sondant le gué de bien loin; et puis, le trouvant trop profond pour ma taille, je me tiens à la rive; et cette recongnoissance de ne pouvoir passer outre, c'est un train de son effet, oui de ceux dont il se vante le plus. Tantôt à un subject vain et de néant, j'essaie voir s'il trouvera de quoy luy donner corps, et de quoy l'appuyer et l'estançonner; tantôt je le promène à un subject noble et tracassé auquel il n'a rien à trouver de soy, le chemin en estant si frayé qu'il ne peut marcher que sur la piste d'autruy: là il fait son jeu à eslire la route qui luy semble la meilleure et, de mille sentiers, il dit que cettuy-cy ou celuy là a esté le mieux choisy. Je prends, de la fortune, le premier argument; ils me sont esgalement bons et ne desseigne jamais de les traiter entiers: (*c*) car je ne vois le tout de rien; ne font pas ceux qui nous promettent de nous le faire veoir. De cent membres et visages qu'a chaque chose, j'en prends un, tantôt à lécher seulement, tantôt à effleurer, et parfois à pincer jusqu'à l'os; j'y donne une pointe, non pas le plus largement, mais le plus profondément que je sais, et aime plus souvent à les saisir par quelque lustre inusité. Je me hasarderois de traiter à fond quelque matiere si je me connoissois moins et me trompois en mon impuissance. Semant ici un mot, ici un autre, eschantillons dépris de leur piece, escartés, sans dessein, sans promesse, je ne suis pas tenu d'en faire bon, ny de m'y tenir moy-mesme, sans varier quand il me plaist, et me rendre au doute et incertitude, et à ma maistresse forme, qui est l'ignorance. (I, 1)[6]

The passage is obviously a cardinal one, for it sets out the role Montaigne has assigned to judgement; but it also stresses the extent to which the older Montaigne asserts his refusal to be held to any fixed position, and ends in the important link he establishes between his *maistresse forme* and ignorance, the significance of which he noted earlier. These last points occur in the passage added to the original text and replacing a much shorter, undeveloped statement. Montaigne also tells us that the essays are essays in judgement and that any topic is of considerably less importance in its own right than as something on which the judgement may sharpen its teeth.

Stylistically, one of the first things to strike us is the imagery, so necessary to exteriorise the operations of his mind. Different fields of imagery are introduced, perhaps in part because there is a considerable time interval between the writing of (*a*) and (*c*). In (*a*), as so often, Montaigne describes his mental processes in terms of the journey, the road, the countryside; this imparts movement to the presentation, but in some contexts it allows him to introduce other travellers in the country of the mind (the ancients or contemporaries, as in I, xxv). Attached to this main set of images is that of the essayist himself, seen as a body along the road. When Montaigne comes to add passage (c), the transition to the image of the dog attacking a bone offers little trouble (the dog is not mentioned specifically, of course); and towards the end, images of pattern and fabric are inserted, images that tend to recur in the *Essais*. The passage, taken as a whole, is by definition rather self-conscious, and Montaigne contrasts himself with others who comport themselves differently in such situations. Though the sentences are carefully constructed to convey a sense of ease and flow, they serve also to induce a binary rhythm and to prepare us for the final sentence, with its near-conceit and a lapidary formulation of a *leitmotiv*. Montaigne has a marked liking for pairs of adjectives and verbs: this structure may be associated in some measure with his legal training, where the doublet is common in the terminology, but other considerations come into play: sometimes a search for the exact, complementary epithet, but also a concern with rhythms and balance.[7] Montaigne often develops binary and even ternary sentence structure: a main clause may be followed by a binary subordinate scheme. When one reads a passage such as this, one may well be struck by the conscious balance and artistry rather than by any apparent spontaneity that Montaigne claims is a feature of his writing. One has only to compare the text of the *essais* with that of the *Journal du Voyage*, undoctored for public consumption, to note how artistically contrived is the search for a natural freedom of style.

In making acquaintance with Montaigne, we have stressed some of the permanent features of his masterpiece, and this has meant playing down the evolution of ideas and attitudes that occurs as he meditates and writes. Basically this evolution is characterised by the transition from a relatively external, normative outlook to something more existential, more concerned with experience, particular and concrete. This growing awareness of self – there is little evidence of any crisis or *moment privilégié* in his progress – though on occasion and in the earlier days it may have led him to stress the 'différence essentielle' of his being, comes to recognise its close relationship with the non-self, and the later essays constitute a dialectic between the self and others, in which the common humanity of both is brought into view. Though Montaigne has rightly been praised for his exceptional insight into the operation of the human mind, he is really more of a *moraliste*, for his observation is an applied one. Somewhere he remarks that 'nous sommes nés pour agir', and we cannot become ourselves except in time and in action, so that he runs little risk of succumbing to the difficulties that beset an Amiel; nor do we detect any marked anguish in the face of existence. As he writes with increasing self-awareness, Montaigne's style begins to blossom, and his essays move into the broader dimensions where a richer and more flexible expression may be attained. His tempo is seldom more than an *andante*, and in order to come to terms with him we must adopt the same movement as himself. Any attempt to take him by storm will fail; he demands of his reader something of the relationship he experienced with La Boétie, a particular friendship in which neither author nor reader seeks to crowd the other out or to imprison the other in constricting categories. Montaigne may affect our outlook on various points – his essential humanity (witness his view of torture) is infectious – and he manages to insinuate into his reader the nagging feeling that nothing should be taken for granted. Few authors have known how to combine serenity with so intense an enjoyment of life, and even fewer have succeeded in imparting so open an attitude to living in their works. Montaigne will remain the target of the fanatic, the reformer, the totally involved; he comes into his own when experience, richly assimilated, asks to be garnered before it loses its flavour and becomes a husk.

NOTES

1. First edition of the *Essais* (Books I and II) 1580 (further editions, 1582, 1587). Fourth edition, including Book III, 1588. In 1595, a posthumous edition, based on additions by Montaigne, is published by Mlle de Gournay. Modern editions: the so-called Bordeaux 'municipal' edition, ed. Strowski, Gébelin, Villey, 5 vols., 1906–33; also those by P. Villey, Alcan, 1922 (reprinted 1967); Thibaudet (Pléiade), 1934; A. Micha (Garnier-Flammarion), 1969; and Thibaudet-Rat ed. of *Œuvres complètes* (Pléiade). *Biography*: D. M. Frame, *Montaigne. A Biography*, New York, 1965. *Critical Studies*: E. Auerbach, *Mimesis*, Berne, 1946; M. Baraz, *L'Etre et la connaissance selon Montaigne*, 1968; A. M. Boase, *The Fortunes of Montaigne*, 1935 (reprinted New York, 1970); F. P. Bowman, *Montaigne: Essais*, 1965; D. M. Frame, *Montaigne's Discovery of Man*, New York, 1955; H. Friedrich, *Montaigne*, Berne, 1949, 2nd ed. 1967; F. Gray, *Le Style de Montaigne*, 1958; F. Jeanson, *Montaigne par lui-même*, 1951; R. C. La Charité, *The Concept of Judgment in Montaigne*, The Hague, 1968; E. Marcu, *Répertoire des idées de Montaigne*, Geneva, 1965; A. Micha, *Le Singulier Montaigne*, 1964; G. Poulet, *Etudes sur le temps humain*, Edinburgh, 1951; R. A. Sayce, 'L'Ordre des Essais de Montaigne', *BHR*, 1956; 'Montaigne et la peinture du passage', *Saggi e ricerche di letteratura francese*, 1963, also *The Essays of Montaigne*, 1972; A. Thibaudet, *Montaigne*, 1963; W. E. Traeger, *Aufbau und Gedankenführung in Montaignes Essays*, Heidelberg, 1961. P. Michel, *Montaigne*, 1969, gives a summary of the essayist's fortunes down the centuries and provides a fairly extensive bibliography; useful information is also to be found in the *Bulletin de la Société des Amis de Montaigne*. Dr R. A. Sayce is engaged on a bibliography of the early eds. of Montaigne. Of the editions mentioned at the beginning of this note, all are available in BM, BN except 1587 (not BM). NLS has 1582 and 1595; it also possesses Montaigne's copy of George Buchanan's *History of Scotland*. On the different *issues* of the early eds. see R. A. Sayce, *The Essays of Montaigne*, chapter 2.

2. W. G. Moore, 'Montaigne's Notion of Experience', *The French Mind: Studies in Honour of Gustave Rudler*, 1952.

3. Frieda S. Brown, *Religious and Political Conservatism in the Essais of Montaigne*, Geneva, 1963.

4. M. Dreano, *La Pensée religieuse de Montaigne*, 1937; C. Sclafert, *L'Âme religieuse de Montaigne*, 1951.

5. M. Metzschies, *Zitat und Zitierkunst in Montaignes 'Essais'*, Geneva, 1966.

6. In many standard eds., the signs *a*, *b*, and *c* denote the text of 1580, 1588, and 1595 respectively.

7. R. A. Sayce, 'The Style of Montaigne; word-pairs and word-groups', *Literary Style: a Symposium*, ed. S. Chatman, London–New York, 1971.

LE JOURNAL DU VOYAGE[1]

In 1580 and 1581 Montaigne undertook a journey which opened his eyes to Germany, Switzerland, and Italy, and kept a log-book of his experiences. The first half, roughly, was dictated to a secretary, and is presented in the third person; the second half was set down by Montaigne himself, partly in Italian and partly in French. In consequence, one may detect a certain stylistic difference from the *Essais* on more than one occasion. The extent to which this journey may have had some effect on the composition of the *Essais* has been a matter of speculation among scholars, but it has an interest in its own right. It was, however, not published until 1774, and if it took time to establish its own claims, it was greatly appreciated by Chateaubriand who refers to it several times in the *Mémoires d'Outre-Tombe*, when he recalls his own peregrinations in the peninsula. Two reasons at least prompted Montaigne to this journey: on the one hand, a desire to get out of the rut and see other people, and on the other, the hope that he would find some alleviation for the renal colics to which he was becoming more and more prone. Thus it is not surprising that the matter of medical treatment and baths crops up fairly often in the text, or that, during his stay in Rome, he should tell us something of the Vatican's reactions to the first edition of the *Essais*. What is perhaps more striking is the greater sociability and curiosity displayed by Montaigne, who, far from wanting to 'promener son moi' through the landscapes, seeks to understand the ways of others: 'M. de Montaigne, pour essayer tout à faict la diversité des mœurs et façons, se laissoit partout servir à la mode de chaque pays, quelque difficulté qu'il y trouvast' (M. Rat, ed., 23). He is very observant of behaviour, and likes to compare the *mœurs* of one town or district with those of another. He is impressed by the buildings he sees, and notes down features in considerable detail; and he has special predilection for mechanical designs and complexities. He draws attention to fountains and their hydraulic action, and is fascinated by the workings of an organ operated by water:

La musique des orgues, qui est une vraie musique et d'orgues natureles, sonans tousjours toutefois ne mesme chose, se faict par le moyen de l'eau qui tumbe aveq grand violance dans une cave ronde, voutée, et agite l'air qui y est, et le contreint de gaigner pour sortir les tuyaux des orgues et lui fournir de vent. Un' autre eau poussant une roue atout certenes dents, faict battre par certain ordre le clavier des orgues; on y oit aussi le son de trompetes contre-faict. . . . De toutes ces invantions ou pareilles, sur ces mesmes raisons de nature, j'en ai veu ailleurs. (ibid., p. 131)

But Montaigne takes an equally lively interest in local economy, agricultural produce, and geographical features, not to speak of the cost of living. There are moments of introspection, more particularly when he is suffering pain, but generally this is the record of a man looking at the outside world, alert, discriminating, and good-humoured. On the other hand, one will notice Montaigne's pre-occupation with things religious, in a manner that seems more pro-nounced than in the *Essais*. In short, though the *Essais* remain in a class of their own, it is a pity to ignore the *Journal* which sheds a pleasant light on the author and, in its own way, is something of a pioneer work in the genre.

NOTE

1. See I. Buffum, *L'Influence du Voyage de Montaigne sur les Essais*, Princeton, 1946; C. Dédéyan, *Essai sur le Journal de voyage de Montaigne*, 1946. The *Journal* may be read in the second Pléiade ed. of Montaigne's works, or in M. Rat's ed. for the Garnier series.

RETROSPECT AND PROSPECT

The period we have been surveying marks the opening stages of the transition from the medieval world to new patterns of life and new structures of society which is becoming more and more urbanised, in which the merchant class is acquiring its identity, and a sense of nationalism is on the way to influence political behaviour – though too much of this point should not be made before the end of the sixteenth century in France, for it is during these decades that the monarchy, for all its failings and the disruptions of the religious wars, is on the ascendant. Theories on the nature of the Renaissance are numerous, but several things stand out clearly. In the first place, there is in reality no violent break with the past, though contemporaries are often aware of a certain distance between themselves and that past – and indeed to think of the past as the past is in itself a significant attitude. Second, the process of development is often much slower than has sometimes been suggested, partly because human nature is remarkably conservative, partly because in France the political and economic factors in play not only encourage attitudes that may imply fidelity to an imagined past, but also because events crowding in on the Renaissance mind often compelled men to act in an *ad hoc* spirit; in France the maturity of Renaissance humanism more or less coincides with the serious prospect of the break-up of the known world, a prospect that may be inhibiting as often as stimulating; and contemporaries may have to devote less time to thoughts about the development of their culture than to solving the immediate and urgent problems with which they are incessantly faced. In any case, cultural progress occurs in disjointed fashion and at different levels: very few people are original and pioneering in all registers of their mental activity, and the application of 'new' principles will vary in effect according to the area concerned: the appeal to early authority makes sense in the field of religion, but hardly so in that of scientific observation and experiment, and it is no coincidence that certain scientific advances are made by men not classically trained, while pre-Copernican attitudes persist in colleges right into the seventeenth century. Learning acts as both a spur and as a brake, and only to a limited extent does the individual let himself go beyond the frameworks of reference with which he is familiar.

Nevertheless, there is a feeling abroad that the old structures are not adequate to emerging situations, that there is a screen between the self and experience. This sense of 'gap' is more marked at certain levels than at others: for instance in the domain of religion where fundamental principles, overgrown with various accretions through the centuries, seem no longer to meet the needs of the community, so that scholasticism and obscurantism becomes closely associated in many minds; in the economic and social fields pressures of a financial and urban nature set up new stresses and strains; and contemporaries sense that recent inventions will alter perspectives, such as the discovery of printing, gunpowder, or the New World. In the fullness of time nationalism will stress certain differences and man is more aware of standing in a different relation to the world about him. In France these tensions come to the surface in part through outside pressures, at any rate at cultural level, at a time when the Italian Renaissance has already passed its zenith; and one must recognise that France's contribution to philosophical and scientific debate in the sixteenth century is a very modest one, as the perusal of any general history of thought will quickly indicate – more original minds show themselves in the field of political theory and jurisprudence (e.g., Jean Bodin). With the acceleration of the Habsburg-Valois conflict and the explosion of the Reformation, the French Renaissance unfolds in an atmosphere of urgency and instability. In consequence, from the middle of the sixteenth century onwards, the world appears to have lost its identity and the individual to have lost the bearings he had known previously. With the polarisation of political and religious principles, there emerges a remarkable range of attitudes and moods, dictated in part by the immediate context but stimulated and enriched by the ferment of the classical revival, which itself will come under searching scrutiny by the minds it had helped to form. Moods will range from exhilaration and optimism to fears about an uncertain future; the enthusiasm for wide-ranging polymathy and experience will be matched by an instinctive urge to order and classify – Pierre de La Ramée is a good example of such a state of mind; and at political and religious level the spectrum is equally wide. To the right there are the die-hard conservatives who fear that the loosening of even one brick in their intellectual fabric will threaten its total structure; to the left there are those who can see no solution but the root-and-branch one, the return to a pure, unsullied authority – just as in the Romantic nineteenth century *Paradise Lost* becomes a major theme, so in Renaissance France do we regularly come across the nostalgia for the Age of Gold. The dignity of man moving towards considerable self-sufficiency is countered by a sombre awareness of his *miseria*. In between, we have all the varieties of tentative solutions. Some will try to synthesise the best elements of different currents that seemed to offer hope and guidance – here again, the parallel with the nineteenth century is suggestive, for syncretism had its Victor Cousins; others hope for gradual improvement from within the system, fearful of breaking completely with the past in case the unknown future should prove even less fruitful. Contemporaries sense the distance that separates them from the medieval past, but whereas some see all evolution as a further detachment from an Eldorado never to be recaptured, others look forward more confidently to a future in which they may make a meaningful contribution and bring man nearer to a realisable ideal. Needless to say, all these shades of opinion have their correlatives in the theological discussions of the times.

But what is particularly striking is the ambivalent attitude of so many humanists to the central problems with which they were faced. There is no *leitmotiv* of Renaissance man that does not immediately conjure up its counterpart – in the literary field look at the fortunes of the themes of glory, of the Court, of Petrarchism; the balance of contraries in Nature seems to find its correspondence in the field of ideas, and it is no coincidence that, at a time when these polarities are exacerbated in the context of a dislocated world-picture, the Neoplatonic theme of unity in diversity should command so much sympathy (as for instance in Ronsard). At all events, it is during the Renaissance that paradox, irony, ambiguity, dialogue, drama of debate become widespread vehicles of expression, that the figure of the fool or clown acquires notable currency; there is talk of *docta ignorantia*, of the wisdom of fools and sucklings. At literary level, this ambivalency finds splendid utterance in the divers *personæ* that inform Rabelais's world, but also in the poetry of Ronsard, where imagery acquires a curiously ambiguous role to express central areas of human experience. A not unconnected phenomenon, it seems, is the tendency for the Renaissance humanist to blur the normal categories of thought, and for the man of letters, for all the lip-service paid to definition of genre, to cut across the boundaries of literary categories, as witness Ronsard's handling of the elegy, or the extraordinarily discursive and often non-committal character of prose-writing, where short story, dialogue, essay, *exemplum*, and *histoires*, whether *tragiques* or *prodigieuses*, crowd in upon one another, trying to obtain some grip upon the human condition they are describing. At this level and also in the theological domain, humanists return to fundamental questions – the debates of the Synod of Arles (*c.* 473) are refought with undiminished intensity.

One of the most important issues, inevitably, is the epistemological one: what are man's sources of knowledge and what validity can he attach to them? These are issues which will be hotly debated long beyond our period. The age-long conflict between the belief in innate ideas coupled with the non-intellectual means of knowing, and the conviction that knowledge can be acquired only through the senses, becomes all the sharper for the social and political context within which the problem becomes relevant, and the positions of Aristotle, Plato, St Thomas, and St Augustine are scrutinised with renewed fervour. In the literature we have considered, the problem appears before Montaigne in the philosophical dialogues more especially, not very often elsewhere; but it will raise acute searchings in the Counter-reformation world in the discussions of man's fallen state, synergism, the relations between the will and the intellect, the status of the passions. The most impressive literary discussion of the epistemological problem is of course Montaigne's *Apologie de Raymond Sebond*, where doubt is cast on all means of knowledge. Montaigne for his part is prepared to accept, as did Bishop Berkeley, a sort of divine underwriting of our means of knowledge, but the wedges inserted by a fideist attitude may work ultimately against a religious solution of the problem; and the placing of the *Essais* upon the Index in the middle of the seventeenth century is, among other things, a sign of the way in which attitudes have evolved.

With all these perplexities, man finds himself face to face with Nature: for most of our period, the humanist attitude remains essentially religious, and Nature, though functioning along certain lines and laws, is none the less controlled by the Will of God. At the same time, there are signs of some loosening of attitudes. At one level, discussion ranges on the predictability of natural phenomena and therefore on the problem of predetermination – hence in part the interest taken in prophecy, astrology, demons, necromancy. At another level, Nature is examined in a more objective fashion – to use the term 'scientific' to distinguish this approach would be inaccurate and anachronistic – and we have careful descriptions of fauna and flora; though even here credulity and hearsay evidence are present, scrutiny is less invested with the trappings of tradition. Nevertheless, attitudes to Nature are rarely devoid of emotion: on the one hand, we have varying views of human nature seen outside the European context, so that some develop the theme of the noble savage unspoiled by corrupt society, whereas others will be impressed by his cruelty; and on the other hand, the forces of Nature will be apprehended variously, partly because man appears to be more aware of his existential difference. As in the Romantic period, two features show themselves: first, man's awareness of Nature becomes more acute, and he sees phenomena in visual and often dramatic terms; and second, he apprehends the vital forces of Nature in a fresh manner, so that in a poet, such as Ronsard, who expresses very forcibly the desire of man *not* to be isolated, Nature takes on from time to time almost a pantheist or vitalist character. In other words, the awareness of Nature acquires a deeper and wider resonance, though at conscious level humanists will have little difficulty in keeping their intuitions within orthodox bounds.

Inside this framework, man's own position and status are under review. His place at the crossroads between God and the animal world is still accepted – he is the microcosm of the larger Universe – but here again the traditional categories have perhaps become less firm: the discussion of man's psychological structures, for instance, may affect his standing in relation to animals. The debate on his greatness and *miseria*, brought to masterly literary expression in Montaigne, is a polarised example of the need to rethink man's place in the scheme of things. There is also much speculation on the relations between nature and custom or habit – yet another theme that will not be lost on Pascal! These ideas will reverberate in the field of jurisprudence, where relativist ideas begin to percolate, in that discussion often hangs on the value of Roman law, representing a fixed authority, in contrast to common law which may well reflect more accurately the spirit and ethos of a nation. A similar mobility is apparent in another area of debate, the problem of wisdom: there are distinctions to be made between *sapientia*, *scientia*, and *prudentia*. In certain domains wisdom belongs solely to God, but man's search for knowledge is also seen as part of his role upon earth (Pico della Mirandola, Bouelles, Scève), and this touches closely on the concept of life as active participation in existence *hic et nunc* or as contemplation and a gradual drawing-nearer to God. In the means of attaining knowledge, new factors come into play: we have already seen how renewed contact with the ancients, and the religious debates, stressed the importance of the authority carried by an authentic tradition, but other voices also make themselves heard. Against the weight of classical example and prestige, national pressures count for much, in the development of historiographical attitudes, in the reappraisal of common law, in the affirmation of France's own contribution linguistically and culturally. From the philologists and legists too will come awareness of the importance of comparative studies, thus easing the way towards a more relativist outlook, itself reinforcing the national awareness of the 'différence essentielle'. From the empirical workers in the field, a sense of the value of experience comes to oppose the excessive claims of authority – Paré and Palissy have much to say on this, and the travellers develop the theme long before Montaigne. And in a very different sphere, authors such as Ronsard and Montaigne seem to be feeling their way towards a more favourable view of the imagination as a source of knowledge. One way and another, the *querelle des anciens et des modernes* is already engaged.

The claims on behalf of scientific method are sounded especially in the fields of textual criticism, jurisprudence, historiography, and the biological sciences. Indeed it is perhaps here that French human-ism makes its most lasting contributions, though France produced no one so eminent as Leonardo da Vinci, the Italian thinkers, Vesalius, Copernicus, and even in those fields new attitûdes do not always make for immediate, unimpeded progress. National sentiment may determine a more generous interpretation of the Middle Ages and especially Charlemagne, but it also tolerates for a time the eccentric fortunes of the Francus myth; French scholarship throws up textual critics of the calibre of Lambyn, Muret, Scaliger, Passerat, and yet Vergil and Ovid continue to appear in editions containing comment-aries by foreign authors that are far from up-to-date; Paré defends the experimental method and then publishes *Des Prodiges*; Henri Estienne offers rational principles of method in determining his-torical truth and illustrates his method by recourse to the Bible, the *Decameron*, and Marguerite de Navarre; historiography is well de-veloped in Renaissance Europe, and Frenchmen like Bodin and Louis Le Roy play an important role, but the revamped medieval chronicle remains popular until the end of our period and beyond.

Nevertheless, progress is being made. Man's relation to existence is complex indeed in these decades; aware of the need to readjust that relationship, he collects more and more facts, he acquaints himself more closely with the archetypal philosophical and religious attitudes to life. While the structures of society still seem solid enough, his re-actions are characterised by vast enthusiasm, a wish to synthesise and harmonise, above all a marked broadening of activity. Then other factors come into play: the growing concern with practical problems thrown up by critical situations results in a desire for order and classification, a gradual secularisation of attitude, an increasing wish to harmonise knowledge and living, symbolised in Montaigne by the shift from the normative to the existential, and therefore also a move towards a more relativist view of life. This attitude will be op-posed by the mounting search for stability and authority at political level: Montaigne and the exponents of absolute monarchy are more or less contemporary. In the atmosphere of the religious wars, the polarisation already manifested in the theological discussions of the 1520s becomes acute: the Calvinist elements are circumscribed and isolated, the Counter-reformation absorbs what it can of the evan-gelical yearnings of the first half of the century, and the theory of divine right moves towards an extreme position in the early decades of the next century.

However, in our period, these currents are still fluid enough, and it is significant that men of letters and artists should so often appre-hend life in the peculiar register of *être/paraître*. We have seen certain aspects of this tendency in philosophical debate: where and how can man attain certainty of knowledge? what are the relations between the permanent Absolute and the contingency of appearances? The problem recurs at artistic level in the theory of Imitation: one must imitate reality, yes, but where does reality manifest itself? at simple, descriptive, phenomenal level? or must we try to capture, behind the contingent and apparent, something of the Absolute and ideal reality? In another domain, the social, the problem is accentuated by the need for man to be seen in society, that is by others. There are also political factors that prompt the Court to show itself more and more and play a part: 'on vaut dans la mesure où l'on paraît'. *Paraître/parade* are part and parcel of the Renaissance complex, but in a world of turmoil the relations between appearance and reality take on varying values, and all the more so if reality needs to be disguised or distorted to achieve acceptability. The Neoplatonist contents himself with layers of contingency affording stages towards a higher spirituality; the Court is show, but also an attempt to realise a certain ideal of living – Brantôme in particular grasped its Paradise-lost quality. D'Aubigné, on the other hand, after a period when he was ensnared by courtly appearances that are the hallmark of a *monde cassé* and of *Nature desvoyée*, sees the world as a non-world, as the negation of reality. Ronsard, in a series of startling poetic intuitions, realises that the line between *paraître, être*, and *néant* is a most delicate one and shows by the symbol of glass-blowing how *enflure* and experience recaptured are closely intermingled.

The French Renaissance is essentially an era of reappraisal in times of crisis when the rapid evolution of events force man to rethink his *condition humaine* and reorganise social and political structures: it is an era when 'human sciences' acquire vitality and status, it is also an era marked by the emergence of a greater patriotic awareness. As soon as the sensibility of the century begins to express itself in vernacular poetry under the pressure of new forces – and this means really from Scève onwards – life is apprehended more and more as something not fixed and stable, but fluid, susceptible to change, the negation of tranquillity. It is no coincidence that the Renaissance debate reaches maturity in humanism during the 1550s precisely at the time when poetic sensibility becomes fully-fledged; both phenomena reflect in their own way a crisis of civilisation. Not, of course, that the problems are all resolved or even brought fully to the surface; the debate will be continued long after our period, and it is interesting in this context to see how certain themes or presences accompany the evolution of thought. One may have reservations about the present enthusiasm for *thématique*, but significant themes in poetry and elsewhere do reveal much about the temper of an age; the prominent concern for *wisdom* or *glory* can be used as a yardstick to measure certain shifts of emphasis, but also to show that such central preoccupations persist into the following century which is still coping with the problems thrown up in our period. Another touchstone, perhaps, is the role played by a fresh exploration of classical mythology, a phenomenon that so often reappears in moments of cultural crisis in the West (cf. the Romantic period and even in our days). One final example: the persistent presence of St Augustine, whose personality crops up time and again in the critical decades, in the formation of Erasmus, in the evangelical inspiration of the 1528-33 period, in the spirituality of the Counter-reformation, especially after 1570, in the religious debates of the early 1600s, in the Jansenist experience. A scholar has written that one of the characteristics of the seventeenth century is its Augustinianism; but what is remarkable is the way in which the Church Father has become relevant to the whole Renaissance crisis, touching on so many common problems and expressing them in a language and style that has its own points of contact with poetic developments.

On the other hand, we have to recognise that the crisis of the Renaissance takes a considerable time to attain articulate expression in the vernacular, and even until the end of our period, many currents of thought prefer to show themselves in Latin. Though the Paris of Charles VIII and Louis XII is clearly the centre of much intellectual activity, stimulated in great measure from the Low Countries, it is surprising how little of this filters into the literary field at that time, when genres, conventions, and structures remain entrenched in traditional grooves. Though the *rhétoriqueurs* are often aware of new stirrings and number humanist scholars among their friends, their literary output is strongly conditioned by the demands of the Court and contemporary politics – and this relative stagnation is also abundantly discernible in the field of drama, whether it be *mystère*, morality, or farce.

Under Francis I, a noticeable shift in interest and tone may be detected, but even then the progress is slow. The years before and after 1530, to give a rough date, are crucial for the development of humanism and religion, but how much of this finds its way into vernacular channels immediately? There is, of course, one genius, Rabelais, but two other impressive figures, Marguerite de Navarre and Scève, attain maturity in the 1540s – and they and Clément Marot deepen their sensibilities away from Paris and Francis I's Court, while the claims of Neo-latin poetry are still serious; strengthened by a certain range and richness of composition, it is able to act as an intermediary for foreign poetic currents.

It is nevertheless during the 1540s that a more significant change is perceptible, for it is at this time that the vernacular makes its breakthrough as the recognised vehicle of literary sensibility. Of course, various factors are involved: national sentiment, the ferment of the ancient world, the new lessons to be learned from classical rhetoric, a widening of the educated public, political pressures, but it also occurs at the same time as the sensibility of the period is itself becoming broader and deeper. I have already pointed to differences in poetic language between Clément Marot and Maurice Scève; from 1544 on, poetic utterance seems capable of much greater range, tone, 'body', and resonance, not to mention a greater capacity for what Donald Davie has called 'articulate energy'. It is only once these shifts of sensibility have occurred that the full range of classical harmonics can be exploited by contemporary poets. Prose seems to lag behind for a time – *rhétoriqueur* habits often persist, for many prose fiction is considered to be less 'serious' (the *Heptaméron* has not yet been published) and French as a means of expression for abstract discourse will get under way in the 1550s. In that decade, the need for popularisation and the emergence of writers not trained to any extent in the classics will promote certain developments in the field of prose.

In the middle third of the century, then, changes of sensibility are apparent. Critical explorations into later poetry have elicited certain traits: mobility, metamorphosis, illusion, and so forth, as characteristic of the final years of the century and beyond. Yet much earlier man is aware of a gap between himself and existence, and this, as in Romanticism, provokes various emotions, a sense of the void, of the fluidity of life, of solitude and a desire for fusion, union, perhaps unattainable ideals, an awareness too of the beast in the jungle – historians have often pointed to the exacerbation of emotion in these decades, violence, fear of sinister forces, excitability, hysteria, sexual vehemence. *Titus Andronicus* may symbolise conveniently a certain morbid, 'Baroque' imagination, but the world of cruelty, dissolution, illusion is adumbrated before the outbreak of the religious wars, witness the almost simultaneous appearance of the *Histoires tragiques* adapted from Bandello (and a probable source for Shakespeare) and the *Antiquitez* and the *Regretz*. In a world that is felt to be crumbling the search for knowledge and the *recherche de la sensation* are never far apart. The sense of a fluid world, an 'insaisissable Protée', is already well developed in Ronsard, who creates his own world as a buffer between reality and the *fantasie* of Ariosto, to express the values of his world-picture and to confer upon poetry a special significance.

In the realm of literature three figures stand out: Rabelais, Ronsard, and Montaigne. I have mentioned the relative paucity of original thinkers in Renaissance France, but the strains and pressures of this epoch are expressed in these three writers in a way that is rarely matched by any other country. The glory of the French Renaissance lies in its literature rather than in its contributions to philosophy, science, or medicine. Though these writers express varying degrees of involvement in the world they inhabit, their outlooks are marked by three features that set them apart from the rank and file of their contemporaries. They have a richer apprehension of the issues, so often conflicting and contradictory, in which their age is implicated, they create an authentic literary world in which these issues are expressed in all their vitality and unresolvedness, and finally they have developed to this end a linguistic medium, individual and unique, which no other writer of the time has achieved. They accept the effervescent, elusive, conflicting, non-rectilinear quality of life and their intuitions transcend any attempts to reduce it to some coherent and convenient code; and it is significant that all three seem to have outgrown contemporary categories, formal and conceptual, to give utterance to their intuitions. Close to them, but none the less at a distance, are three other writers: Calvin, Marguerite de Navarre, and Agrippa d'Aubigné. All six were sensitive, briefly or more permanently, to the winds of religious change; the last three turned their backs on certain aspects of the Renaissance, whereas the others, more open-minded, we might think, and more concerned with human values, become associated with important aspects of emerging European civilisation. Rabelais expresses the early enthusiasm (tinged later with more sombre overtones), Ronsard perceives the ambiguity of a crisis of values, Montaigne introduces a greater element of detachment and acceptance. But, all three reflect what is the chief characteristic of our period, its open-endedness. The crisis has set out the elements and areas of debate and discussion; it will be for later generations to offer tidier solutions. Renaissance France brings together resources and riches of mind and sensibility on which later men can build.

FURTHER READING AND STUDY

MODERN editions and critical works take the student so far; there soon comes a moment when he or she wants to look further afield and see sixteenth-century books and manuscripts in their original state. Almost every *seiziémiste* develops a taste for book-collecting and bibliography; there is consequently much to be said for acquiring some knowledge of printing and book production. Reference has already been made to some sixteenth-century publishers and printers (see above, pp. 28–9), and works such as L. Febvre and H.-J. Martin, *L'Apparition du livre*, provide useful lists of books for further reading. The most up-to-date work in English on bibliographical matters is J. P. W. Gaskell, *A New Introduction to Bibliography*, Oxford, 1972. Articles in bibliographical journals, such as *The Library*, *The Bibliotheck*, the *Proceedings of the Cambridge Bibliographical Society*, are worth consulting; to these may be added the journals issued by various libraries (British Museum, John Rylands, etc.) and publications from America and Europe (e.g., *Gutenberg-Jahrbuch*).

Though photographic reprints of Renaissance editions are becoming more common (e.g., Slatkine reprints, *French Renaissance Classics*, the productions of the Scolar Press, etc.), one will wish to inspect the originals in the course of one's study. In France, the resources of the Bibliothèque Nationale seem inexhaustible, in both the printed and the manuscript fields; but one must not forget the remarkable collections in the Arsenal, the Mazarine, the Bibliothèque Sainte-Geneviève, the Sorbonne Library, and the library of the Société de l'Histoire du Protestantisme. Within certain libraries, there are often important Renaissance collections that do not necessarily find their way into the main catalogue (for instance, the Bliss and Rothschild collections in the Bibliothèque Nationale, the latter of which has a printed catalogue by E. Picot for the books). There are also important holdings in the provincial libraries, such as Besançon, Carpentras, Toulouse; but though the manuscripts of these libraries are listed in published catalogues, the printed books have, in most cases, yet to be similarly catered for. One tends to concentrate on Paris in one's early days of research on French resources, and this is understandable and right, but the holdings of libraries in countries affected by the Reformation or in north Italy must not be overlooked; and scholarship may, like charity, begin at home. The

511

British Museum, which has published STCs[1] of French, Italian, and German holdings in the sixteenth century, is impressively rich, and recent accessions (e.g., the library of Holkham Hall) have added valuable material; also in London, the libraries of Dr Williams and of the Warburg Institute hold much in store for the *seiziémiste*. Outside London several types of library are worth exploring.

(i) *University Libraries*. Oxford and Cambridge are remarkably well endowed, and often have works difficult or impossible to find in France; and in addition to the main libraries should be mentioned the holdings of college libraries. H. M. Adams published a few years ago his catalogue of Cambridge college library books printed in the sixteenth century, and information on Oxford holdings is available in the Bodleian. Beyond Cambridge and Oxford, special mention should be made of the John Rylands Library in Manchester and that of Trinity College, Dublin. In Scotland, all the ancient universities, through their Reformation links and the 'auld alliance', have a wealth of material that their printed catalogues, sometimes old enough themselves, do not describe adequately.

(ii) *Special collections* not listed in the general catalogues of university libraries: the Christie collection (Manchester), formed by the biographer of Etienne Dolet, contains many books relating to French humanism during the reign of Francis I and is described in a published catalogue; Edinburgh University possesses the Library of William Drummond of Hawthornden, a catalogue of which has recently been prepared and published by Dr R. H. MacDonald; Glasgow University has several special collections: the Hunterian (of which the catalogue is published), the Stirling-Maxwell collection of emblem books, perhaps the finest in the world (recently catalogued by Miss Hester Black), and the Murray collection, particularly rich in theological literature, but also of wider interest to the Renaissance specialist; St Andrews University has a unique collection of books by George Buchanan, the Scottish humanist who was a friend of Joachim du Bellay and later principal of St Leonards College.

(iii) *Libraries belonging to private families, dioceses, theological colleges*. The holdings of cathedral libraries are being catalogued in the British Museum;[2] outside England, Blairs College (Aberdeen), Kilkenny and Cashel in Ireland have interesting material; and even in a small library such as Innerpeffray (near Crieff, Perthshire), one may find one of the rare known copies of an early edition of Marot's Psalms.

(iv) Finally, the *National Library of Scotland* in Edinburgh, which has recently published a STC of foreign holdings up till 1600.

Many of these libraries are also very rich in manuscript material. Though the manuscripts of many important poets are not extant, bar the occasional fragment – once their works were printed, the hand-written text vanished – there are valuable works that did not reach publication, others are to be found in collections of verse that circulated in manuscript among humanist friends, and there are the private papers of interesting personages. Rasse des Noeux, a Huguenot surgeon, collected six volumes of contemporary verse, militant, humanist, erotic, and these are to be found in the Bibliothèque Nationale, which also houses the indispensable Dupuy collection (of which the catalogue has been printed). Toulouse holds the manuscript letters and poems, Latin and French, of Jean de Boyssonné, while the letters of Antoine Arlier will be found in Aix (Méjanes Library). In the British Museum the Cotton and Harleian collections have a lot of material relevant to sixteenth-century studies (the Harleian has a second manuscript of D'Aubigné's *Tragiques*). Outside France, there are valuable collections in Germany (including the Camerariussammlung in Munich), Switzerland (Bongars collection, Berne, and of course Geneva), and Italy (Turin and the inexhaustible Vatican Library). Both the ramifications of the Renaissance and the vagaries of book-collectors have spread material throughout the length and breadth of Europe, sometimes with unexpected results: one would hardly expect to find a useful collection of Eustorg de Beaulieu editions in Vienna. Nor have I done justice to what is available in the Low Countries or Denmark; and America, with its immense resources, needs a separate description.

One soon learns that much valuable material, original and critical, appears in periodicals and not always in book form. The increase in the number of periodicals over the past few years has been daunting, but the beginner should keep his or her eye on certain areas of periodical literature, in addition to those journals of a general character which deal with more than one modern language over the whole span of European culture (*Modern Language Review, Publications of the Modern Language Association, Studies in Philology, Symposium*, etc.) and which sometimes devote an issue to one single topic or author (e.g., *L'Esprit créateur* on Ronsard, 1970). Among the more specialised journals, the *Bibliothèque d'Humanisme et Renaissance* is indispensable, and one must add *Renaissance News, Studies in the Renaissance, Bulletin de l'Association Guillaume Budé*. Certain periodicals are devoted exclusively to French language and literature: *French Studies, Revue d'Histoire Littéraire de la France, Studi Francesi*. Other categories of journals should not be forgotten: (i) bulletins of societies devoted to one author or topic, e.g., *Bulletin de la Société des Amis de Montaigne*; (ii) journals concerned with the history of ideas; (iii) periodicals in the field of ecclesiastical history, some confined to the Reformation; (iv) specialised journals connected with the history of art and music;

(v) the *Acta* of congresses devoted to Renaissance studies; (vi) *Festschriften* (see General Bibliography, p. 516).

With such a welter of publication, some guidance is welcome, and there are several annual surveys that will prove useful: *The Year's Work in Modern Languages*, the *Bibliographie Internationale de l'Humanisme et de la Renaissance* (published by Droz, Geneva, beginning in 1965), O. Klapp, *Bibliographie der französischen Literaturwissenschaft*, beginning 1960, *Répertoire analytique de Littérature française* (University of Bordeaux). *Studi Francesi* give summaries of work being done in the various centuries, and *Studies in Philology* have also for many years provided bibliographical inventories. Bibliographies useful up to the date of their publication include D. C. Cabeen, *A Critical Bibliography of French Literature*, vol. II, 1956, and A. Cioranescu, *Bibliographie de la littérature française du XVIe siècle*, 1959.

Time and again one comes across names of persons of whom one would like to know more, and it is not always easy to unearth the necessary information. Over and above the dated, but still useful, general biographical dictionaries like the Michaud or the *Biographie nationale générale* of the nineteenth century, there is the more recent *Dictionnaire de biographie française*, from 1933 on; and these can be supplemented by various regional biographical dictionaries (B. Hauréau for the Orléanais, etc.). Invaluable registers of members of the *parlements* have been published; they often give a lot of biographical material about humanists and men of letters who had taken their legal training (e.g., M. Maugis for Paris, F. Saulnier for the *parlement* of Brittany, Fleury Vindry for the others). The *acta* and registers of universities or their faculties often prove useful (Montpellier, Padua, Geneva, Basel, German universities), especially as in a number of instances we have modern editions of these sources. Further material is available in *actes notariés*, such as are found in E. Coyecque's repertory or in the *Minutier Central* (Archives Nationales), whose resources are now being properly explored. In the field of religious history, the extraordinary piece of Benedictine scholarship carried out in the eighteenth century, the *Gallia Christiana*, still renders great service, and on the Calvinist side, over and above Haag's *La France Protestante*, the registers of various churches (e.g., C.-E. Lart's edition of the Loudun register) furnish interesting sidelights and not a few surprises. A mine of information that has yet to be tapped fully is the fund of prefaces and liminary verses written by humanists and poets to one another; these often give dates, an idea of the company kept by a particular writer, his circumstances at some moment of his career, and so forth. No repertory of this material has been compiled and a massive task it would be; nevertheless, certain well-indexed *instruments de travail*, within

limited contexts, are helpful here. On the one hand, there are bio-
graphies of certain printers with detailed descriptions of the books
they published (e.g., P. Renouard's lives of Josse Bade and Simon de
Colines), and the invaluable *Bibliographie lyonnaise* (by Baudrier),
which will soon be matched by the *Bibliographie parisienne* for the
sixteenth century, of which the first two volumes have appeared. And
on the other, a work like F. Lachèvre's *Bibliographie des recueils
collectifs de poésies du XVIe siècle*, by its very nature, tells us a very
great deal about the different groups where literature and learning
flourished. In all this, as the Renaissance believed, it is a case of
veritas filia temporis, but an awareness of the directions in which one
may look for further information is essential and, if gained early, will
save much labour at a later date. Moreover, colleagues in universities
and scholarly libraries are nearly always willing to be consulted.

NOTES

1. This is the accepted abbreviation for *Short-title Catalogue*; in French
bibliographical circles, colleagues refer to 'un short-title', abbreviating according to well-established linguistic principle.
2. Peterborough Cathedral Library has recently been housed on permanent
loan in Cambridge University Library; it contains among other things a
collection of English pamphlets on the French wars of religion and one of
the two known copies (in public libraries) of Ronsard's *Elegies, Mascarades et
Bergerie*, 1565. This copy, though damaged in the last post-liminary pages,
provides a splendid state of the main text.

GENERAL BIBLIOGRAPHY

English titles are published in London, French ones in Paris unless otherwise indicated. A few titles have been shortened, but not beyond the point of identification. For abbreviations used to show periodicals and series, see above, pp. xxiii–xxiv.

GENERAL

Below a selected list of books is given under relevant rubrics; the books in the General Bibliography do not normally include titles relevant to specific authors.

Earlier histories of French literature have still much to offer, even as far back as the *Tableau* by A. Darmsteter and A. Hatzfeld; A. A. Tilley's *The Literature of the French Renaissance*, 2 vols., Cambridge, 1904, is still valuable, as is the same author's *The Dawn of the French Renaissance*, Cambridge, 1918. See also surveys by R. Morçay and A. Müller, *La Renaissance*, 1961; H. Morf, *Geschichte der französischen Literatur im Zeitalter der Renaissance*, Strasbourg, 1914; and J. Plattard, *La Renaissance des lettres en France de Louis XII à Henri IV*, 1931. More recent surveys include A.-M. Schmidt's contribution to the Pléiade history of literatures; *French Literature and its Background*, I. *The Sixteenth Century*, ed. J. Cruickshank, 1968; and D. Stone, *France in the Sixteenth Century*, Englewood Cliffs, 1969. See also the genre surveys in the *Collection U*.

Useful volumes containing material over a wide field include H. Chamard, *Origines de la poésie française de la Renaissance*, 1932; A. Lefranc, *Grands Ecrivains français de la Renaissance*, 1914; and A.-M. Schmidt, *Etudes sur le XVIe siècle*, 1967. Interesting articles crop up in the increasing number of *Festschriften* offered to distinguished scholars: A. Lefranc, P. Laumonier, H. Chamard, E. Huguet, P. Jourda, R. Lebègue, H. W. Lawton, A. M. Boase, W. L. Wiley, Morris Bishop. Use should also be made of the various Dictionaries: *Dictionnaire des lettres françaises. Le Seizième Siècle*, ed. Grente, 1951; *Dictionnaire de biographie française* (ed. J. Batteau, R. Barroux, M. Prévost), in course of publication since 1933; *Dictionnaire de théologie catholique* (ed. A. Vacant and E. Mangenot), 15 tomes, 1909–50. The *Dizionario critico*, ed. F. Simone, 2 vols., Turin, appeared in the autumn of 1972.

There are a number of useful anthologies on the market: F. Gray in the United States, V. E. Graham in Canada; A. Boase, *The Poetry of France, I. 1400–1600*, 1964 and the Pléiade *Poètes du XVIe siècle*; the older collection of *Satires françaises* by Fleuret and Perceau is still valuable, as is that of H. de Montaiglon and J. de Rothschild, *Recueil de poésie française des XVe et XVIe siècles*, 13 vols., 1855–1878. In the field of the theatre, reference will still be made to Viollet-le-Duc, *Ancien théâtre français*, 10 vols., 1854–57, and E. Fournier, *Le Théâtre français avant la Renaissance (1430–1550)*, 1872, and *Le Théâtre français au XVIe et au XVIIe siècle*, 1871, so long as certain plays have not attracted the attention of modern editors.

HISTORY OF FRANCE

F. Braudel, *La Méditerranée et le monde méditerranéen à l'époque de Philippe II*, 2 vols., 1948.

A. Chastel, *The Crisis of the Renaissance*, Geneva, 1968.

J. Delumeau, *La Civilisation de la Renaissance*, 1967.

A. Denieul-Cormier, *La France de la Renaissance, 1488–1559*, 1962.

W. K. Ferguson, *Renaissance Studies*, Toronto, 1962.

A. Franklin, *Paris et les Parisiens au seizième siècle*, 1921.

H. Hauser and A. Renaudet, *Les Débuts de l'âge moderne* (Peuples et Civilisations, VIII), 1956.

H. Hauser, *La Prépondérance espagnole (1559–1600)* (Peuples et Civilisations, IX), 1948.

J. Huizinga, *The Waning of the Middle Ages*, 1924.

E. Lavisse, *Histoire de France depuis les origines jusqu'à la Révolution*, Vols. V, VI, 1906.

P. S. Lewis, *Later Medieval France – The Polity*, 1968.

J. Russell Major, *Representative Institutions in Renaissance France, 1421–1559*, Madison, 1960.

R. Mandrou, *Introduction à la France moderne. Essai de psychologie historique, 1500–1640*, Paris, 1961.

F. Mauro, *Le XVIe Siècle européen. Aspects économiques*, 1966.

R. Mousnier, *Les XVIe et XVIIe siècles. Les progrès de la civilisation européenne et le déclin de l'Orient (1492–1715)* (Histoire générale des civilisations, IV), 1961.

New Cambridge Modern History. I. *The Renaissance c. 1493–1520*; II. *The Reformation c. 1520–1559*.

M. Poëte, *Une Vie de cité. Paris de sa naissance à nos jours*. Vol. II. *La Cité de la Renaissance*, 1927.

H. Sée, *Histoire économique de la France*, 2 vols., 1948.

H. Sée, A. Rebillon, E. Préclin, *Le XVIe Siècle* (Clio), 1950.

J. W. Thompson, *The Wars of Religion in France, 1559–1576*, London–New York, 1958.

M. Venard, *Les Débuts du monde moderne* (Le Monde et son histoire, VI), 1967.

CURRENTS OF THOUGHT

P. Barrière, *La Vie intellectuelle en France du XVI⁰ siècle à l'époque contemporaine*, 1961.

E. Bréhier, *Histoire de la Philosophie*. I. *L'Antiquité et le Moyen Age*, pt. 3. *Moyen Age et Renaissance*, 1945.

H. Busson, *Le Rationalisme dans la littérature française de la Renaissance*, 2nd ed. 1957.

E. Cassirer, *Das Erkenntnisproblem in der Philosophie und Wissenschaft der neueren Zeit*, Berlin, 1906.

——, *Individuum und Kosmos in der Philosophie der Renaissance*, Leipzig, 1927.

F. Dainville, *La Géographie des humanistes*, 1940.

W. K. Ferguson, *The Renaissance in Historical Thought*, New York, 1948.

E. Gilson, *History of Christian Philosophy in the Middle Ages*, 1955.

W. L. Gundersheimer (ed.), *French Humanism 1470–1600*, 1969.

H. Haydn, *The Counter-Renaissance*, 1963.

A. Levi, *French Moralists. The Theory of the Passions 1585 to 1649*, Oxford, 1964.

D. Ménager, *Introduction à la vie littéraire du XVI⁰ siècle*, 1970.

R. H. Popkin, *The History of Scepticism from Erasmus to Descartes*, Leiden, 1960., revised ed. 1968.

E. Rice, *The Renaissance Idea of Wisdom*, Cambridge, Mass. 1958.

F. Simone, *Il Rinascimento francese*, Turin, 1961.

——, *Umanesimo, Rinascimento, Barocco in Francia*, Milan, 1968.

——, *Per una Storia della storiografia letteraria francese*, Vol. I, Turin, 1966.

D. P. Walker, *Spiritual and Demonic Magic from Ficino to Campanella*, 1958.

F. A. Yates, *The French Academies of the Sixteenth Century*, 1967. (See also her *Giordano Bruno and the Hermetic Tradition*, 1964; *The Art of Memory*, 1966.)

L. Zanta, *La Renaissance du stoïcisme au XVI⁰ siècle*, 1914.

HISTORY OF SCIENCE

A. C. Crombie, *Augustine to Galileo. The History of Science* A.D. *400–1650*, 1952.

——, *Robert Grosseteste and the Origins of Experimental Science 1100–1700*, Oxford, 1953.

A. R. Hall, *The Scientific Revolution 1500–1800*, 1954.

C. J. Singer, *A Short History of Science to the Nineteenth Century*, Oxford, 1941.

L. Thorndike, *A History of Magic and Experimental Science*, Vols. V and VI. *The Sixteenth Century*, New York, 1941.

W. P. D. Wightman, *Science and the Renaissance* (Aberdeen University Studies), 2 vols., Edinburgh, 1962.

RELIGIOUS HISTORY

R. H. Bainton, *The Reformation of the Sixteenth Century*, 1953.

O. Chadwick, *The Reformation* (Pelican), Harmondsworth, 1964.

J. Delumeau, *Naissance et affirmation de la Réforme*, 1966.

A. G. Dickens, *Reformation and Society in Sixteenth-century Europe*, 1966.

——, *The Counter-reformation*, 1968.

L. Febvre, *Le Problème de l'incroyance au XVIᵉ siècle*, 1942.

A. Fliche and V. Martin, *Histoire générale de l'Eglise*, Vols. XV–XVI, 1951–52.

H. Hauser, *Etudes sur la Réforme française*, 1909.

A. L. Herminjard, *Correspondance des Réformateurs dans les pays de langue française*, 9 vols., Geneva, 1871–97.

A. Hyma, *The Christian Renaissance*, 1924.

P. Imbart de la Tour, *Les Origines de Réforme*, 4 vols., 1905–35.

H. Jedin, *Geschichte des Konzils von Trient*, 2 vols., Freiburg, 1949–1951. English translation, *History of the Council of Trent*, 2 vols., 1957–61.

B. J. Kidd, *The Counter-reformation*, 1933.

W. G. Moore, *La Réforme allemande et la littérature française: recherches sur la notoriété de Luther en France*, Strasbourg, 1930.

S. Mours, *Le Protestantisme en France au XVIᵉ siècle*, 1959.

A. Renaudet, *Préréforme et humanisme à Paris pendant les premières guerres d'Italie (1494–1517)*, 2nd revised ed. 1953.

H. A. E. Van Gelder, *The Two Reformations in the Sixteenth Century*, The Hague, 1961.

POLITICAL THEORY

J. W. Allen, *A History of Political Thought in the Sixteenth Century*, 1928.

C. Bontemps, L.-P. Raybaud, J.-P. Brancourt, *Le Prince dans la France des XVIᵉ et XVIIᵉ siècles*, 1965 (includes text of Guillaume Budé's *Institution du Prince*).

V. de Caprariis, *Propaganda e pensiero politico in Francia durante le guerre di religione*, I. (1559–1572), Naples, 1959.

R. W. and A. J. Carlyle, *A History of Medieval Political Thought in the West*, Vol. VI, Edinburgh and London, 1936.

W. F. Church, *Constitutional Thought in Sixteenth-century France*, Cambridge, Mass., 1941.

J. C. Lyons, 'Conceptions of the republic in French literature of the sixteenth century', *RR*, 1930.

P. Mesnard, *L'Essor de la philosophie politique au XVIᵉ siècle*, 1936.

V. P. Mortari, *Diritto romano e diritto nazionale in Francia nel secolo XVI*, Milan, 1962.

B. Reynolds, *Proponents of Limited Monarchy in Sixteenth-century France*, New York, 1931.

G. Weill, *Les Théories sur le pouvoir royal pendant les guerres de religion*, 1892.

PRINTING

E. Armstrong, *Robert Estienne, Royal Printer*, Cambridge, 1954.

J. Baudrier, *Bibliographie lyonnaise* . . . , Lyons, 1895–1921 (with *Tables* by G. Tricou, *THR*, 1950, for the 12 vols.).

R. Brun, *Le Livre français*, 1948.

A. Cartier, M. Audin, E. Vial, *Bibliographie des éditions des de Tournes*, 1937.

R. C. Christie, *Etienne Dolet, the Martyr of the Renaissance, 1508–1546*, 1899.

A. Claudin, *Histoire de l'imprimerie à Paris*, 3 vols., 1900–04.

L. Febvre and H.-J. Martin, *L'Apparition du livre*, 1958.

A. de La Bouralière, *L'Imprimerie et la librairie à Poitiers pendant le XVIᵉ siècle*, 1900.

P. Renouard, *Bibliographie des impressions et des œuvres de Josse Bade Ascensius, imprimeur et humaniste, 1462–1535*, 3 vols., 1909.

——, *Bibliographie des éditions de Simon de Colines, imprimeur – libraire à Paris, 1520–1546*, 1894.

——, *Répertoire des imprimeurs parisiens . . . jusqu'a la fin du XVIᵉ siècle*, enlarged ed. by J. Veyrin-Forrer and B. Moreau, 1965.

S. H. Steinberg, *Five Hundred Years of Printing* (Pelican), Harmondsworth, 1955.

J. Veyrin-Forrer and others, *Imprimeurs et libraires parisiens du XVIᵉ siècle*, 1965–, in course of publication.

COURT, CEREMONIES AND OTHER ARTS

M. Aubert, *La Sculpture française du moyen-âge et de la Renaissance*, Paris–Brussels, 1926.

S. Béguin, *L'Ecole de Fontainebleau*, 1963.

R. Blomfield, *History of French Architecture, 1494–1661*, 1911.

A. Blunt, *Art and Architecture in France 1500–1700*, 1953.

E. Bourciez, *Les Mœurs polies et la littérature de cour sous Henri II*, 1886.

J. Chartrou, *Les Entrées solennelles et triomphales de la Renaissance*, 1928.
F. Decrue de Stutz, *La Cour de France et la société du XVIe siècle*, 1888.
L. Dimier, *La Peinture française au XVIe siècle*, Marseilles, 1942.
F. Gébelin, *Le Style Renaissance en France*, 1942.
R. E. Giesey, *The Royal Funeral Ceremony in Renaissance France*, THR, 1960.
L. Hautecœur, *Histoire de l'architecture classique en France*, I, 1943, revised ed. 1965.
T. G. Jackson, *The Renaissance of Roman Architecture*. III. *France*, Cambridge, 1923.
J. Jacquot (ed.), *Les Fêtes de la Renaissance*, I, 1960.
New Oxford History of Music, Vols. II and III.
G. Reese, *Music in the Renaissance*, 1954.
W. L. Wiley, *The Gentleman of Renaissance France*, Cambridge, Mass., 1954.
F. A. Yates, *The French Academies of the Sixteenth Century*, 1947.
——, *The Valois Tapestries*, 1959.

CRITICAL THEORY[1]

In addition to the works mentioned elsewhere in the Bibliography by H. Gmelin, H. W. Lawton, and W. F. Patterson, the following will be found useful:
J. W. H. Atkins, *English Literary Criticism: The Renascence*, 1947.
E. Langlois, *Recueils d'arts de seconde rhétorique*, 1902.
Ramus (P. de La Ramée), *La Dialectique* (1955), ed. M. Dassonville, THR, 1964.
G. Saintsbury, *A History of Criticism* . . . , 3 vols., Edinburgh–London, 1900–04.
L. A. Sonnino, *A Handbook to Sixteenth-century Rhetoric*, 1968.
J. E. Spingarn, *A History of Literary Criticism in the Renaissance*, New York, 1899.
K. Varga, *Rhétorique et littérature*, 1970.
B. Weinberg, *Critical Prefaces of the French Renaissance*, Evanston, 1950.

THEMES

Classical Mythology

General
J. Seznec, *La Survivance des dieux antiques*, 1947.
G. Demerson, *La Mythologie classique dans l'œuvre lyrique de la Pléiade*, THR, 1972.

Bacchus

T. C. Cave, 'The Triumph of Bacchus', *Humanism in France,*
ed. A. H. T. Levi, Manchester, 1970.

——, 'Ronsard's Bacchic poetry: from the *Bacchanales* to the
Hymne de l'autonne', *ECr*, 1970.

Daphne

Y. Giraud, *La Fable de Daphné*, Geneva, 1969.

Diane

F. Bardon, *Diane de Poitiers et le mythe de Diane*, 1963.

Golden Age

E. Armstrong, *Ronsard and the Age of Gold*, Cambridge, 1968.

Hercules

M. R. Jung, *Hercule dans la littérature française du XVIe siècle,*
THR, 1966.

R. Trousson, 'Ronsard et la légende d'Hercule', *BHR*, 1962.

R. Hallmark, 'Ronsard et la légende d'Hercule', *Lumières de la*
Pléiade, 1966.

R. E. Hallowell, 'L'Hercule Gallique: expression et image
poétique', ibid.

Orpheus

E. Kuschner, 'Le personnage d'Orphée chez Ronsard', ibid.

F. Joukovsky, *Orphée et ses disciples . . .* , Geneva, 1970.

F. Gersuny, *Orpheus der Logosträger*, Munich (announced).

Prometheus

R. Trousson, *Le Thème de Prométhée dans la littérature euro-*
péenne, Geneva, 1964.

Court

P. M. Smith, *The Anti-courtier trend in Sixteenth-century French*
Literature, THR, 1966.

Bourgeois

J. V. Alter, *Les Origines de la satire anti-bourgeoise en France–*
Moyen Age–XVIe siècle, THR, 1966.

Death

E. DuBruck, *The Theme of Death in French Poetry of the Middle*
Ages and of the Renaissance, The Hague, 1964.

Glory

F. Joukovsky, *La Gloire dans la poésie française et néo-latine du*
XVIe siecle, THR, 1969.

THEATRE

(i) General

G. Bapst, *Essai sur l'histoire du théâtre* . . . , 1893.

A. Baschet, *Les Comédiens italiens à la cour de France sous Charles IX, Henri III, Henri IV et Louis XIII*, 1882.

L. E. Dabney, *French Dramatic Literature in the Reign of Henri IV*, Austin, 1952.

L.-F. Gofflot, *Le Théâtre au collège du moyen âge à nos jours*, 1947.

M. Horn-Monval, *Traductions et adaptations françaises du théâtre étranger*, 3 vols., 1958–60.

J. Jacquot (ed.), *Le Lieu théâtral à la Renaissance*, 1964.

H. Kindermann, *Theatergeschichte Europas*, Vols. II–IV, Salzburg, 1959–61.

H. W. Lawton, *A Handbook of French Renaissance Dramatic Theory*, Manchester, 1949.

H. C. Lancaster, *The French Tragi-comedy – its Origins and Development from 1552 to 1628*, 1907.

D. Roaten, *Structural Form in the French Theatre 1500–1700*, Philadelphia, 1960.

W. L. Wiley, *The Early Public Theatre in France*, Cambridge, Mass., 1960.

(ii) Tragedy

H. B. Charlton, *The Senecan Tradition in Renaissance Tragedy*, Manchester, 1946.

E. Faguet, *La Tragédie française au XVIe siècle (1550–1600)*, 1883.

E. Forsyth, *La Tragédie française de Jodelle à Corneille (1553–1640)*, 1962.

F. Holl, *Das politische und religiöse Tendenzdrama des sechzehnten Jahrhunderts in Frankreich*, Erlangen, 1903.

G. Lanson, *Esquisse d'une histoire de la tragédie française*, New York, 1920.

G. Lanson, 'L'Idée de la tragédie en France avant Jodelle', *RHLF*, 1904.

R. Lebègue, *La Tragédie française de la Renaissance*, Brussels–Paris, 1954.

——, *La Tragédie religieuse en France. Les Débuts (1514–1573)*, 1929.

——, 'Tableau de la tragédie française de 1573 à 1610', *BHR*, 1944.

K. Loukovitch, *L'Evolution de la tragédie religieuse classique en France*, 1933.

(iii) Comedy

G. Attinger, *L'Esprit de la commedia dell'arte dans le théâtre français*, 1950.

D. C. Boughner, *The Braggart in Renaissance Comedy*, Minneapolis, 1954.

B. C. Bowen, *Les Caractéristiques essentielles de la farce française et leur survivance dans les années 1550–1620*, Urbana, 1964.

E. Chasles, *La Comédie en France au seizième siècle*, 1862.

R. Garapon, *La Fantaisie verbale et le comique dans le théâtre français*, 1957.

H. Haag, *Der Gestaltwandel der Kuppler in der französischen Literatur des sechzehnten und siebzehnten Jahrhunderts*, Marburg, 1936.

M. T. Herrick, *Comic Theory in the Sixteenth Century*, Urbana, 1964.

A. Hindley, *The Development and Diffusion of Farce in France towards the End of the Middle Ages* (Hull thesis).

B. Jeffery, *French Renaissance Comedy 1552–1630*, Oxford, 1969.

R. Lebègue, 'Tableau de la comédie française de la Renaissance', *BHR*, 1946.

E. Lintilhac, *La Comédie: moyen âge et Renaissance*, 1905.

E. Rigal, *De Jodelle à Molière*, 1911.

Irene Weil, *Einige Personen der französischen Renaissance Komödie. Ihre Herkunft und Entwicklung*, Heidelberg, 1965.

GENRES (NON-DRAMATIC)

Blason

R. Pike, 'The Blasons in French literature of the 16th century', *RR*, 1936.

D. B. Wilson, *Descriptive Poetry in France from Blason to Baroque*, Manchester, 1967.

Cantique

Erika Keil, *'Cantique' und 'Hymne' in der französischen Lyrik*, Bonn, 1966.

Conte and Novel

W. F. J. De Jongh, *A Bibliography of the novel and short story in French from the beginning of printing till 1600*, Albuquerque, 1944.

W. Pabst, *Novellentheorie und Novellendichtung, zur Geschichte ihrer Antinomie in der romanischen Literatur*, Hamburg, 1967.

W. Redenbacher, 'Die Novellistik der französischen Hochrenaissance', *ZFSL*, 1927.

J. M. Ferrier, *Forerunners of the French Novel*, Manchester, 1954.

W. Söderhjelm, *La Nouvelle française au XVᵉ siècle*, 1910.

G. Reynier, *Les Origines du roman réaliste*, 1912; *Le Roman sentimental avant L'Astrée*, 1908.

Devotional Poetry
 T. C. Cave, *Devotional Poetry in France c. 1570–1613*, Cambridge, 1969.

Eclogue
 A. Hulubei, *L'Eglogue en France au XVIe siècle*, 1938.
 ——, *Répertoire des Eglogues en France au XVIe siècle*, 1938.

Elegy
 R. Mahieu, 'L'Elégie au XVIe siècle. Essai sur l'histoire du genre', *RHLF*, 1939.
 C. M. Scollen, *The Birth of the Elegy in France 1500–1550*, *THR*, 1967.

Hymn
 M. Dassonville, 'Eléments pour une définition de l'hymne ronsardien', *BHR*, 1962.

Ode
 D. Janik, *Geschichte der Ode und der 'Stances' von Ronsard bis Boileau*, Berlin–Zurich, 1968.
 C. Maddison, *Apollo and the Nine. A History of the Ode*, 1960.

Psalm Paraphrase
 M. Jeanneret, *Poésie et tradition biblique au seizième siècle*, 1969.

Satire
 C. Lenient, *La Satire en France ou la littérature militante au XVIe siècle*, 2 vols., 1877.
 C. A. Mayer, London thesis on Satire 1500–1550.

Sonnet
 M. Jasinski, *Histoire du sonnet en France*, Douai, 1903.
 E. V. Olmsted, *The Sonnet in French Literature*, New York, 1897.
 H. Vaganay, *Le Sonnet en Italie et en France au XVIe siècle*, 2 vols., Lyons, 1902–03.

VERSIFICATION

H. Chatelain, *Recherches sur le vers français au XVe siècle*, 1907.

W. Th. Elwert, *Französische Metrik*, Munich, 1961.

L. E. Kastner, *A History of French Versification*, Oxford, 1903.

W. F. Patterson, *Three Centuries of French Poetic Theory*, 2 vols., Ann Arbor, 1935.

P. Martinon, *Les Strophes*, 1912.

A. Tobler, *Vom französischen Versbau alter und neuer Zeit*, Leipzig, 1921.

LITERARY INFLUENCES

(i) *Classical*

Catullus

M. Morrison, 'Catullus in the Neo-latin poetry of France before 1550', *BHR*, 1955.
——, *Catullus in France before 1560*, Cambridge thesis.

Greek Anthology

J. Hutton, *The Greek Anthology in France and in the Latin Writers of the Netherlands to the Year 1800*, Ithaca, 1946.

Horace

R. Lebègue, 'Horace en France pendant la Renaissance', *HR*, 1936.

Lucian

C. A. Mayer, London thesis on Satire 1500–50.
L. C. Stevens, 'The reputation of Lucian in XVIth-century France', *SFr*, 1967.

Lucretius

E. Belowski, *Lukrez in der französischen Literatur der Renaissance*, Berlin, 1934.
S. Fraisse, *L'Influence de Lucrèce en France au seizième siècle*, 1962.
C. A. Fusil, 'La renaissance de Lucrèce au XVIᵉ siècle en France', *RSS*, 1928.

Ovid

E. K. Rand, *Ovid and his Influence*, 1926.

Platonism

R. V. Merrill and R. J. Clements, *Platonism in French Renaissance Poetry*, New York, 1957.

Terence

H. W. Lawton, *Térence en France au XVIᵉ siècle*, 1926, Tome II. **Imitation et influence*, Geneva, 1927. This valuable sequel is important for its discussion of the French comedy of the period.

Vergil

L. Comparetti, *Vergil in the Middle Ages*, London–New York, 1895.
A. Hulubei, 'Virgile en France au XVIᵉ siècle', *RSS*, 1931.
H. Raul, *Französische Vergilübersetzungen in der zweiten Hälfte des sechzehnten Jahrhunderts*, Cologne, 1966.

See also more general surveys:

R. R. Bolgar, *The Classical Heritage and its Beneficiaries*, Cambridge, 1954.
J. E. Sandys, *A History of Classical Scholarship*, 3 vols., Cambridge, 1931.

(ii) Modern

Ariosto
A. Cameron, *The Influence of Ariosto's Epic and Lyric Poetry on Ronsard and his Group*, Baltimore, 1930.
A. Cioranescu, *L'Arioste en France, des origines à la fin du XVIIIe siècle*, 2 vols., 1939.

Boccaccio
L. Sozzi, *Boccaccio in Francia nel Cinquecento*, Florence, 1971.

Petrarchism
L. Forster, *The Icy Fire*, Cambridge, 1969.
J. Vianey, *Le Pétrarquisme en France au XVIe siècle*, Montpellier, 1909.

Platonism (Ficinian)
J. Festugière, *La Philosophie de l'amour de Marsile Ficin et son influence sur la littérature française au XVIe siècle*, 1941.
W. Mönch, *Die Italienische Platonrenaissance und ihre Bedeutung für Frankreichs Literatur- und Geistesgeschichte*, Berlin, 1936.

Tasso
C. B. Beall, *La Fortune du Tasse en France*, Eugene, 1942.
See also:
H. Gmelin, 'Das Prinzip der Imitatio in den romanischen Literaturen der Renaissance', *RF*, 1932.

NOTE

1. On Poetic Theory see above, p. 17, note 8. See also C. G. Dubois, *Mythe et langage au XVIe siècle*, Bordeaux, 1970.

GLOSSARY

Adunaton: Figure involving description as something impossible: e.g., opening of Scève, *Délie*, xvii: Plus tost seront Rhosne, & Saone desjoinctz,/Que d'avec toy mon cœur se desassemble.

Anadiplosis: (or *reduplicatio*). Repetition of a word ending a clause, and beginning the next.

Anagogical: Spiritual, elevating reading of the sacred texts (from Greek ἀναγωγικός, mystical).

Anaphora: Repetition of the word at the opening of successive clauses (also termed *repetitio*). In verse, this figure may occur at the start of a line or at the hemistich.

Annates: Normally the first-year income of an ecclesiastical benefice which went to the Papal Chest.

Annexée: Rhyme in which the root of the word involved is used in the word opening the following line (Kastner quotes Fabri: Ainsi se faict rithme annexée,/Annexant vers à aultre vers).

Antonomasia: (or *pronominatio*). The use of something other than the proper name to designate a person: this might be an epithet or some reference to one of his most distinctive characteristics.

Ballade: Usually in our period a poem of three stanzas and the *envoi* (=half-stanza). The stanzas were 8 or 10 lines long, according as to whether the lines were octo- or decasyllabic.

Basoche: Originally the name of a court set up to rule on differences between the *clercs* of the Paris *Parlement*, and by extension, name given to the *clercs* as a social group, or class.

Bâtelée: Rhyme in which the word used at the end of the line recurs at the cæsura of the following line.

Black-letter: Gothic type.

Blason: In poetry, a form of descriptive poetry (see also D. B. Wilson *Descriptive Poetry...*, pp. 6 ff.).

Caractères de civilité: A printing type associated with Lyons towards the end of the 1550s. So-called because it was used in two books called *Civile Honnesteté pour les Enfans* and *La Civilité puerile*, it imitated a form of Gothic script; though attractive, it did not catch on, with the growing convenience of roman and italic.

Cartel: Challenge in joust or tourney; a feature of court poetry (examples in Ronsard).

Chant royal: Rhétoriqueur form of *ballade* usually addressed to some august personage (e.g., Blessed Virgin Mary), and couched in five stanzas of 10 or 11 decasyllables + the *envoi* of six or seven lines; the last line of the stanzas and the *envoi* was always the same.

Cheville: Padding in line of poetry.

Chiasmus: Reversal of word or part of speech in the consecutive pattern *abba* (cf. Du Bellay: ... quel est celuy qui si bien se desguise,/ Qu'il semble homme de guerre entre les gens d'eglise,/Et entre gens de guerre aux prestres est pareil?).

Chronogram: Poem, usually in Latin, in which the letters denoting numerals (M,D,I, etc.), when detached and set out, give the year of birth or some other important date relevant to the person to whom the poem is addressed.

Compar: (or *isocolon*). The balancing of two clauses of equal length. Cf. *Délie,* xiv: Elle me tient par ces cheveulx lyé,/Et je la tien par ceulx là mesmes prise.

Contaminatio: Mingling of various sources to form the pattern of a poem or passage of poem.

Coq-à-l'âne: Sebillet's definition of this genre is given up on p. 110.

Correctio: Substitution of a more suitable word for one just used (e.g., *Délie,* li: Si grand beaulté, mais bien si grand merveille). The figure is also termed *epanorthosis.*

Couronnée: Rhyme which doubles the last syllable of the line.

Devotio moderna: A movement of religious reform associated with the Low Countries in the fifteenth century, and more especially with the Brothers of the Common Life at Windesheim, it laid great stress on inner devotion and was an important aspect of the pre-Reformation.

Emblem: In poetry a symbolic picture accompanied by a motto and a short poem; related to but distinct from the *devise,* which for instance allows only a limited number of figures in its picture and may have a more particular reference to some person (often of noble origin).

Emperiere: Rhyme in which the sound is repeated thrice at the end of the line.

Erastian: Refers to Erastus who denied the power of excommunication to the Anglican Church; also defines the view that the Church should be subordinate to the state.

Euhemerist: View that considers the pagan gods to be mortals elevated by man to the status of deities.

Evangelical: In our period an attitude, rather than a precise doctrine, of humanists who, influenced by Erasmus, sought a liberalisation and interiorisation of religious outlook. This attitude is very much abroad around 1530 and leaves its mark on authors such as Marguerite de Navarre and Rabelais.

Exclamatio: Used to play upon varying emotions (admiration, grief) in the listener.

Exemplum: Illustration of argument by reference to deeds of illustrious personages.

Figure: General word to denote a type of rhetorical device.

Fratrisée: (or *enchaînée*). Describes a rhyme used at the end of a line and at the beginning of the following line.

Gallican(ism): Attitude that favours a certain national autonomy in the administration of church affairs, as opposed to Ultramontanism which asserts the central authority of the Pope.

Genethliacon: Birthday poem.

Gradatio: A chain-sequence of words in the form of *anadiplosis*: e.g., *Délie*, xliii: Moins je la voy, certes plus je la hays:/Plus je la hays, & moins elle me fasche./Plus je l'estime, & moins compte j'en fais:/Plus je la fuys, plus veulx, qu'elle me sache. Also termed *climax*.

Greek Anthology: A compilation of Greek verse stretching over a number of centuries, and coming down to us through two main traditions (in the early Renaissance, the Planudean tradition is known). A source of humanist inspiration (love verse, epitaphs, epigrams, pattern poems, verse to patrons, etc.).

Hesuchist: Used of humanists who maintain a discreet silence about their true (evangelical) convictions.

Hexameric: Refers to poems treating of the six days of Creation.

Icon: A poem which celebrates a personage of note, and therefore combines elements of the *blason, exemplum,* and epitaph. It may be accompanied by a picture of the person in question, but this is by no means obligatory.

Léonine: (or *renforcée*). Rhyme which occurs at the cæsura and at the end of the same line.

Macaronic: Burlesque, often mock-epic poetry in which Latin endings are tagged on to vernacular words. In France, only a few sixteenth-century authors try their hand at the genre: Antoine Arena, Belleau, Bèze, and perhaps Etienne des Accords (Tabourot).

Mascarade: Poetry written for noblemen acting in this court genre, which also involved dancing.

Musica reservata: Refers to a certain kind of music recognisable to contemporaries in the Low Countries, France, Germany, and Italy, but not easily identified today. G. Reese, *Music in the Renaissance,* lists current theories about its nature, p. 514: (i) music expressive of the emotions suggested by the text, (ii) music reserved in expression, (iii) music with improvised ornamentation, (iv) music reserved in its use of figuration, (v) music reserved for an élite.

Numerology: The mystical science of numbers.

Paronomasia: Play on similar sounds of words.

Pasquier: Originally a satire affixed to the statue of Pasquino in Rome; then, by extension, a certain form of satiric verse.

Pelagian: Refers to the views of Pelagius (fifth century), who believed that Original Sin was not transmitted down the generations and that God's grace was granted according to individual man's achievement.

Philautia: Self-love.

Poetrie: May be used of the *rhétoriqueur* mixed form of prose and verse.

Prosopopœia: Speech by an absent or imaginary figure (e.g., la France éplorée during the civil wars) or a dead person addressing the passing traveller reading an epitaph on a tomb (*Viator*).

Protatio: Refers to a character appearing only in the prologue or opening part of a play.

Sententia: Lapidary generalisation.

Stance: The term appears to have been first used by Héroët in 1550 *à propos* of a translation from the Italian; but the *stance* rarely corresponds to the *stanza* or *ottavarima*; in the plural *stances*, it is difficult to distinguish from the *ode*. The term becomes popular in the last decades of the century, being used not only by Desportes and later Malherbe, but by a number of poets with Calvinist leanings.

Stichomythia: Originally in Greek a conversation in alternate lines, the term describes conversation in alternate lines or couplets in tragedy.

Style: In rhetoric, style is divided into three divisions: grand (*magniloquens*), medium (*mediocre*), and low (*humile*). See, for instance, Scaliger's *Poetice*, or D'Aubigné's preface to the *Tragiques*.

Syndérèse: Theological term denoting remorse, penitence.

Synergism: Refers to the view according to which divine grace and human will co-operate in the progress of man towards his salvation.

Topos: A commonplace theme.

Traductio: A word repeated in a variety of forms or parts of speech.

Trope: A figure of rhetoric that involves the substitution of one or more words for others.

Tropological: From the Greek τροπολογικός, denotes the figurative interpretation of the Bible.

Vers mesurés à l'antique: Poetry written according to the quantitative principles of classical poetry (e.g., Baïf's experiments in elegiac couplets or Tennyson's use of the hendecasyllable).

Vers mesurés à la lyre: Verse written in such a way as to be suitable for musical setting.

Vers rapportés: Poetry in which a series of words are related not to each other, but respectively to a series of other parts of speech enumerated subsequently. W. T. Elwert quotes as an example a sonnet by the sieur de Porchères, of which this is the beginning:

> La grandeur et l'amour, le destin, la victoire
> D'un Dieu, d'une beauté du Ciel et des soldats
> Conduise, enflamme, anime et pousse en mille parts
> Tes pas, ton cœur, ton âme et la vertu notoire . . .

Zeugma: Figure in which one verb does service for more than one clause; but other parts of speech may serve for the series (e.g., she left in her carriage and high dudgeon).

A NOTE ON DATING

Some confusion arises in dates given by sixteenth-century sources as a result of the fact that there were different ways of reckoning the beginning of the calendar year: the dates varied from 25 December or 1 January to 25 March or Easter. Therefore, this means that a book whose preface or privilege is dated, say, 22 February 1521 (old style) would be reckoned, by the 'new style', to belong to 1522; but difficulties will naturally arise from the lack of standardised practice, and only in 1563 does Charles IX decree that in future the calendar year will begin on 1 January; the decree was not registered by the *Parlement* until January 1567. There is of course a further modification in that Pope Gregory XIII reforms the calendar in 1582: in France, a decree orders that the ten 'lost' days in the Julian calendar shall be made up by dating 9 December as the twentieth day of the month.

INDEX

The Index is divided into three sections; it covers the main text but not the section on further reading (pp. 511–15).

I. INDEX OF NAMES

(Includes names of persons, biblical and mythological figures, anonymous works, some collective volumes, places, and historical events. Contemporary critics are not listed and names of characters in sixteenth-century texts discussed in the book are omitted, apart from one or two rare exceptions.)

Abel, 354, 355
Academies, 15, 203, 208, 209, 213, 219, 281, 283, 312, **366**, 395, 415
Actæon, 412
Adam, 382, 383
Adamson, P., 279
Aeneas, 171
Aeneas, Sylvius (Piccolomini), 39, 168
Aeschylus, **426–7**
Africa, 225
Agrippa, C., 181, **207**, 222
Aix-en-Provence, 368, 397
Alaigre, A., 422, 439
Alberti, L.-B., 137, 149
Alciat, A., 3, 81, **92**, 148, 150, 156, 201, 369, 398
Aléandre, J., 27, 79
Alexis, G., 65
Almain, J. (*Almanus*), 54, 469
Alsace-Lorraine, 2
Amadis de Gaule, 50, 99, 137, 199, 234, **236–7**, 255, 365, 464
Amboise, conjuration d', 332
Amboise: A. d', 455; F. d', 137, 294, 444, 448, **450**, 451, 455; G. d' (Cardinal), 23; M. d', 98
America, 3, 77, 225, 229
Amiel, H., 496
Amy, P., 172
Amyot, J., 76, **138**, 199, 200, 205, 386
Anacreon, 276, 299
Andrelinus, F., 30, 369
Aneau, B. (*Anulus*), 136, 142, **150–1**, 268, 398: *Lyon Marchant*, 150–1; *Picta Poesis*, 92, 150; *Quintil Horatien*, 14, 141, 150
Anet, castle of, 199
Angeriano, G., 75, 98
Angier, P., **121**
Anjou, 282
Anjou, F. duc d' (*formerly* duc d'Alençon), 333, 335, 368, 384, 385, 416, 456 n10, 466, 467
Anne de Beaujeu, 22

Anne of Brittany, 1, 30, 40, 41, 48, 53, 91, 94, 168, 465
Annecy, 381
Apollo, 157–8, 162, 203
Appian, 53
Arabian Nights, 254
Aratus, 207
Arcadelt, J., 198
Ardillon, A., 99
Aretino, P. B., 131, 410
Ariosto, L., 131, 137, 147, 199, 236, 292, 320, 375, 410, 442, 446, 447, 450, 452, 464, 509
Aristophanes, 443, 451, 452
Aristotle, 8, 25, 84–5, 86, 101, 118, 141, 142, 202, 206, 294, 424, 430, 431, 432, 435, 504
Arles, Synod of, 503
Arlier, A., 190
Armagnac family, 21
Artemidorus, 145 n46
Athens, 49
Attaingnant, P., 14, 15, 90
Aubert, G., 213, 220, 237
Aubigné, A. d', 115, 237, 273, 279–80, 314, 316, 335, 348, 351, 366, 368, 369, 387, 389, 397, 399, 403, 406, 410, 420, 460, 472, 507, 510: *Le Printemps*, **376–9**; *Les Tragiques*, 128, 285, 335, **352–62**, 367, 370, 378, 413, 416, 417
Audebert, G., 381
Augurelli, G. A., 207
Augustine, St, 46, 87, 138, 175, 399, 422 n31, 504, **508**
Aurigny, G. d', 98, 99, 121–2, 236
Auriol, B. d', 66
Ausonius, D. M., 90, 108, 109, 132, 304, 327 n6
Auton, J. d', **47–8**, 65, 99
Auvergne, Martial d', 122, 236
Averroes, 206
Avignon, 2, 147

Babinot, C., 433
Bacchus, 163, 203, 324

Bade: C., 61, 196, 345; J., 28–9, 34, 75, 80, 86, 424
Baïf: J.-A. de, 15, 136, 203, 219, 220, 260, 281–4, 288, 289, 311, 312, 366, 369, 385, 386, 395, 447, 455 (see also under Academies); L. de, 137, 281, 424, 454
Bailly, B., 412, 417
Balzac, H. de, 362
Bandello, M., 137, 252–3, 427, 509
Barrès, M., 484
Barricades, Journée des, 334
Basil, St, 85
Basoche, 57, 58, 59, 98, 106
Bathsheba, 279
Bayart, Histoire de, 53, 462
Bayle, P., 491
Beaubreuil, J., 442, 455
Beaulieu, E. de, 14, 97, 98, 110
Beauvais, collège de, 446
Bectoz, Claude (Scolastique) de, 148
Beda, N., 85, 173
Béhourt, 456
Belleau, R., 207, 303, 348, 366, 394, 402, 416: poetry, 276–81; La Reconnue, 446–7, 455
Belleforest, F. de, 137, 233 n13, 370, 395, 427, 459: Histoires tragiques, 242, 252–3
Belliard, G., 137
Belon, P., 200, 227, 228–9
Bembo, P., 118, 137, 162, 213
Benedictines, 47, 83, 172
Bérault, N., 83, 196
Béreau, J., 294
Bergerac, peace of, 334
Bergson, H., 189, 481
Bering(h)en brothers, 148
Berni, F., 271, 410
Beroaldo, Ph., 26, 76, 236
Berquin, L., 240
Bétholaud, R., 289
Béthune, 32
Bèze, Th. de, 82, 141, 150, 255, 262–3, 287, 292, 337, 348–9, 352, 398, 411: Abraham sacrifiant, 344, 345–6, 432, 455
Bibbiena, Divizio da (Cardinal), 365, 443
Bible, 6, 62, 80, 85, 137, 177, 180, 230, 244, 246, 270, 338, 339, 340, 342, 344, 355, 357, 369, 396, 397, 407, 408, 435, 490, 506: Old Testament, 56, 128, 158, 177, 279, 280, 292, 347, 348, 354, 356, 370, 371, 399, 401, 402, 407, 432; Psalms (and Psalm paraphrases), 15, 62, 85, 91, 96, 107, 114, 115, 122, 138, 231, 296 n10, 346, 347, 348, 361, 370, 371, 387, 394,

407; New Testament, 79, 80, 85, 87, 175, 180, 343
Bigothier, C., 150
Billy: Jacques de, 350, 384, 399–402; Jean de, 399
Binet: C., 294; J., 190
Birague, F. de, 373, 410
Bissipat, G. de, 33, 79
Blake, W., 319
Blarru, P. de (Blarrorivus), 46
Blois, 300, 442
Blondel, 45
Boaistuau, P. de, 137, 230, 243, 252–3, 427
Boccaccio, G., 147, 169, 170, 235, 236, 238, 242, 243, 249, 256, 447, 464, 506
Bodin, J., xvi, 208, 352, 368, 458, 460, 468–9, 502, 506
Boece, H. (Boethius), 458
Bohier family, 74
Boileau, N., 115
Boissard, J.-J., 398
Boissières, C. de, 141
Boleyn, Anne, 151
Bologna, 131
Boncourt, collège de, 200, 260
Bonefons, J., 372
Bordeaux, 3, 81, 424, 477
Borromeo, St Charles, 336
Boteauville, 283
Boton, P., 370
Bouchet: G., 240, 256; J., 56, 67 n26, 99–101, 102, 115, 138, 233 n13, 459, 460
Bouelles C. de (Bovillus), 27, 28, 63, 76, 77, 78, 87, 382, 394, 505
Boulogne, Edict of, 333
Bounyn, G., 368, 416, 428, 431–2, 454
Bourbon: family, 2; cardinal de, 334; connétable de, 153; Jean de, 83; Nicolas (Borbonius), 79, 103, 125, 152, 172
Bourdin, G., 448
Bourgeois, L., 15
Bourges, 3, 56, 81, 82, 150, 201, 337, 338
Bourgogne, hôtel de, 67 n28
Bourgouync, S., 65
Bousy, 455
Boyssières, J. de, 294, 402, 410
Boyssonnée, J. de, 107, 166 n11, 190
Brach, P. de, 294
Brant, S., 34
Brantôme, P., seigneur de Bourdeilles, 59, 69 n39, 91, 234, 237, 364, 369, 442, 462, 464–5, 466, 507
Bretog, J., 455
Breton: F., 294; R. (Britannus), 190

Briçonnet: family, 26; G. de, 24, 85, 126
Brie, G. de (*Brixius*), 30, 40
Brigade, la, 260, 293, 424, 427
Brinchamel, R. de, 236
Brinon, J. de, 101, 200, 263, 284, 427
Brissot, R., 455
Brittany, 1, 22
Brizard, N., 143 n19
Bruès, G. de, 205, 211, 212, 213, 220–1
Brunetière, F., 172
Bucer, M., 214
Buchanan, G., 47, 81, 104, 162, 196, 200, 224, 260, 263, 268, 280, 348, 352, 366, 371, 379, 410, 424, 425, 430, 454, 468, 497 n1
Budé, G., 14, 27, 29, 54, 63, 71, 74, 79, 82–3, 84, 87, 152, 190, 196, 313, 386, 459, 467
Buillon, B. de, 236
Bullant, J., 198
Bunel, P., 190
Bungnyon, Ph., 294
Buonaparte, N., 449
Bur, P. de, 27
Burgundy, 1, 14, 21–2, 23, 31, 64
Bussy, 466
Buttet, M.-C., 288–9

Cabedius, M., 443
Caen, 26, 30
Cahors, 97
Cain, 354, 355, 356, 382, 383
Calais, 1, 197
Calepinus, 80
Calignon, J. de, 410
Calvin, J., 72, 75, 77, 81, 148, 177, 185, 186, 189, 195, 337–43, 345, 351, 474, 510: *Institution chrestienne*, 195, 337, 338–43
Cambrai, peace of, 24
Cardano, G., 207, 222, 223
Carle, L. de, 267, 394
Caron, A., 365
Carpentras, 74, 148
Castel, J., 100
Castel-Jaloux, battle of, 353
Castiglione, B., 72, 91, 116, 118, 119, 123, 147, 162, 199, 212, 235, 243, 244, 412
Cateau-Cambrésis, peace of, 197, 311
Catherine de Medici, 195, 207, 261, 331–2, 353–6, 358–60, 364–7, 412, 426, 442, 466
Catholics, 185, 186, 195, 208, 213, 332, 333, 335, 338, 340, 345, 348, 350, 415, 426, 440, 466, 468
Cato, M. P., 100, 143 n19, 222, 369

Catullus, 78, 86, 101, 200, 261, 278, 299
Caviceo, G., 123, 137, 169, 170
Celestina, La, 249, 451
Cent Nouvelles Nouvelles, 236
Certon, P., 15
Chambord, treaty of, 196
Champier, S., 40, 148–50, 225
Chantelouve, F. G., 455
Chappuys, G., 88 n2, 237, 255, 459
Chariteo, Il, 155
Charlemagne, 47, 506
Charles: VII, 2; VIII, 1, 22, 31, 47, 53, 72, 80, 168, 508; IX, 142, 198, 262, 281, 310–13, 332–3, 336, 364, 370, 375, 415, 444, 456 n6, 460; the Bold of Burgundy, 21, 50; V, emperor, 23, 24, 72–3, 151, 177, 178, 186, 195, 196, 197
Charron, P., 78
Chasse et depart d'amours, La, 64
Chassignet, J.-B., 275, 402, 404, 405, 406–9
Chastelaine de Vergi, La, 169, 235
Chastellain, G., 39, 45, 65, 149, 310
Châtillon, O. de, 196
Chenier, A., 414
Cholières, N. de, 223, 255, 256–7
Chrétien, F., 372, 455, 469, 472
Christ, 83, 98, 101, 102, 126, 128, 129, 176, 246, 338, 382, 393, 395, 396, 398, 490
Chrysostom, St John, 399
Church, Roman Catholic, 4, 5, 24, 25, 31, 34, 54, 57, 58, 59, 82, 83, 86, 107, 113, 127, 175, 223, 240, 247, 249, 251, 314, 350, 357, 384, 411, 445, 468, 470
Church Fathers, 26, 28, 77, 79, 84, 85, 87, 336, 363 n9, 379, 384, 396, 398, 399, 422 n31
Cicero, 13, 83, 86, 91, 101, 124, 150, 205, 212, 223, 349, 395, 493
Clamanges, N. de, 25
Claude de France, 105
Claudel, P., 357, 362
Claudian, 91, 413
Clément, J., 335
Clermont, collège de, 336
Clopinel, *see* Meung
Cluny, 83
Cognac, league of, 23
Coignac, J. de, 61, 454
Coimbra, 81
Col, G. and P., 25
Colet, C., 98, 122
Coligny, G. de, 196, 332, 333, 415
Colin, J., 88 n2
Colines, S. de, 29, 75, 79, 415
Collerye, R. de, 59, 97–8, 102

Colonna, F. (author of *Songe de Poliphile*), 137
Commynes, Ph. de, 22, 50–1, 64, 459
Complainte du nouveau marié, 34
Compte du Rossignol, 123
Comptes du monde aventureux, 242–3
Concordat, 5, 23
Condamnacion de Banquet, La, 57, 58
Condé: family, 196, 314; prince de, 279, 311, 331, 332
Confrérie de la Passion, 56, 67 n28
Cop, G., 72
Copernicus, N., 77, 224, 389, 506
Coqueret, collège de, 260, 443
Coquillart, G., 65
Cordier, M., 81
Corneille, P., 205, 426, 453
Corrozet, G., 92, 98, **123**, 171
Cossé, Ph. de, 74
Cottereau, C., 99, 219
Courcelles, P. de, 141
Court, B., 236
Courville, Thibault de, 15, 366
Cousin, V., 502
Coustau, P. (*Costalius*), 92
Coutras, battle of, 334
Crenne, Helisenne de, 49, 94, 99, **169–70**, 190, 217
Crépy, peace of, 73
Crete, 228
Crétin, G., 21, **32–4**, 38, 39, 44, 65, 73, 93
Cujas, J., 201
Cupid, 122, 131, 153, 154, 213
Cusa, N. de, 28, 85
Cyclops, 324
Cyprian, St, 87, 399
Cyprières, M. de, 442
Cyril, St (of Alexandria), 85

Dampierre, Mme de, 464
Danès, P., 29, 74, 79, 199
Daniel, John, 92
Dante, 40, 43, 127, 147, 386, 396
Danville, 333
Dauphiné, 1
David, 279
Davie, Donald, 509
Deguileville, G. de, 30, 127
Democritus, 485
Demosthenes, 86
Denisot, N. (*Comte Alsinois*), 134, 170, 260, **394**
Denys the Areopagite, 85
De profundis des amoureux, 35
Des Autelz, G., 136, 141, 142, **237–8**, 260, 288, 294

Deschamps, E., 14, 32, 39
Des Essarts, H., 137, 168–9, 236
Des Masures, L., 294, **344**, 345, **346–7**, 371, 432
Des Périers, B., 129, 151, 211: *Contes*, 234, 238, 240, 242, 244, **249–51**, 255, 257; *Cymbalum Mundi*, **213–15**; Poetry, **102**
Des Pins, J., 28, 74
Desportes, Ph., 138, 286, 312, 317, 327 n16, 348, 366, 369, **374–6**, 378, 393, 402, 410
Des Prés, Josquin, 14
Des Roches, dames, 11, 191, 368
Diana, **157**, 377
Dido, 171
Dieppe, 3, 32, 96
Digne, 118
Dijon, 368, 397
Dioscorides, 280
Dolet, E., 11, 80, 88, 103, **136**, 151, **152**, 156, 205, 338
Donatus, A., 443
Dorat, J. (*Auratus*), 79, 200, 208, 260, 263, 277, 281, 295 n2, 366, 368, 371, 384, 415, 469
Douai, 336, 372
Doubert, J., 410
Dryden, John, 272
Du Bartas, Saluste, 203, **224**, 256, 351, 352, 368, 372, **387–9**, 392, 402
Du Bellay: family, 29, 74, 172; Guillaume, 30, 74, 151, 178, 186, 462; Jean, 74, 268; Joachim, 14, 40, 104, 160, 200, 222, 260, 261, 265, **266–76**, 287, 288, 367, 379, 402, 410, 462: *Antiquitez* (and *Songe*), **269–70**, 272, **274–5**, 509; *Deffense*, 5, 10–11, 12, 13, 37, 111, 129, 139, **140–1**, 150, 160, 199, 260, 266, 281, 283, 287, 289, 297, 311, 344, 418, 436, 443; *Jeux Rustiques*, 273–4; *Olive, L'*, 158, 261, **266–7**, 271, 300; *Poemata*, 263, 269, 270, 272; *Regretz, Les*, 112, 269, **270–3**, 285, 401, 411, 509; René, 249
Dubledier, 453
Du Bois, A. (*Sylvius*), 200
Du Bos, Charles, xiv
Du Buys, G., 413
Du Chastel, A., 74
Ducher, G., 150, 152
Du Chesne, J., 389
Duchesne, Léger (*Leodegarius à Quercu*), 415, 468
Du Duc, F., 455
Du Fail, N., 208, 212, 223, 230, 235, **240–1**, 255, 257, 367, 414, 418
Dugast, 466

Du Guillet, P., 121, **161–2**
Du Haillan, B., 475 *n*10
Du Monin, E., 208, 294, 389, 455
Dumoulin, A., 71, 121, 468
Duparc, H., 16
Duplessis-Mornay, Ph., 348, 349, 407
Du Pont, Gratien, seigneur de Drusac, 60, 116, 139, 221
Du Prat, A., 3, 74
Du Puis, Jacques I, 29
Dupuys, N. (*Bonaspes*), 29, 37
Du Tronchet, E., 190–1, 413, 414
Du Vair, G., 205, 395
Duval: P., 57; P., 379
Du Verdier, A., 411, 412, 417–18

East Indies, 96
Ebreo, L. (Abravanel), 118, 213, 215
Elbeuf, marquis d', 442
Elizabeth of England, 125, 353
Ellain, N., 294
Empiricus, Sextus, 200, 206, 479
Endor, witch of, 208
Enfants sans souci, 58, 67 *n*28
England(*and* English), 22, 30, 51, 73, 92, 137, 151, 171, 256, 295, 447
Epictetus, 395, 433
Epicurus, 119, 218, 291
Erasmus, D., 14, 29, 34, 64, 71, 75, 84, **86–8**, 92, 98, 122, 124, 150, 152, 162, 171, 172, 173, 174, 177, 178, 181, 190, 206, 212, 214, 215, 222, 234, 253, 282, 313, 337, 386, 424, 454, 508
Erastus, Histoire pitoyable . . . du prince, 254
Espence, C. d', 395
Espinay, C. d', 294
Estienne (*Stephanus*): family, 29, 79; Charles, 424, **443**, 454; Henri I, 291; Henri II, 6, 29, 80, 212, 213, 282, 283, 367, 412, 506: *Apologie pour Herodote*, **251–2**, **460**; Robert I, 29, 74, 75, 79, 80
Estouteville, cardinal d', 25
Euripides, 424
Eusebius, 80
Evreux, 395

Fabri, P., 138
Faguet, E., 172
Farce de Maistre Jehan Janin, 59
Farce morale de troys pelerins et Malice, 59
Fauchet, C., 461
Fauré, G., 16
Favre, A., 455
Fénelon, F. de S. de L., 247

Ferdinand: of Aragon, 22, 23; of Naples, 22
Fernel, J., 200, 386
Ferrault, J., 54
Ferrier, A., 207
Ferron, A., 458
Fichet, G., 28
Ficino, M., 63, 84, 85, 117, 149, 202, 208, 246, 384, 386
Filleul, N., 294, 365, 442, 454
Finé, O., 74, 200, 386
Firenzuola, A., 213
Flaminio, Marcantonio, 397, 398
Fleix, peace of, 334
Flore, Jeanne, 170, **238–9**
Florence, 268
Flores, Juan de, 168
Foclin, A. (*or* Fouquelin), 141, 142
Folengo, G., 173, 236
Fontaine: C., 87, 90, 116, 117, **120–121**, 125, **129–30**; J., 208
Fontainebleau, 71, 74, 311, 442, 456 *n*6
Fontenelle, B. de, 35
Forcadel: E. (*Forcatulus*), **287–8**, 387; P., 200, 287, 386
Forestier, A. (*Sylviolus*), 30
Fourvières, 44
Franc Archier de: Bagnolet, 60; *Cherré*, 60
France: culture, 44, 45, 49, 76, 133, 135, 139; geography, 1–2; political structures, 2–5, 469; theme in prose and poetry in wars of religion, 14, 49, 168, 353, 373, 414, 416
Francis: I, 2, 3, 5, 11, 14, 21, **23–5**, 29, 36, 47, 54, 61, **71–3**, 79, 80, 81, **91**, 95, 104, 105, 107, 116, 121, 125, 128, 129, 133, 148, 151, 167, 177, 178, 195, 198, 199, 206, 235, 236, 243, 277, 364, 386, 456 *n*6, 458, 468, 508; II, 310, 322
Franciscans, 60, 83, 108, 172, 173, 225, 238, 246, 249
Francus, 459, 506
Froissart, J., 459
Frusius, A. (*Freux*), 371

Gaguin, R., 25, 26, **27**, 28, 30, 31, 33, 40, 45, 49, 63, 74, 84, 86, 148, 458
Galen, 8, 226
Ganges, 158
Gargantua, Grandes et inestimables chronicques de, 172
Garnier, R., 205, 427, 435, **437–42**, 455: *Antigone*, **439–40**; *Bradamante*, 437, **452–3**; *Les Juifves*, 433, 434, 438, 439, **440–2**; *Marc-Antoine*, **437–9**

Gasparino (di Barzizza), 28
Gauchet, C., 294, 418
Gaul, 49
Gawain, 53
Gélida, J., 190
Geneva, 72, 148, 195, 196, 263, 287, 337, 345, 351, 352, 411
Genius, 44, 163
Genoa, 95
Gentillet, I., 468
Germany, 23, 24, 71, 84, 85, 147, 196, 197, 399, 499
Gide, A., 481, 491
Gilles de Delft (*Aegidius*), 26
Gilles, N., 459
Gillot, J., 472
Gilmer, C., 371
Giorgio, F., 215, 384
Giovio, P. E., 458
Girard: C., 443; J., 148, 398
God, 8, 50, 77, 78, 96, 99, 119, 149, 171, 176, 177, 180, 186, 205, 208, 216, 223, 231, 246, 253, 268, 306, 307, 338, 344, 345, 346, 349, 353, 354, 355, 356, 359, 382, 388, 390, 393, 398, 433, 435, 440, 446, 467, 479, 490, 504, 505
Godard, J., 455
Goethe, J. W. von, 189, 297
Gohorry, J., 207, 208, 237
Gomer, 385
Goudimel, C., 15, 198
Goujon, J., 199
Goulart, S., 352, 387
Gouvea family, 81
Granada, L. de, 395
Greece, 30, 49, 135, 137, 277, 283, 292, 381, 383, 385, 424, **426–7**, 430, 431, 433, 437, 453
Greek Anthology, 11, 30, 37, 79, 90, 109, 284, 304, 397
Gregory XIII, 334, 533
Grenoble, 256
Grévin, J., 260, 294, 427, 435, 446, 454; comedies, **445–6**, 454; *Jules César*, **430–1**
Gringore, P., 58, 59, 65
Grouchy, N. de, 81, 133, 138, 196, 201, 469
Gruget, C., 191, 243, 246, 253
Gryphius, S., 75, 80, **152**
Guérente, G., 81
Guéroult, G., 348
Guersens, J., 455
Guevara, A. de, 115, 116, 241, 412, 413
Guicciardini, F., 459
Guise: family, 195, 196, 199, 314, **331–5**, 350, 416, 470, 473; François duc de, 371, 414, 415
Gutenberg, J., 28

Guyenne, collège de, 81, 104, 387, 424
Guyon, Mme de, 247

Habert: F., **100–1**, 102, **122–3**, 199, 207; Isaac, 208, 294, **392–3**
Habsburgs, 24, 502
Hamel, 200
Hardy, A., 453, 457 *n*27
Hecate, 157
Heliodorus, 145 *n*54
Hell, 56, 126, 247
Henry: II, 2, 53, 71, 101, 131, 133, 135, 142, 163, **195–7**, 211, 237, 268, 309, 331, 336, 364, 367, 428, 443, 459, 460; III, 203, 263, 278, 281, 289, 310, 311, 312, 331, **333–5**, 336, 350, 367, 370, 371, 373, 375, 395–7, 412, 415–16, 464, 466, 467; of Navarre, *later* Henry IV, 4, 334–335, 352, 353, 387, 416, 466, 472, 473, 477; VII of England, 22; VIII, 73
Hercules, 49, 380, 385, 439, 451
Héroet, A., 115, 117, **118–20**, 121, 125, 127, 130, 142, 204, 267, 387
Hervet, G., 200, 206
Heynlin, J., 28
Hieronymus, G., 79
Hilary, St, 87
Hippocrates, 8
Homer, 101, 131, 133, 137
Horace, 35, 74, 90, 92, 143 *n*19, 100, 103, 108, 131, 132, 133, 134, 139, 200, 262, 272, 297, 299, 300, 369, 410, 413, 418, 425, 430
Horry, N. (*Horius*), 27
Horus Apollo, 137
Hotman, F., 201, 352, 470
Hugo, V., 357, 362
Huguenots, 4, 10, 54, 57, **196**, 307, 313, 314, 351, 353, 354, 359, 387, 426, 433, 434, 436, 447, 468, 469, 470, 472, 489, 490

Imitation of Christ, 395
Italy, 1, 2, 22, 23, 25, 30, 33, 40, 46, 54, 59, 72, 73, 147, 178, 195, 196, 197, 198, 276, 365
Ivry, Jean d', 65

James: Henry, 357; William, 492
Jamyn, A., 137, 366, **373–4**, 410, 412
Jannequin, C., 15
Jardin de plaisance, Le, 38, 64–5
Jarnac, battle of, 332
Jason, 272
Jeanne d'Albret, 387, 398
Jehan de Paris, **167–8**, 170, 464

Jerome, St, 87
Jesuits, 77, 81, 335–6, 395, 411
Jews, 243, 253
Jodelle, E., 200, 219, 260, 283, 288, 365, 394, 406, 415, 424, 431, 435, 437, 448: comedy, 443, 444–5, 447, 455; poetry, 284–7; tragedies, 260, 427–30, 436, 454, 455
John Casimir, 333
Joinville: castle, 276; treaty of, 334
Josephus, 435
Journal d'un bourgeois de Paris, 462
Joyeuse, A. duc de, 334, 371
Julius: II, 22, 58, 82; III, 196
Juno, 324
Jupiter, 121, 131, 162, 213, 301, 438, 451
Juvenal, 34, 108, 272, 410

Kabbala, 206–7, 208
Koran, 229

Labé, Louise, 162–5
La Boderie, G. Lefèvre de, 12, 32, 207, 208, 224, 291, 368, 384–7, 395
La Boétie, E. de, 352, 470–2, 477, 485, 488, 497
La Borderie, A. de, 116–17, 119, 120, 121
La Bruyère, J. de, 250, 448
La Chesnaye, N. de, 58
Lactantius, 342
La Farge, T. de, 283
La Fontaine, J. de, 250, 251
La Fosseuse, 466
La Gessée, J. de, 368
La Grange, 455
Lallemant, J., 424, 454
La Marche, O. de, 45, 65
La Marck, R. de, 475 n16
La Mare, G. de (*Mara*), 27, 30
Lamartine, A. de, 274
Lambyn, D., 190, 200, 206, 379, 506
La Motte Roullant, seigneur de, 239–40
Landor, W. S., 35
La Noue, O. de, 237, 433
La Perrière, G. de, 455
La Péruse, J. de, 289, 294
La Popelinière, H. de, 351, 460–1
La Primaudaye, P. de, 223
La Ramée, P. de (*Ramus*), xvi, 6, 14, 141, 142, 196, 200, 202, 206, 291, 293, 294–5, 349, 386, 502
Larivey, P., 444, 448–9, 450, 451, 455, 456
La Rochelle, 3, 333
Lascaris, J., 27, 74, 79
Lasso, O. di, 198, 279, 285, 395

La Taille: Jacques de, 434; Jean de, 116, 352, 413, 414, 427, 434–7, 455: comedy, 447–8; *Saül*, 208, 435–6
La Tayssonnière, G. de, 208, 294
La Tour Landry, G. de, 236
Lausanne, 196, 345
Lavardin, J. de, 455
La Vigne, A. de, 37, 58, 65
Le Blanc, R., 207
Le Breton, G., 456 n5
Le Caron, L. (*Charondas*), 141, 203–204, 211, 217–20
Le Coq, T., 57, 455
Le Digne, N., 367
Le Duchat, F. (*Ducatius*), 200, 262, 263, 454
Lefèvre d'Etaples, J., 24, 27, 28, 29, 74, 75, 79, 84–5, 86, 87, 117, 126, 128, 386
Le Franc, M., 65
Légende de Pierre Faifeu, La, 236
Le Havre, 3, 447
Le Jars, L., 455, 447 n27
Le Jeune, C., 15, 366
Le Loyer, P., 209, 451–2, 455
Le Maçon, A., 236, 243
Lemaire de Belges, J., 30, 32, 33, 35, 45, 47, 53, 63, 64, 73, 94, 100, 105, 135, 148, 153, 174, 467: *Illustrations de Gaule*, 49–50; poetry, 40–5
Lemaitre, J., 37
Le Masle, J., 294, 423
Leo X, 23
Le Roy: L. (*Regius*), 472; (co-author of *Satyre Menippée*), 472
Le Saulnyer, G., 399
Le Saulx, M., 402
L'Escot, P., seigneur de Clagny, 199
L'Estoile, P. de, 475 n16
Lethanie des bons compagnons, La, 35
Levant, 3, 225, 233 n16
L'Hôpital, M. de, 3, 199, 203, 263, 298, 313, 332, 335, 369, 372, 395, 415, 418, 468, 473
L'Hostal, P. de, 211, 222
Libytina, 157
Ligny, comte de, 40
Ligue, 334–5, 350, 371, 416, 468, 470, 472–4
Lille, 32
Limoges, 93, 442
Lipsius, J., 205, 349, 395
Livre du faulcon, Le, 35
Livy, 46
Lizet, P., 410–11
Longueil, C. de, 109
Longus, 145 n54
L'Orme, Ph. de, 199

Lorraine, 196
Lorraine: J. cardinal de (d. 1550), 74, 151; J. cardinal de, 276, 309, 310, 353, 354, 355, 357; *see also* Guise
Louis: XI, 1, 21-2, 31, 50; XII, 1, 2, 14, 22-3, 30, 37, 39, 47, 48, 51, 53, 59, 75, 80, 91, 99, 103, 295 n2, 508
Louise de Savoie, 24
Louvre, 198
Loynes, Antoinette de, 368, 394
Loyola, Ignatius, 75, 337, 395
Lucan, 437
Lucian, 34, 84, 86, 105, 110, 137, 162, 171, 174, 181, 182, 206, 212, 214, 222, 223, 251, 412
Lucretius, 200, 206, 223, 251, 305, 308, 319, 379
Lull, R., 28, 85
Lunette des Princes, La, 72
Luther, M., 24, 59, 75, **84,** 85, 87, 107, 114, 126, 177, 214, 245
Lutheran princes, 72
Lycophron, 208
Lyège, J. de (*Lygæus*), 379
Lyons, 2, 15, 25, 28, 40, 44, 74, 80, 81, 92, 93, 103, 104, 107, 117, 120, 129, 131, 142, **147-66,** 191, 198, 202, 207, 208, 219, 238, 239, 241, 242, 260, 365, 368, 369, 398, 443

Machaut, G. de, 32
Machiavelli, N., 459, 467
Macrin, Jean Salmon, 21, 74, 75, 83, 91, 100, **103,** 104, 121, 125, 133, 152, 292, 297
Magny, O. de, 163, 269, 287
Maillard, O., 60, 83
Mailles, J. de, 67 n23
Maillezais, 172
Maisonfleur, E. de, 348, 402
Major, J. (*or* Mair), 54, 469
Malherbe, F. de, 13, 368, 375, 420
Mallarmé, S., xv, 160, 262, **324**
Malvyn, G. de, 371, 414
Mantuan, *see* Spagnuoli
Manutius, Aldus, 79
Marcel, G., 486
Marconville, J. de, 253
Margaret of Austria, 33, 40, 41
Marguerite de France (sister of Henry II), 196, 199, 200, 288-9, 298
Marguerite de Navarre, 3, 24, 57, 73, 74, 81, 84, 85, 90, 92, 102, 114, 117, 118, 120, 130, 131, 133, 151, 167, 177, 198, 202, 214, 260, 506, 508: *Heptaméron*, 125, 126, 169, 212, 217, 234, 235, 242,

243-8, 249, 250, 252, 253, 257, 509; poetry, **125-8**; theatre, **61-3**
Marguerite de Valois, 376, **465-7**
Margues, N. de, **412-13**
Marie de Clèves, 312
Marot: Clément, 5, 21, 35, 37, 40, 42, 73, 87, 91, 93, 97, 101, 102, **104-15,** 129, 130, 131, 132, 134, 139, 141, 152, 153, 154, 156, 163, 165, 189, 250, 264, 284, 285, 314, 364, 387, 419, 428, 508, 509, 510; Jean, 30, 33, 35, 39, 73, 93, **94-6,** 105
Marquets, Anne des, **397-8**
Marseilles, 3
Martial, 12, 34, 90, 104, 107, 108, 109, 131, 132, 288, 387, 410
Martin, J., 118, **137,** 267, 290, 456 n6
Marullus, M. T., 27, 75, 299, 303, 305
Mary, Blessed Virgin, 24, 37, 56, 96, 176, 186, 246
Mary queen of Scots, 310, 311, 332, 366, 371
Mary I Tudor, 197
Mary of Burgundy, 21-2
Masuccio da Guardati, 242
Matheolus, 34
Mathurins, 26
Matthieu, P., 455
Mauburn, John of, 85
Maugin, 199
Mauro, L., 269
Maximilian of Austria, 21, 22, 23
Meaux, 24, 85, 117
Medea, 272
Medici, L. de, 449
Meigret, L., 6, 136, 289
Menot, M., 60, 83
Mercury, 162, 213-14, 324
Mermet, C., 455
Meschinot, J., 65, 100
Mesmes: H. de, 417; J.-P. de, 454
Metz, 196
Meung, J. de, 100, 102, 161
Mexia, P. (*Messie*), 253, 258 n23
Michelet, J., 314
Milan, 22, 73
Milhaud, agreement of, 333
Millanges, S., 477
Minerva, 43, 44, 45, 214
Mirandola, P. della, 77, 88, 96, 394, 505
Mizault, A. (*Mizaldus*), 200, 379
Moderne, J., 15, 148
Monsieur, paix de, 333
Monstrelet, E. de, 459
Montaigne, M. de, xv, 5, 7, 52, 77, 78, 116, 205, 217, 221, 226, 230, 234, 248, 257, 343, 407, 461, 465, 471, 473, **477-98,** 504, 505, 506,

509: *Journal du Voyage*, 487, 496, **499–500**
Montaigu, collège de, 26, 75, 83, 337, 395
Montchrétien, A. de, 455
Montdoré, P. de (*Montaureus*), 133, 196, 200, 371
Montenay, Georgette de, 92, **398–9**
Montluc, B. de, 7, **462–4**
Montmorency, A. de, 73, 331, 332
Montmoret, H. de (*Mommoretus*), 30
Montpellier, 3
Montreux, N. de, 237
More, Thomas, 150
Morel, J. de, 200, 368
Morocco, Moors, 3, 72
Muret, M.-A., 15, 141, 200, 262, 263, 289, 303, 394, 424, 425, 430, 454, 506
Muse chrestienne, La, 348, 402
Musset, A. de, 189
Mystère des Apôtres, Le, 56

Nancy, battle of, 21
Nantes, 3
Naples, 22
Narbonne, 149, 254
Navagero, A. (*Naugerius*), 273
Navarre, 1, 23; collège de, 25
Nemours: family, 21; treaty of, 334
Nérac, 376, 466
Netherlands, 14, 27, 28, 63, 92, 196, 333, 334, 508
Neufville, N. de, 105
Nice, truce of, 73
Nicolay, N. de, **227–8**
Nicot, J., 220
Nîmes, 81
Nivernais, 2
Nostradamus, M. de, 207
Nuysement, Hesteau de, 368, 373, 410, 416

Obrecht, W., 14
Obrizius, R., 372
Ockham, William of, 25
Œuvre Chrestienne, L', 402
Ogier, S., 372
Okeghem, J. (Ockeghem), 14, 33
Olivetan, F., 114
Olivier, F., 3
Opuscules d'amour, 115
Origen, 85
Orléans: family, 21; duc d', 73; town, 2, 3, 27, 79, 81, 149, 151, 238, 337, 338
Orpheus, 324
Ovid, 26, 35, 90, 98, 143 *n*19, 100, 101, 107, 110, 112, 130, 137, 168, 191, 270, 280, 292, 322, 372, 393, 506

Padua, 206, 268
Palingenius, 292
Palissy, B., 212, **231–2**, 505
Pallet, J., 213
Palsgrave, F., 6
Pan, 132
Papillon: Almanque, 116, 120, **121**; Marc, 418, 456
Parabosco, G., 191
Paracelsus, P., 207
Paradin, C., **92–3**
Parangon des nouvelles, Le, 238
Paré, A., 7, 200, 207–8, **229–31**, 240, 253, 462, 505, 506
Paris, **2**, 6, 15, 25, 26, 27, 28, 30, 49, 56, 57, 58, 67 *n*28, **74**, 78, 79, 80, **81**, 83, 85, 103, 104, 107, 117, 118, 121, 141, 142, 147, 148, 149, 151, 152, 173, 195, 196, 197, 198, 200, 202, 209, 232, 260, 270, 276, 288, 289, 293, 334, 336, 337, 338, 364, 365, 383, 395, 419, 425, 442, 443, 447, 448, 466, 472, 473, 508
Parmentier, J., 76, **96–7**, 102
Pascal, B., xiv, 505
Paschal, P., 459
Pasquier, E., 5, 11, 12, 49, 51, 219, 223, 237, 249, 294, 368, 369, 372, 411, 415, 474, 494: *Lettres*, 190, **217**; *Monophile, Le*, 171, 180, 211, **216–17**; *Recherches de la France*, 255, 458, **461**
Passerat, J., 200, 294, 372, 414, 415, **417**, 472, 506
Patrenostre des verollez, Le, 35
Paul, St, 180, 202, 209 *n*8, 245
Paul IV, 196, 197
Pavia, battle of, 23
Péguy, C., 172, 187
Peletier du Mans, J., 129, **132–7**, 138, **139**, 200, 255, 282, 298, 382, 384, 386, 387, 419: *Art poétique*, 141, **142**, 424, 425; *Amour des amours*, **379–81**; *Œuvres poétiques*, **132–135**; *La Savoye*, **381**
Perréal, J., 148
Perrin, F., 294
Persius, 34
Petit Jehan de Sainctré, Le, 170, 236
Petrarch, F., 39, 105, 131, 132, 133, 137, 147, 154, 155, 158, 161, 264, 267, 270, 287, 288, 427, 450
Phalaris (letters of), 191
Philip II of Spain, 197, 333, 334
Philippe-Emmanuel of Savoy, 199
Pibrac, G. de Faur, seigneur de, 16, 282, 294, 370, 396, 418
Picardy, 73
Piccolomini, 271
Piedmont, 73
Pionnier de Seurdre, Le, 68 *n*37

Pithou, P., 472
Placards, Affaire des, 72, 82, 148, 174, 178
Plato, 83, 117, 120, 137, 149, 200, 202, 204, 212, 218, 380, 504
Plautus, 282, 283, 443
Pléiade, 3, 5, 10, 13, 15, 38, 50, 81, 87, 90, 91, 100, 103, 104, 108, 113, 115, 117, 118, 120, 123, 129, 130, 133, 134, 136, 139, 141, 142, 151, 156, 157, 160, 163, 165, 195, 198, 199, 200, 202, 204, 207, 217, 219, 220, 260–96, 297, 298, 325, 336, 344, 345, 352, 363 n10, 369, 370, 375, 387, 393, 394, 397, 402, 409, 410, 416, 418, 419, 422 n28, 424, 427, 432, 437, 443, 444, 447, 470, 471, 472
Pliny, 214, 486
Plutarch, 76, 138, 199, 200, 205, 422 n39, 427, 428, 479, 485
Poissenot, B., 254–5
Poissy, colloque de, 332, 397
Poitiers, 3, 11, 27, 30, 67 n26, 71, 138, 201, 208, 240, 256, 260, 289–293, 303, 368, 397, 442; Diane de, 195, 198
Politiques (or modérés), 201, 283, 333, 334, 335, 372, 416, 469, 472–4
Poliziano, A., 386
Poltrot de Méré, 414
Poltrotus Meræus, 371
Pomponazzi, P., 223
Poncher, E., 26
Pont-à-Mousson, 336
Pontanus, J. J., 75, 132, 282, 380
Ponte, P. de, 26
Pontoux, C. de, 294
Popes, 2, 5, 24, 25, 84, 114, 350, 354, 356, 411, 468, 473; see also under individual names
Portugal, 138
Postel, G., xvi, 206, 207, 209, 233 n16, 251, 384, 386
Poupo, P., 363 n10
Press, J., 155
Priapus, 163
Propertius, 74, 101, 200, 287, 300, 417
Protestants, 72, 92, 185, 186, 195, 206, 213
Proust, M., 342
Provence, 1, 73, 110
Prudentius, 86
Pulci, L., 173, 236

Quintil Horatien, see Aneau
Quintilian, 13
Quinze joyes de mariage, Les, 34, 236

Rabelais, F., xiv, 7, 9, 26, 39, 40, 61, 74, 77, 87, 99, 102, 110, 113, 124, 152, 162, 163, 171–89, 206, 207, 214, 219, 222, 235, 237–8, 239, 240, 249, 250–1, 254, 256, 273, 284, 285, 343, 358, 411, 451, 467, 473, 485, 503, 508, 509: Pantagruel, 172–4, 176; Gargantua, 172, 173, 174–8; Tiers Livre, 172, 173, 178–85, 186, 189, 246; Quart Livre, 182, 185–7, 188, 237; Fifth Book, 171, 187–8
Racine, J., 426, 431
Raemond, F. de, 368
Ramoneur, Le, 60
Ramus, see La Ramée
Rapin, N., 283, 294, 357, 418, 469, 472
Raulin, J., 83
Raynier, J. (Raenerius), 150
Rebeyne, La, 148
Recueil de plusieurs chansons spirituelles, 348
Régnier, M., 410
Renan, E., 87
Retz, maréchale de, 265, 286, 368, 374
Reuchlin, J., 24, 63, 79, 84
Rhétoriqueurs, 10, 11, 12, 13, 14, 16, 21, 30, 31–9, 40, 51–3, 73, 79, 90, 91, 93–102, 103, 104, 105, 106, 108, 109, 110, 111, 112, 113, 114, 115, 121, 122, 123, 131, 132, 136, 138, 149, 151, 153, 154, 156, 157, 173, 174, 199, 229, 239, 254, 277, 285, 295 n2, 309, 364, 367, 384, 459, 508, 509
Rhône, 2
Rivaudeau, A. de, 432–4, 454
Robelin, J., 455
Robertet: F. de, 42, 114; J., 39, 65
Rochechouart, G. and G., 26
Roigny, J. de, 29
Roillet, C., 371, 432, 454
Roman de la rose, Le, 53, 101, 105, 132
Rome, 49, 71, 82, 135, 268, 269, 270, 350, 354, 356, 357, 385, 438, 499
Rondelet, G., 200, 230
Ronsard, P. de, 5, 13, 14, 16, 40, 43, 44, 45, 49, 77, 104, 115, 120, 132, 140, 141, 160, 198, 199, 208, 213, 219, 220, 223, 233, 237, 238, 255, 256, 260, 262, 263, 264, 266, 269, 270, 275, 276, 277, 280, 281, 282, 283, 284, 287, 288, 289, 293, 295 n2, 297–327, 344, 361, 364, 365, 366, 368, 369, 373, 374, 375, 376, 378, 379, 386, 392, 394, 402, 410, 413, 415, 416, 419–20, 428, 444, 467, 468, 473, 474, 503, 504, 505,

507, 509: *Amours*, 12, 15, 157, 158, 200, 261, 299, **300–5**, 310, 333; court poetry, 309–13; *Folastries*, 304; *Franciade*, 310, **311–12**, 316, 318, 415, 470; *Hymnes*, 224, **305–9**, 310, 379; *Institutions*, **313–14**; *Odes*, 156, 203, **261–2**, 266, **298–300**, 301, 305, 309, 310, 311; *Sonets pour Hélène*, 204, **316–18**, 323, 324; *Variants*, **325–6**
Rosset, P., 30
Rouen, 2, 11, 32, 59, 95, 105, 149, 151, 368, 397, 442
Rouillé (*or* Roville), G., 152

Sadoleto, J., 74, 148, 152, 219
Sailly, Toussaint (*Panagius Salius*), 372
Saint-Barthélemy, massacre of, 333, 351, 353, 355, 371, 415, 466, 468
Saint-Gellais: Mellin de, 11, 14, 88 *n*2, 115, **130–1**, 134, 139, 178, 264, 267, 298, 442, 454; Octovien de, 39, 64, 66, 91, 149, 168
Saint-Germain, peace of, 332–3
Saint-Malo, 3
Saint-Omer, 372
Saint-Pol family, 21
Saint-Victor, 26, 173
Sainte-Barbe, collège de, 75, 81, 337, 395
Sainte-Beuve, C.-A. de, 297, 491
Sainte-Marthe: family, 177; Charles de, **130**, 150; Scévole (*or* Gaucher) de, 11, 289, **291–3**, 299, 357, 368, 372, 418, 442
Salel, Hugues, **131–2**, 134, 137, 139, 264, 284
Sallust, 96
Salviati, Cassandre, 300, 376
Sannazaro, G., 132, 137, 199, 262, 277, 290, 300, 366, 370, 374, 393, 396
San Pedro, D. de, 168
Satan, 345, 346, 354, 355, 356, 359
Satyre Menippée, 201, 237, 335, 350, 415, **472–4**
Saulx-Tavannes, G. de, 475 *n*16
Saumur, 67 *n*26
Sauvage, D., 51, 65, 459
Savoy, 1, 73, 197, 243, 288
Scaliger: J.-C., 142, 424–5, 433; J.-J., 256, 506
Scève: family, 74, 148; Maurice, xvi, 10, 14, 52, 92, 94, 104, 115, 135, 142, 148, 152, **153–61**, 164, 168, 204, 238, 261, 264, 265, 266, 267, 338, 365, 377, 398, 406, 408, 505, 507, 508, 509: *Délie*, 119, **153–60**, 162, 273, 290, 300, 383, 418, 420;

Microcosme, 88, 153, **382–4**
Science et asnerye, 57
Sebillet, T., 57, 58, 91, 109, 135–6, **139–40**, 141, 160, 419, 424, 454
Sebond, R., 137, 477
Second, J. (*Secundus*), 261, 278, 287, 303, 381
Semblançay, Jacques de Beaune, seigneur de, 107
Seneca, 34, 84, 86, 205, 209 *n*8, 337, 349, 395, 397, 485; letters, 191, 205; plays, 424, 425, **426–7**, 430, 432, 433, 435, 437, 440
Sepin, G., 263
Serafino dell'Aquila, 40, 95
Serlio, S., 137, 426
Sermon de l'Endouille, Le, 60
Servet, M., 196
Seyssel, C. de, 23, **53–5**, 71, **135**, 467
Sforza, F., 73
Shakespeare, W., 242, 509
Sienna, 196
Silenus, 163
Sleidan, J., 238
Socrates, **485**
Sophocles, 283, 291, 424, 432
Sorbonne, 24, 25, 28, 74, 79, 80, 81, 84, 85, 106, 125, 173, 410, 473
Spagnuoli, B. (Mantuan), 26, 30
Spain, 23, 72, 74, 197, 335, 472
Speroni, S., 154, 213
Sponde, J. de, 115, 274, 275, 290, 348, **349–50**, 389, 402, **403–6**, 420
Standonck, J., 26, 83
Statius, 41
Straparola, G. F., 255
Strasbourg, 81, 338
Strozzi, E. *and* T., 75
Sturm, J., 81
Suárez, F., 468
Surgères, Hélène de, **317**
Sussannée, H., 103, 152
Switzerland, 499
Syrinx, 132

Tabourot, E., seigneur des Accords, **255**, 369, 411
Tagaut, J., 287
Tagliacarne, B. (*Theocrenus*), 72, 74
Tahureau, J.: *Dialogues*, 211, 213, **221–2**, 290, 494; poems, 281, 289, **290–1**
Taillemont, C. de, 212, 241–2, 294
Talcy, Diane de, 376
Tarascon, 148
Tarsus, 202
Tartaret, P., 173
Tebaldeo, A., 155
Télin, G., 45, **138–9**
Tenebres du mariage, Les, 34–5
Terence, 283, 443, 447

Tesserand, C. de, 253
Testament de Martin Luther, Le, 35
Textor, Ravisius (Tissier), 30
Theocritus, 290, 299, 300
Thevet, A., **225–7**, 228, 230
Thibault, *see* Courville
Thiénaud, J., 206
Thionville, siege of, 197
Thomas, St (Aquinas), 504
Thorigny, Mlle de, 467
Thou, J.-A. de (*Thuanus*), 279, 395
Thucydides, 53
Tibullus, 74
Till Eulenspiegel, 236
Tiraqueau, A., 172
Tory, G., **5**, 6, 80, 135
Toul, 196, 447
Toulouse, 3, 11, 32, 58, 71, 82, 149, 190, 254, 437
Tournes, de (printers), 152
Tournon, cardinal de, 74, 196, 228
Tours, 83
Toussaint, J. (*Tusanus*), 29, 74, 79, 199, 202
Toutain, C., 208, 289, **291**, 384, 430, 454
Tragédie du sac de Cabriere, 456 n3
Trappists, 26
Trechsel, J., 29
Trent, Council of, 196, 335, 394–5
Triboulet, 249
Trinité: collège de la, 130, 148, **150–1**; hôtel de la, 67 n28
Triomphe de . . . Dame Verolle, Le, 35
Trissino, G., 366, 430, 442
Tristan, 53
Trithemius, Johann von, 206, 460
Trivulce family, 148
Troy, 47, 49, 241, 317, 459
Troyes (town), 448
Troyes, N. de, **238**
Turin, 294
Turkey, 24, 72, 73, 196, 227, 229
Turnèbe: Adrien, 5, 80, 141, 200, 202, 289, 371, 372, 485; Odet de, **450–1**, 455
Tyard, P. de, 141, 158, 160, 202, 242, 260, 288, 384: *Dialogues*, **203**, **204**, 211, 213, **215–17**, 229, 282; poetry, **264–6**

Ulysses, 268, **272**
Urfé, H. d', 237
Utenhove, C., 255

Valagre, sieur de, 348, 402
Valentinian, T., **170–1**, 180, 217
Valéry, P., xvi, 38, 160, 262

Valla, L., 28, 87, 138
Valois family, 336, 353, 478, 502
Varanne, V. de, 30
Vascosan, M., 29, 79, 80, 132, 199, 386
Vatel, J., 294, 412
Vaucelles, treaty of, 197
Vauquelin de la Fresnaye, A., **289–290**, 384, 418, 419
Vauzelles family, 74, 148
Venaissin, 2, 5
Venice, 22, 47, 95, 200, 268
Venus, 43, 44, 121, 126, 153, 155, 203, 307, 380
Verdun, 196
Vergil, 26, 43, 52, 90, 91, 101, 105, 107, 133, 137, 277, 290, 300, 315, 366, 371, 387, 430, 431, 439, 506
Vergil, Polydore, 458
Verlaine, P., 274
Verville, B. de, **290–2**
Vesalius, A., 506
Vicomercato, F., 206
Vida, H., 396
Vieilleville, F. de Scépeaux, 475 n16
Vienne, Ph. de, **123–4**
Vigenère, B. de, 207
Vigneulles, Ph. de, 238
Villeroy, maréchal de, 368, 374
Villers-Cotteret, edict of, 6
Villiers, H.-Ph., **417**
Villon, F., 22, 34, 35, 113
Vinci, L. da, 506
Vinet, E., 133, 200
Vingle, J. de, 40
Vintimille, J. de, 368
Viret, P., 223
Virey, J. de, 456
Visagier, J. (*Vulteius*), 81, 103, 104, 108, 125, 129, 152, 153
Viterbo, J. of, 49
Vitruvius, 137, 426
Vivre, G. de, 455
Voltaire, 312
Volusenus, F. (*Voluzene*; ? Wilson), 219
Voron, B., 455

Wechel, C., 80, 278
Wier, J., 230
Windesheim (Brothers of the Common Life), 26, 150, 337
Wolmar, M., 82, 150, 337

Xenophon, 53

Yver, J., 239, 240, **253–4**, 255

Zacaire, D., 207

II. INDEX OF SUBJECTS

(Includes matters relevant to the background of the French Renaissance and topics treated by the authors of the period.)

absence, 158, 272, 274, 286, 291
absolutes, 220–1, 223, 507
absolutism, 3, 4, 47, 54, 71, 201, 331, 335, 351, 459, 467, 469, 478, 506; see also Divine right; kingship
agriculture, 383
alchemy, 206, 249, 389, 390
Alexandrian poetry, 278, 283, 284
ambition, 126, 128, 414
anacreontic poetry, 261, 282, 303
androgyne, 118, 119, 204, 217, 246, 264, 390
angels, 8
animals, 34, 41–2, 213, 214, 220, 223, 250, 266, 307, 480, 505
anti-feminism, 34, 116–17, 410, 446
anti-italianism, 44, 53, 71, 251, 367, 411, 412, 413, 446, 461
anti-petrarchism, 117, 120, 238, 261, 268, 286, 317, 367, 411, 418
appearance (paraître), 124, 127, 215, 241, 271, 285, 322–3, 344, 355–6, 365, 368, 402, 405, 409, 412, 418, 420, 449, 480, 488, 493, 506
architecture, 72, 175, 198–9, 365, 383, 386
aristocracy (as form of government), 54, 469
astrology, 8, 124, 206, 207, 208, 215, 221, 222, 253, 256, 305, 306, 307, 325, 366, 388, 390, 465, 504
astronomy, 8, 84, 134, 266
atheism, 8, 205, 226, 251, 384, 490
atomism, 222
Aumônier, Grand, 3
authority (and tradition), xv, 12, 54, 55, 163, 175, 200, 206, 214, 224, 225, 228, 229, 230, 231, 338, 342, 343, 352, 462, 501, 502, 504, 505
avarice, 101, 128, 250, 446, 461, 463

bailliages, 4, 197
banking, 77, 147
Baroque, xv, 293, 356, 408, 509
beauty, 119, 126, 204, 219, 246, 268, 484; see also Neoplatonism
braggart, 412, 445, 446, 447, 448, 450, 453, 473

Calvinism, 10, 15, 61, 77, 81, 83, 114, 120, 138, 141, 150, 171, 176, 190, 195–6, 200, 201, 209, 218, 231, 251, 263, 279, 285, 293, 294,

310, 315, 316, 331, 336–7, 339, 343–52, 357, 363 n10, 367, 368, 370, 371, 394, 395, 397, 398, 402, 410, 411, 412, 414, 415, 416, 424, 430, 433, 453, 460, 468, 469, 470, 474, 506; see also Calvin; Huguenots
castles, Renaissance, 175, 197
celibacy, 77, 180
censorship, 59
Chain of Being, 118, 306
Chambre ardente, 196
Chambre des Comptes, 187
Chambrier, Grand, 4
chameleons, 228
Chancelier de France, 3
charity, 182
chivalry (chivalric ideals), 22, 47, 50, 53, 167, 199, 236, 365, 464
Christianity, 117, 118, 128, 182, 202, 205, 222, 241, 270, 305, 453, 490
Ciceronianism, 7, 86, 174, 263, 474, 493
circle, 321
classical world (and its heritage), 6, 13, 39, 46, 74, 77, 81, 83, 84, 86, 90–1, 106, 114–15, 123, 133, 138, 139, 140, 200–2, 212, 218, 223, 225–6, 228, 262, 344, 345, 346, 379, 384, 396, 436, 443, 463, 505, 508
Classicism, French, 51, 138, 189, 250, 274, 293, 336, 343, 344, 373, 375, 376, 418, 420, 454, 474
clergy, 241, 243, 249, 350, 411
cloud, 322
colleges, Paris, 13, 15, 74, 81, 91, 103–4, 107, 117, 212, 224, 336, 364, 368, 371, 424, 425, 426, 443, 444, 501; see also Sorbonne; and under individual names
comic, 116, 173, 188, 221, 222
Connétable de France, 3, 4, 73
Conseil, Grand, 4
cosmography, 172, 208, 253
cosmology, 118
Counsellors, 34, 218, 223, 425; see also flatterers
Counter-Reformation, 16, 77, 78, 128, 137, 197, 205, 266, 270, 334, 335, 336, 352, 370, 395, 396, 398, 468, 504, 506, 508
country life (rus/urbs, etc.), 133,

Counter-Reformation—*cont.*
235, 240, 249, 299, 367, 369, **413**, 414, 416, 418, 422 *n*39
courage, 205
Court, 3, 6, 10, 11, 14, 27, 30, 31, 46, 55, 62, 64, 68 *n*39, **71–2**, 73–4, 77, **91–2**, 96, 101, 102, 103, 106, 116, 117, 123, 125, 128, 131, 132, 133, 148, 151, 167, 195, 196, 197, **198–9**, 212, 237, 240, 241, 256, 261, 262, 268, 271, 277, 300, 317, 331, 335, 336, 350, 353, 356, **364–368**, 370, 373, 374, 375, **412–14**, 418, 422 *n*39, 426, 430, 442, 443, 464, 465, 503, 507, 508
courtiers, **116**, 127, 221, 271–2, 347, 430; *see also* Counsellors; flatterers; nobility
coutumiers, 197
cowardice, 60
creation, 205, 223
cruelty, *see* violence
cryptography, 172
curiosity, 132, 225, 380, 383, **480**
currency, 2
custom, 54, 217, 223, 481, 505

dancing, 15, 57, 221
dauphin, death of (1536), 151, **152**
death, 38, 41, 42–3, 77, 119, 128, 164, 186, 305, 309, 313, 314, 318, 320, 372, 380, 396, 403, **404–6**, 407–9, 428, 479, 481, 486, 490
decay, 228, 275, 279, 350, 358, 389, 396, 404
democracy (democratic themes), 54, **351–2**, 469, 489; *see also* kingship
demonology, demons, 207, 208, 306, 504
determinism, 9, 307, 438, 462
devotio moderna, 83, 395
Dignitas hominis, 76, 77, 96, 205, 232, 252, 427, 462, 480, 502, 505
divination, 183–4, 203, 206, 207, 208, 307
Divine right, 4, 51, 54, 177, 314, 335, 471, 504; *see also* absolutism; kingship
doctors, 62, 108, 148, 180, 221, 235, 252, 410, 448, 485; *see also* medicine
dreams, 181, 208, 223, 305, 325, 465, 482
dress, 185, 356, 365, 382–3, 412

education, 25, **26**, 27, 30, 59, 75, **78**, **80–2**, 84, 86, 87, **92–3**, 99, 103, 150, 173, 174, 175, 176, **177**, 212, 241, 295, 471, 480, 482, **484**
elegists, Roman, 86, 90, 103, 110, 261, 287, 303

elements, **8**, 390
elephants, 230
encyclopædias, 76
entendement, 219, 223
Entries, Royal, 33, 199, 365, 442
envy, 38, 40, 111, 264
Epicureanism, 119, 218, 291; *see also jouissance*
Euhemerism, 222, 251
evangelism, 24, 61, 62, 74, 84, 88, 90, 98, 102, 113, 114, 118, 125, 126, 128, 129, 143 *n*13, 151, 175, 178, 180, 181, 185, 221, 246, 395, 422 *n*28, 506, 508
evil, 46, 205, 338, 354, 355, 356, 440; *see also* Fall; sin
experience, 54, 55, 78, 127, 150, 223, 224, 225, 226, 227, 228, **229–30**, 231, 462, 479, 480, **482–3**, 484, 485, 496, 505

fairs, 1, 22, 147
faith, 62, 114, 246, 338, 398
Fall, 8, 9, 217, 245, 338, 355, 382–3, 393, 504; *see also* evil; sin
fame, *see* glory
fate (*fatum*), 8, 205, 223, 266, 426, 427, 429, 434, 438, 439
fear, 264
Fideism, 206, 222, 232, 504
finances (*and* taxation), 2, 3, 34, 54, 82, 86
flatterers, 47, 221, 367, 412; *see also* Counsellors; courtiers; nobility
folly, 86, 162–3, 181, 189, 485, 503
fortune, 8, 9, 50, 51, 223, 245, 249, 254, 264, 266, 324, 373, 390, 415, 427, 428, 438, 440, 465, 466, 482, 484; Fortune's Wheel, 38, 46, 270, 425, 430, 436
free-thinkers, 205, 251
free-will, 8, 9, 77, 99, 118, 175, 176, 186, 205, 223, 308, 438
friendship, 171, 221, 438, 448, 471, **487–8**
fureurs, 118, 139, **202–4**, 215, 219, 265, 298

Gallicanism, 4, 5, 23, 25, 83, 84, 186, 468
gardens, 393, 420
ghosts, 208, 253
glory, 45, 48, 124, 162, 219, 265, 270, 275, 288, 289, 300, 318, 320, 323, **324**, 463, 464, 485, 487, 502, 507
Golden Age, 229, 241, 306, 320, 386, **391**, 415, 416, 502
golden mean (*mediocritas*), 9, 185, 369, 486
grace, 9, **175**, 181, 246, 247, 345, 347, 395, 396, 398, 490

grammar, 136
Grands Jours, 4, 11, 368
Great Year, 204
Greek, study of, 27, 30, 75, **78–9**, 81,
  82, 172, 200, 427

habit, 470, 481, 484, 505; *see also*
  custom
harmony, universal, 203, 208, 231,
  380, 384, 386
Hebrew, study of, 24, 79, 80, 84,
  206, 384, 385
historians, Roman, 46, 137
historical outlines, **21–5**, **71–3**, **195–**
  197, **331–6**
historiography, **45–53**, 201, 211, 216,
  217, 223, 351, **458–62**, 505, 506
Humanism, 10, **25–8**, 29, 31, 39, 54,
  57, 61, **63**, **74–5**, 80, 82, 87, 102,
  103, 135, 142, 152, 172, 173, 175,
  198, **199–202**, 224, 260, 262, 293,
  297, 315, 331, 365, 379, 390, 393,
  411, 419, 459, 461, 467, 469, 501,
  506, 508
humours, **8**
hunting, 132, 134, 366, 370, 374,
  379
hypocrisy, 99; *see also* flatterers

ideas, innate, 220, 222, 223, 226,
  503
idleness, 227
ignorance, 11, 78, 86, 107, 120, 140,
  181, 215, 222, 268, 284, 291, 299,
  484–5, 495, 503
imagination, 9, 10, 219, 223, 319–20,
  323, **390–1**, 479, 490
individual(ism), *see* self
indulgences, 82
Italian culture, humanism, literature, 26, 27, 28, 39, 43, 44, 45,
  49, 63, 71, 74, 75, 79, 82, 83, 85,
  90, 91, 95, 103, 118, 120, 124, 131,
  137, 139, 140, 148, 149, 153, 161,
  162, 167, 169, 171, 192, 199,
  202, 205, 212, 213, 215, 217, 223,
  225, 236, 242, 251, 254, 263, 268,
  269, 273, 277, 281, 289, 311, 336,
  365, 366, 375, 385, 396, 410, 411,
  442, 443, 444, 447, 448, 449, 451,
  453, 454, 459, 477, 478, 499, 502,
  506

Jansenism, 508
jealousy, 268
jewellery, 365
jouissance, 77, 219, 220, 486
journey, 187, 270, 272, 382, 494,
  495
jousting, 50, 53, 365

judgement, 9, 78, 124, 218, 219,
  220, 227, 477, **482–4**, 495
jurisprudence, *see under* law
justice (legal structures), **4**, 26, 240
Justice (moral virtue, Astræa), 124,
  205, 218, 223, 240, 309, 355,
  367, 415, 447, 473, 489

kingship, 46, 50, **54**, 59, **71**, 82, 86,
  99–100, 122, 133, **173**, 176, **177–**
  178, 218, 223, 313–14, 335, 350,
  351–2, 365, 388, 434, 452, 459,
  460, **467–72**, 489
knowledge, 62, 120, 126, 127, 128,
  132, 140, 142, 181, 230, 232, 246,
  393, 462, **479**, 480, 485, 503–4,
  505, 506; *see also* wisdom

language, 78, 116, 207, 251
language, French: general remarks,
  5–7; vernacular emerging as
  literary medium, 43, 44, 49, 55,
  75, 116, **133**, **135–8**, 139, **140**,
  149, 189, 198, 200–1, 202, 207,
  209, 211, 217, 225, **228–9**, 252,
  260, 292, 293, 297, 338, 339, 343,
  348, 367, 419, 437, 444, 448, 450,
  458, 459, 460–1, **474**, **492–3**, 507,
  508
lapidaries, 392
Latin culture, **74**; *see also* classical
  world
Latinity, 25, **26**, 29, 81
Latin language, 5, 82, 113, **135**, 137,
  141, 151, 229, 232, 269, 346, 419,
  458, 459, 467, 473, 492, 508
laughter, 222
law: study of law, 4, 82, 172, **201**,
  459, 502, 505; common law, 4, 22,
  459, 460, 461, 505; Roman law, 4,
  71, 459, 461, 467, 469, 505
laws, 54, 71, 217, 218, 220, 223,
  353
lawyers, 58, 108, 172, 174, 176, 185,
  221, 235, 410, **417**
learning, 11, 62, 85, 107, 126, 127,
  128, 141, 150, **174**, 181, 184, 215,
  229, 231, 249, 250, 288, 299, 380,
  384, 480, 484, 485; *see also*
  education; ignorance; knowledge;
  wisdom
lettres de civilité, 80
liberty, 114, 127, 306, 438, 470, 483,
  486
love, 38, 43, 53, 60, 61, 62, 116,
  117, **118**, **121**, 122, 123, 125, 126,
  127, 128, **162–3**, 169, **170**, **171**,
  204, 213, **216–17**, 221, 239, 240,
  243, **244–5**, 254, 256, 261, 268,
  277, **318**, 320, 322, 372, 374,
  380, 390, 429, 438, 446, **453**

lute, 163, 164
Lutheranism, 3, **24**, **84**

macabre (morbid *and* melodramatic),
253, 279, 354, 360, 361, 376, 378,
509
magic, 207, 208, 209, 223, 226
magistrature, 3, 72, 201, 335, 353,
368, 386, 409–10, 414, 419; *see
also* law; lawyers
magnanimity, 124
Maître, Grand, 4
man: human condition (place in
Nature, society, etc.), **8**, 76–7, 174,
175, 189, 200, 201, **214**, 218, 220,
221, **223–4**, 226, 246, 350, 355,
369, 379, 381, **382–3**, 393, 418,
439, 461, 479, 480, 481, **487**, 505,
507; man as microcosm, **77**, 116,
381, **382–3**, 505; psychology, 7,
8–9, 77, 154, 175, 176, 205, 219,
223, **481**–2, 505; *see also* reason;
passions
Marotic school, 161, 165, 287
marriage, 34, 77, 117, 119, 121,
122–3, 170–1, **179**–80, 181, 182,
216–17, 221, 239, **245**, 256, 286,
390, 410, 453
mask, 356
Mass, 114, 411
mathematics, 78, 84, 134, 200, 218,
382, 386
matter, 8, 223, 322, 390
medicine, 6, 149, 172, 225, 229, 252,
379, 499; *see also* doctors
medieval elements, persistence of,
33, 46, 47, 50, 54, 62, 63, 76, 83,
86, 102, 105, 115, 122, 123, 125,
127, 134, 162, 167, 212, 236, 344,
345, 351, 365, 398, 426, 435, 442,
443, 444, 452, 453, 457 *n*27, 469;
see also chivalry; romances, medieval
memory, 9, 118, 119, 219, 480
merveilleux, 234, 237, 355
metamorphosis, 270, 274, **322**, 402,
509
metempsychosis, 118, 204, 208, 305,
308
Middle Ages, 50, 459, 460, 501, 506
mignardise, 278, 303
miracles, 56, 176, 206, 490
miseria hominis, 76, 77, 126, 215,
252, 349, 396, 399–400, 462, 502,
505
monarchy, *see* kingship
monastic orders (*and* monks), 5, **25**,
77, 113, 172, **175**–7, 235, 243,
251, 256, 411
monde cassé, 274, 306, 314, 356,
372, 420, 478, 509

moon, 8, 157, 380
music, 8, **14–16**, 32, 41, 44, **56**, 62,
90, 91, 97, 114, 115, 116, 131,
148, 162, 198, 200, 203, 215, 219,
264, 277, 279, 283, 285, 297,
300, 310, 320, 324, 365, 368,
383, 386, 394, 395
mutability, 218, 266, 308, **321–3**,
359, 393, 396, 408, 420, 422 *n*39,
480–1, 484, 489, 507, 509; *see
also* fortune
mysticism, 28, 55–7, 67 *n*28, 85, 99,
118, 126, 127, 128
mythology, 33, 43, 49, 122, 155,
158, 163, 199, 204, 247, **262**, 265,
266, 267, 268, 270, 280, 284, 299,
309, 324, 377, 380, 392, 432,
508

natives, 226, 227, **229**, 504
Nature, 8, **44**, 50, 99, 102, 103, 124,
132, **133–4**, 207, 208, 219, **221**,
225, 226, 231, 232, 234, 249–50,
253, 263, 265, 267, 268, 275, 278,
282, 283, 284, 286, 289, 291, **299**–
302, 304, 305, 306, **307**, 315, 318–
319, 320, **321**, **355**, 360, 376–7,
378, 380, 381, 383, 385, 388, 390,
429, 438, 466, 470, 471, 483, 484,
486, 490, 503, 504–5, 507
necromancy, 436, 504
Neo-catullan idiom, 103, 282, 303,
372
Neo-latin literature, 5, 10, 21, 27,
29–31, 63, 75, 81, 87, 92, 93, 94,
103–4, 107, 108, **125**, 130, 131,
132, **151–2**, 156, 165, 199, **205**,
208, 217, 224, 238, 260, 261,
262–3, 277, 279, 280, 283, 284,
287, 288, 289, 291, 292, 297, 299,
348, 350, 366, 369, **370–3**, 379,
381, 387, 389, 395, 399, 410, 414,
416, 424, 508
Neoplatonism, 8, 10, 15, 26, 77, 85,
117–18, 123, 125, 126, **149**, 150,
154, 157, 161, **162**, 169, **202–4**,
208, 212, 215, 217, 220, 237, 242,
245, 246, 261, 262, 298, **302**, 307,
366, 376, 377, 379, 385, 395, 412,
503, 507
neo-stoicism, 9, 202, **205**, **395–6**,
418, 433
night, 163
nobility, 58, 72, 195, 218, 240–1,
254, 331, 365, 367, 391, **412**, 413,
416, 469; *see also* Court; courtiers; anti-aulic poetry
noblesse de robe, 72
nominalists, 25
nostalgia, 270, 272
numerology, 175, 207, 208, 388

occultism, **206–9**, 241, 379, 393
old age, 44, 304, 318
opinion, 214, 280, 316

pagan elements (in poetry), 44, 140,
    241, 284, 314, 344
painting, 41, 297, 303; *see also* visual
    arts
palingenesis, 264
pantheism, 307, 504
Paradise lost, 502, 507
paraître, see appearance
parlement(s), 3, 4, 22, 23, 24, 71,
    148, 187, 197, 368, 386
passions, 9, 77, 116, 203, 205, 219,
    223, 429, 479, 481, 482, 486,
    503
patriotism, cultural, 6, 46, 47, 50,
    53, 55, 71, 82, 103, 121, 142, 149,
    177, 217, 242, 309, 371, **385–6**,
    415, 459, 461
patronage, 11, 23, 31, 47, 72, **74**, 82,
    136, 148, 199, 271; *see also* Court
perspective, 56, 365, 443
Petrarchism, 10, 12, 91, 94, 103, 107,
    115, 116, 118, 119, 120, 122, 130,
    132, 144 *n*26, 148, 153, **154–5**, 156,
    157, **158**, 159, 163, 165, 169, 195,
    202, 204, 238, **261**, 264, 265, 267,
    268, 277, 278, 281–2, 286, 288,
    290, 291, **300**, 301–2, 303, **317**,
    320, 321, 345, 367, 372, 373, 375,
    376, 377, 378, 380, 383, 393, 396,
    404, 434, 446, 447, 453, 503
philautia, 173, 174, 181, 214, 241,
    245, 344, 372, 465
philology, 63, 75, 79, 81, 83, 84, 87,
    505; *see also* scholarship
philosophy, 63, 78, 81, 82, 101, 124,
    211, 222, 232, 340, 379, 384, 385,
    390, 461
pilgrimages, 176
Platonism, 117, 118, 130, 132, 139,
    188, 205, 212, 214, 217, 219, 244,
    248, 264, 265, 268, 284, 286
pluralism, 25, 82
political thought, 4, 51, **53–5**, 71, 78,
    201, 211, 217, 222, **350–2**, 437,
    460, **467–72**
poverty, 121
preciosity, 11, 161, 261, 265, 266,
    286, 369
precious stones, 253, 280
predestination, 46, 114, 176
predetermination, 307, 504
présidiaux, 4, 197
Prévôt des marchands, 4
pride, 128, 214, 215, 221, 222, 245,
    270, 323, 324, 399, 415, 438, 440,
    479, **480**, 481, 484, 489
printing, 6, 7, 22, 27, **28–9**, 63, 75,

79–80, 82, 84, 92, **147–8**, **152**,
    227, 228, 471, 502
prodiges, 207, 231–2, 253
pronunciation, 136
prophecy, 206, 207, 208, 222, 223,
    253, 305, 325, 504
providence, 8, 9, 205, 206
provinces, 6, 73, 74, 81, 103, 195,
    263, 287–8, 333, 364, 368, 372,
    376, 387, 397, 424, 426, 442, 452,
    453
psychology, *see* man
punctuation, 136
Purgatory, 114
Pyrrhonism, 180, 479

querelle: *des amyes*, 93, **115–23**,
    129, 422 *n*39; *des anciens et des
    modernes*, 226, **228**, **230**, 241,
    251, 460, 505; *des femmes*, 115,
    180, 242

rationalism, **206**, 220
Readers, Royal, 3, 71, 74, 79, 81,
    199, 206, 368
realism (theol.), 25
reason, 9, 77, 116, 123, 205, 218,
    219, 220, **221**, 223, 230, 231, 245,
    314, 372, 396, 429, 469, 470, **479**,
    480, 481, 483, 490
rebellion, theory of, **351**, 440, 471
Reformation, 6, 29, 78, 80, 502
relativism, 201, 217, 220, 223, 226,
    251, 460, 461, 468, 505
religion, wars of, 57, 72, 76, 151,
    203, 205, 219, 229, 241, 253, 263,
    279, 285, 310, 318, **331–5**, 337,
    350, 353, 364, 365, 370–1, 381,
    393, 395, 411, 412, 419, 426, 437,
    448, 452, 468, 472, 489, 506, 509
religious issues, 24–6, 72, **83–4**, 85,
    86, 113–14, 123, 176–7, 186,
    195–6, 198, 217, 223, 374, 375,
    489–91, 510
Renaissance, xiii–xvi, 5, 6, **7–9**, 10,
    12, 13, 21, 27, 29, 33, 39, 45, **46**,
    49, 50, 55, 56, 61, 63, 74, **75–8**,
    80, 91, 93, **103**, 104, 124, 127,
    128, 137, 152, 154, 162, 175, 189,
    190, 198, 200, 201, 205, 206, 209,
    215, 224, 326, 342, 350, 362, 383,
    418, 444, 458, 459, 478, 485, 494,
    501, 502, 503, 507, 508, 509, 510
renommée, 109; *see also* glory
Requêtes: *de l'Hôtel*, 4; *du Palais*, 4
Romanticism, 10, 76, 171, 502, 504,
    508, 509

Sacraments, 246
saints, 56, 176, 186, 393

Salic law, 459, 473
salons, 11, 200, 212, 266, 286, 292,
  293, 317, **368–9**, 373, 375, 376,
  420, 467, 474
salvation, 244–5, 246, 338, 354
scepticism, **205–6**, 212, 215, 220
scholarship, French, 81, 198, **199–
  200**, 368, 506
scholasticism, 25, 28, 177, 337, 502
science(s), scientific method, 7, 77,
  78, 200, 211, **224–32**, 305, 504,
  505, 506
Scotism, 25
Secretaries of State, 197
self (anthropocentricity, individualism, themes centring on self-
  reliance, etc.), 220, 223, 226, 245–
  246, 372, 394, 441, 464, 465, 480;
  also ch. 15 *passim*
self-knowledge, 9, 124, 223, 372,
  479–80, 482, 484, **487**
sénéchaussées, 4
senses, sense data, 9, 220, 223, 479,
  503, 504
silence, 214, 215, 286, 291, 320
sin, 107, 205, 245, 251, 306, 338,
  354, 359, 383, 393, 398, 440;
  see also evil; Fall
society, 244, 245, **470–1**, 487; *see
  also* laws; man; travellers
soldier, 60, 98, 134, 221, **417**, 445,
  463–4
solitude, 78, 163, 264, 267, 282, 286,
  301, 319, 509
soul, **9**, 119, 120, 126, 128, 203, 205,
  206, 222, 223, 226, 306, 307, **308**,
  481; *see also* man; psychology
Spanish literature, 137, 147, 165,
  167, **168–9**, 171, 236, 253, 363 n9,
  370
spelling, 6, 80, 136, 281, 289, 380
spheres, 8
spirits, 8–9
spirituality, 350, 363 n9, 395, 396
stage, world as, 405, 422 n39
staging of plays, **56**, 426, 436, 443,
  454
States General, 59, 71, 334, 363, 417,
  469, 470
Stoicism, 119, 162, 218, 220, 222,
  256, 270, 291, 307, 369, 372, 396,
  407, 413, 426, 427, 429, 441, 463,
  479, 489; Christian, 372, 395; *see
  also* neo-stoicism; Seneca
suicide, 438
sun, 157, 163, 264, 265, **320**, 394,
  398, 438, 452
supernatural, 207–8
superstition, 253, 307, 342
syncretism, 7, 76, 82, 202, 308, 384,
  502

synergism, 9, 77, **176**, 177, 504

Table de Marbre, 4
tapestries, 365
tears, 400
temperance, 124, 205
themes, Renaissance, **75–8, 103**
theology, 71, 78, 81, 201, 206, 224,
  338
Tiers Etat, 472
time, 134, 154, 266, 270, 272, 274,
  300, 303, **304**, 306, 318, 323, 355,
  356, 482
toleration, 114, 468, 469
torture, 114, 489, 497
tranquillité, **219**, 484, 486
travel(lers), 121, 127, 138, 208, 224,
  225–9, 253, 379, 468, 479, 487,
  499, 500, 505
troupes (actors), 56, 442, 443, 454
tyranicide, 351, 352, 430, 435, 436
tyrant, 86, 177, 218, 441, **470–1**;
  see also kingship

unicorns, 230
Universe, 8, 10, 15, 119–20, 222,
  223, 224, 231, 305, 306, 307, 380,
  389
universities, *see* Sorbonne; *and
  under* names of colleges, *and*
  relevant towns
usage, 116

vanity (of life), 270, 271, 272, 396,
  402, 405–6, 409, 509
violence, 242, 252, **253**, 256, 267,
  270, 274, 360, 376, 377, 378, 404,
  426, 427, 431, 441, 453, 509
virtue, **9**, 121, 124, 132, 205, 215,
  218, 220, 246, 264, 425
visual arts, 72, 91, 198–9, 200, 364,
  365
Vita: activa, 75, **77**, 78, 82, 116,
  176, 201, 218, 219, 491, 496;
  contemplativa, **77**, 116, 218

war, 34, 51, 54, 82, 86, 98, **173**, 175,
  177–8, 218, 221, 265, 417, 436,
  445, 459, 468
water, **321**, 323–4
will, 9, 77, 123, 220, 223, 245, 504
wisdom, 43, **78**, 86, 101, 119, 120,
  138, 204, 205, 215, **218**, 231, 298,
  384, 486, **505**, 507; *see also* ignorance; knowledge; learning
witches, witchcraft, 181, 208, 253,
  307, 359–60, 429
woman, 9, 35, 59, **115–17**, 130, 204,
  216–17, 221, 235, 240, 242, **245**,
  249, 267, 410, 418, 446; *see also*

anti-feminism; love; Neoplatonism; Petrarchism
works, justification by, 114, 246
world-picture, 7–9, 220, 305–6

xenophobia, 335, 367, 412, 415, 472

zodiac, 380

III. INDEX OF LITERARY GENRES, RHETORICAL TERMS, AND MATTERS CONCERNING VERSIFICATION AND SYNTAX

accumulation, 397, 406, 409
adunaton, 14, 155, 397, 406, 409
adverb, 52, 131, 157, 170, 350
adverbial phrase, 343
alexandrine, 13, 38, 44, 101, 125, 139, 265, 266, 268, 269, 270, 282, 308–9, 311, 316, 317, 353, 375, 383, 413, 426, 428, 431, 432
allegory (*and* allegorical features), 33, 38, 43, 47, 56, 57, 58, 61, 62, 94, 98, 99, 105, 106, 111, 125, 132, 151, 162, 175, 262, 277, 280, 306, 309, 311, 316, 361, 416
alliteration, 37, 43, 275, 397, 404
allusio, 255
alternance, 13, 15, 38, 100, 101, 325
amoureuse, 32
anadiplosis, 14
anagram(matic poetry), 208, 366, 369, 384, 386
anaphora, 155, 264, 265, 275, 358, 405, 409, 439
anthologies, 76, 86, 93–4, 274, **348**, **402**, 418
anti-aulic poetry (*and* prose), 116, 120, **123–4**, 134, 168, 268, 271, 299, 310, 312, 347, 350, 356, 367, 390, **412–13**, 445, 446
antithesis, 108, 155, 158, 264, 275, 282, 301, 346, 355, 360, 377, 397, 404, 406
antonomasia, 14, 140, 265
apposition, 157
archaism, 6, 131, 140, 493
article, 6, 7, 51, 157

ballade, 14, 32, 34, 36, 59, 93, 97, 101, 419
ballet de cour, 15, 366, 442, 452
basium (*baiser*), 103, 163, 290; *see also* Second, J.
biblical paraphrase, 114, 279, 348, 370, 384, 394, 395, 399, 407, 416; *see also* Bible
binary patterns (words *and* phrases), 37, 40, 43, 52, 134, 155, 170, 275, **343**, 366, 397, 401, 432, 496
blason, 11, 34, 39, **92**, 97, 134, 264, 271, 280, 287, 309, 379, 380, 381, 411

caesura, 13
cantique, 394, 402
caricature, 59, 112, 184, 272, 279, 316, 355, 357, 358, 413, 473
cartel, 131, 277, 310, 365
chanson, 15, 62, 90–1, 97, 105, 111, 114, 303, 373, 375, 414, 416
chansons spirituelles, 126
chant royal, 12, 32, 34, 36, 94, 105, 129, 287, 384, 395, 399, 419
chants: mesurés, 266; *non mesurés*, 264
chap books, 236
chiasmus, 14, 159, 268, 358, 360, 397, 439
chorus, 346, **425**, 427, **428**, 429, 430, 431, 432, **434**, 436, 438, **440**
chronicle, 11, **45–53** *passim*, 63, 64, 459, 506
chronogram, 208, 366
collective verse, 93, 152, **368–9**, 416; *see also* anthologies; *tumulus*
comedy: plays, 137, 208, 237, 417, 432, 437, **442–52**; theory, **443–4**, 447, **448–9**; language, 445, 446, 448, 449, 450, 451; *see also* farce; *sottie*
commedia erudita, 443
committed poetry, **313–16**, 369, 370, 371–2, **414–16**, 467
compar (*isocolon*), 134, 275, 346
comparison, 14, 48, 52, 134, 235, 248, 272, 275, 278, 282, **315**, 343, 389, 396, 399, 404, 406, 407, 408, 413, 430, 439, 448, 471
complainte, 33, 90, 105, 287, 375, 414, 416
compound words, 289, 389, 432
confidant, 346, 425, 427, 428, 438, 443, 445, 449
conjunctions, 52, 342
conte, 51, 60, 108, 137, 147, 189, 206, 223, 234, 235, 464, 467; *and* ch. 8 *passim*
contrepéterie, 255
coq-à-l'âne, 36, 97, 109–10, 174
correctio, 14, 264
coupe, 140
court poetry, **33**, 94, 262, 270, 284, 285, 289, 297, 299, **309–13**, 388
cry, 57, 106

débat, 34, 35, 46, 62, 76, 98, 109,
116, 122, 125, 131, 133, 162, 212
decasyllable, 13, 41, 111, 115, 151,
268, 269, 311, 399, 413, 428,
432, 444
décor simultané, 56
demonstratives, 378, 397, 404, 405
déploration, 33, 34, 101, 109, 114, 277
désespoir, 161, 268
devis, 234
devisants, 212, 234, 235, 243, 244,
247, 254, 467
devise, 92, 398
devotional: literature, 28, 84, 137,
336, 396, 399, 404; poetry, 367,
390, 402, 408
dialectal elements, 6, 13, 80, 250, 389,
443, 463, 493
dialogue: school dialogue, 86, 212;
literary genre, 76, 116, 137, 141,
202, **211–24, 232**, 235, 242, 257,
390, 394, 503, 504; literary technique, 62, 168, 179, 247, 250, 252
didactic poetry, 205, 282–3, **369**,
372, 373, 379, 388, 390–1, 396;
see also gnomic poetry
diminutives, 131, 278, 303, 401
dizain, 12, 101, 108, 126, 132, **155–6**,
157, 158–60, 261
doctrinal, 34, 94
drama, *see* theatre
dream (literary device *or* genre), 33,
38, 131, 270, 302, 382, 427, 431

eclogue, 13, 30, 38, 61, 90, 91, 103,
109, 131, 277, 280, **283**, 288, 289,
310–11, 366, 371, 374, 387, 393,
416
elegy, 12, 13, 90, 103, 110–11, 130,
266, 287, 305, 309, 312, 318, 503
emblem, 12, **92**, 109, 151, **155–6**,
396, **398**
encomiastic poetry, 101, 151, 179,
182, 199, 263, 271, 288, 366, 370,
374, 416; *see also* court poetry
enigma, 36, 110, 182, 215, 369, 372
enjambement, 13, 43, 157, 159, 282,
285, 301, 397, 401, 408, 409
enumeration, 37, 38, 40, 43, 112,
113, 134, 164, 222, 249, 265, 271,
273, 278, 285, 316, 358, 360, 383,
393, 397, 402, 404, 405, 430, 465
epic (*and* epic style *or* elements), 33,
46, 63, 126, 142, 209, 293, 311–
312, 316, 371, 385, 387
epigram, 32, 90–1, 93, 103, 106, 114,
130, 131, 132, 264, 271, 283, 372,
375, 387, 410, 411, 472
epistle, 13, **35**, 38, 90, 94, 97, 101,
105, **111–13**, 114, 130, 234, 271,
287, 305, 309, 373

epistolary genre (prose), 190–1, 217
epitaph, 90, 103, 109, 132, 271, 303
epithalamium, 277
epithet, 12, 38, 40, 48, 52, 100, 131,
134, 140, 165, 170, 267–8, 273,
275, 289, 316, 343, 358, 360,
378, 393, 397, 408, 432, 496
equivocque, 255
essay, 86, 234, 257, 467, 477; *and*
ch. 15 *passim*
étrennes (xenia) 103, 108, 372
exclamation, 155, 397, 401, 406
exemplum (*and* exemplary literature), 46, 50, 51, 53, 109, 128,
235, 239, 244, 436, 459, 461, 463,
478, 479, 481, 503
extempore verse, 36, 93, 369

fable, 50, 112, 203, **204**, 219
fabliau, 34, 59, 249
facétie, 240, 249
farce, 55, 57, 58–60, 61, 67–8 *n*34,
345, 410, 443, 444, 445, 446, 447,
449, 451, 508
fatras, 36
fatrasie, 74, 110
fourteen-syllable line, 432

genethliacon, 34, 277
genres, 11, **12–13**, 90–1, 103, 107,
138, **139**, 140, 142, 165, 344, 419,
503
gnomic poetry, 12, 92, 148, 396, 418
gradatio, 155

hexameric poetry, 385, 387
hiatus, 13, 140
huitain, 108, 110, 399
hyperbole, 51, 53, 248, 397

icon, 12, 92, 109, 398
imagery, 14, 16, 113, 130, 134, 155,
157–8, 159, 160, 164, 261, 264,
270, 272, 273, 283, 300, 302,
304, 305, 312, **321–2**, 343, 350,
355, 376, 377–8, 380, **396**, 399,
400, 404, 406, 407, 408, 419,
439, 465, 482, 493, **494, 495–6**,
503, 505
imitation, 12, 140, 141, 219, 281,
427, 507
incise, 52, 157, 159, 164, 264, 265,
383, 403, 409
infinitive, 157, 264
innutrition, 140
Institution du Prince, 177
interrogation, 341, 346, 350, 358,
397, 401, 405, 406, 409
invective, 353
invocation, 159, 165, 316, 346, 358,
397, 425, 430

irony, 112, 114, 124, 174, 184, 248, 503
irony, dramatic, 346, 426, 427, 429, 431, 436, 440, 441
Italianisms, 157, **367**

lai, 33
latinisms, 43, 44, 52, 131, 140, 156–157, 158, 170, 239, 289, 493
liminary verse, 11
locus amœnus, 102, 105, 127, 131
love-poetry, 33, 36, 94, 98, 99, 103, 108, 110–11, 118, 132, 133, **153**–**161**, 165, 261, 267, 278, **286**, 290, 292, 298, 321, 323, 366, 369, 372, **373**–**9**, 380, 392, 393, **403**–**4**

macaronic verse, 280, 371, 416, 489
mascarades, 131, 277, 310, **365**
meditation: (prose), **248**–**50**; (verse), 372, 374, 402
memoirs, 234, 458, **462**–**7**
messengers, 425, 429, 431, 436, 439, 441
mignardise (genre), 290
miracle plays, 56, 57
Miroirs des princes, 46, 55
mock epic, 179
monologue: separate genre, **60**, 112, 174; dramatic device, 425, 447, 450; in *Satyre Menippée*, 473–474
moralité, **57**–**8**, 61, 96, 446, 447, 456 *n*2, 508
mystère, **55**–**6**, 99, 118, 173, 345, 346, 347, 508

negative presentation, 38, 112, 343, 355, 357, 360, 397, 399
neologisms, 6, 13, 140, 289, 290, 493
nouns, 157, 361, 397
nouvelle, 59, 169, 189, 212, 234, **235**, 237, **238**, **240**, 410, 464
novel, 50, 137, **167**–**71**, 199, 410

octosyllable, 58, 59, 60, 63, 111, 353, 431, 443, 445
ode, 103, 104, 115, 132, 139, 262, 266, 290, 373, 376; *see also* Pindaric ode

paean, 310, 366, 387
palinod, 32, 93, 125
paradox, 124, 214, 397, 503; (literary genre), 213
parody, 35, 355, 372
participial phrases, 37, 131, 157, 360
participles, 71, 275, 403
pasquil, pasquin, 397–8, 411
pastoral (genre *and* features), 37–8,

56, 61, 137, 161, 199, 254, 262, 276, **277**, 280, 283, **289**–**90**, 311, **370**, 374, 376, 381, 392, 393, 394, 410, 474
pastourelle, 32
pathetic (effects on reader), 252, 254, 256, 346, 353, 358, 360, 371, 396, 414, 417, 426, 436, 441, 473
periphrasis, 140, 142, 170, 267, 270
peripetia, 453
Pindaric ode (*and* style), 139, **298**, 380, 392, 428, 451
poetry *and* poetic theory, **10**–**16**, **138**–**42**, 419; craftsmanship, **12**, 14; functions *and* status, **10**, 29, **31**–**2**, 38, 91–2, 103, 118, 132, 136, 140, 142, 152, 156, **202**–**3**, 219, 262, 270, **292**, 297, 298, 309, 314, 315, **324**, 325, 381, 384, **386**–**7**, 388, 394, 397; inspiration, 138, 140, 141, 270; language, **14**, 113, 156, 325, 420; obscurity, 142, 284; originality, **12**, 16; poetry *and* music, **14**–**16**, 203, 283, 366, 386; public ('elitist' or 'democratic' attitudes), **10**, 11, 32, 61, 91, 103, 135, 140, 141, 142, 156, 160, 219, 267, 292, 293, 314, 396, 435; versification, *see under* separate heading
pointe, 155, 156, 264, 273, 275, 325, 404, 408
prepositions, 360
pro-aulic poetry, 116
pronouns, 51, 140, 343
prose style, 51–3, 55, 138, 139, 227, 234, 237, 239, 357, 458, 467, 474–5, 509; *also* ch. 7, 8, and 14 *passim*
prosopopœia, 14, 109, 127, 275, 280, 288, 316, 371, 374, 414
protatic characters, 425, 431, 441
proverbs, 222
provignement, 140
pseudo-encomium, 162, 182
puys, 11, 30, 32, 93, 95, 105, 125, 395, 399

quadrisyllable, 111
quaternary patterns, 350, 397
quatrain, 16, **92**–**3**, 101, 148, 151, 282, 370, 418
quotation, 342, **494**–**5**

realism, 47, 50, 56, 134, 169, 235, 236, 238, 244, 247, 254, 270, 271, 280, 443, 444, 446, 447
recapitulation, 275
regional reference (in poetry), 103, 155, 158, 289, 291, 299
relative clauses, 7, 52

religious poetry, 30, 32, 113–14, 118, 122, 125–8, 129, 151, 274, 279, 292, 293, 348, 369, 370, 371–2, 378, 384, 392, **394–409**

repetition, 157, 164, 248, 264, 265, 266, 269–70, 271, 273, 275, 278, 285, 303, 304, 313, 346, 349, 350, 358, 360, 377, 378, 382, 397, 398, 400, 404, 405, 406, 408, 409, 432, 439

rhetoric, 12, 13, 27, 51, 78, 81, 91, 95, 98, 105, 131, 134, 135, 139, 140, 141, 165, 189, 261, 264, 265, 267, 271, 273, 282, 295, 316, 339, 344, 346, 349, 357, 376, 392, 396, 401, 408, 409, 416, 417, 419, 425, 426, 430, 441, 453, 473, 492, 493–494, 509

rhyme, 6, 36, 140

rime équivoquée, 411

rimes croisées, 100

rimes plates, 41, 60, 110, 111

romances, medieval, 28, 50, 51, 105, 122, 167, 168, 169, 172, 235, 237, 241, 242, 255

rondeau, 32, 33, 36, 37, 58, 59, 93, 94, 97, 101, 105, 129, 139, 151, 419

satire (genre *and* elements), 13, **34–5**, 55, 57, 58–9, 60, 86, 97, 99, **106–107**, 124, 128, 162, 177, 178, 180, 181, 185, 186, 187, 189, 213, 214, 221, 235, 237, 248, 252, 268, 270, 271, 272, 273, 280, 285–6, 313–16, 317, 346, 350, 358, **410–14**, 416, **417–18**, 445, 447, 451, 467, **472–474**

satire or *discours*, 369

satire française, 151

satire (satura), 59

scientific poetry, 13, 132, 207, 208, 224, 262, **305–9**, 351, 370, **379–394**, 396

sentence structure, 6, 51, 164, 170, 250, 261, 264, 266, 267, **342**, 408, 467; *see also* binary; ternary; quaternary

sententia, 12, 14, 33, 38, 46, 51, 59, 92, 155, 282, 397, 404, 425, 431, 432, 435, 450, 467, 471, 494

sermon, 396, 397; Calvinist, 337, 349, 396, 404; Franciscan, 60, 172, 173; (literary genre), 35, **60**

serventois, 32

sonnet, 12, 15, **115**, 131, 132, 139, 142, 155, **163–5**, 261, 264–8, 269, **270**, 275, 282, 285, 373, 375, 376, 391–2, 396, 397, 399, **403–5**, 407, 411

sottie, 57, **58–9**, 64, 68 *n*34, 110, 444

speeches (in prose), 46, 48, 51, 52, 53, 446, **473–4**

stances, 373, 375, 376, 378, 396, 407

style (rhetorical levels, etc.), 7, 12, 14, 46, 47, 52, 114, 142, 270, 271, 303, 354, 474, 493

superlative, 48, 51, 52, 53, 248, 466

symbol(ism), 42, 62, 99, 111, 273, 321, 324, 325, 355, 356, 357, 358, 359–60, 361, 367

symmetry, 43, 165, 300, 304, 317, 343, 349, 350, 375, 377, 382, 449

syndérèse, 407

syntax, **140**, 157

système entrecoupé, 451

technical vocabulary, 96, 131, 140

temple, 35, 43, 44, 101, **105**

ternary patterns, 120, 131, 133, 155, 159, 275, 285, 382, 397, 400, 432, 496

terza rima, 38, 44, 100, 115, 125, 131, 161, 266, 285

testament, 35

theatre, 12, 14, **55–63**, 64, 76, 139–140, 150–1, 209, 263, 283, 338, 339, 344, **345–7**, 365, 394, 412, **424–57**, 508; college, 61, **103–4**, 424–5; *see also under* separate genres

tombeau (tumulus), 11, 277, 368, 371, 397, 416; *du Dauphin* (1536), 11, 132, 152; of Marguerite de Navarre, 260, 295 *n*2, 422 *n*28

topoi (commonplaces), 12, 16, 38, 40, 47, 109, 110, 112, 121, 133, 162, 218, 230, 270, 289, 291, 301, 304, 310, 367, 378, 399, 405, 413, 427, 429, 430, 432, 434, 441

traductio, 275

tragedy: theory, **425–7**, 430, 432, **434–5**; plays and general references, 103, 131, 137, 205, 260, 263, 336, 344, 366, 370, 395, **424–42**, 444, 467; Calvinist tragedy, **345–7**; *tragédie irrégulière*, 242, 425, 426, 452, 453

tragicomedy, 366, 437, 442, **452–3**, 457 *n*27

translation, 6, 12, **39**, 54, 98, 105, 107, 130, 132, 133, **136–8**, 139, 140, 147, 150, 200, 201, 202, 207, 213, 225, 236, 243, 253, 263, 268, 273, 276, 281, 282, 292, 370, 372, 375, 389, 395, 397, 407, 414, 418, 424, 431, 433, 447, 544–5, 547

trisyllable, 111, 428

unities, dramatic, 346, 347, 425, 427, 431, **432**, 433, 435, 437, 442

verb, 57, 264, 275, 285, 302, 360, 397, 404
versification, 13, 100, 114, 134, 140, 271, 282, 283, 285, 289, 290, 299, 369, 380, 425–6
vers mesurés, 285, 296; *à la lyre*, 15; *à l'antique*, 15, 139, 283, 291, 366

vers rapportés, 285, **286**
vœu (votum), 103

witness technique, 274, 405
word order, 158, 383
word play, 37, 40, 43, 94, 97, 100, 101, 109, 110, 222, 286, 369, 372

xenia, see étrennes

zeugma, 14, 358, 397

Printed in Great Britain
by Western Printing Services Ltd
Bristol